Revolutionary Soldiers
and the
Wives of Soldiers
with Ties to
Switzerland County
Indiana

Compiled and Edited by
Marlene Jan McDerment

HERITAGE BOOKS
2013

HERITAGE BOOKS
AN IMPRINT OF HERITAGE BOOKS, INC.

Books, CDs, and more—Worldwide

For our listing of thousands of titles see our website at
www.HeritageBooks.com

Published 2013 by
HERITAGE BOOKS, INC.
Publishing Division
5810 Ruatan St.
Berwyn Heights, MD 20740

Copyright © 2013 Marlene Jan McDerment

All rights reserved. No part of this book may be reproduced or transmitted in any form or by any means, electronic or mechanical, including photocopying, recording or by any information storage and retrieval system without written permission from the author, except for the inclusion of brief quotations in a review.

International Standard Book Numbers
Paperbound: 978-0-7884-5477-6
Clothbound: 978-0-7884-6926-8

THIS BOOK IS DEDICATED TO GRIFFITH DICKINSON
REVOLUTIONARY WAR SOLDIER, EARLY SETTLER,
THE FIRST LAND OWNER IN SWITZERLAND COUNTY,
AND HIS WIFE SUSAN

CONTENTS

ABNEY, GEORGE	1
ANDREWS, ARTHUR	5
AYER, THOMAS	10
BASSETT, JOSPEH	13
BLADES, JOHN LEVY	17
BOISSEAUX, JEAN BAPTISTE	22
BRAY, JOHN	28
BROWN, SAMUEL	36
BUCK, WILLIAM	41
BURNS, JOHN	45
BUTLER, RICHARD	51
CARVER, CHRISTIAN	55
CHANDLER, WILLIAM	59
CHRISTY, JAMES	63
CONINE, ANDREW	67
COTTON, RALPH	70
COY, CHRISTOPHER	75
COY, WILLIAM	79
CRITCHFIELD, JOHN	84
CROSS, EBENEZER	88
DAVIS, DAVID	90
DAVIS, WILLIAM	96
DEISKY, LEIMAN	98
DEWITT, WILLIAM	104
DICKINSON, GRIFFITH	111
DRAKE, BENJAMIN	118
DUMONT, PETER	124
ELLIS, ROBERT	127
FANCHER, WILLIAM	128
FIELD, DANIEL	131
FOSTER, THOMAS	134
FROMAN, PAUL	135
GAZLEY, JAMES	136
GODDARD, JOSEPH	138
GOOKINS, SAMUEL	142
GRAY, MOSES	146
GREEN, RICHARD	149
GRIFFITH, WILLIAM	151
GULLION, JEREMIAH	154
GULLION, JOHN	157
GULLION, ROBERT	164
HALL, BENJAMIN	171
HAMMOND, LEWIS	174
HANNIS, HENRY	177
HARRIS, DANIEL	183

CONTENTS

HARRIS, ROBERT	187
HAYCOCK, DANIEL	193
HEATH, DANIEL JR	198
HUFMAN, HENRY	205
HUMPHREY, EBENEZER	209
JENNINGS, SOLOMON	214
KELLY, WILLIAM	218
KNOX, ROBERT	225
LANCASTER, WILLIAM	229
LANDRES, KIMBROW	236
LANHAM, HENRY	242
LEAP, JOHN W	246
LEE, JOHN	252
LEVI, ISAAC	257
LEWIS, THOMAS	265
MAGRUDER, NORMAN BRUCE	271
McKAY, ROBERT	278
MELLEN, JOHN	282
MOORE, RODERICK	285
MORGAN, DANIEL	292
MORGAN, NATHAN	293
MOSS, ZEALLY	298
MOUNTS, THOMAS	304
NEAL, CHARLES	311
NIGHSWONGER, SOLOMON	316
NORRIS, DANIEL	319
NORTH, ABIJAH	322
NORTH, LOT	325
NORTH, THOMAS	329
PARKINSON, ABRAHAM	333
PEABODY, STEPHEN G	337
PEAKE, NATHAN	340
PENMETENT, JOHN	346
PICKETT, HEATHCOTE	349
PIERCE, JAMES	352
PORTER, THOMAS	354
POTTER, DAVID	358
PRESTON, WILLIAM	362
PROTSMAN, JOHN	364
RANSTEAD, JAMES	370
REMER, DAVID	376
RENNO, GEORGE	382
RICKETTS, NATHAN	384
RICKETTS, ROBERT	391
RICKETTS, WILLIAM	399
ROBERTS, HEZEKIAH	404

CONTENTS

ROBERT(S), JOHN ... 409
ROBERTS, JOHN ... 415
ROBINSON, WINTHROP ... 423
ROGERS, STEPHEN ... 429
SCUDDER, ABNER ... 435
SHADDAY, JOHN ... 441
SHADDY, WILLIAM ... 448
SHAVER, JOHN ... 449
SHUPE, JOHN ... 453
SIX, JOHN ... 460
SMYTH, PHILLIP D. ... 465
STEPLETON, ANDREW ... 469
STEWART, CHARLES ... 474
TODD, JOSEPH ... 479
TODD, OWEN ... 485
TOWER, GIDEON ... 488
TRAINER, ISAAC ... 492
TURNER, ROBERT ... 494
TURNER, SMITH ... 497
WARDEN, BARNARD ... 502
WEIST, HENRY ... 506
WILSON, MICHAEL ... 511
WHITTEKER, JOHN ... 514
WOOLCOTT, JOSEPH ... 518
Appendix A ... 523
Appendix B ... 525
Appendix C ... 526

PREFACE

While researching my Revolutionary War ancestor, Griffith Dickinson, it came to my attention that his pension application is located at the Switzerland County Courthouse, but it is not located in the War Department holdings. I began to wonder whether records for other soldiers would only be found at the courthouse. In order to determine if this had occurred, it was necessary to identify all of the soldiers who had ties to the county.

There have been earlier published compilations of soldiers who lived and died in Switzerland County. By combining those lists (totaling sixty-six soldiers), consulting county histories to identify names of men who might have served, and combing through the ledgers in the court house, an additional forty-nine men and five wives of Revolutionary Soldiers were identified.

The next task was to verify that the identified men had actually served in the American Revolution. Pension records located at the National Archives, National Society Daughters of the American Revolution ancestor records, Revolutionary War muster and payroll records, and dozens of published records were consulted.

In the final analysis there were a total of eight pension applications recorded in Switzerland County that do not appear anywhere else. There are actually ninety-eight soldiers who lived in Switzerland County, four other soldiers who had ties to Switzerland County, and eight men listed in earlier compilations that either did not live in the county or did not serve in the Revolutionary War.

Records compiled for all of these men and women are included in this volume.

MARLENE JAN McDERMENT

ACKNOWLEDGMENT

I wish to express my gratitude to the many people who have assisted in the compilation of this work by sharing their time, information, and encouragement.

I appreciate the courteous hospitality offered by Judy Kappes during my research trips to Switzerland County. She has been generous with her time, knowledge, connections, and her enthusiasm for this project.

The Ohio Genealogical Society Library provided access to their many records and books. To Tom Neel, Library Director, I am especially grateful for his knowledge and suggestions.

History-genealogy expert Barry Brown, Switzerland County Public Library, who provided copies of newspaper articles about the soldiers. He was the first to recognize the challenge involved in this project. His kind words have been a motivation.

To other researchers who have kindly provided family records I am most grateful: to Bill Farnsworth (Arthur Andrews data); Alan Fisher (Paul Froman data); Gary Lehman (Heathcote Pickett data); and Helen Einhas (William Lancaster data).

Thanks to my friend and fellow family genealogist, James Edge, for his assistance in editing these pages, and for sharing his publishing knowledge.

Most of all, I am grateful to my daughter, Kelly Collene (McDerment) Prostor who never doubted my ability to prepare this volume.

INTRODUCTION

The purpose of this book is to bring into one volume the various records pertaining to the Revolutionary War soldiers, and wives who have ties to Switzerland County. Included are Switzerland County inhabitants who have not previously been identified as having served in the Revolutionary War. Recognition is given to the widows who settled in Switzerland County after the death of the widow's soldier husband. Their contribution to the establishment of the area should not be forgotten.

Earlier works did not provide the source of the information presented about the patriots and the wives. This volume attempts to provide evidence placing them in Switzerland County and to prove or, in some cases, disprove the soldier's Revolutionary service.

In order to trace the county's earliest settlers the land records of the Northwest Territory, State of Ohio, Indiana Territory, and Switzerland County, Indiana need to be consulted. This is because some of these individuals settled (squatted) in the current Switzerland County area when it was still a part of the Northwest Territory. Therefore, records are scant and most often non-existent. In 1803, when Ohio gained statehood, the Ohio land encompassed a portion of land west of the Ohio River (most of current Switzerland County). Several early settlers made their way to Cincinnati to enter their land. In doing so they became citizens of Ohio. After the War of 1812, the Greenville Treaty changed the western boundary of Ohio to the present state line. Switzerland County was now in the Indiana Territory. In the year 1816, Indiana became a state with Switzerland County being a part. With each change the range, township, and section numbers were adjusted so the land descriptions are not consistent. Keep these changes in mind when reviewing the records.

Several dozen sources were consulted to determine the service of these Revolutionary soldiers. Citation of each source is identified in these pages. If you find your subject herein, the listed sources provide direction to the original records.

When genealogical information was provided in the source material it is included. This work is not intended as a genealogical work. However, the family genealogist may find some useful clues within these pages.

Every attempt has been made to present complete and accurate information. In a few cases the several records shown may be for another man with the same name. Even though the various spellings of surnames were used in searching records, as with any publication of this kind, some errors and omissions are unavoidable.

It is my sincere hope that this book serves as a useful guide for readers interested in joining lineage societies such as DAR, SAR, First Families of Indiana, First Families of Ohio, and others, as well as supplementing family records.

ABNEY, GEORGE

Patriot: George Abney
Birth: 10 Feb 1752 Lunenburg Co., VA
Married Spouse 1: 1790 Sarah X (b. 1756 d. 1822 Hamilton Co., IN)
Married Spouse 2: Sally X [living in 1830, Hamilton Co., IN]
Service State(s): South Carolina
Service description: 1) Capts. Henry Foster, Wm. Butler;
Sinquefield & Towles, Col. Leroy Hammond
Rank: Private, Sergeant
Proof of Service: Pension application S16591
Pension application No.: S16591
Residences: Ninety Six District, SC; GA; TN; the last 9 yrs in State of Indiana (Switzerland Co. in 1821); last 4 yrs [1828-1832] in Hamilton County, IN.
Died: Hamilton Co., IN   Last pension payment 5 Apr 1838
Buried: Hamilton Co., IN
DAR Ancestor No.: A135145

Pension Application Abstracted from National Archives microfilm Series 805, Roll 2, File S16591; and *Switzerland County, Indiana Complete Records, Circuit Court, Vol. ?, Sep 3, 1821-Apr 18, 1827; p.248-9.*

Pension abstract for– George Abney   Service state(s): SC
Date: 12 Feb 1821
County of: Switzerland   State of: Indiana
Declaration made before the Circuit Court
Age: 71
Statement of service-

Period	Duration	Names of General and Field Officers
Not stated	18 months	Captain Samuel Sinfield, regiment commanded by Samuel Hammond; brigade commanded by General Pickins; SC Continental establishment

Battles: Siege of Ninety-Six Fort, Battle of Augusta, GA
Evidence: None
Where discharged: Edgefield, Ninety-six district, South Carolina; Indiana
&
Date: 12 Feb 1822
County of: Switzerland   State of: Indiana
Declaration made before an open Circuit Court.
Filing of personal property schedule & declaration of service.
Age: 71 years
Residence when he entered service: South Carolina
Statement of service-

Period	Duration	Names of General and Field Officers
Not stated	18 months	Capt. Samuel Sinfield, Regt. commanded

1

by Col. Samuel Hammond, Brigade commanded by Gen. Pickins in the line of South Carolina, Continental establishment.
Battles: Siege of Ninety-Six; Battle of Augusta
Discharge received: At Edgefield, Ninety-Six District, SC
Statement is supported by –
Documentary proof: Has none
Clergyman:
Persons in neighborhood who certify character:
Occupation: A laborer
Wife: Not named   Wife's age: 66 years old
&
Date: 7 Nov 1832
County of: Hamilton   State of: Indiana
Declaration made before the Circuit Court
Residence when he entered service: Within 18 miles of Ninety Six, SC
Volunteer or Drafted or Substitute: Volunteer; served 8 mos. as 2nd Sergeant, 4 mos. as Private, 16 mos. as a Private Minuteman.
Statement of service-

Period	Duration	Names of General and Field Officers
3 July 1775	4 months	Capt. Henry Foster, 1st Lieut. Morris Gwyne, 2nd Lieut. William Abney (uncle of the applicant),

Regiment commanded by Col. Andrew Perkins; South Carolina Militia.
Battles: 2 engagements against the Indians invading the frontiers of South Carolina. Expedition commanded by Gen. Andrew Williams, SC Militia.
Discharge received: a written discharge
Signed by: his Captain, about the 1st of November
Also -

Period	Duration	Names of General and Field Officers
1779	12 months	Same officers as before

Battles: siege of Augusta, siege of Ninety-Six
Discharge received: a written discharge
Signed by: Capt. Joseph Tolls
Also -

Period	Duration	Names of General and Field Officers
1780 or 1781	16 months	Capt. William Butler; frequently marched in Until close of war company with Capts. Sinfield and Tolls.

Battles: Served as a Minuteman
Discharge received: at the blockhouse at Andersons Mill near Ninety-Six.
What became of discharge papers: Lost
Where and year born: Halifax Co., VA 10 Feb 1752
Residence(s) since the war: SC, GA, TN, the last 9 years in State of Indiana, last 4 years in Hamilton County, IN
Residence now: Hamilton Co., IN
Statement is supported by – Traditionary evidence

Person now living who can testify to service: Knows of no person
Documentary proof: none
Persons in neighborhood who certify character: John Helms - known for 15 yrs, James Brown.
Clergyman: No resident clergyman in the county
Wife: Not named   Wife's age: 66 in 1823
Names and ages of children: Not stated

Switzerland County, Indiana Civil Order Book 4, 1820 – 1823; pg. 314.
Feb. term, 1822
George Abney, a revolutionary soldier now files his schedule made the declaration and took the oath required by a late act of Congress relative to pensioners which are ordered to be recorded and it is ordered to be certified that the property contained in said schedule is valued by the court at six dollars.

Abstract of Final Payment Voucher; General Services Administration, Washington, DC

NAME	ABNEY, GEORGE
AGENCY OF PAYMENT	INDIANA
DATE OF ACT	1832
DATE OF PAYMENT	3rd QUARTER 1833
DATE OF DEATH	-

LAST ~~FINAL~~ PAYMENT VOUCHER RECEIVED FROM THE GENERAL ACCOUNTING OFFICE   Form
General Services Administration   GSA DA 70-7035 GSA Dec 69 7068

1830 U.S. Census, Indiana, Hamilton, No Twp., Series: M19 Roll: 26, page 244.
Abney, George – age 70-80.

Roster of Soldiers and Patriots of the American Revolution Buried in Indiana, Vol. I; compiled by Mrs. Roscoe C. O'Byrne; Indiana Daughters of the American Revolution, 1981; p.33.

Abney, George   Hamilton County
Born – Feb. 10, 1752, Lunenburg, now Halifax Co., Virginia
Service – While residing within 18 miles of Ninety-Six, S.C., he enlisted July 3, 1775, served as pri. in Capt. Henry Foster's CO., Col. LeRoy Hammond's S.C. Regt. He was marched through the mountains to the head of Savannah River against the Indians who were then invading the frontiers of S.C., and while on this tour was in two engagements with the Indians and was discharged after having served 4 mos. Later served as pri. and 2nd Sergeant in Capt. Henry Foster's CO., Col. LeRoy Hammond's S.C. regt., length of this tour not less than 12 mos. Enlisted in 1780 or 81 as pri. under Capts. William Butler, Samuel Sinfield and Tolls in the S.C. troops, scouting and ranging against the Tories. In the siege of Augusta and Ninety-Six and was discharged after having served on this tour 16 mos.
Proof – Pension claim S. 16591.
Died – Last payment of pension was made April 5, 1838. In 1822 he referred to his wife, then aged 66, but does not give name.

The Vevay Reveille-Enterprise; Vol. 122, No. 37, 15 Sep 1938, p. 1, col. 4.
Roster of Revolutionary Soldiers Who Resided in Switzerland County
By Mrs. Effa M. Danner

GEORGE ABNEY - He appears in open court of Switzerland County 1826 to make his petition for pension for service in the Revolutionary War, age 71 (D. Order Book, p. 248). He enlisted in South Carolina under the command of Samuel Sinfield, Col. Samuel Hammond, and General Pickins, Continental Establishment. Discharged at Edgefield 96 District. He was in the siege of 96 Fort and the Battle of Augusta, Ga. He has no evidence of service.

His pension was granted and last paid 1838. He is buried in Hamilton County, Indiana.

Undocumented family information:
Wife: Sarah "Sally" GRIFFITH, b. c1756
Children: Joshua b. c1784 SC, d. 3 Aug 1851 Hamilton Co., IN, m. 28 May 1806 in Jackson Co., TN Mary Ann HELMS b. c1785; Isaac b. c1771 SC, d. aft 1850, m. Dicy (?); George m. Macah Baney; William; Ann m. BROWN.

ANDREWS, ARTHUR
aka ANDRUS

Patriot: Arthur Andrews
Birth: 2 Feb 1762 Lancaster Co., PA
Married Spouse 1: Christiana or Christana (d. bet. 1835-1849)
Service state(s): PA
Service description: Company of Riflemen - Capt. John Marshall, C.A. Boyd, Maj. Steele, Capt. James Lewis.
Rank: Private
Proof of Service: Pension application – Switzerland Co., IN
Pension application No.: Not located in War Dept. records
Residences: Lancaster Co., PA; Chester Co., PA; Redstone [Fayette Co.], PA; Butler Co., OH; Switzerland Co., IN
Died: c. 1849 Boone Co., IN
Buried: Hopewell Cemetery, Lebanon, Boone Co., IN
DAR Ancestor No.: None

Author's notes: There were two men by the name of Arthur Andrews who were born in Lancaster Co., PA. Both men served in the Revolutionary War; both men moved to Chester Co., PA. Pension applications and census records support these facts.

The Pension Application of the subject, Arthur Andrews b. 2 Feb 1762 in Lancaster Co., PA, is recorded in Switzerland County. (*Switzerland County, Indiana Probate Order Book 2, 1831-1837;* p. 134.& *Switzerland County, Indiana Probate Record Book Vol. A, Mar 1827-Nov 1834;* p. 397-398.)
The War Department records contain the Pension Application for Arthur Andrews, b. 10 May 1753, Lancaster Co., PA, d. 6 May 1837 in Chester Co., PA. (Pension Application No. S23517; DAR ancestor No. A002576).

As a result of the Switzerland County pension record not being with the War Department records, the service records for Arthur Andrews, buried at Hopewell Cemetery, Lebanon, Boone Co., IN, have been erroneously attributed to the man who actually died in Chester Co., PA.

The land records (*Switzerland County Land Records, Volume C, pages 159-160* and *Crawfordsville, Indiana Land Office, Receipt No. 24923*) provide evidence (based on the dates of these transactions) that the Arthur Andrews who applied for pension in Switzerland County is the man buried in Boone County.

The date of death in the DAR Rosters I and II (citations follow) gives a death date of 1834. This date is incorrect. Arthur Andrews is found in the 1840 Boone County, IN census (*1840 U.S. Census, Indiana, Boone, No Twp Listed, Series: M704 Roll: 74 Page: 149*). Family records indicate he died in early1849, Boone Co., IN. This date is based on his sale of land to his son in 1849. His wife does not relinquish dower rights indicating she was no longer living (*Boone County, Indiana Deed Book 5*).

Thank you to Bill Farnsworth, a descendant, who has graciously shared his information and confirmed the preceeding analysis.

Switzerland County, Indiana Probate Record Book Vol. A, Mar 1827-Nov 1834; p. 397-398.
Pension abstract for – Arthur Andrews
Service state(s): Pennsylvania
Date: 12 Aug 1833
County of: Switzerland   State of: Indiana
Declaration made before Open Court.
Age: 71 years   Record of age: In father's Bible
Where and year born: 2 Feb 1762 in Lancaster Co., PA
Residence when he entered service: Lancaster, PA
Residence(s) since the war: Lancaster Co., PA for 8 years, Chester Co., PA 7 years, Redstone, PA for 6 years, Butler Co., Ohio 20 years, Indiana for 12 years.
Residence now: Switzerland Co., IN
Volunteer or Drafted or Substitute: Enlisted
Rank(s): Private
Statement of service-

Period	Duration	Names of General and Field Officers
7 or 8 Sep 1776	2 yrs, 4 mos.	Company of Riflemen commanded by Capt. John Marshall, commanded by C.A. Boyd of the 7th Regt. of Pennsylvania Troops; Boyd left detachment, Major Steele took command; then under command of Capt. James Lewis.

Battles: Engagement at Chadd's Ford
Discharge received: He was on furlough at the time his company was discharged. Therefore he received no discharge.
Statement is supported by – none
Person now living who can testify to service: Knows no one.
Clergyman: Samuel Pavy, Switzerland Co., IN
Persons in neighborhood who certify character: Henry Banta, William Richards, Presley Renno, John Carr, Clark Jakeways, etc.
Wife: Not stated
Names and ages of children: Not stated

Switzerland County, Indiana Probate Order Book 2, 1831-1837; p. 134.
12 Aug 1833 – In the Matter of Arthur Andrews
An applicant for a Pension under the act of Congress of the 7 June 1832
       Now on this day personally appears in open Court before the Probate Court of Switzerland County now sitting Arthur Andrews a resident of Switzerland County State of Indiana, who being duly Sworn according to the provisions made by the act of Congress passed the 7th of June AD 1832. (here insert it) And the Said Court, do hereby declare their opinion, after the investigation of the matter, and after putting the interrogations prescribed by the war department that the above named Arthur Andrews was a Revolutionary

Soldier, and served as he states & the Court further Certifies that it appears to them that Samuel Pavy who has Signed the preceding Certificate is Clergyman resident in Switzerland County and State of Indiana. And that Henry Banta who Signed the same is a resident of Switzerland County State of Indiana, and is credible, and their Statement is entitled to Credit.

Early Ohio Settlers, Purchasers of Land in Southwestern Ohio, 1800-1840; Compiled by Ellen T. Berry & David A. Berry; Genealogical Publishing Co., Inc., Baltimore, MD, 1986. p. 7.

Purchaser	Year	Date	Residence	R – T - S
Andrews, Arthur (B)	1818	Sept. 17	Butler	03-03- 04

(B) Indiana Survey: Land lying west of a meridian drawn west of the Great Miami (known as the "Gore"). Switzerland, Dearborn, Franklin, Ohio, Union and Randolph Counties (all or only a part of each county) – all in Indiana.

Early Settlers of Indiana's "GORE" 1803-1820; Compiled and Edited by Shirley Keller Mikesell; Heritage Books, Inc., 1995. p. 187.
Switzerland County - Township 3, Range 3W
Section 4 – Arthur Andrews – 1818 – pg. 10.

Indiana Land Entries Vol. 1 Cincinnati District, 1801-1840; Margaret R. Waters; Originally Published Indianapolis 1948, Second Reprint 1979 by The Bookmark, P.O. Box 74, Knightstown, In 46148. p. 70.
CINCINNATI LAND DISTRICT – VOL. 1.   SWITZERLAND CO.
Arthur Andrews   NE ¼ -S4; 9-17-1818

U.S. Department of Interior, Bureau of Land Management, General Land Office Records; Land Patent Search – accessed 27 June 2012.
ANDREWS, ARTHUR
Accession Nr. CV-0050-389; Document Type – Credit Volume Patent; State – Indiana; Issue Date – 3/14/1820; Cancelled – No
Land Office – Cincinnati; Authority – April 24, 1820 – Cash Entry (3 Stat. 566); Document Nr – 0; Total Acres – 164.44
Land Descriptions: State – IN; Meridian – 1st PM; Twp-Rng – 003N-003W; Aliquots – NE1/4; Section 4; County – Switzerland
&
Accession Nr. IN1370; Document Type – State Volume Patent; State – Indiana; Issue Date – 3/20/1837; Cancelled – No
Land Office – Crawfordsville; Authority – April 24, 1820 – Sale – Cash Entry (3 Stat. 566); Document Nr. – 24923; BLM Serial Nr. – IN NO S/N; Total Acres – 80.00
Land Descriptions: State – IN; Meridian – 2nd PM; Twp-Rng – 020N – 001E; Aliqouts E1/2SW1/4; Section – 31; County - Boone

1830 U.S. Census, Indiana, Switzerland, No Twp., Series: M19 Roll: 32, Pg: 28.
Andrews, Arthur   Age 60-70   [Calculated age – b. 1762 = 68 y/o]

Switzerland County Land Records, Volume C, pages 159-160.
Dated: 12 August 1835
Grantor: Arthur Andrews and Christina his wife of Switzerland County
Grantee: Arnold Potter of Allensville in said County
Conveyance: Sum of four hundred dollars food and lawful money of the United States
Land description: that certain piece or parcel of land being and lying in Switzerland County and Pleasants Township being the south half of the North East quarter of Section four in Township Three of Range three west of the Meridian line drawn from the mouth of the Great Miami River containing Eighty-two acres of land.

Crawfordsville, Indiana Land Office, Receipt No. 24923
Dated: 20 August 1835
Conveyance: It is herby certified, that in pursuance of law, Arthur Andrews of Switzerland county, Indiana on this day purchased of the Register of this Office, at Crawfordsville.
Land description: The lot or East Half of the Southwest quarter of section number thirty one in township number twenty North of range number One East containing eighty acres, at the rate of $1.25 per acre, amounting to $100.00 for which said Arthur Andrews has made payment in full, as required by law.
Now therefore let it be known, that on presentation of this certificate to the Commissioner of the General Land Office, the said Arthur Andrews shall be entitled to receive a patent for the lot above described.

1840 U.S. Census, Indiana, Boone, No Twp., Series: M704 Roll: 74 Pg: 149.
Andrews, Arthur, age 70-80. [Calculated age – b. 1762 = 78 y/o]

Boone County, Indiana Deed Book 5, p. 27-29.
Date: 15 Jan 1849
Grantor: Arthur Andrews, Senior of county aforesaid [Boone]
Grantee: Arthur Andrews, Junior
Conveyance: For consideration of the natural love and affection for which the said Arthur leaves
to said Arthur, as for the better maintenance and support of the said Arthur has given granted, conveyed and confirmed …to the said Arthur Junior, his heirs and assigns forever.
Land description: All that tract of parcel of land lying and being in the County aforesaid, bounded and described as follows to wit: It being the south half of the East half of the South West quarter of Section thirty one in township twenty North of range one East, in the district of lands subject to sale at Crawfordsville Indiana, containing forty acres….

Abstract of Graves of Revolutionary Patriots (4 volumes); by Patricia Law Hatcher; Pioneer Heritage Press, Dallas, TX, 1987. Vol. 1, p. 21.
This is an abstract and an index to information reported to the Daughters of the American Revolution and published in their annual reports to the Smithsonian

Institution, printed as Senate Documents (1900-1974) and published annually in the DAR magazine (1978-1987).
Published 1972 (Senate Doc. 54)
Andrews, Arthur   Hopewell Cem, Boone Co IN 72

Note: The data in the following citations from DAR Rosters and SAR Graves Register is for the "other" Arthur Andrews who died 1837 in Chester County, PA. There was a "Last Final Payment Voucher" paid 2nd quarter 1837, Agency of Payment was Philadelphia, PA.

Roster of Soldiers and Patriots of the American Revolution Buried in Indiana, Vol. I; compiled by Mrs. Roscoe C. O'Byrne; Indiana Daughters of the American Revolution, 1981; p.399.
List of Men Whose Service in Revolutionary War Has Not Been Verified At Present Time
ANDREWS, ARTHUR   Boone County
Born – Mr. 10, 1753, Lancaster Co., Penn.
Died – 1834.   Buried Hopewell Cemetery. Stone.
Collected by Mrs. C. M. McClaine, Lebanon, Indiana

Roster of Soldiers and Patriots of the American Revolution Buried in Indiana, Vol. II; 1966; p. 12.
ANDREWS, ARTHUR   Boone County
Born – March 10, 1753, Lancaster Co., Penn.
Service – Pri. and Lieut. under Capts. McDowel, Hayes, Evans, and Ball, Penn.
Proof – DAR No. 33564; Pensioned April 26, 1833, aged 81 yrs.
Died – 1834. Buried Hopewell Cemetery. Stone.
Married – (1) Ruth Douglas and (2) Anna Cooper 1753-1817. Ch. Isabelle B. 170 m. Thos. Clendening; James b. 1781 m. Margaret Clendening; Arthur b. 1782 m. (1) Jane Andrews, (2) Frances Patterson; Ruth b. 1784; Phoebe b. 1786; Anne b. 1795; Lettice b. 1797.

National Society of the Sons of the American Revolution - Revolutionary War Graves Register; Compiled and Edited by Clovis H. Brakebill, Published by db Publications, Dallas, TX, 1993. p.13.
Andrews, Arthur: 1753-1834; Hopewell Cem; Lieutenant; Ruth Douglas, Ann Cooper.

Monument in Hopewell Cemetery, Lebanon, Boone Co., IN
Inscription across top of tombstone –   Inscription in center of stone -
ARTHUR ANDREWS   1776
REVOLUTIONARY SOLDIER

AYER (AYRES), THOMAS

Patriot: Thomas Ayer
Birth: 31 Aug 1755   Somerset Co., NJ
Married Spouse 1: Mary X (b. 1777) in PA
Service state(s): NJ & NY
Service description: Capts. Jackson Smith, Faulkner, Reeder;
                        Cols. Lamb, Pawling
Rank: Private, Artificer
Proof of Service: Pension application S17245
Pension application No.: S17245
Residences: NY; NJ; OH 25 yrs; Posey Twp, Switzerland Co., IN
Died: 28 Jan 1844 Switzerland Co., IN
Buried: "Old Yard", Patriot, Switzerland Co., IN
DAR Ancestor No.: A004145

Pension Application Abstracted from National Archives microfilm Series 805, Roll 34, File S17245; Switzerland County, Indiana Probate Record Book Vol. A, Mar 1827-Nov 1834; p. 320.
Pension abstract for – Thomas Ayers   Service state(s): NJ, NY
Alternate spelling(s): Thomas Ayre
Date: 7 Sep 1832
County of: Switzerland   State of: Indiana
Declaration made before a Judge at applicant's home. He was unable to attend court, in consequence of Bodily Infirmity caused by general debility.
Age: 77   Record of age: None
Where and year born: Somerset Co., NJ 3 Aug 1755
Residence when he entered service: Sussex Co., NJ
Residence(s) since the war: Sussex Co., NJ, Pennsylvania about 5 years, to Cincinnati, OH for about 25 years and no more, since then in Switzerland Co.
Residence now: Posey Twp., Switzerland Co., IN
He was Drafted, and he Enlisted, and in 1780 he served as a Substitute for Robert Brooks.
Statement of service – was with General Lafayette, Gen. Poor was buried while with Lafayette; General Wellington; General Wayne; General Dickinson.

Period	Duration	Names of General and Field Officers
1776	2 mos.	Capt. Countryman - NJ
1777	1 mos.	Capt. Keykendall - NJ
1777 or 1778	1 mos.	Capt. Westfall - NJ
1778	1 mos.	Capt. Keykendall - NJ
1778	1 mos.	Capt. Shaver or Sheafer (a miller) - NJ
1779	1 mos.	Capt. Keykendall - NJ
1780	3 mos.	Capt. Gano – NY Militia (enlisted at Goshen, NY)
1781	9 mos.	Capt. Haskins - NJ
1782	6 mos.	Capt. Bunnell - NJ

Battles: None specified in application.
Discharge received: Yes

Signed by: Gen. Dickinson
What became of it?: Lost due to age
Statement is supported by – Traditional evidence
Person now living who can testify to service: Knows of no one.
Clergyman: George A. Dugan, residing in Dearborn Co., IN; Aribert Gazley resident of Switzerland Co. signed Certificate.
Persons in neighborhood who certify character: Aribert Gazley, Bela Heanick, Dennis Quigley, Samuel Jack. Colin McNutt, etc. etc.
Family members were not listed in this application.

Revolutionary Soldiers of Switzerland County; Copied by Mary Hill, John Paul Chapter-Daughters of the American Revolution, January, 1958; http://www.ingenweb.org/inswitzerland/switzrevsoldiers.html- Viewed June 2012.
AYRES, THOMAS
Switzerland County, Indiana   Pension Claim S.17245
Born Aug. 31, 1755, Somerset Co. N.J. Entered service from Somerset Co. N.J., 2 months private under Capt. Countrymon; 1777, 1 month private under Capt. Key Kendall; 1778, 1 month under L. Westfall; 1778 - 1779, 1 month under Capt. Key Kendall; 1778, 1 month under Capt. Sheaver; 1779, 1 month under Capt. Key Kendall; 1780, 1 month under Capt. Kane; 1721, 1 month under Capt. Harkness, 1782, 1 month under Capt. Bunnell.
Lived at Patriot, Posey twp. Probably buried there.
Married after Revolution in Penn. and continued to live in Penn. for 5 years.
Lived in Ohio 25 years and then moved to Indiana.

Roster of Soldiers and Patriots of the American Revolution Buried in Indiana, Vol. I; compiled by Mrs. Roscoe C. O'Byrne.; Indiana Daughters of the American Revolution, 1981; p.*1981;* p.47.
AYRES (AYERS), THOMAS   Switzerland County
Born – Aug. 31, 1755, Somerset Co., N.J.
Service – Entered from Sussex Co., N.J., 1776, 2 mos. Pri. under Capt. Countrymon; 1777, 1 mo. Pri. under Capt. Key Kendall; 1778, 1 mo. under L. Westfall; 1778-79, 1 mo. under Capt. Key Kendall; 1778, 1 mo. under Capt. Sheaver; 1779, 1 mo. under Capt. Key Kendall; 1780, 1 mo. under Capt. Kane; 1781, 1 mo. under Capt. Harkness; 1782, 1 mo. under Capt. Bunnell.
Proof – Pension claim S17245. Lived at Patriot, Posey Twp., and is probably buried there.
Married – After the Rev. in Penn., and continued to live in Penn. 5 yrs. Lived in Ohio 25 yrs., then moved to Indiana.

American Militia in the Frontier Wars, 1790-1796; by Murtie June Clark; Genealogical Publishing Co., Inc., 1990. p. 134
Muster Roll, Detachment of Infantry under the Command of Ensign James Kenney in the Green Regiment of Washington District Militia, Commander Daniel Kennedy, Esquire, Protecting the Frontiers, southwest Territory, for the Period Nov 1 to Nov 30, 1794.

Nr	Rank	Name	Remarks
6	Private	Akers, Thomas	-

Author's note: The Southwest Territory, was an organized incorporated territory of the United States that existed from May 26, 1790, until June 1, 1796, when it was admitted as the State of Tennessee.

Register of Certificates Issued by John Pierce, Esquire, Paymaster General and Commissioner of Army Accounts for the United States, to Officers and Soldiers of the Continental Army Under Act of July 4, 1783; Originally Published as Senate Documents, Vol.9, No. 988, 63rd Congress, 3d Session, Washington, 1915; Seventeenth report of the National Society of the Daughters of the American Revolution; Genealogical Publishing Co., Inc, Baltimore, MD, 1984. p. 24. Men listed in this volume with the same name.

No. of Certificate	To whom issued	Amount
85016	Ayers, Thomas	80.00
87398	Ayers, Thomas	80.00

History of Switzerland County Indiana 1885; Reproduced by the Switzerland County Historical Society, Vevay, Indiana, 1999. The portion of the book relating to Switzerland County in the 1885 printing of the "History of Dearborn, Ohio, and Switzerland Counties, Indiana". p. 1173.

"Thomas Ayres, a Revolutionary veteran, is held in vivid remembrance as a teacher who regularly took his nap each afternoon while his pupils were supposed to be preparing their lessons, but in reality were amusing themselves by catching flies and tossing them into his open mouth. His institution was located above the creek where William Lukie now lives. This was in 1829."

The Vevay Reveille-Enterprise; Vol. 122, No. 37, 15 Sep 1938, p. 1, col. 4-5.
Roster of Revolutionary Soldiers Who Resided in Switzerland County
By Mrs. Effa M. Danner

THOMAS AYERS – Veterans Administration, Washington, D.C. He was the son of Peter Ayers, born August 3, 1758 in Somerset County, New Jersey. He enlisted in Sussex County, N.J. for 2 months under Capt. Countryman. He re-enlisted for one or two months continuously and was discharged in 1782. He was pensioned 1822, No. S17245. He was married in Pennsylvania, family not mentioned. He was a tanner by trade and while living in Patriot he taught school in his cabin near the present school building.

It is supposed he lies in an unmarked grave in the "Old Yard" at Patriot. His name is not listed in the 1840 U.S. Military Census so he died before that date.

BASSETT, JOSEPH

Patriot: Joseph Bassett
Birth: 1759   MA   (DAR records indicate 1 Jan 1760)
Married Spouse 1: 1783   Lydia Jones
Married Spouse 2: 30 Sep 1806, Jefferson Co., OH   Mary Milligan
(b. 1776 MD d. Jun 1852)

Service state(s): MA
Service description: Capts. Perry & Callender;
   Cols. Sergeant, Crane; Cont. Artillery
Rank: Private
Proof of Service: Pension application S35770
Pension application No.: S35770
Residences: Taunton, Bristol Co., MA (Enlisted)
Died: 8 Sep 1822   Switzerland Co., IN
Buried: Pleasant Twp. Cemetery, Bennington, Switzerland Co., IN
DAR Ancestor No.: A007250

Ohio Marriage; Jefferson County; 13 Sep 1806   - Spouse 2, Mary Milligan
N° 227 . . . . .Robert Moodey & Grant
   It is hereby certified that Marriage was Solemnized by one Jas
   Snodgrass a Minister of the Gospel on the 11th of September 1806
   between Robert Moody & Jean Grant each of the County of Jefferson,
   State of Ohio on a License granted them by
   The Clerk of the Court of sd County...   By me
N°228 . Also between Joseph Bassett & Polly Milligan }   Jas. Snodgrass
on the thirteenth of September 1806 on a License, each of the County of Jefferson
& State of Ohio
   Rec'd and duly Recorded the 10th day of December Anna
   Domini 1806
   Jn. Ward (Clerk)

*Pension Application Abstracted from National Archives microfilm Series 805,
Roll 60, File S35770*
Pension abstract for – Joseph Bassett   Service state(s): MA
Continental
Date: 13 Sep 1821
County of: Switzerland   State of: Indiana
Declaration made before a Court.
Age: about 62
Residence when he entered service: Taunton, Bristol Co., MA
Residence now: Switzerland Co., IN
Volunteer or Drafted or Substitute
Statement of service-

Period	Duration	Names of General and Field Officers
Spring 1776	1 year	Capt. Perry, Col. Sergeant – MA Continental Line
	3 years	Capt. Perkins company, Col. Crane's

regiment, Gen. Knox brigade; & Capt. Callendar.
Battles: Brandywine, Monmouth, Rhode Island
Discharge received: At Morristown, NJ from Maj. Shaw aide to Gen. Knox
Wife: Mary   Wife's age: abt. 45
Names and ages of children: Ebenezer 24 yrs., Polly 11 yrs., Ard 7 yrs.
Occupation: Farming

Switzerland County, Indiana Civil Order Book 4, 1820 – 1823; pg. 278.
Sept. 12, 1821
Joseph Bassett, Revolutionary soldier---$40.00; and *Switzerland County, Indiana Civil Order Book 4, 1820 – 1823*; pg. 442 June 1822 Joseph Bassett came to court, Sept. 13, 1821 and applied for pension---value of property, $40.00; still a resident of this county.

Switzerland County, Indiana, Probate Order Book 1, Nov. 1814 – Sept. 1824, pp. 210-220, 248-252, and *Switzerland County, Indiana, Probate Order Book 2, 1831-1837, p. 42*
Abstract of will and/or administration for: Ebenezer Bassett, deceased of
                                              Pleasant Township
State & county where recorded: Switzerland Co., Indiana
Book/volume where recorded: Probate Order Book 1, Nov. 1814-Sept. 1824; Probate Order Book 2, 1831-1837.
Date entered in probate: 22 Sep AD 1823
Name of administrator(s): William C. Mitchell
Appraisers: Clark Jakeways, Arthur Andrews, Levi Orum.
Bonded by: William C. Mitchell with Zermeon Slawson and William Richards.
Amount of bond: $1,200.00
Date of final return: 5 Jan 1832 - estate settled

Abstract of Final Payment Voucher; General Services Administration, Washington, DC
NAME   Bassett, Joseph
AGENCY OF PAYMENT   Indiana
DATE OF ACT   1818
DATE OF PAYMENT   3rd Qr. 1823
DATE OF DEATH   Sept 8, 1822
GENERAL SERVICES ADMINISTRATION
National Archives and Records Service
GSA-WASH DC 54-4891

Massachusetts Soldiers and Sailors of the Revolutionary War, A Compilation from the Archives; prepared and published by the Secretary of the Commonwealth in accordance with Chapter 100, Resolves of 1891, Vol. I; Wright & Potter Printing co., State Printers, Boston, MA, 1904. p. 760.
BASSETT, Joseph. Private, Capt. James Perry's co., 16th regt.; enlisted Dec. 13, 1775 (service not given).
&

BASSETT, Joseph. Raynham. Matross, Capt. John Ca Callender's co., Col. Crane's (Artillery) regt.; Continental Army pay accounts for service from April 10, 1777, to Dec. 31, 1779; also, Capt. William Perkins's co., Col. Crane's regt.; muster rolls for Sept.-Dec., 1777; reported sick in hospital at Trenton; also, Lient. John Callender's co., Col. Crane's regt.; muster rolls for Nov., 1778, and April, 1779 dated Providence; reported on command at Tiverton in April, 1779; also, Capt. Slewman's co., Col. Crane's regt.; Continental Army pay accounts for service from Jan. 1, 1780, to April 10, 1780.

Revolutionary Soldiers of Switzerland County; Copied by Mary Hill, John Paul Chapter-Daughters of the American Revolution; January, 1958; http://www.ingenweb.org/inswitzerland/switzrevsoldiers.html- Viewed June 2012.
BASSETT, JOSEPH   Pension S. F. 355770
Born in 1760, Raynham, Mass. Enlisted in spring of 1776 for 1 year, under Capt. Perry in Col. Sargeant's Reg. Mass Line, Cont'l Establishment. Enlisted within 2 or 3 months after his term expired in Capt. Perkins Co. Col. Cranes's Regt. in Gen Knox's Brigade of artillery on the Cont'l Establishment for 3 years. Discharged at Morristown, N. J. under Capt. Calendear from the hands of Major Shaw; aid to Gen Knox. Was in Brandywine, Monmouth and Rhode Island. Died Sept. 8, 1822. Probably buried in Pleasant twp. near Bennington.
He married Mary _____.
Children; Ebenezer m Elizabeth Mapes
Mary m 1823 David Blodgett (Roster of Soldiers and Patriots of the American Revolution Buried in Indiana; 1938; p. 53)
D.A.R. Lineage, Vol. 32 pg. 249 gives a wife Lydia Jones and son, Daniel
Switz. Co. Records: Civil Order bk. A 1811 – 1824; pgs. 177 - 202 - 220
Ebenezer Bassett, adm of Joseph Bassett Jan. 28, 1823. Inventory Feb. 1, 1823
Oct. 20, 1823 Adm. Wm. Hunter; bondsman, Wm. C. Mitchell & William Cotton
Ebenezer Bassett; pgs. 219, 248, 249, 250, 251, 251, 252, 250
Wm. C. Mitchell signs bond Sept. 25, 1823 W. C. Mitchell appraises property of Eben. Bassett
List of property. Oct. 7, 1823, signed by John Burns

Roster of Soldiers and Patriots of the American Revolution Buried in Indiana, Vol. I; compiled by Mrs. Roscoe C. O'Byrne.; Indiana Daughters of the American Revolution, 1981; p.52.
BASSETT, JOSEPH   Switzerland County
Born – 1760, Raynham, Mass.
Service – Enlisted in spring of 1776 for 1 yr. under Capt. Perry in Col. Sargeant's Regt. Mass Line, Cont'l. Establishment. Enlisted within 2 or 3 mos. after this term expired in Capt. Perkins CO., Col. Crane's Regt. in Gen Knox's Brigade of artillery on the Cont'l Establishment for 3 yrs. Discharged at Morristown, N.J., under Capt. Calendar from the hands of Maj. Shaw; aid to Gen. Knox. Was in Brandywine, Monmouth, and Rhode Island.
Proof – Pension claim S. F. 35770.
Died – Sept. 8, 1822. Probably buried in Pleasant Twp., near Bennington.
Married – Mary ____.

Ch. Ebenezer, m. Elizabeth Mapes; Mary, m. 1823 David Blodgett; Ard. D.A.R. Lineage, vol. 32, p. 249, gives wife, Lydia Jones and son, Daniel.
Collected by Mrs. A. V. Danner, Vevay, Indiana

Abstract of Graves of Revolutionary Patriots (4 volumes); by Patricia Law Hatcher; Pioneer Heritage Press, Dallas, TX, 1987. Vol. 1, p. 59.
This is an abstract and an index to information reported to the Daughters of the American Revolution and published in their annual reports to the Smithsonian Institution, printed as Senate Documents (1900-1974) and published annually in the DAR magazine (1978-1987).
Published 1956, Serial set 11999, Volume 8.
BASSETT, Joseph   Pleasant Twp. Cem, Benington IN

The Vevay Reveille-Enterprise; Vol. 122, No. 37, 15 Sep 1938, p. 1, col. 5.
Roster of Revolutionary Soldiers Who Resided in Switzerland County
By Mrs. Effa M. Danner
JOSEPH BASSETT - Born 1766 at Raynham, Mass. Enlisted in 1776, one year. Capt. Perry, Col. Sargent's regiment Mass Line 1777; enlisted in Capt. Perkins Co., Col. Crane's regiment, in General Knox brigade of artillery in Continental Establishment for three years. Discharged at Morristown, New Jersey under Capt. Calender, hand of Major Shaw, aid of General Knox. He was in the battles of Brandywine, Monmouth, and Long Island. Pensioned No. 35770. Died September 8, 1822. Wife Mary, Children, Ebenezer, Polly and Ord. Probate Court, Switzerland County Estate p. 166, Wm. Keenad, 1822.
Early marriages Switzerland Co., Ebenezer Bassett to Elizabeth Mapes, February 26, 1822. Mary Bassett to David Blodgett, February 4, 1823. Lydia Ann Bassett to Henry Drury, December 29, 1846. Ebenezer Bassett, Estate, January 1832, Zennas Sisson appointed guardian of Lydia Bassett. Joseph Bassett resided in Pleasant Township near Bennington.
Historical reference – major Gen. Henry Knox was the most noted artillery man in the Rev. He was at Princeton, Brandywine, Germantown and Monmouth where he directed the artillery with wonderful effect and his artillery spent the winter at Valley forge. He continued all through the war and Knox's artillery was in the heaviest cannonading to thee last at Yorktown. (Electric Hist. U.S., Pg. 178 note).

Undocumented family information:
He married (1) Lydia Jones (2) Elizabeth Taylor (3) Mary Milligan who was mother of Mary Milligan Bassett, born in 1809. Bassett lived in Jefferson Co IN when his daughter Mary Milligan Bassett was born. He died 5 Nov 1822 in Vevay, Switzerland Co., IN.

BLADES, JOHN LEVY

John Levy Blades died in 1784 in Maryland. His wife Sarah and their son Zadock Blades, contributed to the beginning of Switzerland County. Sarah later married William Lancaster, another Revolutionary soldier.

Patriot: John Levy Blades
Birth: c. 1756   Somerset Co., MD
Married Spouse 1: 17 Feb 1776, Worcester Co., MD   Sarah X
(b. 1753 MD d. 18 Feb 1848 IN) After the death of John she married William Lancaster (see his record)
Service state(s): MD
Service description: Col. Gunbey, Howard's 2nd Regiment; Capts. Deshield, Vance; Prisoner
Rank: Private; Patriotic Service
Proof of Service: Pension application W9502
Pension application No.: W9502
Residences: Worcester Co., MD
Died: 1 Jan 1784   Worcester Co., MD
Buried: Worcester Co., MD
DAR Ancestor No.: A124293

National Archives microfilm Series 805, Roll 94, File W9502.
Pension Application
A handwritten note on the cover of this file says "This woman's last husband was pensioned. See William Lancaster, VA, S16912."
Letter from War Dept. in Pension File – William Lancaster   S.16912
Mrs. W. A. Barber   John Levy Blades
Madison, Indiana   W.9502
   BA-J/AWF

Dear Madame:
   Reference is made to your letter in which you request the Revolutionary War record of William Lancaster of Switzerland County, Indiana.
   The record of William Lancaster follows as found in pension claim, B.16912, based upon his service in the Revolutionary War. The Revolutionary War record of John Levy Blades is given herein, also, which may be of interest to you, as William Lancaster married his widow.
   William Lancaster was born November 17, 1745 in Hanover County, Virginia; he was christened in King William County, Virginia. The names of his parents were not given.
   While residing in Orange County, Virginia, William Lancaster enlisted, January 20, 1779, served two months as private in Captain William Buckner's company, Colonel Harvey's Virginia regiment and guarded the British and Hessian prisoners at Albemarle Barracks. He enlisted in 1780, served ninety days in Captain Benjamin Johnson's company, under Major Nathaniel Welsh. He enlisted sometime in July of August, 1781, served four months under Abner Porter, commissary, and was engaged in collecting cattle for the army.

He moved about fifteen years after the Revolution from Orange County, Virginia, to Kentucky and lived there about twenty-eight years, then moved to Indiana.

The soldier, William Lancaster, was allowed pension on his application executed, November 12, 1832, at which time he was living in Switzerland County, Indiana.

....

John Levy Blades – W.9502

The date which follow were obtained from pension claim, W.9502, based upon the service of John Levy Blades in the Revolutionary War.

The date and place of birth of this soldier are not shown, nor are the names of his parents given. He was named "after his uncle" John Levy.

John Levy Blades of Worcester County, Maryland, enlisted March 10, 1777, served as a private in Captains DeShields' and Vance's companies, and in Colonels Gunbey's and John E. Howard's 2nd Maryland regiment; he was in several battles, was taken prisoner by the British, January 28. 1780 and was discharged November 15, 1783. It was not stated how he was released from prison.

John Levy Blades married, January 17, or February 17, 1776 in either Somerset or Worcester County, Maryland, Sarah; her maiden name is not given, nor is it stated when and where she was born.

He died in January of February, 1784 in Worcester County, Maryland.

Their son, Zadock Blades, was born in the month of May, 1777. He, with his widowed mother, Sarah Blades, moved to Kentucky and lived in Mason and Bracken Counties.

The widow, Sarah Blades, married September 11, 1813 in Bracken County, Kentucky, William Lancaster. He was a soldier in the Revolution and a pensioner, and died November 4, 1843 in Switzerland County, Indiana. The said Sarah was his second wife.

Sarah Lancaster was allowed pension, on account of the service of her husband, John Levy Blades, on her application executed June 26, 1845, then living in Craig Township, Switzerland County, Indiana, aged ninety years.

In 1844, Catherine, the wife of Mallory Lancaster (son of William Lancaster by his first wife, name of this wife not given) was a resident of Switzerland, County, Indiana.

William and Catherine J. Lancaster were of Switzerland County, Indiana in 1845; it is not stated that they were related to each other or to the soldier, William Lancaster.

Very truly yours,

D. HILLER
Executive Assistant
To the Administrator

Maryland Revolutionary Records; Harry Wright Newman; Tuttle Publishing, Rutland, VT, 1928. p.10.
Revolutionary Pensioners
Blades, John L.   Pvt.   Maryland Line

The Maryland Militia in the Revolutionary War; by S. Eugene Clements and F. Edward Wright; Published by Family Line Publications, Westminster, MD 21157, 1987. p. 220.
Somerset County – Princess Anne Battalion
1780/Pocomoke Company
John Blades (in list)

Muster Rolls and other records of service of Maryland Troops in the American Revolution; Archives of Maryland, reprinted with permission by Genealogical Publishing Co., Inc., Baltimore, 1972.

p. 293.
A Roll of John Eccleston's Company in the 2nd Maryland Regiment. Commanded by Col. Thomas Price. John Eccleston, Capt.; John Gale 1 Lieut; John Rodd, Ensign.
John Blades in included in the list of privates.

p. 353.
Return of the Names Commissioned and Non Commissioned Officers and Privates of the 2nd Company wch. have been in the Service from 1st Aug., Year '80 to the 1st Jan., '81.
John Blades in included in the list of privates.

p. 385
A List of Recruits and Drafts belonging to Caroline County. 13th Aug., 1781 Drafts to the 10th Dec. next.
Those that are excused are marked.
In the list – John Blades, (sick)

p. 387
Talbot County. August 30th, 1781.
A List of Person draughted to raise two Battalions of Militia to reinforce the American Army, to serve 'till the 10th of December, 1781.
John Blades included in this list.

p. 394
The following members of the 3rd, 4th and 5th Maryland Regiments received from Robert Denny, in Bills of Credit and in Specie pay due them for the present Campaign. 3rd Regt., Aug. 28th, 1781.
4th Company, 3rd Regiment.
John Blades in list of privates.

p. 462
4 Co., 4 B. Capt. George, Richard, Bird. Lt. john Brevet. Ensign Thos. A. Dyson.

Name and Rank		When Commenced	When Left Service and the Reasons.	Remarks
John Blades	P.	1 Jan '82	-	-

p. 487
Pay Roll of the Maryland Line for 1783.
Service is from Jan 1, to Nov 15, 1783.

Names and Rank		When Left Service and the Reasons	Remarks
John Blades	P.	-	-

p. 524
Records of Maryland Troops in the Continental Service

Rank	Names	Served Between 1 Aug 80 1 Jan 82	Served between 1 Jan '82 1 Jan '83	Served between 1 Jan 83 15 Nov 83	Served between 15 Nov 83 10 July 84
Private	John Blades	"	"	"	

Revolutionary War Bounty Land Grants Awarded by State Governments; Lloyd DeWitt Bockstruck; Genealogical Publishing co., IN, Baltimore, MD, 1996. p.45.
Blades, John. Md. Private – 50 acres

Register of Certificates Issued by John Pierce, Esquire, Paymaster General and Commissioner of Army Accounts for the United States, to Officers and Soldiers of the Continental Army Under Act of July 4, 1783; Originally Published as Senate Documents, Vol.9, No. 988, 63rd Congress, 3d Session, Washington, 1915; Seventeenth report of the National Society of the Daughters of the American Revolution; Genealogical Publishing Co., Inc, Baltimore, MD, 1984. p. 51.
Men listed in this volume with the same name.

No. of Certificate	To whom issued	Amount
81115	Blades, John	43.30
81945	Blades, John	80.00
85053	Blades, John	80.00
87296	Blades, John	80.00

Revolutionary Solders of Switzerland County; Copied by Mary Hill, John Paul Chapter-Daughters of the American Revolution; January, 1958;
http://www.ingenweb.org/inswitzerland/switzrevsoldiers.html- Viewed June 2012.
BLADES, JOHN LEVY   W.9502
Widow applied in Switzerland Co.
The date & place of birth of this soldier are not shown, nor the names of his parents given. He was named after his uncle John Levy.
March 10, 1777 ,John Levy Blades of Worchester Co. Maryland, enlisted, served as private in Captain De Shield's & Vance's companies, and in Col. Gunby's & John E. Howard's 2d Maryland regiment; he was in several battles, was taken prisoner by the British, Jan. 28, 1780. It was not stated how he was released from prison.
Discharged, Nov. 15, 1783. It.
Married: Jan. 17, or Feb. 17, 1776 Sarah _____, in Somerset or Worchester Co. Md.
Children: Zadock Blades, was born in the month of May, 1777. He with his widowed mother, Sarah Blades, moved to Kentucky and lived in Mason and Bracken Counties.
Died: Jan. or Feb. 1784 in Worchester Co. Md.
The widow, Sarah Blades, married September 11, 1813 in Bracken Co. Ky. William Lancaster. [See record for William Lancaster] He was a Rev. soldier & pensioner, and died Nov. 4, 1843 in Switzerland Co. Ind. Said Sarah was his 2d

wife. She was allowed pension, on account of her husband, John Levy Blades, on application executed June 26, 1845, then living in Craig twp. Switz. Co. Ind. aged 90 years.
In 1844, Catherine, wife of Mallory Lancaster (son of Wm. by his 1st. wife, name of wife not given) was a resident of Switzerland Co. William and Catherine J. Lancaster were of Switz. Co. Ind. were of Switz. Co. Ind. in 1845; it is not stated that they were related to each other or to the soldier.

Revolutionary Soldiers Buried in Indiana A Supplement; 485 Names Not Listed in the Roster of Soldiers and Patriots of the American Revolution Buried in Indiana (1938) nor in Revolutionary Soldiers Buried in Indiana (1949); Margaret E. Waters; Indianapolis, 1954. p.131.
BLADES, JOHN LEVY & SARAH   Switzerland
He d. Jan.-Feb. 1784, Worcester Co. Md. Pens. W.9502 Md. She m. (2) William Lancaster (Pens. S.16912 Va.) who d. 11-4-1843 ("Roster—" p. 226.)

Revolutionary Soldiers Buried in Indiana (1949) With Supplement (1954) Two Volumes in One; Margaret R. Waters; Genealogical Publishing Company, Baltimore, MD, 1970. p. 140, 141.
p. 140 - In list of spouses buried in Indiana for Switzerland Co. – Blades, Sarah- w. Blades, John Levy & Lancaster, William.
p. 141 – In list of "Soldiers Who Died in Other States" (husbands of widows on list of spouses) – Maryland – Blades, John Levy.

BOISSEAUX, JEAN BAPTISTE
aka Bosso, Boseau, Boso

Patriot: Jean Baptiste (John) Boisseaux
Birth: 1756   France
Married Spouse 1: c. 1786   Barbara Frick (b. 1761 Ft. Pitt, PA (DAR)
    or b. 1770 Germany (1860 census), d. 1866 Switzerland Co., IN)
Service state(s): Unknown
Service description: Unknown
Rank: Unknown
Proof of Service:
Pension application No.: None – served under Lafayette
Residences: Came with Lafayette; Ft. Pitt, PA; WV; Switzerland Co., IN.
Died: 1835   Switzerland Co., IN
Buried: Unknown
DAR Ancestor No.: A011802 - Future applicants must prove correct service.
Lineage for these children has been proven: Charles, John.
Family researchers, to date, have not found direct evidence of his service.

Les Combattants Francais de la Guerre Americaine (1778-1783); *France, du Ministere des Affaires Etrangeres; Genealogical Publishing Co., Baltimore, MD, 1969.*
This is a register of the men (not a complete listing of individuals) who came from France to serve in the American Revolution. There are five citations for men with his name having various surname spellings (pages 53, 66, 80, 175, 343. The soldier listed on page 343 died in the conflict in Savannah (not shown here). Following are the other four citations, in page number order. According to family tradition he was born near Paris, France. He may not have been living there when he enlisted. Tradition also says he was at the battle of Yorktown. Crew members from all of the following ships served at or near Yorktown.
p. 53.
French: L'Artésien. (1778-1781) M. De Peynier, Capitaine de vaisseau, Commandant; Etat – Major.
English: The Artesian [ship]. (1778-1781) Mr. De Peynier, Navy Captain, Commander; State – Major.
Commander   DePeynier
Lieutenants de vasseau [Lieutenant of Navy] Vicomte de Montault; De Villevielle; De la Tournerye; De Chavagnac
Matelots [Sailors] from Libourne - <u>Bossuet (Jean)</u>.
[Libourne is in the Aquitaine region, in southwestern France, northeast of Bordeaux]
p. 66.
French: Le Cesar ou Cezar; M. le Comte de Broves, Chef d'escadre, Commandant;
Jean-Joseph de Rafelis, comte de Broves, Lieutenant general des armees navales du 1 mars 1779, ne au chateau de Borves pres de Frejus le 8 juillet 1715, mort le 12 novembre 1782; Etat – Major.

English: The Cesar or Cezar [ship]; Count of Broves, Chief of Wing Commander; Jean-Joseph de Rafelis, Earl of Broves, Lieutenant General of the armed naval March 1, 1779, not in the castle of Borves near Frejus Jul7 8, 1715, died November 12, 1782; State – Major.
Captaine de vasseau [Naval Captain], DeRaimondie
Lieutenants de vasseau [Lieutenant of Navy] Le Chevalier de Framont de Greze; DeVenet; DeGotho; DeCambray
Matelots [Sailors] - <u>Beaussier (Jean), de la Seyne</u> [Beaussier (John) of Seyne]. [La Seyne is a community in the Provence-Alpes-Côte d'Azur region in southeastern France]
p. 80.
French: L'Annibal; Mm de Ternay, puis de la Motte-Picquet, Chefs d'escadre, Commandants; Etat – Major.
English: The Annibal [ship]; Mr. de Ternay and La Motte-Picquet, Heads of Wing Commanders; State Major.
Chefs d'escadre [Wing Chiefs] Le Chevalier de Ternay; Le Chevalier de la Motte-Piquet
Capitaines de vaisseau [Captains of Navy] De Medine; Le Comte de La Croix.
Lieutenants de vaisseau [Lieutenants of Navy] Granchin de Senneville; De Saint-Felix; Le Large
Hamitton; Duloup; De Rivierre; De Montluc de la Bourdonnaye; De Chavagnac; Marguery
Matelots [Sailors] - <u>Bossuet (Jean), de Marennes.</u>
[Marennes is located in Poitou-Charentes in southwestern France.]
p. 175
French: Le Sagittaire; De janvier 1781 a septembre 1782; M. de Castelanne Majastre, Capitaine de vaisseau, Commandant; Etat-Major
English: Sagittarius [ship]; From January 1781 to September 1782; Mr. Castellanne Majastre, Captain Commander; State Major
Lieutenants de vaisseay [Lieutenants of the Navy] De Montluc de la Bourdonnaye; De Beaurepaire; Des Porcellets.
Matelots [Sailors] - <u>Beausse (Jean), de Bordeaux.</u> [Beausse (Jean), of Bordeaux]. [Bordeaux (Gascon: Bordèu; Basque: Bordele) is a port city on the Garonne River in the Gironde department in southwestern France.]

<u>U.S. Department of Interior, Bureau of Land Management, General Land Office Records; Land Patent Search</u> – accessed 27 June 2012.
BOISSEAU, JOHN
Accession Nr. CV-0059-475; Document Type – Credit Volume Patent; Issue Date 10/5/1824; Cancelled – No
Names On Document – Droz; Frederick; Boisseau, John; Land Office – Cincinnati; Authority – April 24, 1820 – Sale-Cash Entry (3 Stat. 566); General Remarks – Patent Record Imperfect
Document Nr – 626; Total Acres – 160.00
Land Descriptions: State – IN; Meridian – 1st PM; Twp-Rng – 002N-002W; Aliquots – SE1/4; Section 28; County - Switzerland
&

Accession Nr, CV-0067-023; Document Type – Credit Volume Patent; State – Indiana; Issue Date – 2/18/1826; Cancelled - No
Names On Document – Agniel; Camille Boisseau, John; Land Office – Cincinnati; Authority – April 24, 1820 – Sale-Cash Entry (3 Stat. 566); Document Nr. 1747; Total Acres – 159.60
Land Descriptions: State – IN; Meridian -= 1st PM; Twp-Rng – 001N-002W; Aliquots – SE14; Section – 5; County – Switzerland

Switzerland County, IN, Will Book Vol. 1, 3 Jan 1823-10 Nov 1847, p. 232.
Abstract of will and/or administration for: John Boisseaux
Probate of estate is not indexed in Probate Order Book 2.
State & county where recorded: Switzerland Co., Indiana
State & county where will was made: Jefferson Twp., Switzerland Co., IN
Book/volume where recorded: Will Book 1.
Date will made: 25 November 1820
Date entered in probate: 27 March 1835
Witnesses: William C. Keen, Rawleigh Day
Names of heirs and others mentioned in will and relationship if shown: Beloved wife Barbary Boisseaux.

Indiana Land Entries Vol. 1 Cincinnati District, 1801-1840; *Margaret R. Waters; Originally Published Indianapolis 1948, Second Reprint 1979 by The Bookmark, P.O. Box 74, Knightstown, In 46148. p. 40, 42.*
CINCINNATI LAND DISTRICT – VOL. 1.
Page 38. Twp 1 North, Range 2 W of 1st Principle Meridian SWITZERLAND
John Boisseau – SE ¼ - S5; 5-27-1814.
and-
Page 38. Twp 1 North, Range 2 W of 1st Principle Meridian SWITZERLAND
James Burke NW ¼ - S6; 7-14-1814. Relinquished W ½ to John B. Bosseau and Mary Peters, 2-26-1831.
and-
Page 40, Twp. 2 North, Range 2 W of 1st Principle Meridian SWITZERLAND
John Boisseau – SE ¼ S28; 6-6-1817.
-- Note: The tract books for the land offices in Indiana are deposited in the office of the Auditor of State, Indianapolis. They and are in the custody of the State Land clerk. --

Early Settlers of Indiana's "GORE" 1803-1820; *Compiled and Edited by Shirley Keller Mikesell; Heritage Books, Inc., 1995. p. 184.*
Switzerland County - Township 1, Range 2W
Section 5 – John Boisseau – 1814 – pg. 4.

1820 U.S. Census, Indiana, Switzerland, Posey, Series: M33 Roll: 14 Page: 262
John Boisseaux 45 and up; others in household 1 male 101-6, 1 female 45 and up.

1860 U.S. Census, Indiana, Switzerland Co., Jefferson Twp., Series: M653 Roll: 299 Page: 272, Family 910. Barbary Bosso, age 90, Female, Place of Birth Germany

Revolutionary Soldiers of Switzerland County; Copied by Mary Hill, John Paul Chapter-Daughters of the American Revolution; January, 1958; http://www.ingenweb.org/inswitzerland/switzrevsoldiers.html- Viewed June, 2012.

JEAN BAPTISTE BOISSEAU Was a Frenchman, who came to the United States to fight in the revolutionary war. He was under the leadership of Lafayette, and fought at Yorktown and was a witness to the surrender of Cornwallis at Yorktown. He had also seen service At Brandywine and Germantown.

He stayed in the United States and married a woman of German Decent Barbara Frick.

They finally came to Switzerland County Indiana where they owned property and his will was probated in about 1835. they had a farm on Plum Creek and although it has never been proved he may be buried on that property. This is from the Boso Book by James L. Boso on which I helped with the research in Switzerland county.

He is approved for membership in DAR.

Jo Orem Green, jogreen@orvcomm.com

I want to Thank Jo Orem Green for sending in this information, I checked the census records and Jean Boisseaux is listed in the 1820 & 1830 census in Switzerland County. The name is spelled creatively by the census taker and is Americanized by the first name Jean being listed as John.

Sheila

Parkersburg News, Parkersburg, WV, Feb.1,1959

" The progenitor of the Boso family in America was a Frenchman, Jean Baptiste Boisseaux. The American name is John Bates Boso.

"This man, John Boso, was born and reared in a small village on the outskirts of Paris, France. The American colonies had resolved upon their independence and during their struggle in the Revolutionary war, our patriot and statesman, Benjamin Franklin, was sent to France to secure that country's help. Through the wisdom and untiring efforts of Franklin, France became our ally in the year of 1778.

"The French army that came to the aid of the colonies was under the leadership of a young Frenchman named Lafayette and in his army was a young and tender soldier named Jean Baptiste Boisseaux. This soldier saw service at Brandywine and Germantown and witnessed the surrender of Cornwallis at Yorktown on October 19, 1781.

"At the close of the conflict the French army returned to their native land, but a few, John Boisseaux among them, remained to become citizens of western Pennsylvania. At, or near Pittsburgh he married an American lady of German decent, whose name was Barbra Frick.

"John Boisseaux and his family left Fort Pitt by boat and floated down the Ohio river to Fort Belleville. The trip was thrilling and exciting and was fraught with great danger all along the way.

"Indians caused them much trouble from the Little Kanawah river on down the Ohio, the warlike Indians struck with increasing fury and the Boisseaux family was forced to pole their flatboat to the opposite shore. At the mouth of the Little Hocking River they tied fast and there remained until the Indian menace was over. During the hectic days that they spent at the mouth of this river their son Charles was born. They then dropped down the river to the fort at Belleville and took refuge there. This was the year of 1792.

"They were the parents of six children, John, Joseph, Charles, Jacob, Mary and Wickware. Joe married a girl in Indiana, several boys and girls were born to them and they remained in that state, never coming to West Virginia to live. John Boso, grandfather of Green and Sam, married a Miss Jensey Coleman, she was of the old pioneer Coleman family.

"John Boisseaux in 1797, with his family, settled on the South Fork of Lee Creek, one and a half miles back of Belleville, West Virginia, near Buckley Chapel Church. He operated a keel boat and flat boat and farmed around Belleville, he also worked with William Anderson who owned and operated a grist mill on Lee Creek. When Charlie, the boy born on the journey down the river from Pittsburgh, was ten years of age he went with his father and William Anderson to Cincinnati with a keel boat load of products to sell. At that time Cincinnati was only a village of fifty houses, some of log and some frame. Later John Boisseaux moved to Switzerland County, Indiana".

The Swiss Settlement of Switzerland County; by Perrett Dufour; published by the Indiana Historical Commission, Indianapolis, IN, 1925.

p. 83. This article is about the sons of Jean Baptise Boisseau.

About the years 1813, 14, 15, Barges and keel boats were used in transporting produce, Iron, and salt along the Ohio & Mississippi rivers. Joseph Bosseau who came to this place in 1813, together with his brother John were regularly engaged in keel boating.[1] Joseph Bosseau is still living 2-1/2 miles from Vevay, and is in his 84th or 85th year [2] – he Bosseau made one or two trips to New Orleans and back, Several trips to Saint Louis and back – on one of the trips to Saint Louis, he came across on foot by land being six or seven days on the way. He made one trip up the Mississippi river to Prairie du Chein (Chien) with provisions for the garrison stationed there. He also made trips up the Cumberland river to Nashville and up the Tennessee river to the Muscle Shoals – and the Kentucky river to Subletts ferry, to which latter point iron and groceries were taken, and from which tobacco whiskey and bacon were brought on the return trip.

[1] Dufour in his manuscript of 1869 speaks of Joseph Bosseau as 'being at this time 78 years of age, and residing on Bee-Tree Run, 2-1/2 miles from Vevay, and his brother John, being his senior by 5 years, resides in Wood County, West Virginia."

[2] The sentence "Joseph Bosseau....year" is crossed out.

p. 394

"John and Joseph Bosseau are said to be the only survivors of those who were engaged in navigating the western waters in those early days, with Keel boats. "These facts and incidents are here related, as related the writer by 'Uncle Joe' himself, some days since, not for any worth or merit attaching them but with the thought, that perhaps fifty years hence some of those who may then be on the stage of action, may chance to read them and learn what those who preceded them in the Voyage of life had been called upon to do and to suffer that the necessaries of life might be conveyed from one point to another in this now great and prosperous valley of the 'father of Waters', and his numerous tributaries.

"It is said that John Bosseau is to visit this county soon and if so, let any who are curious, to hear from his and his brother Josephs own lips a recital of their trials, hardships, privations, and pleasures too, call and perhaps what is here written of them and much more may be learned." 1869 MS, pp.147-50.

BRAY, JOHN

Patriot: John Bray
Birth: 28 Apr 1761 Hampshire Co., VA
Married Spouse 1: Nancy Morgan
Married Spouse 2: Mrs. Elizabeth X Coonies   (b. 1798/1802, Kentucky;
　　　　　　　　　　　　　　　　　　　　　　d. abt. Jan 1877, Switzerland Co., IN)
Service state(s): VA
Service description: Capt. Wm. Vause, Col. James Woods,
　　　　　　　　　　Gen. Charles Scott, VA Line
Rank: Private
Proof of Service: Pension application W4145
Pension application No.: W4145/BLWT89502-160-55
Residences: Romney, Hampshire Co., VA; Indiana Territory; Switzerland Co, IN
Died: 10 Jun 1832 Switzerland Co., IN
Buried: McKay Cemetery, Craig Twp., Switzerland Co., IN
DAR Ancestor No.: A013894
Child: Samuel Bray (b. 1797 KY d. 23 May 1885 Switzerland Co., IN)

Gallatin County, Kentucky Marriages 1799-1820; Dorothy Merrifield; Cook & McDowell Publications, Owensboro, KY, 1980. p. 3.
Bray, John to Elizabeth Cooney, widow, April 13, 1820. Bond: James Ball. Min. William Morgan.

National Archives microfilm Series 805, Roll 117,
File W4145/BLWT89502-160-55
Letter from War Dept. in Pension File – John Bray

Mrs. E. T. Andres
311 South Mulberry Street
Madison, Indiana
Dear Madame:

　　　　　　　　　　　　　　　　　　　June 14, 1935
　　　　　　　　　　　　　　　　　　　JOHN BRAY
　　　　　　　　　　　　　　　　　　　W.4145
　　　　　　　　　　　　　　　　　　　BA-J/MLB

　　Reference is made to your letter in which you request the record of John Bray (Br.), who received pension for service in the Revolutionary War while residing in Switzerland County, Indiana.
　　The record of John Bray follows as obtained from the papers on file in pension claim, W.4145, based upon his service in the Revolutionary War.
　　The date and place of soldier's birth and names of his parents are not given.
　　John Bray enlisted in September, 1777, in "Romley", evidently meant for Romney, Hampshire County, Virginia, served as a private in Captain William Voss' company, Colonel James Wood's Virginia regiment, was in the battles of Brandywine in which he was wounded, Monmouth and at the taking of Stony Point, also in several small skirmishes, and was discharged after having served three years, the term for which he enlisted.
　　The soldier was allowed pension on his application executed June 20, 1818, at which time he was aged fifty-six years. His application was executed in Switzerland County, Indiana, his place of residence not given.

John Bray married April 15, 1820, at the home of one Jacob Hunter (no relationship to soldier shown), in Gallatin County, Kentucky, Mrs. Elizabeth Coonies, also referred to as Betsey, a widow of that county (the given name of her husband and date of his death no stated). Their marriage was recorded in the County Clerk's Office of said Gallatin County, Kentucky.

In 1821, the soldier was residing in Craig Township, Switzerland County, Indiana. He died in that county June 10, 1832.

John Bray's widow, Elizabeth, married October 4, 1834, Robert Bakes and their marriage was recorded in the office of the County Clerk of Switzerland County, Indiana. Robert Bakes died March 19, 1847.

Said Elizabeth, while a resident of Switzerland County, Indiana, aged fifty-five years, applied October 3, 1853, for pension due her as the former widow of John Bray. Her claim was allowed and she was pensioned under the name of Elizabeth Bray. In 1859, she was still residing in Switzerland County, Indiana, with post office at Vevay, same county. In 1858, her place of residence and post office were the same, Mount Sterling, Switzerland County, Indiana. In 1873, she was living in Jefferson Township, Switzerland County, Indiana, with post office at Vevay which was still her post office in 1874. She did not sign as Elizabeth Bakes but Elizabeth Bray.

The only names designated as children of the soldier, John Bray, were two daughters, Carolina aged two years and Amelia aged three months, in 1821, and Daniel, who in 18?4 made affadavit in soldier's behalf in Switzerland County, Indiana, and referred to one Samuel Bray but did not state his relationship.

In 1870, one John Bakes witnessed the signature by mark of soldier's widow, Elizabeth, in Madison, Indiana, but his relationship to her was not shown.

> Very truly yours,
> A.D. HILLER
> Executive Assistant to the Administrator

Switzerland County, Indiana Civil Order Book 4, 1820 – 1823; pg. 191.
June term 1821
John Bray, Revolutionary soldier & U.S. pensioner---$139.00

Switzerland County, Probate Order Book 2, 1831-1837; pp.70, 89, 99, 110, 123, 138,164, 165, 178, 204, 255, 288, 325, and *Switzerland County, IN, Will Book Vol. 1, 3 Jan 1823-10 Nov 1847, p. 51.*
Abstract of Will and Administration for: JOHN BRAY
State & County where recorded: Switzerland Co., Indiana
Book/Volume where recorded: Probate Order Book No._2 1831-1837; Page No. 89
Date Will made: 14 May 1832
Witnesses to Will: Samuel Culver, Tubman Malcom, Joshua Culver.
Date entered in Probate: 13 Nov 1833
Entered by Samuel Bray who made oath "John Bray late of Switzerland County a Revolutionary Petitioner parted his life on the 10th day of June AD 1832. That at the time of the death of the said John Bray he left Elizabeth Bray his widow who

was his lawful wife. Said John Bray and Elizabeth were married. Said marriage was solemnized in Gallatin County Kentucky on the 13th day of April 1820".
Guardianship:
-13 Nov 1833, Elizabeth Bray filed petition praying court appoint her the Guardian of Nelly Bray, age 11 on the 11th Feb 1832; George Bray, age 9 on the 2nd of April last; Sophia Bray, age 7, on the 22nd of May last. Minors have property which should be saved for them. Court appointed Elizabeth to be Guardian of person and property of the said Sophia, George and Nelly Bray until they shall arrive at the age of 14 years.
-16 Nov 1832, Caroline Bray, age 14, filed petition praying court appoint her mother Elizabeth Bray as her Guardian until she comes of full age. Court appointed Elizabeth to be Guardian of Caroline upon her entering into Bond for $75.00.
-9 Nov 1833, Elizabeth Bray petitions praying court appoint Joseph Malin as Guardian of George W. Bray, her son. Court appointed Joseph Malin as Guardian of person and estate of George W. Bray until he shall arrive at age of 14, upon his entering into Bond in the sum of $150.00. On the same day Elizabeth petitions for Guardianship of Amelia & Sophia Bray, the minor children of John Bray. Court granted Guardianship upon her entering into Bond in the sum of $200.00.
Name of Executor: John Pavy (not dated – after 10 June 1832)
Administration: Date began- not dated   Name of Administrator- John Pavy
Date of Death: (specifically mentioned): 10 June 1832
Bonded by and Amount of Bond:
Guardianship - Elizabeth Bray for Nellie (Amelia), George, Sophia Bray, $200.00.
Guardianship – Elizabeth Bray for Caroline Bray, $50.00
Guardianship – Joseph Malin for George W. Bray, $150.00
Names of Heirs: Elizabeth Bray (wife), John Bray, Daniel Bray, Samuel Bray, Jane Bray, Nancy Bray, Betsey, Caroline Bray, Amelia (aka Nelly/Nellie) Bray; George W. Bray, Sophia Bray (minor children).
Date of Division & disbursement, or Final Return: Estate settled and closed: 11 Feb 1834
References to other files – Books & Pages Nos. (orphans, minors, inventories, petitions, deeds, etc.)
Deeds pertaining to this estate - Purchaser David Leweyllen & wife (see Order Book 2, pg. 204).

The Vevay Reveille-Enterprise, Thurs. 1 Feb 1877, Vol. LX, No.5, p. 2., Col. 3.
Caroline M. Thompson vs. Wm. M. Patton, Administrator of the Estate of Elizabeth Bray alias Elizabeth Bakes – claim of $315.; dismissed by claimant at her costs.

The Vevay Reveille-Enterprise ,Thur. 8 Nov 1877, Vol. LX, No.45, p. 2., Col. 2.
William Sealf vs. William M. Patton, Adm'r of Elizabeth Bray alias Bakes – account; submitted to the Court, and finding for defendant.

The Vevay Reveille-Enterprise, Thurs. 17 May 1888 , Vol.71, No.20, p. 4. Col. 3.
W. M. Patton, Administrator of the estate of Elizabeth Bray, deceased, field a partition report and resignation and was discharged.

Abstract of Final Payment Voucher; General Services Administration, Washington, DC
NAME   Bray, Elizabeth Widow of John
AGENCY OF PAYMENT   Indiana
DATE OF ACT   1853 2nd Sect.
DATE OF PAYMENT   March 1862
DATE OF DEATH
LAST ~~FINAL~~ PAYMENT VOUCHER RECEIVED FROM
THE GENERAL ACCOUNTING OFFICE   Form
General Services Administration   GSA DA 70-7035   GSA Dec 69   7068

Revolutionary War Records – Virginia; Virginia Army and Navy Forces with Bounty Land Warrants for Virginia Military District of Ohio, and Virginia Military Script, from Federal and State Archives; by Gaius Marcus Brumbaugh, M.D, M.s., Litt.D; Genealogical Publishing Co., Inc., Baltimore, 1995. p. 399. Virginia Military Land Warrants, Virginia District of Ohio, Granted for Revolutionary War Services, State Continental Line, Beginning August 8, 1872.

Number	Warrantees	Rank & Service	
3556	Bray, John (Joseph Van Meter, assnee.	Soldier	3 years

Revolutionary War Bounty Land Grants Awarded by State Governments; Lloyd DeWitt Bockstruck; Genealogical Publishing co., IN, Baltimore, MD, 1996. p.60.
Bray, John. Va. Private. 2 Sep 1786. 100 acres.

Early Ohio Settlers, Purchasers of Land in Southwestern Ohio, 1800-1840; Compiled by Ellen T. Berry & David A. Berry; Genealogical Publishing Co., Inc., Baltimore, MD, 1986. p.34.

Purchaser	Year	Date	Residence	R – T - S
Bray, John (B)	1816	March 05	Franklin Ind	04-02-25

(B) Indiana Survey: Land lying west of a meridian drawn west of the Great Miami (known as the "Gore"). Switzerland, Dearborn, Franklin, Ohio, Union and Randolph Counties (all or only a part of each county) – all in Indiana.

Early Settlers of Indiana's "GORE" 1803-1820; Compiled and Edited by Shirley Keller Mikesell; Heritage Books, Inc., 1995. p. 189.
Switzerland County - Township 2, Range 4W
Section 25 – John Bray – 1811 – pg. 14.

Indiana Land Entries Vol. 1 Cincinnati District, 1801-1840; Margaret R. Waters; Originally Published Indianapolis 1948, Second Reprint 1979 by The Bookmark, P.O. Box 74, Knightstown, In 46148. p.79.
CINCINNNATI LAND DISTRICT – VOL. 1.
Page 76. Twp. 1 N, Range 4 W of 1st Principle Meridian SWITZERLAND CO.
John Bray - NE ¼ S25; 3-15-1816.

-- Note: The tract books for the land offices in Indiana are deposited in the office of the Auditor of State, Indianapolis. They and are in the custody of the State Land clerk. --

U.S. Department of Interior, Bureau of Land Management, General Land Office Records; Land Patent Search – accessed 27 June 2012.
BRAY, JOHN
Accession Nr. CV-0052-462; Document Type – Credit Volume Patent; Issue Date – 8/8/1820; Cancelled – No
Land Office – Cincinnati; Authority – April 24, 1820 Sale-Cash Entry (3 Stat. 566); Total Acres – 159.44
Land Descriptions: State – IN; Meridian – 1st PM; Twp-Rng – 002N-004W; Aliquots – NE1/4; Section – 25; County – Switzerland

A Partial Census For Indiana Territory 1810; Compiled by John D & E. Diane Stemmons; Census Publishing LC, Sandy, UT, 2004. p. 63.
Bray, John, Historical Locality: Indiana Territory, Current State: Indiana, Whitewater – Name on petition, 10 Oct 1809, to Jared Mansfield, surveyor general, by inhabitants of Whitewater asking that Emmanuel "vantrees Esqr" be appointed to survey land on & near Whitewater where he lives so they may be able to purchase the land (pages 675-77). – Territorial Papers of the US, vol. 7 pg. 676.
Bray, John, Male

The Pension List of 1820 [U.S. War Department]Reprinted with an Index; by Murtie June Clark; Genealogical Publishing Co., Inc., Baltimore, 1991. Originally published 1820 as Letter from the Secretary of War. p. 656.
Names of the Revolutionary Pensioners which have been placed on the Roll of Indiana, under the Law of the 18th of March, 1818, from the passage thereof, to this day, inclusive, with the Rank they held, and the Lines in which they served, viz.

Names	Rank	Line
John Bray	private	Virginia

1830 U.S. Census, Indiana, Switzerland, No Twp., Series: M19 Roll: 32 Page: 32
Bray, John age 60 & under 70; others in household 2 males under 5, 1 female under 5, 2 females 5-10, 1 female 10-15, 1 female 30-40.

1870 U.S. Census, Indiana, Switzerland, Jefferson Twp., Series: M593 Roll: 361 Page: 313 Family No. 515. Bakes, Elizabeth, Age: 72, Female, Race: White, Born: KY

Revolutionary Soldiers of Switzerland County; Copied by Mary Hill, John Paul Chapter-Daughters of the American Revolution; January, 1958; http://www.ingenweb.org/inswitzerland/switzrevsoldiers.html- Viewed June 2012.
BRAY, JOHN   Pension claim W. 4143
Born about 1762.

John Bray enlisted in September 1777, in "Romley" evidently meant for Romney, Hampshire Co. Virginia, served as a private in Captain William Voss's company, Colonel James Wood's Virginia Regiment, was in the battles of Brandywine, in which he was wounded, Monmouth, and at the taking of Stony Point, also in several small skirmishes, and was discharged after serving three years, the term for which he enlisted.

The soldier was allowed pension on his application executed June 20, 1818, at which time he was aged 56 years. His application was executed in Switzerland County, his place of residence not given.

Married first wife unknown, children: John, Daniel, Samuel, Jane, Nancy, Elizabeth.

John Bray married April 13, 1820, at the home of one Jacob Hunter (no relationship to soldier shown), in Gallatin County, Ky. Mrs. Elizabeth Coonies, also referred to as Betsey, a widow of that county (the given name of her husband and date of his death not shown) Their marriage was recorded in the County Clerk's office of said Gallatin County, Kentucky. Children: Amelia, George Washington, Sophia.

In 1821, the soldier was residing in Craig township, Switzerland County, Indiana. He died in that county, June 10, 1832.

John Bray's widow, Elizabeth, married October 4, 1834, Robert Bakes, and their marriage was recorded in the office of the County Clerk of Switzerland County, Indiana. Robert Bakes died March 19, 1847.

Said Elizabeth, while a resident of Switzerland Co. Ind. aged 55 years, applied Oct. 3, 1853, for pension due her as the former widow of John Bray. Her claim was allowed and she was pensioned under the name of Elizabeth Bray. In 1859, she was still residing in Switz. Co. Ind. with post office at Vevay, same county. In 1863, her place of residence were the same, Mount Sterling, Switz. Co. Ind. with post office at Vevay, which was still her post office in 1874. She did not sign as Elizabeth Bakes but Elizabeth Bray.

The only names designated as children of the soldier, John Bray, were two daughters, Carolina, aged two years, and Amelia, aged three months in 1821, and Daniel, who in 1824 made affidavit in the soldier's behalf in Switz. Co. Ind. and referred to one Samuel Bray, but did not state his relationship.

In 1870 one John Bakes witnessed the signature by mark of soldier's widow, Elizabeth, in Madison, Indiana, but his relationship to her was not shown.

Died 10 Apr 1832.

Buried in McKay cemetery, Craig twp. A stone. (read by Wanda Morford in 1980 as follows - John Sr., d. Jun. 10, 1832 aged 71 y 4 m 12 d)

Land Warrant 8178

1st wife unknown. Ch; John; Daniel; Samuel; Jane; Nancy, Elizabeth.

2nd wife, Mrs. Elizabeth Coonies; ch; Amelia, George Washington, Sophia.

Roster of Soldiers and Patriots of the American Revolution Buried in Indiana, Vol. I; compiled by Mrs. Roscoe C. O'Byrne.; Indiana Daughters of the American Revolution, 1981; p.70.

BRAY, JOHN   Switzerland County

Born – About 1762

Service – Enlisted Sept., 1777, in Romney, Hampshire Co., Vir. Private in Capt. William Voss' CO., Col. James Wood's Regt. Was in battles of Brandywine (wounded), Monmouth and Stoney Point. Discharged at end of three yrs. service.
Proof – Pension claim W. 4145. Land warrant No. 8178.
Died – April 10, 1832. Buried McKay Cemetery, Craig Twp. Stone.
Married – First W. unknown. Ch. John; Daniel; Samuel; Jane; Nancy; Elizabeth.
 - Second W., Mrs. Elizabeth Coonies. Ch. Amelia; George Washington; Sophia.
Collected by Mrs. A.. V. Danner, Vevay, Indiana.

Switzerland County Indiana Cemetery Inscriptions 1817-1985; Wanda L. Morford; Cincinnati, Ohio, 1986, p. 74.
McKay Cemetery, Craig Township, Switzerland Co., IN
Bray   John Sr. d. Jun. 10, 1832 aged 71y 4m 12d

Abstract of Graves of Revolutionary Patriots, 4 volumes; by Patricia Law Hatcher; Pioneer Heritage Press, Dallas, TX, 1987. Vol. I, p. 108.
This is an abstract and an index to information reported to the Daughters of the American Revolution and published in their annual reports to the Smithsonian Institution, printed as Senate Documents (1900-1974) and published annually in the DAR magazine (1978-1987).
Published 1972 (Senate Doc. 54)
BRAY, JOHN   McKay Cem., Craig Twp., Switzerland Co., IN

National Society of the Sons of the American Revolution - Revolutionary War Graves Register; Compiled and Edited by Clovis H. Brakebill, Published by db Publications, Dallas, TX, 1993. p.76.
Bray   John Sr; 1761-1831; McKay Cem, Vevay, IN; Private, VA; Nancy Morgan, Elizabeth Coones.

Tombstone at McKay Cemetery
Inscription –   JOHN BRAY, SR.
                                 DIED
                             June 1o, 1832
                                 AGED
                             71 yrs 4 mo's
                                & 12 d's
                        He served 3 years as
                            a Revolutionary
                         Soldier under Gen.
                              Washington

The Vevay Reveille-Enterprise; Vol. 122, No. 37, 15 Sep 1935, p. 3, col.2-3.
Roster of Revolutionary Soldiers Who Resided in Switzerland County
By Mrs. Effa M. Danner
JOHN BRAY - Pension No. W4045. His birth and place and parents not given in pension claim. He enlisted September 1777 in Romney, Hampshire County, Virginia and served as a private in Captain Wm. Voss's Co., Colonel James Wood's Virginia regiment and he was in the Battle of Brandywine in which he

was wounded, also at the Battle of Monmouth and at the taking of Stony Point and in several other small skirmishes. He was discharged after having served three years, his time of enlistment. He was allowed pension June 30, 1818, age 56, executed in Switzerland County, Ind.
He married his second wife, Mrs. Elizabeth Coonies, April 15, 1820 in Gallatin County, Ky. His U.S. Land Patent was issued March 8, 1816 for N.E. Qt. Sec. 25, T. 2, R. 4W, 159 acres, No. 8178 Switzerland County.
He died June 10, 1832 and is buried in the McKay cemetery, Craig Township, stone marker.
Braytown is named for this family. Children, first wife unknown, John, Daniel, Samuel, James, Nancy, Betsy. Second wife, Elizabeth Coonies; children, Amelia, Sophia and George Washington.
Last will, Book E, p. 52. All the children mentioned. Witnesses, Samuel Culver and Tubman Malcolm. Probated June 26, 1832.
Nancy Bray married Jas. Culver, April 6, 1819. Betsy Bray married Cotton.

The Battle of Stony Point was one of the most important of the war and as several of our men were in this battle I include this description from *Pioneer and Patriot, p. 54*, Dickson.

    Stony Point, July 15, 1779, General Washington laid the plans in utmost secrecy for this battle. The task was to be given to the light infantry made up of picked men from various regiments. The flower of the army, the finest of the troops. Every officer had been hand selected by Washington himself and for their leader had been chosen Gen. Anthony Wayne. The attack on the fort was to be made July 15th at midnight.

    Previous order was given the men to be "fresh shaven and well powdered", for troops poorly equipped grew careless of personal appearance. Every man was given a strip of white paper to fasten on his hat so he might be recognized as an American. No man was to load his gun as the attack was to be a bayonet charge, except a small division to fire in front.

    The moment a man got into the fort he was to shout "the fort is ours". The men had to wade through a marsh waist deep and were seen by the enemy. Straight the two columns went climbing the rough sides of the hill, meeting the fire of musket and cannon but firing never a shot. Gen. Wayne was wounded. Major Murfree's two companies made a great show in front and the British rushed to attack them. The Americans rushed into the fort from either side "the Fort is ours", with 500 British and valuable cannon and supplies.

BROWN, SAMUEL

Patriot: Samuel Brown
Birth: c. 1755   VA
Married Spouse 1: 1780   Susan Bacon
Service state(s): VA
Service description: VA Cont. Line; Lincoln Co., VA Militia
Rank: Private
Proof of Service: Land grants
Pension application No.: None
Residences: Virginia; Lincoln Co., KY District, VA; Indiana Territory; Ohio; Switzerland Co., IN
Died: abt. 1829   Switzerland Co., IN
Buried: Slawson Cemetery, Switzerland Co., IN
DAR Ancestor No.: A015862

<u>Virginia Revolutionary Militia, A List of Non-Commissioned Officers and Soldiers of the Virginia Line on Continental Establishment, Whose names appear on the Army Register, and who have not received Bounty Land</u>; Printed by Samuel Shepherd, Printer to the Commonwealth, Richmond, VA. 1835. p. 6.
Doc. No. 44.
Brown, Samuel   Soldier   Artillery

<u>Revolutionary War Records – Virginia</u>; Virginia Army and Navy Forces with Bounty Land Warrants for Virginia Military District of Ohio, and Virginia Military Script, from Federal and State Archives; by Gaius Marcus Brumbaugh, M.D, M.s., Litt.D; Genealogical Publishing Co., Inc., Baltimore, 1995.
p. 187
Bounty Land Warrants, United States January 16, 1828 (See Senate Documents, 1st Session 20th Congress, Vol. 2, Doc. 42 &c. 1827-'28)
69. Brown, Samuel, r, Private
p. 223
List of non-commissioned officers and soldiers of the Continental Line. List may contain names of individuals who received bounty land for services in the State Line.
Brown, Samuel
p. 399.
Virginia Military Land Warrants, Virginia District of Ohio, Granted for Revolutionary War Services, State Continental Line, Beginning August 8, 1872.

<u>Number</u>	<u>Warrantees</u>	<u>Rank & Service</u>	
1785	Brown, Samuel	Soldier	3 years

<u>Revolutionary War Bounty Land Grants Awarded by State Governments</u>; Lloyd DeWitt Bockstruck; Genealogical Publishing Co., Inc, Baltimore, MD, 1996.
p. 68.
Brown, Samuel. Va. Private. 24 Sep 1783. 200 acres.

Catalogue of Revolutionary Soldiers and Sailors of the Commonwealth of Virginia to Whom Land Bounty Warrants Were Granted by Virginia for Military Service in the War for Independence, From Official Records in the Kentucky State Land Office at Frankfort, Kentucky; compiled by Samuel M. Wilson; Southern Book Company, Baltimore, MD, 1953. p. 8.

Number of Warrant	Name of Officer or Soldier	Number of Acres	Dept. of Service: Continental or State Line or Navy	Number of Years in Service	Date of Warrant
1785	Brown, Samuel	200	Private Va. Cont. Line	war	Sep. 24'83

Possible record for this man – place he resided & enlisted not known, however this record is Samuel Brown who served in the Continental establishment.

Virginia Revolutionary Publick Claims in three volumes; compiled and transcribed b Janice L. Abercrombie and Richard Slatten; Iberian Publishing Co., Athens, GA, 1992. p. 417.

Greenbrier County – Green Brier County Court Booklet. At a court held for Greenbrier County June 18, 1782. Present Samuel Brown, William Ward, Michael Woods, John Henderson and John Anderson, Gent. The following claims allowed and ordered to be certified to wit:

Andrew Donnally & Samuel Brown for 1 horse 5 years £85; 1 horse 6 years £48; 1 horse 7 years £45; 1 horse 6 years £42; 1 horse 6 years £52; 1 horse 7 years £45; 1 horse 7 years £45; 1 horse 4 years Cont. use £50.

Register of Certificates Issued by John Pierce, Esquire, Paymaster General and Commissioner of Army Accounts for the United States, to Officers and Soldiers of the Continental Army Under Act of July 4, 1783; Originally Published as Senate Documents, Vol.9, No. 988, 63rd Congress, 3d Session, Washington, 1915; Seventeenth report of the National Society of the Daughters of the American Revolution; Genealogical Publishing Co., Inc, Baltimore, MD, 1984. p. 71.
Men listed in this volume with the name Samuel Brown.
Author's note: Due to the large number (34) of men with this name they are not listed here. "Pierce's Register" is available in most large libraries.

Second Census of Kentucky, 1800; Clift G. Glenn; Genealogical Publishing Co., Baltimore, MD, 1954.
An alphabetical list of 32,000 taxpayers based on original tax lists on file at the Kentucky Historical Society. Information given includes the county of residence and the date of the tax list in which the individual is listed.
There are nine entries for Samuel Brown – entry (entries) for this man have not been identified.

Brown, Samuel	Fayette (Lexington)	8/19/1800
Brown, Samuel, Dr.	Fayette (Lexington)	8/19/1800
Brown, Samuel	Harrison	1800
Brown, Samuel	Madison	8/12/1800
Brown, Samuel	Nelson	7/7/1800
Brown, Samuel	Nelson	8/30/1800
Brown, Samuel	Nelson	8/30/1800

Brown, Samuel	Nelson	8/30/1800
Brown, Samuel	Scott	1800

A Partial Census For Indiana Territory 1810; Compiled by John D & E. Diane Stemmons; Census Publishing LC, Sandy, UT, 2004. p. 69.
Brown, Samuel, Historical Locality: Indiana Territory, Current State: ?, - Name on petition, 12 Dec 1809, to Congress by citizens of the territory asking for voting rights for all white males over 21 who paid taxes or fulfilled militia duty. They also ask to be allowed to choose their own civil & militia officers (pages 690-92). – Territorial Papers of the US, vol. 7 pg 692.
Brown, Samuel, Male
&
Brown, Samuel, Historical Locality: Indiana Territory, Current State: Indiana, Dearborn, Franklin & Wayne Cos, - Name on petition, 22 Jan 1811, to Congress by inhabitants of Dearborn, Franklin, & Wayne Counties, the latter two of which were recently formed from the north end of Dearborn County, asking that post offices & post roads be established (pages 102-03). Territorial Papers of the Us, vol. 8, pg. 103.
Brown, Samuel, Male

1820 U.S. Census, Indiana, Switzerland, Jefferson, Series: M33 Roll: 14 Pg: 264
Samuel Brown 45; and others in household 1 female 45 and up.

Pensioners of the Revolutionary War Struck Off the Roll with an Added Index to States; Reprinted by Genealogical Publishing Co., Baltimore, MD for Clearfield Company, Inc., 1989. p. 94.
Pensioners in Ohio who have been dropped under the act of 1st May, 1820; prepared in conformity with a resolution of the House of Representatives of the United States of the 17th December, 1835.

Names	Acts under which restored	Remarks
Samuel Brown	March 1, 1823	-

Early Settlers of Indiana's "GORE" 1803-1820; Compiled and Edited by Shirley Keller Mikesell; Heritage Books, Inc., 1995.
p. 194. [Witness – Switzerland County Deeds]
Deed dated 1817. Even Brock & Betsy, his wife, to Joseph Nelson. S32, T2, R1. Signed Evan Brock, Betsy (x) Bock. Witness: Wm. Campbel, John 9x) Nelson, Sam'l Brown, pp. 70, 71.
p. 215 [Witness – Switzerland County Deeds]
Deed dated 1818. Evan Brook & Betsey, his wife, to Amos Brown. S32, T2, R1. Signed Evin Brock, Bets (x) Brosk. Witness: Robert McCorkhill, Samuel Brown, pp. 361, 362.

Revolutionary Soldiers of Switzerland County; Copied by Mary Hill, John Paul Chapter-Daughters of the American Revolution; January, 1958; http://www.ingenweb.org/inswitzerland/switzrevsoldiers.html- Viewed June, 2012.

BROWN, SAMUEL

Born 1756, probably in Virginia.

Service: 3 years in Continental line of Virginia; served in Kentucky, which was then part of Virginia, under General George Rogers Clark; See Vol. 1, pg. 133, same. Samuel Brown had received bounty land before 1828, as indicated by "R" pg. 187;

pg. 395 Samuel Brown was in Va. Military Dist. of Ohio. Also photostats of Muster Roll of Captain James Downings Co. of Militia in Lincoln Co. Ky.; on actual service on an expedition against enemy Indiana(s) under General George Rogers Clark, dated Nov. 24, 1782.

Revolutionary soldiers of Switzerland Co. Indiana

References for family history

2. Bible and Court records; Switz. Co. Marriages estates 1901 - 1920; Mortuary reports of Morrisons.

3. Bible; history of Dearborn, Ohio & Switz. Co. Indiana. Photostat of original of Consent & Marriage returns, Protzman.

4. Photostat notice of Polly Brown Campbell, which states that William R. Protzman was her grandson.

5. Old family letter by Wm. L. Campbell, born 1836 - d 1922. Supp. National No. 293,046, Nellie Protzman Waldemaier.

Children of Samuel Brown and Susan Bacon:

1. Jemima Brown b. abt. 1781,
    m Oct. 19, 1813 in Green Co., Ohio to Isaac Shingledecker
    d 1873, buried Weslayan Cemetery, 4003 Colrain Ave. Cincinnati, Ohio,.
2. Polly Brown b June 17, 1783, Harroldsburg, KY
    m. June 17, 1800 William Campbell
    d. Sept. 4, 1869, Vevay, IN, buried Florence, Switz. Co. Ind.
    sp. William Campbell, b. Aug. 1776, Rowan Co. N. C. d Feb. 10, 1832 Florence, Switz. Co. Ind. Their dau. Polly Campbell b Nov. 13, 1889, Vevay, Ind. m Nov. 29, 1826 to William Protzman, b Feb. 1, 1801, Danville, Ky. d Nov. 5, 1866, Vevay, Ind.
    Their dau, Flora Protzman Betts Morrison
3. Elizabeth (Betsy) Brown, m Evan Brock, Dec. 25, 1812, Green Co. Ohio

Samuel Brown's wife died in Cincinnati, Ohio

Samuel Brown died in Switz. Co. date 1816 given in his estate, he was allowed 44.50 for schooling the children of Caleb Hayes.

Revolutionary Soldiers Buried in Indiana (1949) With Supplement (1954) Two Volumes In One; Margaret R. Waters; Genealogical Publishing Company, Baltimore, MD, 1970. p. 18.

BROWN, SAMUEL   Switzerland
d. 1816 (estate record); m. Susan Bacon;

chn. Jemima d. 1873, bur. Wesleyan Cem., 4003 Colrain Ave., Cincinnati, O. , m. 10-19-1813 Greene Co., O., Isaac Shingledocker; Polly b. 6-17-1783, Harroldsburg, Ky., d. 9-4-1869, Vevay, Ind., bur. Florence, Switzerland Co., Ind., m. 6-17-1800, William Campbell, b. Aug. 1776, * Rowan Co., N.C., d. 2-10-1832, Florence, Ind.; Elizabeth m. 12-25-1812, Greene Co., O., Evan Brock; Samuel m. (wife d. Cincinnati , O.); William b. Aug. 1776, Rowan Co., N.C., d. 2-10-1832, Florence, Ind. (note discrepancy with Polly's husb. above *), m. & had dau. Polly Campbell (*), b. 4-9-1809, Greene Co., O., d. 11-13-1889, Vevay, Ind., m. 11-29-1825, William Protzman, b. 2-1-1801, Danville, Ky., d. 11-5-1866, Vevay, Ind. (& had dau. Flora Protzman Betts Morrison).
Service: 3 yr. in Va. Cont. Line; with Geo. Rogers Clark in Ky.; bounty land given.
REF: Brumbaugh—"Rev. War Rec. of Va.", v. 1, pp. 135, 187, 395; photostat of Capt. James Downing's Comp. of Lincoln Co., Ky., Mil. , 11-24-1782; "Hist of Dearborn, Ohio & Switzerland Cos., Ind."; DAR #293046; Miss Mary Hill, Madison, Ind.

Roster of Soldiers and Patriots of the American Revolution Buried in Indiana, Vol. II; 1966; p. 22.
BROWN, SAMUEL   Switzerland County
Born – Ca. 1755, probably Virginia
Service – Private Lincoln County Militia, and Virginia Continental Line.
Proof – Brumbaugh, "Rev. War Records of Vir.", V.1, pp. 135, 187, 395; Photostat of Capt. James Downing's Comp. of Lincoln Co., Ky. Mil., Nov. 24, 1782; DAR No. 293046 and 293331.
Died – Before 1829, Switzerland Co., Ind.
Married – Susan Bacon. Ch. Jemima, b. ca. 1781, d. 1873, m. Oct.19, 1813, to Isaac Shingledecker; Polly, b. June 17, 1783, d. Sept. 4, 1869, m. June 17, 1800, William Campbell; Elizabeth (Betsy), m. Dec. 25, 1812, Evan Brock; Samuel; William.
Ref. Water's Sip. Rev. S. p. 118.

History of Switzerland County Indiana 1885; Reproduced by the Switzerland County Historical Society, Vevay, Indiana, 1999. The portion of the book relating to Switzerland County in the 1885 printing of the "History of Dearborn, Ohio, and Switzerland Counties, Indiana". p. 1038.
"A squirrel hunt took place in Craig Township March 17 and 18, 1824, and on the 19th they met at Johnson Brown's, on Long Run, to count the game with the following result:"
-Included on this list is Samuel Brown with the count of 167.-

Author's note: Effa M. Danner, who has done remarkable research on the Revolutionary Soldiers of Switzerland County, descends from this man.

BUCK, WILLIAM
aka William Sherman BUCH

Patriot: William Sherman Buck (Buch)
Birth: 1764   prob. Litchfield Co., CT
Married Spouse 1: 1787 in Bradford County, PA Barentha York
(b. 1770, d. 1827)
Her father, Amos York, served in the Revolution. He was taken prisoner in Quebec.
Married Spouse 2: 30 Dec 1830 Elizabeth Hamilton of Switzerland County
28 Feb 1836 William S. Buck petitioned for divorce.
She abandoned him on 31 Dec 1831.
Marriage annulled 22 March 1836.
Service state(s): CT – Wyoming Valley (now Luzerne Co., PA)
Service description: Enlisted Capt. Robert Durkee's Company at Wyoming, PA
Rank: Private
Proof of Service: Connecticut Men in the Military and Naval Service During the War of the Revolution 1775-1783.
Pension application No.: None
Residences: CT; NY; Hamilton Co., OH; Switzerland Co., IN
Died: 1844   Switzerland Co., IN
Buried: "Old Graveyard", Patriot, IN
DAR Ancestor No: See papers for Barentha's father, Amos York (No. A129644)
Children: Hiram Buck (Buch) m. Mercy Karr

The Record of Connecticut Men in the Military and Naval Service During the War of the Revolution 1775-1783. Vol. I-III; Henry P. Johnston, ed.; Hartford, CT, USA: 1889. p. 264.
Chapter - Connecticut in the Revolution
p. 264. The following additional names appear on a list of Durkee's Co., In Penn. Rev. Records, vol. ii, p. 112.
Corporal Edward Setter, Privates ..(list includes) William Buck, Jr. ..

Author's notes:
Officers of Capt. Robert Durkee's Company
1st. Lieut. James Wells; 2nd Lieut. Asahel Buck (Wyoming-Commissioned 26 Aug 176, killed by Indians 10 Feb 1779); Ensign Heman Swift; Sergeants Solomon Johnson, Samuel Cole, Thomas McClure, Ebenezer Skinner; Corporals Perigrene Gardner, Stephen Preston .

William was known as "Jr" because his older uncle, William Buck, resided in the same community, that being Westmoreland which is now known as Wyoming. The older William served as a Captain in the Militia and was killed at the Battle of Wyoming in 1776.

According to family lore William Sherman Buck was the son of James Buck and Elizabeth Sherman.

A Census of Pensioners for Revolutionary or Military Services with their Names, Ages, and Places of Residence Under the Act for Taking the Sixth Census in 1840; Genealogical Publishing Co., Inc., Baltimore, Maryland, 1965. p.185.

INDIANA, SWITZERLAND, POSEY Names of Pensioners for Revolutionary or Military services	Ages	Names of heads of families with whom pensioner resided June 1, 1840
William Buck	77	Morton Buck

Register of Certificates Issued by John Pierce, Esquire, Paymaster General and Commissioner of Army Accounts for the United States, to Officers and Soldiers of the Continental Army Under Act of July 4, 1783; Originally Published as Senate Documents, Vol.9, No. 988, 63rd Congress, 3d Session, Washington, 1915; Seventeenth report of the National Society of the Daughters of the American Revolution; Genealogical Publishing Co., Inc, Baltimore, MD, 1984. p.74.
Man listed in this volume with the same name.

No. of Certificate	To whom issued	Amount
16638	Buck, William	19.82

Roster of Soldiers and Patriots of the American Revolution Buried in Indiana, Vol. I; compiled by Mrs. Roscoe C. O'Byrne.; Indiana Daughters of the American Revolution,1981; p.399.
LIST OF MEN WHOSE SERVICE IN REVOLUTIONARY WAR HAS NOT BEEN VERIFIED AT PRESENT TIME
BUCK, WILLIAM   Switzerland County
Born – 1764.
Died – 1844. Buried at Patriot, Ind. Stone. Is listed on 1840 census as pensioner, but name cannot be found by Vet. Adm.

Indiana Land Entries Vol. 1 Cincinnati District, 1801-1840; Margaret R. Waters; Originally Published Indianapolis 1948, Second Reprint 1979 by The Bookmark, P.O. Box 74, Knightstown, In 46148. p.4.
CINCINNNATI LAND DISTRICT – VOL. 1
Page 3. Twp. 2 N, Range 1 W of 1st Principle Meridian SWITZERLAND CO.
William Sherman Buck SE ¼ - S22; 9-14-1818. Relinquished E ½ to William B. Chamberlain, no date. (Vol. II, p. 4, says 8-21-1827) W ½ to George Teague, 8-21-1817. Note adds to George Teague 8-21-1827.
-- Note: The tract books for the land offices in Indiana are deposited in the office of the Auditor of State, Indianapolis. They and are in the custody of the State Land clerk. --

Early Settlers of Indiana's "GORE" 1803-1820; Compiled and Edited by Shirley Keller Mikesell; Heritage Books, Inc., 1995. p. 183.
Switzerland County - Township 2, Range 1W
Section 22 - Wm. Sherman Buck – 1818 – pg. 3.

Early Ohio Settlers, Purchasers of Land in Southwestern Ohio, 1800-1840; Compiled by Ellen T. Berry & David A. Berry; Genealogical Publishing Co., Inc., Baltimore, MD, 1986. p.42.

Purchaser	Year	Date	Residence	R – T - S
Buck, William Sherman (B)	1818	Sept. 14	Hamilton	01-02-22

(B) Indiana Survey: Land lying west of a meridian drawn west of the Great Miami (known as the "Gore"). Switzerland, Dearborn, Franklin, Ohio, Union and Randolph Counties (all or only a part of each county) – all in Indiana.

Switzerland County, Indiana Civil Complete Record, Vol. G, 23 Sept 1835-29 Jun 1836. p.75.
28 February 1836, William S. Buck vs. Elizabeth Buck, petition for Divorce. William S. Buck of Switzerland County represents about the last of December 1830 he was intermarried with Elizabeth Hamilton of Switzerland County, that they lived together as husband and wife for the space of one year which was about the last of December 1831, all which time he treated her kindly, affectionately, and provided everything necessary for her comfort & happiness. And that some time about the last of December 1831 the said Elizabeth Hamilton left the bed and board of out petitioner in said County without any cause known to petitioner and has ever since refused to live with your petitioner but has ever since lived in County of Switzerland and doth still live separate and apart from said Buck, with the intention of abandonment forever. Petitioner has been a resident of state & county for more than twelve months to wit for the space of seven years. He therefore prays the Court that he may be divorced from the said Elizabeth according to the statute in such cases made and provide and the bonds of matrimony now existing between them be fully dissolved.
                                  A. Buck, Attorney for Petitioner.
&

Switzerland County, Indiana Civil Order Book Vol., A, Oct. 19, 1829-April 16, 1837, p. 408.
22 March 1836, William S. Buck vs. Elizabeth Buck, On Petition for Divorce. On petition by Marshall & Buck his atty's and it appearing to the satisfaction of the Court that the proofs had been duly ---, said defendant according to law, and the said defendant being three times solemnly called comes not, but made default, and the Court after hearing the evidence 7 argument of consul do order, adjudge & decree that the bonds of matrimony heretofore solemnized between the said Wm. S. Buck & Elizabeth Buck be & the same are hereby dissolved, annulled, & set aside, as fully and completely as though the same had never been entered into or solemnized.

1830 U.S. Census, Indiana, Switzerland, No Twp Listed, Series: M19 Roll: 32 Page: 31
Buck, William S. age 60-70; others in household 1 male 15-20.

Switzerland County Health Department, Switzerland County Cemeteries 1800-1980; Church of Latter Day Saints Microfilm No. 1460119302. p. 78.
Old Patriot Cemetery, Posey Twp., Switzerland Co., IN
Buck, William S. , d. 8/4/1841 aged 80 yrs.

<u>Switzerland County Indiana Cemetery Inscriptions 1817-1985</u>; Wanda L. Morford; Cincinnati, Ohio, 1986, 438.
Patriot Cemetery, Posey Twp., Switzerland Co., IN
Buck   William S.,   d. Aug. 4, 1844 in the 80th year of his age

<u>The Vevay Reveille-Enterprise</u>; Vol. 122, No. 37, 15 Sep 1935, p. 3, col. 2.
Roster of Revolutionary Soldiers Who Resided in Switzerland County
By Mrs. Effa M. Danner
William Buck – Born 1764. Lived in Patriot, received pension for service. He is listed in U.S. Military Census 1840, being 75 years old, Morton Buck, guardian. His grave was located by H. F. Emerson in the Old graveyard at Patriot where the head stone is in position and inscription legible, "William Buck, Born 1764, Died 1844 in the 80th year of his age."
We have been unable to find his military service.

BURNS, JOHN

Patriot: John Burns
Birth: 12 Jul 1763
Married Spouse 1: 13 June 1810 in Warren Co., Ohio   Lucretia Vanosdol
(b. c1781, d. 31 Aug1860, Switzerland Co.)
Service state(s): VA – Continental Line
Service description: Capt. Phillip Taliphro; 2nd VA Regt., Col. Richard
Parker, Capt. Alexander Parker's company.
Rank: Private
Proof of Service: Pension application W9772
Pension application No.: W9772/BLWT71127-160-55
Residences: King & Queen Co., VA; Indiana Territory; Switzerland Co., IN
Died: July 13, 1827   Switzerland Co., IN
Buried: Slawson Cemetery, Pleasant Twp., Switzerland Co., IN
DAR Ancestor No.: None

Pension Application Abstracted from National Archives microfilm Series 805, Roll 145, File W9772/BLWT71127-160-55

Pension Application for - John Burns   Service state(s): Virginia - Continental Line

Under Act of 18 March 1818
Date: 12 Feb 1819
County of: Jefferson   State of: Indiana
Declaration made before a Circuit Court.
Age: 56
Residence now: Switzerland Co., IN
Volunteer or Drafted or Substitute: Enlisted in King and Queen Co., VA
Statement of service-

Period	Duration	Names of General and Field Officers
Spring 1777	to May 1780	Capt. Phillip Talafro, col. Richard Parker's regt.

Battles: Battle of Savannah in GA; Battle at Charles Town, SC.
Discharge received: May 1780 in Charles Town, SC
&
Pension abstract – John Burns   Service state(s): VA
Date: 15 Sep 1820
County of: Switzerland   State of: Indiana
Declaration made before a Court.
Age: 57
Where and year born: 12 July 1763
Residence now: Switzerland Co., IN
Volunteer or Drafted or Substitute: Enlisted in King & Queen Co., VA
Statement of service-

Period	Duration	Names of General and Field Officers
	3 years	Capt. Phillip Taliphro, then was detached to 2nd VA Regt. under Col. Richard Parker in Capt. Alexander Parker's co.

Wife: Lucretia   Wife's age: 31 & a weakly woman
Occupation: House painter – unable to make a living in consequence of little work of the kind in the Western country.
Names and ages of children: David Burns age 9; Robert Burns between 7 &8; Jane Burns between 5&6; Elizabeth Burns between 4&5 years; George Burns between 2&3; John M. Burns about 4 months.
Notes: Under the Act of Congress of 18 March 1818, he received Pension No. 16.255.
&
Widow's Bounty Land Application Under Act of Congress 3rd February 1853
Soldier: John Burns   Service state(s): VA
Date: 1 Apr 1853
County of: Switzerland   State of: Indiana
Declaration made before a Justice of the Peace
Widow's residence now: Switzerland Co., IN
Widow's name: Lucretia   Her name before marriage was: Vanosdol
Marriage date and place: 13 June 1810 in Warren Co., Ohio
&
Widow's Bounty Land Application – Under Act of Congress 3rd March 1855
Soldier: John Burns   Service state(s): VA
Continental Line
Date: 7 July 1857
County of: Carroll   State of: Kentucky
Declaration made before a Judge.
Age of widow: 72
Widow's residence: Carroll Co., KY

Abstract of Final Payment Voucher; General Services Administration, Washington, DC
[There are two cards on file for John Burns]
NAME   Burns, John
AGENCY OF PAYMENT   Kentucky
DATE OF ACT   1818
DATE OF PAYMENT   1st qtr. 1827
DATE OF DEATH
LAST ~~FINAL~~ PAYMENT VOUCHER RECEIVED FROM
THE GENERAL ACCOUNTING OFFICE   Form
General Services Administration   GSA DA 70-7035   GSA Dec 69 7068

Virginia Revolutionary Militia, A List of Non-Commissioned Officers and Seamen and Marines of the State Navy, Whose names appear on the Army Register, and who have not received Bounty Land; Printed by Samuel Shepherd, Printer to the Commonwealth, Richmond, VA. 1835. p. 5.
Doc. No. 48.
Burns, John   Soldier   Calvary

Possible record for this man -
American Militia in the Frontier Wars, 1790-1796; by Murtie June Clark; Genealogical Publishing Co., Inc., 1990. p.18.
Muster Roll of a Company of Mounted Volunteers under the Command of Captain Henry Bartlett, Lieut. Colo. Horatio Hall's Regiment, in the service of the United States, Commanded by Major General Scott from Oct 10 to Nov 11, 1793.

Nr	Rank	Name	Remarks
24	Private	Burns, John	enlisted Oct 10

U.S. Department of Interior, Bureau of Land Management, General Land Office Records; Land Patent Search – accessed 27 June 2012.
BURNS, JOHN
Accession Nr. CV-0038-031; Document Type – Credit Volume Patent; State – Indiana; Issue Date – 3/21/1818; Cancelled – No
Land Office – Jeffersonville; Authority – April 24, 1820 Sale-Cash Entry (3 Stat. 566); Total Acres – 00.00
Land Descriptions: State – IN; Meridian – 2nd PM; Twp-Rang – 004N-010E; Aliquots – SE1/4; Section – 6; County - Jefferson
&
Accession Nr. CV-0038-031; Document Type – Credit Volume Patent; State – I; Meridian – 2nd PM; Twp-Rng – 004N-010E; Aliquots – SE1/4; Section 6; County - Jefferson
&
Accession Nr. IN0240_.309; Document Type – State Volume Patent; State – Indiana; Issue Date – 12/5/1831; Cancelled – No
Land Office – Jeffersonville; Authority – April 24, 1820 Sale-Cash Entry (3 Stat. 566); Document Nr. – 2330; BLM Serial Nr. IN NO S/N; Total Acres – 80.00
Land Description: State – IN; Meridian – 2nd PM; Twp-Rng – 005N-009E; Aliquots – W1/2-NE1/4; Section 25; County - Jefferson

Switzerland County, Indiana Civil Order Book 4, 1820 – 1823; pg. 76.
Sept. term 1820
John Burns, a Revolutionary soldier and U.S. Pensioner filled his schedule of property, as above---property valued at $62.25.

Catalogue of Revolutionary Soldiers and Sailors of the Commonwealth of Virginia to Whom Land Bounty Warrants Were Granted by Virginia for Military Service in the War for Independence, From Official Records in the Kentucky State Land Office at Frankfort, Kentucky; compiled by Samuel M. Wilson; Southern Book Company, Baltimore, MD, 1953. p. 10.

Number of Warrant	Name of Officer or Soldier	Number of Acres	Rank	Dept. of Service: Continental or State Line or Navy	Number of Years in Service	Date of Warrant
2708	Burns, John	100	Private	Va. Cont. Line	3 yrs.	Mch. 5, 1784

Revolutionary War Bounty Land Grants Awarded by State Governments; Lloyd DeWitt Bockstruck; Genealogical Publishing Co., Inc., Baltimore, MD, 1996.

p. 77.
Burns, John. Va. Private. 26 Mar 1784. 100 acres.

Register of Certificates Issued by John Pierce, Esquire, Paymaster General and Commissioner of Army Accounts for the United States, to Officers and Soldiers of the Continental Army Under Act of July 4, 1783; Originally Published as Senate Documents, Vol.9, No. 988, 63rd Congress, 3d Session, Washington, 1915; Seventeenth report of the National Society of the Daughters of the American Revolution; Genealogical Publishing Co., Inc, Baltimore, MD, 1984. p.79.
Men listed in this volume with the same name.

No. of Certificate	To whom issued	Amount
67870	Burns, John	50.00
68994	Burns, John	110.00
69025	Burns, John	120.00
70080	Burns, John	31.37
70326	Burns, John	83.54
70625	Burns, John	88.00
74380	Burns, John	26.60
74941	Burns, John	24.84
75304	Burns, John	80.00
81104	Burns, John	80.00
81989	Burns, John	43.30
85139	Burns, John	25.40

Possible record – was he in Union County?
Early Ohio Settlers, Purchasers of Land in Southwestern Ohio, 1800-1840; Compiled by Ellen T. Berry & David A. Berry; Genealogical Publishing Co., Inc., Baltimore, MD, 1986. p.46.

Purchaser	Year	Date	Residence	R – T - S	
Burns, John (B)	1815	Feb. 3	Clermont	02-11-35	Union Co.

(B) Indiana Survey: Land lying west of a meridian drawn west of the Great Miami (known as the "Gore"). Switzerland, Dearborn, Franklin, Ohio, Union and Randolph Counties (all or only a part of each county) – all in Indiana.

Census of Indiana Territory for 1807; Indiana Historical Society, 1980. p. 21.
A list of free males above the age of twenty one in Dearborn County in March 1807 ~~
27   John Burns

The Pension List of 1820 [U.S. War Department] Reprinted with an Index; by Murtie June Clark; Genealogical Publishing Co., Inc., Baltimore, 1991. Originally published 1820 as Letter from the Secretary of War. p. 630.
Names of the Revolutionary Pensioners which have been placed on the Roll of Ohio, under the Law of the 18th of March, 1818, from the passage thereof, to this day, inclusive, with the Rank they held, and the Lines in which they served, viz.

Names	Rank	Line
John Burns	sergeant	Virginia

1860 U.S. Census, Kentucky, Carroll, Carrollton, Series: M653 Roll: 361 Page: 10 Family No. 79.
Burns, Lucretia Age: 74, Female, Race: White, Born: KY

The Vevay Reveille, Wed. 5 Sep 1860 , Vol. XLIII, No. 36, p.2., Col. 6.
Deaths
In this place, on the 31st August, at the residence of James E. Byram, Mrs. Lucretia Burns, consort of John Burns, deceased, in the 79th year of her age.

Revolutionary Soldiers of Switzerland County; Copied by Mary Hill, John Paul Chapter-Daughters of the American Revolution; January, 1958; http://www.ingenweb.org/inswitzerland/switzrevsoldiers.html- Viewed June 2012.
BURNS, JOHN   Switzerland County
Switzerland County, Indiana. Pension claim W.9372, B.L. Wt. 71127 - 160 - 55.
Born about 1763
Entered service 1777 in King and Queen Co., Virginia under Col. Richard Parker. Served until 1780. In battles of Savannah and Charlestown.
Died July 13, 1827, Switzerland Co. Probably buried Slawson cemetery.
Married Lucretia Vanosdol, 1810
Children: David; Robert; Jane; Elizabeth m Harrison Harris; George; John.
Collected by Mrs. A. V. Danner, Vevay, Indiana

Roster of Soldiers and Patriots of the American Revolution Buried in Indiana, Vol. I; compiled by Mrs. Roscoe C. O'Byrne.; Indiana Daughters of the American Revolution, 1981; p. 79.
BURNS, JOHN   Switzerland County
Born – About 1763.
Service – Entered service 1777, in King and Queen Co., Vir., under Col. Richard Parker. Served until 1780. In battles of Savannah and Charleston.
Proof – Pension claim W. 9372, B.L.Wt. 71127-160-55.
Died – July 13, 1827, Switzerland Co. Probably buried Slawson Graveyard.
Married - Lucretia Vanosdol, 1810. Ch. David; Robert; Jane; Elizabeth, m. Harrison Harris; George; John.
Collected by Mrs. A. V. Danner, Vevay, Indiana.

The Vevay Reveille-Enterprise; Vol. 122, No. 37, 15 Sep 1935, p. 3, col. 2.
Roster of Revolutionary Soldiers Who Resided in Switzerland County
By Mrs. Effa M. Danner
John Burns – Virginia line W9373, pension, 1818, Jefferson County, Ind., February 12, 1819. John Burns age 56, resident of Switzerland County. Entered service 1777 in King and Queens Co., VA. Reg. of Col. Richard Parker, served until 1780. Battles of Savannah and Charleston, S.C. Lived in Switzerland Co., Ind., 1820, received pension under Act of 1818. Children, David, age 9; Robert 7, Jane 5, Elizabeth 4, George 2 and John 4 months. Wife Lucretia, age 31.
April 1843 Lucretia, widow, applies for pension; married in Warren County, Waynesville, Ohio, June 13, 1810. Maiden name, VanOsdol.

He died July 15, 1827. He states he is a house painter. He is the "cryer" of Ebenezer Bassett's sale October 1823 and made sworn statement of amount sold, p. 252, vol. 1818-24.

Probate Court, p. 287-382 John Burns estate, comes Lucretia Burns, widow, petitioning to be administrator. Jacob VanOsdol security. Appraisers, Levi Orem, Simeon Slawson, Gabriel Johnson, Justice of the Peace, Lucretia Burns.

Funeral expenses p. 382- shroud, coffin, grave digging $9.50.

Lucretia Burns b. 1792. Consort of John Burns died August 3, 1860 at the home of James E. Bryson. (Reveille 1860.)

Crawfordsville, Ind., November 9, 1809. Letter to Commissioner of Pensions states Elizabeth Harris, aged daughter of John Burns asks for pension due Lucretia. Her last pension drawn about 1861 or 2. Elizabeth, only living child of John Burns. Marriage Switzerland Co., Elizabeth Burns to Harrison Harris, March 15.

Author's note: A John Burns is listed in the DAR graves records. He was massacred near the mouth of Lochrey Creek, (now Dearborn Co., IN), in 1781. This is not the same man.

BUTLER, RICHARD

Patriot: Richard Butler
Birth: abt. 1755
Married Spouse 1: Unknown
Service state(s): NJ
Service description: Capt. Daniel Piatt's company, Col. Winan in the NJ state
                    line; To sea on schooner commanded by
                    Lord Sterling.
Rank: Private
Proof of Service: Pension application S35804
Pension application No.: S35804
Residences: Elizabethtown, NJ, Boone Co., KY, Switzerland Co., IN
Died: 21/31 Jan 1826   Boone Co., KY
Buried: prob. Boone Co., KY
DAR Ancestor No.: None
Child: Ida E. Butler

Pension Application Abstracted from National Archives microfilm Series 805, Roll 149, File S35804

Pension abstract for– Richard Butler, Private   Service state(s): NJ
Date: 2 June 1818
County of: Switzerland   State of: Indiana
Declaration made before a Court.
Age: 63 [Born abt. 1755]
Residence now: Switzerland Co., IN
Volunteer or Drafted or Substitute: Enlisted near Elizabethtown, NJ
Statement of service-

Period	Duration	Names of General and Field Officers
1775	1 year	Captain Daniel Piat, of the First Regt. New Jersey line, Regt. commanded by Colonel Winans; others are named.

Battles: Monmouth; Long Island; several skirmishes
Discharge received: 1776
Signed by: Col. Winans
What became of it?: Lost thirty years since.
Occupation: Shingle maker but not able to do much of any kind of business
Notes: Lives with John Ellis his son-in-law.
&

Date: 2 Oct 1820
County of: Boone   State of: Kentucky
Declaration made before a Court.
Age: about 64
Residence now: Boone Co., KY
Volunteer or Drafted or Substitute
Statement of service-

Period	Duration	Names of General and Field Officers

Fall of 1775 12 months Capt. Daniel Piatt's company, Comm. by
Col. Winan in the NJ state line
Feb. 1776 To sea in a schooner commanded by Lord Sterling.
Battles: Several skirmishes; when at sea took the British vessel called Blue Mountain Valley
Discharge received: Elizabethtown, NJ
Names and ages of children: Son-in-law John Ellis

Abstract of Final Payment Voucher; General Services Administration, Washington, DC
NAME   Butler, Richard
AGENCY OF PAYMENT   Ky.
DATE OF ACT   1818
DATE OF PAYMENT   1st qtr. 1826
DATE OF DEATH   Jan 21, 1836 [typing error on card – should be 1826]
FINAL PAYMENT VOUCHER RECEIVED FROM
THE GENERAL ACCOUNTING OFFICE   Form
General Services Administration   GSA DA 70-7035 GSA Dec 69 7068

Official Register of the Officers and Men of New Jersey in the Revolutionary War; Compiled Under Orders of His Excellency Theodore F. Randolph, Governor; by William S. Stryker, Adjutant General, Printed by the Authority of the Legislature; Wm. T. Nicholson & Co., Printers, Trenton, NJ, 1872, Facsimile Reprint by Heritage Books, Inc., Bowie, MD, 1993; p.160.
Private - Butler, Richard

Register of Certificates Issued by John Pierce, Esquire, Paymaster General and Commissioner of Army Accounts for the United States, to Officers and Soldiers of the Continental Army Under Act of July 4, 1783; Originally Published as Senate Documents, Vol.9, No. 988, 63rd Congress, 3d Session, Washington, 1915; Seventeenth report of the National Society of the Daughters of the American Revolution; Genealogical Publishing Co., Inc, Baltimore, MD, 1984. p. 81-82.
Men listed in this volume with the same name.

No. of Certificate	To whom issued	Amount
68136	Butler, Richard	$460.00
68320	Butler, Richard	293.46
70285	Butler, Richard	923.59
70573	Butler, Richard	750.00
71460	Butler, Richard	45.00
71802	Butler, Richard	1,200.00
71803	Butler, Richard	$1,200.00
71804	Butler, Richard	1,525.00
81984	Butler, Richard	43.30
85056	Butler, Richard	80.00
86584	Butler, Richard	80.00
93010	Butler, Richard	80.00

Family Records of Revolutionary War Pension Applicants, Extracted from the Revolutionary War Pension and Bounty-Land-Warrant Application Files of the National Archives, Vol. I, Butler; by Robert A. Butler; Heritage Technical Services, Kent, Washington,, 1983. Roll 438.
No. 21: RICHARD BUTLER
1. Rank: Private
2. Service: NJ Cont. Line
3. Application File Number: S35804
19. Children: dau. (unnamed), m. Jonathan Ellis (see item 20.)
20. Other relatives: Jonathan Ellis, son-in-law, res. Boone Co., Ky (1820)
21. Places of residence   Switzerland Co., IN (1818); Boone Co., Ky (1820)
23. Revolutionary Service: Enl. 1775 near Elizabethtown, NJ pvt. in Capt. Daniel Piatt's co., Col. Wind's 1st NJ regt., in battles of Monmouth, Long Island, and several minor skirmishes , assisted in capture of British sloop "Blue Mountain Valley" Jan, 1776, disch. at Elizabethtown, NJ, served 1 yr.
24. Survivor/Invalid
Pension Information: $8.00/mo., cert. no. 18857, issued 4 Jan 1823, Roll of KY
27. Other records in file: Subj. res. with son-in-law Jonathan Ellis Oct. 1820 (see item 20).
Author's note: The author, Robert A. Butler, applied numbers to events such as birth, death, etc. Missing numbers in this list occur because he did not provide further information.

Revolutionary Soldiers in Kentucky, containing a roll of the officers of Virginia line who received land bounties, a roll of the Revolutionary pensioners in Kentucky, a list of the Illinois regiment who served under George Rogers Clark in the Northwest campaign, also a roster of the Virginia Navy. Reproduction of the original which appeared in Sons of the American Revolution Kentucky Society Year Book, Louisville, 1896.; Anderson Chenault Quisenberry; Southern Book Co., Baltimore, MD, 1959. p. 111.
Revolutionary Pensioners Living in the County in 1840 (Collins, Vol. I, p. 5.)
Boone County Pensioners Under the Act of March 18, 1818 (All began March 4, 1831)
Butler, Richard, private   New Jersey line
January 4, 1823; October 2, 1820 $96   Died Jan. 31, 1826

National Society of the Sons of the American Revolution - Revolutionary War Graves Register; Compiled and Edited by Clovis H. Brakebill, Published by db Publications, Dallas, TX, 1993. p. 100.
Butler   Richard; 1756-1826; Boone Co, KY; Private, KY.

The Vevay Reveille-Enterprise; Vol. 122, No. 37, p. 3, col.3.
Roster of Revolutionary Soldiers Who Resided in Switzerland County
By Mrs. Effa M. Danner
Richard Butler – made his application for pension while a resident of Switzerland Co., 1818. 1820 he is listed in Boone County, Ky. New Jersey Record, p. 61, Richard Butler enlisted in New Jersey under Captain Pratte. They went in a sloop

under Lord Sterling and captured a British vessel named "Blue Mountain Valley" and brought her to port of Elizabethtown, New Jersey.
Property, one gray mare, one silver watch.
He was a shingle maker, son-in-law, John Ellis.
"Samuel Butler and his father built the first log house in original Vevay. Mrs. Butler, his mother was the second person buried in the Vevay graveyard in 1814. Samuel Butler was a pupil of Nathan Peak's school. Peak was also a Revolutionary Soldier. Samuel Peak married Peggy Butler, December 25, 1815. "Swiss Settlement of Switzerland County", Perret Dufour.

Author's note: This citation establishes the name of Richard Butler's daughter: *Kentucky death record for John W. Ellis, Certificate No. 29145.* John W. Ellis died 1833 in Louisville, Jefferson Co., KY. The death record shows his spouse is Ida E. Butler Ellis.

CARVER, CHRISTIAN

Patriot: Christian Carver
Birth: 1759 Northampton Co., PA
Married Spouse 1: 1785 Magdalina Ziegler Older sister of Mary/Polly
Married Spouse 2: 18 Sep 1801 North Carolina Mary/Polly Siegler/Ziegler
 (b. 25 Dec 1778, d. 1869)
 Younger sister of Magdalina
Service state(s): NC
Service description: Capts. Henry Smith, John Crouse
Rank: Private
Proof of Service: Pension application S27516
Pension application No.: S27516
Residences: Northampton Co., PA; Surry Co., NC; Montgomery Co., Ohio; Indiana Territory; Switzerland Co., Indiana; Sangamon Co., IL
Died: 14 March 1836 Sangamon Co., IL.
Buried: Carver Cemetery, Clear Lake Twp., Sangamon Co., IL
DAR Ancestor No.: A020127

Pension Application Abstracted from National Archives microfilm Series 805, Roll 168, File W27516/BLWT73542-160-55

Pension abstract for – Christian Carver, Private Service state(s): NC
Date: 17 October 1832
County of: Sangamon State of: Illinois
Declaration made before a Judge or Court.
Age: not stated Record of age: Know of no record
Where and year born: in 1759, North Hampton County, Pennsylvania; Removed when twelve years of age to Surry County, North Carolina
Residence when he entered service: Surry County, NC
Residence(s) since the war: Surry County, NC; in 1802 to Montgomery County, Ohio; in 1809; to Switzerland County, Indiana; in 1823 to Sangamon County, Illinois.
Residence now: Sangamon Co., IL
Volunteer or Drafted or Substitute: Drafted
Statement of service-

Period	Duration	Names of General and Field Officers
Abt. Last of 1777		Capt. Henry Smith's company of militia, Lt. John Cooner; then a regt. of Continental Troops commanded by Col. Armstrong; then a company commanded by Capt. Jas. Crouse, Lt. Peter Pinkley.

Battles: none stated
Discharge received: Yes
What became of it?: It is lost.
Clergyman: Charles R. Macking resident of Sangamon Co., IL
Persons in neighborhood who certify character: Thomas M. Neale a resident of Sangamon Co., IL
Soldier died: 14 March 1836 at Sangamon Co., IL.

Widow, Mary Carver, was awarded pension 18 February 1856, County of Dallas, Texas. Aged about 77 years.
Wife: Her name before marriage was Mary (Polly) Segler
Marriage date and place: 19 Feb 1798 in Forsythe County, North Carolina
Names and ages of children: There is no data in the file regarding children.

Abstract of Final Payment Voucher; General Services Administration, Washington, DC
LAST ~~FINAL~~ PAYMENT VOUCHER RECEIVED FROM
THE GENERAL ACCOUNTING OFFICE
NAME   Carver, Christian
AGENCY OF PAYMENT   Illinois
DATE OF ACT   1832
DATE OF PAYMENT   1st qtr. 1836
DATE OF DEATH
GENERAL SERVICES ADMINISTRATION
National Archives and Records Service   NA-286
GSA-WASH DC 54-4891   November 1953

Indiana Land Entries Vol. 1 Cincinnati District, 1801-1840; Margaret R. Waters; Originally Published Indianapolis 1948, Second Reprint 1979 by The Bookmark, P.O. Box 74, Knightstown, In 46148. p. 4.
CINCINNNATI LAND DISTRICT – VOL. 1
Page 3. Twp. 2 N, Range 1 W of 1st Principle Meridian Switzerland Co.
William Carver SW 1/4 - S20; 7-28-1815.
Note: --The tract books for the land offices in Indiana are deposited in the office of the Auditor of State, Indianapolis. They and are in the custody of the State Land clerk. --

Early Settlers of Indiana's "GORE" 1803-1820; Compiled and Edited by Shirley Keller Mikesell; Heritage Books, Inc., 1995. p. 183.
Switzerland County - Township 2, Range 1W
Section 28 – Christian Carver – 1814 – pg. 3.

Early Ohio Settlers, Purchasers of Land in Southwestern Ohio, 1800-1840; Compiled by Ellen T. Berry & David A. Berry; Genealogical Publishing Co., Inc., Baltimore, MD, 1986. p.52.

Purchaser	Year	Date	Residence	R – T - S
Carver, Christian (B)	1813	June 11	Dearborn Ind	01-02- 28

(B) Indiana Survey: Land lying west of a meridian drawn west of the Great Miami (known as the "Gore"). Switzerland, Dearborn, Franklin, Ohio, Union and Randolph Counties (all or only a part of each county) – all in Indiana.

U.S. Department of Interior, Bureau of Land Management, General Land Office Records; Land Patent Search – accessed 27 June 2012.
CARVER, CHRISTIAN
Accession Nr. CV-0044-346; Document Type – Credit Volume Patent; State – Indiana; Issue Date – 4/14/1819; Cancelled – No

Names on Document: Carver John; Carver, Christian
Land Office – Cincinnati; Authority – April 24, 1820 Sale-Cash Entry (3 Stat. 566); Total Acres – 0.00
Land Descriptions: State – IN; Meridian – 1st PM; Twp-Rng – 002N-001W; Section 28; County - Switzerland

1820 U.S. Census, Indiana, Switzerland, Posey, Series: M33 Roll: 14 Page: 265
Christian Carver 45 and up; others in household 4 males under 10, 3 males 10-16, 1 female under 10, 1 female 26-45.

Soldiers of the American Revolution Buried in Illinois; Illinois State Genealogical Society, Springfield, IL, 1976. p.34-5.
CARVER, CHRISTIAN
Born: 1759, in Northampton County, Pennsylvania
Died: March 14, 1836
Buried: Carver Cemetery, Clear Lake Township, Sangamon County, Illinois
Spouses: (1) Magdalina Ziegler
(2) Mary Siegler
Service: Private, North Carolina Continental Troops. He entered the service in Surry County, North Carolina, serving three months from August 1777 in Capt. Henry Smith's Company; and for three months in November 1777 in Capt. John Crouse's Company.
Pension: Mary, North Carolina Continental Troops. He entered the service in Surry County, North Carolina, serving three months from August 1777 in Capt. Henry Smith's Company; and for three months in November 1777 in Capt. John Crouse's Company.
Marker: His name is on a bronze plaque in the south mall of the Old State Capitol, Springfield, placed by Springfield Chapter DAR and SAR, October 19, 1911.
Sources: DAR, NSDAR, PI, PENSION, W.

National Society of the Sons of the American Revolution - Revolutionary War Graves Register; Compiled and Edited by Clovis H. Brakebill, Published by db Publications, Dallas, TX, 1993. p. 113.
Carver, Christian; 1759-1836; Carver Cem, Clear Lake Twp, Sangamon Co, IL; Private, NC; (1)Magdalena Ziegler (2)Mary Siegler.

The Vevay Reveille-Enterprise; Vol. 122, No. 37, 15 Sep 1935, p. 3, col. 3.
Roster of Revolutionary Soldiers Who Resided in Switzerland County
By Mrs. Effa M. Danner
Christian Carver – born 1759 Northampton County, Pa., son of Michael Carver who landed in Philadelphia 1727, entered land in Bucks County, Pa. Michael Carver removed to Surry County, N. Carolina, 1771 where Christian Carver enlisted as a private in Captain Henry Smith's Co., N. Carolina, August 1777 for three months. Enlisted again November 1777, three months, enlisted February 1778 three months. Received pension, removed to Montgomery Ohio 1802, to Switzerland County, Indiana 1809. Land Patent No. 6907 – 158 acres June 11, 1813 near Florence where he lived until 1823 he removed to Sangannon County,

Ill. Died, Springfield, Ill., March 14, 1836. He married Magdalina Ziegler in 1785. Children: George, Jacob, Michael, Elvira and Elizabeth. First wife died and he married her younger sister Mary (Polly) Ziegler in N. Carolina, September 18, 1801. She was born December 25, 1778, died in 1869. Her children, Abraham, Richard, born 1804 in Ohio, married Mary J. Simmons. Solomon married Mary Bromfield. Moses born August 29, 1812, Switzerland County, married Susan Blue. Mary Polly born 1814 Switzerland County, married Samuel McDaniel. Christian.

George Carver married Sallie Hoover, November 1, 1819, Switzerland County. Research Effa M. Danner.

CHANDLER, WILLIAM

Patriot: William Chandler
Birth: c. 1746
Married Spouse 1: XX (b. abt. 1772, d. 6 May 1822 Madison Co., KY)
Married Spouse 2: Mrs. Mary (X) Goff
Service state(s): VA
Service description: Capts. James Franklin, Clough Shelton,
　　　　　　　　　　Cols. Edward Stevens; John Green, William
　　　　　　　　　　Russell, Lt. Col. Samuel Hawes [Amherst County officers]
　　　　　　　　　　10th Regt., 6th Regt. VA Line.
Rank: Private
Proof of Service: Pension application S35832
Pension application No.: S35832
Residences: Buckingham Co., VA; Oldham Co., KY; Garrard Co., KY; Switzerland Co., IN; Orange Co., IN.
Died: 10 Feb 1837 Orange Co., IN
Buried: Danner's Chapel Cemetery, Orange Co., IN
DAR Ancestor No.: A207596

National Archives microfilm Series 805, Roll 175, File S25832.
CHANDLER, WILLIAM　　　　　　　　　　　　　Switzerland Co., IN
Letter from War Dept. in Pension File –
May 23, 1927

　　　　　　　　　　　　　　　　　　　　BA-J/???/???
　　　　　　　　　　　　　　　　William Chandler – S35832

Virginia H. Buck
417 E. 2d Street
Madison, Indiana
Dear Madam
　　　Reference is made to you letters in which you request the Revolutionary War records of John Austin, who received pension in Oldham County, Kentucky; William Chandler, who was pensioned in Garrard County, Kentucky and in 1828, was living in Switzerland County, Indiana; Thomas McCarty, who was pensioned in Fayette County, Pennsylvania; Thomas Carson, of Butler County, Indiana; and Robert Turner, who served in the Pennsylvania troops and later lived in Switzerland County, Indiana.
Because of the great demand for Revolutionary War data and the limited, trained clerical force available for furnishing such information, it is impossible to comply in full with each request pertaining to soldiers of that war. You are furnished herein the record of William Chandler as found in the papers on file in his claim for pension, S.35832, based upon his military service in the Revolutionary War.
　　　The date and place of birth and names of the parents of William Chandler are not shown.
　　　William Chandler enlisted in Buckingham County, Virginia, in 1775, served as a private in Captain Franklin's and Clough Shelton's Companies, Colonel Stevens' Virginia Regiment, was in the battles of Brandywine,

Germantown, Monmouth and others not named and was discharged after having served three years and six months.

He was allowed pension on his application as executed June 22, 1818, while residing in Garrard County, Kentucky.

In 1822, he was living in Madison County, Kentucky, aged between seventy and eighty years, and stated that his wife was then aged over fifty years, that all of his children had married and moved away from him except a daughter, aged about nineteen years and a son, aged about seventeen years. He gave no names of wife or children.

In 1826, William Chandler was living in Posey Township, Switzerland County, Indiana.

In order to obtain the date of last payment of pension, the name and address of persons paid and possibly the date of death of the Revolutionary War pensioner, William Chandler (S.35832), you should address the Comptroller General, General Accounting Office, Records Division, this city, and cite the following data:

William Chandler
Certificate No. 6825
Issued February 5, 1819
Rate $8 per month
Commenced June 22, 1818
Act of March 18, 1818
Indiana Agency.

Very truly yours
A. D. HILLER
Executive Assistant
to the Administrator.

Abstract of Final Payment Voucher; General Services Administration, Washington, DC
FINAL PAYMENT VOUCHER RECEIVED FROM
THE GENERAL ACCOUNTING OFFICE
NAME   Chandler, William
AGENCY OF PAYMENT   Indiana
DATE OF ACT   1818
DATE OF PAYMENT   2d qtr. 1837
DATE OF DEATH   Feb 10, 1837
GENERAL SERVICES ADMINISTRATION
National Archives and Records Service   NA-286
GSA-WASH DC 54-4891   November 1953

Virginia Revolutionary Militia, A List of Non-Commissioned Officers and Soldiers of the Virginia Line on Continental Establishment, Whose names appear on the Army Register, and who have not received Bounty Land; Printed by Samuel Shepherd, Printer to the Commonwealth, Richmond, VA. 1835. p. 9. Doc. No. 44.
Chandler, William   Soldier   Infantry

Revolutionary War Records – Virginia; Virginia Army and Navy Forces with Bounty Land Warrants for Virginia Military District of Ohio, and Virginia Military Script, from Federal and State Archives; by Gaius Marcus Brumbaugh, M.D, M.s., Litt.D; Genealogical Publishing Co., Inc., Baltimore, 1995.p. 228. List of non-commissioned officers and soldiers of the Continental Line. List may contain names of individuals who received bounty land for services in the State Line.
Chandler, William

Historical Register of Virginians in the Revolution, Soldiers, Sailors, Marines, 1775-1783; John H. Gwathmey; The Dietz Press, Richmond, VA, 1938. p. 143.
Chandlor, William (Chandler) 6CL.

The Pension List of 1820 [U.S. War Department] Reprinted with an Index; by Murtie June Clark; Genealogical Publishing Co., Inc., Baltimore, 1991. Originally published 1820 as Letter from the Secretary of War. p. 602.
Names of the Revolutionary Pensioners which have been placed on the Roll of Kentucky, under the Law of the 18th of March, 1818, from the passage thereof, to this day, inclusive, with the Rank they held, and the Lines in which they served, viz.

Names	Rank	Line
William Chandler	private	Virginia

1830 U.S. Census, Indiana, Switzerland, No Twp., Series: M19 Roll: 32 Page: 35
Chandler, William age 70-80; others in household 2 males under 5, 2 males 10-15, 1 female under 5, 1 female 5-10, 1 female 30-40.

Roster of Soldiers and Patriots of the American Revolution Buried in Indiana, Vol. I; compiled by Mrs. Roscoe C. O'Byrne.; Indiana Daughters of the American Revolution, *1981;* p. 93.
CHANDLER, WILLIAM   Orange County
Service – Enlisted in Buckingham Co., Vir., in 1776, and served as a pri. under Capt. Franklin and Capt. Shelton, Col. Steven's Virginia regt. Was in the battles of Brandywine, Germantown, Monmouth and others. Discharged, having served 3-1/2 yrs.
Proof – Pension record.
Died – Feb. 10, 1837. Burial graveyard at Danner's Chapel, Stampers Creek Twp. [Orange Co.]
Married – First wife unknown. Ch. Elizabeth; Robin; Catherine; Sarah; Isaac; Rachel; William.
Second W., Polly Goff, a widow.
Collected by Mrs. N. B. Mavity, French Lick and Mrs. Harvey Morris, Salem.

The Vevay Reveille-Enterprise; Vol. 122, No. 37, 15 Sep 1935, p. 3, col. 3.
Roster of Revolutionary Soldiers Who Resided in Switzerland County
By Mrs. Effa M. Danner
William Chandler – Enlisted in Buckingham County, Va., 1776; served as private under Captain Franklin and Capt. Clough Shelton and Col. Stevens' Virginia

regiment. He was in the Battles of Brandywine, Germantown, Monmouth and others. Discharged after serving 3 years and 6 months. Pension all owed June 22, 1818, Garrard County, Ky. July 4, 1826 he transferred pension to Switzerland County, Ind., William Chandler's name shown on 1830 census Switzerland County and 1835 in Orange County, Ind. Died there in 1837. Burial at Danner's Chapel cemetery.

His widow, Polly Chandler is paid arrears of pension due May 19, 1837 at Bedford, Ind. In 1822 he reports his children married except one daughter 19 and son 17. Daughter, Sarah Chandler married John A. Perry, 1836. Their daughter, Fanny Perry married John Lewis Care. Their daughter, Sudie Rebecca Care married A.S. Dolch, Attica, Ind. This record and the William Coy record obtained by research of Mrs. A.S. Dolch, D.A.R. Regent of Attica, Ind. Elizabeth Chandler, Henry Fesler, 1827.

Danner's Chapel, Stampers Creek Twp., Orange Co., IN
Tombstone inscription –
      WILLIAM
      CHANDLER
      VIRGINIA
      PVT
    CAPT. SHELTON'S CO.
    10 REGT. VA LINE
    REVOLUTIONARY WAR
    FEBRUARY 10, 1837

CHRISTY, JAMES
aka (CHRISTIE)

Patriot: James Christy
Birth: 1751   Londonderry, Ireland
Married Spouse 1: 1785   Elizabeth McFee (d. Aug 1822)
Service state(s): PA
Service description: Capt. William Willson
Rank: Private
Proof of Service: Pennsylvania Archives
Pension application No.: Not located in War Dept. records
Residences: Cumberland Co., PA; Shelby Co., KY; Switzerland Co., IN
Died: 22 Aug 1822 Vevay, Switzerland Co., IN
Buried: Switzerland Co., IN
DAR Ancestor No.: A021783

Pennsylvania Archives, Series 3, Volume XX, First State Tax of Cumberland County for the Year 1778, pg. 30.
First State Tax

Freemen	Amount of Tax
James Christy	1.10.0

Pennsylvania Archives, Series 3, Volume XX, Transcript of Supply Rates for the County of Cumberland, for the Year 1779, pg. 145.
County of Cumberland – 1779

Freemen	Amount of Tax
James Christy	5.0.0

Pennsylvania Archives, Series 5, Volume VI, Muster Rolls Relating to the Associators and Militia of the County of Cumberland, pg. 563.
County of Cumberland - 1781
Captain Joshua Brown's Return of His Class Roll, Eighth Battalion of Cumberland County Militia, Commanded by Alex. Brown, for the Years 1780, 1781, 1782. (b.)
Captain Joshua Brown, Lieutenant John Wakefield, Ensign John Bell.
Eighth Class – James Christy

Pennsylvania Archives, Series 3, Volume XX, Transcripts and Taxables of the County of Cumberland, for the Year 1781, pg. 417.

County of Cumberland – 1781	Amount of Tax
James Christy	45.0.0

Pennsylvania Archives, Series 3, Volume XXIII, Muster Rolls of the Navy and Line, Militia and Rangers, 1775-1783. with List of Pensioners, 1818-1832, p. 807.
Cumberland County Militia – 1782

Captain Joshua Brown's Return of His Class Roll, Eighth Battalion of Cumberland County Militia, Commanded by Alex. Brown, for the Years 1780, 1781, 1782.
Captain Joshua Brown, Lieutenant John Wakefield, Ensign John Bell.
Eighth Class – James Christy

Pennsylvania Archives, Series 3, Volume XX, Transcripts and Taxables of the County of Cumberland for the Year 1782, pg. 682.
Transcript of Taxables 1782

Freemen	Amount of Tax
James Christie	5.0.0

Pennsylvania Archives, Series 3, Volume XXIII, Muster Rolls of the Navy and Line, Militia and Rangers, 1775-1783. with List of Pensioners, 1818-1832, pg. 275.
Rangers on the Frontiers 1778-1783
Cumberland County
James Christie is listed

Pennsylvania in 1780, A Statewide Index of Circa 1780 Pennsylvania Tax Lists, Compiled by John D and E. Diane Stemmons; Self published, 1978. p 35.
Christey, James   CUMB:DR [Derry Twp]

Virginia Militia in the Revolutionary War; J.T. McAllister, McAllister Publishing Co., Hot Springs, VA, 1913. p. 267.
Part V, Pensioners Residing Outside of Virginia in 1835 who Received Pensions as Virginia Militiamen.
Christie, James   85 [age]   Shelby   Kentucky

Register of Certificates Issued by John Pierce, Esquire, Paymaster General and Commissioner of Army Accounts for the United States, to Officers and Soldiers of the Continental Army Under Act of July 4, 1783; Originally Published as Senate Documents, Vol.9, No. 988, 63rd Congress, 3d Session, Washington, 1915; Seventeenth report of the National Society of the Daughters of the American Revolution; Genealogical Publishing Co., Inc, Baltimore, MD, 1984. p. 99.
Men listed in this volume with the same name.

No. of Certificate	To whom issued	Amount
8615	Christey, James	$ 102.60
56124	Christey, James	23.00
70833	Christie, James	111.69
70854	Christie, James	234.00
71157	Christie, James	436.19
71316	Christie, James	400.00
72979	Christie, James	24.00
73295	Christie, James	800.00
73296	Christie, James	800.00
73297	Christie, James	447.30
84434	Christie, James	300.00

9096	Christy, James	80.00
24624	Christy, James	44.66
25270	Christy, James	80.00
72260	Chrystie, James	36.60

Second Census of Kentucky, 1800; Clift G. Glenn; Genealogical Publishing Co., Baltimore, MD, 1954.
An alphabetical list of 32,000 taxpayers based on original tax lists on file at the Kentucky Historical Society. Information given includes the county of residence and the date of the tax list in which the individual is listed.
Christy, James   Fleming   8/11/1800

Early Kentucky Householders 1787-1811; Compiled by James F. Sutherland; Genealogical Publishing Co., Inc., Baltimore, MD, 1986. p. 32.

Lincoln County Tax Lists	Date	bk. pg.	
Christy, James	14 JUN 03	3.04	1 taxable male over 21

Roster of Soldiers and Patriots of the American Revolution Buried in Indiana; 1980; p. 15.
JAMES CHRISTY
Born about 1751, Londonderry, Ireland.
Died 22 Aug 1822, Vevay, Switzerland Co., IN
Married about 1785 Cumberland Co., PA to Elizabeth McFee.
Children:
1. James Matthew married 26 Jul 1820, Switzerland Co., IN to Nancy McGinnis;
2. Robert born 6 Dec 1786 Cumberland Co., PA, died 22 Jul 1850 of Cholera in Pittsburgh, PA, married 4 Oct 1810 to Anne Gilchrist born about 1789, died 24 Jun 1780 Allegheny Co., PA.

Roster of Soldiers and Patriots of the American Revolution Buried in Indiana, Vol. III; 1980; p. 15.
CHRISTY, JAMES   Switzerland County
Born – ca. 1751 Londonderry, Ireland
Service – Pvt. In Capt. Wilson's CO., Cumberland Co., Pa. Militia. Tour of duty in Penn's Valley Apr. 11, 1781.
Proof – Genesis of Mifflin Co.; Pa. Archives, Series 3, Vol. 23, p. 725; 1790 Census, Mifflin Co., Pa. portion south of River Juniata, p. 150; Patriot Index, p. 130.
Died – Aug. 22, 1822 Vevay, Switzerland Co., Ind.
Married – ca. 1785 Cumberland Co., Pa. Elizabeth McFee.
Children – James Matthew m. July 26, 1820 Switzerland Co., Ind. Nancy McGinnis; Robert b. Dec. 6, 1786 Cumberland Co., Pa. d. July 22, 1850 of Cholera in Pittsburgh, Pa. m. Oct. 4, 1810 Anne Gilchrist b. ca. 1789 d. June 24, 1780 Allegheny Co., Pa.
By Mrs. Adena Charlton, 310 Sunnyside Avenue, Aurora, Indiana 47001.

Revolutionary Soldiers Buried in Indiana (1949) With Supplement (1954) Two Volumes in One; Margaret R. Waters; Genealogical Publishing Company, Baltimore, MD, 1970. p.141.

p. 140 – In list of spouses buried in Indiana for Ripley Co., - Christie, Sarah-w. James.

p. 141 – In list of "Soldiers Who Died in Other States" (husbands of widows on list of spouses) – Kentucky – Christie, James.

Rejected or Suspended Applications for Revolutionary War Pensions; Reprinted for Clearfield Company Inc. by Genealogical Publishing Co., Inc., Baltimore, MD, 1998. p.360.

A list of the names of persons residing in Kentucky who have applied for pensions under the act of June 7, 1832, whose claims have been rejected; prepared in conformity with the resolution of the Senate of the United States of September 16, 1850.

Names	Residence	Reasons for rejection
CHRISTY, JAMES	-, Morgan Co.	Not under competent military authority.

Revolutionary Soldiers in Kentucky, containing a roll of the officers of Virginia line who received land bounties, a roll of the Revolutionary pensioners in Kentucky, a list of the Illinois regiment who served under George Rogers Clark in the Northwest campaign, also a roster of the Virginia Navy. Reproduction of the original which appeared in Sons of the American Revolution Kentucky Society Year Book, Louisville, 1896.; Anderson Chenault Quisenberry; Southern Book Co., Baltimore, MD, 1959. p. 225.

Shelby County - Pensioners Under the Act of March 18, 1818
Christie, James, private   Virginia militia [Note: Rangers on the
February 11, 1833; $56. Age 76   Frontier were Virginia militiamen.]

Undocumented family lore
Robert's parents were involved in the 'Siege of Derry' and immigrated to the US in 1763/5 and lived on the Juniata River, near McVeightown, Mifflin County, PA.

A son, James Paul Christy was born in 1751 in Londonderry, Ireland and died in Vevay, IN in 1822/3. James Paul Christy died there. James Paul had 6 children with Elizabeth McFee.

Author's note: There were two men named James Christy/Christie who served in the Revolutionary War. The other man was a Captain in the 3rd Pennsylvania Regiment. He was born in Edinburgh, Scotland in 1755, immigrated to America at age 5, died in 1823 near Delmont, (now Montgomery Co.), PA.

CONINE, ANDREW
aka Carnine

This soldier did not live in Switzerland County. His wife (widow), and some of his children were found here in early records.

Patriot: Andrew Conine
Birth: 22 Oct 1761 NJ
Married Spouse 1: Sep 1785, Yorktown, VA   Lydia (d. 1 Mar 1845)
Service state(s): VA
Service description: See pension abstract
Rank: Private
Proof of Service: Pension application W9809
Pension application No.: W9809
Residences: Berkley Co., VA; Henry Co., KY; widow in Switzerland Co., IN
Died: 11 Jun 1836 Henry Co., KY
Buried: Henry Co., KY
DAR Ancestor No.: None

Pension Application Abstracted from National Archives microfilm Series 805, Roll 162, File W9809

Pension abstract for – Andrew Conine   Service state(s): VA
Alternate spelling(s): Carnine
Date: 3 Dec 1832
County of: Henry   State of: Kentucky
Declaration made before a Court.
Age: 71   Record of age: Father's Bible now in his possession.
Where and year born: New Jersey on 22 Oct 1761
His father moved to Berkley Co., VA in 1767.
Residence when he entered service: Berkley Co., VA
Residence(s) since the war: To KY sometime after the war where he has resided 33 years
Residence now: Henry Co., KY
Statement of service-

Period	Duration	Names of General and Field Officers
Drafted Apr 1776	Discharged 1 Sep 1776	VA Militia under Ensign David Sewel, Lt. William Nestel, Capt. Robert Letter, Maj. William Morgan.
Enlisted additional three months on the Frontier, for 3 mos., does not recall dates.		
Drafted Oct 1780	4 mos.	VA Militia under Lt. ???, Capt. Anderson, Col. Williams.
Remained in the army until April 1781		Capt. Anderson
Drafted 6 Jul 1781	3 mos.	VA Militia under Capt. McEntire, Lt. Thornberry.
Enlisted 1781	Discharged 6 Oct 1781	Col. Dark (near Williamsburg)

Battles: Sent out to guard the Frontier against the Indians. Was sent to Union Town, Pitsburg, Wheeling, Holoways Cove all in PA. No fighting but on soldier was taken prisoner.
During last tour (1781) Gen. Washington & Lafayette joined the troops where he was. Under their command marched to Little York at the siege of Cornwallis.
Discharge received: Yes – Apr 1776 tour; Yes Oct 1780 tour; 1781 tour by Col. Dark (verbal).
Signed by: April 1776 tour by Maj. Morgan; Oct 1780 tour by Capt. Anderson.
What became of them?: Lost
Clergyman: John Jones
Persons in neighborhood who certify character: Samuel Dumaree
Soldier died: 11 Jun 1836, Henry Co., KY (Recorded in Jacob Bier's Bible)
Widow's applied for pension 7 Jul 1838, Switzerland Co., IN; she lived in Switzerland Co, IN since death of her husband.
Wife: Lydia
Marriage date and place: Sep 1785, Yorktown, VA
Proof of marriage: No record of marriage
Proof of children: Family Bible record in the handwriting of Jacob Bier now in her possession
These Bible pages are included in the application papers.
Names and ages of children: From John Bier's Bible -
Richard   2 Oct 1786
Anna   3 Feb 1788
Mary   10 Feb 1790
Sarah   19 Dec 1791
Ally   27 Dec 1793
John   22 Nov 1795   d. 23 Jun 1835 or 1836
Cornelius   22 Oct 1797
Cornelius   28 Sep 1800   d. 28 Sep 1839
Dennis   Apr 1802
Andrew   8 May 1804
David Damaree   2 Apr 1809
Mary   4 Jul 1810

Abstract of Final Payment Voucher; General Services Administration, Washington, DC
NAME   Conine, Lydia widow of Andrew
AGENCY OF PAYMENT   New Albany
DATE OF ACT   1838, 1843 & 1844
DATE OF PAYMENT   March 1, 1845
DATE OF DEATH
LAST ~~FINAL~~ PAYMENT VOUCHER RECEIVED FROM
THE GENERAL ACCOUNTING OFFICE   Form
General Services Administration   GSA DA 70-7035   GSA Dec 69   7068

Virginia Militia in the Revolutionary War; J.T. McAllister, McAllister Publishing Co., Hot Springs, VA, 1913. p. 267.

Part V, Pensioners Residing Outside of Virginia in 1835 who Received Pensions as Virginia Militiamen.
Conine, Andr.   [no age]   Henry   Kentucky

<u>Historical Register of Virginians in the Revolution, Soldiers, Sailors, Marines, 1775-1783</u>; John H. Gwathmey; The Dietz Press, Richmond, VA, 1938. p. 172.
Conine, Andrew, Henry Co., Ky., mpl.

<u>Revolutionary Soldiers in Kentucky</u>, containing a roll of the officers of Virginia line who received land bounties, a roll of the Revolutionary pensioners in Kentucky, a list of the Illinois regiment who served under George Rogers Clark in the Northwest campaign, also a roster of the Virginia Navy. Reproduction of the original which appeared in Sons of the American Revolution Kentucky Society Year Book, Louisville, 1896.; Anderson Chenault Quisenberry; Southern Book Co., Baltimore, MD, 1959. p. 166.
Henry County – Pensioners Under the Act of June 7, 1832 (Began March 4, 1831)
Conine, Andrew, private   Virginia militia
    May 11, 1833; $40.   Age 73

<u>Revolutionary Soldiers Buried in Indiana (1949) With Supplement (1954) Two Volumes in One</u>; Margaret R. Waters; Genealogical Publishing Company, Baltimore, MD, 1970. p.132, p. 140, 141.
CONINE, ANDREW   Switzerland
p. 132 - He d. 6-11-1836, Henry Co., Ky. Pens. W.9809 Va.
p. 140 - p. 140 – In list of spouses buried in Indiana for Switzerland Co. – Conine, Lydia-w. Conine, Andrew.
p. 141 – In list of "Soldiers Who Died in Other States" (husbands of widows on list of spouses) – Kentucky – Conine, Andrew.

<u>National Society of the Sons of the American Revolution - Revolutionary War Graves Register</u>; Compiled and Edited by Clovis H. Brakebill, Published by db Publications, Dallas, TX, 1993. p. 141.
Conine   Andrew; 1762-1835; Henry Co, KY; Private, KY; Lydia.

COTTON, RALPH

Patriot: Ralph Cotton
Birth: 10 Jan 1742 VA
Married Spouse 1: 1762   Elizabeth Kitchen
    (1747, d. 12 Jan 1832, Mt. Sterling, Switzerland Co., IN)
    Her father, William Kitchen, has been recognized as a Patriot by DAR – he provided supplies.
Service state(s): PA
Service description: Capt. Timothy Dawning,
    Washington Co., PA Militia, 3rd Battalion
Rank: Private
Proof of Service: Pennsylvania Archives, 6TH SER, VOL 2, PP 104, 118.
Pension application No.: None
Residences: Washington Co., PA; Indiana Territory; Switzerland Co., IN
Died: 1817   Vevay, Switzerland Co., IN
Buried: Cotton Graveyard, near Mt. Sterling, Jefferson Twp., Switzerland Co., IN
DAR Ancestor No.: A026389

Pennsylvania Archives, Series 6, Volume II. p. 104.
Third Battalion Washington County Militia
A Return 6th, 7th and 8th Classes, Captn. Timy. Downings Compy. 3D Battn. Washington County Militia, Ordered to Rendevouze May 18th, 1782.
6th Class – list includes Ralph Cotton.

Pennsylvania Archives, Series 6, Volume II. p. 118
Third Battalion Washington County Militia
Associators and Militia
Class Roll of Capt. Timothy Downings Compy, 3D Batt. W. County Militia.
Ralph Cotton in 6th class list.

Census of Indiana Territory for 1807; Indiana Historical Society, 1980. p. 22.
A list of free males above the age of twenty one in Dearborn County in March 1807 ~
88   Ralph Cotton   (Ralph Cotton, Jr. is #90 on this list.)

A Partial Census For Indiana Territory 1810; Compiled by John D & E. Diane Stemmons; Census Publishing LC, Sandy, UT, 2004. p. 116.
Cotton, Ralph, Sen. Historical Locality: Indiana Territory, Current State: Indiana, Jefferson County, - Name on recommendation list, 1813, to the President asking that Elijah Sparks be appointed to fill the vacancy on the General Court that existed because of the death of Judge Vanderburgh (pages 244-50). – Territorial Papers of the US, vol. 8 pg. 247.
Cotton, Ralph, Sen, Male
Author's note: Ralph Cotton, Junr. also sighed this document.

Indiana Territory, Switzerland Circuit Court Records, Order Book, October Term 1814 to March Term 1815. p.7.

He is listed in county records for the first time on 27 March 1815, as a juror. Court held at the house of John Francis Dufour in the Town of Vevay.

Early Settlers of Indiana's "GORE" 1803-1820; Compiled and Edited by Shirley Keller Mikesell; Heritage Books, Inc., 1995. p. 186.
Switzerland County – Township 3, Range 2W
Section 36 – Ralph Cotton SR – 1818 – pg. 8.
and on same page
Township 2, Range 3W
Section 1 – Ralph & Nathaniel Cotton – 1812 – pg. 8.

Early Ohio Settlers, Purchasers of Land in Southwestern Ohio, 1800-1840; Compiled by Ellen T. Berry & David A. Berry; Genealogical Publishing Co., Inc., Baltimore, MD, 1986. p.69.

Purchaser	Year	Date	Residence	R – T - S
Cotton, Ralph (B)	1815	Nov. 01	Switzerland	03-03-09
Cotton, Ralph Jr. (B)	1812	Nov. 02	Jefferson	03-02-01

(B) Indiana Survey: Land lying west of a meridian drawn west of the Great Miami (known as the "Gore"). Switzerland, Dearborn, Franklin, Ohio, Union and Randolph Counties (all or only a part of each county) – all in Indiana.

Indiana Land Entries Vol. 1 Cincinnati District, 1801-1840; Margaret R. Waters; Originally Published Indianapolis 1948, Second Reprint 1979 by The Bookmark, P.O. Box 74, Knightstown, In 46148. p.46, 68, 70.
CINCINNNATI LAND DISTRICT – VOL. 1
Page 43. Twp. 3 North, Range 2 W of 1st Principle Meridian Switzerland Co.
Ralph Lotton, Sr. SW ¼ - S36; 6-5-1818.
and –
Page 63. Twp. 2 North, Range 3 W of 1st Principle Meridian Switzerland Co.
Ralph Cotton, Jr. & Nathan Cotton NW ¼ - S1; 11-2-1812.
and –
Page 65. Twp. 3 North, Range 3 W of 1st Principle Meridian Switzerland Co. Ralph Cotton SE ¼ - S9; 1-1-1815.
-- Note: The tract books for the land offices in Indiana are deposited in the office of the Auditor of State, Indianapolis. They and are in the custody of the State Land clerk. --

U.S. Department of Interior, Bureau of Land Management, General Land Office Records; Land Patent Search – accessed 27 June 2012.
COTTON, RALPH
Accession Nr. CV-0050-315; Document Type – Credit Volume Patent; State – Indiana; Issue Date – 2/24/1820; Canceled – No
Names on Document: Karr, John; Cotton, Ralph
Land Office – Cincinnati; Authority – April 24, 1820 Sale-Cash Entry (3 Stat. 566); Total Acres – 165.30
Land Descriptions: State – IN; Meridian – 1st MP; Twp-Rng – 003N-003W; Aliquots – SE1/4; Section - 9; County - Switzerland
&

Accession Nr. CV-0036-401; Document Type – Credit Volume Patent; State – Indiana; Issue Date – 5/20/1825; Cancelled – No
Names on Document: Cotton, Nathaniel; Cotton, Ralph
Land Office – Cincinnati; Authority – April 24, 1820 Sale-Cash Entry (3. Stat. 566); Document Nr. 1200; Total Acres – 167.00
Land Descriptions – State – IN; Meridian – 1st PM; Twp-Rng – 002N-003W; Aliquots – NW1/2; Section – 1; County – Switzerland

Revolutionary Soldiers of Switzerland County; Copied by Mary Hill, John Paul Chapter-Daughters of the American Revolution; January, 1958; http://www.ingenweb.org/inswitzerland/switzrevsoldiers.html- Viewed June 2012.
COTTON, RALPH
Born Jan. 10, 1742
Service: Served as a private in 6th Class, in Capt. Timothy Downing's Company, 3rd Batt. of Washington Co. Pa. Militia; ordered to
rendezvous May 18, 1782
Proof: Pa. Archives, 6th Series, Vol. 2, pg. 104 - 105. pg. 117 - 118
Died 1817
Buried Cotton graveyard, near Mt. Sterling, Switz. Co. Ind. Died 1817
Married about 1761 Elizabeth Kitchen (b. 1747,, died 12 Jan 1832)
Children: Henry Smith, b 1763, m Mary Harrold; Susana, b. 1765; Peggy, b 1767; Jemima b 1769; Mary b 1772; John b 1774; William b 1776 m Christina Froman; Sarah b 1778; Nathaniel, b 1783; Ralph b 1786; Robert b 1788.
-More on COTTON, RALPH
Ralph Cotton, born Jan. 10, 1742, was a Revolutionary soldier; served as a private of the 6th class in Captain Timothy Downing's company, 3d Battalion of Washington Co. Militia, Pa. ordered to rendezvous May 18, 1872. This muster roll is published in the Pennsylvania archives, 6th Series; Vol. 2 pg. 104 - 105. Another muster roll of this company in which Ralph Cotton served as above stated is published also in the Vol. and series referred to pages 117 - 118 and the original roll is in the possession of Division of Arch. belonging to period of 1782 - 1783; Commonwealth of Penn. State Library of museum, Harrisburg.
Parents; John Ralph Cotton married Susan Smith, Feb. 17, 1741;
Children of above:
Ralph born Jan. 10, 1742 died Switz. Co. Ind. 1817.
John " Sept. 20, 1744
Mary " Mar. 5, 1746
Elizabeth born Apr. 15, 1749
Sarah March 26, 1751
Nathaniel March 8, 1753
Susana May 7, 1756
Robert Dec. 30, 1759

Vevay Switzerland County Indiana 1795-1999; no author or publisher. p. 1.
The first settler in the county of whom any definite account is given was Heathcoat Pickett, a Revolutionary War veteran, who located here is 1795, followed in 1798 and 1799 by the Cotton, Dickason and Gullion families.

Virginia Magazine of History and Biography; Richmond, VA; Jul 1902, Vol. 10, Iss. 1., p. 107-108.
pg. 107 - COTTON, TALBOT. – Cotton from old Bible. Ralph Cotton, son of John Ralph Cotton, born January 10th, 1742 married Elizabeth, daughter of William Kitchen, Loudoun county, Va.
Henry, born September 4th, 1763; Susannah, born February 14th, 1765; Peggy, born August 4th, 1767; Jemima, born August 8th, 1769; Mary Jane, born January 27th, 1772; John, born February 12th, 1774; William, born March 13th, 1776; Sarah, born May 10th, 1778; Nathaniel,
pg. 108 - born April 7th, 1783; Ralph, born January 17th, 1786; Robert, born September 4th, 1788.

Roster of Soldiers and Patriots of the American Revolution Buried in Indiana, Vol. II; 1966; p.29.
COTTON, RALPH   Switzerland County
Born – Jan. 16, 1742, Penn.
Service – Pri. in 6th class in Capt. Timothy Downing's Co., 3rd Battalion of Washington Co., Penn., Militia, ordered to rendezvous May 18, 1782.
Proof – Penn. Archives, 6th Series, Vol. 2, pp. 104-105; 117-118.
Died – 1817. Buried Cotton graveyard near Mt. Stirling.
Married – 1761, Elizabeth Kitchen, b. 1747, d. Jan. 12, 1832. Ch, Henry Smith; Susana; Peggy; Jemima; Mary; John; William; Sarah; Nathaniel; Ralph Robert. Collect by John Paul Chapter, Madison, Indiana.

Revolutionary Soldiers Buried in Indiana (1949) With Supplement (1954) Two Volumes in One; Margaret R. Waters; Genealogical Publishing Company, Baltimore, MD, 1970. p. 25.
COTTON, RALPH   Switzerland
b. 1-10-1748, Pa.; d. 1817; bur. Cotton Cem. near Mt. Stirling, Ind.; m. ca. 1761, Elizabeth Kitchen, b. 1747; d. 1832; chn.: Henry Smith b. 1763, m. Mary Harrold; Susanna b. 1765; Peggy b. 1767; Jemima b. 1769; Mary b. 1772; John b. 1774; William b. 1776, m. Christina Froman; Sarah b. 1778; Nathaniel b. 1783; Ralph b. 17886; Robert b. 1788. Service: pvt. 6th class, Capt. Timothy Downing, 3rd Batt., Washington Co., Pa., Mil. 5-18-1782. (Note: A Ralph Cotton (son?) was appt. J.P. for Jefferson Co., Ind. (from Switzerland Co., was formed in 1814) on 12-14-1810; on 6-15-1814, Coroner for Switzerland Co.; on 10-6-1814; J.P. for Switzerland Co.; on 12-23-1819, Associate Judge for Switzerland Co. (resigned 9-21-1821); on 8-28-1827, Sheriff; dead by Aug. 1828).
REF: "Pa. Arch.", 6th Ser., v.2., pp. 104-5, 117-8; John Paul Chap., DAR, Madison, Ind; "Exec. Journ. Of Ind. Terr., 1800-1816", pp. 167, 220, 222; "Exec Proc. Of Ind 1816-1836", pp. 121, 193 note, 206, 617 (2).

Switzerland County Indiana Cemetery Inscriptions 1817-1985; Wanda L. Morford; Cincinnati, Ohio, 1986, p.93.
Cotton Cemetery, Jefferson Township, Switzerland Co., IN
"the oldest commercial stone found in the county by the compiler, may be found here, that of Ralph Cotton, Sen., who died March 16, 1817 in the 70th year of his

age. It is down, as so many of the stones in this cemetery are, but it is in surprisingly good condition.
p. 94. Elizabeth, wife of Ralph, Sen., d. Jan 12, 1832 in the 85th year of her age – down

Abstract of Graves of Revolutionary Patriots (4 volumes); by Patricia Law Hatcher; Pioneer Heritage Press, Dallas, TX, 1987. Vol. 1, p. 208.
This is an abstract and an index to information reported to the Daughters of the American Revolution and published in their annual reports to the Smithsonian Institution, printed as Senate Documents (1900-1974) and published annually in the DAR magazine (1978-1987).
Published 1972 (Senate Doc. 54)
COTTON, Ralph   Cotton Graveyard nr Mt. Sterling, Switzerland Co IN

Tombstone photographed by author, Marlene McDerment, October, 2011.
Cotton Cemetery, Mount Sterling, Switzerland Co., IN
Tombstone inscription -   RALPH COTTON, SEN.
DIED
Mar. 16, 1817.
in the 70th year
of his age.

National Society of the Sons of the American Revolution - Revolutionary War Graves Register; Compiled and Edited by Clovis H. Brakebill, Published by db Publications, Dallas, TX, 1993. p. 148.
Cotton   Ralph; 1742-1817; Cotton Graveyard, Mt. Sterling, IN; Private, IN; Elizabeth Kitchen.

COY, CHRISTOPHER

Patriot: Christopher Coy
Birth: c. 1753
Married Spouse 1: April 15, 1773 in MD   Elizabeth (possibly Tucker)
(b. 1754 MD, d. 4 Mar 1847 Lawrence Co., IL)
Service state(s): MD
Service description: Capts. Turner, Hardin, Dixon, Col. Henry Dixon
Rank: Private
Proof of Service: Pension application W9798
Pension application No.: W9798
Residences: Worcester Co., MD; Caswell Co., NC, Garrard Co., KY, Madison Co., KY; Switzerland Co., IN; Lawrence Co., IL.
Died: 12 Oct 1839 Lawrence Co., IL
Buried: Melton Family Cemetery, Lawrence Co., IL
DAR Ancestor No.: A027112

National Archives microfilm Series 805, Roll 673, File W9798.
Letter from War Dept. in Pension File – Christopher Coy
October 27, 1933
Mrs. John C. Miller
Heber Springs
Arkansas
Christopher Coy - W.9798
Dear Madame;
    Reference is made to your letter in which you request information in regard to Christopher Coy, a soldier of the War of the Rebellion.
    The data furnished herein were obtained from the papers on file in pension claim, W.9798, based upon the Revolutionary War service of Christopher Coy.
    The date and place of his birth are not stated, nor are the names of his parents given.
    Christopher Coy enlisted in the State of Maryland, in April, 1779 and served as a private in Captain Henry Gaither's company and in Colonel Smallwood's Maryland regiment; he was in the siege of Yorktown, after which he was discharged.
    In 1807 he was living in Garrard County, Kentucky. He was allowed pension on his application executed, November 6, 1821, then aged sixty years and a resident of Madison County, Kentucky.
    The soldier, Christopher Coy, married in Maryland (probably Worcester County), April 12 or 15, 1773 or in 1775 or 1776, Elizabeth. Her maiden name is not stated, and date and place and names of parents are not shown.
    Christopher Coy died October 12, 1839 in Lawrence County, Illinois. His widow, Elizabeth Coy, was allowed pension on her application executed, November 15, 1839, then aged eighty-five years and a resident of Parks County, Indiana. In 1844 she was living in Lawrence County, Illinois.

Their children were referred to, some living in Indian in 1838. In 1840 their son, John Coy, was forty-seven years of age and then stated that he had three brothers and three sisters living, only names shown being – Samuel aged sixty years in 1840, and Anna or Amy Smith aged sixty-five or sixty-six years in 1843 and living in Lawrence County, Illinois.

Very truly yours
A.D. MILLER
Assistant to Administrator

Author's note: There are 45 pages in this pension application file.

Abstract of Final Payment Voucher; General Services Administration, Washington, DC
LAST ~~FINAL~~ PAYMENT VOUCHER RECEIVED FROM
THE GENERAL ACCOUNTING OFFICE
NAME   Coy, Christopher
AGENCY OF PAYMENT   Indiana
DATE OF ACT   1818
DATE OF PAYMENT   Sept. 3, 1839
DATE OF DEATH
GENERAL SERVICES ADMINISTRATION
National Archives and Records Service   NA-286
GSA-WASH DC 54-4891   November 1953

Maryland Revolutionary Records; Harry Wright Newman; Tuttle Publishing, Rutland, VT, 1928. p. 16.
Revolutionary Pensioners
Coy, Christopher   1761   Pvt.   Maryland Line

The Maryland Militia in the Revolutionary War; by S. Eugene Clements and F. Edward Wright; Published by Family Line Publications, Westminster, MD 21157, 1987. p. 196.
Montgomery County, Middle Battalion, 4th Company
Christopher Coy (in list)
Author's note: Served in the same unit as William Coy

Muster Rolls and other records of service of Maryland Troops in the American Revolution; Archives of Maryland, reprinted with permission by Genealogical Publishing Co., Inc., Baltimore, 1972.
p. 419.

Names	When Inlisted	Term	Remarks
Christ. Coye	20 March	3 years	recruited by Capt. Anderson 4 Regt.

p. 470.
Records of Maryland Troops in the Continental Service 1782

Name and Rank		When Commenced	Left Service and the Reasons	Remarks
Christopher Coy	P	20 March	-	-

p. 509.

Names and Rank		When left service and the reason	Remarks
Christopher Coy	C	dischd. 1 Aug '83	-

p. 530.
Records of Maryland Troops in the Continental Service

Rank	Names	Served between 1 Aug 80 1 Jan 82	Served between 1 Jan 82 1 Jan 83	Served between 1 Jan 83 15 Nov 83	Served between 15 Nov 83 10 July 84
Private	Christopher Coy (Corpl., Dischd. 12 Aug '83)"				"

Register of Certificates Issued by John Pierce, Esquire, Paymaster General and Commissioner of Army Accounts for the United States, to Officers and Soldiers of the Continental Army Under Act of July 4, 1783; Originally Published as Senate Documents, Vol.9, No. 988, 63rd Congress, 3d Session, Washington, 1915; Seventeenth report of the National Society of the Daughters of the American Revolution; Genealogical Publishing Co., Inc, Baltimore, MD, 1984. p. 122.
Men listed in this volume with the same name.

No. of Certificate	To whom issued	Amount
84584	Coy, Christopher	47.60
86658	Coy, Christopher	62.40
89254	Coy, Christopher	80.00

Early Kentucky Householders 1787-1811; Compiled by James F. Sutherland; Genealogical Publishing Co., Inc., Baltimore, MD, 1986. p. 39.

Lincoln County Tax Lists	Date	bk. pg.	
Coy, Christopher	05 JUL 96	2.04	1 male over 21
Coy, Chris	08 JUN 97	1.05	1 male over 21

Second Census of Kentucky, 1800; Clift G. Glenn; Genealogical Publishing Co., Baltimore, MD, 1954.
An alphabetical list of 32,000 taxpayers based on original tax lists on file at the Kentucky Historical Society. Information given includes the county of residence and the date of the tax list in which the individual is listed.
Coye, Christopher   Madison   1800

Roster of Soldiers and Patriots of the American Revolution Buried in Indiana, Vol. I; compiled by Mrs. Roscoe C. O'Byrne.; Indiana Daughters of the American Revolution, 1981; p. 404.
In the list of "Revolutionary Soldiers Who Were Pensioned in Indiana and Later Transferred to Other States" -
Coy, Christopher   Harrison County   d. in Ill.

Revolutionary Soldiers Buried in Indiana (1949) With Supplement (1954) Two Volumes in One; Margaret R. Waters; Genealogical Publishing Company, Baltimore, MD, 1970. p.132. 140, 141.

COY, CHRISTOPHER & ELIZABETH   Parke Co.
p. 132 -He. d. 10-12-1839, Lawrence Co., Ill. (having liv. prev. in Madison Co,
Ky. & tr. to Ind., Harrison Co. 3-11-1828. R.9798 Md. See Ill. Rev. Sold., 68.
p. 140 – In list of spouses buried in Indiana for Parke Co., - Coy, Elizabeth- w/Christopher.
p. 141 – In list of "Soldiers Who Died in Other States" (husbands of widows on list of spouses) – Illinois – Coy, Christopher.

Soldiers of the American Revolution Buried in Illinois; Illinois State Genealogical Society, Springfield, Il, 1976. p. 51.
COY, CHRISTOPHER
Born: After 1753 in Maryland
Died: October 12, 1839.
Buried: Melton or Spring Hill Cemetery, Bridgeport, Lawrence County, Illinois.
Spouse: Elizabeth
Residences: He removed to Kentucky and from there to Lawrence County.
Service: Private Maryland. He enlisted in 1779 under Capt. Henry Gaither and Col. William Smallwood, serving to the close of the war. He was in the siege of Yorktown.
Pension: Elizabeth W9798 (Md)
Marker: His name appears on a bronze tablet in the Lawrenceville Court House placed by Toussaint du bois Chapter DAR in 1921.
Sources: DAR, HR, PI, PENSION, W

National Society of the Sons of the American Revolution - Revolutionary War Graves Register; Compiled and Edited by Clovis H. Brakebill, Published by db Publications, Dallas, TX, 1993. p. 151.
Coy,   Christopher; 1753-1839; Melton or Spring Hill Cem, Bridgeport, Lawrence Co, Il; Private, MD; Elizabeth.

The Vevay Reveille-Enterprise; Vol. 122, No. 37, p. 3, col.3-4.
Excerpt from the Roster of Revolutionary Soldiers Who Resided in Switzerland County
By Mrs. Effa M. Danner.
"William Coy article - I annex affidavit of my brother Christopher Coy, sworn to 25th day of October 1831 while living in Switzerland County, Ind. Christopher Coy, pensioner No. W9798 died in Lawrence County, Illinois."

COY, WILLIAM

Patriot: William Coy
Birth: 10 Mar 1756 Somerset Co., MD
Married Spouse 1: 25 Nov 1779 Montgomery Co., MD   Mary Ann Dennis
                           (b. abt. 1760 MD d. 1832 Switzerland Co., IN)
Service state(s): MD
Service description: Capt. Nathaniel Pigman, Col. Mordock, Gen. Smallwood
Rank: Private
Proof of Service: Pension application S21614
Pension application No.: S31614
Residences: Montgomery Co., MD; Switzerland co., IN
Died: 10 Jul 1833 Switzerland Co., IN
Buried: Ted Carver Farm on Hominy Ridge, near Delhi School, York Twp., Switzerland Co., IN, tree marks grave.
DAR Ancestor No.: A027119

National Archives microfilm Series 805, Roll 26, File S31614.
War Dept. letter in Pension File –
Rev. & 1812 Wars Section.
September 4, 1938
Mrs. A. S. Dolch
204 Avenue Two,
Attica, Indiana
Madam:
  I advise you from the papers in the Revolutionary War pension claim, S. 31614, it appears that William Coy was born March 10, 1756 in Somerset County, Maryland.
  While residing in Montgomery County, Maryland, he enlisted in July or August 1777 and served five months as private in Captain Nathaniel Pigman's Company, Colonel Mordock's Maryland Regiment and was in battle of Germantown; he enlisted in October 1781, and served five months as a private in Colonel Mordock's Regiment.
  He was allowed pension on his application executed September 18, 1832, at which time he was living in Switzerland County, Indiana.
  He died July 10, 1833. His wife, her name is not given, died prior to this time.
  Children: Thomas, Nancy, Susannah, Samuel, Esther, Elizabeth, Ann, William, Sarah, Mary, Seely, and Frances. The dates of their births are not stated.
  The War of 1812 records of this bureau fail to afford any information in regard to pension having been claimed on account of the service of Samuel Coy.

                Respectfully,
                WINFIELD SCOTT,
                Commissioner.
                  Copied by ADY

Switzerland County, Indiana Civil Order Book Vol., A, Oct. 19, 1829-April 16, 1837, p. 178.
In the matter of Robert Ricketts, Thomas Mounts, Ebenezer Humphrey, Daniel Heath, William Coy and Isaac Levi, An application to obtain a pension.
    Personally appeared in open Court before the Switzerland Circuit Court now Sitting The above named applicants who being first duly Sworn doth in their several oaths make their several declarations in order to obtain the benefit of the Act of Congress of the 7th June Ad 1832 that they entered the Service of the United States under the Officers named in their several declarations (here insert them) And the said Court do hereby declare their opinion after the investigation of the matter and after putting the interrogations prescribed by the War Department that the above named applicants were Revolutionary Soldiers and Served as they have stated And the Court further certifies that is appears to them that John Pavy who signed the several Certificates is a Clergyman resident in Switzerland County and State of Indiana and the other persons who has also signed the same are credible persons and that their Statement is entitled to credit.

Abstract of Final Payment Voucher; General Services Administration, Washington, DC
FINAL PAYMENT VOUCHER RECEIVED FROM
THE GENERAL ACCOUNTING OFFICE
NAME   Coy, William
AGENCY OF PAYMENT   Indiana
DATE OF ACT   1832
DATE OF PAYMENT   2nd qr. 1834
DATE OF DEATH   July 10, 1833
GENERAL SERVICES ADMINISTRATION
National Archives and Records Service   NA-286
GSA-WASH DC 54-4891   November 1953

Maryland Revolutionary Records; Harry Wright Newman; Tutile Publishing, Rutland, VT, 1928. p. 16.
Revolutionary Pensioners
Coy, William   1756   Pvt.   Militia

The Maryland Militia in the Revolutionary War; by S. Eugene Clements and F. Edward Wright; Published by Family Line Publications, Westminster, MD 21157, 1987.
p. 196.
Montgomery County, Middle Battalion, 4th Company
Wm. Coy (in list)
Author's note: Served in the same unit as Christopher Coy.
p. 202
A List of the different companies in the middle Battn. of Montgomery County with the classes as returned by Coll. Archibald Orme the 15th of July 1780 – Wm. Coy. 3rd company.

Register of Certificates Issued by John Pierce, Esquire, Paymaster General and Commissioner of Army Accounts for the United States, to Officers and Soldiers of the Continental Army Under Act of July 4, 1783; Originally Published as Senate Documents, Vol.9, No. 988, 63rd Congress, 3d Session, Washington, 1915; Seventeenth report of the National Society of the Daughters of the American Revolution; Genealogical Publishing Co., Inc, Baltimore, MD, 1984. p. 122.
Men listed in this volume with the same name.

No. of Certificate	To whom issued	Amount
26077	Coy, William	13.44

Second Census of Kentucky, 1800; Clift G. Glenn; Genealogical Publishing Co., Baltimore, MD, 1954.
An alphabetical list of 32,000 taxpayers based on original tax lists on file at the Kentucky Historical Society. Information given includes the county of residence and the date of the tax list in which the individual is listed.

Coye, William   Madison   1800

1830 U.S. Census, Indiana, Switzerland, No Twp., Series: M19 Roll: 32 Page: 34
Coy, William Senr. age 60-70; others in household 1 female 60-70.

Switzerland County, Indiana, Probate Order Book 2, 1831-1837, pp. 133, 139, 144, 169, 197, 203, 219, 239, 261, 277, 283, 301, 305, 307.
Abstract of will and/or administration for: William Coy, Sr.
State & county where recorded: Switzerland Co., Indiana
Book/volume where recorded: Probate Order Book 2, 1831-1837
Date entered in probate: 31 July 1833
Administration:
Date began- 31 Jul 1833
Name of administrator- Joseph S. Lillard
Date of death: 10 July 1833
Notations: 15 Aug 1833, William Coy, Senr. Who made application for a pension under the Act of Congress of 7 June 1832 (on the 18th day of September 1832 in Switzerland Circuit Court) departed his life on the 10th of July last past, and that the widow of said Wm. Coy, Senr. has since that time also departed this life, leaving sundry children in this county. – Thos., Wm. & Elizabeth.
Witnesses/appraisers: Christopher Coy, the witness, whose affidavit is dated 25th October 1831, is a credible person.
Bonded by and amount of bond: Joseph S. Lillard, $200.00.
Names of heirs and relationship if shown: Thomas Coy, son
William coy, son
Elizabeth Webb, daughter
Date of division & disbursement, or final return: Insolvent estate.
Estate settled 15 may 1835. The sum of $12.00 was to be distributed to the descendants at $1.00 each (indicates there were 12 heirs). Named in records were William Coy, Edward Patton.

Revolutionary Soldiers of Switzerland County; Copied by Mary Hill, John Paul Chapter-Daughters of the American Revolution; January, 1958; http://www.ingenweb.org/inswitzerland/switzrevsoldiers.html- Viewed June 2012.
COY, WILLIAM
Pension S.31614
Born 10 Mar 1756, Somerset, MD
Enlisted July 1777, Montgomery Co. Maryland, under Capt. Nathaniel Pigman, Col. Mordock, Gen. Smallwood's Brigade, served 5 months in the battle of Germantown; discharged. Drafted Oct. 1781, served 5 months guard over Cornwallis' men, Hessians at Fredricktown.
Died July 10, 1833 Buried on Ted Carver farm on Hominy Ridge near Dalhi School. Tree marks grave.
Married Mary Ann Dennis on Nov. 25, 1779.
Pension gives children: Thomas, Ann, Nancy, William, Susannah, Sarah, Samuel, Mary, Esther, Seely, Elizabeth, Francis
Indianapolis Star; April 6, 1930: William Coy, Rev. soldier, born Mar. 10, 1756, Somerset Co. Maryland and married Nov. 25, 1779 Mary Ann Dennis; moved to Garrard Co. Ky. where he lived till 1826; moved to Switz. Co. Ind.
Pension gives children; Thomas, Nancy, Susannah, Samuel, Esther, Elizabeth, Ann, William, Sarah, Mary, Seely (Celia) and Francis, who was born Dec. 4, 1802 and married in Garrard Co. Ky. Aug. 18, 1824 to William Chandler.
William Coy died in Switz. Co. Ind. July 10, 1833. His brother Christopher Coy, also a Rev. soldier, died in Lawrence Co. Oct. 12, 1839. (See Star, July 3, 1932 for record of Christopher Coy).
Indianapolis Star of June 1, 1930 gives grave of William Coy: Unmarked grave on the Carver farm, Hominy Ridge, York twp. 21-2-1. This is near the town of Florence.

Roster of Soldiers and Patriots of the American Revolution Buried in Indiana, Vol. I; compiled by Mrs. Roscoe C. O'Byrne.; Indiana Daughters of the American Revolution, 1981; p.107.
COY, WILLIAM   Switzerland County
Born – March 10, 1756, Somerset Co., Md.
Service – Enlisted July, 1777, Montgomery Co., Md., under Capt. Nathaniel Pigman, Col. Murdock, Gen. Smallwood's Brigade, served 5 mos. in the battle of Germantown, discharged. Drafted Oct., 1781, served 5 mos. Guard over Cornwallis' men, Hessians at Frederickstown.
Proof – Pension claim s. 31614.
Died – July 10, 1833. Buried on Ted Carver farm on Homeney Ridge, near Delhi School. Tree marks grave.
Married – Mary Ann Dennis, n. Nov. 25, 1779. Pension gives children, Thomas; Nancy; Susannah; Samuel; Esther; Elizabeth; Ann; William; Sarah; Mary; Seely; Francis.
Collected by Mrs. Raymond Carnine and Mrs. A. V. Danner, Vevay, Indiana.

Abstract of Graves of Revolutionary Patriots (4 volumes); by Patricia Law Hatcher; Pioneer Heritage Press, Dallas, TX, 1987. Vol. 1, p. 212.

This is an abstract and an index to information reported to the Daughters of the American Revolution and published in their annual reports to the Smithsonian Institution, printed as Senate Documents (1900-1974) and published annually in the DAR magazine (1978-1987).
Published 1972 (Senate Doc. 54)
COY, William   Carver farm, Homeney Ridge, Switzerland Co IN

Indianapolis Star of June 1, 1930
Grave of William Coy: Unmarked grave on the Carver farm, Hominy Ridge, York twp. 21-2-1. This is near the town of Florence.

The Vevay Reveille-Enterprise; Vol. 122, No. 37, 15 Sep 1935, p. 3, col.3-4.
Roster of Revolutionary Soldiers Who Resided in Switzerland County
By Mrs. Effa M. Danner
William Coy – Born March 10, 1756, Somerset Co., Maryland. Enlisted July 1777, Montgomery Co., Md. Commanded by Captain Nathaniel Pigman, Col. Moredock's regiment, Gen. Smallwood's brigade, served as private full term, five months. Was in battle of Germantown, October 4th discharged October 1781. Drafted in Montgomery county and served five months guard over Cromwell. Men consisting of Hessians, at Fredericktown.
I annex affidavit of my brother Christopher Coy, sworn to 25th day of October 1831 while living in Switzerland County, Ind. Christopher Coy, pensioner No. W9798 died in Lawrence County, Illinois. Wm. Coy died July 10, 1833. Buried on Ted Carver farm, Hominy ridge, near Delphi school, Sept. 21, R1W [Range 1 W], York Township, located by Mrs. Raymond Carnine. Wife, Mary Ann Dennis of Montgomery County, Md. Married Nov. 25, 1779, moved to Garrard County, Ky., removed to Indiana 1826. Children, Thomas, Nancy, Susan, Samuel, Esther, Elizabeth, Ann, William, Sarah, Mary, Sella (Celia) and Francis.
Frances Coy, born 1802, married Wm. Chandler, August 18, 1824 in Garrard County, Ky. A Revolutionary soldier. William Coy Jr., married Catherine Charmel in Kentucky. Their daughter Sinae Elizabeth Coy in Francis Marion Scott, February 17, 1851 [error in original publication]. His father, William Scott born in Virginia 1785 came to Switzerland Co., 1809, married Rachel Mounts, daughter of Thomas Mounts and Nancy Crawford, Rev. Soldier. Selah Coy married Evan Jones, 1828.

CRITCHFIELD, JOHN

Patriot: John Critchfield (Crutchfield)
Birth: 1754   Sussex Co., NJ
Married Spouse 1: Silvia Nichols (proven for NSDAR) or Sylvia Randolph.
Service state(s): NC
Service description: Capt. Woodridge's Co., County Militia,
  Capt. Wm. Underwood in Surry Co., NC,
  Maj. Winston, Gen. Green
Rank: Private
Proof of Service: Pension application R2547
Pension application No.: R2547
Residences: Surry Co., NC; Claiborne Co., TN; IN; Claiborne Co., TN;
  Garrard Co., KY; Switzerland Co., IN
Died: 31 Dec 1841 Vevay, Switzerland Co., IN
Buried: Vevay Cemetery, Section 1, Jefferson Twp., Switzerland Co., IN
DAR Ancestor No.: A028378
Child: Mary (aka Polly) Critchfield

Pension Application Abstracted from National Archives microfilm Series 805, Roll 232, File R2547 (Rejected claim)
Pension abstract for –   John Critchfield   Service state(s): North Carolina
Date: 3 Dec 1832
County of: Clairborne Co.   State of: Tennessee
Declaration made before a Court.
Age: 77   Record of age: None
Where and year born: Sussex Co., NJ in 1762. He moved to Surry Co., NC when age 16.
Residence when he entered service: Surry Co., NC
Residence(s) since the war: Surry Co. for about 36 yrs., lived in Clairborne Co., TN, moved to Indiana, and back to Clairborne Co., TN.
Residence now: Clairborne Co., TN
Statement of service-

Period	Duration	Names of General and Field Officers
Volunteered	6 mos.	Capt. Woodridge's Co., County Militia Capt. Wm. Underwood in Surry Co., NC Capt's name forgotten, Maj. Winston, Gen. Green

Battles: Battle of Cowpens, Battle of Guilford Courthouse
Discharge received: Never applied because he was sick.
Persons in neighborhood who certify character: Jacob Cloud, Joseph Hamilton, Elisha Wallen, Peter Huf???, John Ousiley, and indeed all of his neighbors.
Wife: Not named
Names and ages of children: None named

Switzerland County, Indiana Probate Order Book 3, p. 435.
Abstract of will and/or administration for: John Critchfield
State & county where recorded: Switzerland Co., Indiana

Book/volume where recorded: Probate Order Book 3, 1837-1843, p. 435
Date entered in probate: 18 Feb 1842 – Satisfactory proof is this day made in open court by the oath of Perret Dufour and Julius Dufour that John Critchfield late a Revolutionary pensioner of the United States departed this life on the 31st day of December ad 1841 and that he was the identical person named in the pension certificate now produced in court granting to the said John Critchfield a pension of twenty dollars pension numbered 1701 dated the 9th day of November 1832 and signed by Lewis Cass Secretary of War, and it is further proved to the satisfaction of the court that John Critchfield left no widow.
Name(s) of executors: Perret Dufour
Administration:
Date began- 18 Feb 1842
Name of administrator- Perret Dufour
Date of death: 31 December 1841
Place of death: Switzerland County
Bonded by and amount of bond: Julius Dufour for $100.00.

1830 U.S. Census, Tennessee, Clairborne, No Twp, p. 134.
John Critchfield, Age 60-70.

Rejected or Suspended Applications for Revolutionary War Pensions; Reprinted for Clearfield Company Inc. by Genealogical Publishing Co., Inc., Baltimore, MD, 1998. p. 382.
A list of the names of persons residing in Tennessee who have applied for pensions under the act of June 7, 1832, whose claims have been rejected; prepared in conformity with the resolution of the Senate of the United States of September 16, 1850.

Name	Residence	Reason for rejection
Crutchfield, John	Tazewell, Claiborne	Not six months of service

1840 U.S. Census, Kentucky, Garrard, No Twp Listed, p. 51.
John Crutchfield Age 87, He is listed in household of Mordicea Critchfield, in the column Pensioners for Revolutionary or Military Services Included in the Foregoing.

Revolutionary Soldiers of Switzerland County; Copied by Mary Hill, John Paul Chapter-Daughters of the American Revolution; January, 1958;
http://www.ingenweb.org/inswitzerland/switzrevsoldiers.html- Viewed June 2012.
CRITCHFIELD, JOHN   Switzerland Co. Ind. Pension claim R.2547.
Pension rejected because he did not serve six months.
D.A.R. Lineage, Vol. 50, pg. 294
Born 1752 Sussex Co. N.J. Entered service in Capt. Wm. Underwood's Co. Surry Co. N.J. then Capt. Woolridges county Militia.
Died Dec. 31, 1841 Buried Vevay Cemetery. Stone.
Married Sylvia Randolph.
Daughter Mary married John Francis Dufour.
Collected by Mrs. A. V. Danner, Vevay, Indiana

Roster of Soldiers and Patriots of the American Revolution Buried in Indiana, Vol. I; compiled by Mrs. Roscoe C. O'Byrne.; Indiana Daughters of the American Revolution, 1981; p.108.
CRITCHFIELD, JOHN   Switzerland County
Born – 1752, Sussex Co., N.J.
Service – Entered
Capt. Wm. Underwood's CO., Surry Co., N.C., then Capt. Woolridge's CO. county militia.
Proof – Pension claim R. 2547. Pension rejected because he did not serve 6 mos. D. A. R. Lineage, vol. 50, p. 294.
Died – Dec. 31, 1841. Buried Vevay Cemetery. Stone
Married – Sylvia Randolph.
Daughter Mary, m. John Francis Dufour.
Collected by Mrs. A. V. Danner, Vevay, Indiana.

Switzerland County Indiana Cemetery Inscriptions 1817-1985; Wanda L. Morford; Cincinnati, Ohio, 1986, p. 119.
The Vevay Cemetery, Section 1, Jefferson Twp., Switzerland Co., IN
Critchfield   John, a soldier of the Revolution born in New Jersey 1752, immigrated to North Carolina 1763 and to Ky, in 1803 d. at Vevay Dec. 31, 1841 in the 88th year of his age – this stone is with the Dufours'.

Contributed by Judy Kappes –
Tombstone photographed, and transcribed, 12 May 2012.
Dufour plot, Vevay Cemetery, Vevay, Jefferson Twp., Switzerland Co., IN.
        Inscription –   John Critchfield
                                A Soldier of
                                the Revolution
                            Born New Jersey 1752
                                Imigrated to
                              North Carolina in
                                    1762
                              and to KY in 1803
                                  Died at
                            Vevay Dec 31, 1841
                              In the 88yr of
                                  His age

Abstract of Graves of Revolutionary Patriots (4 volumes); by Patricia Law Hatcher; Pioneer Heritage Press, Dallas, TX, 1987.
This is an abstract and an index to information reported to the Daughters of the American Revolution and published in their annual reports to the Smithsonian Institution, printed as Senate Documents (1900-1974) and published annually in the DAR magazine (1978-1987). p. 217.
Published 1972 (Senate Doc. 54)
CRITCHFIELD, John   Vevay Cem, Switzerland Co IN

The Vevay Reveille-Enterprise; Vol. 22, No. 37, 15 Sep 1935, p. 3, col.2.
Roster of Revolutionary Soldiers Who Resided in Switzerland County
By Mrs. Effa M. Danner

John Critchfield – B. 1752 in New Jersey. "Emigrated to North Carolina, 1763, Surry Co. Died Dec. 31, 1841, buried at Vevay on J. F. Dufour lot. Grave stone inscribed "revolutionary Soldier".

He moved to Kentucky 1803 to a farm on the Kentucky River Hill above Hickman Creek. Daughter Polly born 1789, married John Francis Dufour 1806. His wife ---Randolph.

Military record, North Carolina. Claborne Co., Tenn., applied for pension. He entered Captain Wm. Underwood's Co., Surry Co., N. Car. Then Capt. Wooldridge's Co., County Militia. Born Sussex Co., N.J., 1762, moved to Surry Co., N. Car. When 16 years old, then moved to Claeborne Co., Tenn., then to Indiana, back to Claeborne Co., then to Indiana. Claim rejected – did not serve 6 months. Pension granted Nov. 9, 1832, No. 1701. Signed by Lewis Cars, Secretary Wr. Probate Court, Estate p. 582 – 1844. Perret Dufour, Administrator.

CROSS, EBENEZER

Patriot: Ebenezer Cross
Birth: 2 May 1754
Married Spouse 1: Hannah
Service state(s): CT – Continental Line
Service description: Capt. Nathaniel, Regt., Col. Levi Wells;
          Jonathan Little, conductor of teams
Rank: Private
Proof of Service: Pension application – Switzerland Co., IN
Pension application No.: Not located in War Dept. records
Residences: CT, Switzerland Co., IN
Died: aft 1820   Switzerland Co., IN
Buried: Unknown
DAR Ancestor No.: None

Document contributed by Judy Kappes
Switzerland County, Indiana Complete Records, Circuit Court, Vol. C, 5 Nov 1818 - 8 Feb 1821; p. 375-6.
Pension abstract for – Ebenezer Cross   Service state(s): CT
Continental Establishment
Date: 19 Sep 1820
County of: Switzerland   State of: Indiana
Declaration made before a Court.
Age: 56 [or 66] on the second day of May last.
Volunteer or Drafted or Substitute: Enlisted
Statement of service-

Period	Duration	Names of General and Field Officers
March 1780	9 mos.	Capt. Nathaniel in Regt. commanded by Col. Levi Wells, Line of Connecticut, Continental establishment.
In 1781	9 mos.	Jonathan Little, conductor of teams

Battles: at Hanks Front near West Point in NY
Discharge received: Yes, by Little near West Point, NY.
Signed by: Little
Occupation: Farmer but not able to labor.
Statement is supported by – no other evidence of service
Wife: Hannah   Wife's age: 50

Switzerland County, Indiana Civil Order Book 4, 1820 – 1823; pg. 102.
Sept. 1820
Ebenezer Cross, Revolutionary soldier and U.S. pensioner---$30.00

Indiana Territory, Switzerland Circuit Court Records, Order Book, October Term 1814 to March Term 1815. p.90.
He is listed in county records for the first time on 14 September 1815, as a juror.

Revolutionary Soldiers of Switzerland County; Copied by Mary Hill, John Paul Chapter-Daughters of the American Revolution; January, 1958; http://www.ingenweb.org/inswitzerland/switzrevsoldiers.html- Viewed June 2012.
CROSS, EBENEZER
Born about 1754. Enlisted May 1780 in Conn. Capt. Nathaniel's Co. Col. Levi Will's Regt. Continental Establishment. Served 9 months. In 1781 under Jonathan Little, conductor of teams, for 9 months. Discharged by Little.
See Switzerland Co. Ind. Civil Order bk. 1820 pg. 373.
Married Hannah _____.

Roster of Soldiers and Patriots of the American Revolution Buried in Indiana, Vol. I; compiled by Mrs. Roscoe C. O'Byrne.; Indiana Daughters of the American Revolution, 1981; p.110.
CROSS, EBENEZER   Switzerland County
Born – About 1754
Service – Enlisted May, 1780 in Conn. Capt. Nathaniel's CO., Col. Levi Will's Regt., Continental Establishment, served 9 mos. In 1781, under Jonathan Little, conductor of teams, for 9 mos. Discharged by Little.
Proof – Switzerland County, Ind.
Married – Hannah _____
Collected by Mrs. A. V. Danner, Vevay, Indiana

The Vevay Reveille-Enterprise; Vol. 122, No. 37, 15 Sep 1935, p. 3, col.3.
Roster of Revolutionary Soldiers Who Resided in Switzerland County
By Mrs. Effa M. Danner
Ebenezer Cross – Switzerland Co. Order Book 1820, p. 375, Book C. Age 56. Enlisted in Revolutionary War in May 1780 in Conn. Company of Capt. Nathaniel, Col. Levi Wills regiment, Line of Continental Establishment, served nine months. In 1781 under Jonathan Little conductor of teams he served nine months and discharged by Little conductor of teams, at Blanks Point, now West point, N.Y. No further evidence of service. Farmer by trade. Wife, Hannah age 50. Miles Eggleston, President Judge of Court.

DAVIS, DAVID

Patriot: David Davis
Birth: abt. 1757
Married Spouse 1: bef. 1805   Unknown
Married Spouse 2: Anne (b. abt. 1775)
Service state(s): PA – Pennsylvania Line
Service description: Capt. Amos Wilkinson, Regt., Col. Thomas Proctor, Pennsylvania Line.
Rank: Matross
Proof of Service: Pension application S35878; Pennsylvania Archives
Pension application No.: S35878
Residences: Lancaster Co., PA; Switzerland Co., IN
Died: 1 Mar 1829
Buried: Unknown (poss. Ohio Co., IN)
DAR Ancestor No.: None

Pension Application Abstracted from National Archives microfilm Series 805, Roll 250, File S35878/BLWT252-100.
Pension abstract for – David Davis, Private/Montross   Service state(s): PA
Date: 18 May 1818
County of: Switzerland   State of: Indiana
Declaration made before a Court.
Residence(s) since the war: Pennsylvania; Switzerland Co., IN
Residence now: Switzerland Co., IN
Discharge received: Yes, at Carlisle, PA
Signed by: Maj. Dickens
What became of it?: Voucher is filed with the Honorable Secretary of War [PA] having been allowed 100 acres of land by the United States in 1806.
&
Date: 7 Jun 1821
County of: Switzerland   State of: Indiana
Declaration made before a Court.
Age: 64
Residence when he entered service: Lancaster Co., PA
Residence now: Switzerland Co., IN
Volunteer or Drafted or Substitute: Enlisted
Statement of service-

Period	Duration	Names of General and Field Officers
10 May 1777		Capt. Amos Wilkinson, Regt. Commanded by Col. Thomas Proctor, the Pennsylvania Line.

Rolls: Certification of Land award is in the file. Certificate states the record is in the Rolls Office of the Commonwealth of Pennsylvania, Patent Book 55, Page 343.
Occupation: Farmer – am old and frail and cannot make a living.
Wife: Anne   Wife's age: 46

Names and ages of children: "My family consists of" Alace aged 16 years; David aged 14 years; John aged 11 years; Spencer aged 7 years; Malinda aged 14 years, a step daughter, nearly blind; Manda aged 10 years.
&
Letter from War Dept. in this Pension File –
Rev. & 1812 Wars Section
Mr. James W. Liggett,   December 30, 1926
Labaratoriegntan No. 10,
Stockholm, Sweden
Sir:
     I have to advise you, that from the papers in the Revolutionary War pension claim, S. 35878, it appears that David Davis enlisted at Lebanon, Lancaster County, Pennsylvania on May 10, 1777, as a Matross, in Captain Amos Wilkinson's Company, Colonel Thomas Proctor's Regiment of Continental Artillery and served until discharged at Carlisle, Pennsylvania in the year 1783.
     He was allowed pension on his application executed May 18, 1818, while living in Switzerland County, Indiana.
     In 1821, he was sixty-four years old and stated that his family consisted of his wife, Anne, aged forty-six years, Alace aged sixteen years, David aged fourteen years, John aged eleven years, Spencer aged seven years, Malinda aged ten years, a step daughter nearly blind, Manda aged ten years. Relationships not stated. The date and place of soldier's birth are not on record.
                Respectfully,
                WINFIELD SCOTT
                Commissioner

Switzerland County, Indiana Civil Order Book 4, 1820 – 1823; pg. 195.
June 1821
David Davis, Revolutionary soldier & U.S. pensioner---$114.50

Abstract of Final Payment Voucher; General Services Administration, Washington, DC
LAST ~~FINAL~~ PAYMENT VOUCHER RECEIVED FROM
THE GENERAL ACCOUNTING OFFICE
NAME   Davis, David
AGENCY OF PAYMENT   Indiana
DATE OF ACT   1818
DATE OF PAYMENT   March 1, 1829
DATE OF DEATH
GENERAL SERVICES ADMINISTRATION
National Archives and Records Service   NA-286
GSA-WASH DC 54-4891   November 1953

Pennsylvania Archives, Series 5, Volume VII. p. 403
County of Lancaster
A Return of Capt. James Murray's Compy. of the First Class of the Fourth Battalion Lancaster County Militia for the Year 1779. Captn. James Murray, 1st. [Lt.] Geo. Chchran, 2nd

[Lt.] Geo. Bell.
Second Class - 19. David Davis

Pennsylvania Archives, Series 3, Volume XXIII. p. 249.
Rangers on the Frontiers – 1778-1783
James Murray, Capt.(p. 246) – in the list on the following pages is David Davis (p. 249).

Pennsylvania Archives, Series 5, Vol. VII. p. 1098
Lancaster County Militia – Battalions not Stated
January 8th, 1778. Rec'd from Joseph Barnet three Pounds ten Shillings it Being for the Poor families of Hanover Township who have Been in actual Service Belonging to Capt. W'm McCullough's Comp'y of Militia of Lancaster County, Rec'd by David Davis.

Pennsylvania Archives, Series 2, Volume XIII. p. 51.
Alphabetical List of Revolutionary Soldiers 1775-1783.
Davis, David.

Pennsylvania Archives, Series 3, Vol. XVII. p. 700
Returns and Valuations – Year 1792.
David Davis, 1 Cattle   Tax – 3.9

Pennsylvania Archives, Series 5, Vol. VII. p. 540.
A Return of the 1st Compy. of the 4th Battalion of Militia of Lancaster County for the Year 1778 and 1779.
Captain Wm. McCallough – Served in Middleton; First Lt. Isaac Hanna, Serv'd Volinteer; Second Lt. John Barnet, Serv'd North'd; Ensign James Wilson, Serv'd Volenteer.
First Class listing - 6. David Davis, Serv'd Middleton.

Pennsylvania Archives, Series 5, Vol. VII. p. 397
Fourth Battalion Lancaster County Militia
A Return of Capt. Jas. Murray's Compy. of the First Class of the Fourth Battalion, Lancaster County Militia, Oct. 21st, 1779. Capt. Jas. Murray; 1st Lieut. Geo. Cochran; 2nd Lieut. George Ball; Ensign John Ryan.
2nd Class – David Davis in this list

Pennsylvania Archives, Series 5, Volume VII. p. 1038.
Associators and Militia
Tenth Battalion Lancaster County Militia
A True and Exact List of the Names of each and every Male white person, inhabiting or residing, within my district, in the Fifth Company of the Tenth Battalion of Lancaster County, Militia, between the age of eighteen and fifty-three years. Taken for the Year 1782. Capt. Andrew Stewart.
Fifth Class – David Davis in this list.

Pennsylvania Archives, Series 5, Vol. VII. p. 998.
Associators and Militia
Upper Patang, April 12th, 1781.
A List of the Male White Inhabitants Between the ages of Eighteen and fifty-three Residing within the District of Capt. James Murray's Company of Militia, the first Class of the tenth Battalion of Lancaster County Militia, commanded by Col. Robert Elder.
Second Class – David Davis in this list.

Pennsylvania Archives; Series: Series 3; Volume: XXIII; Chapter: Muster Rolls of the Navy and Line, Militia and Rangers, 1775-1783. with List of Pensioners, 1818-1832.; Page: 596.
Statement showing the Names of Pennsylvanians Residing in the State of Indiana, who have been Inscribed on the Pension List Under the Act of Congress Passed March 8, 1818
-Shelby County-
Davis, David, matross, P.L., April 19, 1819; 77.

Register of Certificates Issued by John Pierce, Esquire, Paymaster General and Commissioner of Army Accounts for the United States, to Officers and Soldiers of the Continental Army Under Act of July 4, 1783; Originally Published as Senate Documents, Vol.9, No. 988, 63rd Congress, 3d Session, Washington, 1915; Seventeenth report of the National Society of the Daughters of the American Revolution; Genealogical Publishing Co., Inc, Baltimore, MD, 1984. p 136.
Men listed in this volume with the same name.

No. of Certificate	To whom issued	Amount
56988	Davis, David	43.38
58108	Davis, David	80.00
69490	Davis, David	76.00
69770	Davis, David	80.00
73863	Davis, David	33.30

Revolutionary War Bounty Land Grants Awarded by State Governments; Lloyd DeWitt Bockstruck; Genealogical Publishing co., IN, Baltimore, MD, 1996. p. 135.
Davis, David. Pa. Private. 30 Mar 1805. 200 acres.

Early Ohio Settlers, Purchasers of Land in Southwestern Ohio, 1800-1840; Compiled by Ellen T. Berry & David A. Berry; Genealogical Publishing Co., Inc., Baltimore, MD, 1986. p.78.

Purchaser	Year	Date	Residence	R – T - S
Davis, David D. (B)	1833	Jan 21.	Dearborn Ind	02-07-36 [Son?]

(B) Indiana Survey: Land lying west of a meridian drawn west of the Great Miami (known as the "Gore"). Switzerland, Dearborn, Franklin, Ohio, Union and Randolph Counties (all or only a part of each county) – all in Indiana.

1820 U.S. Census, Indiana, Switzerland, Posey, Series; M33 Roll: 14 Page: 265
David Davis 45 and up; others in household 1 male under 10, 2 males 10-16, 3 males 16-18, 4 males 16-26, 1 female under 10, 2 females 10-16, 4 females 16-26, 1 female 26-45.

The Pension List of 1820 [U.S. War Department] Reprinted with an Index; by Murtie June Clark; Genealogical Publishing Co., Inc., Baltimore, 1991. Originally published 1820 as Letter from the Secretary of War. p.656.
Names of the Revolutionary Pensioners which have been placed on the Roll of Indiana, under the Law of the 18th of March, 1818, from the passage thereof, to this day, inclusive, with the Rank they held, and the Lines in which they served, viz.

Names	Rank	Line
David Davis	matross	Pennsylvania

Revolutionary Soldiers of Switzerland County; Copied by Mary Hill, John Paul Chapter-Daughters of the American Revolution; January, 1958; http://www.ingenweb.org/inswitzerland/switzrevsoldiers.html- Viewed June, 2012.
DAVIS, DAVID   Switzerland Co. Indiana.
Pension claim S. 35878 B.L. Wt. 252 - 100
Born about 1754.
Enlisted at Lebannon, Penn. as private May 10, 1777 under Capt. Amos Wilkinson, of Col. Thomas Proctor's Artillery.
Discharged at Carlisle, Penn. in 1783, by Major Lukens.
Allowed 100 acres land 1801.
Last payment of pension made Mar. 27, 1829.
Married Anne _____.
Children; Alace; David; John; Spencer.

Roster of Soldiers and Patriots of the American Revolution Buried in Indiana, Vol. I; compiled by Mrs. Roscoe C. O'Byrne.; Indiana Daughters of the American Revolution, 1981; p.114.
DAVIS, DAVID   Switzerland County
Born – About 1754
Service – Enlisted at Lebanon, Penn., as pri. May 19, 1777, under Capt. Amos Wilkinson of Col. Thos. Proctor's Artillery. Discharged at Carlisle, Penn., in 1783, by Major Lukens. Allowed 100 acres of land, 1801.
Proof – Pension claim S. 35878., B. L. Wt. 252-100
Died – Last payment of pension made March 27, 1829.
Married – Anne _____. Ch. Alace; David; John; Spencer.

The Vevay Reveille-Enterprise; Vol. 122, No. 37, 15 Sep 1935, p. 3, col.3.
Roster of Revolutionary Soldiers Who Resided in Switzerland County
By Mrs. Effa M. Danner
David Davis – No. S35-878. Pension granted while residing in Switzerland County, Ind., May 15, 1818. Enlisted May 10, 1777 Continental, Pa. under Captain Amos Wilkinson and Col. Thomas Proctor's artillery. Discharged at

Carlyle, Pa., in 1783 by Major Lukens. Vouchers are filed in office of Secretary of War, having been allowed 100 acres of land 1801. David Davis enlisted at Lebanon, Pa. Family, himself 64, wife, Ann, 76; Children, Alace 16, David 14, John 11, Spencer 7, Melenda 14, step-daughter nearly blind, Manda, age 10. Indiana certificate 9471R, Switzerland County, $8.00 per month in Matross regiment. Command Col. Proctor of Pennsylvania line 6 years, 1777-1783. Certificate issued April 19, 1819. Switzerland County census 1820. He was a resident of Jefferson Township family not listed 1830. Early marriages, David Davis, Ann Roan, January 28, 1819. Alice Davis, Richard Roan, November 24, 1821. "Daughter of David Davis, certificate of consent of parents being produced."

DAVIS, WILLIAM

William Davis was erroneously listed, in the Report of the Secretary of War printed in 1835, as having served in the Virginia troops and pensioned in Switzerland County, Indiana.

Virginia Militia in the Revolutionary War; J.T. McAllister, McAllister Publishing Co., Hot Springs, VA, 1913. p. 109, 140, 207, 269.
p. 269. Part V. Alphabetical List of Pensioners Residing Outside of Virginia in 1835, whose Pensions were Granted for Services as Virginia Militiamen. This list was compiled from a report made by the Secretary of War in 1835. The ages are those given in that report, and are believed to be the ages of the pensioners in 1835.

Name	Age	County	State
Davis, William	70	Switzerland	Indiana

From Kentucky March 4, 1834

The erroneous information was repeated in this work.
Historical Register of Virginians in the Revolution, Soldiers, Sailors, Marines, 1775-1783; John H. Gwathmey; The Dietz Press, Richmond, VA, 1938. p.213.
Davis, William, 70, Switzerland, Ind. mpl*.
*mpl. – Militia Pension List. Compiled from a report of the Secretary of War in 1835,
"pension", Volume II, of men receiving pensions for services as Virginia Militiamen. Approximate ages in 1833 and counties of residence at that time given.]

The following transcript from the War Department Pension File clears up the confusion.
National Archives microfilm Series 805, Roll 255, File S32202.

January 4, 1937   BA-J/FEL
Viola McX. Coleman   William Davis – S.32202
Foster Apartments
Madison, Indiana
Dear Madam;

    Reference is made to your letter in which you request the Revolutionary War record of William Davis, who received pension in Switzerland County, Indiana, in 1834.

    The data which follows are obtained from the papers on file in Revolutionary War pension claim, S.32202, based upon the military service in that war of William Davis, the only soldier of that name, who was receiving pension in 1834, while residing in the state of Indiana. He served in the Maryland troops and received pension while residing in Bourbon County, Kentucky, and in 1834, was transferred to Indiana, being then a resident of Parke County, that state. He was erroneously listed in the Report of the Secretary of War, printed in 1835, as having served
in the Virginia troops and pensioned in Switzerland County, Indiana.

William Davis was born January 12, 1761, in Worcester County, Maryland. The names of his parents are not shown.

While residing in Worcester County, Maryland, William Davis enlisted in march, 1780, and served three years as a private under Captains John Stewart and Bartley Townsend, Colonel Samuel Handy's Maryland Regiment. He stated that he served as a ranger guarding the shores of the rivers and protecting the inhabitants of Worcester and adjoining counties from the Tories.

He was allowed pension on his application executed November 28, 1833, while residing in Bourbon County, Kentucky. In 1834, he moved to Parke County, Indiana, to be near "his only sister and son". He gave no names and there is no reference to a wife.

In 1834, on John G. Davis resided in Parke County, Indiana and was clerk of the court for said county. No relationship to the soldier was shown.

Very truly yours,
A.D. Hiller
Executive Assistant
to the Administrator.

DEISKY, LEIMAN
aka surname: DEASTY; DESKY; DEASKY; DUSTY
aka given : LEEMAN; LEAMAN; LEEMON

Patriot: Leiman Deisky
Birth: 1757/ 1758
Married Spouse 1: Hannah
Service state(s): NJ
Service description: Capt. Cummings, Capt. Cyrus DeHart, 2nd Regt.,
  Col. Barber, New Jersey Line.
Rank: Private
Proof of Service: Pension application S35886
Pension application No.: S35886
Residences: NJ, Switzerland Co., IN
Died: 15 Jan 1829 Jefferson Twp., Switzerland Co., IN
Buried: prob. near Old Bethel Church, Craig Twp. (now York Twp.),
  Switzerland Co., IN
DAR Ancestor No.: None

Pension Application Abstracted from National Archives microfilm Series 805, Roll 259, File S35886; Switzerland County, Indiana Complete Records, Circuit Court, Vol. C, 5 Nov 1818 - 8 Feb 1821; p. 374.
Pension abstract for – Leaman Deisky, Private   Service state(s): NJ
Alternate spelling(s): Leeman Desky
  Leiman Deisky
Date: 16 June 1818
County of: Switzerland   State of: Indiana
Declaration made before a Court.
Age: nearly 61
Residence when he entered service: Cape May Co., New Jersey
Residence now: Jefferson Twp., Switzerland Co., IN
Volunteer or Drafted or Substitute: Enlisted
Statement of service-

Period	Duration	Names of General and Field Officers
In 1780	For the duration	Capt. Cummings

Battles: Capture of Cornwallis
Discharge received: Yes, on 5 June 1783.
Signed by: Gen. Washington, at headquarters.
He was awarded a Badge of Merit for his faithful service.
What became of it?: Herein enclosed.
&
Date: 14 September 1820
County of: Switzerland   State of: Indiana
Declaration made before a Court.
Age: about 61
Residence now: Switzerland Co., IN
Volunteer or Drafted or Substitute: Enlisted
Statement of service-

98

Period	Duration	Names of General and Field Officers
		Capt. Cyrus DeHart of the 2nd Regt., commanded by Col. Barber of the New Jersey Line.

Note: He received a pension from the United States, No. 12806, dated 4 July 1819.

Occupation: Farmer – unable to pursue his occupation in consequence of being lame from a wound received in his right knee.

Wife: Hannah   Wife's age: abt. 58 in weak health

Names and ages of children: Daughter Malinda abt. 16 yrs.; Son Samuel abt. 19, very weakly; daughter Emily abt. 12 years.

&

Date: 17 Oct 1826
County of: Switzerland   State of: Indiana
Declaration made before a Court.
Age: 68
Residence when he entered service: New Jersey
Residence now: Switzerland Co, IN
Volunteer or Drafted or Substitute: Enlisted
Statement of service-

Period	Duration	Names of General and Field Officers
March 1780	Duration of the War (3 years)	Cyrus Dehart in Regt. commanded by Col. Barber (who was killed by a tree falling on him), in the Line of the State of New Jersey, and the Continental Establishment.

Discharge received: Yes at New Herndon, NJ
Signed by: Gen. Washington
What became of it?: Discharge on file
Occupation: Farmer – am feeble and not able to make a living.
Wife: not named   Wife's age: 68 – see feeble that she is not able to do anything for the maintenance of herself or family.
Names and ages of children: Daughter Sally aged about 23 years, subject to fits, has been considerably disfigured from falling in the fire, her face, head and legs very much burned; Emily, about 17 years of age, a cripple, the fingers of her right hand cut off, and of a very weakly constitution; Samuel age about 19, in the last stages of consumption; Malinda and her two children, deserted by her husband about one year, and is weakly; Polly age about 24 years and able to make her own living and to contribute some labor for the maintenance of the balance of the family.

&

Letter from War Dept. in this Pension File –

May 14, 1937
Mrs. Carrie Crozier   BA-J/EEL
405 West 3rd Street   Leiman Deisky-S.35886
Madison, Indiana
Dear Madame;

Reference is made to your letters in which you request the record of Leman Deasky, a soldier of the Revolutionary War, who received pension in Switzerland County, Indiana.

The data which follow are obtained from the papers on file in Revolutionary pension claim S.35886, based upon the military service in the war of Leiman Deisky, the name is shown, also, as Leamon Deasky and Leeman Desky.

The date and place of birth and the names of the parents of Leiman Deisky are not shown.

Leiman Deisky enlisted in Cape May County, New Jersey, served in Captain Cumming's New Jersey Company and in Captain Cyrus DeHart's Company, Colonel Barber's 2nd New Jersey Regiment, was at the surrender of Lord Cornwallis and was discharged June 5, 1783, having served three years. Soldier stated that he received a badge of merit for "faithful service".

He was allowed pension on his application executed June 16, 1818, at which time he was aged nearly sixty-one years and resided in Jefferson Township, Switzerland County, Indiana. He signed by mark. Leeman Desky, was borne on the pension roll as Leiman Deisky.

The soldier died February 15, 1829; place not shown.

In 1820, 1825, and 1826, soldier's family was referred to as wife, Hannah, date of marriage and maiden name not given, aged between fifty-eight and sixty-eight years; children, Malinda, Emily, Sarah, Polly, James and Samuel, and niece, Emila, aged about eighteen years in 1825, names of parents not shown. In 1826, Malinda had two children and her husband had deserted her; name of husband and children not shown.

                Very truly yours
                A.D. HILLER
                Executive Assistant
                to the Administrator

Switzerland County, Indiana Civil Order Book 4, 1820 – 1823; pg. 78.
Sept. Term 1820
Leiman Deasky, Revolutionary soldier and U.S. pensioner files his schedule--$94.87 1/2.

Switzerland County, Indiana Civil Order Book Vol. 6, Oct. 17, 1825-Apr. 25, 1929, p. 162.
17 Oct 1826 -
Leiman Deasky a Revolutionary soldier now comes, and files his Schedule of property And made the Declaration, and took the Oath required by the Act of Congress relative to pensioners, which are Ordered to be Recorded, and it is further Ordered to be Certified that the property Contained in the Said Schedule is Valued at One hundred and sixty three Dollars and twenty five cents.

Official Register of the Officers and Men of New Jersey in the Revolutionary War; Compiled Under Orders of His Excellency Theodore F. Randolph, Governor; by William S. Stryker, Adjutant General, Printed by the Authority of

the Legislature; Wm. T. Nicholson & Co., Printers, Trenton, NJ, 1872, Facsimile Reprint by Heritage Books, Inc., Bowie, MD, 1993; p. 181.
Deaskey, Leman. Second Battalion, Second Establishment; Second Regiment.

Switzerland County, Indiana Probate Record Book Vol. A, Mar 1827-Nov 1834; p. 106.
Abstract of will probate record for: Leiman Deasky
State & county where recorded: Switzerland Co., Indiana
State & county where will was made:
Date: 2 Mar 1829 – submittal of Inventory
Administration:
Name of administrator - William Scudder
Place of death: Jefferson Twp., Switzerland Co., IN
Occupation of deceased: Farmer as evidenced by goods and chattels
Appraisers: William Campbell & Robert Gullion
Bonded by and amount of bond: John Miller for $400.00.
Names of heirs and others mentioned in will (also signed receipts of division of estate) and relationship if shown: wife not named; heirs not named
Date of division & disbursement, or final return: 3 May 1830

Abstract of Final Payment Voucher; General Services Administration, Washington, DC
FINAL PAYMENT VOUCHER RECEIVED FROM
THE GENERAL ACCOUNTING OFFICE
NAME   Deasky, Leiman
AGENCY OF PAYMENT   Indiana
DATE OF ACT   1818
DATE OF PAYMENT   2d qtr. 1829
DATE OF DEATH   Jan 15, 1829
GENERAL SERVICES ADMINISTRATION
National Archives and Records Service   NA-286
GSA-WASH DC 54-4891   November 1953

Register of Certificates Issued by John Pierce, Esquire, Paymaster General and Commissioner of Army Accounts for the United States, to Officers and Soldiers of the Continental Army Under Act of July 4, 1783; Originally Published as Senate Documents, Vol.9, No. 988, 63rd Congress, 3d Session, Washington, 1915; Seventeenth report of the National Society of the Daughters of the American Revolution; Genealogical Publishing Co., Inc, Baltimore, MD, 1984. p.144.
Men listed in this volume with the same name.

No. of Certificate	To whom issued	Amount
9581	Deskey, Leamon	80.00
9340	Deskey, Leamon	40.60
8989	Deskey, Leamon	80.00

The Pension List of 1820 [U.S. War Department]Reprinted with an Index; by Murtie June Clark; Genealogical Publishing Co., Inc., Baltimore, 1991. Originally published 1820 as Letter from the Secretary of War. p. 656.

Names of the Revolutionary Pensioners which have been placed on the Roll of Indiana, under the Law of the 18th of March, 1818, from the passage thereof, to this day, inclusive, with the Rank they held, and the Lines in which they served, viz.

Names	Rank	Line
Leiman Deasky	private	New Jersey

1820 U.S. Census, Indiana, Switzerland, Jefferson, Series: M33 Roll: 14, p. 264
Leimen Deasky 45 and up; others in household 1 male 10-16, 1 male 16-26, 1 female 10-16, 4 females 16-26, 1 female 45 and up.

Revolutionary Soldiers of Switzerland County; Copied by Mary Hill, John Paul Chapter-Daughters of the American Revolution; January, 1958; http://www.ingenweb.org/inswitzerland/switzrevsoldiers.html- Viewed June 2012.
LEMAN DEASKY.(LEIMAN DEISKY)   S. 35886
Name is shown as Leamon Desky, also.
The date and place of birth and names of Parents are not shown.
Born about 1758
Leiman Deisky enlisted in Cape May County, New Jersey, served in Captain Cummings's New Jersey Company and in Captain Cyrus De-Hart's company, Colonel Barbers's 2d New Jersey Regiment, was at the surrender of Lord Cornwallis and was discharged June 5th, 1783, having served three years. Soldier stated that he received a badge of merit for "faithful service."
He was allowed pension on his application executed June 16, 1818, at which time he was aged nearly sixty-one ears and resided in Jefferson Township, Switzerland County, Indiana. He signed by mark, Leeman Desky, was born on the pension roll as Leiman Deisky.
The soldier died February 15, 1829, place not shown.
In 1820, 1825, 1826, soldier's family was referred to as wife, Hannah, date of marriage and maiden name not given, aged between fifty-eight and sixty-eight years:
Children, Malinda, Emily, Sarah, Polly, James and Samuel, and niece, Emila, age about eighteen in 1825, names of her parents not shown.
n 1826, Malinda had two children and her husband had deserted her; names of husband and children not shown.
Switz. Co. records; Probably buried near Old Bethel church now in York Township.
Malinda married 1824 to Joel Heron
Polly married Chas. F. Krutz 1830
Sarah married 1823 Thomas Hatton

Roster of Soldiers and Patriots of the American Revolution Buried in Indiana, Vol. I; compiled by Mrs. Roscoe C. O'Byrne.; Indiana Daughters of the American Revolution, 1981; p.118.
DEISKY (DEASTY, DESKY), LEIMAN (LEAMON, LEEMON)
                                                                Switzerland County
Born – About 1758.

Service – Enlisted 1780 as pri., N.J. Battalion, 3 yrs. Discharged by Gen. Washington, June 5, 1783. He was honored by a badge of merit for faithful service.
Proof – Pension claim S. 35886.
Died – Feb. 15, 1828. Probably buried near Old Bethel Church,
                       now in York Twp.
Married – Hannah _____. Ch. Malinda, m. Joel Heron 1824; Samuel; Polly, m. Chas. F. Krutz 1830; James; Sarah, m. Thomas Hatton 1823.
Collected by Mrs. A. V. Danner, Vevay, Indiana.

The Vevay Reveille-Enterprise; Vol. 122, No. 37, 15 Sep 1935, p. 3, col.3.
Roster of Revolutionary Soldiers Who Resided in Switzerland County
By Mrs. Effa M. Danner
Leiman Deasky – Pension No. S35885, allowed 1818. Leiman Deasky enlisted at Cape May County, N. Jersey in Captain Cummings Co., and in Capt. Cyrus Deharts Co. Col. Barber's 2nd New Jersey regiment. He was at the siege of Yorktown and stood on the parade ground at the surrender of Cornwallis. He was discharged at Yorktown, June 5, 1783 having served three years. (He received a "Badge of Merit" for faithful service. The discharge certificate of Leiman Deasky signed by Gen. Washington dated June 5, 1783 has been removed from the regular files and claims, Washington, and locked up for safe keeping in the record division. It is badly mutilated. Veterans Administration Indiana Certificate 12806, Jefferson Township, Switzerland County July 14, 1819. Sent to Vevay. Wm. Keen writes Washington, he thinks applicant should be dropped because he has enough to support himself. Suspended – Suspension removed 1826 – Invalid No. 35886. Index Vol. 2, p. 108.
Wife Hannah in weak health, family consumptive. Children, Melinda, Mece, Emily, Sarah, Polly, James, Samuel.
Marriages, Sarah Ducky, Thomas Hatton, Dec. 20, 1823. Melinda Dusky, Joel Herron, Feb. 19, 1824. Polly Dusky, Chas. F. Krutz, Mar. 27, 1830.
Switzerland County census 1820, Leiman Deasky has a wife, 3 boys and 5 girls.
Land Patents T2, R2W – N.W. Sec. 35, 160 acres, Sept. 17, 1817. This tract is now York Township and joins the Scudder tract.
The Revolutionary soldiers held a mutual bond in their experience and there were quite a number in a neighborhood or none at all.
Probate Court, March 2, 1829, Estate of Leiman Deasky who died 15 days earlier. Wm. Scudder administrator $400 bond. List of estate p. 438-440.
Robert Gullem [Gullion], Revolutionary soldier, Wm. Scudder and Wm. Campbell both 1812 soldiers are appraisers.
Hannah Deasky, widow took her $100 share, p. 441. The sale was attended by the above soldiers, also Daniel Haycock and Isaac Levi. Wm. Campbell bought two small books, 30c; log chain $1.31 ¼. Daniel Haycock bought 6 pewter plates $2.00, a brindled cow and bell $10.00, page 442. This sale is quite interesting but too long to copy.
He was probably buried on his farm or at Old Bethel church. If anyone knows anything concerning the exact location of this soldier's grave that Washington honored, I would be very glad to hear from you.

DEWITT, WILLIAM
aka DE WITT

Patriot: William Dewitt
Birth: 18 Mar 1763 Frederick Co., MD
Married Spouse 1: 4 Dec 1804   Mrs. Elizabeth (White) Connor
                                (d. 1835 Switzerland Co., IN)
Service state(s): PA
Service description: Capt. Thomas Clugedge
Rank: Private
Proof of Service: Pension application W729
Pension application No.: W729
Residences: aft. war – Bedford Co., PA; KY; Indiana Territory; Switzerland Co.
Died: 31 Jan 1838 Cotton Twp., Switzerland Co., IN
Buried: prob. in Cotton Twp., Switzerland Co., IN
DAR Ancestor No.: A032505

Switzerland County, Indiana Complete Records, Circuit Court, Vol. A, Apr ?, 1827-Mar 10, 1832; p. 62.; Switzerland County, Indiana Probate Record Book Vol. A, Mar 1827-Nov 1834; p. 325. ;Pension Application Abstracted from National Archives microfilm Series 805, Roll 267, File W729/BLWT26609-160-55.

Pension abstract for – William Dewitt   Service state(s): PA
Date: 17 Oct 1827
County of: Switzerland   State of: Indiana
Declaration made before a Circuit Court.
Schedule of property valued at $114.50, and declaration of service.
Age: 64 years on 18 March last.
Residence when he entered service: Huntingdon Co., PA
Residence now: Switzerland Co., IN
Volunteer or Drafted or Substitute: Enlisted
Rank(s): not stated
Statement of service-

Period   Duration   Names of General and Field Officers
1780 or 1781   9 mos.   Thomas Cluedege, Maj. Robert Cluedege,
                               Pennsylvania Line, Continental establishment.

Family: None stated
&
Date: 14 November 1832
County of: Switzerland   State of: Indiana
Declaration made before a Judge or Court.
Age: 69 years   Record of age: Bible presented by father.
                          Showed very old Bible to the Court.
Where and year born: 18 March 1763 in Fredericktown, Maryland
Residence when he entered service: Bedford Co., PA
Residence(s) since the war: Bedford Co., for 20 years; Kentucky 18 years,
                            since in Indiana.
Residence now: Switzerland Co., IN

Volunteer or Drafted or Substitute Enlisted
Statement of service-

Period	Duration	Names of General and Field Officers
1 Apr 1780	9 months	Pennsylvania Militia commanded by Thomas Clugedge, Major Robert Clugedge, Col. Piper.

Discharge received: No written discharge
Clergyman: John Pavy
Persons in neighborhood who certify character: Samuel Pavy, John Dickinson, Peter Lock, William Dickinson, and many others.
Soldier died: 31 January 1838
&
Widow's Pension Application
Date: 8 March 1853
County of: Switzerland   State of: Indiana
Declaration made before a Court of Common Pleas
Wife: Elizabeth Conner, a widow whose maiden name was White.
Wife's age: 75 years
A resident of Cotton Township, Switzerland Co., IN
Marriage date and place: 4 December 1804 at Newport, Campbell Co., KY
Proof of marriage: Copy of Marriage Bond dated 23 April 1853 is in this pension file
Campbell Co., KY; William Dewitt to Elizabeth Conner, widow
Names and ages of children: No reference to children.

Switzerland County, Indiana Civil Order Book Vol. 6, Oct. 17, 1825-Apr. 25, 1929, p. 317.
17 Oct 1827 -
William DeWitt a Revolutionary Soldier now comes in open Court, and files his Schedule of Property, and made the Declaration and took the Oath required by the Act of Congress relative to Pensioners, which are ordered to be Recorded; and it is further ordered by the Court to be Certified that the property contained in Said Schedule is Valued at One hundred and fourteen Dollars and fifty cents.

Switzerland County, Indiana Probate Order Book 2 1831-1837; p. 91,
14 November 1832
In the matter of   } An applicant for a Pension under the act of Congress of the
William Dewitt   } 7th June 1832
                                       And the Court do hereby declare their opinion, after the Investigation of the matter, and after putting the interrogations prescribed by the war department, that the above named William Dewitt was a Revolutionary Soldier and served as he states, and the Court further certifies that it appears to them that John Pavy who has Signed the preceeding certificate is a clergyman resident in Switzerland County State of Indiana and that John Dickinson who also Signed the Same is a resident of Switzerland County and State of Indiana and is a credible person and their Statement is entitled to Credit.

Pennsylvania Archives, Series 3, Volume XXIII. p. 600.
Muster Rolls of the Navy and Line, Militia and Rangers, 1775-1783. with List of Pensioners, 1818-1832.
Switzerland County
DeWit, Wm., pr. P.M., April 13, 1833; 78.

Index to U.S. Invalid Pension Records 1801-1815; by Murtie June Clark; Genealogical Publishing Co., Inc., 1991; p. 57.
This book is an index to the ledger titled: "Revolutionary War and Acts of Military Establishment, Invalid Pensioners Payments, March 1801 through September 1815, containing pensions paid by the United States to invalid soldiers who served in the Revolutionary War and the frontier wars after 1783."
Description : "This ledger is an important substitute for lost claim files, composed of evidence and testimony of Revolutionary War soldiers together with judicial certification and War Department confirmation, that perished in the catastrophes in the capital city."
PENNSYLVANIA

Name	Rank	Page	Remarks
Dewitt, William	Private	40, 106	-

Revolutionary Pensioners, A Transcript of the Pension List of the United States for 1813; Southern Book Company, Baltimore, 1959. p. 30.

		No on Roll	Rank or Quality	Annual Stipend
Pennsylvania	William Dewitt	56	Private	30

Abstract of Final Payment Voucher; General Services Administration, Washington, DC
FINAL PAYMENT VOUCHER RECEIVED FROM
THE GENERAL ACCOUNTING OFFICE
NAME   Dewitt, William
AGENCY OF PAYMENT   Indiana
DATE OF ACT   1832
DATE OF PAYMENT   2d qtr. 1838
DATE OF DEATH   Jan 31, 1838
GENERAL SERVICES ADMINISTRATION
National Archives and Records Service   NA-286
GSA-WASH DC 54-4891   November 1953
&
Abstract of Final Payment Voucher; General Services Administration, Washington, DC
NAME   Dewitt, Elizabeth widow of William
AGENCY OF PAYMENT   Indiana
DATE OF ACT   1853 2d Sect.
DATE OF PAYMENT   Sept. 4, 1863
DATE OF DEATH
LAST ~~FINAL~~ PAYMENT VOUCHER RECEIVED FROM

THE GENERAL ACCOUNTING OFFICE   Form
General Services Administration   GSA DA 70-7035 GSA Dec 69 7068

Switzerland County, Indiana Probate Order Book 3, p. 83.
16 May 1838
In the matter of the Proof of the }
Death of William Dewitt, Dec'd.}
                      Now on this day comes into Court Elizabeth Dewitt widow of the said Decedent and Exhibited to the Said County Satisfactory evidence that William Dewitt late of Switzerland County, Indiana who was a pensioner of the United States at the rate of thirty dollars per annum, died in Cotton Township County aforesaid on the 31st day of January 1838, that he left a widow whose name is Elizabeth Dewitt.

Switzerland County, IN, Will Book Vol. 1, 3 Jan 1823-10 Nov 1847, p. 130.
Abstract of will and/or administration for: William Dewitt
State & county where recorded: Switzerland Co., Indiana
State & county where will was made: Switzerland Co., IN
Book/volume where recorded: Will Book 1.
Date will made: 1 April 1835
Date entered in probate: 19 May 1838
Witnesses/appraisers: (in some cases, purchasers at sale of estate may be listed on another page and attached hereto): Witnesses to Will – John K. Walker & Amasa Hyde.
Names of heirs and others mentioned in will (also signed receipts of division of estate) and relationship if shown: Wife Elizabeth; Children named in the will are Polly Bradford, Nancy, Betsey, Palmerton, John married Mary Jane Potter, Pheoby married John Johy, Judith married Simeon Shattick, Marie and Isabelle.

Switzerland County, Indiana Probate Order Book 3, 12 Jan 1863-20 Sep 1867; p.314, 322.
Abstract of will and/or administration for: Elizabeth Dewitt
State & county where recorded: Switzerland Co., Indiana
Witness to Will: James Dickason
Date entered in probate: 28 June 1865 – Proof of Will

Second Census of Kentucky, 1800; Clift G. Glenn; Genealogical Publishing Co., Baltimore, MD, 1954.
An alphabetical list of 32,000 taxpayers based on original tax lists on file at the Kentucky Historical Society. Information given includes the county of residence and the date of the tax list in which the individual is listed.
Dewitt, William   Bracken   11/22/1799

Census of Indiana Territory for 1807; Indiana Historical Society, 1980. p. 22.
A list of free males above the age of twenty one in Dearborn County in March 1807 ~~
127   William Dewitt

A Partial Census For Indiana Territory 1810; Compiled by John D & E. Diane Stemmons; Census Publishing LC, Sandy, UT, 2004. p. 147.
Dewit, William, Historical Locality: Indiana Territory, Current State: Indiana, Dearborn County, Randolph Township – Name on list of electors of election held 3 August 1812 at the house of Daniel Aikens at John James Saw Mill. – Election Returns, 1809, 1812 (Indiana Historical Society), Coll. #M98 Box 32, Folder 10 pg. 12.
Dewit, William, Male

1820 U.S. Census, Indiana, Switzerland, Jefferson, Series: M33 Roll: 14 Pg: 267
William Dewitt 45 and up; others in household 2 males 10-16, 4 females under 10, 1 female 16-26, 1 female 45 and up.

1830 U.S. Census, Indiana, Switzerland, No Twp, Series: M19 Roll: 32 Page: 38.
William Dewitt, Age 60-70

Revolutionary Soldiers of Switzerland County; Copied by Mary Hill, John Paul Chapter-Daughters of the American Revolution; January, 1958;
http://www.ingenweb.org/inswitzerland/switzrevsoldiers.html- Viewed June 2012.
DEWITT, WILLIAM   Pension W.729
William Dewitt was born March 18, 1763 in Fredericktown, Frederick County, Maryland. Names of Parents not shown.
While residing in Bedford County, Pennsylvania, William Dewitt enlisted April 1, 1780, served nine months as a private in Captain Thomas Cluggage's company, Colonel Piper's Pennsylvania Regiment; Marched to a fort at the lead mines in Bedford county, where he was stationed during the whole time of his enlistment. After the Revolution, he continued to reside in Pennsylvania for twenty years, then moved to Kentucky, and lived eighteen years, then to Indiana.
He died in Switzerland County, January 31, 1838.
Is probably buried in Cotton Twp., Switzerland Co.
The soldier married in December, 1804, Elizabeth Conner, a widow, whose maiden name was White.
The date and place of her birth was not given.
The widow stated that she was married to William Dewitt in Newport, Campbell County, Kentucky, also in Scott County, Ky. The marriage bond was dated Dec. 5, 1804 in Campbell Co. Ky.
Elizabeth, widow of William Dewitt, was allowed pension on her application executed April 8, 1855, at which time she was aged seventy-five years and resided in Cotton township, Switzerland County, Indiana.
There is no reference to children
Pr. bk. A pg. 91 Switz. Co. Ind.: William Dewitt, revolutionary soldier. John Pavy & John Dickerson, sign

Roster of Soldiers and Patriots of the American Revolution Buried in Indiana, Vol. 1; compiled by Mrs. Roscoe C. O'Byrne.; Indiana Daughters of the American Revolution, 1981; p.122.
DEWITT, WILLIAM   Switzerland County
Born – March 18, 1763, Frederick Co., Maryland

Service – Enlisted and served in a company of Penn. Militia, under Capt. Thos. Clugedge, Maj. Poper. Was drafted in Bedford Co., Penn. Served 9 mos.
Proof – Pension claim w. 729 B. L. Wt. 26609-160-35.
Died – Jan 31, 1838. Probably buried in Cotton Twp., Switzerland Co..
Married – Elizabeth White Connor, m. Dec. 4, 1804. Ch. (named in soldier's will) Polly Bradford; Nancy; Betsey; Palmerton; John m. Mary Jane Potter; Phoebe b. John Johy; Judith m. Simeon Shattick; Marie; Isabelle.
Collected by Mrs. A V. Danner, Vevay, Indiana

The Vevay Reveille-Enterprise Vol. 122, No. 37, 15 Sep 1935, p. 3, col.4-5.
Roster of Revolutionary Soldiers Who Resided in Switzerland County
By Mrs. Effa M. Danner
The data which follows are obtained from the papers on file in Revolutionary War pension claim W.729, based upon the military service in that war of William Dewitt.
William Dewitt- was born March 18, 1763, in Fredericktown, Frederick County, Maryland. The names of his parents are not shown.
While residing in Bedford County, Pennsylvania, William Dewitt enlisted April 1, 1780, served nine months as a private in Captain Thomas Cluggage's Company, Col. Piper's Pennsylvania Regiment, marched to a fort at the lead mines in Bedford County, where he was stationed during the whole time of his enlistment.
After the Revolution he continued to reside in Pennsylvania for twenty years then moved to Kentucky and lived eighteen years; thence to Indiana.
He was allowed pension on his application executed November 14, 1832 while residing in Switzerland County Indiana.
He died in said Switzerland County, January 31, 1838.
The soldier married in December 1804, Elizabeth Conner or Connor, a widow whose maiden name was White. The date and place of her birth was not given. The widow stated that she was married to William Dewitt in Newport, Campbell County, Kentucky, also, in Scott County, Kentucky. The marriage bond was dated December 5, 1804, in Campbell County, Kentucky.
Elizabeth widow of William Dewitt, was allowed pension on her application executed April 8, 1853, at which time she was aged seventy-five years and resided in Cotton Township, Switzerland County, Ind.
There is no reference to children.
Switzerland County Records – Wm. Dewitt's petition for pension, June 7, 1832, page 91, probate court. Rev. John Pavy and John Dickason, witnesses, both creditable citizens.
Last will, Book H, p. 89, April 1, 1835. Probated Mary 1838 – "I, Wm. Dewitt, yeoman, etc., to my beloved daughters, Polly Bradford $1.00; Nancy Dewitt $1.00; Betsy Palmerton $1.00; son, John Dewitt $1.00, Phoeby Irby $1.00, Judith Shattuck $1.00, to Marie Dewitt, a cow, one bed $1.00, Isabelle Dewitt, a cow, one bed and bedding and $1.00, to my wife Elizabeth the residue of my real and personal property, she being executrix. April 1, 1835.
William Dewitt   witnesses, John K. Walker, Amasy Hyde. He died 15 days prior to May 18, 1838.

Cotton Township marriages: John Dewitt, Mary Jane Potter, 1824. Phoebe Dewitt, John Irby, Dec. 20, 1881. Judith Dewitt, Simeon Shaddock, Nov. 4, 1834. Mariah Dewitt, John Moore, Jr., Feb. 20, 1837. Belle Dewitt, George F. Garlinghouse, Apr. 5, 1840.

DICKINSON, GRIFFITH
aka DICKASON

In 1798, or before, Griffith Dickison and his wife Susan moved from Logan Co., KY to the Northwest Territory. On 1 March 1803, the land they settled became a part of the State of Ohio. On 30 Nov 1804, Griffy Dickison and his neighbor Stillwell Heady, entered their land at the Cincinnati Land Company. The land, located on Indian Creek, was described as Range 03W, Township 02, Section 02. Griffith Dickinson and Stillwell Heady are the first proven land owners in what later became Switzerland County, Indiana.

Patriot: Griffith Dickinson
Birth: 25 Dec 1762 Hanover Co., VA
Married Spouse 1: 1785/1786 VA   Susan X (b. bef. 1767, VA
                                            d. 1830-1833, Switzerland Co., IN)
Service state(s): VA
Service description: Capt. Richard Anderson's 5th Virginia Regiment
            commanded by Col. Ball and Gen. Hand's Brigade.
Rank: Private
Proof of Service: Pension application – Switzerland Co., IN
Pension application No.: Not in War Department records
Residences: Hanover Co., VA; Lincoln & Logan Co., KY; Northwest Territory;
            Ohio; Indiana Territory; Switzerland Co., IN.
Died: aft. 1840 census   Switzerland Co., IN
Buried: Unknown
DAR Ancestor No.: A207752

Switzerland County, Indiana Civil Complete Record, Vol. F, Sept. 1831-Sept. 1835, Page 68-69.
September Term 1832
Pleas in the Circuit Court of the County of Switzerland and the State of Indiana
Pension abstract for – Griffith Dickinson   Service state(s): Virginia
Date: 17 September 1832
County of: Switzerland   State of: Indiana
Declaration made before Circuit Court.
Record of age: Lost it
Where and year born: 25 December 1862 in Hanover Co., Virginia
Residence when he entered service: Hanover Co., VA
Residence(s) since the war: Hanover Co., Virginia about 6 years, Kentucky about 14 years, Indiana 22 or 23 years. "I entered the first land in this county."
Residence now: Switzerland Co., IN
Volunteer or Drafted or Substitute: Drafted First tour, Volunteered Second tour.
Rank(s): Private
Statement of service-

Period	Duration	Names of General and Field Officers
1777	3 years	Capt. Richard Anderson's 5th Virginia Regiment commanded by Col. Ball and Gen. Hand's Brigade.

Battles: White Plains, Monmouth, at Valley Forge over winter. Had camp fever at Valley Forge and was left behind. Recovered, pursued the army, overtook it between Philadelphia and Germantown, then sent to Valley Forge by May 1778. Discharge received: At Williamsburg, VA (he thinks). Had a written discharge, at my house and it burned about 30 years ago.
Person now living who can testify to service: Know of none living who can testify to service.
Clergyman: John Pavy
Persons in neighborhood who certify character: William Cotton, Samuel Beal, Stilwell Heady, Thomas Gilliand, John F. Dufour.

Switzerland County, Indiana Civil Order Book Vol., A, Oct. 19, 1829-April 16, 1837, p. 171.
In the matter of Robert Moore, Griffith Dickinson, Nathan Ricketts, Gideon Tower, and John Shaddy, An application to obtain a pension under the Act of Congress of the 7th June AD 1832.
      Personally appeared in open Court, before the Switzerland Circuit Court now sitting the above named applicants who being first duly Sworn doth on their several oaths make their several declarations in order to obtain the benefit of the Act of Congress of the 7th June AD 1832 that they entered the Service of the United States under the officers named in their several declarations (here insert them) And the said Court do hereby declare their opinion after the investigation of the matter and after putting the interrogations prescribed by the War department that the above named Applicants were revolutionary Soldiers and Served as they have stated and the Court further Certifies that it appears to them that John Pavy who Signed their several Certificates is a Clergyman Resident in Switzerland County and State of Indiana and the other persons who has also Signed the Same are credible persons and that their Statements in entitled to credit.

American Militia in the Frontier Wars, 1790-1796; by Murtie June Clark; Genealogical Publishing Co., Inc., 1990. p.5.
Kentucky Militia
Pay Roll of a Company of Volunteers Under the Command of Captain John Dyall in 1792, Mar 22 to Mar 29, 1792, 8 days.

Nr	Rank	Name	Remarks
31	Private	Dickeson, Griffley	-

Early Ohio Settlers, Purchasers of Land in Southwestern Ohio, 1800-1840; Compiled by Ellen T. Berry & David A. Berry; Genealogical Publishing Co., Inc., Baltimore, MD, 1986. p.87.

Purchaser	Year	Date	Residence	R – T - S
Dickinson, Greffy (B)	1804	Oct. 09	Kentucky	03-02-02

(B) Indiana Survey: Land lying west of a meridian drawn west of the Great Miami (known as the "Gore"). Switzerland, Dearborn, Franklin, Ohio, Union and Randolph Counties (all or only a part of each county) – all in Indiana.

Early Ohioans' Residences From the Land Grant Records; Compiled by Mayburt Stephenson Riegel; Published by the Ohio Genealogical Society, Mansfield, OH, 1976. p. 4.
Land Grants Recorded by Residents of the Indiana Territory at the Cincinnati Land Office. The original Land Grant records are in the Archives of the Ohio Historical Society. They are from the Auditor of the State of Ohio Land Office.

NAME	DATE	SEC	TWP	RANGE	VOL	PG
DICKISON, Griffy	11-30-1804	S2	T2	R3W	B	198

Cincinnati Land Office records from the Land Office of the Auditor of State of Ohio, for the period 1801-1806; in the Archives of the Ohio Historical Society, Columbus, OH, copy at the Ohio Genealogical Society, Bellville, OH; Microfilm #411, Vol. B, pg. 198.

Dr.
Stilwel Heady and Griffy Dickerson of Indiana Territory

1804	Nov. 30	569	To Sales of public Lands		36	640.00
1807 June 3		8306	Interest Accompt	O	228	42.28
" "		7	Sales of Lands	O	28	10.68
			Int. corrected from 8.76 by order of Recr.			
			In Jny 1818			692.96

Cr.
from the West Half of Section No. 2 of Township No. 2 of Range No. 3 West

1804	Nov. 30	578	By Cash & Stock			160.00
1806	Sept. 30	1534	"	ditto	4	220.00
1807	Oct. 6	2121	"	ditto	21	80.00
1808	Sept. 29	2706	"	ditto	-	80.00
1810	Oct. 9	3593	"	ditto	-	124.20
18§7	June 3	8306	s"	ditto O	127	18.76
						692.96

Early Settlers of Indiana's "GORE" 1803-1820; Compiled and Edited by Shirley Keller Mikesell; Heritage Books, Inc., 1995. p. 186.
Switzerland County – Township 2, Range 3W
Section 2 – Stillwell, Heady & Griffy Dickison – 1804 – pg. 8.

Indiana Land Entries Vol. 1 Cincinnati District, 1801-1840; Margaret R. Waters; Originally Published Indianapolis 1948, Second Reprint 1979 by The Bookmark, P.O. Box 74, Knightstown, In 46148. p.68.
CINCINNNATI LAND DISTRICT – VOL. 1
Page 63. Twp. 2 North, Range 3 W of 1st Principle Meridian SWITZERLAND Georg Craig & Griffin Dickinson W ½ - S2; 10-9-1804. Vol. II, p. 114, says to Stillwell Heady & Griffy Dickison.
-- Note: The tract books for the land offices in Indiana are deposited in the office of the Auditor of State, Indianapolis. They and are in the custody of the State Land clerk. – [see next entry]

U.S. Department of Interior, Bureau of Land Management, General Land Office Records; Land Patent Search – accessed 27 June 2012.
DICKISON, GRIFFY
Accession Nr. CV-0038-590; Document Type – Credit Volume Patent; State – Indiana; Issue Date – 4/29/1818; Cancelled – No
Names on Document: Heady, Stilwell; Craig, George; Dickison, Griffy
Land Office – Cincinnati; Authority – April 24, 1820 Sale-Cash Entry (3 Stat. 566); Total Acres – 0.00 Land Descriptions – State – IN; Meridian – 1st PM; Twp-Rng – 002N-003W; Aliquots – W1/2; Section – 2; County - Switzerland
&
DICKASON, GRIFFITH
Accession Nr. CV-0062-272; Document Type – Credit Volume Patent; State – Indiana; Issue Date 4/1/1825; Cancelled - No
Names On Document: Dickason, Griffith; Lamberson, Samuel
Land Office – Cincinnati; Authority – April 24, 1820 Sale-Cash Entry (3 Stat. 566); General Remarks – Patent Record Imperfect; Document Nr. 837; Total Acres – 160.88
Land Descriptions: State – IN; Meridian – 1st PM; Twp-Rng – 002N-003W; Aliquots – NE1/4; Section – 5; County - Switzerland

Census of Indiana Territory for 1807; Indiana Historical Society, 1980. p. 22.
A list of free males above the age of twenty one in Dearborn County in March 1807 ~
113   Griffy Dickerson

A Partial Census For Indiana Territory 1810; Compiled by John D & E. Diane Stemmons; Census Publishing LC, Sandy, UT, 2004.
p. 147.
Dickarson, Griffeth, Historical Locality: Indiana Territory, Current State: Indiana, Dearborn County, First Township – Name on list of electors of election held 3 April 1809 at the house of Daniel Dufour. – Election Returns, 1809, 1812 (Indiana Historical Society), Coll. #M98 Box 32, Folder 1 pg 9.
Dickarson, Griffeth, Male
p. 148.
Dickson, Griffith, Historical Locality: Indiana Territory, Current State: Indiana, Jefferson County, - Name on recommendation list, 1813, to the President asking that Elijah sparks be appointed to fill the vacancy on the General Court that existed because of the death of Judge Vanderburgh (pages 244-50).- Territorial Papers of the US, vol. 8 pg. 247.
Dickson, Griffith, Male

Indiana Territory, Switzerland Circuit Court Records, Order Book, October Term 1814 to March Term 1815. p.6.
He is listed in county records for the first time on 27 March 1815, as a juror. Court held at the house of John Francis Dufour in the Town of Vevay.

1820 U.S. Census, Indiana, Switzerland, Posey, Series: M33 Roll: 14 Page: 265
Griffith Dickinson 45 and up; others in household 1 male 0-16, 1 female under 10, 2 females 10-16, 1 female 26-45.

1830 U. S. Census, Indiana, Switzerland, No Twp., Series M19, Roll 32. p. 37.
Dickinson, Griffith (Sr)
Males   70-80 = 1   Griffith; Females 60-70 = 1 Susan

Revolutionary Soldiers of Switzerland County; Copied by Mary Hill, John Paul Chapter-Daughters of the American Revolution; January, 1958; http://www.ingenweb.org/inswitzerland/switzrevsoldiers.html- Viewed June 2012.
DICKENSON, GRIFFITH
Born Dec. 25, 1762, Hanover Co. Virginia
Enlisted 1777 under Capt. Richard Anderson, 5th Virginia Regt. Col. Fall, Gen. Hand's Brigade, for 3 years. Was at Valley Forge.
Discharged near Williamsburg.
See Switzerland County, Ind. Civil Order bk. Sept. 1832, pg. 68
Collected by Mrs. A. V. Danner, Vevay, Indiana

Roster of Soldiers and Patriots of the American Revolution Buried in Indiana, Vol. I; compiled by Mrs. Roscoe C. O'Byrne.; Indiana Daughters of the American Revolution, 1981; p.122.
DICKENSON, GRIFFITH   Switzerland County
Born – Dec. 25, 1762. Hanover Co., Virginia
Service – Enlisted 1777 under Capt. Richard Anderson, 5th Vir. Regt., Col. Ball, Gen. Hand's Brigade, for 3 yrs. Was at Valley Forge. Discharged near Williamsburg.
Proof – Switzerland County, Ind., Civil Order Book, Sept. 1832, p. 68.
Collected by Mrs. A. V. Danner, Vevay, Indiana.

History of Switzerland County Indiana 1885; Reproduced by the Switzerland County Historical Society, Vevay, Indiana, 1999. The portion of the book relating to Switzerland County in the 1885 printing of the "History of Dearborn, Ohio, and Switzerland Counties, Indiana". p. 990.
"In 1798 the Cotton and Dickason families settled on Indiana Creek, a few miles back from the Ohio River, and in 1799 Robert Gullion settled on the Ohio River bottom, above the mouth of Log Lick Creek."

Indiana Historical Collections VOL. XIII, The Swiss Settlement of Switzerland Co., Indiana; Peret Dufour; Indianapolis 1923; p. 7.
"The first settlers, of the county, or rather of the territory embraced in the limits of the county, were the Cottons, <u>Dickason</u>, Ricketts, Drakes, Maguire, Rayl, David and Stewart, who severally settled within a few miles of the present location of Vevay. William Cotton, and <u>Griffith Dickason settled on Indian Creek sometime in 1798 or 1799</u>, Heathcoat Pickett above the mouth of Hunts Creek about the year ------ Robert and Benjamin Drake two brothers about 1799 or 1800. Maguire whose Christian name is not known about 1800, John Rayl about

1801, and James Stewart about the year 1799 or 1800, and then a part [of] the Swiss colony became their neighbors in the spring of 1803...."

Vevay Switzerland County Indiana 1795-1999; no author or publisher. p. 1.
The first settler in the county of whom any definite account is given was Heathcoat Pickett, a Revolutionary War veteran, who located here is 1795, followed in 1798 and 1799 by the Cotton, Dickason and Gullion families.

The Vevay Reveille-Enterprise; Vol. 122, No. 37, 15 Sep 1935, p. 3, col.4.
Roster of Revolutionary Soldiers Who Resided in Switzerland County
By Mrs. Effa M. Danner
Griffith Dickinson – Switzerland Co., Record Book F, p. 68 – 1832 Order Book. He entered service in Rev. War under the following named officers, enlisted A.D. 1777 Company commanded by Capt. Richard Anderson, 5th Va., Reg., Col. Ball's and Gen. Hand's brigade, served 3 years. He was born in Hanover Co., Va., December 25, A.D. 1762. He resided in Hanover County when called to service. After the war he lived six years in Virginia, Kentucky 14, Indiana 22. "I entered the first land in this (Switzerland) County. Drafted first, volunteered 2nd term. Drafted as private Capt. Richard Cluff Anderenis Co., and Gen. Muslenberg's brigade. Col. Ball was killed at the Battle of Monmouth, N.J. Company was reorganized September A.D. 1777, marched to Middlebrook, N.J. for short time, marched to White Plains 1778. I was in the battle of Monmouth, Capt. Bently belonged to our regiment. Marched to York as a guard and in December to Valley Forge in Pennsylvania and lay there all winter. I had camp fever there and was left behind when the army marched to White Horse, but overtook them near Germantown. Capt. Bently took command in place of Anderson, one year. Was discharged at Williamsburg, Va. Discharge burned when house burned 30 years ago. "Character witnesses, Wm. Cotton, Samuel Beal, Stillwell Heady, John F. Dufour, Rev. Samuel Pavy, Miles C. Eggleston, Pres. Judge, Joseph Malin and Elisha Golay, Associate Judges.

Records of Marlene McDerment, NSDAR Member# 738197.
DICKASON (DICKERSON, DICKINSON), GRIFFITH
Married Susan _____ (1767-1830/1833), about 1785, VA
On 21 Oct 1790, he signed a petition requesting the grant of a County to be laid off from Lincoln Co. [Virginia]- this was later granted as Logan Co., VA.
See *Petitions of the Early Inhabitants of Kentucky to the General Assembly of Virginia 1769 to 1792, No. 27, by James Rood Robertson, M.A, Ph.D.; Filson Club Publications , Louisville, KY 1914, reprinted by Genealogical Publishing co., Inc., Baltimore, MD, 1998; p. 141*-142. Petition Number 74.
Children: John A. married Mary "Polly" White, William Perry married Anna Holdcraft, Daniel David married Hannah C. Kiger, Hanna "Anna" married John Hugh Holdcraft, Elizabeth married John Buttles, Sarah "Sally" married Christopher Waltz, Ruth married 1)David F. Gerrard 2)James Froman, Griffith married Nancy _____, Mary "Polly" married John McMakin, Elijah married Martha Heady.
Griffith Dickason died aft. 1840, Switzerland Co.

Buried place Unknown – It is supposed that he, and others, were buried on or near his property, or in Cotton Cemetery, along Indian Creek. During the flood of 1937 the gravestones were washed out.

DRAKE, BENJAMIN

Patriot: Benjamin Drake
Birth: Unknown
Married Spouse 1: Hannah McCullough (d. aft. 16 Sep 1822)
Service state(s): VA
Service description: Beverly Daniels; Major Jesse Daniels;
                        Captain Vivion Daniels
Rank: Private
Proof of Service: Bounty Land Warrants
Pension application No.: None
Residences: prob. Caroline Co., VA; Clark Co., KY; Indiana Territory;
                Switzerland Co., IN
Died: bet. 2 Mar 1820 - 18 Mar 1820 Switzerland Co., IN
Buried: prob. Drake Cemetery, Switzerland Co., IN
DAR Ancestor No.: None

Revolutionary War Records – Virginia; *Virginia Army and Navy Forces with Bounty Land Warrants for Virginia Military District of Ohio, and Virginia Military Script, from Federal and State Archives; by Gaius Marcus Brumbaugh, M.D, M.s., Litt.D; Genealogical Publishing Co., Inc., Baltimore, 1995. p.615.*
Bounty Land Warrants, Va. Military District in Ohio, Original Bounty Land Warrants Located in Virginia Military District in Ohio
Drake, Benjamin

American Militia in the Frontier Wars, 1790-1796; *by Murtie June Clark; Genealogical Publishing Co., Inc., 1990. p.187,*
Virginia Militia
The Expedition Against the Insurgents in Pennsylvania.
[These troops were raised to quell the "Whiskey Insurrection" in southwestern (Washington County) Pennsylvania .]
Pay Roll of Lieutenant Robert Walters' Company of Militia, of General Carrington's Brigade, Pittsylvania County, Virginia, from Sept 25 to Nov 21, 1794, 58 days.

Nr	Rank	Name	Remarks
5	Private	Drake, Benj:n	-

Historical Register of Virginians in the Revolution, Soldiers, Sailors, Marines, 1775-1783; *John H. Gwathmey; The Dietz Press, Richmond, VA, 1938. p. 236.*
Drake, Benjamin, Ky. Mil., C

Probable record for Benjamin -
Virginia Revolutionary Publick Claims in three volumes; compiled and transcribed b Janice L.
Abercrombie and Richard Slatten; Iberian Publishing Co., Athens, GA, 1992.
Caroline County – Caroline County Court Booklet I. At a Court held for Caroline County on Thursday 11 July 1782 continued by several adjournments

till Thursday 12 Sept. 1782. The Court proceeded to examine the claims for horses provisions &c furnished the Army, Oct. 1780-Aug. 1782.
p. 187.
Page 8 - Dan'l Coleman assne of Ben. Drake 106½# bacon £6-13-1½
p. 188.
Page 10 – Drake, Benja. Cartage 9 days £2-1-10
p. 195.
Page 1 - Benja. Drake 5-52#
p. 202.
Page 33 – Certificates issued by John Broaddus D. Comr. of Caroline County for bacon collected for publick use, May to June 1781.
Benj. Drake 106½# £639
p. 209.
Certificates for Sundry Expenses price in paper money, Oct. to Dec. 1781.
Benja. Drake cartg. Wheat & brandy £2160

Census of Indiana Territory for 1807; Indiana Historical Society, 1980. p. 22.
A list of free males above the age of twenty one in Dearborn County in March 1807 ~~
117   Benjamin Drake

A Partial Census For Indiana Territory 1810; Compiled by John D & E. Diane Stemmons; Census Publishing LC, Sandy, UT, 2004. p.153.
Drake, Benjamine, Historical Locality: Indiana Territory, Current State: Indiana, Dearborn County, Loglick Township – Name on list of electors of election held 3 august 1812 at the house of Lewis Jones Esqr. – Election Returns, 1809, 1812 (Indiana Historical Society), coll. M98 Box 32, Folder 10 pg 11.
Drake, Benjamine, Male, - He was election "Judge".
[He was also listed on this page, with the same description, as Benjamon Drake.]

Indiana Territory, Switzerland Circuit Court Records, Order Book, October Term 1814 to March Term 1815. p.115.
He is listed in county records for the first time on 26 June 1815, as a juror.

U.S. Department of Interior, Bureau of Land Management, General Land Office Records; Land Patent Search – accessed 27 June 2012.
DRAKE, BENJAMIN
Accession Nr, CV-0044-030; Document Type – Credit Volume Patent; State – Indiana; Issue Date – 4/18/1819; Cancelled – No
Names On Document: Drake, Benjamin; Nelson, Joseph
Land Office – Cincinnati; Authority – April 24, 1820 Sale-Cash Entry (3 Stat. 566); Total Acres – 0.00
Land Descriptions: State – IN; Meridian – 1st PM; Twp-Rng – 002N-001W; Aliquots - SW1/4; Section – 31; County - Switzerland
&
Accession Nr. CV-0045-116; Document Type – Credit Volume Patent; State – Indiana; Issue Date 4/27/1819; Cancelled - No
Names On Document: Drake, Benjamin; Miles, Benjamin

Land Office – Cincinnati; Authority – April 24, 1820 Sale-Cash Entry (3 Stat. 566); Total Acres – 0.00
Land Descriptions: State – IN; Meridian – 1st PM; Twp-Rng – 004N-002W; Aliquots – SW1/4; Section – 36; County - Ohio

Early Ohio Settlers, Purchasers of Land in Southwestern Ohio, 1800-1840; Compiled by Ellen T. Berry & David A. Berry; Genealogical Publishing Co., Inc., Baltimore, MD, 1986.
(B) Indiana Survey: Land lying west of a meridian drawn west of the Great Miami (known as the "Gore"). Switzerland, Dearborn, Franklin, Ohio, Union and Randolph Counties (all or only a part of each county) – all in Indiana.

Purchaser	Year	Date	Residence	R – T - S
Drake, Benj'm (B)	1814	July 16	Dearborn (Ind	01-02-31

(B) Indiana Survey: Land lying west of a meridian drawn west of the Great Miami (known as the "Gore"). Switzerland, Dearborn, Franklin, Ohio, Union and Randolph Counties (all or only a part of each county) – all in Indiana.

Early Settlers of Indiana's "GORE" 1803-1820; Compiled and Edited by Shirley Keller Mikesell; Heritage Books, Inc., 1995.
p. 183.
Switzerland County - Township 2, Range 1W
Section 31 – Benj. P. Drake & Jas. Nelson – 1814 – pg. 3,
p. 191.
Switzerland County Deeds; Book A.
Deed dated 1815. John Buchanon & Rachel his wife of Jefferson Co. to Benjamin Drake.
S6, T1, R1. Signed John Buchanon, Rachel (x) Buchanon. Witness: George Teague, Amos Brown. pp. 18, 19.
p. 196.
Switzerland County Deeds; Book A.
New York * plat map dated 1817. Benjamin Drake, proprietor. Witness: William C.
Keen. Pp. 88, 89. (*Bk A. pp. 121, 122, 123 – in S6, T1, R1)
p. 199.
Switzerland County Deeds; Book A.
Deed dated 1818. Benjamin Drake & Hannah, his wife, to Harry Pierson. New York town lots S6, T1, R1. Signed Benjamin Drake, Hannah (x) Drake. Witness: Martin Adkins, Robert McCorkle. pp. 121, 122, 123.

Indiana Land Entries Vol. 1 Cincinnati District, 1801-1840; Margaret R. Waters; Originally Published Indianapolis 1948, Second Reprint 1979 by The Bookmark, P.O. Box 74, Knightstown, In 46148. p 4.
p. 4 – Switzerland Co. - Benjamin Drake & Joseph Nelson SW 1/4-S31; 7-16-1814

Author's note: Benjamin Drake, and his wife Hannah, sold land on 2 March 1820. See *Switzerland County, Indiana Deeds, Vol. A., p. 510*. This indicates he was still living on this date.

Switzerland County Probate Order Book 1, Nov 1814 - Sept 1824; pp. 86, 87, 88.
Abstract of will and/or administration for: Benjamin Drake
State & county where recorded: Switzerland Co., Indiana
State & county where will was made: Switzerland Co., Indiana
Book/volume where recorded: Probate Order Book 1, Nov 1814 – Sept 1824
Date will made: 18 March 1820
Date entered in probate: 13 April 1820
Name(s) of executors: Jaba Moore
Administration:
Date began – 13 April 1820
Place of death: Switzerland Co., Indiana
Witnesses to the will: John Gibson
George Hutchison
William Clancey
Jaba Moore
Names of heirs and others mentioned in will (also signed receipts of division of estate) and relationship if shown: Hannah Drake, wife; Nancy Nelson, daughter; Sally Brasheart, daughter; John Drake, son; Betsy Adkins, daughter.

Author's note: Hannah Drake, late wife of Benjamin Drake, sold land on 16 Sep 1822. This indicates she was still living at this date. See *Switzerland County, Indiana Deeds, Vol. B., p. 319.*

Switzerland County, Indiana Cemetery Locator; *By Ellyn R. Kern; Published by Switzerland County Historical Society, Vevay, IN, 1998 (2011). p. 3.*
"Drakes were among the original settlers of Switzerland County."

History of Switzerland County Indiana 1885; Reproduced by the Switzerland County Historical Society, Vevay, Indiana, 1999. The portion of the book relating to Switzerland County in the 1885 printing of the "History of Dearborn, Ohio, and Switzerland Counties, Indiana".
p. 1002.
"In 1817 Benjamin Drake laid out the town of New York, the name has since been changed to Florence."
p. 1178.
"As regards to the early settlers of York Township little definite information can be obtained. Benjamin Drake seems to have been among the first both in time and prominence. In 1817 he laid out the town of Florence (then New York) in the vicinity of which the first settlement of the township seems to have been made. He was a man of considerable moral worth, and who did much to build the interests of the place. "

Indiana Historical Collections VOL. XIII, The Swiss Settlement of Switzerland Co., Indiana; Peret Dufour; Indianapolis 1923; p. 7.
"The first settlers, of the county, or rather of the territory embraced in the limits of the county, were the Cottons, Dickason, Ricketts, Drakes, Maguire, Rayl, David and Stewart, who severally settled within a few miles of the present location of Vevay. William Cotton, and Griffith Dickason settled on Indian Creek sometime in 1798 or 1799, Heathcoat Pickett above the mouth of Hunts Creek about the year ------ Robert and Benjamin Drake two brothers about 1799 or 1800. Maguire whose Christian name is not known about 1800, John Rayl about 1801, and James Stewart about the year 1799 or 1800, and then a part [of] the Swiss colony became their neighbors in the spring of 1803...."
p. 42.
Benjamin Drake who owned the land where the town of Florence now stands, made a proposition to the Commissioners to have the seat of Justice fixed on Fractional Section 6 T2 R1 west.
p. 48.
Among the early settlers in the upper end of the county were James McClure who was Judge of the courts, Ezekiel and Joshua Petty, Peter Lostutter, Lewis Jones, George and Elisha Wade, Caleb Mounts, Williams Pierson, <u>Benjamin and Robert Drake</u>,.....etc.
p. 95.
Benjamin Drake who was the proprietor of New York now Florence had a Brother Robert Drake, who married a sister of Heathcoat Picket – lived in Plum Creek for some time removed to Arnolds Creek and came to Pleasant Township and purchased part of Section 16, or the School Section – while living on Plum Creek in the year 1800 he had a daughter born who is now living and is 76 years of age. She is no doubt the oldest person now living in the County born within its bounds. She is the mother of Asa Newton.
p. 144.
In 1817 Benjamin Drake laid out the town of New York, the name has since been changed to Florence.

Land of Our Fathers, History of Clark County, Kentucky; A. Goff Bedford; Self-published,1958. p. 205.
The second deed was from John and Rachel Quisenberry to Benjamin Drake for the sale of some land on Two Mile Creek.

Contributed by Alan L. Fisher
Benjamin F.[2] Drake (Drake[1]) died 1820 in Switzerland CO, IN. He married Hannah McCullough.
Notes for Benjamin F. Drake: *Westmoreland County, Virginia Wills, 1654-1800;* Drake, Sarah, 5 Feb. 1784; 29 June 1784, Entire estate to son Benjamin.
Citation: *American Revolutionary War Veterans;* Page 63 D.
[Author's note – I have not been able to locate this citation.]
"Beverly Daniels; Major Jesse Daniels; Captain Vivion Daniels; ... John Douglas; Benjamin Drake; ... 1st Virginia Line; First Lt. Jacob Duty."
Citation: *Land of our Fathers, History of Clark County, Kentucky;* A. Goff Bedford; Mt. Sterling, KY.

"Dearborn County was organized in 1803. It included land which is now Switzerland County, Ross Township of Ripley County; the area below Grant's Creek in 1809 became Jefferson County. Ohio County and Switzerland counties were formed about 1810; Ripley County was formed about then."

"The first families in the area were: Cottons, Dickasons, Picketts, Drakes, Maguires, Rahl, David and Stuart. William Cotton, Griffin Dickson settled at Indian Creek 1798/99. Heathcoat Pickett above Hunts Creek 1796/97. David near Hunts Creek, Drakes 1799/1800. Maguire about 1800. John Rayl about 1801, near James Stuart 1799/1800.

"Benjamin Drake bought land for a settlement called 'New York' - present day Florence in Switzerland County. Benjamin and Robert owned land on what is now the upper end of Switzerland County."

DUMONT, PETER

Patriot: Peter Dumont
Birth: 1 Oct 1744   Staten Island, Richmond Co., NY
Married Spouse 1: 25 Oct 1770   Mary Lowe (b. 3 Jun 1750 Shamoken, NJ
     d. 25 Jan 1841 Switzerland Co., IN)
Service state(s): NJ
Service description: 2nd Battalion, Somerset County Militia
Rank: Captain
Proof of Service: Stryker's Official Register of the Officers and Men of New
     Jersey in the Revolutionary War
Pension application No.: None
Residences: Somerset Co., NJ, Switzerland Co., IN
Died: 1821   Vevay, Switzerland Co., IN
Buried: Vevay Cemetery, Section 2, Jefferson Twp., Switzerland Co., IN
DAR Ancestor No.: A034612

Official Register of the Officers and Men of New Jersey in the Revolutionary War; Compiled Under Orders of His Excellency Theodore F. Randolph, Governor; by William S. Stryker, Adjutant General, Printed by the Authority of the Legislature; Wm. T. Nicholson & Co., Printers, Trenton, NJ, 1872, Facsimile Reprint by Heritage Books, Inc., Bowie, MD, 1993; p. 389.
DUMONT, Peter   Captain, Second Battalion, Somerset.

Indiana Territory, Switzerland Circuit Court Records, Order Book, October Term 1814 to March Term 1815. p.24 .
He is listed in county records for the first time on 8 April 1818, as a plaintiff.
Author's note: There are entries in this volume that are not within the range of dates shown on the binder cover.

Roster of Soldiers and Patriots of the American Revolution Buried in Indiana, Vol. I; compiled by Mrs. Roscoe C. O'Byrne.; Indiana Daughters of the American Revolution, 1981; p.129-130.
DUMONT, PETER   Switzerland County
Born – 1744, New York.
Service – Captain in 2nd Battalion Somerset, N.J. His services in the cause were even more outside the ranks than as a soldier, Gen. Washington often consulted him. Certain accounts still in existence indicate that he may have been in the commissary department. It is also said that at Washington's request he ran the mills day and night to help the soldiers at Valley Forge and that this resulted in irretrievable loss financially. Due to over-work his health failed and he became blind. He refused to apply for a pension.
Proof – Tales of Our Forefathers by Eugene McPike, pp. 55-152; Stryker's Register of N.J. Officers and Soldiers, p. 289.
Died – 1821. Buried Cemetery at Vevay, Ind.
Married – Mary Lowe, 1750-1841. Ch. Lydia Guest; Catherine Anderson; Jane Murphy; John; Abraham.

Collected by Mrs. A. V. Danner, Vevay and Miss Ellen Graydon, Indianapolis, Ind.

Revolutionary Soldiers of Switzerland County; Copied by Mary Hill, John Paul Chapter-Daughters of the American Revolution; January, 1958; http://www.ingenweb.org/inswitzerland/switzrevsoldiers.html- Viewed June, 2012.

DUMONT, PETER   See National No. 138, 632

Peter Dumont, born Staten Island, N.Y. 1744; died Vevay, Indiana 1821. Stone in Vevay, Ind. cemetery.

Married Mary Lowe (1750-1841) in 1770.

Children: Lydia Guest; Catherine Anderson; Jane Murphy; John 1787 -1871 who married Julia Louise Carey, in 1812; Abraham.

Capt. in 2d Batt. Somerset, N.J. Services in the cause were even more outside the ranks than as a soldier. Gen. Washington often consulted him. Certain accounts still in existence indicate that he may have been in the commissary department. It is also said that at Washington's request that he ran his mills day and night to help the soldiers at Valley Forge and that this resulted in irretrievable loss financially. Due to overwork his health failed and he became blind. He refused to apply for a pension.

See Tales of Our Forefathers by Eugene McPike, pg. 55 - 152.

Stryker's Register of N.J. Officers and Soldiers, pg. 229

Children; Lydia Guest; Catherine Anderson; Jane Murphy; John; Abraham .

Switzerland County Indiana Cemetery Inscriptions 1817-1985; Wanda L. Morford; Cincinnati, Ohio, 1986, p. 134.

The Vevay Cemetery, Section 2, Jefferson Twp., Switzerland Co., IN

Dumont   Peter, a soldier in the Revolution, died A.D. 1821   aged 91y

Mary, consort of Peter, died A.D. 1840 aged 91y

Vevay Cemetery, Vevay, Switzerland County, IN

Tombstone inscriptions -

Peter Dumont	Mary Dumont
A soldier of theRevolution	Consort of Peter Dumont
Died AD 1821	Died AD 1840
Aged 77 Years	Aged 91 years

The Vevay Reveille-Enterprise; Vol. 122, No. 37, 15 Sep 1935, p. 3, col.5.

Roster of Revolutionary Soldiers Who Resided in Switzerland County

By Mrs. Effa M. Danner

Captain Peter Dumont – He was born 1744 in New York, removed to New Jersey, he served as Captain in 2nd battalion of Somerset. He was requested by Washington to run his mills day and night to relieve the suffering of the soldiers at Valley Forge, which he did. Pension No. 138632.

He removed to Vevay, Switzerland County, 1814. His wife, Mary Lowe born in New Jersey 1750, married in 1770. He died 1821, age 77, buried at Vevay. She died 1840, age 90, burial at Vevay. Their children, Mary Dumont, born 1771, Lydia Demont, born 1773, Catherine Dumont, born 1775, Hendrick Dumont, born 1778, Peter Dumont, born 1780, Jane Dumont, born 1782, Anna Dumont, born 1784, John Dumont, born 1787, Abraham B. Dumont, born 1789. All baptized by Domine Hardenburgh.

Family history notes:
History of the Dumont family, early Huguenot settlers in New York and New Jersey from Holland, and later in Vevay: Eugene F. McPike, "Dumont and allied families", *New York Genealogical and Biographical Record* 29:103-109, 161-164, 237-240, and 30:36-40 (1898-1899). McPike also published a book including further details, *Tales of our forefathers and biographical annals of families allied to those of McPike, Guest and Dumont* (Albany: J. Munsell's Sons, 1898). McPike quotes many documents from families of Vevay, such as Morerod and Detraz.

ELLIS, ROBERT

The only information about this man comes from the book *Revolutionary Soldiers Buried in Indiana (1949) With Supplement (1954) Two Volumes in One;* by Margaret R. Waters; Genealogical Publishing Company, Baltimore, MD, 1970. p.31.

ELLIS, ROBERT   Switzerland
"Said to be Rev. sold. bur. there. (Could not be the same man above.)"
[The 'man above' is the Robert Ellis who died in Dec 1848 in Greene Co., IN. He served in South Carolina, lived in various parts of Georgia, various parts of Tennessee, and his last years in Greene Co., IN]
REF: Mr. Schrum
[Mr. Schrum seems to have been a member of the Sons of the American Revolution. The source of Robert Ellis being buried in Switzerland County is not known.]

Author's note: There were at least 8 men named Robert Ellis who served in the American Revolution. One (1) man served in NJ and died there; another (2) served in North Carolina and died there; another (3) served in New Hampshire and died in Maine; another (4) served in Virginia as evidenced by muster rolls; another (5) served in Maryland as evidenced by muster rolls; another (6) is found in Bounty Rights records for New York; two received Bounty Land Warrants for their service in Georgia (7) and Pennsylvania (8). Evidence has not been located to establish that any of these men ever resided in Switzerland County. I am convinced that Mr. Schrum is in error. Documentation is available from the author.

Patriot: Robert Ellis
Birth: u/n
Married Spouse 1: u/n
Service state(s): u/n
Service description: u/n
Rank: u/n
Proof of Service: u/n
Pension application No.: none
Residences: u/n
Died: u/n
Buried: u/n
DAR Ancestor No.: none

FANCHER, WILLIAM
aka FANCIER

Patriot: William Fancher
Birth: 9 Oct 1744 NJ
Married Spouse 1: 20 Jul 1815 Switzerland Co., IN   Elizabeth Ryal
Service state(s): NJ
Service description: New Jersey Militia,
Rank: Private
Proof of Service: Pension application – Switzerland County, IN
Pension application No.: Not in War Department records
Residences: Residence(s) since the war: New Jersey; Virginia; Pennsylvania;
            Ohio; KY; IN.
Died: 19 Oct 1859 [This would make him 115 years old - ?]
            May not have died in Switz. Co.
Buried: Rayl's Farm, Plum Creek Rd., Switzerland Co., IN
(from a LDS submission – not confirmed)
DAR Ancestor No.: None

Switzerland County Indiana Marriage Licenses 1814-1830, Part I-Grooms, Part II-Brides; Compiled by Louise Antoinette LeClerc Knox of Vevay, Indiana; self published 1970. p. 8 – Part I - Grooms.
Rayl, Elizabeth   7-20-1815   Fancier, William

Document contributed by Judy Kappes
Pension Application Abstracted from Switzerland County, Indiana Probate Record Book Vol. A, Mar 1827-Nov 1834; p. 330.
Pension abstract for – William Fancher, Sen.   Service state(s): NJ
Date: 17 Nov 1832
County of: Switzerland   State of: Indiana
Declaration made before a Probate Court.
Age: 90 years   Record of age: No record
Residence when he entered service: Sparktown, NJ
Residence(s) since the war: New Jersey 1 yr; Virginia 2 or 3 yrs; Pennsylvania
                 abt. 20 yrs; Ohio 1 yr; KY 8 yrs; since in IN.
Residence now: Switzerland Co., IN
Volunteer or Drafted or Substitute: Volunteered
Rank(s): Private
Statement of service-

Period	Duration	Names of General and Field Officers
1775 or 1776	1 year	Capt. Jacob Shuler, Col. Winans or Wine, Maj. Gaskins, NJ Militia. Part of time Capt. John Start, same Maj., same Col.

Battles: None stated
Discharge received: Yes
Signed by: Gen. Sullivan
What became of it?: Destroyed by fire a few years ago.
Statement is supported by –

128

Documentary proof: None
Person now living who can testify to service: Knows of no person living by whom I can prove the same.
Clergyman: John Pavy
Persons in neighborhood who certify character: Isaac Nash, John Rayle, Joseph Hayes, Elisha Golay, David Dufour.
No family information stated

Switzerland County, Indiana Probate Order Book 2 1831-1837; p. 101.
17 November 1832
In the matter of   }   An Applicant for a Pension under the act of
William Fancher, Sr.}   Congress of the 7th June 1832
          Now on this day comes the said William Fancher before the Probate Court of Switzerland County now Sitting and under Oath makes the following declaration in order to obtain a pension under the act of congress of the 7th June 1832 And the Said Court do hereby declare their opinion after the investigation of the matter and after putting interrogations prescribed by the war department that the above named William Fancher was a Revolutionary Soldier and Served as he states and the Court further certifies that it appears to them that John Pavy who has Signed the preceding Certificate is a Clergyman resident in Switzerland County State of Indiana and that Isaac Nash who also Signed the Same is a resident of Switzerland County and State of Indiana, and is a credible person and that their statement is entitled to Credit.

New York in the Revolution as Colony and State, Volume II, 1901 (Supplement);
Compiled by Frederick G. Mather; Genealogical Publishing Co., Baltimore, MD.
p. 204.
The names of all persons who appear in connection with the Land Bounty Rights have been classified; and they may be found in the six lists given below: -
          <u>Assignees</u> – Fansher William (on this listing) [Listed here as spelled.]
p. 208.
The names of all persons who appear in connection with the Land Bounty Rights have been classified; and they may be found in the six lists given below: -
          <u>Assignees</u> – Fansher William (on this listing) [Listed here as spelled.]

Second Census of Kentucky, 1800; Clift G. Glenn; Genealogical Publishing Co., Baltimore, MD, 1954.
An alphabetical list of 32,000 taxpayers based on original tax lists on file at the Kentucky Historical Society. Information given includes the county of residence and the date of the tax list in which the individual is listed.
Fancher, William   Bracken   11/22/1799

1830 U.S. Census, Ohio, Delaware, Harlem, Series: M19 Roll: 130 Page: 74.
William Fancher, Age 30-40 (listed below Sam'l Fancher).

Revolutionary Soldiers Buried in Indiana A Supplement; 485 Names Not Listed in the Roster of Soldiers and Patriots of the American Revolution Buried in

Indiana (1938) nor in Revolutionary Soldiers Buried in Indiana (1949); Margaret E. Waters; Indianapolis, 1954. p.117.
FANCHER, WILLIAM   Switzerland
(Uncertain). This name was received too late for me to check. His appl. for a pens. was accompanied by affidavits signed by John Pavy & Isaac Nash. William Fancher signed the pens. appl. of Jemima Nighswonger, wid. of Solomon Nighswonger (see later in this Suppl.). The soldier may not have died in Switzerland Co.
REF: Switzerland Co., Ind., Probate Bk. A. p. 330 (name has Sr.); Probate Ord. Bk. A (1831-1837), p. 101; Mary Hill, Madison, Ind.

The Hoosier Genealogist; Fifth year (issue unknown); Switzerland county Marriages 1814-1830, Credited to Louise A. L. Knox.
Fancier, William – Elizabeth Rayl 7-20-1815.
also –
http://genealogytrails.com/ind/switzerland/marriages1.html
William Fancier married Elizabeth Rayl 20 July 1815
also –
Switzerland County, Indiana Early Marriage Records 1814-1825; by. Colleen Alice Ridlen; Copyright by Walter R. Gooldy, Ye Olde Genealogie Shoppe, Indianapolis, IN, 2001. p. 8.
Fancier, William   Elizabeth Rayl   July 20, 1815

The Indiana Reveille, 2 Nov 1859 , Vol. XLII, No. 44, p. 4, column 3.
DIED
In Vevay, October 19th, WILLIAM FANCHER – an old citizen of Switzerland county, and a soldier in the last war with Great Britain.

FIELD, DANIEL

This man apparently served in the Revolutionary War. He appeared in Switzerland County Civil Court where he made his declaration of service and filed his property schedule. Although his declaration and schedule were ordered to be recorded this may not have happened. The schedule and declaration have not been located in the courthouse records. Also, his filing was not recorded in the War Department. Therefore, record(s) of his military service have not been located.

Patriot: Daniel Field
Birth: Unknown
Married Spouse 1: Unknown
Service state(s): Unknown
Service description: Unknown
Rank: Unknown
Proof of Service: Switzerland Co., IN Civil Order Book, Vol. 5, p. 121.
Pension application No.: Not in War Department
Residences: Unknown; Switzerland County, IN
Died: Unknown
Buried: Unknown
DAR Ancestor No.:

Switzerland County, Indiana, Civil Order Book - Vol.5, Feb 10, 1823 - Jun 21, 1826, September Term, 1823, p.121.
10 Sept 1823 - David Field a revolutionary Soldier who wishes to obtain the benefit of the acts of Congress concerning pensions Now files his Schedule makes the Declaration and took the oath required by the acts of Congress provided for persons engaged in the Land and Navel Services of the United States in the revolutionary war which are ordered to be recorded and it is Ordered that the property Contained in Said Schedule is valued by the Court at Sixteen Dollars and fifty cents.

Author's note: I researched every man by this name who served in the Revolutionary War. Soldiers who served in Massachusetts and Rhode Island have been eliminated because they died in those states. This leaves possible service states of Vermont, and Virginia. Those records are shown below.

VERMONT Service record for Daniel Field –
Rolls of the Soldiers in the Revolutionary War, 1775 to 1783; comp. and ed. by John E. Goodrich, pub. by authority of the legislature; The Tuttle Company, Rutland, VT, 1904. p.273.

Names & Rank	When Joined	When Discharged	Days Service	Wages Amt. per Mo.	Miles Wgs	Amt. Travld	Amt. milage	Total Rations
Daniel Field	16 Oct 1780	17 Oct 1780	2	£2	2.8	22	0.7.4	2.8 0.7.4

VIRGINIA Service records for Daniel Field –
Virginia Revolutionary Militia, A List of Non-Commissioned Officers and Seamen and Marines of the State Navy, Whose names appear on the Army Register, and who have not received Bounty Land; Printed by Samuel Shepherd, Printer to the Commonwealth, Richmond, VA. 1835. p. 8.
Doc. No. 48.
Field, Daniel   Matross Infantry

Revolutionary War Records – Virginia; Virginia Army and Navy Forces with Bounty Land Warrants for Virginia Military District of Ohio, and Virginia Military Script, from Federal and State Archives; by Gaius Marcus Brumbaugh, M.D, M.s., Litt.D; Genealogical Publishing Co., Inc., Baltimore, 1995.
p.171
List of non-commissioned Officers and Soldiers of the Illinois regiment, and the Western Army, Under Command of General G. R. Clarke, Who Are Entitled to Bounty Land, Richmond, August, 1833.
205.   Field, Daniel (died) Entitled to land for service of 3 years.
p. 203
Names may be found on this list which are the same with those of non-commissioned officers and soldiers, &c. who have received bounty land. It may be generally presumed that there were as many different persons of the same name as there were time of the occurrence of the name on the army register.
Field, Daniel, Matross, Inf.

Historical Register of Virginians in the Revolution, Soldiers, Sailors, Marines, 1775-1783; John H. Gwathmey; The Dietz Press, Richmond, VA, 1938. p. 270.
Field, Daniel, Clark's Ill. Reg.
Field, Daniel, Matross, Art.
Field, Daniel E. -

Virginia Revolutionary Publick Claims in three volumes; compiled and transcribed b Janice L. Abercrombie and Richard Slatten; Iberian Publishing Co., Athens, GA, 1992.
Culpeper County – Culpeper County Court Booklet I. At a court held for Culpeper County 19 aug. 1782 the Court proceeded to adjust claims for property impressed or taken for public service and made the following valuations.
p.262   Pg. 17 - Daniel Field Jan. 1781 for 350# beef, driving for same.
p.273   Pg. 40 – Daniel Field Nov. 1781 for 325# beef for Greensby Waggoner.
p.278   Culpeper County - At a court appointed and held for the said County 29 May 1782 for the purpose of adjusting claims for property impressed or taken for publick use, the court proceeded and made the following valuations.
Daniel Field Dec. 1781 for 325# beef.
p.282   Culpeper County – Culpeper County Court Booklet I. Pg. 15 At a court held for Culpeper County 18 July 1785. The Court proceeded to adjust claims for property impressed or taken for publick use and made the following allowances.
Daniel Field for 207 day waggonage pr. Cert.
p.386   Frederick County – Frederick County Court Booklet – Pg. 32 for wagon hire for Cont.   Daniel Fields for 122 days do.

Author's note: On 3 September 1821 a Daniel Field, and Elizabeth his wife, sold land in Switzerland County. *Switzerland County Deed Records, Vol. B, May 1820-Jan 1825, p. 198*. They were residing in Polk County, Illinois. This Daniel Field is not found in the 1830 census for Pope County. However, a younger man of that name is found there (age 30-40).

FOSTER, THOMAS

No one by the name of Thomas Foster, a Revolutionary soldier, lived in Switzerland County. Records for every soldier named Thomas Foster have been thoroughly searched. None can be connected to Switzerland County.

This citation is obviously an error. The pension application number S17640 is actually the application of Thomas Porter (see his record).
Revolutionary Soldiers of Switzerland County; Copied by Mary Hill, John Paul Chapter-Daughters of the American Revolution; January, 1958;
http://www.ingenweb.org/inswitzerland/switzrevsoldiers.html- Viewed June 2012.
FOSTER, THOMAS
Switzerland Co. Indiana Pension claim S.17640
Private in company under Capt. Chapman, in Connecticut Line for 9 months.

FROMAN, PAUL

Paul Froman, Jr., who lived in Switzerland County, is not the man who served in the Revolutionary War. Paul Froman, Jr., of Switzerland County, is the son of Paul Froman the Revolutionary Soldier. The soldier died sometime after 29 Sep 1807 in Nelson Co., KY. Records have not been located to place the soldier in Switzerland County for any period of time. Alan Fisher, a descendant, has thoroughly researched this family. Alan has generously provided his records and evidence regarding these men.

There are a large number of records pertaining to the service of the soldier Paul Froman, and also numerous Switzerland County records about the early settler Paul Froman. This is the record for the Revolutionary War solder –

Patriot: Paul Froman, Jr.
Birth: 16 Oct 1734 NJ
Married Spouse 1: Unknown
Married Spouse 2: Mary McCarty
                 (b. 10 Dec 1738 d. abt. 1793 Nelson Co., KY)
Service state(s): VA
Service description: Jefferson Co. VA Militia, Gen. George Rogers Clark
Rank: Captain
Proof of Service: Gwathmey's Hist. Reg. of VA in the Revolution, p. 290.
Pension application No.: Not in War Department records
Residences: Kentucky Co., VA; Jefferson Co., Kentucky District, VA
Died: aft. 29 Sep 1807   Nelson Co., KY
Buried: Unknown
DAR Ancestor No.: A042816

The John Paul Chapter DAR had erroneous recorded Paul Froman, the Revolutionary War soldier as being in Switzerland County. This is the erroneous record -
Revolutionary Soldiers of Switzerland County; Copied by Mary Hill, John Paul Chapter-Daughters of the American Revolution; January, 1958.
FROMAN, PAUL, JR.   Switzerland Co. Indiana
Born Oct. 17, 1734 in New Jersey
Service; Captain in Virginia on "Pittsburg Pay Roll" for 176 days. Also a Captain at Fort Nelson in Jefferson Co. Virginia in 1781.
Proof; Va. State Library "Pittsburg Pay Roll" pg. 56; Echenrode, List of Revolutionary soldiers; Virginians in Revolution War Department; Adjutant General's office
Wife: Mary Cartmell [1]
Daughter Christina, mar. William Cotton, she was born Sept. 24, 1775 in Pa. mar. Jan. 7, 1796, buried in Cotton cemetery near Mt. Stirling. [2]

Author's notes: Early DAR records show wife Mary Cartmell. Later DAR records correct the wife to Mary McCarthy. See National Society Daughters of the American Revolution web site.

GAZLEY, JAMES
aka GAZLAY

Patriot: James Gazley
Birth: 23 Jan 1758 Dutchess Co., NY
Married Spouse 1: Huldah Carter (b. 1767, d. 1844)
Service state(s): NY
Service description: 4th Regt.
Rank: Ensign, Quartermaster
Proof of Service: Military Minutes of the Council of Appointment of New York
Pension application No.: None
Residences: Dutchess Co., NY, [poss. Hamilton Co., OH], Switzerland co., IN
Died: 6 Aug 1823 Patriot, Switzerland Co., IN
Buried: Unknown
DAR Ancestor No.: A043866

Military Minutes of the Council of Appointment of the State of New York, 1783-1821. N.Y; State of New York, 1901-1902.
New York Militia - Dutchess County
In Lieutenant Colonel Commandant Isaac Bloom's regiment:
John Lothrup, surgeon; Isaac DeLauvergne, surgeon's mate; James Gazley, quartermaster, Daniel Ward, paymaster.

Revolutionary War Service Records, New York; www.Footnote.com, accessed 20 Jun 2012.
p. 1 - Gazley, James   Ensign   Card Numbers 37265696
p. 2 - G1 NY   James Gazley   Ensign
Appears as shown below on a Certificate Of Arch'd Campbell, Dep. Secretary, State of New York, stated as follows:
State of New York, Secretary's Office
I certify that it appears by the minutes of the Council of Appointment of this State in this office, that on the 28th of May 1778, the following officers were appointed in the Regiment of Militia in the County of Dutchess whereof John Freer was Colonel, viz.
(Revolutionary War)
That on the 4th day of March 1780 the following officers were appointed in the said Regiment, viz.   James Gazley, Ensign
    Arch'd Campbell, dep. Secretary
Certificate dated   Albany   Jany 20, 1838
Number of record: 69
    Hamilton Copyist

Roster of Soldiers and Patriots of the American Revolution Buried in Indiana; 1966; p.44.
JAMES GAZLEY   Switzerland County
Born 23 Jan 1758, Duchess Co., NY
Married Huldah Carter

Children: James; William married Rebecca Williams; Ann; Julia married Garnett Van Arsdale; Elizabeth married Charles Kellogg; Knight; Kavenda married David Swing; Cornellia married William Chamberlain; Theodore married Jane E. Fitch.
Died 6 Aug 1823, Patriot, Switzerland Co., IN

Roster of Soldiers and Patriots of the American Revolution Buried in Indiana, Vol. II; 1966; p. 44.
GAZLEY, JAMES   Switzerland County
Born – Jan. 23, 1758. Dutchess Co., N.Y.
Service – 1780 served as Ensign in Capt. Reuben Spencer's Co., Col. Tobias Stroughtenburg's Regt., Dutchess Co., N.Y., Militia.
Proof – N.Y. in the Revolution, p. 231; DAR No. 131373.
Died – Aug. 6, 1823, Patriot, Ind., Switzerland Co., Ind.
Married – Huldah Carter. Ch. James; William, m. Rebecca Williams; Ann; Julia, m. garnet Van Arsdale; Elizabeth, m. Charles Kellogg; Inyers, m. Susan Hay; Arabert, m. Elizabeth Buck; Della, m. Albert Knight; Kavenda, m. David Swing; Cornella, m. William Chamberlain; Thoedore, m. Jane E. Fitch.

National Society of the Sons of the American Revolution - Revolutionary War Graves Register; Compiled and Edited by Clovis H. Brakebill, Published by db Publications, Dallas, TX, 1993. p. 234.
Gazley   James; 1758-1823; Patriot, IN; Ensign, IN; Huldah Carter.

The Vevay Reveille Enterprise; Vol. 122, No. 37, 15 Sep 1935, p. 3, col.5.
Roster of Revolutionary Soldiers Who Resided in Switzerland County
By Mrs. Effa M. Danner
Ensign James Gazlay – or Gazley, 1758-1823. Pension Certificate M1783. He enlisted in Captain Ruben Spencer's Co., Col. Tobias Stooughtenburgh's Regiment, Duchess Co., N.Y., Militia. He was born in Duchess Co., N.Y. and died at Patriot, Switzerland County, Ind. Wife, Hulda Carter, 1767-1844. D.A.R. No. 131-373.
Gazley's mentioned on Switzerland County records. Aribert Gazley was a county supervisor and Justice of the Peace of Posey Township in 1831. Aribert and Elizabeth Gazley were members of the Universalist church, Patriot 1835. Sayer Gazley entered land grant 1832. Mary E. Gazley married Gen. Wm. C. Keene, November 17, 1821. He was a General in the War of 1812.

Author's note: I have not been able to locate the Pension Certificate No. M1783 as referred to in this article.

GODDARD, JOSEPH

This soldier died in Fleming Co., KY. His wife (widow), Frances Goddard, moved to Switzerland County after his death. She became one of the early settlers of Switzerland County. She died here.

Patriot: Joseph Goddard
Birth: 27 Sep 1761
Married Spouse 1: 20 Sep 1780 Fauquier, VA   Frances Glasscock
                 (b. 30 Sep 1762/3 Fauquier Co., VA d. 5 Jul 1845
                 Switzerland Co., IN; buried Vevay Cemetery)
Service state(s): VA
Service description: Capts. Thomas Blackwell, James Williams,
                      Cols. Edward Stevens, John Green
Rank: Private; Corporal
Proof of Service: Pension application R4078
Pension application No.: R4078 Rejected widow's pension
Residences: Fauquier Co., VA; Red Stone Country; Fleming Co., KY
Died: 28 Jun 1844 Fleming Co., KY
Buried: Fleming Co., KY
DAR Ancestor No.: A045870

Pension Application Abstracted from National Archives microfilm Series 805, Roll 361, File R4078.
Pension abstract for – Joseph Goddard   Service state(s): VA
Date: 9 Aug 1832
County of: Fleming   State of: Kentucky
Declaration made before a Court.
Age: 71 on the 27 Sept next .
Residence when he entered service: 1st enlistment - Fauquier Co., VA; 2nd enlistment – Middlebrook, NJ.
Residence(s) since the war: Fauquier Co., VA until 1783, then to Red Stone country, after several years to Fleming Co., KY
Residence now: Fleming Co., KY
Volunteer or Drafted or Substitute: Enlisted
Rank(s): Private & Corporal in Capt. Thomas Blackwell's company
Statement of service-

Period	Duration	Names of General and Field Officers
16 Jan 1777	Until Dec 1778	6th VA Continental Regt. commanded by Capt. Thomas Blackwell, Col. Edward Stephens; then in Capt. James Williams' company, Col. John Green's VA regt..
Apr 1779	Sep 1779	10th VA company commanded by Col. John Green's VA regt.

Battles: 1st enlistment - Brandywine. 2nd enlistment - Monmouth, Stony Point.
In Sep 1779 he enlisted a man by the name of John Higgins to serve in his place.
Discharge received: Yes
Signed by: Col. John Green

What became of it?: It is misplaced.
&
Widow's application for pension
Date: 22 March 1845
County of: Switzerland   State of: Indiana
Declaration made before Jonathan M. Froman, J.P.
Wife: Frances (maiden name not stated)   Wife's age: 83
Marriage date and place: 20 Sep 1780, Fauquier Co., VA
Living witness, name(s): Burtis Ringor, a revolutionary soldier, and his wife Hannah who reside in Fleming Co., KY. Hannah states she is a cousin of Frances and they lived as neighbors in Fauquier Co., VA, and KY.
Soldier died: 28 Jun 1844, Fleming Co., KY
Names and ages of children: 12 children – none named.
Shortly after death of soldier the widow went with one of her sons to IN; a daughter Sarah's petition follows.
&
Date: 1 Apr 1853
County of: Switzerland   State of: Indiana
Petition to prosecute against the government of the United States for any claims(s) to arrears of pension money.
Petitioner: Sarah Smithson, daughter and heir-at-law of Frances Goddard dec'd late of Switzerland Co., IN, widow of Joseph Goddard. Widow died 5 Jul 1845.

Historical Register of Virginians in the Revolution, Soldiers, Sailors, Marines, 1775-1783; John H. Gwathmey; The Dietz Press, Richmond, VA, 1938. p. 312.
Goddard, Joseph, Corp., 6 CL, 10 CL, Ky. pens.

Revolutionary Soldiers in Kentucky, containing a roll of the officers of Virginia line who received land bounties, a roll of the Revolutionary pensioners in Kentucky, a list of the Illinois regiment who served under George Rogers Clark in the Northwest campaign, also a roster of the Virginia Navy. Reproduction of the original which appeared in Sons of the American Revolution Kentucky Society Year Book, Louisville, 1896.; Anderson Chenault Quisenberry; Southern Book Co., Baltimore, MD, 1959. p. 142.
Revolutionary Soldiers in Kentucky – Roll of Pensioners – Fleming County Pensioners Under the Act of June 7, 1832 (Began March 4, 1831)
Goddard, Joseph, private   Virginia line
    March 25, 1833; $80.   Age 73.

Rejected or Suspended Applications for Revolutionary War Pensions; Reprinted for Clearfield Company Inc. by Genealogical Publishing Co., Inc., Baltimore, MD, 1998.
A list of the names of persons residing in Indiana who have applied for pensions under the act of July 7, 1838, whose claims have been rejected; prepared in conformity with the resolution of the Senate of the United States of September 16, 1850, p. 417..

Names	Residence	Reasons for rejection
GODDARD, FRANCES widow of Joseph	Vevay, Switzerland	Not a widow at the date of the act.

A Census of Pensioners for Revolutionary or Military Services with their Names, Ages, and Places of Residence Under the Act for Taking the Sixth Census in 1840; Genealogical Publishing Co., Inc., Baltimore, Maryland, 1965. p. 162.
KENTUCKY, FLEMING COUNTY, 3RD DIVISION

Names of Pensioners for Revolutionary or Military services	Ages	Names of head families with whom pensioner resided June 1, 1840
Joseph Goddard	79	Joseph Goddard

Second Census of Kentucky, 1800; Clift G. Glenn; Genealogical Publishing Co., Baltimore, MD, 1954.
An alphabetical list of 32,000 taxpayers based on original tax lists on file at the Kentucky Historical Society. Information given includes the county of residence and the date of the tax list in which the individual is listed.

Godard, William	Henry	8/6/1800

Revolutionary Soldiers Buried in Indiana (1949) With Supplement (1954) Two Volumes in ne; Margaret R. Waters; Genealogical Publishing Company, Baltimore, MD, 1970. p.133, 140, 141.
GODDARD, JOSEPH & FRANCES   Switzerland
p. 133 - He. d. 6-28-1844, Fleming Co., Ky.   Pens. R.4078 Va.
p. 140 – In list of spouses buried in Indiana for Switzerland Co., - Goddard, Frances-w. Joseph.
p. 141 – In list of "Soldiers Who Died in Other States" (husbands of widows on list of spouses) – Kentucky – Goddard, Joseph.

National Society of the Sons of the American Revolution - Revolutionary War Graves Register; Compiled and Edited by Clovis H. Brakebill, Published by db Publications, Dallas, TX, 1993. p. 242.
Goddard (Godard) Joseph; 1761-1844; Goddard Methodist Church Cem, Goddard, Fleming Co, KY; Corporal, VA; Frances Glasscock.

Switzerland County Indiana Cemetery Inscriptions 1817-1985; Wanda L. Morford; Cincinnati, Ohio, 1986, p. 146.
Vevay Cemetery, Section 2, Jefferson Twp., Switzerland Co., IN
Goddard, Frances, d. Jun. 6, 1845   aged 82y 9m 6d – is a large above ground mausoleum with the Northcotts'

Abstracts of obituaries in the Western Christian Advocate, 1834-1850; Compiled by Margaret R. Waters, Dorothy Riker, and Doris Leistner, in observance of the Northwest Ordinance of 1787; Indiana Historical Society, Indianapolis, IN, 1988. p. 130.
9 May 1845 – Daughter Fanny's obituary.

Northcut, Fanny L.; b. 28 Jun 1807, Fleming Co., KY; d. prob. early in 1845, in 38th yr.; dau. of Goddard, Joseph & Frances; mar. 22 Dec 25, Northcut, William, Rev. [Reverend]. Issue 6 chn. Signed A. Bussey {12-16; 9 May 45}.

Cemetery/Tombstone-Joseph Goddard
Goddard Methodist Church Cemetery, Poplar Plains, Fleming Co., KY
Tombstone inscription –   SACRED
In the memory of
JOSPEH GODDARD
who Departed this life June 28
1844 in the 85th year of his Age
Passenger is thou art a Soldier
Remember the distinguished and gallant
Services rendered in the Cuntry by the Patriot
Who sleeps beneath this tomb

GOOKINS, SAMUEL

It appears that Samuel Gookins did not have ties to Switzerland County. The *Roster of Soldiers and Patriots of the American Revolution Buried in Indiana, Vol. 1* (citation below) indicated that he was of Switzerland County. No other records have been located placing him in Switzerland County. His record is included here for evidence purposes only.

Patriot: Samuel Gookins
Birth: 19 Sep 1762 CT
Married Spouse 1: 13 Mar 1786 Pawlet, VT   Polly/Mary Andrus
                                                    (b. 4 Mar 1764 Norwich, CT
                                    d. 13 Jun 1848 Delaware Twp., Ripley Co., IN)
Service state(s): CT
Service description: Capt. Samuel Granger, Col. S. B. Webb
Rank: Private
Proof of Service: Pension application W10064
Pension application No.: W10064
Residences: Danbury, Fairfield Co., CT; Rutland Co., VT; Ontario Co., NY; Ripley Co., IN
Died: 4 Dec 1842 Ripley Co., IN
Buried: Gookins Family cemetery, Delaware Twp., Ripley Co., IN
DAR Ancestor No.: A045930

Pension Application Abstracted from National Archives microfilm Series 805, Roll 365, File W10064.

Pension abstract for – Samuel Gookins   Service state(s): Connecticut
Date: 19 Aug 1820
County of: Ontario   State of: New York
Declaration made before a Court of the Common Pleas
Age: 58
Residence(s) since the war: Sussex, Hartford Co., CT, now Ontario Co., NY
Residence now: Freeport, Ontario Co., NY
Volunteer or Drafted or Substitute: Not stated
Rank(s): Private
Statement of service-

Period	Duration	Names of General and Field Officers
Spring 1777	until June 1783	Capt. Samuel Granger, Col. Clarke Webb's regt. of Connecticut line. Transferred to Col. Samuel B. Webb's regt. CT line.

Battles: Stony Point
Discharge received: Regularly discharged
&
Widow's application for pension –
Date: 19 May 1843
County of: Ripley   State of: Indiana

Declaration made before a Judge. Due to bodily infirmity she is unable to appear in court.
Soldier died: 4 Dec 1842, in Delaware Twp., Ripley Co., IN.
Widow's name: Polly Gookins   Age: 79
Marriage date and place: 1 March 1886 in Pollet, Rutland Co., VT
Proof of marriage: On 1 Sep 1843, Asa Gookins, resident of Ripley Co., IN, makes oath that he is the fourth child of Samuel & Polly Gookins, they had seven children all living. He provides a copy of Family Record from a Bible now in his hands. Record lists these children –

Naomi	Gookins	Born	Oct. 11, 1785
Lydia	Gookins	Born	Aug'st. 19, 1788
Anna	Gookins	Born	March 10, 1791
Asa	Gookins	Born	August 26, 1795
Samuel	Gookins	Born	January 25, 1797
Polley	Gookins	Born	May 21st, 1801
Olive	Gookins	Born	March 22th, 1803

Abstract of Final Payment Voucher; General Services Administration, Washington, DC
FINAL PAYMENT VOUCHER RECEIVED FROM
THE GENERAL ACCOUNTING OFFICE
NAME   Gookins, Samuel
AGENCY OF PAYMENT   Indiana
DATE OF ACT   1818
DATE OF PAYMENT   3rd Qr. 1843
DATE OF DEATH   Dec. 11, 1842
GENERAL SERVICES ADMINISTRATION
National Archives and Records Service   NA-286
GSA-WASH DC 54-4891   November 1953

Register of Certificates Issued by John Pierce, Esquire, Paymaster General and Commissioner of Army Accounts for the United States, to Officers and Soldiers of the Continental Army Under Act of July 4, 1783; Originally Published as Senate Documents, Vol.9, No. 988, 63rd Congress, 3d Session, Washington, 1915; Seventeenth report of the National Society of the Daughters of the American Revolution; Genealogical Publishing Co., Inc, Baltimore, MD, 1984. p. 207.
Men listed in this volume with the same name.

No. of Certificate	To whom issued	Amount
4092	Gookin, Samuel	49.26
4461	Gookins, Samuel	80.00
2421	Gookins, Samuel	4.52

U.S. Department of Interior, Bureau of Land Management, General Land Office Records; Land Patent Search – accessed 27 June 2012.
GOOKINS, SAMUEL
Accession Nr. CV-0087-396; Document Type – Credit Volume Patent; Issue Date – 9/6/1831; Cancelled – No
Names on Document: Crowley, Ellis; Gookins, Samuel; Craig, George

Land Office – Jeffersonville; authority – April 24, 1820 Sale-Cash Entry (3 Stat. 566); Document Nr. 2644; Total Acres – 160.00
Land Descriptions: State – IN; Meridian – 2nd PM; Twp-Rng – 009N-012E; Aliquots – SW1/4; Section – 28; County - Ripley
&
Accession Nr. IN2750_.005; Document Type – State Volume Patent; State – Indiana; Issue Date – 8/1/1839; Cancelled – No
Names on Document: Gookins, Samuel
Land Office – Jeffersonville; Authority – April 24, 1820 Sale-Cash Entry (3 Stat. 566); Document Nr. 1346; BLM Serial Nr. – In No S/N; Total Acres – 80.00
Land Descriptions:

State	Meridian	Twp-Rng	Aliquots	Section	County
IN	2nd PM Ripley	009N-012E	SW1/4NW1/4		32
IN	2nd PM Ripley	009N-012E	NW1/4SW1/4		32

&
Accession Nr. IN2330_.326; Document Type – State Volume Patent; State – Indiana; Issue Date – 10/1/1840; Cancelled – No
Names on Document: Gookins, Samuel B.
Land Office – Vincennes; Authority – April 24, 1820 Sale-Cash Entry (3 Stat. 566); Document Nr. 25313; Total Acres – 80.00
Land Descriptions: State – IN; Meridian – 2nd PM; Twp-Rng – 012N-008W; Aliquots – W1/2SE1/4; Section – 23; County - Vigo

A Census of Pensioners for Revolutionary or Military Services with their Names, Ages, and Places of Residence Under the Act for Taking the Sixth Census in 1840; Genealogical Publishing Co., Inc., Baltimore, Maryland, 1965. p.184 .
INDIANA, RIPLEY COUNTY, DELAWARE

Names of Pensioners for Revolutionary or Military services	Ages	Names of heads of families with whom pensioner resided June 1, 1840
Samuel Gookins	78	Asa Gookins

Roster of Soldiers and Patriots of the American Revolution Buried in Indiana, Vol. I; compiled by Mrs. Roscoe C. O'Byrne.; Indiana Daughters of the American Revolution, 1981; p.160.
GOOKINS, SAMUEL   Switzerland County
Born – Sept. 19, 1762, Suffolk, Connecticut
Service – Enlisted April 26, 1777, for the term of the war in Capt. Samuel Granger's CO., 2nd Regt. Conn. Line, Col. Chas. Webb. Was later in Cpt. Roger Well's CO., 3rd Conn. Line, Col. Samuel B. Webb.
Proof – Family records furnished by Mrs. Clara Gookins Scherer.
Died – Dec. 4, 1842. Buried in family cemetery, Delaware Twp., Ripley Co. Stone. Name on bronze tablet in Versailles Court House.
Grandchildren of Soldier – Samuel; Lydia; William.
Collected by Mrs. A. B. Wycoff, Batesville, Indiana.

Abstract of Graves of Revolutionary Patriots (4 volumes); by *Patricia Law Hatcher; Pioneer Heritage Press, Dallas, TX, 1987. Vol. 2, p. 83.*
This is an abstract and an index to information reported to the Daughters of the American Revolution and published in their annual reports to the Smithsonian Institution , printed as Senate Documents (1900-1974) and published annually in the DAR magazine (1978-1987).
Published 1977.
GOOKINS, Samuel Fam cem, Rt 48, Delaware Twp., Ripley Co IN

National Society of the Sons of the American Revolution - Revolutionary War Graves Register; Compiled and Edited by *Clovis H. Brakebill, Published by db Publications, Dallas, TX, 1993. p. 246.*
Gookins Samuel;   ?-?; Old Gookins Family Cem, W fr Lookout, [Ripley Co.],IN

GRAY, MOSES

Patriot: Moses Gray
Birth: Unknown
Married Spouse 1: Unknown
Service state(s): PA
Service description: Captain John McDaniel (or Donald),
   Col. John Piper's Regt., Continental line,
Rank: Private
Proof of Service: Switzerland County, Indiana, Civil Order Book - Vol.5, , p.67.
Pension application No.: Not in War Department records
Residences: Bedford Co., PA; Switzerland Co., IN
Died: aft Jun 1832 Indiana (poss. Jefferson Co.)
Buried: Unknown
DAR Ancestor No.: None

Switzerland County, Indiana, Civil Order Book - Vol.5, Feb 10, 1823 - Jun 21, 1826, p.67.
5 June 1823 - Moses Gray, a revolutionary soldier and United States Pensioner now files his schedule and declaration, and took the oath required by the several acts of congress, providing for certain persons engaged in the land and navel service of the United States in the revolutionary war, and it is further ordered by the court that the schedule and declatation aforesaid be recorded and it is further ordered that it be certified that the property contained in the schedule aforesaid is valued by the court at Sixty Seven Dollars and fifty cents.
Author's note: His schedule and declaration have not been located in the courthouse records.

Pennsylvania Archives, Series 5, Vol. 5. p. 53.
Associators and Militia County of Bedford
A Return of Capt. Thomas Paxton's Company of Rangers in Bedford County
Moses Gray   Commencing Sept. 18th; Ending Nov'r 13th; Days in pay 57; Rations drawn 57.

Pennsylvania Archives, Series 5, Vol. V. p. 55
Muster Rolls and Papers Relating to the Associators and Militia of the County of Bedford.
Captain Paxton's Ranging Company
A Return of Captain Thomas Paton's company of Rangers at Bedford, the 12th of September, and discharged November the 13th, 1776.
Moses Gray, September 18, 1776

Pennsylvania Archives, Series 2, Vol. XIV. p. 639.
Muster Rolls and Papers Relating to the Associators and Militia of the County of Bedford.
Associated Battalions and Militia of the Revolution
Captain Paxton's Ranging Company.

A Return of Captain Thomas Paxton's company of Rangers, of Bedford, the 12th of September, and discharged November the 15th, 1776.
Moses Gray, September 18, 1776.

Early Settlers of Indiana's "GORE" 1803-1820; Compiled and Edited by Shirley Keller Mikesell; Heritage Books, Inc., 1995. p. 207.
Switzerland County Deeds; Book A
Agreement dated 1819. Stephen C. Stevens, Moses Gray & Lewis Houghman. S10, T2, RW. Lists work to be done by Gray & Houghman for lease of land lately occupied by William Brandenburgh. Signed S.C. Stevens, Moses Gray, Lewis (x) Huffman. Witness: E. Harrell. Pp. 243, 244.

Indiana Territory, Switzerland Circuit Court Records, Order Book, October Term 1814 to March Term 1815. p.66.
He is listed in county records for the first time on 16 February 1820.
Author's note: There are entries in this volume that are not within the range of dates shown on the binder cover.

U.S. Department of Interior, Bureau of Land Management, General Land Office Records; Land Patent Search – accessed 27 June 2012.
GRAY, MOSES
Accession Nr. CV-0087-417; Document Type – Credit Volume Patent; State – Indiana; Issue Date – 9/6/1831; Cancelled – No
Names on Document: Ormsby, Oliver; Gray, Moses
Land Office – Jeffersonville; Authority – April 24, 1820 Sale-Cash Entry (3 Stat. 566); Document Nr. – 2667; Total Acres – 160.00
Land Descriptions: State – IN; Meridian – 2nd PM; Twp-Rng – 003N-008E; Aliquots – NWE1/4; Section – 23; County - Jefferson

Revolutionary Soldiers of Switzerland County; Copied by Mary Hill, John Paul Chapter-Daughters of the American Revolution; January, 1958; http://www.ingenweb.org/inswitzerland/switzrevsoldiers.html- Viewed June, 2012.
GRAY, MOSES   Switzerland County
Revolutionary Soldier.
For service see manifest in Switz. Co. dated June 23, 1823. He enlisted for 1 year, March 1775, Bedford Co. Pa. under Captain John McDaniel (or Donald), Regiment of Col. John Piper, Continental line, State of Pa. He was in battles of Trenton and Brunswick; received gun wound at Trenton and discharged. Family, wife, aged 53, feeble; son William, age 18 years. Estate 1 mare, 8 years old; 3 cows, 3 calves, 10 small hogs, 1 table, 4 chairs, cubboard and ware, 1 kittle, 1 skillet, 1 plough.
Signed
Moses Gray, June 1832
John ?. Dufour
The following Gray marriages are recorded in Switzerland Co. Ind.
Moses ? Gray to Malinda Oberon April 2, 1827
James Gray to Mary Van Dusen April 22, 1820

Isaac Gray to Elizabeth McLean Jan. 6, 1827
John Gray to Mathilda Bellamy Feb. 2, 1827
Joseph Gray to Adaline Smith Oct. 20, 1827
Elizabeth, dau. of James Gray to Joseph Alfrey July 2, 1823
Sallie Gray to Andrew Poland Apr. 9, 1823
Lydia Gray to H. Bright Oct. 23, 1827
See Charles Allfrey in Biog. Souvenir of Jeff. Co. pg. 203 - 204, for record of James Gray

Revolutionary Soldiers Buried in Indiana A Supplement; 485 Names Not Listed in the Roster of Soldiers and Patriots of the American Revolution Buried in Indiana (1938) nor in Revolutionary Soldiers Buried in Indiana (1949); Margaret E. Waters; Indianapolis, 1954. p. 42.

GRAY, MOSES   Switzerland
married (wife ae. 53, 6-23-1823; chn. 9 at least): William, ae. 18 in 1823. (Note a Moses Gray was comm.. J.P. for Scott Co., Ind. 6-14-1820; comm.. Capt. in 6th Regt. Ind. Mil., 8-19-1818 and comm.. Col. In 29th Regt., 8-3-1820; (the 6th Regt. Was Switzerland, Jefferson, Clark, & Scott Co. men; the 29th was Scott Co.)
Service: enl. k [typo in book] yr., Mar. 1775, Bedford Co., Pa., Capt. John McDaniel (sp.? McDonald), Col. Piper, Pa. Cont. Line; in Batt. of Trenton & Brunswick.
REF: Manifest dated 6-23-1823, Switzerland Co., Ind., courthouse; "Exec. Proc. Of Ind., 1816-1836", pp. 139, 110, 143; Miss Mary Hill, Madison, Ind.; 1831 rej. Pens. List, p. 48—serv. In regt. not on cont. establishment.

GREEN, RICHARD

Patriot: Richard Green
Birth: abt. 1747
Married Spouse 1: Unknow
Service state(s): NC
Service description: Capt. Moseley, William Preston, NC line, Continental
Rank: Private
Proof of Service: Switzerland Co. Complete Records, Circuit Court, 1821- 1827
Pension application No.: Not in War Department records
Residences: NC, IN
Died: bef. May 1831   Switzerland Co., IN
Buried: Unknown
DAR Ancestor No.: None

Switzerland County, Indiana Complete Records, Circuit Court, Vol. ?, Sep 3, 1821-Apr 18, 1827; p.494.
Pension abstract for – Richard Green   Service state(s): North Carolina
Date: 20 April 1825
County of: Switzerland   State of: Indiana
Declaration made before a Circuit Court.
Schedule of property valued at $35.00, and declaration of service.
Age: 78 years
Residence when he entered service: North Carolina, Switzerland Co., IN
Residence now: Switzerland Co., IN
Volunteer or Drafted or Substitute: Enlisted
Statement of service-

Period	Duration	Names of General and Field Officers
1782	18 months	Company commanded by Capt. Moseley, Regt. commanded by William Preston, in the North Carolina line on the Continental establishment.

Battles: Battle of Guilford
Discharge received: At Guilford Old Courthouse in North Carolina
Statement is supported by –
Documentary proof: None
Occupation: Farmer but totally unable to maintain himself.
Family: Has no family but himself and is subject to fits.

Switzerland County, Indiana, Civil Order Book - Vol.5, Feb 10, 1823 - Jun 21, 1826, p.289.
20 April 1825 - Richard Green a Revolutionary Soldier now appeared and files his Schedule of Property and made the Declaration and took the Oath required by the Act of Congress relative to Pensioners, which are ordered to be recorded and it is further ordered to be Certified that the Property Contained in Said Schedule is valued at Thirty five Dollars.

Switzerland County, Indiana Probate Order Book 2, 1831-1837; p. 5, 17, 22, 36, 45, 54, 63, 83.; *Switzerland County, Indiana Probate Record Book Vol. A, Mar 1827-Nov 1834;* p. 302.
Abstract of will and/or administration for: Richard Green
State & county where recorded: Switzerland Co., Indiana
State & county where will was made: No will
Book/volume where recorded: Probate Order Book 2
Date entered in probate: May Term 1831
Administration:
Date began - May Term 1831
Name of administrator - Frederick Green
Bonded by and amount of bond: Richard Lock for $100.00.
Date of division & disbursement, or final return: 18 August 1832
References to other files - book & page no. (orphans, minors, inventories, petitions, deeds, etc).: None

Roster of Soldiers from North Carolina in the American Revolution, with an appendix containing a collection of miscellaneous records; North Carolina Daughters of the American Revolution; D.A.R., Durham, NC, 1932. p. 382.
Vouchers – The following are the usual form of vouchers found in the Comptroller's Records.
Vouchers in Box B-1 follow
Militia Richard Green No. 5346 Salisbury Dis[trict]

Possible record for this man –
The North Carolinian : a quarterly journal of genealogy and history.; William Perry Johnson, editor; William Perry Johnson and Russell E. Bidlack publisher, 1955-. p. 623.
Gates County Record Book A (Deeds & Grants), 1776-1783.
87 – 1780 – Richard Green & wife Selah to Jonathan Cullin.

Register of Certificates Issued by John Pierce, Esquire, Paymaster General and Commissioner of Army Accounts for the United States, to Officers and Soldiers of the Continental Army Under Act of July 4, 1783; Originally Published as Senate Documents, Vol.9, No. 988, 63rd Congress, 3d Session, Washington, 1915; Seventeenth report of the National Society of the Daughters of the American Revolution; Genealogical Publishing Co., Inc, Baltimore, MD, 1984. p. 215.
Men listed in this volume with the same name.

No. of Certificate	To whom issued	Amount
12277	Green, Richard	3.54
13118	Green, Richard	51.50
18733	Green, Richard	18.03
19780	Green, Richard	80.00
21021	Green, Richard	80.00
22196	Green, Richard	40.60
25692	Green, Richard	53.30
26376	Greene, Richard	22.00

GRIFFITH, WILLIAM

Patriot: William Griffith
Birth: 1745   Kent Co., MD
Married Spouse 1: Hannah Griffith
Service state(s): MD
Service description: Capts. Simon Wickes, John Moore, Col. Richard
　　　　　　　　　　　Graves, Kent Co., VA
Rank: Private
Proof of Service: The Maryland Militia in the Revolutionary War
Pension application No.: None
Residences: Fairley Creek, Kent Co., MD; Switzerland Co., IN
Died: 1820/1821 Hendricks Co., IN
Buried: Long Run Cemetery, Craig Twp., Switzerland Co., IN
DAR Ancestor No.: A048420

The Maryland Militia in the Revolutionary War; by S. Eugene Clements and F. Edward Wright; Published by Family Line Publications, Westminster, MD, 1987. p. 183.
Kent County, 13th Battalion of Militia under Command of Col. Richard Graves, June 1775
Benj. Chalmers, Lt. Col.; Isaac Perkins, Major; Willm. Frisby, Major.
6th Class - William Griffith (in list)
p. 190.
Kent County, 13th Battalion of Militia under Command of Col. Richard Graves Lowr. Langford Bay, 4th Company – Simeon Wickes, Capt.; Thomas Crow, 1st Lieut.; Samuel Beck, 1st Lieut.
6th Class – Wm. Griffith (in list)

Muster Rolls and other records of service of Maryland Troops in the American Revolution; Archives of Maryland, reprinted with permission by Genealogical Publishing Co., Inc., Baltimore, 1972. p. 408.
Records of Maryland Troops in the Continental Service
An alphabetical List of discharged Soldiers of the two Battalions of Militia raised to serve in the Continental Army in the year 1781.

County	Names
Dorchester	Griffith, William

Register of Certificates Issued by John Pierce, Esquire, Paymaster General and Commissioner of Army Accounts for the United States, to Officers and Soldiers of the Continental Army Under Act of July 4, 1783; Originally Published as Senate Documents, Vol.9, No. 988, 63rd Congress, 3d Session, Washington, 1915; Seventeenth report of the National Society of the Daughters of the American Revolution; Genealogical Publishing Co., Inc, Baltimore, MD, 1984. p. 217.
Men listed in this volume with the same name.

No. of Certificate	To whom issued	Amount
8619	Griffith, William	109.30
74965	Griffith, William	40.60

75271 Griffith, William 80.00

U.S. Department of Interior, Bureau of Land Management, General Land Office Records; Land Patent Search – accessed 27 June 2012.
GRIFFITH, WILLIAM
Accession Nr. CV-0035-184; Document Type – Credit Volume Patent; State – Indiana; Issue Date – 8/5/1817; Cancelled - No
Names on Document: Griffith, William J.; Heath, Samuel
Land Office – Cincinnati; Authority – April 24, 1820 Sale-Cash Entry (3 Stat. 566); Total Acres – 0.00
Land Descriptions: State – IN; Meridian – 1st PM; Twp-Rng – 002N-003W; Section – 6; County - Switzerland
&
Accession Nr. CV-0048-306; Document Type – Credit Volume Patent; State – Indiana; Issue Date – 11/3/1819; Cancelled – No
Names on Document: Rogers, Henry; Griffith, William Jackson
Land Office – Cincinnati; Authority – April 24, 1820 Sale-Cash Entry (3 Stat. 566); Total Acres – 160.94
Land Descriptions: State – IN; Meridian – 1st PM; Twp-Rng – 003N-003W; Aliquots – SW1/4; Section – 30; County - Switzerland

Roster of Soldiers and Patriots of the American Revolution Buried in Indiana, Vol. II; 1966; p.48.
GRIFFITH, WILLIAM   Switzerland County
Born - 1745
Service – Pri. in Capt. S. Wicks Co. and Capt. John Morris Co., Col. Richard Graves' Regt., Kent Co., Maryland.
Proof - Vol. 2, pp. 95 and 129, Kent Co. Md., Militia, unpublished Records DAR No.
Died 1821/2. Bur. in Long Run Cemetery, Switzerland Co., IN. Stone.
Married Hannah _____. Ch, Griffith; Wm. Jackson, married Catherine Sigmond; Benjamin; they had three daus. whose names are not given but they married an Ellis, Ogle, & Lewis

Abstract of Graves of Revolutionary Patriots (4 volumes); by Patricia Law Hatcher; Pioneer Heritage Press, Dallas, TX, 1987. Vol. 2, p. 96.
This is an abstract and an index to information reported to the Daughters of the American Revolution and published in their annual reports to the Smithsonian Institution, printed as Senate Documents (1900-1974) and published annually in the DAR magazine (1978-1987).
Published 1972 (Senate Doc. 54)
GRIFFITH, William   Long Run Cem, Switzerland Co IN

History of Switzerland County Indiana 1885; Reproduced by the Switzerland County Historical Society, Vevay, Indiana, 1999. The portion of the book relating to Switzerland County in the 1885 printing of the "History of Dearborn, Ohio, and Switzerland Counties, Indiana". p. 1148.

Craig Township – "William J. Griffith, who located in this township in 1816, was a native of Milburn in the year 1778, and a son of William and Hannah Griffith (no relation) whose parents were of Welsh extraction. The family became early settlers of Indiana."

GULLION, JEREMIAH

Jeremiah lived in Gallatin Co., KY, across the Ohio River from his brothers, John and Robert. He frequently interacted in Switzerland Co., IN. Therefore his record is included here.

Patriot: Jeremiah Gullion
Birth: 28 Nov 1758 Fort Frederick, MD
Married Spouse 1: bef. 1780, PA   Isabella/Bella/Bell Patty
(b. 30 Mar 1760, Ireland; d. 1 Aug 1843, Carroll Co., KY)
Service state(s): PA
    Service description: Capts. Joseph Erwin, Matthew Jack, Jeremiah Lochney,
            Col. Carnahan
Rank: Private
Proof of Service: Pension application W8879
Pension application No.: W8879
Residences: Westmoreland Co., PA; Carroll Co., KY
Died: 9 Sep 1816 Eagle Creek, Gallatin Co., KY
Buried: prob. Gallatin Co., KY (Family traditions says he is buried in
       Gullion Cemetery, Gallatin Co., KY – now Carroll Co., KY)
DAR Ancestor No.: A048322

National Archives microfilm, Series M805, Roll 383, File W8979.
Letter in Pension Application file – W8879.
Major General Allen W. Gullion   May 28, 1838
Judge Advocate General, U.S.A.   Jeremiah Gullion, W.8879
War Department   RA-J/MGS
Washington, D.C.
Dear Sir:
        Reference is made to your request by telephone for information relative to Jeremiah Gullion who served in the Revolutionary War.
        The data which follows were obtained from papers on file in the pension claim, W.8879, based on the Revolutionary War service of Jeremiah Gullion.
        He was born November 28, 1758. The place of his birth and the manes of his parents were not given.
        While living in Westmoreland County, Pennsylvania, he enlisted about 1776 and served at various times until the declaration of peace in 1783 as private with the Pennsylvania troops under Captains Joseph Erwin, Matthew Jack and Jeremiah Lochrey and Colonel Carnahan, and while at Lexington, Kentucky, in the spring of 1780 he was appointed by Colonel Todd as Indian spy and ranger and served under General Clark in his expedition against the Indiana at Chillicothe and Pickaway. He received two wounds, one in the right foot and the other in the right leg. He was in the battles of Hannahstown and Blue Licks and his entire service amounted to at least three and one half or four years.
        It was stated that he received a pension on account of his wounds while living in Pennsylvania.

He moved to Kentucky about 1786 and he died in April, 1815, or about 1817, or in June or July, 1819. His residence at the time of his death was on the Kentucky River near the mouth of the Eagle Creek in what was later Carroll County, Kentucky.

Jeremiah Gullion married in 1779 or in January, 1780, at her father's house near Hannahstown, Isabella Pattie or Patty who was born March 3, 1760, and was the daughter of George Pattie or Patty. She was born in Ireland and came to America with her father before the Revolution and during the Revolution she lived in Westmoreland County, Pennsylvania.

She applied for pension March 16, 1837, while living in Henry County, Kentucky. The claim was allowed.

Isabella Gullion died August 1, 1843, in Carroll County, Kentucky, and was survived by the following children: Rachael Gullion, resident of Henry county, Kentucky; Jeremiah Gullion, resident of Indiana; William Gullion, resident of Kentucky; Ann Kelly who married Jack Kelly and was living in Kentucky; Jane Cabbin who married William Cabbin and was living in Indiana; and Polly McCreary who married --- McCreary and was living in Indiana.

The following were referred to as the children of Jeremiah and Isabella Gullion:

Thomas	born	April	3, 1781
Rachael	"	February	3, 1783
William	"	July	20, 1787
Mary	"	August	20, 1789
Jeremiah	"	August	11, 1793
George	"	March	27, 1795
Jean	"	January	26, 1798

The following family data also appear: William Gullion was born June 7, 1802; Thomas Gullion's children: William Gullion was born May 28, 1801; Nelly Gullion was born April 18, 1803.

The soldier, Jeremiah Gullion, and his brothers, Robert who was living in Switzerland County, Indiana, in March, 1829, and was "seventy-four years of age and upwards"; and John who was living in Decatur County, Indiana, in October, 1839, and stated that he would be seventy-seven years of age on April 28, 1940. The soldier's sister, Mary Raiborne, was living in Frankfort, Kentucky, in 1838.

In 1837 Mrs. Rachael Gullion made a deposition at the house of one Benjamin Gullion in Henry County, Kentucky, and stated that she was about seventy-four years of age and was a sister of the widow, Isabella Gullion.

The papers in this claim contain no further data relative to the family of Jeremiah Gullion.

Very truly yours,
A.D. HILLER
Executive Assistant
to the Administrator

Included in this pension file are pages from a notebook that belonged to William Gullion, son of, the subject. The content of these pages is interesting because of the first-hand account of the historic Earthquake of 1811 that affected the Ohio River Valley. Transcription of these pages -

First page - On Monday morning the 16th day of Decm 1811 Thee was a Small Shock or Colvulsion in the Earth Which G(hole in page) minutes, about (hole in page) in the morning lasted nearly 15 minutes, then another Small Shock the 23th of Jany 1812 , at, 8 O'(illegible) It lasted about twenty minutes.

Second page – George Gullion was born in the Year of our Lord William Gullion his Book

On Monday morning the 16 day 1811 thar was a Small Shock or Colvince about (illegible) ninety Earth which came up

George Gulliion was Born March 27 1795

Pennsylvania Archives, Series 6, Vol. II., p. 331.
Battalions Not Stated Westmoreland County Militia. County of Westmoreland Penn's Volunteer's - Accounts of the Company Commanded by Capt'n Jeremiah Lochrey. Stationed in Westmoreland County for Defence of the Frontiers.

```
                         1780 Commencement          Ending
Jeremiah Gullion     April 17th               Oct'r April 21st, 1781
```
[John Gullion also on this list]

Gallatin County Kentucky, Will Book A; Abstract of Estate
GULLION, Jeremiah
Inventory, Sept. 1, 1816
Administrator: Belle Gullion
Appraisers: John Brown, Jerry Gullion, John Gullion.

Abstract of Final Payment Voucher; General Services Administration, Washington, DC
NAME   Gullion, Isabel (Jeremiah)
AGENCY OF PAYMENT   Ky
DATE OF ACT   1836
DATE OF PAYMENT   2nd qtr. 1844
DATE OF DEATH   Aug 1, 1843
FINAL PAYMENT VOUCHER RECEIVED FROM
THE GENERAL ACCOUNTING OFFICE   Form
General Services Administration   GSA DA 70-7035   GSA Dec 69 7068

Second Census of Kentucky, 1800; Clift G. Glenn; Genealogical Publishing Co., Baltimore, MD, 1954.
An alphabetical list of 32,000 taxpayers based on original tax lists on file at the Kentucky Historical Society. Information given includes the county of residence and the date of the tax list in which the individual is listed.
Gullion, Jeremiah   Gallatin   4/11/1800

Vevay Switzerland County Indiana 1795-1999; no author or publisher. p. 1.
The first settler in the county of whom any definite account is given was Heathcoat Pickett, a Revolutionary War veteran, who located here is 1795, followed in 1798 and 1799 by the Cotton, Dickason and Gullion families.

GULLION, JOHN
aka O'GULLION, JOHN & JACK/JACKSON

Patriot: John Gullion
Birth: abt. 1763   Fort Frederick, MD
Married Spouse 1: abt. 1797 Mrs. Catherine (Riffel) Tanner
 (d. 11 Feb 1845, Decatur Co., IN; buriedSpillman farm,
 Clinton Twp., Decatur Co., IN)
 She married 1. ? Tanner in Westmoreland Co., PA
Service state(s): PA
Service description: Capts. Joseph Irwin, Matthew Jack, Andrew Hood,
 James Patton
Rank: Private
Proof of Service: Pension application S36567
Pension application No.: S36567
Residences: Westmoreland Co., PA; to Indiana Territory (abt. 1810); Ohio;
 Switzerland Co., IN; Decatur Co., IN; Howard Co., IN
Died: 29 Jun 1850 Howard Co., IN
Buried: Twin Springs Cemetery, near Kokomo, Howard Co., IN
DAR Ancestor No.: A048267

Pension Application Abstracted from National Archives microfilm Series 805, Roll 383, File S36567.
Pension abstract for – Gullion, John O.   Service state(s): PA
Alternate spelling(s): O'Gullion, John
Date: 12 May 1818
County of: Switzerland   State of: Indiana
Declaration made before the Circuit Court.
Residence when he entered service: Hannah's Town, Westmoreland Co., PA
Residence(s) since the war: Lived in Ohio many years, then to Indiana.
Residence now: Switzerland Co., IN
Volunteer or Drafted or Substitute Volunteered
Rank(s): Private
Statement of service-

Period	Duration	Names of General and Field Officers
1775	abt. 18 mos.	Captain Joseph Erwin's company, Colonel Miles' Pennsylvania rifle regiment

Battles: Long Island; skirmish in New Jersey where he was severely wounded.
Discharge received: At Valley Forge in 1777.

Period	Duration	Names of General and Field Officers
1778	6 mos.	Captain Matthew Jack's company, Colonel Bayard's Pennsylvania regiment
Date not given	6 mos.	Captain John Shearer's company, Colonel Davis' Pennsylvania regiment
1783		Captain Andrew Hood's company, Colonel Crawford's regiment

Battles: Defeat in Sandusky in 1782.

Period	Duration	Names of General and Field Officers
Date not given		Captain James Patton's company, Colonel Hardin's Pennsylvania regiment
Date not given		Colonel McMullen's regiment

Battles: Engagements on the Saint Josephs and Mary's Rivers under General Harmer.

Statement is supported by –

Living witness, name(s) who can testify to service: Robert Gullion and
James White.

20 Mar 1919 - Robert Gullion, his brother, deposes that John Gullion was absent from home for about two years in the service of the United Colonies during the Revolutionary War, and that his brother Jeremiah came home severely wounded and he has experienced considerable inconvenience from his wounds since.

22 Mar 1919 - James White deposed that he verifies that John Gullion, now residing in Jefferson Twp., Switzerland Co., served for about two years under Capt. Joseph Irwin of Westmoreland Co., PA.

&

Date: 29 Mar 1852
County of: Howard   State of: Indiana
Declaration made before a Court.

Thomas Gullion declares he is one of the children and heirs of John O'Gullion, late deceased, of Howard Co., IN. John O'Gullion died 29 June 1850 in Howard Co., IN, leaving no widow. His wife, "my mother" died 11 Feb 1845. Father left only two children viz. Thomas and Susan intermarried with Levi Rayls both of whom are living in Howard Co., and claiming the benefit . "I have frequently heard my father say that he never received any benefit in the way of pay while in the service. He once had a considerable amount of "Continental Money" which was worthless but even at nominal value my belief is that he never received his pay. I have heard him also say that he was entitled to bounty land although he never received any.

Marriage of soldier: John O. Gullion or O'Gullion married, date not given, near Lexington, Kentucky, or near Dayton, Ohio, Mrs. Catherine Turner, a widow, of Decatur County, Indiana. Her maiden name was Catherine Riffel; the date of her former marriage not shown, nor was the Christian name and date of death of her former husband given.

Residences of soldier: Ohio, Switzerland Co., IN, Decatur Co., IN, finally to Howard Co., IN.

Thomas, also says "I make this declaration and application for the purpose of obtaining the pension pay, arrears or increase of pay, or pension or the bounty land warrant to which I may be entitled as one of the children and heirs of the above named John O'Gullion deceased under any law or laws of Congress to the benefit of which I may be entitled."

Abstract of Final Payment Voucher; General Services Administration, Washington, DC
LAST FINAL PAYMENT VOUCHER RECEIVED FROM
THE GENERAL ACCOUNTING OFFICE
NAME   Gullion, John O.

AGENCY OF PAYMENT	Indiana
DATE OF ACT	1818
DATE OF PAYMENT	1st Qr. 1851
DATE OF DEATH	June 29, 1850

GENERAL SERVICES ADMINISTRATION
National Archives and Records Service NA-286
GSA-WASH DC 54-4891 November 1953

Pennsylvania Archives, Series 6, Vol. II. p. 331
Battalions Not Stated Westmoreland County Militia
Penna Volunteer's
Accounts of the Company Commanded by Capt'n Jeremiah Lochrey. Stationed in Westmoreland County for Defence of the Frontiers.

	1780 Commencement	Ending
John Gullion	Oct'r 11th	Dec. 15th

[Jeremiah Gullion also listed here]

Pennsylvania Archives, Series 3, Vol. XXIII. p. 337.
Muster Rolls of the Navy and Line, Militia and Rangers, 1775-1783. with List of Pensioners, 1818-1832.
Rangers on the Frontier 1778-1783
Westmoreland County, Capt. Jere Lochry's Rangers Comp
John Gullion is listed here

Pennsylvania Archives, Series 6, Vol. 1. p. 472.
Associators and Militia City of Philadelphia
Muster Rolls Relating to the Associators and Militia of the City of Philadelphia.
John Gullion in this list

Pennsylvania Archives, Series 3, Vol. XXIII. p. 308.
Muster Rolls of the Navy and Line, Militia and Rangers, 1775-1783. with List of Pensioners, 1818-1832.
Rangers on the Frontier 1778-1783
Moses Coe's Company –
John Gullion
[Robert Gullion also on this list]

Pennsylvania Archives; Series: Series 3; Volume: XXIII; Chapter: Muster Rolls of the Navy and Line, Militia and Rangers, 1775-1783. with List of Pensioners, 1818-1832.; Page: 595.
Statement showing the Names of Pennsylvanians Residing in the State of Indiana, who have been Inscribed on the Pension List Under the Act of Congress Passed March 8, 1818.
-Dearborn county-
Gullion, John O., pr. P.L, Jan. 30, 1832; 74.

A Partial Census For Indiana Territory 1810; Compiled by John D & E. Diane Stemmons; Census Publishing LC, Sandy, UT, 2004. p.223.
Gullun, John, Historical Locality: Indiana Territory, Current State: Indiana, Jefferson County,- Name on recommendation list, 1813, to the President asking that Eijah Sparks be appointed to fill the vacancy on the General Court that existed because of the death of Judge Vanderburgh (pages 244-50).- Territorial Papers of the US, vol. 8 pg. 247.
Gullun, John, Male

Indiana Territory, Switzerland Circuit Court Records, Order Book, October Term 1814 to March Term 1815. p.115.
He is listed in county records for the first time on 26 June 1815, as a juror.

Early Settlers of Indiana's "GORE" 1803-1820; Compiled and Edited by Shirley Keller Mikesell; Heritage Books, Inc., 1995. p. 185.
Switzerland County – Township 2, Range 2W
Section 35 – John Gullion – 1810 – pg 7.

U.S. Department of Interior, Bureau of Land Management, General Land Office Records; Land Patent Search – accessed 27 June 2012.
GULLION, JOHN & HENRY
Accession Nr. CV-0044-332; Document Type – Credit Volume Patent; State – Indiana; Issue Date – 4/14/1819; Cancelled – No
Names on Document: Miller, John; Gullion, Henry; Gullion, John; Mosely, James; Hutchinson, Sally
Land Office – Cincinnati; Authority – April 24, 1820 Sale-Cash Entry (3 Stat. 599); Total Acres – 0.00
Land Descriptions: State – IN; Meridian – 1st PM; Twp-Rng – 002N-002W; Aliquots – NE1/4; Section – 27; County – Switzerland
&
GULLION, JOHN
Accession Nr. CV-0012-342; Document Type – Credit Volume Patent; State – Indiana; Issue Date – 2/17/1812; Cancelled – No
Land Office – Jeffersonville, Authority – April 24, 1820 Sale-Cash Entry (3 Stat. 566); Total Acres – 0.00
Land Descriptions – State – IN; Meridian – 2nd PM; Twp-Rng – 005N-011E; Aliquots – NW1/4; Section – 3; County - Jefferson
&
Accession Nr. CV-0020324; Document Type – Credit volume Patent; State – Indiana; Issue Date – 2/11/1814; Cancelled – No
Land Office – Cincinnati; Authority – April 24, 1820 Sale-Cash Entry (3 Stat. 566); Total Acres – 0.00
Land Descriptions: State – IN; Meridian – 1st PM; Twp-Rng – 002N-002W; Aliquots – SW1/4; Section – 35; County – Switzerland
&
Accession Nr. CV-0031-355; Document Type – Credit Volume Patent; State – Indiana; Issue Date – 12/6/1816; Cancelled – No
Names on Document: Gullion, John; Gullion, Henry; Crane, Daniel

Land Office – Cincinnati; Authority – April 24, 1820 Sale-Cash Entry (3 Stat. 566); Total Acres – 0.00
Land Descriptions:
State – IN; Meridian – 1st PM;Twp-Rng – 002N-002W; Aliquots – SE1/4; Section – 35; County – Switzerland

A Census of Pensioners for Revolutionary or Military Services with their Names, Ages, and Places of Residence Under the Act for Taking the Sixth Census in 1840; Genealogical Publishing Co., Inc., Baltimore, Maryland, 1965. p. 182.
INDIANA, DECATUR (NO TWP.)

Names of Pensioners for Revolutionary or Military services	Ages	Names of heads of families with whom pensioner resided June 1, 1840
Gullion, John	77	Thomas Gullion

Early Ohio Settlers, Purchasers of Land in Southwestern Ohio, 1800-1840; Compiled by Ellen T. Berry & David A. Berry; Genealogical Publishing Co., Inc., Baltimore, MD, 1986. p.126.

Purchaser	Year	Date	Residence	R – T - S
Gullion, John (B)	1810	Mar. 16	Dearborn Ind	02-02-35

(B) Indiana Survey: Land lying west of a meridian drawn west of the Great Miami (known as the "Gore"). Switzerland, Dearborn, Franklin, Ohio, Union and Randolph Counties (all or only a part of each county) – all in Indiana.

Indiana Land Entries Vol. 1 Cincinnati District, 1801-1840; Margaret R. Waters; Originally Published Indianapolis 1948, Second Reprint 1979 by The Bookmark, P.O. Box 74, Knightstown, In 46148. p. 43.
CINCINNNATI LAND DISTRICT – VOL. 1
Page 40, Township 2N, Range 2 W of the 1st Principle Meridian
John Gullion, SW 1/4 – S35; 3-16-1810
Note: --The tract books for the land offices in Indiana are deposited in the office of the Auditor of State, Indianapolis. They and are in the custody of the State clerk. --

The Swiss Settlement of Switzerland County; by Perrett Dufour; published by the Indiana Historical Commission, Indianapolis, IN, 1925. p. 37.
In Town[ship] 2, R[ange] 2 W[est] SW qr Sec. 3 entered March 16, 1810 by John Gullion containing 160 acres.

Roster of Soldiers and Patriots of the American Revolution Buried in Indiana, Vol. I; compiled by Mrs. Roscoe C. O'Byrne.; Indiana Daughters of the American Revolution, 1981; p. 167.
GULLION (O'GULLION), JOHN O.   Howard County
Born – 1760
Service – Enlisted from Westmoreland Co., Penn., in April or May, 1776, as pri. in Capt. Joseph Erwin's Co., Col. Miles' Penn. Rifle Regt. Was wounded and discharged at Valley Forge after serving 18 mos. Re-enlisted 1778, served 6 mos.

in col. Bayard's Penn. Regt., and 6 mos. in Col. Davis' Penn. Regt. In 1782 he was in Col. Crawford's Regt.
Proof – Pension claim S.36567. Lived in Switzerland Co., Ind., 1818, 1819. Applied for pension 1831 from Decatur Co., Ind., and was still living there in 1836.
Died – June 29, 1850, in Howard Co., Ind.
Proof – Pension record and Probate Court Records of Howard Co., Ind. Buried Twin Springs Cemetery, S.W. of Kokomo, Ind. Stone. There is also a government marker bearing soldier's name erected on Spillman farm, Clinton Twp., Decatur Co.

Vevay Switzerland County Indiana 1795-1999; no author or publisher. p. 1.
The first settler in the county of whom any definite account is given was Heathcoat Pickett, a Revolutionary War veteran, who located here is 1795, followed in 1798 and 1799 by the Cotton, Dickason and Gullion families.

The Vevay Reveille-Enterprise; Vol. 122, No. 37, 15 Sep 1935, p. 3, col.5-6.
Excerpt from newspaper article - Roster of Revolutionary Soldiers Who Resided in Switzerland County
By Mrs. Effa M. Danner
Robert Gullion article -
His brother, John Gullion entered land in 1810 and was a Revolutionary soldier. He moved to Decatur County, census 1840.
Pension records, John Gullion, age 77, Thomas Gullion, guardian. Wife's name, Kittie. Book G, p. 364.

Tombstone inscription-

JOHN GULLION
MILES' PA. MIL.
REV. WAR
BORN 1760
DIED
June 29, 1850
IN BATTLE OF LONG
ISLAND WOUNDED
IN NEW JERSE
SERVED EIGHTEEN
MONTHS HONORABLY
DISCHARGED AT
VALLEY FORGE
ERECTED B GEN
JAMES COX CHAPTER
OF DAUGHTERS OF
AMERICAN REV.

Abstract of Graves of Revolutionary Patriots (4 volumes); by Patricia Law Hatcher; Pioneer Heritage Press, Dallas, TX, 1987. Vol. 2, p. 100.

This is an abstract and an index to information reported to the Daughters of the American Revolution and published in their annual reports to the Smithsonian Institution, printed as Senate Documents (1900-1974) and published annually in the DAR magazine (1978-1987).
Published 1972 (Senate Doc. 54)
GULLION, John   Twin Springs Cem, nr Kokomo, Howard Co IN

Howard County Genealogical Society Newsletter; Oakford, IN; Fall 2003, Vol. 19, Iss. 3, p. 68.
Two Veterans of Revolution Lie in County
One Sleeps in Twin Springs Cemetery; the other in Oak Mound Cemetery
Within the borders of Howard County reposes the dust of soldier who have borne arms for the Republic in every war in which it has ever engaged.
The soil of Howard County is not even without honor of that kind as regards the war to independence, the Revolution. Two men who fought under Washington, in the long conflict in which the British yoke was thrown off, sleep in Howard County cemeteries.
The grave of one of these, Jack Gullion, is in Twin Springs cemetery, five miles west of Kokomo on the Twin Springs pike. The grave of the other, Abner Clark, is in Oak Mound cemetery, sometimes called the Brown graveyard, just west of Poplar Grove in the northwest corner of the county. Gullion's grave is marked by a government headstone that attests his service in the Revolution.

Author's note: Additional research divulged a third brother Jeremiah (in addition to Robert and John). Jeremiah settled in Henry County, KY where he died in April 1815 or 1817, or in June or July, 1819. He lived on the Kentucky River near the mouth of Eagle Creek in what was later Carroll Co., KY. His wife, Isabella, applied for pension March 16, 1837, claim W8879, while living in Henry Co., KY. The application includes statements that Jeremiah had two brothers, Robert who was living in Switzerland Co., IN, and John who was living in Decatur Co., IN, and a sister Mary Raiborne was living in Frankfort, KY. The three brothers served under Capt. Joseph Erwin, Pennsylvania troops.

GULLION, ROBERT

Patriot: Robert Gullion
Birth: 4 Feb 1764   Fort Frederick, MD
Married Spouse 1: 1784/1786 Washington Co., PA   Barbary/Barbara X
                                    (d. 20 Dec 1832, Switzerland Co., IN)
Service state(s): PA
Service description: Capt. Shearer; Capt. Hood
Rank: Private
Proof of Service: Pension application S16396
Pension application No.: S16396
Residences: Big Sweetly Creek, Westmoreland Co., PA; Indiana Territory;
            Switzerland Co., IN
Died: 3 Sep 1852, or 6 Aug 1853, or 23 Jul 1853 Switzerland Co., IN
Buried: Gullion Cemetery, York Twp., Switzerland Co., IN
DAR Ancestor No.: A048268

Pension Application Abstracted from National Archives microfilm Series 805, Roll 383, File S16396.; Switzerland County, Indiana Probate Record Book Vol. A, Mar 1827-Nov 1834; p. 264.

Pension abstract for – Robert Gullion   Service state(s): PA
Date: 13 August 1832
County of: Switzerland   State of: Indiana
Declaration made before the Probate Court. Recorded in Book A, pg. 256.
Age: 68   Record of age: Never had any record.
Where and year born: Near Fort Frederick on the Potomac River on 4 Feb 1764.
Residence when he entered service: Big Sweety Creek, Westmoreland Co., PA
Residence(s) since the war: After he left PA, 13 or 14 years in KY, for the last 33 years in Indiana. Now live in Switzerland Co.
Residence now: Switzerland Co., IN
Volunteer or Drafted or Substitute: Volunteered both times.
Rank(s): Private
Statement of service-

Period	Duration	Names of General and Field Officers
1780 or 81	Upward of 90 days	Capt. Sheaver, PA Militia
Apr or May 1782	Upward of 3 mos.	Capt. Andrew Hood, Col. William Crawford

Battles and/or general circumstances of your service: Rendezvoused at Mingo Bottom on the Ohio River to the number of about 500 men; crossed the river and took up the line of March for Sandusky but were defeated by the Indians on the 4th day of June 1782. Nicholson, Stover and Zanes were our pilots.
Discharge received: Never received a written discharge.
Statement is supported by –
Living witness, name(s): John Gullion, his brother, makes statement – Decatur Co., Indiana, John Gullion is well acquainted with Robert Gullion; served together during the Revolutionary War for the full term of 6 months on 1781; served in a company of Pennsylvania Militia or Rangers commanded by Capt. Sheaver of Westmoreland Co., PA; stationed at a block house on the waters

of Turtle Creek in PA. In 1782, Robert Gullion served as a private in a company of PA Militia commanded by Capt. Andrew Hood, was in the expedition commanded by Col. William Crawford when it was defeated on the 4th day of June 1782. After defeat was with a number of other soldiers under the command of Major Williams and marched to the Mingo Bottom on the Ohio.
Documentary proof: Have none.
Person now living who can testify to service: My brother, John, of Decatur county, Indiana was with me in all of the foregoing service. William Scudder residing in Switzerland Co., IN.
Clergyman: James Cox residing in Gallatin Co., KY
Persons in neighborhood who certify character: William Scudder, Joseph Malin, Edward Patton, John F. Dufour, Elisha Golay, Newton H. Tapp. &c, &c, &c.

Switzerland County, Indiana Probate Order Book 2 1831-1837; p. 69.
13 Aug 1832
In the matter of Robert Gullion,
An applicant for a pension under the act of congress of June 7, 1832, Said applicant being duly Sworn and examined by the said Court do hereby declare their opinion. After the investigation of the matter & after putting the Interrogations prescribed by the War department that the above named Robert Gullion was a Revolutionary Soldier and Served as he states and the Court further certifies, that it appears to them that James Cox who has Signed the preceding Certificates is a Clergyman, resident of Gallatin county and State of Kentucky, and that William Scudder who also Signed the Same is a resident in Switzerland County and State of Indiana is a credible person, and their Statement is entitled to Credit.

Switzerland County, IN, Will Book Vol. 2, 6 Sept 1847-26 Jul 1859, p. 109.
Abstract of administration for: Robert Gullion
State & county where recorded: Switzerland Co., Indiana
State & county where will was made: Switzerland Co., IN
Book/volume where recorded: Will Book Vol. 2.
Date will made: 21 September 1848
Date entered in probate: 5 August 1853
Name(s) of executors: Sons John, Henry, Charles.
Witness to Will – John McCullough, Robert Burns.
Names of heirs and others mentioned in will (also signed receipts of division of estate) and relationship if shown: Catherine Miller, Sarah McQueston, Polly Miller, Rachael Fulton, Rachael dau. of Henry Gullion, grandson John Gullion; sons John, Henry, Charles.

Abstract of Final Payment Voucher; General Services Administration, Washington, DC
LAST FINAL PAYMENT VOUCHER RECEIVED FROM THE GENERAL ACCOUNTING OFFICE
NAME　　　　　　　　　　Gullion, Robert
AGENCY OF PAYMENT　　Indiana
DATE OF ACT　　　　　　1832

DATE OF PAYMENT   Sept. 3, 1852
DATE OF DEATH
GENERAL SERVICES ADMINISTRATION
National Archives and Records Service   NA-286
GSA-WASH DC 54-4891   November 1953

Pennsylvania Archives, Series 3, Vol. XXIII. p. 308.
Muster Rolls of the Navy and Line, Militia and Rangers, 1775-1783. with List of Pensioners, 1818-1832.
Moses Coe's Company –
Robt. Gullion
[John Gullion also on this list]

Pennsylvania Archives, Series 3, Volume XXIII. p. 600.
Muster Rolls of the Navy and Line, Militia and Rangers, 1775-1783. with List of Pensioners, 1818-1832.
Switzerland County
Gullion, Robt., pr. P.M., July 15, 1833; 73.

American Militia in the Frontier Wars, 1790-1796; by Murtie June Clark; Genealogical Publishing Co., Inc., 1990. p.17.
Kentucky Militia
Muster roll of a Company of Mounted Volunteers under Command of Captain Henry Bartlett, Lieut. Colo. Horatio Hall's Regiment, in the service of the United States Commanded by Major General Charles Scott from Oct 10 to Nov 11, 1793.

Nr	Rank	Name	Remarks
15	Private	Gullion, Robert	enlist Oct 6 – Sep 27 left

Census of Indiana Territory for 1807; Indiana Historical Society, 1980. p. 23.
A list of free males above the age of twenty one in Dearborn County in March 1807 ~~
189   Robert Gullion

A Partial Census For Indiana Territory 1810; Compiled by John D & E. Diane Stemmons; Census Publishing LC, Sandy, UT, 2004. p.223.
Gullun, Robert, Historical Locality: Indiana Territory, Current State: Indiana, Jefferson County,- Name on recommendation list, 1813, to the President asking that Eijah Sparks be appointed to fill the vacancy on the General Court that existed because of the death of Judge Vanderburgh (pages 244-50).- Territorial Papers of the US, vol. 8 pg. 247.
Gullun, Robert, Male

Indiana Territory, Switzerland Circuit Court Records, Order Book, October Term 1814 to March Term 1815. p.6.
He is listed in county records as a member of the Grand Jury at the first court held in the county, on 28 October 1814. Court held at the house of Robert M. Trotter, in the Town of Vevay.

Early Ohio Settlers, Purchasers of Land in Southwestern Ohio, 1800-1840; Compiled by Ellen T. Berry & David A. Berry; Genealogical Publishing Co., Inc., Baltimore, MD, 1986. p.127.

Purchaser	Year	Date	Residence	R – T - S
Gullion, Robert (B)	1816	Sept. 06	Switzerland	02- 02-24

(B) Indiana Survey: Land lying west of a meridian drawn west of the Great Miami (known as the "Gore"). Switzerland, Dearborn, Franklin, Ohio, Union and Randolph Counties (all or only a part of each county) – all in Indiana.

Early Settlers of Indiana's "GORE" 1803-1820; Compiled and Edited by Shirley Keller Mikesell; Heritage Books, Inc., 1995. p. 185.
Switzerland County – Township 2, Range 2W
Section 34 – Robert Gullion & David Miller – 1816 – pg 7.

Indiana Land Entries Vol. 1 Cincinnati District, 1801-1840; Margaret R. Waters; Originally Published Indianapolis 1948, Second Reprint 1979 by The Bookmark, P.O. Box 74, Knightstown, In 46148. p.73, 132.
CINCINNNATI LAND DISTRICT – VOL. 1
Page 60. Twp. 4 N, Range 3 W of 1st Principle Meridian SWITZERLAND CO.
John F. Dufour & Robert Gullion NW ½ - S32; 4-15-1815. Relinquished.
and –
page 67. Twp. 2 N, Range 2 W of 1st Principle Meridian
Robert Gullion & David Miller NE ¼ - S35; 11-2-1818.
-- Note: The tract books for the land offices in Indiana are deposited in the office of the Auditor of State, Indianapolis. They and are in the custody of the State Land clerk. --

U.S. Department of Interior, Bureau of Land Management, General Land Office Records; Land Patent Search – accessed 27 June 2012.
GULLION, ROBERT
Accession Nr. CV-0053-394; Document Type – Credit Volume Patent; State – Indiana; Issue Date – 12/29/1820; Cancelled – No
Names on Document: Gullion, Robert; Miller, David
Land Office – Cincinnati; Authority – April 24, 1820 Sale-Cash Entry (3 Stat. 566); Total Acres – 160.00
Land Descriptions: State – IN; Meridian – 1st PM; Twp-Rng – 002N-002W; Aliqouts – NE1/4; Section – 34; County – Switzerland
&
Accession Nr. CV-0062-244; Document Type – Credit Volume Patent; State – Indiana; Issue Date – 4/1/1825; Cancelled – No; Document Nr. 809; Total Acres – 80.00; General Remarks – Patent Record Imperfect
Names on Document: Gullion, Robert; Capbell, William
Land Descriptions: State – IN; Meridian – 1st PM; Twp-Rng – 002N-002W; Aliqouts – E1/2SE1/4; Section – 20; County - Switzerland

1830 U.S. Census, Indiana, Switzerland, No Twp., Series: M19 Roll: 32 Page: 42
Gullion, Robert age 60-70; others in household 1 male 5-10, 1 male 20-30, 1 female 10-15, 1 female 15-20, 1 female 60-70.

A Census of Pensioners for Revolutionary or Military Services with their Names, Ages, and Places of Residence Under the Act for Taking the Sixth Census in 1840; Genealogical Publishing Co., Inc., Baltimore, Maryland, 1965. p.185.
INDIANA, SWITZERLAND, YORK

Names of Pensioners for Revolutionary or Military services	Ages	Names of heads of families with whom pensioner resided June 1, 1840
Robert Gullion	76	Robert Gullion

Revolutionary Soldiers of Switzerland County; Copied by Mary Hill, John Paul Chapter-Daughters of the American Revolution; January, 1958; http://www.ingenweb.org/inswitzerland/switzrevsoldiers.html- Viewed June, 2012.

GULLION, ROBERT   Pension S. 16396
Born Feb. 4, 1764, near Frederick on the Potomac
Enlisted 1780 or 1781 in a company of militia or rangers under Capt. Shearer of Westmoreland Co. Penn. Was stationed at a block house on the waters of Turtle Creek in Penn. for 90 days. In 1782 under Col. Wm. Crawford marched against the Indians on the Ohio River.
Married Barbara _____.
Children; Henry
John m 1815 Elizabeth Jones & 1824 Betsy Scudder
Charles D. m Lena Dillman
Polly m David Miller
Rachel m Joseph Fulton
Sallie m Wm. McQuiston
Robert m Dolly Fulton
Died July 23, 1853.
Probably buried York township.
Abstracted Switzerland Co. Will Bk. 2, p. 109 - Robert Gullion.
Sons; John, Henry, Charles.
Daughters; Catherine Miller, Sarah McQuiston, Rachel Fulton, Rachel Gullion.
Probate Bk. A - pg. 69 - Robert Gullion, revolutionary soldier. Signed by Jas. Cox of Gallatin Co. Ky. and William Scudder.

Roster of Soldiers and Patriots of the American Revolution Buried in Indiana, Vol. I; compiled by Mrs. Roscoe C. O'Byrne.; Indiana Daughters of the American Revolution, 1981; p.168.
GULLION, ROBERT   Switzerland County
Born – Feb. 4, 1764, near Frederick on the Potomac.
Service – Enlisted 1780 or 81 in a company of militia or rangers under Capt. Shearer of Westmoreland Co., Penn. Was stationed at a blockhouse on the waters of Turtle Creek in Penn. For 90 days. In 1782 under Col. Wm. Crawford marched against the Indians on the Ohio River.
Proof – Pension claim R. 16396.
Died – July 23, 1853. Probably buried in York Twp.

Married – Barbara _____. Ch. Henry; John m. 1815 Elizabeth Jones and 1824 Betsy Scudder; Charles D., m. Lena Dillman; Polly, m. David Miller; Rachael, m. Joseph Fulton; Sallie, m. Wm. McQuiston; Robert, m. Dolly Fulton. Collected by Mrs. A. V. Danner, Vevay, Indiana.

History of Switzerland County Indiana 1885; Reproduced by the Switzerland County Historical Society, Vevay, Indiana, 1999. The portion of the book relating to Switzerland County in the 1885 printing of the "History of Dearborn, Ohio, and Switzerland Counties, Indiana".
p. 990.
"In 1798 the Cotton and Dickason families settled on Indiana Creek, a few miles back from the Ohio River, and in 1799 Robert Gullion settled on the Ohio River bottom, above the mouth of Log Lick Creek."
p. 998.
Robert Gullion is listed on this page as being among the early settlers in the upper end of the county.

The Swiss Settlement of Switzerland County; by Perrett Dufour; published by the Indiana Historical Commission, Indianapolis, IN, 1925. p. 48.
Among the early settlers in the upper end of the county were James McClure who was Judge of the courts, Ezekiel and Joshua Petty, Peter Lostutter, Lewis Jones, George and Elisha Wade, Caleb Mounts, Williams Pierson, Benjamin and Robert Drake, the Vandoren family, John Kilgore, William Campbell, <u>Robert Gullion</u>, Amos A. Brown…….etc

Vevay Switzerland County Indiana 1795-1999; no author or publisher. p. 1.
The first settler in the county of whom any definite account is given was Heathcoat Pickett, a Revolutionary War veteran, who located here is 1795, followed in 1798 and 1799 by the Cotton, Dickason and Gullion families.

Switzerland County Indiana Cemetery Inscriptions 1817-1985; Wanda L. Morford; Cincinnati, Ohio, 1986, p. 485.
Gullion Cemetery, York Twp., Switzerland Co., IN
Robert, d. Jul. 10, 1854 in the 89 year of his age
Barbary Gullian?, consort of Robert, d. Dec. 20, 1832 aged 67
Note: This small family cemetery is located on the South side of Log Lick creek near the Markland bridge. All of the stones are down and it is now used as pasture land.

Weekly Reveille-Enterprise, 8 Sep 1853, Vol.I, No. 12, p.3, column 3.
NOTICE
Notice is hereby given that the undersigned have been appointed Executors of the last will of Robert Gullion, late of Switzerland county, deceased. Said estate is supposed to be solvent.
Henry Gullion, John Gullion, Executors. Sept. 1, 1853.

The Vevay Reveille-Enterprise; Vol. 122, No. 37, 15 Sep 1935, p. 3, col.5-6.
Roster of Revolutionary Soldiers Who Resided in Switzerland County

By Mrs. Effa M. Danner

Robert Gullion – Pension No. S16-396. Birth February 4, 1764 near Frederick on Potomac river. Service: Enlisted 1780 or 81 in a Company of Militia or rangers commanded by Capt. Shearer of Westmoreland Co., Pennsylvania. Stationed at a block house on the waters of Turtle Creek in Pennsylvania. Served 90 days. In April or May 1782 in Company of militia commanded by Col. Wm. Crawford marched through Mingo Bottom on the Ohio river against the Indians. Served three months. Lived in Big Sweetly Creek, Westmoreland County, Penn. Since he left Pennsylvania lived 13 or 14 years in Kentucky, for 33 years in Indiana 91799) arrived in Switzerland County. Applied for pension Aug. 13, 1832, Switzerland County, Ind. My records: U.S. census 1840, age 76. Served on first Grand Jury 1814, Switzerland Co., also Daniel Mount to land grant, T2, R2W, N.E. Sec. 34, 160 acres, York Township, No. 8379, Robert Gullem and David Miller, Sept. 6, 1816.

Reveille, Robert Gullion dies York Township, John and Henry Gullion administrators, sale, Nov. 19, 1853.

Switzerland County Probate Court, p. 69, Aug. 1832 manifest for pension signed by Rev. James Cox of Gallatin County, Ky., and by William Scudder of Switzerland County, Ind.

He settled above the mouth of Log Lick Creek in 1799. His brother, John Gullion entered land in 1810 and was a Revolutionary soldier. He moved to Decatur County, census 1840.

Pension records, John Gullion, age 77, Thomas Gullion, guardian. Wife's name, Kittie. Book G, p. 364. Robert Gullion deed to John Boyd, Nov. 2, 1830. Signed Robert Gullion and wife, Barbara Gullion. Book D, p. 225 Will put to probate August 6, 1853, heirs, p. 115, Rachel Fulton, Joseph Fulton, Polly Miller, David Miller, Sallie McQuinston, Henry Gullion, John Gullion, Chas. Gullion and heirs of Kate Miller are Aaron Miller, John Miller, Henry Miller, William Miller, Massalenus Miller, Polly Dillman, Nancy, Ellison and Catherine Miller. Final report p. 458.

Author's note: Additional research divulged a third brother Jeremiah (in addition to Robert and John). Jeremiah settled in Henry County, KY where he died in April 1815 or 1817, or in June or July, 1819. He lived on the Kentucky River near the mouth of Eagle Creek in what was later Carroll Co., KY. His wife, Isabella, applied for pension March 16, 1837, claim W8879, while living in Henry Co., KY. The application includes statements that Jeremiah had two brothers, Robert who was living in Switzerland Co., IN, and John who was living in Decatur Co., IN, and a sister Mary Raiborne was living in Frankfort, KY. The three brothers served under Capt. Joseph Erwin, Pennsylvania troops.

HALL, BENJAMIN

Patriot: Benjamin Hall
Birth: 1753　　　Hopkinton, Washington Co., RI
Married Spouse 1: Unkonwn
Service state(s): RI
Service description: See pension application
Rank: Private, Sergeant & substitute
Proof of Service: Pension application R5362 & S32295
Pension application No.: S32295
Residences: Hopkinton, [current Washington Co.], RI; Switzerland Co., IN;
　　　　　　Ripley Co., IN
Died: July 1837 Switzerland Co., IN or 1850 Jefferson Co., IN
Buried: Unknown
DAR Ancestor No.: A049461

Pension Application Abstracted from National Archives Microfilm Series 805, Roll 388, File S32295.
Pension abstract for – Benjamin Hall, Private　　Service state(s): Rhode Island
Date: 18 Sep 1832
County of: Switzerland　　　　　　　　　　　　State of: Indiana
Declaration made before a Court.
Age:　　80 years　　　　　　　　　　　Record of age: None
Where and year born: estimate 1752/1753
Residence when he entered service: Hopkinton, Little Neck Co., Rhode Island
Residence(s) since the war: none stated
Residence now: Ripley Co., IN
Volunteer or Drafted or Substitute: Volunteered (4th term as a substitute
Statement of service-

Period	Duration	Names of General and Field Officers
1st May or June 1775	8 mos	Gen. Greene, Capt. Sam Wood, 1st Regt Rhode Island Line
2nd April 1776	9 mos	Gen Correll, Capt. Wm. Parker, Col. Pritchard
3rd 12 May 1777　1 year		Col. Geo. Tappan, 1st Regt. Rhode Island Line
4th 1778　　3 years		Capt. Elijah Lewis, Col. Angel

Battles: Battle of Rhode Island known as Sullivan's Expedition, Bunker Hill, White Plains, Saratoga, Monmouth, Battle of Red Banks on the Delaware.
He was wounded in the shoulder in 1776 in Sullivan's Expedition.
Discharge received & signed by: 1st 8 Dec 1775; 2nd Jan 1777 by Col. Hitchcock; 3rd by Col. Tappan; 4th in 17881 by Col. Angel.
No family information is given.

Author's note: Benjamin Hall has been proven as a patriot for the National Society Daughters of the American Revolution. Their records show that Benjamin Hall died in Jefferson Co., IN. The death place (Jefferson County), and death year (1850) may be in error.

1 - Benjamin Hall does not appear in the 1840 Revolutionary War Census therefore it can be supposed that he died before then. Also, the final payment voucher for Benjamin Hall is dated 3Sep 1838.
2 - The following will abstract from 1837 is likely for Benjamin Hall, who resided in Switzerland County, and served in the Revolutionary War. Perhaps the death record located by the DAR member was for the son of this man or another Benjamin Hall.

Switzerland County, Indiana Probate Order Book 3, Aug 1837-Sep 1841; p. 1, 15, 42, 67, 114, 127, 144, 189, 207, 295.
Abstract of administration for: Benjamin Hall
State & county where recorded: Switzerland Co., Indiana
Book/volume where recorded: Probate Book 3, Aug 1837-Sep 1841.
Date entered in probate: 14 Aug 1840
Administration:
Date began - 13 Aug 1837
Name of administrator – Martha Hall and George Hall
Date of death: Not recorded
Bonded by and amount of bond: George Hall, $500.00, Benjamin Wilson his security.
Names of heirs and others mentioned in will (also signed receipts of division of estate) and relationship if shown: None
Date of division & disbursement, or final return: 16 Aug 1839

Abstract of Final Payment Voucher; General Services Administration, Washington, DC
LAST FINAL PAYMENT VOUCHER RECEIVED FROM
THE GENERAL ACCOUNTING OFFICE
NAME   Hall, Benjamin
AGENCY OF PAYMENT   Indiana
DATE OF ACT   1832
DATE OF PAYMENT   Sept. 3, 1838
DATE OF DEATH
GENERAL SERVICES ADMINISTRATION
National Archives and Records Service   NA-286
GSA-WASH DC 54-4891   November 1953

Register of Certificates Issued by John Pierce, Esquire, Paymaster General and Commissioner of Army Accounts for the United States, to Officers and Soldiers of the Continental Army Under Act of July 4, 1783; Originally Published as Senate Documents, Vol.9, No. 988, 63rd Congress, 3d Session, Washington, 1915; Seventeenth report of the National Society of the Daughters of the American Revolution; Genealogical Publishing Co., Inc, Baltimore, MD, 1984. p. 222.
Men listed in this volume with the same name.

No. of Certificate	To whom issued	Amount
45069	Hall, Benjamin	64.80
83743	Hall, Benjamin	56.58

Rejected or Suspended Applications for Revolutionary War Pensions; Reprinted for Clearfield Company Inc. by Genealogical Publishing Co., Inc., Baltimore, MD, 1998. p. 407.
A list of the names of persons residing in Indiana who have applied for pensions under the act of June 7, 1832, whose claims have been rejected; prepared in conformity with the resolution of the Senate of the United States of September 16, 1850.

Names	Residence	Reasons for rejection
HALL, BENJAMIN	Vevay, Switzerland	Caveat to this claim from Wm. C. Keen, Printer's Retreat, August 23, 1832.

Roster of Soldiers and Patriots of the American Revolution Buried in Indiana, Vol. I; compiled by Mrs. Roscoe C. O'Byrne.; Indiana Daughters of the American Revolution, 1981; p.170.

HALL, BENJAMIN   Ripley County
Service – Enlisted from Rhode Island in May or June, 1775. Discharged on Dec. 8, 1775. Re-enlisted April, 1776. Discharged Jan., 1777. Re-enlisted May 12, 1777. Served 1 yr., total service 2 yrs. 5 mos.
Proof – Pension claim S 32295.
Died – Jan., 1850. Name on bronze tablet in Versailles Court House. Collected by Mrs. A. b. Wycoff, Batesville, Indiana.

Revolutionary Soldiers Buried in Indiana A Supplement; 485 Names Not Listed in the Roster of Soldiers and Patriots of the American Revolution Buried in Indiana (1938) nor in Revolutionary Soldiers Buried in Indiana (1949); Margaret E. Waters; Indianapolis, 1954. p.44, 119.

p. 44-
HALL, BENJAMIN   Ripley (?)
(Note: this man is not the one of Ripley Co., Ind, "Roster" p. 1170, Pens. S.32295. However, this man's res. is uncertain; see below). b. 1749. Pens. appl. 10-16-1819, ae. ca. 70, Switzerland Co., Ind.; again 2-28-1820, ae. 70. Letter 8-23-1838 from William C. Keen, Printer's Retreat, Switzerland Co., Ind., says that sold. may make another appl. from Ripley, Dearborn, or Jefferson Co., Ind. Service: enl. Apr.-May 1776 for 3 yr., Lexington, Conn., Capt. Elijah Lewis, Col. John Angle, Conn. Line; disch. At White Plains, N.Y.; again enl. Sept. 1780, Easton, Pa., Maj. Ebenezer Adams, Artillery, & serv. till end of War. REF: Pens. R.5362-1/2 R.I.; Rej. Pens. List, p. 407—Caveat to this claim from William C. Keen, Printer's Retreat, 8-28-19832. (See p. 119 later).

p. 119 –
HALL, BENJAMIN – p. 44. Confusion between a Rev. sold., Benajah Hall, d. 11-4-1840, Cuyuga Co., N.Y., who liv. After Rev. at Hartford, Conn., & Dutchess Co., N.Y.; had pens.; had son Benajah who is incorrectly given as Benjamin Hall, 61, Conn.; wife Margaret, 54, N.Y.; chn.: Simon, 26, N.Y; George W., 19, N.Y.; Margaret C., 16, N.Y.; Lewis, 12, Ohio; in 1850 Cens., Ripley Co., Ind., Washington Twp., p. 312-1/2, fam. 70. The Rhode Island man in "Roster", p. 170, should be Benjamin and not Benajah.

HAMMOND, LEWIS
aka HAMMON, LEWIS

Patriot: Lewis Hammond
Birth: abt. 1759
Married Spouse 1: Unknown
Service state(s): VA
Service description: VA Militia, Capt. Reynold, Col. Holmes; Capt. Samuel
                        Glass; Capt. Nighswonger, Lieut. Jenkins.
Rank: Private
Proof of Service: Pension application R4535
Pension application No.: R4535
Residences: Winchester Co., VA; [Scott Co..] KY, Indiana Territory;
                Switzerland Co., IN
Died: Switzerland Co., IN
Buried: Unknown Switzerland Co., IN
DAR Ancestor No.: None

Pension Application Abstracted from National Archives microfilm Series 805, Roll 393, File R4535.
Note on file cover - Regiment did not serve but 5 mos. [His application was denied.]

Pension abstract for – Lewis Hammond	Service state(s): VA
Date: 14 October 1842	
County of: Switzerland	State of: Indiana

Declaration made before a Justice of the Peace
Age: 83 years   [b. abt. 1759]
[It appears he applied earlier, in Kentucky, under the Act of 1832. There are no papers in the file regarding this application.]
Rank(s): Private
Statement of service-

Period	Duration	Names of General and Field Officers
1781	3. mos.	VA Militia Capt. Reynold under Col. Holmes at Winchester, VA. Guarding prisoners taken by Col. Morgan.
No date	2 mos.	Capt. Samuel Glass. Guarding prisoners on move toFredericktown, MD.
No date	3 mos.	Capt. Nighswonger, Lieut. Jenkins.

Wife: None indicated in pension file

Early Ohio Settlers, Purchasers of Land in Southwestern Ohio, 1800-1840; Compiled by Ellen T. Berry & David A. Berry; Genealogical Publishing Co., Inc., Baltimore, MD, 1986. p.130.

Purchaser	Year	Date	Residence	R – T - S
Hammond, Lewis (B)	1815	Sept. 07	Hamilton 01	03-34-

(B) Indiana Survey: Land lying west of a meridian drawn west of the Great Miami (known as the "Gore"). Switzerland, Dearborn, Franklin, Ohio, Union and Randolph Counties (all or only a part of each county) – all in Indiana.

Early Settlers of Indiana's "GORE" 1803-1820; Compiled and Edited by Shirley Keller Mikesell; Heritage Books, Inc., 1995. p. 185.
Switzerland County – Township 3, Range 1W
Section 34 – Lewis Hammond – 1815 – pg. 4.

Indiana Land Entries Vol. 1 Cincinnati District, 1801-1840; Margaret R. Waters; Originally Published Indianapolis 1948, Second Reprint 1979 by The Bookmark, P.O. Box 74, Knightstown, In 46148. p.6.
CINCINNNATI LAND DISTRICT – VOL. 1
Page 5. Twp. 3 N, Range 1 W of 1st Principle Meridian SWITZERLAND CO.
Lewis Hammond NW ¼ - S34; 9-7-18185.
-- Note: The tract books for the land offices in Indiana are deposited in the office of the Auditor of State, Indianapolis. They and are in the custody of the State Land clerk. --

U.S. Department of Interior, Bureau of Land Management, General Land Office Records; Land Patent Search – accessed 27 June 2012.
HAMMOND, LEWIS
Accession Nr. CV-0065-458; Document Type – Credit Volume Patent; State – Indiana; Issue Date – 8/27/1825; Cancelled – No
Names on Document : Woodward, William; Hammond, Lewis
Land Office – Cincinnati; Authority – April 24, 1820 Sale-Cash Entry (3 Stat. 566); General Remarks – Patent Record Imperfect
Land Descriptions: State – IN; Meridian – 1st PM; Twp-Rng – 003N-001W; Aliquots – NW1/4; Section – 34; County - Switzerland

Rejected or Suspended Applications for Revolutionary War Pensions; Reprinted for Clearfield Company Inc. by Genealogical Publishing Co., Inc., Baltimore, MD, 1998. p. 407.
A list of the names of persons residing in Indiana who have applied for pensions under the act of June 7, 1832, whose claims have been rejected; prepared in conformity with the resolution of the Senate of the United States of September 16, 1850, p. 407.

Names	Residence	Reasons for rejection
HAMMON, LEWIS	Vevay, Switzerland	Only five months' service.

1840 U.S. Census, Indiana, Switzerland, Posey, Series: M704 Roll: 95 Page: 172
Lewis Hammond age 70-80, others in household 1 female 10-15, 1 female 50-60.

Roster of Soldiers and Patriots of the American Revolution Buried in Indiana, Vol. II; 1966; p.49.
HAMMOND, LEWIS   Switzerland County
Born – Oct. 14, 1760
Service – Va. Militia, 1781, Winchester, Va., under Capt. Reynolds, Col. Holmes.
Proof – Pens. R. 4535, Va; only 5 mos. service. Pens. Appl. May 25, 1843, Switzerland Co., Ind.
From Waters' Sip., p. 44.

Revolutionary Soldiers Buried in Indiana A Supplement; 485. Names Not Listed in the Roster of Soldiers and Patriots of the American Revolution Buried in Indiana (1938) nor in Revolutionary Soldiers Buried in Indiana (1949); Margaret E. Waters; Indianapolis, 1954. p. 44.

HAMMOND, LEWIS   Switzerland
b. 10-14-1762. Pens. Appl. 5-25-1843, Switzerland Co., Ind., ae. 80 last Oct. 14. Service: Va. Mil., 1781, Winchester, Va., Capt. Reynolds, Col. Holmes.
REF: Pens. R.4535 Va.; Rej. Pens. List, p. 407—only 5 mo. service.

HANNIS, HENRY
aka HANNAS

Patriot: Henry Hannis
Birth: 12 May 1757 Ulster Co., NY
Married Spouse 1: Hannah X
Married Spouse 2: Gilly X
Service state(s): NY
Service description: Capts. Akers, Deyo, Hardenbergy, Conklin,
  Cols. Rawlings, Pawling, Owens
Rank: Private
Proof of Service: Pension application S3228
Pension application No.: S3228
Residences: Ulster Co., NY; VA; KY; Indiana Territory; Switzerland Co., IN
Died: 23 Sep 1835 Vermillion Co., IL
Buried: Unknown
DAR Ancestor No.: A051226

Pension Application Abstracted from National Archives microfilm Series 805, Roll 396, File S3228.;Switzerland County, Indiana Probate Record Book Vol. A, Mar 1827-Nov 1834; p. 329.

Pension abstract for – Henry Hannis   Service state(s): NY & VA
Various spelling: Henry Hanns. When serving in NY he was called 'Hanns" for short.
Date: 14 Nov 1832
County of: Switzerland   State of: Indiana
Declaration made before a Probate Court.
Age: 75 years   Record of age: I have it home in my Bible copied
                              from my father's Bible.
Where and year born: Ulster Co., NY on 12 May 1757
Residence when he entered service: Ulster Co., NY, served in NY; Removed to VA in 1780, Served in VA..
Residence(s) since the war: In VA 9 or 10 years; in Kentucky about 30 years;
                            in Indiana since.
Residence now: Switzerland Co., IN
Volunteer or Drafted or Substitute: Volunteered
Rank(s): Private
Statement of service-

Period	Duration	Names of General and Field Officers
Sep 1775	9 mos.	Company of NY Militia under Capt. Aker.
Jul 1776	6 mos.	Capt. John Deyo, Col. Paling's Regt. In a skirmish with the British.
Early 1777	6 mos.	Capt. Hardenbergh's Co., Col. Pawling's Regt.
Aug 1777	3 mos.	Capt. Oeleg Ransom's Cp., Col. Hardenbergh's Regt. *
Sep 1779	4 mos.	Capt. Conklin's Co., under Col. Owens.
1781	3 mos.	William Campbell's VA Regt. under Capt. Bowen & Capt. Arthur Campbell.

Battles: * Battle of Saratoga in 1777.
Discharge received: No written discharge.
Statement is supported by –
Documentary proof: None
Person now living who can testify to service: None
Persons in neighborhood who certify character: John Graham, Griffith Dickinson, Grancis Lansdale, John F. Dufour, William Turner, William Jackson, Griffith, John Wright, Henry Banta.
Wife: No reference to wife or children.
Soldier died: 23 September 1835

Switzerland County, Indiana Probate Order Book 2, 1831-1837; p. 92.
In the matter of   } An applicant for a pension under the act of
Henry Hannas   } Congress of 7th June 1832
        Comes now into Court before the Probate court of Switzerland County now Sitting Henry Hannas and in order to obtain a pension under the act aforesaid make the following report (here insert it) And the Said Court, do hereby declare their opinion after the investigation of the matter, and after putting the interrogation prescribed by the war department that the above named Henry Hannas was a Revolutionary Soldier and Served as he States. And the court further certifies that it appears to them that Samuel Pavy who has also signed the preceding Certificate is a Clergyman resident in Switzerland County and State of Indiana, and that Francis Lansdel who also Signed the Same is a resident of Switzerland County State of Indiana, and is a credible person and their Statement is entitled to Credit.

New York in the Revolution as Colony and State, Second Edition, 1898; by James A Roberts, Comptroller; Genealogical Publishing Co., Baltimore, MD. p. 196.
The Militia – Ulster County, Third Regiment
Colonel   Levi Pawling   Quarter Master   Philip Hoornbeeck
          John Cantine   John Van Dusen
          Lieut. Col. Jacob Hoornbeek
Enlisted Men – Hannes Henry (in this listing)

Abstract of Final Payment Voucher; General Services Administration, Washington, DC
FINAL PAYMENT VOUCHER RECEIVED FROM
THE GENERAL ACCOUNTING OFFICE
NAME   HENNIS, Henry
AGENCY OF PAYMENT   Indiana
DATE OF ACT   1832
DATE OF PAYMENT   1st Qr. 1836
DATE OF DEATH   Sept. 25, 1835
GENERAL SERVICES ADMINISTRATION
National Archives and Records Service   NA-286
GSA-WASH DC 54-4891   November 1953

Indiana Territory, Switzerland Circuit Court Records, Order Book, October Term 1814 to March Term 1815. p.6.
He is listed in county records as a member of the Grand Jury at the first court held in the county, on 28 October 1814. Court held at the house of Robert M. Trotter, in the Town of Vevay.

Early Ohio Settlers, Purchasers of Land in Southwestern Ohio, 1800-1840; Compiled by Ellen T. Berry & David A. Berry; Genealogical Publishing Co., Inc., Baltimore, MD, 1986. p.131.

Purchaser	Year	Date	Residence	R – T - S
Hannas, Henry (B)	1814	Jan. 10	Kentucky	04-03-36

(B) Indiana Survey: Land lying west of a meridian drawn west of the Great Miami (known as the "Gore"). Switzerland, Dearborn, Franklin, Ohio, Union and Randolph Counties (all or only a part of each county) – all in Indiana.

Early Settlers of Indiana's "GORE" 1803-1820; Compiled and Edited by Shirley Keller Mikesell; Heritage Books, Inc., 1995.
p. 188.
Switzerland County Township 3, Range 3W
Section 32 – Henry Hannas – 1817 – pg. 12.
p. 189.
Switzerland County – Township 3, Range 4W
Section 36 – Henry Hannas – 1814 – pg. 4.
p. 207.
Switzerland County Deeds; Book A
Deed dated 1819. Henry Hannis & Hannah, his wife, to James Bell. S36, T3, R4W. "to Sarah Bell". Signed Henery Hannis, Hannah (x) Hannis. Witness: Joseph Gilliland, Joseph Todd. pp. 232, 233.
p. 211.
Switzerland County Deeds; Book A
Deed dated 1819. Henry Hannis & Hannah, his wife to Sarah Ball. S36, T3, R4W. Signed Henry Hannas, Hannah (x) Hannis. Witness: John Gilliland, Joseph Todd. pp. 299, 300, 301.

U.S. Department of Interior, Bureau of Land Management, General Land Office Records; Land Patent Search – accessed 27 June 2012.
HANNAS, HENRY
Accession Nr. CV-0039-507; Document Type – Credit Volume Patent; State – Indiana; Issue Date – 7/1/1818; Cancelled – No
Land Office – Cincinnati; Authority – April 24, 1820 Sale-Cash Entry (3 Stat. 566); Total Acres – 0.00
Land Descriptions: State – IN; Meridian – 1st PM; Twp-Rng – 003N-004W; Aloquots - ; Section 36; County - Switzerland
&
Accession Nr. CV-0066-251; Document Type – Credit Volume Patent; State – Indiana; Issue Date – 10/22/1825; Cancelled – No
Names on Document: Garrard, Nathaniel; Hannas, Henry

Land Office – Cincinnati; Authority – April 24, 1820 Sale-Cash Entry (3 Stat. 566); Document Nr. 1507; Total Acres – 170.14
Land Descriptions: State – IN; Meridian – 1st PM; Twp-Rng – 003N-003W; Aliquots – NW1/4; Section – 32; County – Switzerland

1820 U.S. Census, Indiana, Switzerland, Craig, Series: M33 Roll: 14 Page: 248
Henry Hannis 45 and up; others in household 1 female 10-16, 1 female 26-45.

Revolutionary Soldiers of Switzerland County; Copied by Mary Hill, John Paul Chapter-Daughters of the American Revolution; January, 1958; http://www.ingenweb.org/inswitzerland/switzrevsoldiers.html- Viewed June 2012.
HANNIS, HENRY Revolutionary soldier   Pension record S. 32288.
Henry Hannis was born May 12, 1757 in Ulster County, N. Y. Names of parents not stated.
While residing in said Ulster County, Henry Hannis served as a private with the New York troops, as follows; from sometime in September, 1775, nine months with Captain John Aker's company; from early in July, 1776, in Captain John Deyo's company, Colonel Rawlings regiment, was in a skirmish with the British, and was discharged December 25, 1776; from early in 1777, six months in Captain Hardenburgh's company, Colonel Rawling's regiment; from sometime in August, 1777, three months in Captain Peleg Ransom's company, Colonel Hardenbergh's regiment; was in the battle of Saratoga, and guarded the Hessian prisoners to Albany; from sometime in September, 1770 four months in Captain Conklin's company, under Colonel Owens.
The soldier, Henry Hannis moved sometime in 1780 from Ulster Co. New York, to Washington County, Virginia, and served three months under Captain Bowen and Arthur Campbell in Colonel William Campbell's Virginia Regiment.
Henry Hannis continued to live in the state of Virginia for about ten years; then moved to Kentucky, where he lived for about thirty years, then moved to Indiana. He was allowed pension on his application executed November 14, 1832, then a resident of Switzerland Co. Ind. He died September 23, 1835.
The papers on file in this claim contain no reference to wife or children of the soldier, Henry Hannis.
In order to obtain the name of the person paid the last payment of this pension, you should apply to the Comptroller General, General Accounting Office, Records Division, Washington, D. C. and cite the following; Henry Hannis, Certificate #22239, Issued Oct. 18, 1833, Rate $80.00 per annum, Commenced March 4, 1831, Act of June 7, 1832, Indiana Agency
From the General Accounting Office, a letter - Henry Hannis, Certificate 22239, died Vermillion County, State of Illinois, Sept. 23, 1835. survived by a widow, Gilly Hannis
Arrears of Pension due from March 4, 1835 to Sept. 23, 1835 paid on Jan. 11, 1836 at State Bank of Indiana to Calvin Fletcher, as attorney for the widow.
Switzerland Co. Ind. Records:
Deed Bk. B. pg. 457 1826 Henry Hannis and his wife Hannah, to William Hannis part sec. 36-3-4 to the old Indian boundary line from sugar tree, etc
Deed Bk. B. pg. 503 same signatures.
Probate court records, Nov. 14, 1832; pg. 92 Henry Hannis' petition for pension.

He came to Switzerland Co. 1814 from Garrard Co. Kentucky. A Baptist preacher, and lived on Indian Creek, Jefferson Township.
Married Hannah _____
Son William Hannis.
Henry Hannis died July 18, 1846 -- he was a son of William. See bk. 1846 pg. 293; widow, Elizabeth J.
Chancery Court, August 1847; William Hannis, vs. widow & heirs of Henry Hannis; pg. 345 vs. Cecelia Hannis, et al. William E. Elias R., Mahala, John, Mary, minor heirs of William & Ellen, his wife. pg. 296, 1847.

Roster of Soldiers and Patriots of the American Revolution Buried in Indiana, Vol. I; compiled by Mrs. Roscoe C. O'Byrne.; Indiana Daughters of the American Revolution, 1981; p. 176.
HANNIS, HENRY   Switzerland County
Born – May 12, 1757, Ulster, New York
Service – Pvt. In New York Troops as follows: Sept. 1775, 9 mos. Capt. John Aker's CO.; July 1776, Capt. John Deyo's CO., Col. Pawling's Regt., discharged 1776; 1777, 6 mos. in Capt. Hardenbergh's CO.; Aug. 1777, 3 mos. Capt. Peleg Ranson's CO., and was in the battle of Saratoga; Sept. 1779, 4 mos. Capt. Conklin's CO., Col. Owen's Regt.
Proof – Pension claim S. 32288.
Died – Sept. 23, 1835.
Married – Hannah _____. Ch. Sarah, m. James A. Stewart; William (War of 1812), m. Ellen Burns; Hannah, m. Wm. Griffith; Lydia, m. Wilson Crandell; Polly, m. Thomas Huston; Margaret, m. ____ Ferguson.
Collected by Mrs. A. V. Danner, Vevay, Indiana

History of Switzerland County Indiana 1885; Reproduced by the Switzerland County Historical Society, Vevay, Indiana, 1999. The portion of the book relating to Switzerland County in the 1885 printing of the "History of Dearborn, Ohio, and Switzerland Counties, Indiana".
p. 1008.
"In February, 1814, Henry Hannis came to the county with his family, consisting of his wife, son William, and three daughters. He rented the farm on Indian Creek, where George Tardy lived so long. William Hannis was born in Garrard County, Ky, September 18, 1797."
p. 1140.
Jefferson Township, Center Square, Indian Creek Church, aka Center Square Church (Baptist), organized 1810 –
"The names of Paul Froman, Henry Hannis and John Hawkins were among the early members who all lived to old age."

The Swiss Settlement of Switzerland County; by Perrett Dufour; published by the Indiana Historical Commission, Indianapolis, IN, 1925. p. 103.
In Feb 1814 Henry Hannas Came to the county, with his family consisting of his wife, son William and three daughters. He rented of John Francis Dufour the farm on Indian Creek where George Tandy lived so long.

The Vevay Reveille-Enterprise; Vol. 122, No. 38, 22 Sep 1935, p. 3, col. 1-2.
Roster of Revolutionary Soldiers Who Resided in Switzerland County
By Mrs. Effa M. Danner

Henry Hannis – Certificate S32288. He was born may 12, 1757 in Ulster County, N. York. While residing there he served as private in New York troops. September 1775 – nine months in Capt. John Aker's Company, July 1776 in Capt. John Deyo's Company, Col. Pawling's Regiment. Was in a skirmish with British; was discharged December 26, 1776. 1777, six months in Capt. Hardenbergh's Company, Col. Pawling's Regiment. August 1777, three months in Capt. Pelog Ransom's Company, Col. Hardenbergh's Regiment. Was in the Battle of Saratoga and guarded Hessian prisoners at Albany. September 1779, four months in Capt. Cnkling's Company under Col. Owens. Henry Hannis moved in 1780 from Ulster Co., New York to Washington County, Virginia and served 1781, three months under Capt. S. Bowen and Capt. Arthur Campbell in Col. William Campbell's Regiment, serving 2 years and 7 months.

Switzerland County Record p. 92, 1832 November 14, Henry Hannis petition for pension. Rev. Samuel Pavy and Francis Lansdel creditable witnesses. Indiana Agency No. 22239, rate $80.00 per annum. He came to Switzerland County in 1814 from Garrard County, Kentucky where his son William was born. They lived on Indian Creek where he built a horse mill. He was a Baptist preacher. He died September 23, 1835.

Henry Hannis' wife, Hannah.

Children, one son and seven daughters.

William Hannis was a soldier of 1812. He married (Ellen) Burns – Records, Sallie Burns, August 28, 1819. John Six, step-father of lady present, Wm. J. Stewart, Justice of Peace.

Polly Hannis, Thomas Huston, September 4, 1817. Sarah Hannis, Jas. A. Stewart, November 24, 1814. Margaret Hannis, Ferguson. Lydia Hannis, Wilson Crandell, September 1, 1819, father present. Hannah Hannis, Wm. J. Griffith, Jr., February 22, 1822.

Children, Wm. Hannis and (Ellen) Sallie Burns. Henry d. 1846, married Eliza Vernon; second, Todd. Elias unmarried. William E. married Orr. John married Mrs. Gray. Margaret married George J. Taylor, Dec. 24, 1842. Cecelia married W. P. Taylor. Mahala, Patrick, Keziah.

Book B, p. 497, deeds 1826 signed, Henry Hannis and wife Hannah X Hannis to Wm. Hannis.

HARRIS, DANIEL

Patriot: Daniel Harris
Birth: c. 1737
Married Spouse 1: Elizabeth Demarest
Service state(s): PA
Service description: Continental Line,
Rank: Private
Proof of Service: Pension application S36575
Pension application No.: S36575
Residences: Conewago, York Co., PA; Shepherdstown, VA; Switzerland Co., IN
Died: 6 Jul 1821   Switzerland Co., IN
Buried: prob. Allensville Cemetery, Cotton Twp., Switzerland Co., IN
DAR Ancestor No.: A051563

Pension Application Abstracted from National Archives microfilm Series 805, Roll 401, File S36575; Switzerland County, Indiana Complete Records, Circuit Court, Vol. C, 5 Nov 1818 - 8 Feb 1821; p. 370.

Pension abstract for – Daniel Harris   Service state(s): Continental VA & PA
Date: 26 May 1818; 14 Sep 1820
County of: Switzerland   State of: Indiana
Declaration made before a Circuit Court.
Age: 83 years in 1820 [Estimated birth year 1737]
Residence when he entered service: Sheppardstown (Shepherdstown), Virginia
Residence(s) since the war: Not stated
Residence now: Switzerland Co., IN
Volunteer or Drafted or Substitute: Volunteered
Rank(s): Private
Statement of service-
1st Enlistment

Period	Duration	Names of General and Field Officers
2 April 1777	Upwards of 3 yrs.	Capt. James Kearney's Co., in Col. Thomas Hartley's Regt. of Gen. Hand's Brigade in York, PA; Also, Gen. Wayne's Brigade in NJ; in Indian Expedition with Gen. Sullivan, Col. Hoobly's Regt.

Battles: 1st enlistment - Was in Sullivan's Indian Expedition
Discharge received: by Gen. Gates in Berkley Co., VA, 1 Jun 1780
                    from Col. Adam Enbley's PA Regt.
Occupation: Carpenter
Wife: Elizabeth Harris, is nearly blind   Wife's age: 81 yrs. in 1820
Names and ages of children: Reside with our children (1820)

Switzerland County, Indiana Civil Order Book 4, 1820 – 1823; pg. 71.
Sept. 1820
Daniel Harris, Revolutionary soldier & U.S. pensioner---$99.75

Pennsylvania Archives; Series: Series 3; Volume: XXIII; Chapter: Muster Rolls of the Navy and Line, Militia and Rangers, 1775-1783. with List of Pensioners, 1818-1832.; Page: 596.
Statement showing the Names of Pennsylvanians Residing in the State of Indiana, who have been Inscribed on the Pension List Under the Act of Congress Passed March 8, 1818.
PENNSYLVANIA PENSIONERS
-Switzerland County-
Harris, Daniel, pr. P.L., April 15, 1819; 85; d. June 7, 1821.

Author's note: The only records located for a Daniel Harris were in Westmoreland Co., PA.

Register of Certificates Issued by John Pierce, Esquire, Paymaster General and Commissioner of Army Accounts for the United States, to Officers and Soldiers of the Continental Army Under Act of July 4, 1783; Originally Published as Senate Documents, Vol.9, No. 988, 63rd Congress, 3d Session, Washington, 1915; Seventeenth report of the National Society of the Daughters of the American Revolution; Genealogical Publishing Co., Inc, Baltimore, MD, 1984. p. 231.
Men listed in this volume with the same name.

No. of Certificate	To whom issued	Amount
29512	Harris, Daniel	18.30
30442	Harris, Daniel	40.00
35687	Harris, Daniel	78.42
43576	Harris, Daniel	20.43
44174	Harris, Daniel	80.00
45018	Harris, Daniel	64.24
54052	Harris, Daniel	47.75

Revolutionary Soldiers of Switzerland County; Copied by Mary Hill, John Paul Chapter-Daughters of the American Revolution; January, 1958; http://www.ingenweb.org/inswitzerland/switzrevsoldiers.html- Viewed June 2012.
HARRIS, DANIEL   Pension S.36575
Born about 1737.
Enlisted Sheperdstown, Virginia, Mar. 2d or Apr. 2d, 1777 in Capt. James Kearney's co. Col. Thomas Hartley's Regt. Was in Sullivan's Indian campaign. Discharged June 1, 1780, from Colonel Adam Hubley's Pennsylvania Regiment.
Married Elizabeth _____
Children: Several including Robert, a Revolutionary Solider.
Allowed pension on his application executed May 26, 1818, at which time he was residing in Switzerland Co. Ind. In 1820 he stated that he was 85 years of age and that his wife Elizabeth was 81 years of age and that they resided with their children but did not give their names.
Died June 7, 1821, Probably buried in Allensville, Cotton Twp.

Roster of Soldiers and Patriots of the American Revolution Buried in Indiana, Vol. I; compiled by Mrs. Roscoe C. O'Byrne.; Indiana Daughters of the American Revolution, 1981; p.179.

HARRIS, DANIEL   Switzerland County
Born – About 1737.
Service - Enlisted Sheperdstown, Vir., March 2 or April 2, 1777, in Capt. James
Kearney's CO., Col. Thomas Hartley's Regt. Was in Sullivan's Indian
campaign. Discharged June 1, 1780, from Col. Adam Hubley's Penn. Regt.
Proof – Pension claim S. 36575.
Died June 7, 1821. Probably buried Allensville, Cotton Twp.
Married – Elizabeth _____. Has several children.
Collected by Mrs. A. V. Danner, Vevay, Indiana.

The Vevay Reveille-Enterprise; Vol. 122, No. 38, 22 Sep 1935, p. 3, col.
Roster of Revolutionary Soldiers Who Resided in Switzerland County
By Mrs. Effa M. Danner
Daniel Harris – Born 1737. Pension S36575. He enlisted at Shepherdstown, Va.,
March 2, 1777 in Captain James Kearney's Company, in Col. Thomas Hartley's
Regiment. Was in Sullivan's Indian expedition and was discharged June 1, 17809
from Col. Adams Hubley's Pennsylvania Regiment. He was allowed pension on
his application executed May 26, 1818, at which time he lived in Switzerland
County, Ind.
In 1820 he stated he was 83 years of age and that his wife, Elizabeth, was 81
years of age; that they resided with their children, but did not give their ages or
names.
Daniel Harries died June 7, 1821.
Col. Sullivan's Campaign, August 22, 1779 was organized by Gen. Jas. Clinton,
5000 men against the Iroquois Indians in revenge of the massacres of Wyoming,
Pa., and Cherry Valley, N.Y. Indians were under Brant and Red Jacket and
Butlers. The forces met at Newton and the Indians were routed. The Americans
then destroyed their villages, orchards and crops and laid waste as the Indians had
done. Sullivan resigned his commission and returned from the army in 1779-80,
the coldest winter in New York; harbor frozen solid enough to bear up troops and
cannon. Life of Washington, by Irving 466, page 310 Sears.

Author's note: The following information, from The Genealogy of Nine Early
Families in the Ohio River Valley, differs from the other records herein for
Daniel Harris. It has been supposed that Robert Harris, the other Revolutionary
Soldier in this publication, was the son of this Daniel Harris. This is probably not
the case. Further research is needed to determine if these men were related.

The Genealogy of Nine Early Families in the Ohio River Valley; Compiled by
Thomas L. Byram; 405 Westminster Road, Brooklyn, NY, November 1969. p. 36.
5-24   DANIEL HARRIS (son of Daniel 5-22)
Born: June 17, 1743, Preston, Conn.
Married: Dorothy Rudo (daughter of Jacob Rudo)
Marriage Date and Place: December 19, 1765, Plainfield, Conn.
Died: August 28, 1828, Kartright, New York (Delaware County)
Children:
5-36   Robert Harris, 1766
         John Searle Harris, August 14, 1769

Daniel Harris, June 19, 1771
Elizabeth Harris, October 25, 1773
Jacob Harris, October 17, 1775
James Harris, October 14, ?

Undocumented family information:
Daniel HARRIS b. abt. 1737; lived in Nine Partners, Dutchess Co. NY; died 7 June 1821, age 83, probably in Switzerland Co., IN; married Elizabeth Demarest, abt. 1757. Member Dutch Reformed Church. After the war was a member of the Conewago settlement in Adams, PA; then to the Dutch Colony near Harrodsburg.; abt. 1810, with a son Peter, to Switzerland Co. IN. Children: John m. Phebe Van Cleave; Peter m. Rachel Van Arsdale; Eleanor m. John Kephart; Samuel m. Elizabeth Van Cleave; Lena; George; Daniel Jr.; Polly m. John Teague; Annie m. Samuel Duree; (possibly others)

HARRIS, ROBERT

Patriot: Robert Harris
Birth: 12 Dec 1766 Preston, New London Co., CT
Married Spouse 1: 15 Feb 1787 in CT   Lucretia Kennedy
            (b. 28 Apr 1773 d. 16 Apr 1848, IL)
Service state(s): CT
Service description: Capt. Benjamin Durkee, Col. Samuel McClellan
Rank: Private, Matross
Proof of Service: Pension application W10076
Pension application No.: W10076
Residences: Preston, New London Co., CT; Kartright [Kortright, Delaware Co.],
            NY; in 1817 to Switzerland Co., IN
Died: 22 Jul 1826 Switzerland Co., IN
Buried: Quercus Grove Cemetery, Posey Twp., Switzerland Co., IN
DAR Ancestor No.: A051844

Pension Application Abstracted from National Archives microfilm Series 805, Roll 402, File W10076.
Pension abstract for – Robert Harris   Service state(s): Connecticut
Note: There is a large hole in the middle of the page.
Date: 14 December 1819
County of: Switzerland   State of: Indiana
Declaration made before a Circuit Court.
Age: 53
Residence(s) since the war: He, his father, and Daniel to Kartright [Kortright], New York in 1786 to clear land, wife to Kartright in 1788. To Switzerland Co., IN about 1818.
Residence now: Switzerland Co., IN
Rank: Matross
Statement of service-

Period	Duration	Names of General and Field Officers
March 1782	1 year	Capt. Benjamin Durkee's Company, Col. Samuel McClellan's Connecticut regt.

Discharge received: in New London, State of Connecticut
Wife: Not named, always weakly   Wife's age: Not stated
Names and ages of children: Children not named – they were listed as –
One son eighteen years old; one son nine years old and weakly; one son of two years old; one daughter fifteen years old; one daughter thirteen years old; one daughter eleven years old. Daughters also weakly and not able to support themselves.
&
Widow's Pension Application by: Lucretia Harris
Date: 26 August 1839
County of: Switzerland   State of: Indiana
Declaration made before a Judge.
Where and year soldier was born: 12 December 1766 (Family Record), son of Daniel Harris.

Residence when he entered service: Preston, Lew London, Connecticut
Residence(s) since the war: Connecticut, Switzerland Co., IN
Rank(s): Private in Rhode Island or Connecticut State Troops
Soldier died: 22 July 1826
Widow: Lucretia Harris
Widow's age, date, place of birth: Age 66, 28 April 1773, Northerntown, CT. (Family Record)
Widow's maiden name: Lucretia Kennedy
Resident of: Switzerland Co., IN
Marriage date and place: 15 February 1787, place not stated
Proof of marriage: Family Record pages from Bible, in the possession of Jacob R. Harris. Family Record is in the pension application file.
Names and ages of children: : Robert b 1793; Daniel Kennedy, b 1797; James Hiram b 1800; Jacob Rude b 1802; Josiah John Nelson b 1811; Westley b 1818; Lucretia b 1789; Dorothy b 1791; Alice b 1795; Lucretia Whipple b 1804; Fanny Morial b 1808; Mary Zelphia Anny b 1813 (Family Record) Note: Marriages and deaths of some children are in the Family Record.

Switzerland County, Indiana Civil Order Book 4, 1820 – 1823; pg. 192.
June term, 1821
Robert Harris, Revolutionary soldier and U.S. pensioner ---$47.50.
Note: Widow's pension application lists children & Family Bible Record is with application.

Abstract of Final Payment Voucher; General Services Administration, Washington, DC
LAST FINAL PAYMENT VOUCHER RECEIVED FROM
THE GENERAL ACCOUNTING OFFICE
NAME   Harris, Lucy (Robert)
AGENCY OF PAYMENT   Illinois
DATE OF ACT   1836
DATE OF PAYMENT   4th qtr. 1850
DATE OF DEATH   April 16, 1848
GENERAL SERVICES ADMINISTRATION
National Archives and Records Service   NA-286
GSA-WASH DC 54-4891   November 1953

Register of Certificates Issued by John Pierce, Esquire, Paymaster General and Commissioner of Army Accounts for the United States, to Officers and Soldiers of the Continental Army Under Act of July 4, 1783; Originally Published as Senate Documents, Vol.9, No. 988, 63rd Congress, 3d Session, Washington, 1915; Seventeenth report of the National Society of the Daughters of the American Revolution; Genealogical Publishing Co., Inc, Baltimore, MD, 1984. p. 232.
Men listed in this volume with the same name.

No. of Certificate	To whom issued	Amount
72213	Harris, Robert	60.20
72235	Harris, Robert	221.70
72235	Harris, Robert	432.00

72835	Harris, Robert	369.57
74379	Harris, Robert	25.18
88151	Harris, Robert	100.00
88152	Harris, Robert	54.15
89848	Harris, Robert	26.00
93614	Harris, Robert	930.46

Early Ohio Settlers, Purchasers of Land in Southwestern Ohio, 1800-1840; Compiled by Ellen T. Berry & David A. Berry; Genealogical Publishing Co., Inc., Baltimore, MD, 1986. p.134.

Purchaser	Year	Date	Residence	R – T - S
Harris, Robert (B)	1817	Nov. 10	Switzerland	01-02-06

(B) Indiana Survey: Land lying west of a meridian drawn west of the Great Miami (known as the "Gore"). Switzerland, Dearborn, Franklin, Ohio, Union and Randolph Counties (all or only a part of each county) – all in Indiana.

Early Settlers of Indiana's "GORE" 1803-1820; Compiled and Edited by Shirley Keller Mikesell; Heritage Books, Inc., 1995. p. 182.
Switzerland County - Township 2, Range 1W
Section 6 – Robert Harris – 1817 – pg. 2.

Indiana Land Entries Vol. 1 Cincinnati District, 1801-1840; Margaret R. Waters; Originally Published Indianapolis 1948, Second Reprint 1979 by The Bookmark, P.O. Box 74, Knightstown, In 46148. p.2.
CINCINNNATI LAND DISTRICT – VOL. 1
Page 2. Twp. 2 N, Range 1 W of 1st Principle Meridian SWITZERLAND CO.
Robert Harris   SW ¼ - S 6; 11-10-1817.
-- Note: The tract books for the land offices in Indiana are deposited in the office of the Auditor of State, Indianapolis. They and are in the custody of the State Land clerk. --

U.S. Department of Interior, Bureau of Land Management, General Land Office Records; Land Patent Search – accessed 27 June 2012.
HARRIS, ROBERT
Accession Nr. CV-0065-434; Document Type – Credit Volume Patent; State – Indiana; Issue Date – 8/12/1825; Cancelled – No
Land Office – Cincinnati; Authority – April 24, 1820 Sale-Cash Entry (3 Stat. 566); Document Nr. 1309; Total Acres – 160.32
Land Descriptions: State – IN; Meridian – 1st PM; Twp-Rng – 002N-002W; Aliquots – SW1/4;
Section – 6; County - Switzerland

1820 U.S. Census, Indiana, Switzerland, Posey, Series: M33 Roll: 14 Page: 260
Robert Harris 45 and up; also in household 2 males under 10, 1 male 16-26, 3 females 10-16, 1 female 26-45.

Revolutionary Soldiers of Switzerland County; Copied by Mary Hill, John Paul Chapter-Daughters of the American Revolution; January, 1958; http://www.ingenweb.org/inswitzerland/switzrevsoldiers.html- Viewed June 2012.
HARRIS, ROBERT   Pension W.10076
Born 12 Dec 1766, Preston, CT. (see Hist. of Switz. Co. pg. 1222)
Son of Daniel Harris (Revolutionary Soldier)
Married in 1787 Lucretia Kennedy (b. 1773 CT, died 1844 age 72)
Children: Robert b 1793; Daniel Kennedy, b 1797; James Hiram b 1800; Jacob Rude b 1802; Josiah John Nelson b 1811; Westley b 1818; Lucretia b 1789; Dorothy b 1791; Alice b 1795; Lucretia Whipple b 1804; Fanny Morial b 1808; Mary Zelphia Anny b 1813.
Rev. soldier moved to Indiana 1817
Died 1827, age 60 yrs.
Roster, pg. 179: Born Dec. 12, 1766, Preston, Conn. Son of Daniel Harris. Matross in company under Captain Durkee in Conn. Line for 1 year. Died July 22, 1826 buried in Quercus Grove, Switz. Co. Married Lucretia Kennedy, 1787, born 1773.
Source: Roster of Soldiers and Patriots of the American Revolution Buried in Indiana; 1938; p. 179.

Roster of Soldiers and Patriots of the American Revolution Buried in Indiana, Vol. I; compiled by Mrs. Roscoe C. O'Byrne.; Indiana Daughters of the American Revolution, 1981; p.179.
HARRIS, ROBERT   Switzerland County
Born – Dec. 12, 1766, Preston, Conn. (Son of Daniel)
Service – Matross in company under Capt. Durkee in Conn. Line, 1 year.
Proof – Pension claim W. 10076.
Died – July 22, 1826. Buried in Quercus Grove, Switzerland Co.
Married – Lucretia Kennedy, 1787, b. 1773. Ch. Robert, b. 1793; Daniel Kennedy, b. 1797; James Hiram, b. 1800; Jacob Rude, b. 1802; Josiah John Nelson, b. 1811; Wesley, b. 1818; Lucretia, b. 1789; Dorothy, b. 1791; Alice, b. 1795; Lucretia Whipple, b. 1804; Fanny Morial, b. 1808; Mary Zelphia, b. 1813.

History of Switzerland County Indiana 1885; Reproduced by the Switzerland County Historical Society, Vevay, Indiana, 1999. The portion of the book relating to Switzerland County in the 1885 printing of the "History of Dearborn, Ohio, and Switzerland Counties, Indiana".
p. 1154.
Pleasant Township -
"Nelson Harris, born in New York in 1811, came to this county with his father, Robert Harris, about 1818, and subsequently located in this township, where he has since resided."
p. 1222.
In the passage about Rev. Harvey Harris – "His grandfather, Robert Harris, was born in Connecticut and died in 1827, aged sixty years. His grandmother, Lucretia (Kennedy) Harris, was also a native of Connecticut, and died in 1844, aged seventy-two years. The former was a Revolutionary soldier and moved to Indiana in 1817."

The Genealogy of Nine Early Families in the Ohio River Valley; Compiled by
Thomas L. Byram; 405 Westminster Road, Brooklyn, NY, November 1969. p. 38.
5-36 ROBERT HARRIS (son of Daniel 5-24)
Born: December 12, 1766, Preston, Conn.
War Service: Served under Captain Durkee, one year, in the Revolutionary War, from March 5, 1782, to March, 1783.
Married: Lucretia Kennedy (born April 28, 1773, Conn. Died 1855, daughter of Lucretia Whipple and Daniel Kennedy
Marriage Date: February 15, 17887, Kartright, New York (Delaware Co.)
Moved: Robert Harris and some of his family left Kartright, New York on September 8, 1817, for the State of Indiana. They traveled by land to a place then called Robbstown, Penna. There they built a boat and then traveled by water (Ohio River). They stopped off at Cincinnati, Ohio, for two weeks then traveled on to Grants Creek, Switzerland County, Indiana. Two of Robert Harris' sons, Jacob R. and James, traveled by land (instead of boat), and each drove a team of horses pulling a wagon. The sons reached the destination about two weeks before Robert Harris and his family.
Resided: Posey Township., Switzerland Co., Indiana
Died: July 22, 1826, Switzerland County, Indiana
Buried: Quercus Grove Cemetery, Switzerland County, Indiana
Children: Lucretia Harris, October 23, 1789. Died in infancy.

5-38	Dorothy Harris, 1791
5-39	Robert Harris, 1793
5-40	Alice Harris, June 16, 1795
5-41	Daniel Kennedy Harris, 1797
	James Hiram Harris, March 31, 1800. Never married.
5-42	Jacob Rudo Harris, 1802
5-43	Lucretia Whipple Harris, 1804
5-44	Cynthia Lydia Hill Harris, 1806
5-45	Fannie Mariah Harris, 1808
5-46	Josiah John Nelson Harris, 1811
	Mary Zelpha Ann Harris, June 1, 1813
5-47	Westley Harris, March 12, 1818

Switzerland County Indiana Cemetery Inscriptions 1817-1985; Wanda L. Morford; Cincinnati, Ohio, 1986, p.450.
Quercus Grove Cemetery, Posey Twp., Switzerland Co., IN
Harris   Robert d. Jul. 23, 1826 in the 60th year – Masonic emblem } single
Lucretia, consort of Robert, d. Sep. 22, 1845 in the 73 year of her age } stone

Abstract of Graves of Revolutionary Patriots (4 volumes); by Patricia Law Hatcher; Pioneer Heritage Press, Dallas, TX, 1987. Vol. 2, p. 122.
This is an abstract and an index to information reported to the Daughters of the American Revolution and published in their annual reports to the Smithsonian Institution , printed as Senate Documents (1900-1974) and published annually in the DAR magazine (1978-1987).
Published 1972 (Senate Doc. 54)
HARRIS, Robert   Quercas Grove, Switzerland Co IN

Tombstone inscription –   IN MEMORY OF
ROBERT HARRIS
-MASONIC EMBLEM-
DEPARTED THIS LIFE
JULY 23, 1826
60 YEARS OF HIS AGE

The Vevay Reveille-Enterprise; Vol. 122, No. 37, 22 Sep 1935, p. 3, col.2.
Roster of Revolutionary Soldiers Who Resided in Switzerland County
By Mrs. Effa M. Danner
Robert Harris – Lucretia Harris W10076; Switzerland County, Ind., August 26, 1839 Lucretia filed application for pension, widow of Robert Harris, a private volunteer in Connecticut troops, Rev. War. She married, February 15, 1787. Robert died July 22, 1826 and is buried at Quercus Grove.
In 1841 she appears again, age 67, April 28, 1840. Born near Farmington, Conn. Allensville, Switzerland Co., Ind., her address. She is granted a pension certificate 6168 for service of Robert Harris who was a matross, (soldier in the Artillery) in Company commanded by Capt. Durkee of Regiment in Connecticut line one year {error in original publication]. Inscribed on rolls of Indiana $50.00 per annum.
Family – Robert Harris born Dec. 12, 1766, Preston, Conn. Lucretia Kennedy born April 28, 1773, Farmington, Conn.
Children – Robert Harris, born May 5, 1793; Daniel Kennedy, born Dec. 12, 1797; James Hiram Harris, born Mar. 31, 1800; Jacob R Dec. 12, 1797; James Hiram Harris, born Mar. 31, 1800; Jacob R. Harris, born May 20, 1802; J.J. Nelson Harris, born Mar. 13, 1811; Lucreetia Harris, born Oct. 23, 1789; Dorothy Harris, born April 15, 1791; Alice Harris, born June 16, 1795; Lucretia W. Harris, born Mar. 5, 1804; Fanny M. Harris, born May 11, 1808; Maranny M. Harris, born May 11, 1808; Mary Z. A. Harris, born June 1, 1813; Westley Harris, born Mar. 12, 1818, Posey Township.

HAYCOCK, DANIEL

Patriot: Daniel Haycock
Birth: Unknown
Married Spouse 1: Jane X (b. abt. 1779)
Service state(s): NJ
Service description: See pension abstract
Rank: Private
Proof of Service: Pension application S35999
Pension application No.: S35999
Residences: Clarkstown, NY; Franklin Co., KY; Indiana Territory;
        Switzerland Co., IN; Pope Co., IL
Died: 15 Sep 1840 Pope Co., IL
Buried: prob. Pope Co., IL
DAR Ancestor No.: None

Pension abstracted from Switzerland County, Indiana Civil Order Book 4, 1820 – 1823; pg. 101, Sept. 1820; Switzerland County, Indiana Complete Records, Circuit Court, Vol. ?, Sep 3, 1821-Apr 18, 1827; p.614-615; National Archives microfilm Series 805, Roll 411, File S35999.

Pension abstract for – Daniel Haycock   Service state(s): New Jersey
Date: 2 June 1818
County of: Switzerland   State of: Indiana
Declaration made before a Circuit Court.
Where he entered service: Clarkstown, New York
Residence now: Switzerland Co., IN
Volunteer or Drafted or Substitute : Enlisted
Rank: Private
Statement of service-

Period	Duration	Names of General and Field Officers
March 1777	until Dec. 1880	Lieut. William Martin, 5th regiment of New Jersey, Capt. William Britton's Company, commanded by Oliver Spencer. Transferred to Capt. William Bull's Company. Later to Capt. Bonnell's Company in the Light Infantry under command of Gen. Lafayettte.

Battles: Brandywine, Germantown, Monmouth, Springfield, in Gen. Sullivan's Campaign.
&
Date: 4 March 1820
County of: Switzerland   State of: Indiana
Declaration made before a Court.
Schedule of property submitted to the court.
&
Date: 30 March 1820
County of: Switzerland   State of: Indiana
Declaration made before a Court.

Occupation: Farmer. He is a cripple because of a fall.
Wife: Jane   Wife's age: about 41 years
Names and ages of children: Daughter Elinor abt. 13 yrs.; daughter Polly abt. 11 yrs.; son Robert abt. 10 yrs.; daughter Lucretia abt. 8 yrs.; son Thomas abt. 6 yrs. daughter Elizabeth abt. 1 yr.
&
Date: 16 Sep 1820
County of: Switzerland   State of: Indiana
Declaration made before a Court.
Schedule of property value $1.92-1/2 cents and declaration of service.
Age: Not stated
Residence now: Switzerland Co., IN
Volunteer or Drafted or Substitute: Was enlisted by Lt. Martin of Capt. Williams battalion.
Rank(s): Not stated
Statement of service-

Period	Duration	Names of General and Field Officers
		Lt. Martin, Capt. Williams battalion, Col. Oliver Spencer, 5th Jersey Regiment in Jersey Line; transferred to Capt. William Ball – same regt.; thence to Capt. James Bonnell's company in the Marquis de Lafayette's infantry.

Battles: Not stated
Discharge received: by Capt. Bonnell at Stony Point.
Statement is supported by –
Documentary proof: None
He is a cripple because of a fall.
Wife: Jane   Wife's age: abt. 41 yrs.
Names and ages of children: Elinor, abt. 13; Polly abt. 11; Robert abt. 10; Thomas abt. 6; Elizabeth abt. 1 yr.
&
Date: 17 Oct 1826
County of: Switzerland   State of: Indiana
Declaration made before a Circuit Court.
Field schedule of property valued at $67.50, and declaration of service.
Age: about 68 years
Residence when he entered service: Albany Co., NY
Residence(s) since the war:
Residence now: Switzerland Co., IN
Volunteer or Drafted or Substitute: Enlisted all tours
Rank(s): Third Sergeant (1st tour); First Sergeant (2nd tour); Lieutenant (3rd tour).
Statement of service-

Period	Duration	Names of General and Field Officers
Mar or Apr 1777	9 mos.	Capt. John McCalebs, Col. - , Lt. Col.

		John Blair; after death of Col. Lt. Co. Gersham Woodworth, Line of New York, Continental establishment.
Mar 1779	9 mos.	Capt. John Smith, Brigade commanded by Gen. Schyler, NY line, Cont.
Mar 1780		Hiram Woodworth, Gen. Schyler's brigade.

Discharge received: 1st tour - end of December in Saratoga, NY; 2nd tour – last day of December 1779 in Saratoga, NY; 3rd tour – Jan 1781 at headquarters in Saratoga, NY by Gen. Schyler.

Occupation: I am crippled in my right arm and left leg occasioned by wounds received at Fort Ann[?] while in the service.

Wife: Not named   Wife's age: 51 years

Family: Consists of myself, my wife (not named), one son (17 yrs and lame of the left leg), and one daughter (13 yrs. and healthy).

Names and ages of children: Until within a few months ago I had four able bodied sons who lived with me and maintained the family who are now married and three of them removed back to the Eastward and the fourth one living by himself about a mile from me.

&

Application for a transfer of pension to Illinois
Date: 8 July 1840
County of: Pope   State of: Illinois
Declaration made before a Justice of the Peace

Abstract of Final Payment Voucher; General Services Administration, Washington, DC

FINAL PAYMENT VOUCHER RECEIVED FROM
THE GENERAL ACCOUNTING OFFICE
NAME   Haycock, Daniel
AGENCY OF PAYMENT   Illinois
DATE OF ACT   1818
DATE OF PAYMENT   4th qtr. 1841
DATE OF DEATH   Oct 8, 1841
GENERAL SERVICES ADMINISTRATION
National Archives and Records Service   NA-286
GSA-WASH DC 54-4891   November 1953

Official Register of the Officers and Men of New Jersey in the Revolutionary War; Compiled Under Orders of His Excellency Theodore F. Randolph, Governor; by William S. Stryker, Adjutant General, Printed by the Authority of the Legislature; Wm. T. Nicholson & Co., Printers, Trenton, NJ, 1872, Facsimile Reprint by Heritage Books, Inc., Bowie, MD, 1993; p. 209.
Haycock, Daniel. "Spencer's Regiment," Continental Army/

Register of Certificates Issued by John Pierce, Esquire, Paymaster General and Commissioner of Army Accounts for the United States, to Officers and Soldiers of the Continental Army Under Act of July 4, 1783; Originally Published as Senate

Documents, Vol.9, No. 988, 63rd Congress, 3d Session, Washington, 1915; Seventeenth report of the National Society of the Daughters of the American Revolution; Genealogical Publishing Co., Inc, Baltimore, MD, 1984. p. 237.
Men listed in this volume with the same name.

No. of Certificate	To whom issued	Amount
1257	Haycock, Daniel	33.30

Early Ohio Settlers, Purchasers of Land in Southwestern Ohio, 1800-1840; Compiled by Ellen T. Berry & David A. Berry; Genealogical Publishing Co., Inc., Baltimore, MD, 1986. p.139.

Purchaser	Year	Date	Residence	R – T - S
Haycock, Daniel (B)	1815	July 22	Kentucky	01-02-30

(B) Indiana Survey: Land lying west of a meridian drawn west of the Great Miami (known as the "Gore"). Switzerland, Dearborn, Franklin, Ohio, Union and Randolph Counties (all or only a part of each county) – all in Indiana.

Indiana Territory, Switzerland Circuit Court Records, Order Book, October Term 1814 to March Term 1815. p.90.
He is listed in county records for the first time on 14 September 1815, as a juror.

1820 U.S. Census, Indiana, Switzerland, Jefferson, Series: M33 Roll: 14 Pg: 261
Daniel Haycock 45 and up; also in household 2 males under 10, 1 male 10-16, 2 females under 10, 2 females 10-16, 1 female 26-45.

Author's note: Switzerland County Pension Roll 2 - Jun 1818
30 March 1820 moved to Pope Co., IL

Revolutionary Soldiers of Switzerland County; Copied by Mary Hill, John Paul Chapter-Daughters of the American Revolution; January, 1958; http://www.ingenweb.org/inswitzerland/switzrevsoldiers.html- Viewed June, 2012.
HAYCOCK, DANIEL
Revolutionary soldier & U.S. pensioner---$31.92 1/2
Enlisted in Clarkstown, NY, March 1877

Switzerland County Courthouse Records
HAYCOCK, DANIEL
Daniel Haycock lived on Tapps Ridge; wife, Janie. A Revolutionary soldier. See Adv. in Village Times, 1837. Lived in Franklin Co. Ky. A private in New Jersey. pension in 1818. Deed bk. E-280. Switz. Co. Dau. Lucretia Boyd.
&
HAYCOCK, DANIEL
Married Jane _____
Children of HAYCOCK, DANIEL – Elinor, Polly, Robert, Lucretia, Thomas, Elizabeth

Roster of Soldiers and Patriots of the American Revolution Buried in Indiana, Vol. I; compiled by Mrs. Roscoe C. O'Byrne.; Indiana Daughters of the American Revolution, 1981; p.404.
REVOLUTIONARY SOLDIERS WHO WERE PENSIONED IN INDIANA AND LATER TRANSFERRED TO OTHER STATES
Haycock, Daniel   Switzerland Co.   Trans to Ill.

History of Switzerland County Indiana 1885; Reproduced by the Switzerland County Historical Society, Vevay, Indiana, 1999. The portion of the book relating to Switzerland County in the 1885 printing of the "History of Dearborn, Ohio, and Switzerland Counties, Indiana". p. 1097.
Practical Jokes - "As a candidate for representative at one time, Daniel Haycock, a Revolutionary Soldier, was Samuel Merrill's opponent, and by some means, in Ross Township, a man by the name of Laycock was voted for instead of Haycock, which was the cause of Merrill's election, as the votes of Laycock added to Haycock's would outnumber the votes cast for Mr. Merrill."

The Vevay Reveille-Enterprise; Vol. 122, No. 37, 22 Sep 1935, p. 3, col. 2.
Roster of Revolutionary Soldiers Who Resided in Switzerland County
By Mrs. Effa M. Danner
Daniel Haycock – is listed in the New Jersey line. His record is to be found p. 377, Order Book C. Sept. 1820, Switzerland County Court.
He served under Lieut. Martin, Capt. Wm. Bretten, Col. Oliver Spinoen, 5th New Jersey Regiment, Jersey Line, Continental establishment, transferred to Capt. William Ball's Co., same Regiment to Capt. James Bonnell's Co. General Marquis De la Fayette's infantry. Served 3 years and 9 months. Honorable discharge signed by Capt. Bonnel at Stony Point. Received pension 1818, No. 16620.
Family, wife, Jane age 41. Children, Eleanor 13, Polly 11, Robert 10, Lucretia 8, Thomas 6, Elizabeth 1 year old. His home on Tapps Ridge was a "Private Post" for the neighborhood in 1837 and he distributed the "Village Times", (Vevay).
He was a candidate for Indiana Representatives against Samuel Mervill of Vevay, 1817. He was called the People's Candidate and was quite popular, but the name was written Laycock on the ballot in Ross township by the voters and he was defeated by the Yankee. He was a juryman with John Shupe and Daniel Bray, November 1818. Swiss Settlement p. 81-397, Perret DuFour.
He removed to Pope County, Illinois and is listed there in the U.S. Military Census of 1840.
Early marriages, Switzerland County – Eleanor Haycock, Nathan Haddock, June 26, 1826. Polly Haycock, Elijah Boyd, August 3, 1829. Lucretia Haycock, Thomas Henry Boyd, April 7, 1832. Thomas M. Haycock, Elizabeth Sullivan, June 9, 1833. Elizabeth Haycock, Samuel Gibson, June 28, 1833. Robert Haycock, Catherine Sullivan, July 11, 1834.

HEATH, DANIEL JR

Patriot: Daniel Heath, Jr.
Birth: 26 May 1760 Coventry, Windham Co., CT
Married Spouse 1: Hannah Gates
Married Spouse 2: Azuba Reynolds
Service state(s): NY
Service description: Capts. Gilmore, McCaleb, John Brown, John Smith, Cols. Blair, Younglove
Rank: Private, Sergeant
Proof of Service: Pension application W7711
Pension application No.: W7711
Residences: Albany Co., NY; OH; Switzerland Co., IN
Died: 1 Oct 1841 Rising Sun, IN
Buried: Private burying ground near Enterprise, Cotton Twp., Switzerland Co., IN or Rising Sun, Ohio Co., IN.
DAR Ancestor No.: A053929

Pension Application Abstracted from National Archives microfilm Series 805, Roll 415, File W711/BLWT40013-160-55; Switzerland County, Indiana Complete Records, Circuit Court, Vol. ?, Sep 3, 1821-Apr 18, 1827; p. 614.

Pension abstract for – Daniel Heath   Service state(s): New Hampshire
Date: 14 October 1826
County of: Switzerland   State of: Indiana
Declaration made before a Circuit Court.
Age: about 57
Residence when he entered service: Albany, New York (both terms)
Residence now: Switzerland Co., IN
Volunteer or Drafted or Substitute: Enlisted for all terms
Rank(s): Third sergeant (first term), First sergeant (second term), Lieutenant (third term)
Statement of service-

Period	Duration	Names of General and Field Officers
March or April 1777	9 months	Capt. John McCaleb, regiment commanded by Lieut. Col. John Blair.
March 1779	9 months	Capt. John Smith, brigade commanded by General Schyler in the Continental Establishment.
March 1780	1 year	Company commanded by Hiram Woodworth, brigade commanded by General Schyler, in the Continental Establishment,

Battles: none indicated
Discharge received: December 1777 at Saratoga, NY (first term), 31 December 1779 at Saratoga, NY (second term), February 17781 at Saratoga County, NY by Gen. Schyler.
Applicant is crippled in his right arm and left leg.
Wife: Azubah   Wife's age: 51 years

Names and ages of children: Family consists of myself, my wife, a son Almon age 17, and daughter Angelina age 13. Also, 4 sons, 3 married and moved back to Easterland, 4th son lives by himself about a mile from applicant.
&

Date: 18 September 1832
County of: Switzerland   State of: Indiana
Declaration made before a Judge or Court.
Recorded in Book F, page 85.
Age: 62 years   Record of age: At home in my Bible copied from my mother's Bible which was burned at Buffalo, last war.
Where and year born: Coventry, Connecticut on 26 March 1760
Residence when he entered service: Albany Co., NY
Residence(s) since the war: New York for about 25 years, to Ohio in 1819 for about 5 years, about 14 years in Indiana.
Residence now: Switzerland Co., IN
Volunteer, Drafted or Substitute: Drafted then Enlisted 3 times and served as a substitute for William Johnson.
Statement of service-

Period	Duration	Names of General and Field Officers
April 1776 (drafted)	3 months	Capt. George Gilmore, in a regiment of New York Militia, company commanded by Col. John Blair

[see above pension application for other service]
Battles: Battle against Burgoyne when he surrendered. Was wounded at Fort Ann.
Discharge received: Several discharges signed by Gen. Schyler
What became of them?: Lost them all.
Statement is supported by –
Documentary proof: Has none
Person now living who can testify to service: None
Clergyman: John Pavy
Persons in neighborhood who certify character: Thomas Cole, Esq., Joseph McHenry, Benjamin Potter, Nicholas Sedam, John Dickason, William Dickason, Joseph Lapeler, William Smith.
Wife: Azubah
Marriage date and place: 29 May 1797 by Judge Bazeley in Cayuga County, NY
Proof of marriage: Bible record (copy in file)
Names and ages of children: Arden Heath b. 28 May 1801 in Cayuga Co., NY; Sebrina Heath b. 4 October 1802 in Cayuga Co., NY; Filinda Heath b. 24 July 1804 in Cayuga Co., NY; Charles Heath b. 13 December 1806 in Cayuga Co., NY; Philo Almand Heath b. 24 June 1810 in Niagara Co., NY; Angeline Heath b. 21 December 1812 in Niagara Co., NY
&

Widow, Azubah Heath's application for pension
Date: 12 June 1850
County of: Switzerland   State of: Indiana
Declaration made before a Court.
Soldier died 1 October 1841.

Age of widow: 72
Marriage date and place: 29 May 1797
Proof of marriage: Showed the record of births of her children, verified by her son Charles Heath age 43.
&
Date: 21 May 1856
Widow, Azubah Heath's application for Bounty Land which she is entitled to under the act of 3 March 1855.
Age of widow: 77 years
Residence of applicant: Enterprise, Switzerland Co., IN.
Persons who verified the appearance and statements of applicant: William R. Richmond & William Dickason.

Switzerland County, Indiana Civil Order Book Vol. 6, Oct. 17, 1825-Apr. 25, 1929, p. 163.
17 Oct 1826 -
Daniel Heath a Revolutionary soldier, Now comes, and files his Schedule of property, and made the Declaration, and took the Oath required by the Act of Congress relative to pensioners, which is ordered to be recorded: And it is ordered to be Certified that the Said property Contained in said Schedule is Valued at Sixty Seven Dollars and fifty cents.

Switzerland County, Indiana Civil Order Book Vol., A, Oct. 19, 1829-April 16, 1837, p. 178.
In the matter of Robert Ricketts, Thomas Mounts, Ebenezer Humphrey, Daniel Heath, William Coy and Isaac Levi, An application to obtain a pension.
   Personally appeared in open Court before the Switzerland Circuit Court now Sitting The above named applicants who being first duly Sworn doth in their several oaths make their several declarations in order to obtain the benefit of the Act of Congress of the 7th June AD 1832 that they entered the Service of the United States under the Officers named in their several declarations (here insert them) And the said Court do hereby declare their opinion after the investigation of the matter and after putting the interrogations prescribed by the War Department that the above named applicants were Revolutionary Soldiers and Served as they have stated And the Court further certifies that is appears to them that John Pavy who signed the several Certificates is a Clergyman resident in Switzerland County and State of Indiana and the other persons who has also signed the same are credible persons and that their Statement is entitled to credit.

Switzerland County, Indiana Probate Order Book 3,1837, 1843; pp. 404, 412, 425, 447, 450, 465, 497; Switzerland County, IN, Will Book Vol. 1, 3 Jan 1823-10 Nov 1847, p. 184.
Abstract of will and/or administration for: Daniel Heath
State & county where recorded: Switzerland Co., Indiana
State & county where will was made: Switzerland County, Indiana
Book/volume where recorded: Probate Order Book 3, 1837-1843.
Date will made: 2 March 1841
Witnesses to Will: Joseph Culp & Abijah H. Seymour

Date entered in probate: 1 November 1841
Name(s) of executors: Hezekiah Seymour
Administration: Will proven 1 November 184
Name of administrator: Hezekiah Seymour
9 November 1841 –Inventory of Goods & Chattels & Bills of Sale were filed.
14 February 1842 - Estate being insolvent, all heirs being out-of-state, court was petitioned by
executor to sell Real Estate funds to discharge the debts of the estate. Same to be published in the weekly newspaper three weeks before the Second Monday of May next.
9 May 1842 - Administrator proves notice of pendency of sale of Real Estate has been published for three successive weeks in the Western Statesman & Democratic Whig a weekly newspaper printed and published in Switzerland County, Indiana.
8 August 1842 - Administrator presented accounting of receipts & disbursements. Same were recorded.
Place of death: Switzerland County
Bonded by and amount of bond: William Kirby & William Melick for $400.00.
Names of heirs and others mentioned in will (also signed receipts of division of estate) and relationship if shown: Philo Almon Heath & Angeline Lockwood & J. S. Lockwood, resident heirs. Sobrina Ann Byrington & Phillinder McBeth, heirs of Ann Buckingham late Ann Heath; the heirs of Ira Heath; the heirs of Ada Heath; the heirs of Jeremiah Heath; Mary Halford late Mary Heath; Daniel Heath; James Heath; Orra Babbitt late Orra Heath, heirs at law are not residents of the State of Indiana.
Date of division & disbursement, or final return: 1843

Abstract of Final Payment Voucher; General Services Administration, Washington, DC
LAST FINAL PAYMENT VOUCHER RECEIVED FROM
THE GENERAL ACCOUNTING OFFICE
NAME   Heath, Daniel
AGENCY OF PAYMENT   Indiana
DATE OF ACT   1832
DATE OF PAYMENT   2d Qr. 1843
DATE OF DEATH   Oct. 1, 1841
GENERAL SERVICES ADMINISTRATION
National Archives and Records Service   NA-286
GSA-WASH DC 54-4891   November 1953

New York in the Revolution as Colony and State, Second Edition, 1898; by James A Roberts, Comptroller; Genealogical Publishing Co., Baltimore, MD. p. 131.
Albany County Militia – Sixteenth Regiment
Colonel   John Blair   Adjutant   John McClong
          Lewis Van Woert   Joseph Younglove
Major   James Ashton   Quarter Master   Joseph Younglove
Capt.   George Gilmore (among others in the list)
Additional Names on State Treasurer's Pay Books

Enlisted Men – Heath Daniel
Heath Daniel, Jr.
Other Heath names on this list are –
Elijah, Joseph, Samuel, Simeon, Stephen, Timothy, Windslow

1830 U.S. Census, Indiana, Switzerland, No Twp., Series: M19 Roll: 32 Page: 46
Heath, Daniel age 70-80; others in household 1 male under 5, 1 male 20-30, 1 female 10-15, 1 female 15-20, 1 female 50-60.

Early Ohio Settlers, Purchasers of Land in Southwestern Ohio, 1800-1840; Compiled by Ellen T. Berry & David A. Berry; Genealogical Publishing Co., Inc., Baltimore, MD, 1986. p.140.

Purchaser	Year	Date	Residence	R – T - S
Heath, Dan'l (B)	1833	Sept. 16	Switzerland	02-03-34

(B) Indiana Survey: Land lying west of a meridian drawn west of the Great Miami (known as the "Gore"). Switzerland, Dearborn, Franklin, Ohio, Union and Randolph Counties (all or only a part of each county) – all in Indiana.

Indiana Land Entries Vol. 1 Cincinnati District, 1801-1840; Margaret R. Waters; Originally Published Indianapolis 1948, Second Reprint 1979 by The Bookmark, P.O. Box 74, Knightstown, In 46148. p.132.
CINCINNNATI LAND DISTRICT – VOL. 1
Page 73. Twp. 3 N, Range 2 W of 1st Principle Meridian SWITZERLAND CO. Daniel Heath NW ¼ - NE ¼ - S34; 9-16-1833.
-- Note: The tract books for the land offices in Indiana are deposited in the office of the Auditor of State, Indianapolis. They and are in the custody of the State Land clerk. --

A Census of Pensioners for Revolutionary or Military Services with their Names, Ages, and Places of Residence Under the Act for Taking the Sixth Census in 1840; Genealogical Publishing Co., Inc., Baltimore, Maryland, 1965. p.185.
INDIANA, SWITZERLAND, COTTON

Names of Pensioners for Revolutionary or Military services	Ages	Names of heads of families with whom pensioner resided June 1, 1840
Daniel Heath	83	Daniel Heath

Revolutionary Soldiers of Switzerland County; Copied by Mary Hill, John Paul Chapter-Daughters of the American Revolution; January, 1958;
http://www.ingenweb.org/inswitzerland/switzrevsoldiers.html- Viewed June 2012.
HEATH, DANIEL
Born 26 Mar 1760, Coventry, CT
Lived in Albany N. Y. where he enlisted 1777, Private & Serg. in company commanded by Capt. McCalups under Col. Blair, N.Y. Militia for 2 years.
Married 1) Hannah Gates (1765-1797)
Children: James (1794-1864) married Susannah White; Ann Buckingham; Ira; Asa; Ann; Jeremiah; Mary Halford; Daniel; Orra Babit;

Married 2) 1797 Azubah Reynolds
Children: Arden b. 1810; Sebvina b. 1802; Felinda b. 1804 married Frances B. McBeth; Charles b. 1806; Philo Almand b. 1810; Angeline b. 1812;
Pension W.7711, B.L. Wt. 40013-160-55
Died Oct. 1, 1841
Buried near Enterprise, Cotton twp.
Abstracted Will, Switzerland Co. Bk.1, page184:
Written Mar. 2, 1841; recorded Nov. 1, 1841
8 children; Anna Buckingham; Ira Heath; Asa Heath; Jeremiah Heath; Mary Halford; Daniel Heath; James Heath; Orra Babit
Grandsons; Jefferson & Napoleon Bonaparte.
A private burying ground.
His wife, Ozubah Heath and remaining 6 children; Arden, Sobrina, Ann Byington, Philanda McBeth, Charles Philo Almon, Angelina Lockwood.
See DAR Natl Nos. 139, 877; 135, 546; 164, 566.
Daniel Heath 1760 - 1841
Natl No. 139, 877
On pension roll of Switz. Co. Ind. Born Coventry, Conn.
Mar. 20, 1760. Private & sergeant in N.Y. Militia.
Mar. 1st Hannah Gates 1765 -1797. Died Switz. Co.
Children James M. Heath, 1794 - 1864 m 1819 Susannah White (1794 - 1858)

Roster of Soldiers and Patriots of the American Revolution Buried in Indiana, Vol. I; compiled by Mrs. Roscoe C. O'Byrne.; Indiana Daughters of the American Revolution, 1981; p.183.
HEATH, DANIEL   Switzerland County
Born – March 26, 1760, Coventry, Conn.
Service – Lived in Albany, N. Y. when he enlisted 1777. Pri. and Serg. in company commanded by Capt. McCalups of Regt. under Col. Blair, N. Y. Militia for 2 years.
Proof – Pension claim W. 7711.
Died – Oct. 1, 1841. Buried near Enterprise, Cotton Twp.
Married – First W., 1785, Hannah Gates (1765-1797). Ch. James (1794-1864), m. Susannah White; Ann Buckingham; Ira; Ann; Jemima; Mary Harford; Daniel; Prra Babit. Second W., Azubah Reynolds, m. 1797. Ch. Arden, b. 1801; Sebvina Ann, b. 1802; Felinda, b. 1804, m. Frances b. McBeth; Charles, b. 1806; Philo Almand, b. 1810; Angeline, b. 1812.
Collected by Mrs. A. V. Danner, Vevay, Indiana

Abstract of Graves of Revolutionary Patriots (4 volumes); by Patricia Law Hatcher; Pioneer Heritage Press, Dallas, TX, 1987. Vol. 2, p. 138
This is an abstract and an index to information reported to the Daughters of the American Revolution and published in their annual reports to the Smithsonian Institution , printed as Senate Documents (1900-1974) and published annually in the DAR magazine (1978-1987). .
Published 1956, Serial set 11999, Volume 8.
HEATH, Daniel   Rising Sun IN

The Vevay Reveille-Enterprise; Vol. 122, No. 38, 22 Sep 1938, p. 3, col.1.
Roster of Revolutionary Soldiers Who Resided in Switzerland County
By Mrs. Effa M. Danner
Lieut. Daniel Heath – W.7711. Daniel Heath enlisted 1777, March, for nine months in Albany, N.Y. under Capt. John McCaleb's Regiment, Lieut. Col. John Blair. Served until December 1777. Discharged at Saratoga, N.Y. Enlisted again March 1779, Albany, N.Y. for nine months, Capt. John Smith, brigade of Gen. Schuyler. Served until last of December 1779. Enlisted again for 1 year, 1780. Served as Lieutenant in Company commanded by Capt. Hiram Woodsworth. Col. Schuyler served until January 1781. Discharged at Saratoga, N.Y.
Commissioned as Lieutenant signed by Gov. George Clinton, the same being eaten up by mice.
Daniel Heath was born in Coventry, Connecticut, March 26, 1760. Lived in Albany, N.Y. when he enlisted. After the war he lived in N.Y. 25 years, in Ohio 6 years, balance of time in Indiana. Daniel Heath died October 1, 1841.
Will, Switzerland County, book I, p. 184, recorded Nov. 1, 1841. Eight children, Anna Buckingham, Ira, Asa and Jeremiah Heath; Mary Halford, Daniel and James Heath, Orra Babit. Grandsons, Jefferson and Napoleon Bonepart. Second wife, Azubah Heath, six children, Arden, Subrina, Ann Byington, Philanda, McBeth, Charles, Philo, Almon Heath and Angeline Lockwood.
June 13, 1850, Azubah Heath, widow applies for pension. Married May 29, 1797 in Genoa, Cuyuga County, New York. Maiden name, Reynolds. First wife's name was Hannah Gates.
Daniel Heath is buried in a private cemetery near Enterprise.

HUFMAN, HENRY
aka HUFFMAN

Patriot: Henry Huffman
Birth: abt. 1750   Germany
Married Spouse 1: Fanny [aka Mary] (d. mid-1853, IN)
Service state(s): MD
Service description: Capt. McMahon, Col. Nevel
Rank: Private
Proof of Service: Maryland Revolutionary Records; Maryland Militia in the
　　　　　　　　Revolutionary War
Pension application No.: Not in War Department records
Residences: MD; Switzerland Co., IN; Dearborn Co., IN
Died: 1834   Dearborn Co., IN
Buried: Unknown
DAR Ancestor No.: None

Document contributed by Judy Kappes
Pension Application Abstracted from Switzerland County, IN, Circuit Court, Vol. A, Apr 1827-Mar 10, 1832, pg. 117

Pension abstract for – Henry Hufman　　　　　Service state(s): MD
Date: 23 Apr 1828
County of: Switzerland　　　　　　　　　　　State of: Indiana
Declaration made before a Circuit Court.
Age: 78 years
Residence when he entered service: Maryland
Residence now: Switzerland Co., IN
Volunteer or Drafted or Substitute: Enlisted
Rank(s): Private
Statement of service-

Period	Duration	Names of General and Field Officers
Mar 1777-Mar 1781	3 years	Co. commanded by Capt. McMahon, Regt. commanded by Col. Nevil, in Line of State of Maryland of the Continental Establishment.

Battles: None stated
Discharge received: Yes
What became of it?: The reason for not making an earlier application viz. Gen. Dill of Lawrenceburg Indiana refused to sent on his application because his discharge had be burnt about fifteen years ago.
Wife: Not named　　　　　　　　　Wife's age: 56 years old
Names and ages of children: 2 daughters, Ann is about 20 years old, Sarah is about 14 years old.
"we all live with my son Lewis, who is a married man, having small children who depend on him for support".

Switzerland County, Indiana Civil Order Book Vol. 6, Oct. 17, 1825-Apr. 25, 1929, p. 363.
April Term 1828 -
Henry Huffman a Revolutionary Soldier now comes and files his Schedule of property and Made the Declaration and took the Oath required by the Act of Congress relative to pensioners, which are ordered to be Recorded, And it is further Ordered to be Certified that the property contained in Said Schedule is Valued at Forth Dollars.

Abstract of Final Payment Voucher; General Services Administration, Washington, DC

LAST ~~FINAL~~ PAYMENT VOUCHER RECEIVED FROM 1 of 2
THE GENERAL ACCOUNTING OFFICE
NAME   Hoffman, Mary (Henry)
AGENCY OF PAYMENT   Indiana
DATE OF ACT   1848
DATE OF PAYMENT   3rd Quarter 1853
DATE OF DEATH   Form
General Services Administration   GSA DC 70-7035   GSA Dec 69 7068
&
last ~~FINAL~~ PAYMENT VOUCHER RECEIVED FROM 2 of 2
THE GENERAL ACCOUNTING OFFICE
NAME   Hoffman Mary widow of Henry
AGENCY OF PAYMENT   New Albany, Ind.
DATE OF ACT   1848
DATE OF PAYMENT   Sept. 1853
DATE OF DEATH   Form
General Services Administration   GSA DC 70-7035   GSA Dec 69 7068

Maryland Revolutionary Records; Harry Wright Newman; Tuttle Publishing, Rutland, VT, 1928. p. 94.
Non-Pensioners
Huffman, Henry   Pvt., Flying Camp

The Maryland Militia in the Revolutionary War; by S. Eugene Clements and F. Edward Wright; Published by Family Line Publications, Westminster, MD 21157,1987. p. 237.
Washington County
A List of Officers & Men in Capt. Henry Botelers Compy. 1 Lieut. Thomas Odel; 2 Lieut, John Nicholls; Ensign (blank); 1 Sergt. Daniel Giveings; 2 Sergt. Henry Edward Boteler; 3 Sergt. William Nicholls; 4 Sergt. Trail Nicholls.
3rd Class – Henry Hufman (in list)
-farther down on same page -
A List of Capt. Nichodemus's Compy. as now Classed.
Second Batta., No. 6., 4th Class Henry Hufman.

Muster Rolls and other records of service of Maryland Troops in the American Revolution; Archives of Maryland, reprinted with permission by Genealogical Publishing Co., Inc., Baltimore, 1972. p. 47.
List of men enrolled in Capt. Mantz's Company. Passed by C. Beatty, July 13th, 1776.
Henry Huffman [included in list of privates]

Register of Certificates Issued by John Pierce, Esquire, Paymaster General and Commissioner of Army Accounts for the United States, to Officers and Soldiers of the Continental Army Under Act of July 4, 1783; Originally Published as Senate Documents, Vol.9, No. 988, 63rd Congress, 3d Session, Washington, 1915; Seventeenth report of the National Society of the Daughters of the American Revolution; Genealogical Publishing Co., Inc, Baltimore, MD, 1984. p. 250.
Men listed in this volume with the same name.

No. of Certificate	To whom issued	Amount
72176	Hoffman, Henry	40.60

Revolutionary Soldiers of Switzerland County; Copied by Mary Hill, John Paul Chapter-Daughters of the American Revolution; January, 1958; http://www.ingenweb.org/inswitzerland/switzrevsoldiers.html- Viewed June 2012.
HUFFMAN (HUFMAN), HENRY
Born about 1750
Enlisted 3 years March 1777 in Maryland company, under Capt. McMahon, Col. Nevel, to serve till March, 1781.
Discharged at Lancaster, PA
Married Fanny _____.
Children: Ann; Sarah; Lewis m Elizabeth Glenn.
Switzerland Co. Indiana, Civil Order bk. 1828, pg. 117
Collected by Mrs. A. V. Danner, Vevay, Ind.

Roster of Soldiers and Patriots of the American Revolution Buried in Indiana, Vol. I; compiled by Mrs. Roscoe C. O'Byrne.; Indiana Daughters of the American Revolution, 1981; p.199.
HUFFMAN, HENRY   Switzerland County
Born – About 1750.
Service – Enlisted 3 yrs. March, 1777, in Maryland company under Capt. McMahon, Col. Nevel, to serve until March, 1781. Discharged at Lancaster, Penn.
Proof – Switzerland County, Ind. Civil Order Book 1828, p. 117.
Married – Fanny _____. Ch. Ann; Sarah; Lewis m. Elizabeth Glenn.
Collected by Mrs. A. V. Danner, Vevay, Indiana.

The Vevay Reveille-Enterprise; Vol. 122, No. 37, 22 Sep 1935, p. 3, col. 2-3.
Roster of Revolutionary Soldiers Who Resided in Switzerland County
By Mrs. Effa M. Danner
Henry Hufman, Huffman – Resident of Switzerland County, age 78, 1828. He enlisted 3 years, March A.D. 1777 in Maryland, Company of Capt. McMahow,

Col. Nevel, Continental Establishment Md. line. Continued to serve until March A.D. 1781. Discharged from service at Lancaster, Pa.
Family – wife, age 56. Children – Ana, 20, Sarah 14. We live with my son Lewis who is married and has five small children. Renews application made in 1818.
Marriage record – Lewis Huffman to Elizabeth Glenn, April 4, 1818.

HUMPHREY, EBENEZER
aka HUMPHRY, HUMPHREYS

Patriot: Ebenezer Humphrey
Birth: 8 May 1764 Oxford, MA
Married Spouse 1: Hulda Keeney
Service state(s): MA
Service description: Capts. Tucker, Moore
Rank: Private
Proof of Service: Pension application S18040
Pension application No.: S18040
Residences: Oxford, Worcester Co., MA; NH; VT: Switzerland Co., IN
Died: 3 Mar 1840 Switzerland Co., IN
Buried: Quercus Grove Cemetery, Posey Twp., Switzerland Co., IN
DAR Ancestor No.: A059798

Pension Application Abstracted from National Archives microfilm Series 805, Roll 454, File S18040.
Pension abstract for – Ebenezer Humphreys   Service state(s): Massachusetts
Alternate spelling(s): Humphry
Date: 18 September 1832
County of: Switzerland   State of: Indiana
Declaration made before Open Court
Recorded: Book F, pg. 82.
Age: 69 years   Record of age: His name and age is recorded in Oxford, Massachusetts on the Town Books
Where and year born: Oxford, MA on 8 May 1763
Residence when he entered service: Oxford, MA
Residence(s) since the war: New Hampshire about 5 years; then to Vermont about 35 years; then Ohio for 1 year, Indiana last 15 years.
Residence now: Switzerland Co., IN
Volunteer or Drafted or Substitute: Volunteered and enlisted the last 3 times.
Rank(s): Private
Statement of service-

Period	Duration	Names of General and Field Officers
1777	3 months	Company commanded by Capt. William Tucker, in Regiment of Massachusetts Militia commanded by Col. Tyler
1778 or 1779	9 months (3 successive enlistments)	Company commanded by Capt. William Moore, in the Regiment of Massachusetts Militia commanded by (he believes, but is not certain) Brentwood.

Discharge received: at West Point. No written discharge.
Person now living who can testify to service: No one.
Clergyman: John Pavy
Persons in neighborhood who certify character: Samuel Blake, Bela Hearick, Aribet Gazley, William Cunningham, Levi Maples, Wm. B. Chamberlain, Abel C. Pepper, Caleb Craft.

No family data is in the file. However, an enquiry letter in the file claims he married Hulday Kennedy b. Corinth, VT, and had sons - Stephen b. 1791, m. Hannah Barrows; Arthur b. 1796, m. Catherine Tripp. Soldier died 23 March 1841, buried in Switzerland Co., IN.

Switzerland County, Indiana Civil Order Book Vol., A, Oct. 19, 1829-April 16, 1837, p. 178.
In the matter of Robert Ricketts, Thomas Mounts, Ebenezer Humphrey, Daniel Heath, William Coy and Isaac Levi, An application to obtain a pension.
    Personally appeared in open Court before the Switzerland Circuit Court now Sitting The above named applicants who being first duly Sworn doth in their several oaths make their several declarations in order to obtain the benefit of the Act of Congress of the 7th June Ad 1832 that they entered the Service of the United States under the Officers named in their several declarations (here insert them) And the said Court do hereby declare their opinion after the investigation of the matter and after putting the interrogations prescribed by the War Department that the above named applicants were Revolutionary Soldiers and Served as they have stated And the Court further certifies that is appears to them that John Pavy who signed the several Certificates is a Clergyman resident in Switzerland County and State of Indiana and the other persons who has also signed the same are credible persons and that their Statement is entitled to credit.

Switzerland County, Indiana Probate Order Book 3, 1837-1843, pp. 299, 303, 330, 345, 382, 384, 456, 475; and *Switzerland County, Indiana Probate Orders Book, 1843-1849, p. 28.*
Abstract of will and/or administration for: Ebenezer Humphry
Book/volume where recorded: Probate Order Book 3, 1837-1843.
Date will made: Died intestate
Date entered in probate: 21 October 1840
Administration:
Date began - 21 October 1840
Name of administrator - Stephen Humphry
10 August 1841 – Administrator presented account of estate which was ordered filed.
Bonded by and amount of bond: Henry Monroe for $600.00.
Date of division & disbursement, or final return: 13 May 1844

Early Settlers of Indiana's "GORE" 1803-1820; Compiled and Edited by Shirley Keller Mikesell; Heritage Books, Inc., 1995. p. 183.
Switzerland County - Township 2, Range 1W
Section 17 – Ebenezer Humphrey – 1817 – pg. 2.

Indiana Land Entries Vol. 1 Cincinnati District, 1801-1840; Margaret R. Waters; Originally Published Indianapolis 1948, Second Reprint 1979 by The Bookmark, P.O. Box 74, Knightstown, In 46148. p.3.
CINCINNNATI LAND DISTRICT – VOL. 1
Page 2. Twp. 2 N, Range 1 W of 1st Principle Meridian SWITZERLAND CO.

Ebenezer Humphrey (portion illegible) – S17; 5-8-1817. Vol. II, p. 3, says NE ¼ - S17.
-- Note: The tract books for the land offices in Indiana are deposited in the office of the Auditor of State, Indianapolis. They and are in the custody of the State Land clerk. –

U.S. Department of Interior, Bureau of Land Management, General Land Office Records; Land Patent Search – *accessed 27 June 2012.*
HUMPHREY, EBENEZER
Accession Nr. CV-0053-459; Document Type – Credit Volume Patent; State – Indiana; Issue Date – 12/29/1820; Cancelled – No
Land Office – Cincinnati; Authorit – April 24, 1820 Sale-Cash Entry (3 Stat. 566); Total Acres 160.66
Land Descriptions: State – IN; Meridian – 1st PM; Twp-Rng – 002N-001W; Aliquots – NE1/4; Section – 17; County - Switzerland

1830 U.S. Census, Indiana, Switzerland, No Twp., Series: M19 Roll: 32 Page: 46
Humphrey, Ebenezer age 60-70; others in household 1 male under 5, 1 male 10-15, 1 female under 5, 1 female 20-30, 1 female 60-70.

The "Lost" Pensions, Settled Accounts of the Act of 6 April 1838; by Craig R. Scott; Willow Bend Books, Lovettsville, VA, 1996. p. 166.
An Act directing the transfer of money remaining unclaimed [for the term of eight months] by certain pensioners, and authorizing payment of the same at the Treasury of the United States.
Name – Humphrey, Ebenezer; Pension Office – administrator of Ind.; Box - 86; Account - #16806.

Roster of Soldiers and Patriots of the American Revolution Buried in Indiana, Vol. I; compiled by Mrs. Roscoe C. O'Byrne.; Indiana Daughters of the American Revolution, 1981; p.199-200.
HUMPHREY, EBENEZER   Switzerland County
Born – May 8, 1763. Worcester Co., Massachusetts.
Service – Pri. in CO. of Capt. Tucker, Regt. of Col. Tyler in Mass. Militia, 15 mos.
Proof – Pension claim S. 18040.
Died – March 23, 1841. Buried Inercus Grover [Quercus Grove] Cemetery, Posey Twp. Stone.
Married - Hulda Keeney. Ch. Stephen, b. 1791; Arthur, b. 1796; Indianus H., b. 1824. There were two other children.
Collected by Mrs. A. V. Danner, Vevay, Indiana.

Revolutionary Soldiers of Switzerland County; Copied by Mary Hill, John Paul Chapter-Daughters of the American Revolution; January, 1958; http://www.ingenweb.org/inswitzerland/switzrevsoldiers.html- Viewed June 2012.
HUMPHREY, EBENEZER
Born May 8, 1763 Worcester Co. Massachusetts
Private in co. of Capt. Tucker, Regt. of Col. Tyler, in Mass. Militia for 15

months.
Married Hulda Keeney
Children: Stephen b 1791; Arthur b 1796; Indianus H. b. 1824; There were other children.
Switzerland County, Indiana. Pension Claim S.18040
Died March 23, 1841
Buried in Quercus Grove Cemetery, Posey Twp. Stone
Collected by Mrs. A. V. Danner, Vevay, Indiana

History of Switzerland County Indiana 1885; Reproduced by the Switzerland County Historical Society, Vevay, Indiana, 1999. The portion of the book relating to Switzerland County in the 1885 printing of the "History of Dearborn, Ohio, and Switzerland Counties, Indiana". p.
"Arthur Humphrey, was born August 26, 1796, in Corinth, Vt. He was the son of Ebenezer and Huldah (Keeney) Humphrey, also natives of Vermont."
Stephen Humphrey, one of the early settlers of this county, was born in Vermont in 1791. ...His father, Ebenezer Humphrey was a soldier in the Revolutionary war, and all through it."

Switzerland County Indiana Cemetery Inscriptions 1817-1985; Wanda L. Morford; Cincinnati, Ohio, 1986, p.451.
Quercus Grove Cemetery, Posey Twp., Switzerland Co., IN
Humphrey
Ebenezer, born in Mass. May 6, 1762 d. Mar. 23, 1841 – Soldier of}
        Revolutionary War and War of 1812 – Masonic emblem } single
        Huldah Keeney, wife of Ebenezer, no dates   } stone

Tombstone photographed by Marlene McDerment, Oct 1985
Quercus Grove Cemetery, Switzerland Co., IN
Tombstone inscription –
           EBENEZER HUMPHREY
           BORN IN MASSACHUSETTS
           MAY 8, 1762
           DEPARTED THIS LIFE
           MARCH 23, 1841
           SOLDIER OF REVOLUTIONARY
           WAR AND WAR OF 1812

Vevay Times and Switzerland County Democrat, Vol. IV, Saturday, March 7, 1840, pg. 3, col. 5.
OBITUARY
"In the midst of Life we are in Death"
Died – In Posey township, on Tuesday last, the 3d instant, Ebenezer Humphrey, a soldier of the revolution, aged about 81 years.

The Vevay Reveille-Enterprise; Vol. 122, No. 37, 22 Sep 1935, p. 3, col. 3.
Roster of Revolutionary Soldiers Who Resided in Switzerland County
By Mrs. Effa M. Danner

Ebenezer Humphreys – S18040. Born in Worchester County, Oxford, Mass, May 8, 1763. Enlisted as a private in Capt. Tucker's Co., Regiment of Col. Tyler in Mass line for 18 months. Inscribed on rolls of Indiana $50 per annum.
Wife, Huldah Keeney, born in Corinth, Vermont. Sons, Stephen born 1791, married Hannah Barrows. Arthur, born 1796, married Catherine Tripp.
Ebenezer Humphrey – S18040 the War of 1812. He is buried at Quercus Grove. Grave stone inscription – Ebenezer Humphrey, Born Massachusetts May 8, 1762. Departed this life March 23, 1841. Grave located by H. Fenton Emerson.
Record published in Complete Record Book F, p. 81, Switzerland Co., Ind.

JENNINGS, SOLOMON

Solomon Jennings died in Owen Co., Kentucky. His widow, Polly, moved to Switzerland County, Indiana and applied for pension there in 1841.

Patriot: Solomon Jennings
Birth: abt. 1752
Married Spouse 1: 25 Dec 1792, Woodford Co., KY   Polly Reading
                            (d. aft. Apr 1841, Switzerland Co., IN)
Service state(s): NY Continental Line
Service description: Captain Mercer's (?) Company, Col. Van Schoicks
                      NY Continental Line
Rank: Private
Proof of Service: Pension application W10147
Pension application No.: W10147
Residences: NY: Owen Co., KY: Polly in Switzerland Co., 1841
Died: 20/30 Nov 1820   Owen Co., KY
Buried: Unknown
DAR Ancestor No.: None

Pension Application Abstracted from National Archives microfilm, Series M105, Roll 470, File W10147.
Abstracted from pension application – Solomon Jennings
He applied for pension on 6 January 1820, 2nd Circuit Court, State of Kentucky.
Service – New York
He enlisted as a Private at Fishkill on the Hudson River, State of New York, in the spring of the year 1776, in Captain Mercer's (?) Company, belonging to Col. Van Schoicks, being in the New York Continental Line. Served until the end of the war in 1783 when he was honorably discharged at Newburgh on the Hudson River in the State of New York. Was in Battles of: taking of Bourgoyne & Stony Point.
On 9 October 1820, he appeared in Owen County Circuit Court, aged 69, stating he served until the close of the war. He was discharged at New Windsor in New York. He was at the taking of Burgoyne at Saratoga, Stony Point and Little York. Stated that he made application for pension under the act of 18 March 1818, and received a pension certificate No. 16-826. His occupation is a farmer but he is not able to work much on account of rheumatic pains. He has a wife and nine children, William aged 22 years, Mathias age 21 past, Solomon age 18, Winny age 16, Nally age 14, Sally 12, David age 10, Lucy age 8, Nancy 6 years, John age 4, a cripple Madison age 2, and two sons married who have left him. Schedule of property valued $16.37-1/2.
Widow, Polly Jennings, appl. 12 Apr 1841, Switzerland Co. IN, age 65(?), a resident of Switzerland County.
She said his name was on the 1818 pension list Roll of Kentucky. She drew the balance on his pens. at the time of his death, 20 Nov 1820, in Lexington, KY. Sold. was private.
She m. on 25 Dec 1792, Woodford Co., KY. Produced marriage record – her name Polly Reading. Record of marriage included in the application papers.

ch: Minor Jennings accompanied his mother to Lexington, in 1820 or 1821, to receive the balance of pension due to Solomon Jennings at the time of his death.

National Archives microfilm Series 805, Roll 470, File W10147.
Letter from War Dept. in Pension File –
Rev. & 1812 Wars Section
September 17, 1924
Miss Alice Jennings
114 N. Orange St.
Glendale, Calif.
Madame:
   I have to advise you that from the papers in the Revolutionary War pension claim, W.10147, if appears that Solomon Jennings enlisted at Fishkill, New York, in 1776 or 1777, and served until the close of the Revolution in 1783 as a private in Capt. Mercer's Company, Colonel Van Schaick's New York Regiment; he was at the capture of Burgoyne and the battles of Stony Point and Yorktown.
   He was allowed pension of his application executed January 26,, 1820, while residing in Owen County, Kentucky, aged 68 years. He died November 30, 1820.
   He married December 25, 1792, in Woodford County, Kentucky, Polly Reading. She was allowed pension on her application executed April 12, 1841, while residing in Vevay, Switzerland County, Indiana, aged 65 years.
   In 1820 the soldier stated that he had the following children: William aged 22, Mathias aged 21, Solomon aged 18, Winny aged 16, Polly aged 14, Sally aged 12, Daniel aged 10, Lucy aged 8, Nancy aged 6, John aged 4, Madison aged 2 years, and two sons who were married, names not stated. In 1841 a son, Minor was referred to.

              Respectfully,
              Acting Commissioner

Abstract of Final Payment Voucher; General Services Administration, Washington, DC

NAME	Jennings, Solomon
AGENCY OF PAYMENT	KY
DATE OF ACT	1818
DATE OF PAYMENT	2nd qtr. 1821
DATE OF DEATH	Nov. 30, 1820
LAST FINAL PAYMENT VOUCHER RECEIVED FROM THE GENERAL ACCOUNTING OFFICE General Services Administration	Form GSA DA 70-7035 GSA Dec 69 7068

New York in the Revolution as Colony and State, Second Edition, 1898; by James A Roberts, Comptroller; Genealogical Publishing Co., Baltimore, MD. p. 22.
The Line
First Regiment
Colonel Goose Van Schaick   Adjutant John H. Wendell
Lieut. Col. Cornelius Van Dyck   Quarter Master Henry Van Woert

Major John Graham   Pay Master Jeremiah Van Rensselaer
Enlisted Men – Jennings Solomon (on this listing)

American Militia in the Frontier Wars, 1790-1796; by Murtie June Clark; Genealogical Publishing Co., Inc., 1990.
p. 21
Kentucky Militia
Muster Roll of a Company of Mounted Volunteers from Kentucky under the Command of Captain Hezekiel Haydon, Lieut. Colo. Horatio Hall's Regiment, in the service of the United States, under the Command of Major General Charles Scott, mustered July 15, 1793.

Nr	Rank	Name	Remarks
35	Private	Jennings, Solomon	-

p. 22
Kentucky Militia
Pay Roll of Captain Ezekiel Hatdon's Company of Mounted Calvary, Lieut. Colo. Horatio Hall's Regiment in the service of the United States from Kentucky, Commanded by Major General Charles Scott.

Nr	Rank	Name	Remarks
35	Private	Jennings, Solomon	enlisted Sept 20

p. 56
Kentucky Militia
Pay Roll of a Company of Mounted Volunteers, Commanded by Captain John Franciscoe, Major William Price's Battalion, Called into the Service by the President of the United States in 1794.

Nr	Rank	Name	Remarks
45	Private	Jennings, Solomon	Jun 13-Oct 26, 136 days sold horse Sep 9

Revolutionary Soldiers in Kentucky, containing a roll of the officers of Virginia line who received land bounties, a roll of the Revolutionary pensioners in Kentucky, a list of the Illinois regiment who served under George Rogers Clark in the Northwest campaign, also a roster of the Virginia Navy. Reproduction of the original which appeared in Sons of the American Revolution Kentucky Society Year Book, Louisville, 1896.; Anderson Chenault Quisenberry; Southern Book Co., Baltimore, MD, 1959. p. 210.
Roll of Pensioners – Owen County
Jennings, Solomon, private   New York line
May 3, 1820; $96.   Age 69.   Died Nov. 30, 1820

Register of Certificates Issued by John Pierce, Esquire, Paymaster General and Commissioner of Army Accounts for the United States, to Officers and Soldiers of the Continental Army Under Act of July 4, 1783; Originally Published as Senate Documents, Vol.9, No. 988, 63rd Congress, 3d Session, Washington, 1915; Seventeenth report of the National Society of the Daughters of the American Revolution; Genealogical Publishing Co., Inc, Baltimore, MD, 1984. p. 273.
Men listed in this volume with the same name.

No. of Certificate	To whom issued	Amount
65248	Jennings, Solomon	80.00
65895	Jennings, Solomon	40.60
66462	Jennings, Solomon	46.60
66998	Jennings, Solomon	18.71

Revolutionary War Bounty Land Grants Awarded by State Governments; Lloyd DeWitt Bockstruck; Genealogical Publishing co., IN, Baltimore, MD, 1996. p. 276.
Jennings, Solomon. N.Y. Private. 8 Jul 1790. 600 acres.

Revolutionary Soldiers Buried in Indiana (1949) With Supplement (1954) Two Volumes in One; Margaret R. Waters; Genealogical Publishing Company, Baltimore, MD, 1970. p.134.
JENNINGS, SOLOMON & POLLY   Switzerland
He d. 11-30-1820, Owen Co., Ky.   Pens. W.10147 N.Y.

Revolutionary Soldiers Buried in Indiana (1949) With Supplement (1954) Two Volumes in One; Margaret R. Waters; Genealogical Publishing Company, Baltimore, MD, 1970. p. 140, 141.
p. 140 – In list of spouses buried in Indiana for Switzerland Co., - Jennings, Polly-w. Solomon.
p. 141 – In list of "Soldiers Who Died in Other States" (husbands of widows on list of spouses) – Kentucky – Jennings, Solomon.

KELLY, WILLIAM
aka KELLEY

Patriot: William Kelly
Birth: Nov 1755   Chester County, PA
Married Spouse 1: 1 Jan 1794 Westmoreland Co., PA   Sarah Pressor
(d. 1842, IN)
Service state(s): VA
Service description: Capt. Thomas Baldwin, Col. Steel, VA Militia;
   Capt. Calamede, Col. Daniel Morgan
Rank: Private
Proof of Service: Pension application W10165
Pension application No.: W10165
Residences: Winchester Co., VA; PA, KY; Switzerland Co., IN
Died: 21 Jan 1834 Switzerland Co., IN
Buried: prob. Lostetter (aka Grant's Creek) Cemetery, Posey Twp.,
   Switzerland Co., IN
DAR Ancestor No.: None

Pension Application Abstracted from National Archives microfilm Series 805, Roll 490, File W10165.;Switzerland County, Indiana Probate Record Book Vol. A, Mar 1827-Nov 1834; p. 318.

Pension abstract for – William KELLY   Service state(s): Virginia
Alternate spelling(s): William KELLEY
Date: 7 Sep 1832
County of: Switzerland   State of: Indiana
Recorded in Book A, page 318
Declaration made before a Judge at the home of the soldier
Age: 79 years   Record of age: none
Where and year born: Chester County, Pennsylvania, on 2 Nov AD 1755
Residence when he entered service: Winchester, ?????? (Illegible) County, Virginia
Residence(s) since the war: Virginia about 10 years, lived in Pennsylvania about 13 years, then in Kentucky 26 or 27 years, since that time in Indiana.
Volunteered (from widow's application)
Rank(s): Private
Statement of service-

Period	Duration	Names of General and Field Officers
1777	9 mos.	Captain Thomas Baldwin of the Regt. commanded by Col. Steel in the Virginia Militia
1780/1781	3 mos.	Captain Calamede, Col. Daniel Morgan

Names of Regular Officers: General Washington, General Pickins, Col. Howard.
   Col. Morgan was the commander of our regiment.
Discharge received: Yes
Signed by: Capt. Baldwin and Capt. Calamede
What became of it?: Both were destroyed when my house was burnt in (Clark County) KY.

Statement is supported by – Traditional Evidence - Declaration proven by Thomas Kelly and William Kelly whose affidavits are certified by the judge.
Living witness, name(s): My brother, Thomas Kelly whose affidavit is annexed.
Documentary proof: none
Clergyman: George A. Dugan
Persons in neighborhood who certify character: George Dugan residing in Dearborn County; Paschal Early residing in Dearborn County.
Soldier died: 21 Jan 1834, Switzerland Co., IN
Wife: Sarah Pressor (from Widow's application)
&
Widow's Application for Pension according to the Act of 7 July 1838 granting half-pay and pension to certain widows.
Applicant: Sarah Kelly widow of William Kelly
Date: 5 November 1838
County of: Switzerland   State of: Indiana
Declaration made before a Court.
Widow's age: 74 years
William Kelly was awarded Certificate No. 19049 under the Act of Congress 7 June 1832
Widow's maiden name: Sarah Pressor
Widow's residence now: Posey Twp., Switzerland Co., IN
Marriage date and place: 1 January 1794, in Westmoreland Co., PA
Proof of marriage: Handwritten page in pension file; affidavit of Mrs. Nancy Cunningham, and John Brown. Certificate of Marriage was destroyed by fire when home burnt about 40 years ago in Clark Co., KY.
Names of children: Thomas Kelly, of Switzerland Co., declares Sarah Kelly is his mother and that she has never been married since the death of his father, William Kelly.

Marriage record; Revolutionary War Pension Application file W10165(abstracted above).
William and Sarah Kelly was married 14 September 1786, Westmoreland County, Pennsylvania. Marrade by James Finley, Presbyterian minister.

1820 U.S. Census, Indiana, Switzerland, Jefferson, Series: M33 Roll: 14 Pg: 261
William Kelly 45 and up; also in household 1 male 10-16, 3 females 16-26, 1 female 45 and up.

Switzerland County, Indiana Probate Order Book 2, 1831-1837; p.195.
Pensioner's Widow
12 May 1834
Now comes Sarah Kelly and proves to the Satisfaction of the Court that William Kelly late of Switzerland County Departed this life in Said County on the 21st day of January 1834, and that the Said Sarah Kelly is now the widow and was the lawful wife of the Said William Kelly in his lifetime & lived with hi until the time of his death, and that Said decedent is the Identical person inscribed on the Pension list roll of the Indiana agency.

Switzerland County, Indiana Probate Order Book 2, 1831-1837; pp. 250, 258, 296, 322, 353, 391, 416;and *Switzerland County, IN, Will Book Vol. 1, 3 Jan 1823-10 Nov 1847,* p. 71.
Abstract of will and administration for: William Kelly
State & county where recorded: Switzerland Co., Indiana
Book/volume where recorded: Probate Order Book 2, 1831-1837.
Date Will written: 16 January 1834
Witnesses to Will: John Gibbons
Date entered in probate: 10 December 1834
Administration:
Date began- 10 Dec 1834
Name of administrator- Polly Kelly
Date of death: Not stated [21 Jan 1834 is shown in the pension file.]
Bonded by and amount of bond: Peter Lostetter for $628.00
Names of heirs and others mentioned in will and relationship if shown: Sarah (Polly) Kelly, widow. Leaves to said wife his Pension due the Sixth day of March AD 1834 to pay for the cow he bought
Son, Thomas Kelly to be executor.
Date of division & disbursement, or final return: settled 8 August 1836.

Switzerland County, Indiana Probate Order Book 3, 1837-1843; p. 121.
12 November 1838, Kelly, William – Widow of
In the matter of Sarah Kelly widow of
William Kelly Dec'd who was a Pensioner of the U.S.
The Report of the said Sarah Kelly taken by the Judge of this Court in Vacation under the act of Congress of 1838 is now filed, and by the Court ordered of record, which a part reads in the words and figures following to wit (here insert it).

Abstract of Final Payment Voucher: General Services Administration, Washington, DC
LAST FINAL PAYMENT VOUCHER RECEIVED FROM
THE GENERAL ACCOUNTING OFFICE
NAME   Kelly, Sarah
AGENCY OF PAYMENT   Indiana
DATE OF ACT   1838
DATE OF PAYMENT   4th Quarter 1842
DATE OF DEATH   -
THE GENERAL ACCOUNTING OFFICE   Form
General Services Administration   GSA DA 70-7035   GSA Dec 69   7068

Virginia Revolutionary Militia, A List of Non-Commissioned Officers and Soldiers of the Virginia Line on Continental Establishment, Whose names appear on the Army Register, and who have not received Bounty Land; Printed by Samuel Shepherd, Printer to the Commonwealth, Richmond, VA. 1835. p. 28.
Doc. No. 44
Kelly, William   Soldier   Infantry   (3 citations on this page)

Revolutionary War Bounty Land Grants Awarded by State Governments; Lloyd DeWitt Bockstruck; Genealogical Publishing co., IN, Baltimore, MD, 1996. p. 292.
Kelly, William. Va. Private. 8 Nov. 1784. 200 acres.

Catalogue of Revolutionary Soldiers and Sailors of the Commonwealth of Virginia to Whom Land Bounty Warrants Were Granted by Virginia for Military Service in the War for Independence, From Official Records in the Kentucky State Land Office at Frankfort, Kentucky; compiled by Samuel M. Wilson; Southern Book Company, Baltimore, MD, 1953. p.44.

Number of Warrant	Name of Officer or Soldier	Number of Acres	Rank	Dept. of Service: Continental or State Line or Navy	Number of Years in Service	Date of Warrant
3511	Kelly, William	200	Private	Va. Cont. Line	War	Nov. 8, 1784

Revolutionary War Records – Virginia; Virginia Army and Navy Forces with Bounty Land Warrants for Virginia Military District of Ohio, and Virginia Military Script, from Federal and State Archives; by Gaius Marcus Brumbaugh, M.D, M.s., Litt.D; Genealogical Publishing Co., Inc., Baltimore, 1995.
p.189 Bounty Land Warrants, United States January 16, 1828 (See Senate Documents, 1st Session 20th Congress, Vol. 2, Doc. 42 &c. 1827-'28)
204. Kelly, William, *r*, Private
p. 250 (4 listed) List of Non-Commissioned Officers and Soldiers of the Virginia Line on Continental Establishment, Whose Names Appear on the Army register and Who Have Not Received Bounty Land, Richmond, 1835.
Kelly, William, Soldier, Inf.
Kelly, William, Soldier, Inf.
Kelley, William, Soldier, Inf.
Kelly, William, Soldier, Inf.
p. 460 Virginia Military Land Warrants, Virginia District of Ohio, Granted for Revolutionary War Services, State Continental Line, Beginning August 8, 1872.

Number	Warrantees	Rank & Service
3511	Kelly, William	Soldier War

American Militia in the Frontier Wars, 1790-1796; by Murtie June Clark; Genealogical Publishing Co., Inc., 1990. p. 57.
Kentucky Militia
Roll of a Company of Mounted Volunteers Commanded by Captain George Frazier, Major William Price's Battalion, Called into Service by the President of the United States in 1794.

Nr	Rank	Name	Remarks
39	Private	Kelly, William	Sept 3

Virginia Revolutionary Publick Claims in three volumes; compiled and transcribed b Janice L. Abercrombie and Richard Slatten; Iberian Publishing Co., Athens, GA, 1992. p. 380.
Frederick County – Frederick County Court Booklet. At a Court held for Frederick County the 3rd day of April 1782. An act of General Assembly entitled

an act for adjusting claims for property impressed or taken for public service was produced and read. Thereupon, pursuant to the directions thereof the court proceeded to receive the several claims of persons within the county for such articles and on due consideration are of opinion the several claimants ought to receive the several sumes of money for the articles so impressed or taken hereafter mentioned in the annexed lists, which distinguished applications to the Continent from that of the state. Viz.

Pg. 15 – William Kelly for ferriage 10 horses for Cont. £1s-8.

Register of Certificates Issued by John Pierce, Esquire, Paymaster General and Commissioner of Army Accounts for the United States, to Officers and Soldiers of the Continental Army Under Act of July 4, 1783; Originally Published as Senate Documents, Vol.9, No. 988, 63rd Congress, 3d Session, Washington, 1915; Seventeenth report of the National Society of the Daughters of the American Revolution; Genealogical Publishing Co., Inc, Baltimore, MD, 1984. p. 287. Men listed in this volume with the same name.

No. of Certificate	To whom issued	Amount
68372	Kelly, William	33.30
68628	Kelly, William	33.30
68913	Kelly, William	83.54
69076	Kelly, William	88.00
69441	Kelly, William	76.00
69711	Kelly, William	80.00
74688	Kelly, William	40.60
74741	Kelly, William	44.66
75670	Kelly, William	80.00
76864	Kelly, William	68.42
77203	Kelly, William	100.00
77234	Kelly, William	37.20
77775	Kelly, William	50.75
77806	Kelly, William	50.75
77592	Kelly, William	80.00
77532	Kelly, William	80.00

[Possible citation. His residences have not been fully determined.]

Census of Indiana Territory for 1807; Indiana Historical Society, 1980. p. 33.
Randolph County

Names of Persons	No. of free male Inhabitants 21 yrs and above
William Kelly	1

Early Ohio Settlers, Purchasers of Land in Southwestern Ohio, 1800-1840; Compiled by Ellen T. Berry & David A. Berry; Genealogical Publishing Co., Inc., Baltimore, MD, 1986. p. 175.

Purchaser	Year	Date	Residence	R – T - S
Kelly, William (B)	1830	Feb. 13	Switzerland	02-03-25 [Son?]
Kelly, William (B)	1834	May 15	Switzerland	01- 02- 06[Son]

(B) Indiana Survey: Land lying west of a meridian drawn west of the Great Miami (known as the "Gore"). Switzerland, Dearborn, Franklin, Ohio, Union and Randolph Counties (all or only a part of each county) – all in Indiana.

Early Settlers of Indiana's "GORE" 1803-1820; Compiled and Edited by Shirley Keller Mikesell; Heritage Books, Inc., 1995. p. 183.
Switzerland County - Township 3, Range 1W
Section 30 – William Kelly – 1817 – pg. 4.

Indiana Land Entries Vol. 1 Cincinnati District, 1801-1840; Margaret R. Waters; Originally Published Indianapolis 1948, Second Reprint 1979 by The Bookmark, P.O. Box 74, Knightstown, In 46148. p. 6.
CINCINNNATI LAND DISTRICT – VOL. 1
Page 4. Twp. 3 N, Range 1 W of 1st Principle Meridian SWITZERLAND CO. William Kelly, St. NE ¼ - S30; 3-22-1817.
-- Note: The tract books for the land offices in Indiana are deposited in the office of the Auditor of State, Indianapolis. They and are in the custody of the State Land clerk. –

U.S. Department of Interior, Bureau of Land Management, General Land Office Records; Land Patent Search – accessed 27 June 2012.
KELLY, WILLIAM
Accession Nr. CV-0072-555; Document Type – Credit Volume Patent; State – Indiana; Issue Date – 8/2/1833; Cancelled – No
Land Office – Cincinnati; Authority – April 2, 1820 Sale-Cash Entry (3 Stat. 566); Document Nr. 2753; Total Acres – 160.60
Land Descriptions: State – In; Meridian – 1sp PM; Twp-Rng – 003N-001W; Aliquots – NE1/4; Section – 30; County - Switzerland

Revolutionary Soldiers of Switzerland County; Copied by Mary Hill, John Paul Chapter-Daughters of the American Revolution; January, 1958; http://www.ingenweb.org/inswitzerland/switzrevsoldiers.html- Viewed June 2012.
KELLY, WILLIAM
Born Nov. 2, 1755, Chester Co. Penn.
Resided in Winchester, Virginia, when he enlisted.
Private in Virginia Militia, 9 months from 1777, Capt. Baldwin, Col. Steele.
Married 1786 Sarah Preysor.
Children:
Nancy, b. Apr. 13, 1787
Catherine b. Dec. 30, 1789
Mary Ann b. Feb. 17, 1792
Elizabeth b. Sept. 20, 1795
Thomas b July 31, 1798 m Dorthea &Rachel
Lydia Ann b. Nov. 11, 1820 m William Hess
William b Mar. 26, 1802 m Sept. 6, 1837 Mirea Craig
Pension W.10165
Died Jan. 21, 1834 Posey twp. Switzerland Co. Ind.
Probably buried Lostutter Cemetery.

Switz. Co. Probate bk. A - pg. 195;
Comes Sarah Kelly, William Kelly died Jan. 21, 1834.
Sarah, widow, said William is the person in Pension Roll of Indiana Agency/ Was resident of Switz. Polly Kelly, adm.
Will Abstract, Switzerland County, Bk. 1, pg 71.William Kelly Thomas Kelly, executor. Jan. 16, 1832.
Wife, Sarah, 50 acres NE 30-3-1.
Leaves wife pension due March 6, 1834 to pay for cows.
Son, Thomas Kelly, exec.
Witnesses; John Gibbons and John Stockdale

Roster of Soldiers and Patriots of the American Revolution Buried in Indiana, Vol. I; compiled by Mrs. Roscoe C. O'Byrne.; *Indiana Daughters of the American Revolution, 1981; p.218.*
KELLY (KELLEY), WILLIAM   Switzerland County
Born – Nov. 2, 1755, Chester Co., Penn.
Service – Pri. in Virginia Militia, 9 mos. from 1777, Capt. Baldwin, Col. Steele. Resided in Winchester, Vir. when he enlisted.
Proof – Pension claim !. 10165.
Died – Jan. 21, 1834, Posey Twp., Switzerland Co. Probably buried Lostutter Cemetery.
Married – 1786, Sarah Preysor. Ch. Nancy, b. April 13, 1787; Catherine, b. Dec. 30, 1789; Mary Ann, b. Feb. 17, 1792; Elizabeth, b. Sept. 20, 1795; Thomas (m. Dorthea) and Rachael, b. July 31, 1798; Lydia Ann, b. Nov. 11, 1800, m. 1824 Wm. Hess; William, b. March 26, 1802, m. Sept. 6, 1837, Mirea Craig.
Collected by Mrs. O. V. Danner, Vevay, Indiana.

The Vevay Reveille-Enterprise; Vol. 122, No. 37, 22 Sep 1935, p. 3, col. 3.
Roster of Revolutionary Soldiers Who Resided in Switzerland County
By Mrs. Effa M. Danner
Wm. Kelly – Born Nov. 2, 1755, Chester County, Pa. Resided in Winchester, Va. where he enlisted as a private in the Virginia militia for 9 months, in July 1777 in Capt. Baldwins' Company, Col. Steele's Regiment.
Pension allowed, No. W10168.
Wife, Sarah Pressor, married September 14, 1786 in Westmoreland County, Pa.
Children, Nancy, born April 13, 1787; Catherine, born Dec. 30, 1789; Mary Ann, February 17, 1792; Elizabeth, Sept. 20, 1795; Thomas and Rachel, July 31, 1798; Lydia Ann, Nov. 11, 1800; William, March 22, 1802.
Land grant, Posey Township, Switzerland County, T.3, R.N.1.W., N.E. Sec. 30, 160 acres, March 22, 1817.
William Kelly died January 21, 1834, Posey Township.
Probate Court, Vol. 1836-40, p. 121. Sarah Kelly, widow of William Kelly pensioner, allowed pension 1838.
Last will of Wm. Kelly 1834, Book E. p. 491, xx to my wife Sarah, 50 acres of N.E. qt. Sec. 30, T 3, R. 1 W, all my personal goods and my pension due March 1834 to pay for the cow I bought, xxx my son Thomas to be my executor. Wm. Kelly. Thomas Kelly, land grant No. 377, Book 4, p. 378.
Lydia Kelly married Wm. Hess in 1824.

KNOX, ROBERT

Patriot: Robert Knox
Birth: 11 Apr 1758 Ireland
Married Spouse 1: 1785   Elizabeth Gill (d. 1817)
Married Spouse 2: aft 1817   Milly Bohannon (b. 1793 KY, d. 26 Feb 1861, Gallatin Co., KY)
Service state(s): SC
Service description: Capts. Knox, Walker, Whitesides, McClure, Turner, Hanna, Mills
Rank: Private, Sergeant
Proof of Service: Pension application W26190
Pension application No.: W26190
Residences: SC; KY District VA; Switzerland Co., IN
Died: 3 Oct 1836   Gallatin Co., KY
Buried: Unknown
DAR Ancestor No.: A067112

Kentucky Marriage Records, Franklin County. p. 28.
17 Jul 1817, Robt. Knox to Milley Bohannon.

Pension Application Abstracted from National Archives microfilm Series 805, Roll 505, File W26190/BLWT26714-160-55.; Switzerland County, Indiana Probate Record Book Vol. A, Mar 1827-Nov 1834; p. 266.
Pension abstract for – Robert Knox   Service state(s): South Carolina
Date: 13 August 1832
County of: Gallatin Co.   State of: Kentucky
Declaration made before a Court.
Recorded in Book A page 266.
Age: 74   Record of age: Recorded in family Bible that was destroyed in the Revolution.
Where and year born: 11 April 1758 in County Antrim, Ireland
Residence when he entered service: Camden district, South Carolina
Residence(s) since the war: 2 years in SC, last 46-47 years in KY, now live 3 miles from Vevay, Indiana.
Residence now: Switzerland Co., IN
Volunteer or Drafted or Substitute: Substituted for William Miller, was drafted twice, volunteered several times.
Statement of service-

Period	Duration	Names of General and Field Officers
1779 or 1780	about 70 days	Company commanded by Capt. James Knox of Camden district S.C.
1779 or 1780	about 70 days	Company commanded by Capt. Phillip Walker of same district.
1780	4 months	Same captain, same district.
1781	40 days	John McClure

Battles: Rocky Mount; Hanging Rock where he was wounded in the left knee; Eutaw Springs; Siege of Ninety-Six.

Discharge received: Yes
Signed by: Col. Lacey
What became of it?: Lost it
Statement is supported by –
Documentary proof: None is my possession. Refers to documents filed in Jan. 1825 with the War
Clergyman: James Cox, of Gallatin Co., KY
Persons in neighborhood who certify character: Gen. Jesse Lindsey, William Lindsey, Thomas Neal, Lewis Yesterday, and others.
Wife: not named
Names and ages of children: none shown
&
Widow's application for Pension
Widow: Mrs. Milly Knox
Date: 9 January 1854
County of: Gallatin   State of: Kentucky
Declaration made before Open Court
Widow's age: 62 years
Soldier died: 3October 1836
Marriage date and place: 17 July 1817 in Franklin Co., KY by Rev. William Hickman, Jr. a minister of the Baptist Church
Name before marriage: Milly Bohanan
Names and ages of children: None shown
&
Declaration for Pension or for Increase of Pension of Children Under Sixteen Years of Age
Applicant: Amanda Melvina Fuller (nee Knox) only surviving legitimate child who was under 16 at the time of soldier's death.
Soldier died: 3 October 1836. Wounded in knee at Cow Pens and cause of death was from the affects of said wound.
Date: 26 March 1897
County of: Carroll   State of: Kentucky
Declaration made before a Justice of the Peace
Applicant stated the widow drew pension for herself but not for claimant, and she applies for her father's accrued pension due. Geo. Welby Van Pelt, of Vevay, IN her attorney to prosecute the claim.
Age of applicant: 67 years
Residence of applicant: Worthville, Carroll Co., KY
Mother: Mildred Bohanan   She died: 26 February 1861
Names and ages of children:

Mildred Ann	b. 19 March 1819	d. 21 March 1864
Amanda Melvina	b. 30 September 1829	
Robert	b. 19 February 1821	d. July 1884
Margaret Jane	b. 27 July 1827	d. 7 October 1880
Angeline	25 June 1817	Living

Switzerland County, Indiana Probate Order Book 2, 1831-1837;p. 69.
13 August 1832

In the matter of}
Robert Knox } An applicant for a pension under the act of Congress
of June the 7, 1832.
Now comes into Court the Said Robert Knox, And the Said Court do hereby declare their opinion, after the investigation of the matter and after putting the interrogations prescribed by the War department that the above named Robert Knox was a Revolutionary Soldier and Served as he states, And the Court further certifies that it appears to them that James Cox, who has Signed the preceding Certificate is a Clergyman resident in Gallatin County and State of Kentucky and that Robert Gullion who also signed the Same is a resident of Switzerland County and State of Indiana and is a credible person, and their statement is entitled to Credit.

Abstract of Final Payment Voucher; General Services Administration, Washington, DC
NAME Knox, Milly (Robert)
AGENCY OF PAYMENT KY
DATE OF ACT 1853
DATE OF PAYMENT 2nd qtr. 1861
DATE OF DEATH Feb 26, 1861
FINAL PAYMENT VOUCHER RECEIVED FROM
THE GENERAL ACCOUNTING OFFICE Form
General Services Administration GSA DA 70-7035 GSA Dec 69 7068

The "Lost" Pensions, Settled Accounts of the Act of 6 April 1838; by Craig R. Scott; Willow Bend Books, Lovettsville, VA, 1996. p. 188.
An Act directing the transfer of money remaining unclaimed [for the term of eight months] by certain pensioners, and authorizing payment of the same at the Treasury of the United States.
Name – Knox, Elizabeth; Administrator of Pension Office - Madison, Ind.; Box – 130; Account - #7908.

Second Census of Kentucky, 1800; Clift G. Glenn; Genealogical Publishing Co., Baltimore, MD, 1954.
An alphabetical list of 32,000 taxpayers based on original tax lists on file at the Kentucky Historical Society. Information given includes the county of residence and the date of the tax list in which the individual is listed.
Knox, Robert Franklin 8/7/1801

1860 U.S. Census, Kentucky, Gallatin, Warsaw P O, Series: M653 Roll: 368 Page: 569, Family No. 339.
Knox, Milly Age: 67, Female, Race: White, Born: KY

Revolutionary Soldiers Buried in Indiana A Supplement; 485 Names Not Listed in the Roster of Soldiers and Patriots of the American Revolution Buried in Indiana (1938) nor in Revolutionary Soldiers Buried in Indiana (1949); Margaret E. Waters; Indianapolis, 1954. p. 35, 140, 141.
KNOX, ROBERT & MILLY Switzerland

p. 35. - He d. 10-3-1836, Gallatin Co., Ky., but had liv. In Switzerland Co., Ind. She later retd. To Gallatin Co., Ky. Pens. W.26190 S.C. (Switzerland Co. Probate Bk. A, p. 69.

p. 140 – In list of spouses buried in Indiana for Switzerland Co., - Knox, Milly-w. Robert.

p. 141 – In list of "Soldiers Who Died in Other States" (husbands of widows on list of spouses) – Kentucky – Knox, Robert.

History of Switzerland County Indiana 1885; Reproduced by the Switzerland County Historical Society, Vevay, Indiana, 1999. *The portion of the book relating to Switzerland County in the 1885 printing of the "History of Dearborn, Ohio, and Switzerland Counties, Indiana". p. 1288.*
In the passage about James S. Knox – "Robert Knox, the father of George G. Knox, was a native of County Down, Ireland, and immigrated to the United States with his parents, who located in Charleston, S.C. From here, when grown, he enlisted in the Revolutionary war and served during the entire struggle, receiving a bullet wound in his knee in the battle of Cowpens, which eventually caused his death, the leaden missile never being extracted. He removed to Madison County, Ky., and in the fall of 1791 to Carroll County, where he died. He married Elizabeth Gill, a native of South Carolina."

The Vevay Reveille-Enterprise; Vol. 122, No. 37, 22 Sep 1935, p. 3, col.3.
Roster of Revolutionary Soldiers Who Resided in Switzerland County
By Mrs. Effa M. Danner
Robert Knox – was born April 11, 1758 in County Antrim, Ireland. He died October 8, 1836 near Ghent, Ky. He emigrated to South Carolina, Charleston, and there enlisted in Revolutionary War as a Private in Capt. James Knox' Co. militia under Major Joseph Brown and received a bullet in the knee at the Battle of Cowpens. In 1779 under Col. Lacy he was in the battles of Coosawatchee, Rocky Mount and Hanging Rock. He was in the battle of Estan Springs and at the siege of 96 Fort and carried dispatches from Col. Henderson to Gov. Rutledge and received honorable mention.
He resided in Camden Dist. South Carolina. He removed to Switzerland County and lived with his son George G. Knox, and died at his daughter's home and is buried on the Shermer farm 3 miles West of Ghent, Ky. Probate court, Switzerland County, p. 69, June 7, 1832 Robert Knox applied for pension. Rev. James Cox of Gallatin County, Ky., and Robert Gullion, witnesses.
Children of Robert Knox and Elizabeth Gill Knox – George G. Knox, Mary Knox Nighswonger, John Knox, James Knox, Elizabeth Knox.
Record endorsed by D.A.R. Julia LeClere Knox.

LANCASTER, WILLIAM

Patriot: William Lancaster
Birth: 17 Nov 1746 Hanover Co., VA
Married Spouse 1: 1771/2 VA Mary (Polly) Webb (1756-1799) per SAR#97877
Married Spouse 2: 11 September 1813 Bracken Co., KY   Sarah X
                                               (widow of John Levy Blades)
                                               (b. 1753 MD d. 18 Feb 1848 IN)
Service state(s): VA
Service description: Capts. Wm. Buckner, Benj. Johnson,
                      Cols. Harvey, Abner Porter.
                      Furnished supplies
Rank: Private; Patriotic Service
Proof of Service: Pension application S16912; Abercrombie & Slatten, VA Rev.
                                           Publick Claims, Vol. 2, p. 274.
Pension application No.: S16912
Residences: b. King William Co., VA; Orange Co., VA; Switzerland Co., IN
Died: 4 Nov 1843 Switzerland Co., IN
Buried: Napoleon Miller's farm (formerly Mallory Lancaster's farm, the son
        of William Lancaster), Switzerland Co., IN
DAR Ancestor No.: A068365
Child: Henry B. Lancaster (b. 31 Jan 1773 Orange Co., VA d. 20 Jan 1851
                                                                 Boone Co., KY)

Pension Application Abstracted from National Archives microfilm Series 805, Roll 510, File S16912.; Switzerland County, Indiana Probate Record Book Vol. A, Mar 1827-Nov 1834; p. 323.
Pension abstract for – William Lancaster   Service state: VA
Noted on cover page – "This man's widow Sarah was pensioned as the former widow of John Levy Blades, Md., W9502."
Date: 12 Nov 1832
County of: Switzerland   State of: Indiana
Declaration made before a Court. Application recorded in Book A, pg. 323.
Age: 85 years   Born: 17 November 1746 in Hanover Co., VA
Record of age: Was Christened in King William County, Virginia where my
                    age is recorded.
Residence when he entered service: Orange County, VA;
Residence(s) since the war: 15 years in Orange Co., VA; 27 or 28 years in
                                   Kentucky, then to Indiana.
Residence now: Switzerland County, IN
Volunteer or Drafted or Substitute: Drafted
Rank(s): Private
Statement of service-

Period	Duration	Names of General and Field Officers
Abt. 20 Jun 1779	Upwards of two months	Company of Virginia Militia command by William Buckner of Col. Harvey's regiment.

Battles/Service: Stationed as a guard at Albemarle Barracks over British &

Hessian soldiers.
These persons were detailed at the same time: William Proctor, Duncan Campbell, Burle Boton, Richard Allen, William Ingraham, George Petty, John Samuel, Joseph Boston.
&
Volunteer or Drafted or Substitute: Drafted
Rank(s): Private
Statement of service-

Period	Duration	Names of General and Field Officers
1780	90 days	Capt. Benjamin Johnson's company of Virginia Militia of Orange County.
Jul or Aug 1781	4 months	Under command of Abner Porter, company of the Army.

Discharge received: No written discharge.
Documentary proof: None
Clergyman: John Pavy
Persons in neighborhood who certify character: Prescott (?) Harvey, Henry Peters, James N. Taylor, George Craig, Ab??? McKay, Joseph Short, George Munn(?).
1st wife – not named.
Names of children: Mallory Lancaster (in 1844 his wife, Catherine, was living in Switzerland Co.
2nd Wife: Sarah Blades, widow of John Levy Blades
Marriage date and place: 11 September 1813 in Bracken Co., KY
Death of soldier: 4 November 1843

Switzerland County Indiana, Probate Order Book 2, 1831-1837, page 89.
12 November 1832
In the matter of William Lancaster } An applicant for a Pension under the act of Congress of the 7th June 1832.
Now comes the Said William Lancaster in open Court before the Probate Court of Switzerland County now Sitting, and makes Report as follows to witt (here insert it) And the Said Court do hereby declare their opinion after the investigation of the matter, and after putting the interrogations prescribed by the War Department that the above named William Lancaster was a Revolutionary Soldier and Served as he states, And the Court further Certifies that is appears that John Bray who has Signed the preceding Certificate is a Clergyman resident in Switzerland County and State of Indiana, and that Clm. Pruit Harvey who also Signed the same is a resident of Switzerland County and State of Indiana and is a credible person and their Statement is entitled to Credit.

Switzerland County, Indiana Probate Orders Book, 1843-1849, p. 63.
12 November 1844
It has been represented and Proved to the Satisfaction of the Said Switzerland Probate Court that William Lancaster last of Craig township County aforesaid departed this life on the fourth day of December eighteen hundred and forty three leaving his widow who now resides in Craig township aforesaid. That

William Lancaster was a pensioner of the United States and received thirty dollars per annum his Certificate and dates at the War Office of the United States on the 13th day of May 1833 which is ordered to be Certified.
Switzerland County, Indiana Probate Orders Book, 1843-1849, pgs. 376, 379, 429, 430.
15 February 1848
Probate Court Estate records for Sarah Lancaster .

Abstract of Final Payment Voucher; General Services Administration, Washington, DC
FINAL PAYMENT VOUCHER RECEIVED FROM
THE GENERAL ACCOUNTING OFFICE
NAME   Lancaster, William
AGENCY OF PAYMENT   Indiana
DATE OF ACT   1832
DATE OF PAYMENT   4th Q. 1844
DATE OF DEATH   Dec 4, 1843
GENERAL SERVICES ADMINISTRATION
National Archives and Records Service   NA-286
GSA-WASH DC 54-4891   November 1953

Revolutionary War Records – Virginia; Virginia Army and Navy Forces with Bounty Land Warrants for Virginia Military District of Ohio, and Virginia Military Script, from Federal and State Archives; by Gaius Marcus Brumbaugh, M.D, M.s., Litt.D; Genealogical Publishing Co., Inc., Baltimore, 1995. p.252.
List of Non-Commissioned Officers and Soldiers of the Virginia Line on Continental Establishment, Whose Names Appear on the Army register and Who Have Not Received bounty Land, Richmond, 1835.
Lancaster, William, Soldier, Inf.

Historical Register of Virginians in the Revolution, Soldiers, Sailors, Marines, 1775-1783; John H. Gwathmey; The Dietz Press, Richmond, VA, 1938. p. 455.
Lancaster, William. 87, Switzerland, Ind. mpl.

Virginia Militia in the Revolutionary War; J.T. McAllister, McAllister Publishing Co., Hot Springs, VA, 1913. p. 279.
Part V, Pensioners Residing Outside of Virginia in 1835 who Received Pensions as Virginia Militiamen.
Lancaster, Wm.   87 [age]   Switzerland   Indiana

Virginia Revolutionary Publick Claims in three volumes; compiled and transcribed b Janice L. Abercrombie and Richard Slatten; Iberian Publishing Co., Athens, GA, 1992. p. 754.
Orange County – Orange County Court Booklet – At a court held by the justices of Orange County court at the courthouse [var. dates] 1782 for adjusting the claims made to the said court agreeable to an act made and passed the last session of assembly, entitled an act "For adjusting claims for property impressed or taken for public service" The following claims were allowed to be just and reasonable.

Pg. 7 – William Lancaster

Revolutionary Soldiers of Switzerland County; Copied by Mary Hill, John Paul Chapter-Daughters of the American Revolution; January, 1958; http://www.ingenweb.org/inswitzerland/switzrevsoldiers.html- Viewed June 2012.
LANCASTER, WILLIAM
Born November 17, 1745 in Hanover County, Virginia
Christened in King William County, Va.
Names of parents not given
When residing in Orange County Va. William Lancaster enlisted, January 20, 1779, serving two months as private in Captain William Buckner's company, Colonel Harvey's Virginia Regiment & guarded the British and Hessian prisoners at Albemarle Barracks.
He enlisted in 1780 and served 90 days in Captain Benjamin Johnson's company, under Major Nathaniel Welsh.
He enlisted sometime in July or August, 1781, served four months under Abner Porter, commissary, and was engaged in collecting cattle for the army.
Married Unknown
He moved about 15 years after the Revolution from Orange County, Virginia to Kentucky and lived there about 28 years, then moved to Indiana.
He was allowed pension on his application executed November 12, 1832, at which time he was living in Switzerland County, Indiana. Pension S.16912
Married Sarah (d. 18 Feb 1848), the widow of John Levy BLADES a Switzerland County Revolutionary War soldier.
Children: Isabel married Evan Miller; Catherine married Patrick E. Porter
Died 4 Nov 1843
Buried on Napoleon Miller's farm, Switzerland County

Roster of Soldiers and Patriots of the American Revolution Buried in Indiana, Vol. III; 1980; p. 65.
LANCASTER, WILLIAM   Roster I, p. 226   Switzerland County
Additional data or corrections.
Married – (1) Mary (Polly) Webb in Va. D. ca. 1800 probably Mason Co., Ky.
          (2) Sept. 8, 1810 Mason Co., Ky, Mrs. Sarah Blades.
Children – Henry b. Jan 3, 1773, d. Killed by accident in Boone Co., Ky. Aug. 8, 1817 m. Sarah Boothe d. Jan 20. 1851; Edith b. Mar. 12, 1775 m. Joseph Boothe; Robert b. Sept. 12, 1777; Susannah b. Jan. 16, 1780 m. William Young; Sarah b. June 16, 1783/4 m. Christopher Shroufe; Amelia b. May 3, 1786 m. William Reeves; Mallory b. Jan. 9, 1790 (Was in War of 1812) d. Oct. 12, 1844 m. Aug. 10, 1815 Catherine Byars; Nancy b. Sept. 25, 1792 m. (1) James Leak (2) William Glackin.
Note – The listing of Isabelle Miller and Catherine Porter as daughters, is an error. They were granddaughters of the soldier, being daus. of the soldier's son Mallory.
By Col. James Glackin, a descendant, 860 Hinman Avenue, Evanston, Illinois 60202. Col. Glackin has collected a great deal of data on this family.

Roster of Soldiers and Patriots of the American Revolution Buried in Indiana, Vol. I; compiled by Mrs. Roscoe C. O'Byrne.; Indiana Daughters of the American Revolution, 1981; p.226-227.

LANCASTER, WILLIAM   Switzerland County

Born – Nov. 17, 746, Hanover Co., Vir.

Service – Enlisted Orange Co., Vir., in Wm. Buckner's CO., Col. Harvey's Regt.; guarded British and Hessian prisoners at Albemarle Barracks; 1780, was 80 days in Capt. Berry Johnson's CO., Maj. Nathaniel Welsh; July and Aug., 1871, under Abner Oirter, commissary, collecting cattle for army.

Proof – Pension claim S. 16902.

Died – Nov. 4, 1843. Buried on Napoleon Miller's Farm, Switzerland Co.

Married – First W. unknown. Second W. Mrs. Sarah Blades, d. Feb. 18, 1848.

Ch. Isabel, m. Evan Miller; Catherine, m. Patrick E. Porter.

Collect by Mrs. A. V. Danner, Vevay, Indiana.

Notarized document provided by Helen Einhas. The original notarized document and diagram are in the possession of Helen Einhas (2012). Copy of the document and diagram are in the Switzerland County Auditor's Office.

WILLIAM LANCASTER/SARAH LANCASTER BURIAL SITE LOCATION

In the summer of 1972, my parents, Glenn W. and Ruth Holder Todd, and I visited at the home of Ruth's cousin, Ralph T. Miller of Switzerland County, Indiana. My mother and I were preparing our applications for the Daughters of the American Revolution so we were inquiring about our ancestor, William Lancaster (1746-18430, a Soldier of the Revolutionary War.

Ralph Miller told us William Mallory Lancaster, a son of William Lancaster, came to Indiana Territory in 1813 and entered his father's land located on the Old Indian Boundary Line in Craig Township, Switzerland County. Ralph then asked his wife, Harriet Miller, to go with us to the burial site of William and Sarah Lancaster.

Starting at the driveway of the William Mallory Lancaster house, we walked east through the adjoining lot where his parents William and Sarah Lancaster had lived in a small cabin. We crossed over a fence and immediately came upon the mound where William and Sarah Lancaster are buried. I have the diagram where my father measured and wrote down the distance from the Lancaster-Miller home to the site. The Lancaster homestead remains today in the possession of a descendant of William Lancaster but the burial site property is in the name of Ric Louis Parton.

DATE: February 18, 2009   Helen Todd Einhaus

Sworn to and subscribed before me
This 18 day of Feb A.D. 2009
Ruth M. Hulert
Notary Public, State of Indiana
My commission expires 10-26-2016
County of Ripley
The referenced diagram is dated 1972.

Abstract of Graves of Revolutionary Patriots (4 volumes); by Patricia Law Hatcher; Pioneer Heritage Press, Dallas, TX, 1987. Vol. 3, p. 4.
This is an abstract and an index to information reported to the Daughters of the American Revolution and published in their annual reports to the Smithsonian Institution, printed as Senate Documents (1900-1974) and published annually in the DAR magazine (1978-1987).
Published 1972 (Senate Doc. 54)
LANCASTER, William Miller Cem, Switzerland Co IN

The Vevay Reveille-Enterprise; Vol. 122, No. 37, 22 Sep 1935, p. 3, col. 3 & p. 7, col.1
Roster of Revolutionary Soldiers Who Resided in Switzerland County
By Mrs. Effa M. Danner
William Lancaster – Born Nov. 17, 1746 in Hanover County, Virginia. Christened in King Williams County, Virginia.
Enlisted in Orange County, Virginia from January 20, 1779 for 2 months in Capt. Wm. Buckner's Co., Col. Harvey's Regiment. Guarding prisoners, British and Hessans at Albemarle Barracks. In 1780 enlisted for 90 days in Capt. Benj. Johnson's Company, Major Nathaniel Welsh; July or August 1781, four months under Abner Potter, Commissary and was engaged in collecting cattle for the army.
Allowed pension while residing in Switzerland County, Indiana, Sept. 12, 1832, No. S16912.
Married second wife, Sarah, widow of John Levy Blades, a Revolutionary soldier who served in the 2nd Maryland Regiment and was taken prisoner by the British, Jan. 28, 1780. He was discharged Nov. 15, 1783. It was not stated how he was released from prison. John Levy Blades and Sarah were married February 17, 1778 in Somerset County, Md. He died February 11, 17884 in Maryland. Their son Zadock Blades, born in 1777, and his widowed mother moved to Kentucky, Bracken County, where she married William Lancaster, September 11, 1813. He died November 4, 1848 and she was allowed pension on the service of John Levy Blades, June 26, 1848, age 90. Catherine Lancaster, wife of Mallory Lancaster, son of William Lancaster and first wife, her name not given, testifies in Sarah's behalf. She died Feb. 18, 1848.
William Lancaster's son Mallory Lancaster came to Switzerland Co., Indiana 1812 and filed his father's land warrant in Craig Township on the Old Indian Boundary Line. It is still owned by his descendants.
William Lancaster had settled in Orange County, Ky., but moved to Switzerland County in 1819 and lived with Mallory where he died Nov. 4, 1843 and was buried near the house on their farm near Five Points. Mallory Lancaster was a soldier of 1812. He married Catherine Byers at Augusta County, Ky. He died on a flat boat trip of yellow fever and was buried at Memphis, Tenn. In 1850.
Children of Mallory and Christine Lancaster – Eliza married James Vaughn, Dec. 12, 1836. Margaret married Moses McKay, Jan. 18, 1832. Nancy married Daniel McKay, Mar. 16, 1844. Sarah married Honeywell Haskell, May 15, 1843. John married Sarah Johnson, Feb. 5, 1840. William married Jemima Garber, Jan 13, 1849. Isabelle married Evan Miller, May 14, 1854. Laura married Solomon Hubbard Sept. 22, 1858. Lucy. Georgia. Moses S. married Polly Collrus, Nov.

12, 1832. Phoebe married Nelson Johnson, Sept. 1, 1840. Catherine married Patrick Porter, Aug. 6, 1852.

The Lancasters were exiled from England and founded the city of Lancaster, Pa. There are many descendants in this county.

LANDRES, KIMBROW
aka LANDERS, KIMBROW or KEMBROW

Patriot: Kimbrow Landers
Birth: c. 1753
Married Spouse 1: 24 Jul 1782 Mary Branham
Married Spouse 2: 21 July 1798 in Louisa Co., VA   Keziah Humbles
(b. abt. 1770 d. aft. Sep. 1848)
Service state(s): VA
Service description: Capts. Thomas Walker, Robert Barrett, Cols. George
Matthews, Francis Taylor
Rank: Private
Proof of Service: Pension application W1623
Pension application No.: W1623
Residences: Albemarle Co., VA; Louisa Co., VA; Indiana Territory;
Switzerland Co., IN
Died: 26 May 1831   Switzerland Co., IN
Buried: Cotton Cemetery, Jefferson Twp., Switzerland Co., IN
DAR Ancestor No.: A202299

Virginia Marriage Record, Louisa County, No. 85.
21 Jul 1798, Kimbro Landers to Keziah Humbles.
> Know all men by thse presents that we Kimbro Landers & John Michie are held and firmly bound unto James Wood esq. our present Governor and his successors in office in the sum of one hundred & fifty dollars, to which payment will and truly to be made we bind ourselves etc. dated this 21st day of July 1798. The condition of the above obligation is such that whereas there is a marriage suddenly intended to be had ans soleminized, between the above bound Kimbro Landers and Keziah Humbles.
> If therefore there is no lawfull cause to obstruct the said marriage then this obligation to be void.
> Signed & in the presence }   Kimbro Landers (Seal)
> of   John Michie (Seal)
> W. G. Poindexter

Pension Application Abstracted from National Archives microfilm Series 805, Roll 510, File W1623; Switzerland County, Indiana Complete Records, Circuit Court, Vol. C, 5 Nov 1818 - 8 Feb 1821; p. 371.
Pension abstract for – Kimbrow Landres   Service state(s):
Virginia
Alternate spelling(s): Kimbro
Date: 19 May 1818
County of: Switzerland   State of: Indiana
Declaration made before a Circuit Court
Residence now: Switzerland Co., IN
Volunteer or Drafted or Substitute: Enlisted
Rank(s): Private

237

Statement of service-

Period	Duration	Names of General and Field Officers
11 February 1776 or 77	2 yrs.	Capt. Thomas Walker's company, Col. George Matthew's 9th Virginia regiment
16 May 1778 or 1779	3 yrs.	Capt. Powell of the 13th Virginia regiment.

Battles: Germantown, White Marsh near Philadelphia (first term)
&
Date: 16 September 1820
County of: Switzerland   State of: Indiana
Declaration made before a Circuit Court.
Age: 67
Residence now: Switzerland Co., IN
Volunteer or Drafted or Substitute: Enlisted in Albemarle Co., VA
Rank(s): Private
Statement of service-

Period	Duration	Names of General and Field Officers
11 February 1776 or 77	2 yrs.	Capt. Thomas Walker's company, Col. George Matthew's 9th Virginia regiment
16 May 1778 or 1779	3 yrs.	Capt. Robert Barrett's company, Col. Francis Taylor's Virginia regiment

Battles: Germantown, White Marsh near Philadelphia (first term)
Discharge received: On the Schullyhill plains
Signed by: Col. William Russell
Statement is supported by – He received Pension Certificate No. 9470 under the Act of 18 March 1818.
Wife: Keziah   Humbles (Kimbles)   Wife's age: 50 years
Marriage date and place: 21 July 1798 in Louisa Co., VA (date from marriage bond)
Proof of marriage: Marriage bond in file.
&
Widow's Application for Pension
Date: 22 September 1848
County of: Switzerland   State of: Indiana
Declaration made before James Brown, Justice of the Peace
Widow's Residence: Switzerland Co., IN
Rank(s): Private
Statement is supported by – Evidence now on file with the Commissioner of Pensions
Soldier died 28 May 1831 in Switzerland Co., IN
Marriage date and place: 1 January 1799 (date from her statement)

<u>Switzerland County, Indiana Civil Order Book 4, 1820 – 1823;</u> pg. 96.
Sept. 1820
Kimbro Landers, Revolutionary soldier & U.S. pensioner---$789.25

Switzerland County, Indiana Probate Order Book 2, 1831-1837; pp. 10, 18, 27, 37, 46, 55, 65, 83, 87; and *Switzerland County, IN, Will Book Vol. 1, 3 Jan 1823-10 Nov 1847,* p. 33.
Abstract of will and/or administration for: Kimbrow Landers
State & county where recorded: Switzerland Co., Indiana
book/volume where recorded: Probate Order Book 2, 1831-1837.
Date Will written: 14 March 1831
Witnesses to Will: Josiah M. Doan & John F. Doan
Date entered in probate: 13 June 1831
Name(s) of executors: Keziah Laners and Aaron Sturgeon
Administration:
Date began- 13 June 1831
Name of administrator- Keziah Laners and Aaron Sturgeon
Bonded by and amount of bond: Edward Patton for $400.00.
Names of heirs and others mentioned in will and relationship if shown: Wife Keziah;
6 sons - John Landers & Kimbrow Landers who live in the State of Kentucky; Nathaniel Landers, William Landers, Benjamin Landers and Bradley Landers; son-in-law Aron Sturgeon.
Date of division & disbursement, or final return: settled 12 November 1832

Abstract of Final Payment Voucher; General Services Administration, Washington, DC
LAST FINAL PAYMENT VOUCHER RECEIVED FROM
THE GENERAL ACCOUNTING OFFICE
NAME   Landers, Kimbrow
AGENCY OF PAYMENT   Indiana
DATE OF ACT   1818
DATE OF PAYMENT   March 1, 1820
DATE OF DEATH
GENERAL SERVICES ADMINISTRATION
National Archives and Records Service   NA-286
GSA-WASH DC 54-4891   November 1953

Revolutionary War Records – Virginia; Virginia Army and Navy Forces with Bounty Land Warrants for Virginia Military District of Ohio, and Virginia Military Script, from Federal and State Archives; by Gaius Marcus Brumbaugh, M.D, M.s., Litt.D; Genealogical Publishing Co., Inc., Baltimore, 1995. p.251.
List of Non-Commissioned Officers and Soldiers of the Virginia Line on Continental Establishment, Whose Names Appear on the Army register and Who Have Not Received bounty Land, Richmond, 1835.
Landers, Kimbrough, Soldier, Inf.

Virginia Revolutionary Militia, A List of Non-Commissioned Officers and Soldiers of the Virginia Line on Continental Establishment, Whose names appear on the Army Register, and who have not received Bounty Land; Printed by Samuel Shepherd, Printer to the Commonwealth, Richmond, VA. 1835. p. 28.
Doc. No. 44.

Landers, Kimbrough   Soldier   Infantry

Historical Register of Virginians in the Revolution, Soldiers, Sailors, Marines, 1775-1783; John H. Gwathmey; The Dietz Press, Richmond, VA, 1938. p. 456.
Landers, Kimbrough, Inf.
Landes, Kimbrow (Landers, Kimbro) 9 CL.

Early Ohio Settlers, Purchasers of Land in Southwestern Ohio, 1800-1840; Compiled by Ellen T. Berry & David A. Berry; Genealogical Publishing Co., Inc., Baltimore, MD, 1986. p.185.

Purchaser	Year	Date	Residence	R – T - S
Landers, Kimbrow (B)	1814	Apr. 23	Kentucky	03-03-36

(B) Indiana Survey: Land lying west of a meridian drawn west of the Great Miami (known as the "Gore"). Switzerland, Dearborn, Franklin, Ohio, Union and Randolph Counties (all or only a part of each county) – all in Indiana.

Early Settlers of Indiana's "GORE" 1803-1820; Compiled and Edited by Shirley Keller Mikesell; Heritage Books, Inc., 1995. p. 188.
Switzerland County – Township 3, Range 3 W
Section 36 – Kimbraw Landey or Landers – 1814 – pg. 13.

Indiana Land Entries Vol. 1 Cincinnati District, 1801-1840; Margaret R. Waters; Originally Published Indianapolis 1948, Second Reprint 1979 by The Bookmark, P.O. Box 74, Knightstown, In 46148. p.72.
CINCINNNATI LAND DISTRICT – VOL. 1
Page 67. Twp. 3 N, Range 3 W of 1st Principle Meridian SWITZERLAND CO.
Kimbrow Landers NE ¼ - S36; 4-23-1814.
-- Note: The tract books for the land offices in Indiana are deposited in the office of the Auditor of State, Indianapolis. They and are in the custody of the State Land clerk. --

U.S. Department of Interior, Bureau of Land Management, General Land Office Records; Land Patent Search – accessed 27 June 2012.
LANDERS, KIMBRAW
Accession Nr. CV-0042-085; Document Type – Credit Volume Patent; State – Indiana; Issue Date – 12/8/1818; Cancelled – No
Land Office – Cincinnati; Authority April 24, 1820 Sale-Cash Entry (3 Stat. 566); Total Acres – 0.00
Land Descriptions: State – IN; Meridian – 1st PM; Twp-Rng – 003N-003W; Aliquots – NE1/4; Section – 36; County - Switzerland

1820 U.S. Census, Indiana, Switzerland, Jefferson, Series: M33 Roll:14 Pg: 267
Kimbrow Landres 45 and up; others in household 1 male 16-18, 1 female 45 and up.

The Pension List of 1820 [U.S. War Department]Reprinted with an Index; by Murtie June Clark; Genealogical Publishing Co., Inc., Baltimore, 1991.
Originally published 1820 as Letter from the Secretary of War. p. 656.

Names of the Revolutionary Pensioners which have been placed on the Roll of Indiana, under the Law of the 18th of March, 1818, from the passage thereof, to this day, inclusive, with the Rank they held, and the Lines in which they served, viz.

Names	Rank	Line
Kimbrow Landres [Note spelling]	private	Virginia

Revolutionary Soldiers of Switzerland County; Copied by Mary Hill, John Paul Chapter-Daughters of the American Revolution; January, 1958; http://www.ingenweb.org/inswitzerland/switzrevsoldiers.html- Viewed June 2012.
LANDERS, KIMBROW   Pension W.1632 Switzerland Co. Indiana
Born 1757, Albemarle Co. Virginia.
Enlisted 1777, 2 years 9th Virginia Regiment under Col. George Mathews.
Enlisted again under Capt. Powell of 13th Vir. Regiment for 3 years. Discharged at Winchester, Va. In Battle of White Marsh and Germantown.
Married 1) Unknown
Married 2) Keziah Humbles. July 21, 1793
Children: Martha m Aaron Sturgeon, Nathanial, William, Benjamin, John, Kimbrow, Bradley
Died May 26, 1831
Buried Cotton cemetery, Jefferson Twp.
Will Abstract – Switzerland County, Bk.1, p.35 - Kimbro Landers
Written Mar. 14, 1831; Recorded June 10, 1831
Wife Keziah
6 sons: Nathanial, William, Benjamin, John, Kimbro and Bradley. Son-in-law Aaron Sturgeon and wife Martha

Roster of Soldiers and Patriots of the American Revolution Buried in Indiana, Vol. I; compiled by Mrs. Roscoe C. O'Byrne.; Indiana Daughters of the American Revolution, 1981; p.227.
LANDERS, KIMBROW   Switzerland County
Born – 1757, Albemarle Co., Vir.
Service – Enlisted 1777, 2 yrs., 9th Vir. Regt. under Col. George Marthews. Enlisted again under Capt. Powell of 13th Vir. Regt. for 3 yrs. Discharged at Winchester, Vir. In Battles of White Marsh and Germantown.
Proof – Pension claim W. 1623.
Died – May 26, 1831. Buried Cotton Cemetery, Jefferson Twp.
Married - Second W. Keziah Humbles, m. July 21, 1798. Daughter, Martha, m. Aaron Sturgeon. Sons named in soldier's Will are Nathaniel, Benjamin, John, Kimbrow and Bradley.
Collected by Mrs. A. V. Vanner, Vevay, Indiana.

Abstract of Graves of Revolutionary Patriots (4 volumes); by Patricia Law Hatcher; Pioneer Heritage Press, Dallas, TX, 1987. Vol. 3, p. 4.
This is an abstract and an index to information reported to the Daughters of the American Revolution and published in their annual reports to the Smithsonian

Institution, printed as Senate Documents (1900-1974) and published annually in the DAR magazine (1978-1987).
Published 1972 (Senate Doc. 54)
LANDERS, Kimbrow   Cotton Cem, Jefferson Twp, Switzerland Co IN

The Vevay Reveille-Enterprise; Vol. 122, No. 37, 22 Sep 1935, p. 7, col. 1.
Roster of Revolutionary Soldiers Who Resided in Switzerland County
By Mrs. Effa M. Danner
Kimbrow Landers – Pension W1623. He enlisted February 11, 1777 under Capt. Thomas Walker of 9th Virginia Regiment, commanded by Col. George Mathews; served 2 years. Enlisted in 1779 under Capt. Powell of 13 Virginia Regiment for three years. Discharged at Winchester, Virginia. Battles of White Marsh near Philadelphia and Germantown.
Made application for pension May 19, 1818 before William Cotton, associate Judge. Attested by John Francis Dufour. Buried in Cotton cemetery on Indian Creek.

LANHAM, HENRY

Patriot: Henry Lanham
Birth: 28 May 1761 Prince Georges Co., MD
Married Spouse 1: 1801   Eleanor Milli X
            (b. 29 Feb 1765, d. 9 Oct 1837 Switzerland Co., IN)
Service state(s): MD
Service description: Capt. Patrick Sims 2nd Co.
Rank: Private
Proof of Service: Archives of Maryland, Vol. 18, pgs. 7, 8;
            Maryland Historical Mag. June 1919, pg. 110-120
Pension application No.: None
Residences: Prince Georges Co., MD; Indiana Territory; Switzerland Co., IN
Died: 20 Nov 1849 Switzerland Co., IN
Buried: McKay Cemetery, Braytown, Craig Twp., Switzerland Co., IN
DAR Ancestor No.: A069047

Muster Rolls and other records of service of Maryland Troops in the American Revolution; Archives of Maryland, reprinted with permission by Genealogical Publishing Co., Inc., Baltimore, 1972. p. 8.
Records of Maryland Troops in the Continental Service
2nd Company of Maryland Troops, 1776.

Rank	Date of Enlistment	Names	Remarks
Private	Feb. 3	Henry Lanham	present

Switzerland County Probate Orders 1849-52, pp. 26, 31; *Switzerland County, IN, Will Book Vol. 2, 6 Sept 1847-26 Jul 1859*, p. 26.; *Switzerland County, Indiana Probate Order Book 3, 12 Jan 1863-20 Sep 1867*; p. 431, 438.
Abstract of will or administration for: Henry Lanham
State & county where recorded: Switzerland Co., Indiana
State & county where will was made: Switzerland County
Book/volume where recorded: Will Book Vol. 2.
Date will made:
Date entered in probate: 7 Dec 1849
Name(s) of executors: Meshack Lanham
Administration:
Date began - 7 Dec 1849
Name of administrator – Isaac McKay
Date of death: affidavit of death presented 7 Dec 1849,
            date of death not specified.
Place of death: Switzerland County
Witnesses to Will: David Cain, Samuel Bray.
Witnesses/appraisers: Samuel Bray, witness to will.
Bonded by and amount of bond: Shadrack Lanham for $3200.00.
Names of heirs and others mentioned in will (also signed receipts of division of estate) and relationship if shown: Sons Shadrack H., John, Mashack; grandson Morris McKay; daughters Milly McKay, Cloe Sadler, Nancy McCarty; children

of deceased daughter Sarah McKay, children of Mary McKay deceased; grandson of Mary McKay whose mother was Bridjah Phillips.
Date of division/disbursement, or final return: Not in Probate Order 1849-52.
Final settlement of Estate, 25 Jun 1866. Isaac McKay, administrator. Order Book 3, 1863-1867.
Note: the will is in Switzerland Co., Book B, p. 259.

Indiana Territory, Switzerland Circuit Court Records, Order Book, October Term 1814 to March Term 1815. p.92. Henry Langham is listed in county records for the first time on 15 September 1820,as a juror.
Author's note: There are entries in this volume that are not within the range of dates shown on the binder cover.

Early Ohio Settlers, Purchasers of Land in Southwestern Ohio, 1800-1840; Compiled by Ellen T. Berry & David A. Berry; Genealogical Publishing Co., Inc., Baltimore, MD, 1986. p.185.

Purchaser	Year	Date	Residence	R – T - S
Lanham, Henry (B)	1814	Jan. 29	Jefferson Ind	04-02-36

(B) Indiana Survey: Land lying west of a meridian drawn west of the Great Miami (known as the "Gore"). Switzerland, Dearborn, Franklin, Ohio, Union and Randolph Counties (all or only a part of each county) – all in Indiana.

Early Settlers of Indiana's "GORE" 1803-1820; Compiled and Edited by Shirley Keller Mikesell; Heritage Books, Inc., 1995. p. 189.
Switzerland County – Township 2, Range 4W
Section 36 – Henry Lanham – 1814 – pg. 14.

Indiana Land Entries Vol. 1 Cincinnati District, 1801-1840; Margaret R. Waters; Originally Published Indianapolis 1948, Second Reprint 1979 by The Bookmark, P.O. Box 74, Knightstown, In 46148. p.79.CINCINNNATI LAND DISTRICT – VOL. 1
Page 76. Twp. 1 N, Range 4 W of 1st Principle Meridian SWITZERLAND CO.
Henry Lanham NE ¼ - S36; 1-20-1814.
-- Note: The tract books for the land offices in Indiana are deposited in the office of the Auditor of State, Indianapolis. They and are in the custody of the State Land clerk. --

U.S. Department of Interior, Bureau of Land Management, General Land Office Records; Land Patent Search – accessed 27 June 2012.
LANHAM, HENRY
Accession Nr. CV-0033-210; Document Type – Credit Volume Patent; State – Indiana; Issue Date – 2/21/1817; Cancelled – No
Land Office – Cincinnati; Authority – April 24, 1820 Sale-Cash Entry (3 Stat. 566); Total Acres – 0.00
Land Descriptions: State – IN; Meridian – 1st PM; Twp-Rng – 002N-004W; Aliquots – NE1/4; County - Switzerland

1820 U.S. Census, Indiana, Switzerland, Craig, Series: M33 Roll: 14 Page: 248
Henry Lanham 45 and up; others in household 1 male under 10, 1 male 10=16, 1 female 10-16, 1 female 16-26,   1 female 45 and up.

Revolutionary Soldiers of Switzerland County; Copied by Mary Hill, John Paul Chapter-Daughters of the American Revolution; January, 1958; http://www.ingenweb.org/inswitzerland/switzrevsoldiers.html- Viewed June 2012.
LANHAM, HENRY
Born May 28, 1761, Prince Georges Co. Maryland.
Enlisted Feb. 3, 1776
Served in 2d company of Maryland troops in Battle of Long Island, 1776.
Proof: Archives of Maryland, Maryland Troops in Revolution, pg. 8.
Maryland Historical Mag. June 1919, pg. 110-120
Family Bible and Will in Switz. Co. Ind.
Married 1) Eleanor Howell (b. 1765)
Children: (other records have conflicting information about the children) Meshack 1811 - 1883 m Susanna Bray; Shadrick; Thomas b. 23 Feb 1792; Mary b. 1800 m Abisha McKay; Chloe b. 1795 m a Saddler; Sarah b. 1805 m Zachariah McKay; Milley m a McKay; Nancy m a McCarty
Married Millia _____
Died 20 Nov 1849, Switzerland Co.
Buried McKay Cemetery, Braytown, Switzerland Co.
Inscription on stone "Henry Lanham, May 28, 1761 - Nov. 20, 1849"

Roster of Soldiers and Patriots of the American Revolution Buried in Indiana, Vol. II; 1966; p. 64.
LANHAM, HENRY   Switzerland County
Born – MAY 28, 1761, Prince George Co., Md.
Service – Enlisted Feb. 3, 1776, 2nd Co., Md. Troops. In the Battle of Long Island, 1776.
Proof – Md. Archives; "Md. Troops in the Revolution", p. 8; Md. Hist. Mag., v. 14, p. 117; Waters' Supp., p. 62.
Died – Nov. 20, 1849. Bur. In McKay Cem., Braytown, Switzerland Co., Ind. Stone.
Married – Eleanor Howell, b. 1765. Ch. Shadrack; Thomas, b. Feb. 23, 1792, d. April 22, 1864, m. Feb. 28, 1818, Elizabeth Peters, b. June 12, 1802, d. Feb. 9, 1892; John; Chloe, b. 1795, m. ____ Sadler; Mary, b. 1800, m. Abisha McKay; Sarah, m. Zachariah McKay; Meshack, b. 1811, m. Susanna Bray; Milley, m. ____ McKay; Nancy, m. ____ McCarthy.
By Mrs. Herbert R. Hill, DAR No. 318587, R.R. 1, Fountaintown, Ind. 46130.

Revolutionary Soldiers Buried in Indiana A Supplement; 485 Names Not Listed in the Roster of Soldiers and Patriots of the American Revolution Buried in Indiana (1938) nor in Revolutionary Soldiers Buried in Indiana (1949); Margaret E. Waters; Indianapolis, 1954. p. 62.
LANHAM, HENRY   Switzerland
b. 5-28-1761, Prince Charles Co., Md.; d. 11-20-1849; bur. on McKay Cem., Braytown, Ind.;

m. 6-28-1818, Switzerland Co., Ind., Elizabeth Peters, b. 6-12-1802, Va.; d. 2-9-1892, Rush Co., Ind.
ch: John; Chloe b. 1795, m. Mr. Sadler; Mary b. 1800, m. Abisha McKay; Sarah, m. Zachariah McKay; Meshack b. 1811, m. Susanna Bray; Milley, m. Mr. McKay; Nancy, m. Mr. McCarthy.
Service: enl. 2-3-1776, 2nd Co., Md. Troops; batt. of Long Island, 1776.
REF: "Md. Arch.—Md. Troops in the Rev.", p. 8; "Md. Hist. Mag.", v. 14, p. 117; Miss Mary Hill, Madison, Ind.

Switzerland County Indiana Cemetery Inscriptions 1817-1985; Wanda L. Morford; Cincinnati, Ohio, 1986, p. 76.
McKay Cemetery, Craig Twp., Switzerland Co., IN
Lanham   Henry, b. May 28, 1761 d, Nov. 20, 1849
                Milla, wife of Henry, b. ----, broken, reset, dated illegible

Abstract of Graves of Revolutionary Patriots (4 volumes); by Patricia Law Hatcher; Pioneer Heritage Press, Dallas, TX, 1987. Vol. 3, p. 7.
This is an abstract and an index to information reported to the Daughters of the American Revolution and published in their annual reports to the Smithsonian Institution, printed as Senate Documents (1900-1974) and published annually in the DAR magazine (1978-1987).
Published 1972 (Senate Doc. 54)
LANHAM, Henry   McKay Cem, Braytown, Switzerland Co IN

McKay Cemetery, Craig Twp., Switzerland Co., IN
Tombstone inscription –

HENRY LANHAM
BORN
May 28th,1761
DIED
Nov 20th, 1849

LEAP, JOHN W.

Patriot: John W. Leap
Birth: 15 Apr 1745 Near Manheim on Rhine River
Married Spouse 1: 1768 Bucks Co., PA Margaret Crow
Married Spouse 2: Lancaster Co., PA Sarah Barbara Deleow (DeLeon)
Service state(s): PA
Service description: 4th Regiment PA Militia, Capt. John Jameson,
          Col. Arch'd McIllroy.
Rank: Private
Proof of Service: Pension application R6225
Pension application No.: R6225
Residences: Bucks Co., PA; Lancaster Co., PA; Greene Co., IN; Switzerland Co., IN, Boone Co., IN
Died: 16 Sep 1845
Buried: Mount Tabor Cemetery, Fayette, Boone Co., IN
DAR Ancestor No.: None

Switzerland County, Indiana Complete Records, Circuit Court, Vol. ?, Sep 3, 1821-Apr 18, 1827; p. 365.;*Switzerland County, Indiana Probate Record Book Vol. A, Mar 1827-Nov 1834;* p. 269.;*Pension Application Abstracted from National Archives microfilm Series 805, Roll 518, File R6225.*

Pension abstract for – John Leap   Service state(s): Pennsylvania
Date: 20 Apr 1824
County of: Switzerland   State of: Indiana
Declaration made before a Circuit Court.
Schedule of property valued at $62.50, and declaration of service.
Age: near 74 years
Residence when he entered service: State of Pennsylvania
Residence now: Switzerland Co., IN
Volunteer or Drafted or Substitute: Enlisted
Rank(s): Not stated
Statement of service-

Period	Duration	Names of General and Field Officers
15 May 1775	2 yrs	Capt. Valentine Upp, Col. Daniel Clymer, PA Line, Continental est.; transferred to company commanded by Capt. Church, same company.
25 May 1777	2 yrs	Capt. Jacob Bowers, Col. Lutz, PA Line, Cont. est.
5 Jan 1780	18 mos	Capt. John Jameson, Col. McIlroy, PA Line, Cont.
1781	12 mos	Capt. McFeely, Col. David Archy, PA Line, Cont.

Battles: Brandywine, Germantown, Monmouth
Discharge received: (2nd tour) Morristown, NJ, 27 May 1779;
                (3rd tour) Princeton, NJ, 17 Jul 1781; (4th tour) Princeton,

NH (no date stated).
Statement is supported by –
Documentary proof: None in his possession
Occupation: Farmer on rented land, am very infirm.
Wife: Barbara   Wife's age: abt. 48 yrs.
Names and ages of children: Polly, age 15; David, age 11; daughter Jurtia, age 13 yrs; Chancey, age 9 yrs.; Jackson, age 6 yrs.; Sarah, age 3 yrs.
&
Date: 13 August 1832
County of: Switzerland   State of: Indiana
Declaration made in Open Court
Age: 87   Record of age: No record in this country
Where and year born: Near Manheim on the river Rhine on 15 April 1745
Residence when he entered service: Springfield Twp., Bucks Co., Penn.
Residence(s) since the war: 6 years in New Jersey, 29 or 30 in Pennsylvania,
                    last 16 in Indiana.
Residence now: Switzerland Co., IN
Volunteer or Drafted or Substitute: Enlisted voluntarily
Rank(s): Private
Statement of service-

Period	Duration	Names of General and Field Officers
Sep 1775	Jan 1778	4th Regiment Pennsylvania Militia Capt. John Jameson, Col. Arch'd McIllroy.

Battles: Staten Island, crossed the Delaware with Gen. Washington,
          Trenton, Princeton.
Discharge received: Battle Hill near Morristown, NJ
Signed by: Col. McIllroy
What became of it?: Lost it
Statement is supported by –
Evidence: Traditionary evidence
Person now living who can testify to service: Col. John F. Siebert, John D. Miranda, John R. Dufour, and one hundred others.
Clergyman: John Morrill
Note: Soldiers application was Rejected because he failed to prove service of six months.
&
Widow's Application for Pension
Widow's name: Barbara Leap
Date: 24 May 1853
County of: Boone   State of: Indiana
Declaration made before a Justice of the Peace
Widow's residence: Boone Co., IN
No family information in application

Switzerland County, Indiana, Civil Order Book - Vol.5, Feb 10, 1823 - Jun 21, 1826, p.180.

18 Oct 1826 - John Leap a Revolutionary Soldier and United States Pensioner in open court at this present Month, before the Judges of said Court filed his Schedule of Property and made Declaration and took the oath required by a late act of Congress relative to pensioners _which are ordered to be recorded and it is ordered to be Certified that the property contained in the said Schedule is valued by the court to be worth Sixty Six Dollars and twenty five cents.

Switzerland County, Indiana Probate Order Book 2, 1831-1837; p. 70.
13 August 1832
In the matter of   } An applicant for a Pension under the act of
John Leap   } Congress of June 7 AD 1832.
      And this day Court, do hereby declare their opinion after the investigation of the matter, and after putting the interrogations prescribed by the war department, that the above named John Leap was a Revolutionary Soldier and Served as he States, And the Court further Certifies that it appears to them that John Morrill who has signed the preceding Certificate is a Clergyman resident in Switzerland County and State of Indiana, and that Jean D. Moreand who also Signed the Same is a resident in Switzerland County and State of Indiana, and is a credible person, and their statement is entitled to Credit.

Pennsylvania Archives, Series 6, Vol. III; p. 126.
Militia Rolls 1783-1790
Privates 5th Class – John Leap

Pennsylvania Archives, Series 5, Vol. V; p. 604.
Muster Rolls Relating to the Associators and Militia of the County of Chester
Privates 6th Class – John Leap

Pennsylvania Archives, Series 5, Vol. V, p 621.
Muster Rolls Relating to the Associators and Militia of the County of Chester
Privates – 6th Class – John Leap

Pennsylvania Archives, Series 5, Vol. V, p. 877.
Muster Rolls Relating to the Associators and Militia of the County of Chester
Privates – 5th Class – John Leap

Pennsylvania Archives, Series 3, Volume XX, p. 247.
Transcript of Supply Rates for the County of Cumberland, for the Year 1779. »
Page 247

	Acres	Horses	Cattle	Negroes
John Leap -		2	2	-

Pennsylvania Archives, Series 5, Vol. V, p. 880
Muster Rolls Relating to the Associators and Militia of the County of Chester.
Privates 5th Class – John Leap

Indiana Territory, Switzerland Circuit Court Records, Order Book, October Term 1814 to March Term 1815. p.39.
He is listed in county records as a member of the Grand Jury at the first court held in the county, on 8 March 1814.

Rejected or Suspended Applications for Revolutionary War Pensions; Reprinted for Clearfield Company Inc. by Genealogical Publishing Co., Inc., Baltimore, MD, 1998. p.408.
A list of the names of persons residing in Indiana who have applied for pensions under the act of June 7, 1832, whose claims have been rejected; prepared in conformity with the resolution of the Senate of the United States of September 16, 1850.

Names	Residence	Reasons for rejection
LEAP, JOHN	Printer's Retreat, Switzerland	He did not serve six months

1850 U.S. Census, Indiana, Boone, 7-Dist, Series: M432 Roll: 136 Page: 138, Family No. 1112.
Barbary Leap, Age 69, Born PA

Revolutionary Soldiers of Switzerland County; Copied by Mary Hill, John Paul Chapter-Daughters of the American Revolution; January, 1958; http://www.ingenweb.org/inswitzerland/switzrevsoldiers.html- Viewed June, 2012.
LEAP, JOHN W.
Probate bk. A. pg. 70: Swit. Co. Ind. John Leap, revolutionary soldier.
Signed by John Morrill, clergyman and Jean D. Moreod.

Roster of Soldiers and Patriots of the American Revolution Buried in Indiana, Vol. I; compiled by Mrs. Roscoe C. O'Byrne.; Indiana Daughters of the American Revolution, 1981; p.231-232.
LEAP, JOHN   Boone County
Born – 1735, Germany.
Service – Served under Capt. Jameson of 4th Regt. Penn. Militia, Col. Arch. McIlroy, from Sept., 1775, to Jan. 1778, as private. Enlisted while living in Springfield Twp., Bucks Co., Penn. Discharged at Morristown, N. J.
Proof – R. 6225
Died - Sept. 16, 1845.
Buried Mountabor Cemetery, Fayette, Indiana. Government marker.
Married – Barbara Dirth Leap. Ch. David, m. Frances Shandy; Isaac C., m. Sarah Wollen; Andrew J.
Collected by Mrs. J. H. Duchemin, Sheridan, Indiana, and Mrs. Sarah Leap Action, Seattle, Washington.

Roster of Soldiers and Patriots of the American Revolution Buried in Indiana, Vol. III; 1980; p.66.
LEAP, JOHN   Roster I, pp. 231-232   Boone County
Additional data or corrections.

Proof – Probate Court Records, Switzerland Co., Ind. For 1832 and Civil Order Books A and D gives further data on John Leap's service.
Died - 1845 Boone Co., Ind. Buried there.
Married – After the Rev. War, he moved to Switzerland Co., Ind. M. (1) 1814 Margaret Crow and had three sons and one dau. W. d. (2) Sarah Barbara DeLeon. Moved to Boone Co., Ind.
Children – (As given in Switzerland Co. Records) John W.; Samuel; Gabiel; Polly; Sarah. Marriage records show Polly Leap m. July 28, 1824 Ensley Shaddy and Samuel Leap m. May 1, 1821 Hannah Gyles.
By Mrs. A. G. Charlton, 301 Sunnyside Avenue, Aurora, Indiana 47001.

Abstract of Graves of Revolutionary Patriots (4 volumes); by Patricia Law Hatcher; Pioneer Heritage Press, Dallas, TX, 1987. Vol. 3, p. 12.
This is an abstract and an index to information reported to the Daughters of the American Revolution and published in their annual reports to the Smithsonian Institution, printed as Senate Documents (1900-1974) and published annually in the DAR magazine (1978-1987).
Published 1924, Serial set 8399, Volume 7; . Published 1972 (Senate Doc. 54).
LEAP, John   Mountabor Cem, nr Fayette, Boone Co IN

Mountabor Cemetery, Fayette, IN
Tombstone inscription -
                    Inscription on top of stone -
                    John Leap Revolutionary Soldier
Front of stone –   1776

The Vevay Reveille- Enterprise; Vol. 122, No. 37, 22 Sep 1935, p. 7, col. 1.
Roster of Revolutionary Soldiers Who Resided in Switzerland County
By Mrs. Effa M. Danner
John W. Leap – was born in Germany in 1733. After the war he moved to Switzerland County in 1814 and resided here a number of years. He married Margaret Crow. Children, three sons and one daughter. She died and he married Sarah Barbara DeLeon. He moved to Boone County, Indiana. Died in 1845 and is buried at Mt. Tabor cemetery.
His children, Gabriel, John W., Samuel, Polly and Sarah.
Probate Court, Switzerland County, p. 89, June 7, 1832 John Leap applied for pension; vouchers, Rev. John Merrill and Jean D. Morerod.
The history of the Leap family has been written by Lu A. Riley and given to the Vevay Library.
Military service recorded, Vevay, June 1832, Civil Order Book. John Leap, age 87. He was a private in the 4th Regiment of Pa., militia under Capt. John Janurm, Col. Archibald McIlroy 1775-1778. He was in the battle of Staten Island and captured some Hessians, p. 270, Book A.
Book D, p. 365.

Indianapolis Star, Nov. 8, 1931
Newspaper article –

John W. Leap born on Rhine River, Germany, came to America in 1757: born in 1733; settled near families of Washington & Clark. Tradition that he knew George Rogers Clark as a child. He joined the New York militia at outbreak of Revolution and was a quartermaster general. He married before the war but name of wife not shown. After the war they came to Switzerland County, Indiana. Before this they moved to Lancaster Co. Pa. where they lived till 1796. Later came to Switz. Co. Ind. They went back to Virginia and then returned to Switz. Co. probably with 2d wife: Children of 1st marriage were; Gabriel b 1771, died 1866 in Martinsville, W. Va. m Jennie Courtney; John W. m Mahala Wise, died Oct. 1866; Katie m _____ Ferby; Samuel W. b 1795, d Vevay, Ind. 1884 m Henrietta Guile, b 1794.

LEE, JOHN

Patriot: John Lee
Birth: 20 Jul 1760   Flemington, Hunterdon Co., NJ
Married Spouse 1: 15 Mar 1780 Morris Co., NJ   Margaret [possibly Thomas]
(b. 1762 d. prob. 26 Jun 1845)
Service state(s): NJ
Service description: 3rd Regt. Militia, Capts. Maxwell, Chamber
Rank: Private
Proof of Service: Pension application R6254
Pension application No.: R6254
Residences: Flemington, Hunterdon Co., NJ; Indiana Territory;
Switzerland Co., IN; Jefferson Co., IN
Died: 17 Sep 1837 Milton Twp., Jefferson Co., IN
Buried: Unknown – poss. Lee Graveyard, Canaan, Jefferson Co., IN
DAR Ancestor No.: A106214

Pension Application Abstracted from National Archives microfilm Series 805, Roll 520, File R6254
Abstracted pension application – Margaret Lee, widow of John Lee, applied for Widow's Pension in Switzerland Co., IN, on 26 June 1845. Margaret Lee a resident of Cotton Twp., aged eighty-three for the 'act of Congress, July 7, 1838, for half-pay and pensions to certain widows. By reason of old age and consequent loss of memory she cannot swear positively as to the service of her husband, but will according to the best of her recollection narrate what her said husband, and others of the family said upon the subject.
John Lee served various times as a private soldier in the companies of New Jersey militia, commanded by Capt. John Maxwell of Hunterdon Co., Capt. Chambers, in Essex Co.,
and other captains, names not recollected. Served in Col. David Chambers regiment or battalion. Was in service the years 1776, 1777, 1778, 1779, 1780 and 1781. Was in the battles at Vannesto Mills (a John Coleman was killed at Van Host's Mills); Staten Island, Trenton, Princeton, Monmouth and Red Banks. Leiman Deasky [see record for Leaman Deisky] was a private in same companies with him. John Read was a ensign, James Stout and Robert Maxwell wee lieutenants over said John Lee. The battle of Monmouth was a Sunday morning in June; the day was exceptionally warm and sultry – many of the men fainted and died from thirst and heat. Gen. Lee commanded, in the first part of the day; tho Washington opposed the command, and the fighting continued till near nightfall: the American army encamped on the battle ground intending to continue the battle next day, but the enemy retreated in the night leaving their dead and wounded behind them. At various times during the service of said John Lee, David Barnes, Enos Campbell, Henry Dow, James Ivy, Stephen Price, James Welch and William Wright, served as private soldiers.
She further declares that when off duty, under his captain, drove a team for David Cox; he hauled generally from Trenton to Morristown and various other places where American troops were stationed.

Joseph Lee, brother of said John, served with said John Lee the greater part of the time. The widow of Joseph (Eleanor Lee) is now a pensioner of the United States on the Indiana roll.

John Lee resided in the county of Morris, New Jersey, and was generally a volunteer, and done all his service in his native state. She has no documentary evidence in support of her claim and knows of no person, living, by which she can prove the same.

That towards the close of 1776 New Jersey was completely overrun by the enemy – the enemy filling every town and farm house with their hateful troops – the behavior of the Hessians towards the country people was barbarous, in the extreme: they burnt houses, destroyed the furniture, killed the stock and abused the females; and spread consternation and ruin all along their route. Then it was that every Jersey man went cheerfully to avenge the wrong done.

Margaret Lee further declares that she was married to John Lee in Morris County, State of New Jersey on the fifteenth day of March, Seventeen hundred and Eighty, by Justice Emmons – that she believes that no official records of marriages were kept in that state.

Her children, by John Lee, were born and named as follows: Gershom Lee, born Feb. 11, 1781, her daughter Mary, Dec. 9, 1783, Rebecca Feb. 10, 1787, Nathan October 15, 1789, John April 15, 1792, James May 12, 1796, Sarah Feb. 24, 1799, Nancy on the 4th day of August 1801, and her son Nathaniel on the 16th day of May, 1804.

Her husband died on the seventeenth day of September, Eighteen hundred and thirty seven. She has remained a widow.

John Lee was born in Flemingtown, Jersey on the 20th day of July AD 1760. She was married to him before he left the service.

She is not able to attend personally in open court, which is at a distance from her residence, by reason of bodily infirmity incident to old age. Witnessed by David Cain, Nancy Lee. David Cain, Associate Judge.

Abstract of Final Payment Voucher; General Services Administration, Washington, DC

LAST FINAL PAYMENT VOUCHER RECEIVED FROM THE GENERAL ACCOUNTING OFFICE

NAME	Lee (Alias SEE), John
AGENCY OF PAYMENT	Indiana
DATE OF ACT	1832
DATE OF PAYMENT	Jan 1837
DATE OF DEATH	
GENERAL SERVICES ADMINISTRATION	
National Archives and Records Service	NA-286
GSA-WASH DC 54-4891	November 1953

Official Register of the Officers and Men of New Jersey in the Revolutionary War; Compiled Under Orders of His Excellency Theodore F. Randolph, Governor; by William S. Stryker, Adjutant General, Printed by the Authority of

the Legislature; Wm. T. Nicholson & Co., Printers, Trenton, NJ, 1872, Facsimile Reprint by Heritage Books, Inc., Bowie, MD, 1993; p. 663.
Lee, John. Captain Maxwell's Company, Second Regiment, Hunterdon.

<u>Register of Certificates Issued by John Pierce, Esquire, Paymaster General and Commissioner of Army Accounts for the United States, to Officers and Soldiers of the Continental Army Under Act of July 4, 1783</u>; *Originally Published as Senate Documents, Vol.9, No. 988, 63rd Congress, 3d Session, Washington, 1915; Seventeenth report of the National Society of the Daughters of the American Revolution; Genealogical Publishing Co., Inc, Baltimore, MD, 1984. p. 305.*
Men listed in this volume with the same name.

No. of Certificate	To whom issued	Amount
5003	Lee, John	13.30
6950	Lee, John	12.24
7926	Lee, John	66.60
36070	Lee, John	76.18
52558	Lee, John	1.27
54108	Lee, John	54.60
81517	Lee, John	80.00
82288	Lee, John	43.30
85726	Lee, John	80.00
89561	Lee, John	80.00
90831	Lee, John	43.30
91474	Lee, John	80.00
93142	Lee, John	80.00

<u>Early Ohio Settlers, Purchasers of Land in Southwestern Ohio, 1800-1840</u>; *Compiled by Ellen T. Berry & David A. Berry; Genealogical Publishing Co., Inc., Baltimore, MD, 1986. p.188.*

Purchaser	Year	Date	Residence	R – T - S
Lee, John (B)	1806	Feb.24	Hamilton	02-13-36

(B) Indiana Survey: Land lying west of a meridian drawn west of the Great Miami (known as the "Gore"). Switzerland, Dearborn, Franklin, Ohio, Union and Randolph Counties (all or only a part of each county) – all in Indiana.

<u>U.S. Department of Interior, Bureau of Land Management, General Land Office Records: Land Patent Search</u> – *accessed 27 June 2012.*
LEE, JOHN
Accession Nr. CV-0038-413; Document Type – Credit Volume Patent; State – Indiana; Issue Date – 4/2/1818; Cancelled – No
Land Office – Jeffersonville; Authority – April 23, 1820 Sale-Cash Entry (3 Stat. 566); Total Acres – 0.00
Land Descriptions: State – IN; Meridian – 2nd PM; Twp-Rng – 004N-012E; Aliquots – NW1/4; Section – 30; County – Jefferson

Census of Indiana Territory for 1807; Indiana Historical Society, 1980. p. 24.
A list of free males above the age of twenty one in Dearborn County in March 1807 ~~
307   John Lee
&
Census of Indiana Territory for 1807; Indiana Historical Society, 1980. p. 27.
A list of free males above the age of twenty one in Dearborn County in March 1807 ~~
595   John Lee

Rejected or Suspended Applications for Revolutionary War Pensions; Reprinted for Clearfield Company Inc. by Genealogical Publishing Co., Inc., Baltimore, MD, 1998, p. 419.
A list of the names of persons residing in Indiana who have applied for pensions under the act of July 7, 1838, whose claims have been suspended; prepared in conformity with the resolution of the Senate of the United States of September 16, 1850.

Names	Residence	Reasons for rejection
LEE, MARGARET, widow of John	Vevay, Switzerland	Not proved so far as for six months' service.

1840 U.S. Census, Indiana, Jefferson, Milton, Series: M704 Roll: 83 Page: 167.
Margaret Lee, Age 90-100

Revolutionary Soldiers Buried in Indiana A Supplement; 485 Names Not Listed in the Roster of Soldiers and Patriots of the American Revolution Buried in Indiana (1938) nor in Revolutionary Soldiers Buried in Indiana (1949); Margaret E. Waters; Indianapolis, 1954. p. 64.
LEE, JOHN   Jefferson
(Not to be confused with John Lee, a.k.a. See, of Henry Co., Ind.)
"Roster" p. 232, wid. Margaret, Pens. S.17538. b. 7-20-1760, Flemington, N.J.; d. 9-17-1837; m. 3-15-1780, Morris Co., N.J., Margaret -----, b. ca. 1762; chn. Gershom, b. 2-11-1781, m. Elizabeth Ford (dau. of Rev. sold., Warner Ford); Mary, b. 12-8-1783; Rebecca, b. 2-10-1787; Nathan, b. 10-15-1789; John b. 4-15-1792; James b. 5-12-1796; Sarah b. 2-24-1799; Nancy b. 8-4-1801; Nathaniel b. 5-16-1804. Wid's pens. appl. 6-26-1845, ae. 83, Milton Twp., Switzerland Co., Ind. (error: Milton Twp. Is in Jefferson Co., Ind. MRW); her husb. res. in Morris Co., N.J.; fellow solds. In his Comp. were: David Barnes, Enos Campbell, Henry Dow, James Joy, Stephen Price, James Welch, William Wright, and sold's. bro., Joseph Lee, decd. ("Roster" p. 232) whose wid., Eleanor Lee is now a pensr. In Decatur Co., Ind.
Affid. 6-26-1845, Switzerland Co., Ind. of Samuel Bellamy, M.E. clergyman, res. of Craig Twp., Switzerland Co., Ind., and near line dividing Switzerland Co. from Jefferson Co., Ind.; that he knew John Lee & wife well in Jefferson Co., Ind., ca. 14 yr. before John died; liv. within 8 mi. of them for 26 yr. till they mov. onto the waters of Indian-Kentucky (in Jefferson Co., MRW) ca. 3 mi. from where deponent now lives. Affid. of Thomas Mounts ("Roster" p. 262) ae. 82; that he knew John & Margaret Lee since they res. at mouth of Kentucky River since

1790. Same from Robert Poindexter, ae. 78; that he knew them over 50 yr. ago in Woodford Co., Ky; Gallatin Co., Ky; that all 9 chn. Were b. in Gallatin Co., Ky. (I question this; MRW); that wid. Margaret now res. on waters of Indian-Kentucky in Jefferson Co., Ind. Service: N.J. Mil., 1776-1781, incl.; Capt. Maxwell, Hunterdon Co., ; Capt. Chambers, Essex Co. REF: Pens. R.6254 N.J.; Susp. Pens. List (1852) p. 419- - not proved so far for 6 mo. service; Miss Mary Hill, Madison, Ind.; Miss Rose Anne Howe, Chicago, Ill.

Revolutionary Soldiers Buried in Indiana A Supplement; 485 Names Not Listed in the Roster of Soldiers and Patriots of the American Revolution Buried in Indiana (1938) nor in Revolutionary Soldiers Buried in Indiana (1949); Margaret E. Waters; Indianapolis, 1954. p. 64.

Lee, John   Jefferson
(Not to be confused with John Lee, a.k.a. See, of Henry Co., Ind., "Roster" p. 232, wid. Margaret, Pens. S.17538).
b. 7-20-1760, Flemington, N.J.; d. 9-7-1837; m. 3-15-1780, Morris Co., N.J., Margaret ...., b. ca. 1762; chn.: Gershom, b. 2-11-1781; m. Elizabeth Ford (dau. of Rev. sold., Warner Ford); Mary, b. 12-8-1783; Rebecca, b. 2-10-1787; Nathan, b. 10-15-1789; John, b. 4-15-1792; James b. 5-12-1796; Sarah b. 2-24-1799; Nancy b. 8-4-1801; Nathaniel B. 5-16-1804. Wid,'s pens. appl. 6-26-1845, ae. 83, Milton Twp., Switzerland Co., Ind. (error: Milton Twp. is in Jefferson Co., Ind. MRW); her husb. res. in Morris Co., N.J.; fellow sold. in his Comp. were: David Barnes, Enos Campbell, Henry Dow, James Joy, Stephen Price, James Welch, William Wright, and sold.'s bro., Joseph Lee, decd. ("Roster", p. 232) whose wid., Eleanor Lee is now a pensr. In Decatur Co., Ind. Affid. 6-26-1845, Switzerland Co., Ind. of Samuel Bellamy, M.E. clergyman, res. of Craig Twp., Switzerland Co., and near line dividing Switzerland Co., from Jefferson Co., Ind.; that he knew John Lee & wife well in Jefferson Co., Ind., ca. 14 yr. before John died; liv. within 8 mi. of them for 26 yr. till they mov. onto the waters of Indian-Kentucky (In Jefferson Co., MRW) ca. 3 mi. from where deponent now lives. Affid. of Thomas Mounts ("Roster" p. 262) ae. 82; that he knew John & Margaret Lee since they res. at mouth of Kentucky River since 1790. Same from Robert Poindexter, ae. 78; that he knew them over 50 yr. ago in Woodford Co. Ky.; Gallatin Co., Ky.; that all 9 chn. were b. in Gallatin Co., Ky. (I question this; MRW); that wid. Margaret now res. on waters of Indian-Kentucky in Jefferson Co., Ind. Service: J.J. Mil., 1776-1781, incl.: Capt. John Maxwell, Hunterdon Co.; Capt. Chambers, Essex Co. REF: Pens. R6254 N.J.; Susp. Pens. List (1852) p. 419—not proved so far for 6 mo. service; Miss Mary Hill, Madison, Ind.; Miss Rose Anne Howe, Chicago, Ill.

LEVI, ISAAC

Patriot: Isaac Levi
Birth: 1 Feb 1749 Hungary
Married Spouse 1: X X
Married Spouse 2: XX
Married Spouse 3: Mrs. Mary Tucker   (b. 1801/1803, d. 14 Oct 1853, IN)
Service state(s): VA
Service description: Capt. Patterson, VA Militia
Rank: Private
Proof of Service: Pension application W773
Pension application No.: W773
Residences: Lexington, Kentucky Co., VA (enlisted); Switzerland Co., IN; Ripley Co., IN
Died: 21 Sep 1850 Delaware Twp., Ripley Co., IN
Buried: Stone at Myers Cemetery, near Osgood, Ripley Co., IN – Bronze tablet at Versailles Court House - Stone in Perseverance Cemetery says buried Levi Cemetery.
DAR Ancestor No.: A069676
Child: Abraham Levi (b. abt. 1787 d. 1830 Ripley Co., IN) Son of wife #1

Pension Application Abstracted from National Archives microfilm Series 805, Roll 524, File W773.
Pension abstract for – Isaac Levi   Service state(s): Virginia
Date: 18 September 1832
County of: Switzerland   State of: Indiana
Declaration made before a Circuit Court.
Recorded in Book F, pg. 87.
Age: 82   Record of age: No record – was 17 years old when he came to America.
Where and year born: In Hungary in February 1749
Residence when he entered service: Lexington, Virginia (now Kentucky)
Residence(s) since the war: Lived in Lexington and continued in KY for about 40 years, lived in Ohio for 5 or 6 years, in Indiana the balance of time.
Residence now: Switzerland Co., IN
Volunteer or Drafted or Substitute: Enlisted
Rank(s): Private
Statement of service-

Period	Duration	Names of General and Field Officers
June 1780	Upwards of 2 years	Company of Virginia Militia commanded by Capt. Robert Patterson

Battles: Several battles with the Indians in Ohio and Indiana Territory
Discharge received: at the Falls of the Ohio
Signed by: Gen. Clark
What became of it?: Lost it.
Statement is supported by – Has none, and know of no body now living who can prove same.
Person now living who can testify to service: Andrew C. Forbes, Joseph Hayes, Thomas Mounts.

Clergyman: John Pavy
Persons in neighborhood who certify character: Joseph Hayes
&
Mary Levi, late Mary Tucker, Application for Pension
She is the Widow of John Tucker, a pensioner who was a resident of Ripley Co., IN. He drew his pension at the agency in Madison, IN.
Date: 26 March 1853
County of: Jefferson   State of: Indiana
Declaration made before a Judge of the Circuit Court
Widow's age: 50 years
Widow's residence: Jefferson Co., IN
Persons in neighborhood who certify character:
Soldier, John Tucker, died 14 November 1840 in Ripley Co., IN
Marriage date and place: to John Tucker in Scott Co., KY in February 1833.
Reference made to 2 children of John & Mary Tucker.
&
Marriage record for (Mrs.) Polly (aka Mary) Tucker to Isaac Levi, Sr. is in this pension file.
Marriage date and place: 14 November 1841 at Versailles, Ripley Co., IN by R. B. Mitchell, J.P.
In the same year the couple moved to Ripley Co., IN
Soldier, Isaac Levi, died 21 September 1850 in Ripley Co., IN
She was allowed pension on account of the service of her husband Isaac Levi.
Application executed 26 March 1853
Mary (Polly) Levi died 14 October 1853.
She left several children at her death "some of which are not of age".

Switzerland County, Indiana Civil Order Book Vol., A, Oct. 19, 1829-April 16, 1837, p. 178.
In the matter of Robert Ricketts, Thomas Mounts, Ebenezer Humphrey, Daniel Heath, William Coy and Isaac Levi, An application to obtain a pension.
   Personally appeared in open Court before the Switzerland Circuit Court now Sitting The above named applicants who being first duly Sworn doth in their several oaths make their several declarations in order to obtain the benefit of the Act of Congress of the 7th June Ad 1832 that they entered the Service of the United States under the Officers named in their several declarations (here insert them) And the said Court do hereby declare their opinion after the investigation of the matter and after putting the interrogations prescribed by the War Department that the above named applicants were Revolutionary Soldiers and Served as they have stated And the Court further certifies that is appears to them that John Pavy who signed the several Certificates is a Clergyman resident in Switzerland County and State of Indiana and the other persons who has also signed the same are credible persons and that their Statement is entitled to credit.

Abstract of Final Payment Voucher; General Services Administration, Washington, DC
LAST FINAL PAYMENT VOUCHER RECEIVED FROM
THE GENERAL ACCOUNTING OFFICE

NAME   Levi, Isaac
AGENCY OF PAYMENT   Indiana
DATE OF ACT   1832
DATE OF PAYMENT   1st Qr. 1851
DATE OF DEATH   Sept 21, 1850
GENERAL SERVICES ADMINISTRATION
National Archives and Records Service   NA-286
GSA-WASH DC 54-4891   November 1953
&

Abstract of Final Payment Voucher; General Services Administration, Washington, DC
NAME   Levi, Mary Widow of Isaac
AGENCY OF PAYMENT   Indiana
DATE OF ACT   1853 2d Sect
DATE OF PAYMENT   4th Qr. 1853
DATE OF DEATH   Oct 14, 1853
LAST FINAL PAYMENT VOUCHER RECEIVED FROM
THE GENERAL ACCOUNTING OFFICE   Form
General Services Administration   GSA DA 70-7035 GSA Dec 69 7068

American Militia in the Frontier Wars, 1790-1796; by Murtie June Clark; Genealogical Publishing Co., Inc., 1990. p. 23.
Kentucky Militia
Muster Roll of Mounted Volunteers from Kentucky under the Command of Captain John Hall, Lieut. Colo. Horation Hall's Regiment, in the service of the United States Commanded by Major General Charles Scott, Oct 30, 1793.

Nr	Rank	Name	Remarks
7	Sergeant	Levi, Isaac	enlisted Sept 22

Historical Register of Virginians in the Revolution, Soldiers, Sailors, Marines, 1775-1783; John H. Gwathmey; The Dietz Press, Richmond, VA, 1938. p. 470.
Levi, Isaac, IP
Levi, Isaac, 75, Switzerland Co., Ind., mpl.

Virginia Militia in the Revolutionary War; J.T. McAllister, McAllister Publishing Co., Hot Springs, VA, 1913. p. 279.
Part V, Pensioners Residing Outside of Virginia in 1835 who Received Pensions as Virginia Militiamen.
Levi, Isaac   75 [age]   Switzerland   Indiana

Second Census of Kentucky, 1800; Clift G. Glenn; Genealogical Publishing Co., Baltimore, MD, 1954.
An alphabetical list of 32,000 taxpayers based on original tax lists on file at the Kentucky Historical Society. Information given includes the county of residence and the date of the tax list in which the individual is listed.
Levy, Isaac   Harrison 1800

Early Ohioans' Residences From the Land Grant Records; Compiled by Mayburt Stephenson Riegel; Published by the Ohio Genealogical Society, Mansfield, OH, 1976. p. 8.
Land Grants Recorded by Residents of the Indiana Territory at the Cincinnati Land Office. The original Land Grant records are in the Archives of the Ohio Historical Society. They are from the Auditor of the State of Ohio Land Office.

NAME	DATE	SEC	TWP	RANGE	VOL	PG	RESIDENCE
LEVI, Isaac	9-19-1804	S29	T8	R1W	B	141	DN Dearborn

Early Ohio Settlers, Purchasers of Land in Southwestern Ohio, 1800-1840; Compiled by Ellen T. Berry & David A. Berry; Genealogical Publishing Co., Inc., Baltimore, MD, 1986. p.190.

Purchaser	Year	Date	Residence	R - T - S
Levi, Isaac (B)	1817	Sept. 08	Hamilton	02-02-30

(B) Indiana Survey: Land lying west of a meridian drawn west of the Great Miami (known as the "Gore"). Switzerland, Dearborn, Franklin, Ohio, Union and Randolph Counties (all or only a part of each county) – all in Indiana.

Indiana Land Entries Vol. 1 Cincinnati District, 1801-1840; Margaret R. Waters; Originally Published Indianapolis 1948, Second Reprint 1979 by The Bookmark, P.O. Box 74, Knightstown, In 46148. p. 42.
CINCINNNATI LAND DISTRICT – VOL. 1
Page 40. Twp. 2 N, Range 2 W of 1st Principle Meridian SWITZERLAND CO.
Isaac Levi W ½ - NW ½ - S30; 9-8-1817.
-- Note: The tract books for the land offices in Indiana are deposited in the office of the Auditor of State, Indianapolis. They and are in the custody of the State Land clerk. --

U.S. Department of Interior, Bureau of Land Management, General Land Office Records; Land Patent Search – accessed 27 June 2012.
LEVI, ISAAC
Accession Nr. CV-0016-108; Document Type – Credit Volume Patent; State – Indiana; Issued Date – 9/23/1812; Cancelled – No
Names on Document: Jones, James; Levi, Isaac
Land Office – Cincinnati; Authority – April 24, 1820 Sale-Cash Entry (3 Stat. 566); Total Acres – 0.00
Land Descriptions: State – IN; Meridian –1st PM; Twp-Rng – 008N-001W; Aliquots – S1/2; Section – 29; County - Franklin
&
Accession Nr. CV-0069-192; Document Twp – Credit Volume Patent; State – Indiana; Issue Date – 11/10/1827; Cancelled – No
Names on Document: Jackson, Albion; Jackson, George A.; Levi, Isaac
Land Office – Cincinnati; Document Nr. 2163; Total Acres – 99.48
Land Descriptions: State – IN; Meridian – 1st PM; Twp-Rng – 002N-002W; Aliquots – W1/2NW1/4; Section – 30; County – Switzerland
&
Accession Nr. IN2680_.204; Document Type – State Volume Patent; State – Indiana; Issue Date – 8/1/1838; Cancelled – No

Land Office – Jeffersonville; Authority – April 24, 1820 Sale-Cash Entry (3 Stat. 566); Document Nr. 10242; BLM Serial Nr. – IN NO S/N; Total Acres – 80.00
Land Descriptions: State – IN; Meridian – 2nd PM; Twp-Rng – 008N-011E; Aliquots – N1/2SE1/4; Section – 15; County - Ripley
&
Accession Nr. IN2670_.080; Document Type – State Volume Patent; State – Indiana; Issue Date – 8/2/1838; Cancelled – No
Land Office – Jeffersonville; Authority – April 24, 1820 Sale-Cash Entry (3 Stat. 566); Document Nr. 9618; total Acres – 40.00
Land Descriptions: State – IN; Meridian – 2nd PM; Twp-Rng – 008N-011E; Aliquots – SE1/4SE1/4; Section – 15; County - Ripley
&
Accession Nr. IN2780_.206; Document Type – State Volume Patent; State – Indiana; Issue Date – 9/20/1839; Cancelled – No
Land Office – Jeffersonville; Authority – April 24, 1820 Sale-Cash Entry (3 Stat. 566); Document Nr. 15245; BLM Serial Nr. – IN NO S/N; Total Acres – 40.00
Land Descriptions: State – IN; Meridian – 2nd PM; Twp-Rng – 008N-010E; Section – 26; County - Ripley

Indiana Territory, Switzerland Circuit Court Records, Order Book, October Term 1814 to March Term 1815. p. 72.
He is listed in county records for the first time on 8 May 1820, as a defendant.
Author's note: There are entries in this volume that are not within the range of dates shown on the binder cover.

1830 U.S. Census, Indiana, Switzerland, No Twp., Series: M19 Roll: 32 Page: 51
Levi, Isaac age 70-80; others in household 1 make 20-30, 1 female 20-30, 1 female 60-70.

A Census of Pensioners for Revolutionary or Military Services with their Names, Ages, and Places of Residence Under the Act for Taking the Sixth Census in 1840; Genealogical Publishing Co., Inc., Baltimore, Maryland, 1965. p.184.

INDIANA, RIPLEY, JOHNSON

Names of Pensioners for Revolutionary or Military services	Ages	Names of heads of families with whom pensioner resided June 1, 1840
Levi, Isaac	91	Martin Levi

The "Lost" Pensions, Settled Accounts of the Act of 6 April 1838; by Craig R. Scott; Willow Bend Books, Lovettsville, VA, 1996. p. 195.
An Act directing the transfer of money remaining unclaimed [for the term of eight months] by certain pensioners, and authorizing payment of the same at the Treasury of the United States.
Name – Levi, Mary; Pension Office - Ohio; Box - 73; Account - #12743.

Revolutionary Soldiers of Switzerland County; Copied by Mary Hill, John Paul Chapter-Daughters of the American Revolution; January, 1958; http://www.ingenweb.org/inswitzerland/switzrevsoldiers.html- Viewed June 2012.

LEVI, ISAAC   Pension record: W.773
Isaac Levi was born in February, 1749 in Hungary, and when about seventeen years of age arrived in America. The names of his parents were not shown. While a resident of Lexington, "Kentucky" he enlisted sometime in June, 1780, served as a private in Captain Robert Patterson's and Benjamin Harrison's companies with the Virginia troops; went on a expedition against the Indians on the Big Miami under General Clark, was in a battle at Pickaway Town, where the Indians were defeated and the town burned, after which they were stationed for fifteen or eighteen months at Fort Vincent (later Vincennes, Indiana); then returned to the Falls of the Ohio, where he was discharged having served "upwards of two years."
He continued to reside in Kentucky for about forty years, then moved to Ohio and lived five or six years, thence to Indiana.
Isaac Levi was allowed pension on his application executed September 18, 1832, at which time he was living in Switzerland Co. Ind.
He married November 14, 1841, in Ripley County, Indiana Mrs. Mary (Polly) Tucker. She was the widow of John Tucker, to whom she was married in February 1836 in Scott County, Kentucky. In the same year they moved to Ripley County, Indiana, where John Tucker died November 14, 1840.
Isaac Levi died September 21, 1850 in Ripley County, Indiana. His widow, Mary Levi, was allowed pension on account of the services of her husband, Isaac Levi, on her application executed March 26, 1853, at which time she was aged fifty years and a resident of Jefferson County, Indiana. She died October 14, 1853.
Reference was made in 1854 to two children of John & Mary Tucker, and it was stated that the widow, at her death, left several children, "some of which are not of age:. Names of children are not given.
Roster; Buried near Osgood, Ripley Co. John Tucker also served in Revolution.

Roster of Soldiers and Patriots of the American Revolution Buried in Indiana, Vol. I; compiled by Mrs. Roscoe C. O'Byrne.; Indiana Daughters of the American Revolution, 1981; p.235.
LEVI, ISAAC   Ripley County
Born – 1751, Germany
Service – While resident of Lexington, Ky., he enlisted in 1780. Pri. in Capt. Robert Patterson's and Benj. Harrison's CO., a troop on expedition against the Indians on Big Miami under Gen. George Rogers Clark. In the battle of Pickaway Town, defeated the Indians. Stationed at Post Vincennes. Served two years.
Proof – Pension claim W. 773.
Died – Sept. 21, 1850. Buried near Osgood, Ripley, Co. Bronze tablet at Versailles Court House.
Married – Last W. Mary Tucker (widow of John Tucker, a Rev. S.), m. Nov. 14, 1841. Descendants of former marriages settled about Osgood, Indiana.
Collected by Mrs. A. B. Wycoff, Batesville, Indiana.

The Vevay Reveille-Enterprise; Vol. 122, No. 37, 22 Sep 1935, p. 7, col. 1.
Roster of Revolutionary Soldiers Who Resided in Switzerland County
By Mrs. Effa M. Danner

Isaac Levi – Pension certificate No. W773, granted 1834 in Switzerland County. Age 75 granted Va. Born February 1749 in Hungary, Europe, emigrated at the age of 17 to America. While a resident of Lexington, Ky., he enlisted in 1780 as private in Captain Robert Patterson's and Benj. Harrison's Co., of Virginia troops on expedition against Indians on Big Miama under Gen. George Roger Clark. He was in the battle of Pickaway Town, defeated the Indians. Stationed at Fort Vincennes (later Vencennes, Ind.) returned to the falls of the Ohio; served two years and was discharged.
Switzerland County land entry T2, R. 2W, Sect. 30, Sept. 8, 1817.
He is listed in Ripley County, 1840, age 91, guardian Martin Levi. Switzerland County census 1820 he had four boys and one girl.
Pension record, Isaac Levi married Nov. 14, 1841 in Ripley County, Ind., Mrs. Mary Tucker, widow of John Tucker to whom she was married February 1833 in Scot County, Ky. He died in Ripley County, November 14, 1840.
Isaac Levi died September 21, 1850, Ripley County, Ind. Widow, Mary Levi allowed pension March 26, 1856, she being 50 years old and residing in Jefferson County, Oct. 14, 1853. She died leaving minor children. Mary Levi must have been his second wife.

Abstract of Graves of Revolutionary Patriots (4 volumes); by Patricia Law Hatcher; Pioneer Heritage Press, Dallas, TX, 1987. Vol. 3, p. 12.
This is an abstract and an index to information reported to the Daughters of the American Revolution and published in their annual reports to the Smithsonian Institution, printed as Senate Documents (1900-1974) and published annually in the DAR magazine (1978-1987).
Published 1972 (Senate Doc. 54)
LEVI, Isaac   Nr Osgood, Ripley Co IN

Tombstones for John Levi
Perseverance Cemetery
Tombstone inscription –
ISAAC
LEVI
PVT
CONTINENTAL
LINE
REV WAR
FEB 1 1749
SEP 21 1850
BURIED IN LEVI CEM
CENTER TWO
RECORDED P PG 103

Meyers Cemetery
Tombstone inscription –
ISAAC
LEVI
PVT
CONTINENTAL
LINE
REV WAR
FEB 1 1749
SEP 21 1850

Tri-County Genealogical Society Newsletter; Batesville, IN; Oct. 2006, Vol. 14, Iss. 4, p. 6.
Mr. Isaac Levi Revolutionary War Pensioner
The following entry is found on the 1850 Census of Ripley Co., IN, Delaware Twp, p. 206 (House #89):

Isaac Levi,	114,	born in Hungary
Mary Levi,	49,	born in Virginia
Benjamin Tucker,	14,	born in Kentucky
Martha Green	22,	born in Kentucky

At the bottom of the page, the following is written:

Mr. Levi died Sept. 21, 1850, without an hour's sickness. He believed himself to be in his one hundred and fifteenth year. He said he was born in Hungary (Europe) May 10, 1736, crossed the Atlantic May 1758, enlisted in the American Army August, 1776, in his 40th year, served 4 years therein and died as above. He was a pensioner.

If this information is correct, Mr. Levi may well have been the oldest living Revolutionary War pensioner in 1850. Does any reader have more information about Mr. Levi or the three people living in his household in 1850?

Contributed by Charlie Hessler

Author's note: A similar article appeared in the *Ripley County Indiana Historical Society Quarterly Bulletin*; Versailles, IN; Jan 2006, Vol 27, Iss 1, p 2.

LEWIS, THOMAS

Patriot: Thomas Lewis
Birth: 18 Dec 1764 Caroline Co., VA
Married Spouse 1: Nancy Rey (b. 1764 d. 1803)
Married Spouse 2: 4 Aug 1805 Angelica, Allegheny Co., NY Sarah Condly
                (b. 5 Feb 1782, NY; d. 4 Sep 1858, Switzerland Co., IN)
Service state(s): VA
Service description: Capts. Coleman, Sutton/Taylor,
                Col, Thomas Mathews, Maj. Carey
Rank: Private; second sergeant
Proof of Service: Pension application W8032
Pension application No.: W8032
Residences: Caroline Co., VA; Genesee Co., NY; Butler Co., OH;
            Indiana Territory; Switzerland Co., IN
Died: 28 Jul 1832 or 18 Jul 1833 Tapps Ridge, Switzerland Co., IN
Buried: Unknown
DAR Ancestor No.: A070150

Pension Application Abstracted from National Archives microfilm Series 805, Roll 526, File W8032/BLWT27672-160-55;Switzerland County, Indiana Probate Record Book Vol. A, Mar 1827-Nov 1834; p. 275.
Pension abstract for – Thomas Lewis   Service state(s): VA
Alternate spelling(s):
Date: 18 August 1832
County of: Switzerland   State of: Indiana
Declaration made before a Court.
Age: 68 Where and year born: Carolina County, VA, September 1764.
Record of Age: No record of age but believes he was born on the 18th or 20th of
        that year.
Residence when he entered service: Caroline Co., VA
Residence(s) since the war: About 17 years in Genesee Co., NY; about 3 years,
        Butler Co., OH; and 14 years in this county.
Residence now: Switzerland County
Volunteer or Drafted or Substitute: Drafted 3 different times.
Rank(s): Private
Statement of service-

Period	Duration	Names of General and Field Officers
Mar/Apr 1780	2 mos.	Company of Virginia Militia commanded by Coleman, Sutton of Taylor in Regt. commanded by Col. Andrew Thornton.
June 1781	2 mos.	Company of Virginia Militia commanded by Coleman, Sutton of Taylor in Regt. commanded by Col. Thomas Mathews.
Sept 1781	2 mos.	Company of Virginia Militia commanded by Coleman, Sutton of Taylor in Regt. commanded by Major Cary of the Continental Army.

Regular Officers with the troops where you served: Gen. Lafayette, Gen. Washington. Gen. Lafayette commanded me at the Siege of York; Gen. Washington commanded when Cornwallis surrendered.
Battles: Siege of York, Surrender of Cornwallis.
Discharge received: After Cornwallis' Surrender was marched to Winchester, from there to Fredericksburg where we were discharged.
Signed by: Never received a written discharge.
Statement is supported by –
Living witness, name(s):
Documentary proof: None
Person now living who can testify to service: Newton H. Tapp, William Scudder, Allen Wiley, William Cotton, David McCormick, George Markland, Daniel Haycock.
Clergyman: None. Newton H. Tapp certifies he is well acquainted.
Persons in neighborhood who certify character:
Soldier died: 28 July 1832.
Wife: Sarah (Condly) applied for Widow's Pension, age 70 in April 1853); and she applied for Bounty Land in Apr 1855.
Marriage date and place: Angelica, Allegheny Co., NY, 4 August 1805.
Proof of marriage: Family record, she believes Marriage Records were kept by the State of NY.
Names and ages of children: 9 children – names not given.

Switzerland County, Indiana Probate Order Book 2, 1831-1837; p. 84.
In the matter of Thomas Lewis on Declaration in order to obtain the benefit of the act of Congress of The 7th June 1832
    Now in the 18th day of August 1832 personally appears in open Court now Setting Thomas Lewis a resident of Switzerland County in the State of Indiana, aged 68 years, who being first duly sworn according to law doth on his oath make this the following Declaration in order to obtain the benefit of the act of Congress passed the 7 June1832 that he entered the Service of the United States under the following named officers and Served as herein Stated (tour).
    And the Said Court do hereby declare their opinion after the investigation of the matter, and after putting the interrogation prescribed by the War department. That the above named Applicant was a Revolutionary Soldier and Served as he states.
    And the Court further certifies that it appears to them that Newton H. Tapp who has Signed the preceding certificate is a resident of Switzerland County in the State of Indiana a credible person and that his Statement is entitled to Credit.

Switzerland County, Indiana Probate Order Book 2, 1831-1837;, pg. 171.
16 November 1833
In the matter of Sarah Lewis }
widow of Thos. Lewis Dec'd } Comes now here into Court before the Probate Court of Switzerland now Sitting Sarah Lewis widow of Thomas Lewis Late of Said County said deceased Thomas Lewis departed this life on the 28th day of July 1833, that She was the lawful wife of the Said decedent, in his lifetime, that

she lived with him from the time she was married to him until the time of his death in Switzerland County, that Said Thomas Lewis applied for and was placed on the pension rolls of the United States under the act of Congress of the 7th June 1832, all of which is ordered to be Certified.

Abstract of Final Payment Voucher; General Services Administration, Washington, DC
LAST FINAL PAYMENT VOUCHER RECEIVED FROM
THE GENERAL ACCOUNTING OFFICE
NAME   Lewis, Thomas
AGENCY OF PAYMENT   Indiana
DATE OF ACT   1832
DATE OF PAYMENT   2nd Qr. 1844
DATE OF DEATH   July 28, 1833
GENERAL SERVICES ADMINISTRATION
National Archives and Records Service   NA-286
GSA-WASH DC 54-4891   November 1953
&
Abstract of Final Payment Voucher; General Services Administration, Washington, DC
NAME   Lewis, Sarah Widow of Thomas
AGENCY OF PAYMENT   Madison
DATE OF ACT   1853 2d Sect
DATE OF PAYMENT   Sept. 4, 1858
DATE OF DEATH
LAST ~~FINAL~~ PAYMENT VOUCHER RECEIVED FROM
THE GENERAL ACCOUNTING OFFICE   Form
General Services Administration   GSA DA 70-7035   GSA Dec 69 7068

Virginia Soldiers of 1776; Compiled from Documents on File in the Virginia Land Office, Together with Material found in the Archives Department of the Virginia State Library, and Other Reliable Sources, 3 volumes; Compiled and Edited by Louis A. Burgess, Genealogical Publishing Co., Inc., Baltimore, MD, 1973. p. 1251.
Payroll of Capt. Thomas Baytop's Company of Militia "Gloster" country, commencing May 31, the day they joined the army, terminating June 5th, 1781, both days included.
Privates – list includes Thomas Lewis.

Virginia Revolutionary Militia, A List of Non-Commissioned Officers and Soldiers of the Virginia Line on Continental Establishment, Whose names appear on the Army Register, and who have not received Bounty Land; Printed by Samuel Shepherd, Printer to the Commonwealth, Richmond, VA. 1835. p. 29. Doc. No. 44.
Lewis, Thomas   Soldier   Infantry

Historical Register of Virginians in the Revolution, Soldiers, Sailors, Marines, 1775-1783; John H. Gwathmey; The Dietz Press, Richmond, VA, 1938. p.472-3.

Lewis, Thomas, of Levay,[as printed in book] Ind., born in Caroline, dmp.
Lewis, Thoma, 70, Switzerland, Ind., mpl.

Virginia Militia in the Revolutionary War; J.T. McAllister, McAllister Publishing Co., Hot Springs, VA, 1913.
p. 138. Part II, Declarations of Virginia Militia Pensioners, §1 to §250. Section No.158.
Lewis, Thomas. – Vevay, Ind., Aug. 18, 1832. Born in Caroline, Dec. -, 1764. Went out in spring of 1781 under Capt. Coleman Sutton (Taylor?), of Co. Anthony Thornton's regiment. Again in June, 1781, under same captain and Col. Thomas Mathews. Again in September, 1781, same captain and Maj. Carey. Was drafted each time. Served in lower Virginia. At siege of Yorktown was second sergeant. After the surrender guarded prisoners to Winchester. Went to New York, 1798; to Indiana, 1818.
p. 280. Part V, Pensioners Residing Outside of Virginia in 1835 who Received Pensions as Virginia Militiamen.
Lewis, Thos.   70 [age]   Switzerland   Indiana

Register of Certificates Issued by John Pierce, Esquire, Paymaster General and Commissioner of Army Accounts for the United States, to Officers and Soldiers of the Continental Army Under Act of July 4, 1783; Originally Published as Senate Documents, Vol.9, No. 988, 63rd Congress, 3d Session, Washington, 1915; Seventeenth report of the National Society of the Daughters of the American Revolution; Genealogical Publishing Co., Inc, Baltimore, MD, 1984. p. 309.
Men listed in this volume with the same name.

No. of Certificate	To whom issued	Amount
13824	Lewis, Thomas	19.05
14267	Lewis, Thomas	9.07
15085	Lewis, Thomas	36.17
39604	Lewis, Thomas	26.60
40324	Lewis, Thomas	53.30
85727	Lewis, Thomas	80.00
86794	Lewis, Thomas	2.80
88373	Lewis, Thomas	100.00
89701	Lewis, Thomas	30.20

Early Ohio Settlers, Purchasers of Land in Southwestern Ohio, 1800-1840; Compiled by Ellen T. Berry & David A. Berry; Genealogical Publishing Co., Inc., Baltimore, MD, 1986. p.191.

Purchaser	Year	Date	Residence	R – T - S
Lewis, Thomas (B)	1806	Aug. 25	Dearborn Ind	02-12-11
Lewis, Thomas (B)	1806	Aug. 25	Dearborn Ind	02-12-11
Lewis, Thomas (B)	1806	Aug. 25	Dearborn Ind	02-13-35

(B) Indiana Survey: Land lying west of a meridian drawn west of the Great Miami (known as the "Gore"). Switzerland, Dearborn, Franklin, Ohio, Union and Randolph Counties (all or only a part of each county) – all in Indiana.

Census of Indiana Territory for 1807; Indiana Historical Society, 1980. p. 27.
A list of free males above the age of twenty one in Dearborn County in March 1807 ~~
575   Thomas Lewis

1830 U.S. Census, Indiana, Switzerland, No Twp., Series: M19 Roll: 32 Page: 51
Lewis, Thomas age 60-70; others in household 1 male under 5, 2 females under 5, 1 female 5-10, 1 female 40-50.

Revolutionary Soldiers of Switzerland County; Copied by Mary Hill, John Paul Chapter-Daughters of the American Revolution; January, 1958; *http://www.ingenweb.org/inswitzerland/switzrevsoldiers.html-* Viewed June 2012.
LEWIS, THOMAS
Born December 1764, Caroline County, Virginia
Enlisted in March or April 1781; served two months as a private in Captain Coleman Sutton's or Captain Taylor's company, Colonel Andrew Thornton's Virginia Regiment.
Enlisted in June, 1781, served two months as a private in Capt. Coleman Sutton's or Capt. Taylor's company, Colonel Thomas Matthew's Virginia Regiment.
He enlisted in Aug. or Sept., 1781 and served as 2d Sergeant in Capt. Coleman's or Capt. Taylor's Company, under Major Carey, in the Virginia Troops for two months and two weeks.
Married Aug. 4, 1805/6, Sarah Condly, in Angelica, Allegany Co. NY
Children: 9 children
He died in Switzerland Co. Indiana, July 28, 1833
For proof: Veterans Administration, Washington, D. A. Letter to Mrs. Harvey Morris, Salem, Indiana, dated Jan. 14, 1936.
"He was allowed pension Aug. 18, 1832, while residing in Switz. Co. Ind. where he had resided for 14 years.
He married Aug. 4, 1805/6 in Angelica, Allegany Co. N.Y. Sarah Condly. The date and place of her birth not given, nor names of her parents. She was allowed pension April 3 or 5, 1853, while residing in Switz. Co. Ind. age 70 years, in 1854, she stated she was aged 80 years, and in 1855, 74 years. No explanation given for this. Nine children survived Thomas Lewis, names not given. In 1849 a daughter was residing in Cincinnati, and same year a son-in-law, Robert D. Collins, resided in Cincinnati, but name of his wife is not given."
A Joseph Lewis, born 1812, died near Aaron, Feb. 9, 1893; buried in Brushy Fork. (This may be one son.)
Pr. Bk. A-84;
Thomas Lewis, 1832, age 68 yrs. Newton E. Tapp signs.
pg. 171
Sarah, widow of Thomas Lewis. Thomas died July 28, 1832
Applied for pension June 7, 1832. Certified.

Roster of Soldiers and Patriots of the American Revolution Buried in Indiana, Vol. I; compiled by Mrs. Roscoe C. O'Byrne.; Indiana Daughters of the American Revolution, 1981; p.236.
LEWIS, THOMAS   Switzerland County

Born – Dec. 1764, Caroline Co., Virginia.
Service – Enlisted as a pri. in Capt. Coleman Sutton's or Capt. Taylor's CO., Col. Andrew Thornton's Vir. Regt. This was in March or April, 1781, served 2 mos. Enlisted in June, 1781, 2 mos. under Col. Thomas Matthews. In Aug. or Sept., 1781, served as 2nd Serg. Under Major Carey in Vir. Troops for 2 mos. and 2 wks.
Proof – McAllister, Virginia Militia in the Rev. War, p. 138; Pension Claim W. 8032, B. L. Wt. 27672-160-55.
Died – July 28, 1832. Switzerland County.
Married – 1804, Sarah Condly. Had 9 children, name not given in pension papers.
Collected by Mrs. Harvey Morris, Salem, Indiana.

The Indiana Reveille, Wed. 14 Sep 1859, Vol. XLIL, No.37, p. 2., Col. 5.
Obituary
Died, September 3d, at the residence of her son-in-law, (Geo. W. Hagan) in Moorefield, Switzerland county, Indiana, Mrs. Sarah Lewis, in the 79th year of her age. Mrs. Lewis was born in the State of New York, on the 5th of February, 1782. Se emigrated to Indiana forty-one years ago. She joined the Methodist Episcopal Church at Old Bethel, near Jacksonville in this county. She lived a consistent Christian; amiable in her disposition, she won a place in the hearts of all who made her acquaintance. The hope of meeting her in heaven cheers her children and many friends.
                      E.A. Anderson

The Vevay Reveille-Enterprise; Vol. 122, No. 37, 22 Sep 1935, p. 7, col. 1.
Roster of Revolutionary Soldiers Who Resided in Switzerland County
By Mrs. Effa M. Danner
Thomas Lewis, Sergeant – Born on December 18, 1764 in Carolina County, Virginia. Service – while residing in Carolina County, Virginia he enlisted as private in Capt. Coleman Sutton's and Capt. Taylor's Company under Col. Andrew Thornton's command, Virginia Regiment in March or April 1781. Served two months. Enlisted in June 1781; Served two months in Capt. Sutton's or Capt. Taylor's Company, Col. Thomas Mathew's Virginia Regiment. Enlisted August 1781; served as 2nd Sergeant in Capt. Coleman's or Taylor's Co., under Major Carey, Virginia troops for two months and two weeks. Allowed pension Aug. 18, 1832 while residing in Switzerland County where he had lived 14 years. Died in Switzerland County July 18, 1833. Official papers, Washington, D.C. Married August 4, 1805 or 1806 in Angelica, Allegheny Co., New York to Sarah Condly. She was allowed pension in Switzerland County, April 5, 1853, age 70. Nine children survived Thomas Lewis. In 1849 a daughter resided in Cincinnati, son-in-law, Robert Collins.
Thomas Lewis pension petition Switzerland County, Probate Court p. 84, 1832. Witnesses Newton Tapp.
There are a number of Lewis's in this county but I do not know who is who.

MAGRUDER, NORMAN BRUCE
aka McGRUDER

Patriot: Norman Bruce Magruder
Birth: 1754　　MD
Married Spouse 1: 25 Dec 1783　Nancy Paugh
　　　　　　　　(b. 1767 MD d. prob. 1845 Lexington Co., KY)
Service state(s): MD
Service description: Capt. Bell, Col. Murdock
Rank: Private
Proof of Service: Pension application W9542
Pension application No.: W9542
Residences: George Town (now D.C.); MD; Washington Co. (now Allegheny),
　　　　PA; Switzerland Co., IN
Died: 16 Feb 1836 Switzerland Co., IN
Buried: Unknown
DAR Ancestor No.: A073128

Pension Application Abstracted from National Archives microfilm Series 805, Roll 547, File W9542.;Switzerland County, Indiana Probate Record Book Vol. A, Mar 1827-Nov 1834; p. 271.
Pension abstract for – Norman Bruce Magruder　Service state(s): Maryland
Date: 1832 (day/month not shown)
County of: Switzerland　　　　　　　　　　　State of: Indiana
Declaration made before Open Court.
Age: 77 years　　[estimated b. 1755]
Residence when he entered service: George Town (now D.C.)
Residence(s) since the war: In Washington County, that part that was later called
　　　　Allegheny Co., MD for 31 years, about 1814 to Switzerland Co., IN
Residence now: Switzerland Co., IN
Volunteer or Drafted or Substitute: Not stated
Rank(s): Private
Statement of service-

Period	Duration	Names of General and Field Officers
1781	More than 6 mos.	Capt. George Ball's company, Col. William Murdock's and William Dickey's Maryland Regiment.

Wife: Nancy Paugh, daughter of Michael Paugh
Children: Mary or Polly, b. 30 December 1784; James b. 12 February 1786; Sarah or Sally b. 3 May 1789.
&
Widow, Nancy Magruder's, Application for Pension – his Certificate no. 2216.
Date: 16 November 1836
County of: Switzerland　　　　　　　　　　　State of: Indiana
Declaration made before Probate Court.
Widow's age:　　69 years
Where and year (widow) born: in 1777

Persons who stated they were well acquainted with the applicant: Amos Gilbert & John Pavy.
Soldier died: 16 February 1836 in Switzerland Co., IN
Marriage date and place: 25 December 1781 at Cumberland in Maryland
Proof of marriage: Statement of John Keith, dated 8 December 1845, who posted his and Magruder's notices of intended marriage on the door of the meeting house in Washington Co., MD (later Allegheny Co., MD).
Names and ages of children: As stated by John Keith, youngest daughter Sally (also referred to as Sarah) b. 1789.
&
William C. Keen stated he was acquainted with Norman Magruder from 1814 until his death. Nancy removed to Louisville, KY where she lives with her granddaughter. In 1814 all of her children were dead except Sarah (aka Sally) who was married to Amos Gilbert. Nancy Magruder's granddaughter has a son nine years old. The family is Roman Catholics and I have never seen a Bible among them.
&
In 1844, Smith McMillen and Elijah Gilbert, grandchildren of soldier, were living in Vevay. Ages and names of parents not given.
&
In 1845, Isaac Paugh, a half-brother of soldier's widow, was living in Ripley Co., IN.

Switzerland County, Indiana Probate Order Book 2, 1831-1837;, pp. 78, 447.
p. 78
State of Indiana Switzerland County SS
Now on the Seventeenth day of August 1832. Personally appeared in open Court before Probate Court of Said County now Sitting Norman B. Magruder a resident of the County of Switzerland in the State of Indiana aged Seventy Seven years, who boring first duly Sworn according to Law doth in his oat make the following declaration in order to obtain the benefit of the act of Congress passed June 7th 1832. That he entered the Service of the United States under the following named officers and Served as herein Stated (here insert the dictation). And the Said Court do hereby declare their opinion, after the investigation of the matter, and after putting the interrogations prescribed by the War Department that the above named applicant was a Revolutionary Soldier and Served as he States. And the Court further certifies that it appears to them that John Pavy who has Signed the preceding Certificate is a Clergyman resident of Switzerland and State of Indiana, and that Jean D. Morend who also Signed the Same is a resident in the Said County and State and is a credible person , and that their Statement is entitled to Credit.
p. 447
In the matter of the Identity of the widow of N. B. Magruder Dec'd. } Now on this day personally appeared in open Court before the Probate Court of the County of Switzerland Nancy Magruder of County aforesaid aged sixty nine years, who being duly sworn according to law doth on her oath make the following declaration in order to obtain the benefit of the provisions made by the act of Congress passed July 4th

1836 that She is the widow of Norman B. Magruder, who was a private Soldier in the Army of the Revolution, and a pensioner under the act of June the 7th 1832, his Certificate being numbered 2216, that She further declares that She was married to the Said Norman B. Magruder, at Fort Cumberland in Maryland on the 25 day of Dec'mr AD 1787 that her husband, the Said Norman B. Magruder died on the 16th day of February AD 1836, and that She has remained a widow ever since that period as will more fully appear by a reference to the proof hereunto annexed.

       her
Nancy X Magruder
       mark

Sworn to and Subscribed in open Court this 16th day of November 1836
Also personally appeared in open Court at the same time and place Amos Gilbert and John Pavy of lawful age who after being Sworn deposith and Saith, that they are well acquainted with the above named Nancy Magruder, that She is the widow of Norman Magruder who departed this life on the 16th day of Feby AD 1836.

      Amos Gilbert
      John Pavy

Sworn & Subscribed in open Court Nover 16, 1836   }
                                         Edward Patton Clerk   }

It was also proven to the Satisfaction of the Court that Amos Gilbert & John Pavy, who Signed the above, are respectable persons and that their Statement is entitled to Credit.

Switzerland County, Indiana Probate Order Book 3, 1837-1843; p. 132
15 November 1838
In the matter of Nancy Magruder widow   }
of N. B. Marauder a pensioner of the US   }   Now on this day comes into open Court the Said Nancy Magruder and filed her report which She Subscribes and is Sworn to in open Court, under the act of Congress of 1838 providing for the widows of Pensioners of the United States (here insert it) which report is ordered of record and Certificate.

Switzerland County, Indiana Probate Order Book 3, 1837-1843; p. 396.
Pensioners Widow
10 May 1836
In the matter of Nancy Magruder   }
Widow if N.B. Magruder Ded'd.   }   Now on this day comes Nancy Magruder, and proves to the Satisfaction of the Court that Norman B. Magruder late of Switzerland County, departed this life in Switzerland County on the 16th day of February 1836, that Said N.B. Magruder Dec'd was placed on the pension roll of the Indiana agency as a revolutionary soldier, that the Said Nancy Magruder was the lawful wife of and is now the widow of the Said N B Magruder deceased.

Switzerland County, IN, Will Book Vol. 1, 3 Jan 1823-10 Nov 1847, p. 93.
Abstract of will and/or administration for: Norman B. Magruder

Estate papers not found in the Probate Record Book index.
State & county where recorded: Switzerland Co., Indiana
State & county where will was made: Switzerland Co., IN
Book/volume where recorded: Will Book Vol. 1
Date will made: 14 January 1834
Date entered in probate: 26 April 1836
Name(s) of executors: Wife Nancy Magruder
Witnesses/appraisers: (in some cases, purchasers at sale of estate may be listed on another page and attached hereto): Witnesses to Will – John Pavy and Samuel Pavy.
Names of heirs and others mentioned in will (also signed receipts of division of estate) and relationship if shown: Wife Nancy; Daughters Elizabeth White, Sarah Gilbert; Grandchildren Amos Gilbert and Nancy Gilbert.

Abstract of Final Payment Voucher; General Services Administration, Washington, DC
LAST FINAL PAYMENT VOUCHER RECEIVED FROM
THE GENERAL ACCOUNTING OFFICE
NAME   Magruder, Norman B.
AGENCY OF PAYMENT   Indiana
DATE OF ACT   1832
DATE OF PAYMENT   Sept 4, 1835
DATE OF DEATH
GENERAL SERVICES ADMINISTRATION
National Archives and Records Service   NA-286
GSA-WASH DC 54-4891   November 1953
&
Abstract of Final Payment Voucher; General Services Administration, Washington, DC
NAME   Magruder, Nancy
AGENCY OF PAYMENT   Indiana
DATE OF ACT   1844
DATE OF PAYMENT   3rd quarter 1847
DATE OF DEATH
LAST FINAL PAYMENT VOUCHER RECEIVED FROM
THE GENERAL ACCOUNTING OFFICE   Form
General Services Administration   GSA DA 70-7035   GSA Dec 69 7068

The Maryland Militia in the Revolutionary War; by S. Eugene Clements and F. Edward Wright; Published by Family Line Publications, Westminster, MD 21157,1987.
p. 199.
Montgomery County, Lower Battalion
Officers and Privates for the 29th (Lower) Battalion – Coll. John Murdock; Lieut. Wm. Deakins; Maj. George Beall -
4th Co.: 29 Aug 1777 – Norman B. Magruder (in list)
p. 204.
Appendix B: Muster Rolls and Other Lists

A List of the different companies in the lower Battn. of Montgomery county with the different Classes as returned by Coll. John Murdock the 15th of July 1780 – 1st Company: Wm. Bailey, Capt.; Hezh. Magruder, 1st Lieut; Stophel Kiser,, 2nd Lieut; Josiah Magruder, Ensign.
Class No. 7: Norman B. Magruder (in list)

Maryland Revolutionary Records; Harry Wright Newman; Tuttle Publishing, Rutland, VT, 1928. p. 36.
Revolutionary Pensioners
Magruder, Norman (no birth date)   Pvt.   Militia

Virginia Militia in the Revolutionary War; J.T. McAllister, McAllister Publishing Co., Hot Springs, VA, 1913. p. 281.
Part V, Pensioners Residing Outside of Virginia in 1835 who Received Pensions as Virginia Militiamen.
Magruder, Norman B.   79 [age]   Switzerland   Indiana

Indiana Territory, Switzerland Circuit Court Records, Order Book, October Term 1814 to March Term 1815. p.6.
He is listed in county records for the first time on 27 March 1815, as a juror. Court held at the house of John Francis Dufour in the Town of Vevay.

1820 U.S. Census, Indiana, Switzerland, Cotton, Series: M33 Roll: 14 Page: 266
Norman B. Magruder 45 and up; others in household 1 male under 10, 1 female 10-16, 1 female 45 and up.

Revolutionary Soldiers of Switzerland County; Copied by Mary Hill, John Paul Chapter-Daughters of the American Revolution; January, 1958; http://www.ingenweb.org/inswitzerland/switzrevsoldiers.html- Viewed June 2012.
MCGRUDER, NORMAN B.   Pension W.9542
                                                        Switzerland Co. Indiana
The date and place of birth and names of parents of Norman Bruce McGruder are not shown in his Pension Application.
While a resident of Georgetown, now District of Columbia, Norman Bruce McGruder enlisted in 1781 and served as a private in Captain George Bell's company, Colonel William Murdock's and William Dickey's Maryland Regiments: length of service more than six months.
He lived in Washington County, that part which was later called Allegheny County, Maryland, for thirty-one years, and about 1814 moved to Switzerland County, Indiana.
He died February 16, 1836, in Switzerland Co. Indiana.
Married December 25, 1783, Nancy Paugh, in Washington Co. Maryland, Nancy Paugh was born in Allegheny County, Maryland. She was the daughter of Michael Paugh. Name of her mother is not shown.
Norman Bruce McGruder & Nancy had three children; Mary or Polly, born Dec. 30, 1784; James born Feb. 12, 1786; and Sarah or Sally, born May 2, 1789. Said Mary and James died prior to 18?4. Sarah married, date and place not stated Amos Gilbert, his age not given. They were both died in 1845, dates and places

of death not stated.
In 1844 Amity MacMillen and Elijah Gilbert, grandchildren of soldier and Nancy McGruder, were living in Switz. Co. Ind. their ages or names of their parents were not designated.
Soldier's widow, Nancy McGruder, was allowed pension on her application executed Jan. 1, 1845, at which time she was residing in Louisville, Jefferson Co. Ky. with her granddaughter, her name not designated. Various statements were made in regard to Nancy McGruder's age -- that she was born in 1777, that she was aged 69 years in 1836; aged 68 years in 1845; and aged 75 in 1845.
In 1845, a son, nine years old, of a granddaughter of Nancy McGruder soldier's widow, was referred to, no names were designated.
In 1845, Isaac Paugh, a half brother of soldier's widow, Nancy, was living in Ripley Co. Ind. age not given. There is no further family data.
Pro. Bk. A p. 78, Switzerland Co. records
Norman McGruder, age 77 rev. soldier. pg. 447
Pr. Bk. C p.447
Nov. 1836 Nancy McGruder, age 69, widow of Norman B. McGruder, Rev. soldier on pension rolls, Cert. 2216, was married at Ft. Cumberland, Maryland, Dec. 25, 1751. He died Feb. 16, 1836. Signed by John Pavy and Amos Gilbert.
Will abstract - Bk.1 p. 71; Norman Bruce McGruder; pg. 93
Wife, Nancy, daughters Elizabeth White and Sarah Gilbert
Grandchildren; Nancy Gilbert to have bed, etc.
Amos Gilbert, Jr.
Written Jan. 14, 1834
Witnesses; John Pavy and Samuel Pavy

Roster of Soldiers and Patriots of the American Revolution Buried in Indiana, Vol. I; compiled by Mrs. Roscoe C. O'Byrne.; Indiana Daughters of the American Revolution, 1981; p.243.
MAGRUDER, NORMAN BRUCE				Switzerland County
Service – While resident of Georgetown (now D.C.) enlisted 1781 and served as pri. in Capt. George Bell's CO., Cols. Wm. Murdock's and Wm. Dickey's Md. Regt., 6 mos.
Proof – Pension claim W. 9542.
Died – Feb. 16, 1836. Switzerland co.
Married – 1783, Nancy Paugh. Ch. Mary b. 1784; James b. 1786; Sally b. 1789, m. Amos Gilbert.
Collected by Mrs. A. V. Danner, Vevay, Indiana.

The Vevay Reveille-Enterprise; Vol. 122, No. 37, 22 Sep 1935, p. 7, col. 2.
Roster of Revolutionary Soldiers Who Resided in Switzerland County
By Mrs. Effa M. Danner
Norman Bruce Magruder – Certificate No. W9542. Service – While residing in Georgetown, now Dist. of Columbia he enlisted in 1781 and served as private in Capt. George Bell's Co., Col. Wm. Murdock's and Col. William Dickey's Maryland Regiment – service 6 months. He lived in Washington County, that part that was called Allegany Co., Md., 31 years and about 1814 moved to Switzerland County, Ind. He was allowed pension 1832. He died Feb. 16, 1836 in

Switzerland County. Soldier married Dec. 25, 1783 in Washington County, Md., Nancy Paugh who was born in Allegany County, Maryland. She was the daughter of Michael Paugh.

Nancy Magruder, widow, allowed pension January 1, 1845 while residing in Louisville, Ky., with a granddaughter, name not given. Various statements in regard to her age, born 1777, age 69 in 1836; age 68 in 1845; 75 in 1845. Witnesses Amos Gilbert and Rev. John Pavy.

They had three children, Sarah Magruder married Amos Gilbert. Both dead, 1845.

In 1814 Amity MacMillen and Elijah Gilbert, both grandchildren of Nancy were living in Vevay.

In 1845 Isaac Paugh, a half-brother of Nancy was living in Ripley County, Ind. He married a daughter of Thomas Mounts in Switzerland Co.

Norman B. Magruder and Nancy were administrators of John Shupe's estate, 1834, p. 194.

Michael Wilson's estate, Amos Gilbert and Norman B. Magruder are creditors and heirs, p. 275, Vol. 1818-1824.

McKAY, ROBERT

Patriot: Robert McKay
Birth: 12 Feb 1760 Frederick Co., VA
Married Spouse 1: Shenandoah Valley, VA   Lydia Leith (b. 1763
                                                           Shenandoah Valley, VA
                                                           d. 1830 Jefferson Co., IN)
Service state(s): VA
Service description: Capts. William Jennings, George Princee
Rank: Private
Proof of Service: Pension application S16956
Pension application No.: S16956
Residences: Shenandoah Co., VA; Jefferson Co., IN
Died: Sep 1835 Jefferson Co., IN
Buried: McKay Cemetery, Jefferson Co., IN
DAR Ancestor No.: A077394

Virginia Marriages, Shenandoah County, p. 5.
9 Jul 1782, Robt. McKay to Lydia Leath.

Pension Application Abstracted from National Archives microfilm Series 805, Roll 572, File S16956.
Pension abstract for – Robert McKay   Service state(s): Virginia
Date: 2 September 1832
County of: Jefferson   State of: Indiana
Declaration made before Open Court
Age: 73 years on 12 February last   Evidence of age: Has none
Where and year born: 12 February 1760 in Shenandoah Co., VA
Residence when he entered service: Shenandoah Co., VA
Residence(s) since the war: Shenandoah Co., VA until age 50, then to Indiana
Residence now: Jefferson Co., IN
Volunteer or Drafted or Substitute: Enlisted
Rank(s): Private
Statement of service-

Period	Duration	Names of General and Field Officers
Oct 1779	3 months	Capt. William Jenning's Virginia company – guarded prisoners at Albemarle Barracks.
Oct 1780	3 months	Capt. William Jenning's Virginia Company
In 1781	3 months	Capt. George Prince's Virginia Company

Discharge received: Yes
Signed by: Col. John Netherton
What became of it?: Destroyed by time or accident
Clergyman: Samuel Bellamy, resident of Switzerland Co., IN
Persons in neighborhood who certify character: Samuel Bellamy and John E. Gale, William Cotton and Nathaniel Cotton.
No information about soldier's family

Certificate No. 19434 was issued 9 Sep 1833.
Historical Register of Virginians in the Revolution, Soldiers, Sailors, Marines, 1775-1783; John H. Gwathmey; The Dietz Press, Richmond, VA, 1938. *p. 530*.
McKay, Robert, 81, Jefferson Co., Ind. mpl.

Virginia Militia in the Revolutionary War; J.T. McAllister, McAllister Publishing Co., Hot Springs, VA, 1913. *p. 281*.
Part V, Pensioners Residing Outside of Virginia in 1835 who Received Pensions as Virginia Militiamen.
McKay, Robt.   81 [age]   Jefferson   Indiana

Virginia Revolutionary Publick Claims in three volumes; compiled and transcribed b Janice L. Abercrombie and Richard Slatten; Iberian Publishing Co., Athens, GA, 1992. *p. 845*.
Shenandoah County – Shenandoah County Court Booklet – A list of claims produced to Court and ordered to be certified of the county of Shenandoah August 29, 1782. (certificates by Saml. Porter unless otherwise noted.)
Pg. 12 – James and Robert McKay 1 days each driving cattle 12s. [shillings]

Author's note: Robert McKay was age 73 when he applied for pension in Switzerland County in 1832. He was residing in Jefferson County and had been in Indiana for 23 years. He would have arrived in about 1809.

Author's note: There was another man by the name of Robert McKay who resided in Switzerland County. He died before March 21, 1832 when his estate was entered in Switzerland County Probate Court (*Switzerland County, Indiana Probate Record Book Vol. A, Mar 1827-Nov 1834; p. 471; Switzerland County, Indiana Probate Order Book 2, 1831-1837*; p. 56, 70, 97, 109, 122, 138, 170, 186, 200, 223). Some of the following records may be for this other Robert McKay.

Indiana Territory, Switzerland Circuit Court Records, Order Book, October Term 1814 to March Term 1815. p.7.
Robert McKay is listed in county records for the first time on 27 March 1815, as a juror. Court held at the house of John Francis Dufour in the Town of Vevay.

Early Settlers of Indiana's "GORE" 1803-1820; Compiled and Edited by Shirley Keller Mikesell; Heritage Books, Inc., 1995.
p. 34.
Franklin County – Township 12, Range 13E
Section 34 – Robert McKoy -   1816 -1pg. 47.
p. 187.
Switzerland County Original Land Entries Tract Book
Township 2, Range 3W
Section 31 – Robert McKay – 1816 – pg. 10.
p. 190.
Switzerland County Deeds; Book A

280

Deed dated 1815. Isaac Bledsoe of Gallatin co., KY to Robert McKay. R3, T1, S5. "to Sturman Craig's land …to James McKay's corner" Signed by Isaac Bledsoe. Relinquishment of dower rights by Elizabeth Bledsoe, wife of Isaac. Witness: none. pg 1.
p. 193.
Switzerland County Deeds; Book A
Deed dated 1816. Robert McKay to Stuman Craig. S%, T1, R3. Signed Robert (x) McKay, Polly (x) McKay. Witness: John Gilliland. pp. 56, 57.
p. 194.
Switzerland County Deeds; Book A
Deed dated 1816. Stuman Craig to Robert McKay. S6, T1, R3. Signed Stuman Craig, Elizabeth Craig. Witness: none. Note by George Craig, JP: Elizabeth, wife of Stuman. pp. 60, 61, 62.

Indiana Land Entries Vol. 1 Cincinnati District, 1801-1840; Margaret R. Waters; *Originally Published Indianapolis 1948, Second Reprint 1979 by The Bookmark, P.O. Box 74, Knightstown, In 46148. p. 91.*
CINCINNNATI LAND DISTRICT – VOL. 1.
Note: --The tract books for the land offices in Indiana are deposited in the office of the Auditor of State, Indianapolis. They and are in the custody of the State clerk. --
Robt. McKay   SW1/4-S27; 10-2-1816. Vol. II, p. 189. Says McKay
FRANKLIN CO.

U.S. Department of Interior, Bureau of Land Management, General Land Office Records; Land Patent Search – accessed 27 June 2012.
McKAY, ROBERT
Accession Nr. CV-0021-555; Document Type – Credit Volume Patent; State – Indiana; Issue Date – 6/29/1814; Cancelled – No
Names on Document: McKay, Robert; McKay, Abraham
Land Office – Jeffersonville; Authority – April 24, 1820 Sale-Cash Entry (3 Stat. 566); Total Acres – 0.00
Land Descriptions: State – IN; Meridian – 2nd PM; Twp-Rng – 004N-011E; Aliquots – NW1/4; Section – 25; County - Jefferson
&
Accession Nr. CV-0022-463; Document Type – Credit Volume Patent; State – Indiana; Issue Date – 10/3/1814; Cancelled – No
Names on Document: McKay, Robert
Land Office – Jeffersonville; Authority – April 24, 1820 Sale-Cash Entry (3 Stat. 566); Total Acres – 0.00
Land Descrioptions: State – IN; Meridian – 2nd PM; Twp-Rng – 003N-012E; Aliquots - _; Section – 17; County – Jefferson
&
Accession Nr. CV-0066-431; Document Type – Credit Volume Patent; State – Indiana; Issue Date – 2/8/1826; Cancelled – No
Names on Document: McKay, Robert; Culver, Aaron
Land Office – Cincinnati; Authority – April 24, 1820 Sale-Cash Entry (3 Stat. 566); Document Nr. 1644; Total Acres – 80.00

Land Descriptions: State – IN; Meridian – 1st PM; Twp-Rng – 002N-003W; Aliquots – W1/2-NW1/4; Section – 31; County – Switzerland

Roster of Soldiers and Patriots of the American Revolution Buried in Indiana, Vol. I; compiled by Mrs. Roscoe C. O'Byrne.; Indiana Daughters of the American Revolution, 1981; p. 272.

McKAY, ROBERT   Jefferson County
Born – Feb. 12, 1760.
Service – Enlisted from Shenandoah Co., Vir., where he lived, Oct. 1779. Served 3 mos. in Capt. Wm. Jennings' Vir. Co., and guarded prisoners at Albemarle Barracks; enlisted Oct., 1780, and served 3 mos. under same capt.; 3 mos. in Capt. George Prince's Vir. Co.
Proof – Pension claim S. 16956.
Died – Last payment of pension Sept. 28, 1835. Probably buried on his farm.
Married – 1782, Lydia Leith. Ch. David, m. 1804 Sophia Smith; John m. 1801 Isabel Gaines; Enoch, m. 1799 Clary H. Smith.
Collected by John Paul Chapter D.A.R.

History of Switzerland County Indiana 1885; Reproduced by the Switzerland County Historical Society, Vevay, Indiana, 1999. The portion of the book relating to Switzerland County in the 1885 printing of the "History of Dearborn, Ohio, and Switzerland Counties, Indiana".
p. 1072.
At the second term of the circuit court, Robert McKay served on the jury.
p. 1146.
"Up to 1812 the settlement of Craig Township was quite sparse. Among the names from that locality in the early days, we find those of ……. Robert McKay, James McKay, Abisha McKay…."
Author's note: These may be for the other McKay family.

The Swiss Settlement of Switzerland County; by Perrett Dufour; published by the Indiana Historical Commission, Indianapolis, IN, 1925.
p. 50-51.
The first deed recorded in the Recorders office of the County was dated 16th January 1815 executed by Isaac Bledsoe and Elizabeth Bledsoe his wife of Gallatin County Kentucky to Robert McKay for 155 acres of land being part of Frac. Sec. No. 5, Town 1, Range 3: the consideration being $612.00.
p.53.
Among the early settlers in the lower end of the county were George Craig, Stuman Craig, Joshua Cain, <u>Robert McKay</u>, James McKay, Abisha McKay and George Ash.

MELLEN, JOHN
aka Melon, Mellon

Patriot: John Mellen
Birth: Date unknown   Oxford, Worcester, MA
Married Spouse 1: Unknown
Service state(s): MA
Service description: Capt. Samuel Curtis, Col. Ebenezer Learned;
                     Capt. Ebenezer Bilknap,
                     Col. Nath'l Hadis, Capt. Nathan Fisher.
Rank: Private
Proof of Service: Pension application R7015
Pension application No.: R7015
Residences: Oxford, Worcester, MA; Switzerland Co., IN
Died: bef. 1818, prob. Switzerland Co., IN before passage of the Act of Congress
Buried: Unknown
DAR Ancestor No.: None

Pension Application Abstracted from National Archives microfilm Series 805, Roll 580, File R7015.
Application was made by his son John Mellen, age 50. The son's testimony is used in this abstract.
Claim was rejected – File is noted: "he died before the passage of the act"
Pension abstract for – John Mellen   Service state(s): Massachusetts
Alternate spelling(s): Millen
Date: 25 June 1845
County of: Switzerland   State of: Indiana
Declaration made before a Court.
Where and year born: Oxford, Worcester, MA, not date given.
Residence when he entered service: Oxford, Worcester, MA
Rank(s): Private
Statement of service- On the 25th day of June, 1845, in Switzerland County Circuit Court, Indiana, Bila Heavick Esq., acting Justice of the Peace, presented this written affidavit.
Commonwealth of Massachusetts
Secretary's Office, Boston
October 1, 1845
I hereby Certify That, from an examination of the Books and Documents, relating to Military Services in the War of the Revolution, which remain in this Department, it appears that – the name of John Mellen of Oxford is borne upon a Muster roll of Capt. Samuel Curtis's Company, in Col. Ebenezer Learned's regt. as a private from May 15 to August 1, 1775 inclusive. 2 months & 21 days upon a return of said company dated Roxbury, October 1, 1775. Upon a Pay roll of Capt. Ebenezer Bilknap's company in Col. Nath'l Hadis regt for services at R. Island as a private from June 23, 1778 to January 1, 1779. 6 months and 12 days, including allowance of the miles travel. Said company was mustered by Capt. Nathan Fisher and the above is all the evidence of service of anyone of the name as known by records in this office.

No other information is in the file for John Mellen.
And I further Certify That before search made for evidence of said facts, the application hereto annexed was filed in this Office, in the form in which the same now appears: that the search was made by myself and my clerks alone; and that said application, and the certificate above set forth, contain all the facts and circumstances within my knowledge, pertaining to the case.
In Testimony Whereof, I have hereunto affixed the Seal
of the Commonwealth, the date above written.
[Signature uncertain] John ? P??????
Secretary of the Commonwealth
Document –
        New York, Indiana
Oct. 25, 1845
Sir,
I herewith send you some papers at the request of John Mellen, Esq. of Patriot, Indiana not knowing of any law of Congress making any provisions of Pensions or Land to such soldier. I send the same to you. You will please write him upon the Subject.
Most respectfully,
William C. Keen

Massachusetts Soldiers and Sailors of the Revolutionary War, A Compilation from the Archives; prepared and published by the Secretary of the Commonwealth in accordance with Chapter 100, Resolves of 1891, Vol. X; Wright & Potter Printing Co., State Printers, Boston, MA, 1904. p.743.
MILLEN, JOHN, Oxford. Private, Capt. Samuel Curtis's co., Col. Ebenezer Learned's regt.; muster roll dated Aug. 1, 1775; enlisted May 15, 1775; service, 2 mos., 3 weeks, 1 day.
&
Vol. X, p. 787.
MILLINS, JOHN, Oxford. Private, Capt. Samuel Curtiss's co., Col. Ebenezer Learned's (4th) regt.; company return dated Roxbury, Oct. 7, 1775

Register of Certificates Issued by John Pierce, Esquire, Paymaster General and Commissioner of Army Accounts for the United States, to Officers and Soldiers of the Continental Army Under Act of July 4, 1783; Originally Published as Senate Documents, Vol.9, No. 988, 63rd Congress, 3d Session, Washington, 1915; Seventeenth report of the National Society of the Daughters of the American Revolution; Genealogical Publishing Co., Inc, Baltimore, MD, 1984. p. 349.
Men listed in this volume with the same name.

No. of Certificate	To whom issued	Amount
72461	Mellen, John	33.00
74243	Mellen, John	80.00
74024	Mellin, John	70.40
74916	Mellin, John	40.60
7529	Mellon, John	80.00
29146	Meloin, John	80.00

Rejected or Suspended Applications for Revolutionary War Pensions; Reprinted for Clearfield Company Inc. by Genealogical Publishing Co., Inc., Baltimore, MD, 1998. p. 413.

A list of the names of persons residing in Indiana who have applied for pensions under the act of June 7, 1832, whose claims have been suspended; prepared in conformity with the resolution of the Senate of the United States of September 16, 1850, p. 413.

Names	Residence	Reasons for rejection
MELLEN, JOHN (dec'd)	New York, Switzerland	He died before the passage of the act.

and

A list of the names of persons residing in Kentucky who have applied for pensions under the act of June 7, 1832, whose claims have been suspended; prepared in conformity with the resolution of the Senate of the United States of September 16, 1850, p. 362.

MILLION, JOHN	-, Madison	Not six months' service.

MOORE, RODERICK

Patriot: Roderick Moore
Birth: 9 Feb 1761   Salisbury, Litchfield Co., CT
Married Spouse 1: 2 Jun 1787 Chemngo Co., NY Mary Guthrie
                 (b. 24 Dec 1770 CT d. 1849 Switzerland Co., IN)
                 [Note – see Final Payment Voucher Dated Sept. 1854]
Service state(s): CT
Service description: Capt. Roger, Col. Enos, Capt. Roger Moore
Rank: Private
Proof of Service: Pension application W9578
Pension application No.: W9578
Residences: Salisbury, Litchfield Co., CT; NY; OH; Indiana Territory;
             Switzerland Co., IN
Died: 16 Jun 1841 Switzerland Co., IN
Buried: Unknown
DAR Ancestor No.: A087618

Pension Application Abstracted from National Archives microfilm Series 805, Roll 596, File W9578.
Pension abstract for – Roderick Moore   Service state(s): Connecticut
Date: 17 September 1832
County of: Switzerland   State of: Indiana
Declaration made before a Court.
Recorded in Book F, pg. 74.
Age: 71 years
Where and year born: Salisbury, CT on 9 February 1761
Record of age: Age is recorded in the Clerk's Books in the town of Salisbury,
               Litchfield Co., CT
Residence when he entered service: Salisbury Twp., Litchfield Co., CT
Residence(s) since the war: In Salisbury after the war, 3 years in New York
                 about 25 years, in Ohio about 37 years, about 14
                 years in Indiana.
Residence now: Switzerland Co., IN
Volunteer or Drafted or Substitute: Enlisted one tour, volunteered one tour.
Rank(s): Private
Statement of service-

Period	Duration	Names of General and Field Officers
1777	6 months	A Litchfield Co. company Connecticut Militia commanded by Capt. Rogers, regiment commanded by Col. Enos.
Jul or Aug 1778	2 months	Company belonging to same county commanded by Capt. Roger Moore.

Person now living who can testify to service: His brother's, Orson, affidavit is
                                              annexed.
Clergyman: John Pavy
Samuel Blake certifies acquaintance & belief of service.

286

Persons in neighborhood who certify character: Ambert Gazley, Samuel Jack, Amos A. Brown, Bela Hedick, Henry Weist, Col. A.C, Pepper, Wm. Landis, Caleb A. Craft, Colin McNutt.

&

Widow, Mary Moore, Application for Pension
Date: 11 November 1841
County of: Switzerland   State of: Indiana
Declaration made before a Judge. She unable to attend court by reason of bodily disability.
Widow's place and date of birth: (Place not stated) 24 December 1770
Widow's residence: Jefferson Twp., Switzerland Co. IN
Soldier died 16 June 1841 in Switzerland Co., IN
Marriage date and place: 2 June 1787 in Chenango Co., NY
Proof of marriage: Family record is in the file.
Names and ages of children: from Family Record in file.

Cynthia	b. 21 Mar 1788	
Erastus	b. 24 Sep 1790	
Lucretia	b. 20 Nov 1793	
William	b. 14 Feb 1795	d. 22 Jun 1795
Jeremiah	b. 12 Jul 1796	d. 30 Jul 1800
Almon	b. 30 Jun 1800	
Maryann	b. 28 Oct 1802	d. 10 Sep 1823
Philena	b. 16 Jul 1805	
Roderick, Jr.	b. 20 Nov 1808	
Charlotte	b. 18 Jan 1811	

Additional family information: Orson Moore, brother of solder, age 62 in 1832 residing in Switzerland Co., IN

Switzerland County, Indiana Probate Order Book 3, 1837-1843; pp. 375, 376, 408, 417, 450, 475, 499; and *Switzerland County, Indiana Probate Orders Book, 1843-1849, p.152, 199, 248.*
Abstract of will and/or administration for: Roderick Moore
State & county where recorded: Switzerland Co., Indiana
Book/volume where recorded: Probate Order Book 3, 1837-1843
Date entered in probate: 1 July 1841
Administration:
Date began - 1 July 1841
Name of administrator – Widow relinquished her rights to Erastus Moore
8 October 1841 – Erastus Moore since his appointment has departed this life. The Court appoints John Barker as administrator.
10 November 1841 – a note of $46.00 on Erastus Moore payable to Roderick Moore be given up to the widow of the said deceased Roderick Moore. The note compasses part of the hundred dollars for which she accepted administration.
Date of death: (if specifically mentioned):
Place of death: Switzerland County
Bonded by and amount of bond:
Erastus Moore filed bond with Samuel Howard for $1,500.00
John Barker filed bond with George A. Jackson for $1,500.00

Names of heirs and others mentioned in will (also signed receipts of division of estate) and relationship if shown: Widow not named.
Date of division & disbursement, or final return: After November 1846

Abstract of Final Payment Voucher; General Services Administration, Washington, DC
LAST FINAL PAYMENT VOUCHER RECEIVED FROM
THE GENERAL ACCOUNTING OFFICE
NAME   Moore, Roderick
AGENCY OF PAYMENT   Indiana
DATE OF ACT   1832
DATE OF PAYMENT   4th Qr. 1841
DATE OF DEATH   July 16, 1841
GENERAL SERVICES ADMINISTRATION
National Archives and Records Service   NA-286
GSA-WASH DC 54-4891   November 1953
&

Abstract of Final Payment Voucher; General Services Administration, Washington, DC
NAME   Moore, Mary widow of Roderick
AGENCY OF PAYMENT   Madison, Ind.
DATE OF ACT   1848
DATE OF PAYMENT   Sept. 1854
DATE OF DEATH
LAST FINAL PAYMENT VOUCHER RECEIVED FROM
THE GENERAL ACCOUNTING OFFICE   Form
General Services Administration   GSA DA 70-7035   GSA Dec 69   7068

Switzerland County, Indiana Civil Order Book Vol., A, Oct. 19, 1829-April 16, 1837, p. 171.
In the matter of Robert Moore, Griffith Dickinson, Nathan Ricketts, Gideon Tower, and John Shaddy, An application to obtain a pension under the Act of Congress of the 7th June AD 1832.

  Personally appeared in open Court, before the Switzerland Circuit Court now sitting the above named applicants who being first duly Sworn doth on their several oaths make their several declarations in order to obtain the benefit of the Act of Congress of the 7th June AD 1832 that they entered the Service of the United States under the officers named in their several declarations (here insert them) And the said Court do hereby declare their opinion after the investigation of the matter and after putting the interrogations prescribed by the War department that the above named Applicants were revolutionary Soldiers and Served as they have stated and the Court further Certifies that it appears to them that John Pavy who Signed their several Certificates is a Clergyman Resident in Switzerland County and State of Indiana and the other persons who has also Signed the Same are credible persons and that their Statements in entitled to credit.

Early Ohio Settlers, Purchasers of Land in Southwestern Ohio, 1800-1840; Compiled by Ellen T. Berry & David A. Berry; Genealogical Publishing Co., Inc., Baltimore, MD, 1986. p.230.

Purchaser	Year	Date	Residence	R – T - S
Moore, Roderick (B)	1815	Nov. 24	Hamilton	02-06-29

(B) Indiana Survey: Land lying west of a meridian drawn west of the Great Miami (known as the "Gore"). Switzerland, Dearborn, Franklin, Ohio, Union and Randolph Counties (all or only a part of each county) – all in Indiana.

Early Settlers of Indiana's "GORE" 1803-1820; Compiled and Edited by Shirley Keller Mikesell; Heritage Books, Inc., 1995. p. 182.
Switzerland County - Township 2, Range 1W
Section 9 – Roderick & E. Moore – 1817 – pg. 2.

Indiana Land Entries Vol. 1 Cincinnati District, 1801-1840; Margaret R. Waters; Originally Published Indianapolis 1948, Second Reprint 1979 by The Bookmark, P.O. Box 74, Knightstown, In 46148. p.2.
CINCINNNATI LAND DISTRICT – VOL. 1
Page 2. Twp. 2 N, Range 1 W of 1st Principle Meridian SWITZERLAND CO. Roderick Moore & Erastus Moore NE ¼ - S9; 3-24-1817.
-- Note: The tract books for the land offices in Indiana are deposited in the office of the Auditor of State, Indianapolis. They and are in the custody of the State Land clerk. --

U.S. Department of Interior, Bureau of Land Management, General Land Office Records; Land Patent Search – accessed 27 June 2012.
MOORE, RODERICK
Accession Nr. CV-0060-351; Document Type – Credit Volume Patent; State – Indiana; Issue Date – 9/9/1824; Cancelled – No
Names on Document: Moore, Roderick; Moore, Erastus
Land Office – Cincinnati; Authority – April 24, 182 Sale-Cash Entry (3 Stat. 566); Document Nr. 531; Total Aces – 159.60
Land Descriptions: State – IN; Meridian – 1st PM; Twp-Rng – 002N-001W; Aliquots – NE1/4; Section – 9; County - Switzerland
&
Accession Nr. CV-0070-087; Document Type – Credit Volume Patent; State – Indiana; Issue Date – 3/20/1828; Cancelled – No
Names on Document: Stilts, William; Bowers, James W.; Moore, Roderick
Land Office – Cincinnati; Authority – April 24, 1820 (3 Stat. 566); Document Nr. 2356; Total Acres – 80.00
Land Descriptions: State – IN; Meridian – 1st PM; Twp-Rng – 006N-002W; aliquots – E1/2SW1/4; Section – 29; County – Dearborn

1820 U.S. Census, Indiana, Switzerland, Posey, Series: M33 Roll: 14 Page: 262
Roderick Moore 45 and up; others in household 1 male 10-16, 1 male 16-26, 1 male 26-45, 1 female under 10, 1 female 10-16, 1 female 16-26, 1 female 45 and up.

Revolutionary Soldiers of Switzerland County; Copied by *Mary Hill, John Paul Chapter-Daughters of the American Revolution; January, 1958;* http://www.ingenweb.org/inswitzerland/switzrevsoldiers.html- Viewed June 2012.
MOORE, RODERICK   Pension W9578
Born February 9, 1761 in Salidbury, Litchfield County, Connecticut.
While residing in Salisbury, Conn. Roderick Moore enlisted some time in June or July, 1777, and served as a private six months in Captain Roger's company, Colonel Eno's Connecticut regiment.
He enlisted sometime in July or August, 1773, served two months in Captain Roger Moore's Connecticut company: it was not stated that he was related to soldier.
Roderick Moore continued to live in Connecticut for about three years after the Revolution, then moved to New York, where he lived about twenty-five years, then to Ohio, lived about three years, thence to Indiana.
He was allowed pension on his application executed September 17, 1832, at which time he was a resident of Switzerland Co. Indiana.
Roderick Moore married June 16, 1841, Mary Guthery (b. 1770), in Switzerland Co., IN
Children of Roderick Moore & wife, Mary:
Cynthia, born March 21, 1788
Erastus, born Sept. 24, 1790
Lucretia, born Nov. 20, 1792
William, born Feb. 14, 1795, died June 22, 1795
Jeremiah, born July 12, 1796; died July 30, 1800
Almon, born June 30, 1800
Maryann, born Oct. 28, 1802, died Sept. 10, 1823
Philena, born July 16, 1805
Roderick, Jr. born Nov. 20, 1808
Charlotte, born Jan. 18, 1811
His widow, Mary Moore, was allowed pension on her application executed Nov. 11, 1841. at which time she was living in Jefferson two. Switzerland Co. Ind. She was still living in Switzerland Co. in 1849. Certificate #4672, issued April 6, 1849; Rate, $26,66 per annum, commenced Mar. 4, 1848, Act of Feb. 2, 1848, Indiana (Madison) Agency.
Orson Moore, brother of the soldier, Roderick Moore, was aged about 62 yers. in 1832, then a resident of Switz. Co. Indiana.
To get name of person paid & date of death of widow, apply to the Comptroller General, General Accounting Office, Records Division, Washington D.C. and give the following data:
Mary Moore, widow of Roderick Moore; Certificate #4672, issued April 6, 1849; Rate, $26,66 per annum, commenced Mar. 4, 1848, Act of Feb. 2, 1848, Indiana (Madison) Agency.

Roster of Soldiers and Patriots of the American Revolution Buried in Indiana, Vol. I; compiled by *Mrs. Roscoe C. O'Byrne.; Indiana Daughters of the American Revolution, 1981; p.260.*
MOORE, RODERICK   Switzerland County
Born - Feb 9, 1761, Salisbury, Connecticut.

Service – Enlisted from Salisbury in June or July, 1777, pri., 6 mos. in Capt. Roger's CO., Col. Enos' Conn. regt. Enlisted 1778, 2 mos. in Capt. Roger Moore's Conn. CO.
Proof – Pension claim W. 2578.
Died – June 16, 1841, Switzerland Co.
Married – 1787, Mary Guthery b. 1770. Ch. Cynthia b. 1788; Erastus b. 1790; Lucretia (1792-1860, m. Ethel B. Lyon; William b. and d. 1795; Jeremiah (1798-180); Almon b. 1800, m. 1825 Laura Pearson; Mary Ann (1802-1823; Philena b. 1805, m. John Barker; Roderick Jr. b. 1808, m. Mary Phillips; Charlotte b. 1811.
Collected by Mrs. A. V. Danner, Vevay, Indiana.

History of Switzerland County Indiana 1885; Reproduced by the Switzerland County Historical Society, Vevay, Indiana, 1999. The portion of the book relating to Switzerland County in the 1885 printing of the "History of Dearborn, Ohio, and Switzerland Counties, Indiana". p. 1244.
In the passage about E. B. Lyon, his wife Lucretia – "Lucretia Moore was a daughter of Roderic Moore, an early settler at North Bend, where he was employed by Gen. Harrison as dairy man. He settled in Switzerland County about 1818, entering the George Dibble farm, on which still stands the old cabin, built by him. He married Mary Guthery in New York, and they raised seven children, namely: Cynthia, Erastus, Lucretia, Almond, Philena, Roderick and Charlotte. The grandfather, Roderick St., was a Revolutionary soldier."

The Vevay Reveille-Enterprise; Vol. 122, No. 37, 22 Sep 1935, p. 7, col. 3.
Roster of Revolutionary Soldiers Who Resided in Switzerland County
By Mrs. Effa M. Danner
Roderick Moore – No. W9578. Was born February 9, 1761 in Salisbarg, Litchfield Co., Conn. Enlisted there June 1777, served six months, Capt. Rogers Co., Col. Enos, Conn. Regiment. Enlisted August 1778, served two months Capt. Rogers Moore, Conn. co. Not stated if related. He lived in Connecticut three years after the war, in New York 25 years, in Ohio three years and Indiana. Allowed pension September 17, 1832 Switzerland County, Ind. He married June 2, 1797 in Chanango Co., New York, Mary Guthery, born Dec. 24, 1770. He died June 16, 1841.
Mary Moore allowed pension 1841 and still living 1849, New York (now Florence) Switzerland County, Mary Moore waves right of administrator of Roderick Moore estate "to my son Erastus Moore", p. 375 – Erastus Moore's bond $1500, p. 408, John Barker appears stating the death of Erastus Moore and is himself appointed in his place.
Census 1820, Roderick Moore, wife, three boys, four girls. Land grant T2, R. 1W, Sec. 9, N.E. 159 acres, March 1819.
Cynthia born Mar. 21, 1788; Erastus born Sept. 24, 1796; Lucretia born Nov. 20, 1792, married Ethol b. Lyon, July 1, 1818; William born Feb. 14, 1795, died June 23, 1795; Jeremiah born July 12, 1796, died July 30, 1800; Alman born June 30, 1800, married Lauree Pearson 1825; Mary Ann born Oct. 28, 1802, died Sept. 10, 1823; Phelent born July 16, 1806, married John Barker, Sept. 20, 1824; Roderick Jr., born Nov. 20, 1808, married Mary Phillips, Nov. 7, 1838; Charlotte born Jan. 18, 1811.

Orson Moore, brother of Roderick Moore, Sr., resides in Switzerland Co., in 1832.

Author's note: Orson Moore, brother of Roderick Moore, was about age 62 in 1832. He would have been born abt. 1770 therefore he was too young to have participated in the Revolutionary War.

MORGAN, DANIEL

Records have not been identified regarding a man of this name serving in the Revolutionary War or residing in Switzerland County. The only mention of this man is in Margaret Water's *Revolutionary War Soldiers Buried in Indiana* (see below).

Patriot: Daniel Morgan
Birth: -
Married Spouse 1: Unknown
Service state(s): -
Service description: -
Rank: -
Proof of Service: -
Pension application No.: -
Residences: Unknown; Switzerland Co., IN
Died: 1839   Switzerland Co., IN
Buried: Unknown
DAR Ancestor No.: -

Revolutionary Soldiers Buried in Indiana A Supplement; 485 Names Not Listed in the Roster of Soldiers and Patriots of the American Revolution Buried in Indiana (1938) nor in Revolutionary Soldiers Buried in Indiana (1949); Margaret E. Waters; Indianapolis, 1954. p.74.
MORGAN, DANIEL   Switzerland
Rev. sold. who d. 1839.
REF: Mrs. Herbert R. Hill, Indianapolis.

MORGAN, NATHAN

Patriot: Nathan Morgan
Birth: 22 Oct 1752 Delaware
Married Spouse 1: 30 Dec 1775   XX
Married Spouse 2: 1791/1792   Elizabeth Williams (d. 1813)
Service state(s): VA
Service description: Capt. William Love, Co. Preston
Rank: Private
Proof of Service: Pension application S16985
Pension application No.: S16985
Residences: Lynchburg, Bedford Co., VA; GA; SC; KY; Switzerland Co., IN
Died: 1833/1834 Vevay, Switzerland Co., IN
Buried: McKay Cemetery, Craig Twp., Switzerland Co., IN
DAR Ancestor No.: A080563

Pension Application Abstracted from National Archives microfilm Series 805, Roll 598, File S16985.; Switzerland County, Indiana Probate Record Book Vol. A, Mar 1827-Nov 1834; p. 326.

Pension abstract for – Nathan Morgan   Service state(s): Virginia
Date: 14 November 1832
County of: Switzerland   State of: Indiana
Declaration made before Probate Court.
Age: 80 years   Record of age: At home copied from mother's record
Where and year born: State of Delaware on 22 October 1752.
Residence when he entered service: Virginia
Residence(s) since the war: Virginia about 2 years, Georgia about 8 years, South Carolina about 3 years, Kentucky about 2 years, Indiana 20 years.
Residence now: Switzerland Co., IN
Volunteer or Drafted or Substitute: Volunteered
Rank(s): Private
Statement of service-

Period	Duration	Names of General and Field Officers
1777 or 1778	3 tours	Col. Preston's regt., Capt. William Love's company.

Most of service at Chizel's Lead Mine in Montgomery Co., VA.
Battles: None
Discharge received: No written discharge
Statement is supported by –
Evidence: Traditionary
Clergyman: Samuel Pavy
Persons in neighborhood who certify character: Charles B. Freeman, Perrett Harvey, Johnson Brown, Henry Peters, Robert McKay, Jacob Kern.
No data regarding soldier's family in the file.

Switzerland County, Indiana Probate Order Book 2, 1831-1837; p. 91.
14 November 1832
In the matter of } An Applicant for a Pension under the act of Congress of the

Nathan Morgan} 7 June 1832.
   Come the Said Nathan Morgan before the Probate Court of Switzerland County now Sitting and under oath makes the following Report of himself (here insert it) and the Said Court do hereby declare their opinion after the investigation of the matter, and after putting the interrogations prescribed by the war department that the above named Nathan Morgan was a Revolutionary Soldier and Served as he Stated And Said Court further Certifies that it appears to them that Samuel Pavy who has Signed the preceding Certificate is a Clergyman resident in Switzerland County and State of Indiana and that Charles B. Froman who also Signed the same is a resident of Switzerland County and State of Indiana and is a credible person and their Statement is entitled to Credit.

Switzerland County, Indiana Probate Order Book 2, 1831-1837; p. 455.
19 November 1836
   Now comes Lewis H. Morgan of Switzerland County of lawful age and proves to the satisfaction of the Court that Nathan Morgan late of Said County and Revolutionary pensioner departed this life at his late residence in Craig township Switzerland County on the 27th day of August AD 1835 leaving in Said County the following children his Viz. Samuel, Rachel, Nancy, Lewis H. and Willis Morgan and no widow, that the Said Nathan Morgan had some children by another wife what names and residences are not known.

Switzerland County, Indiana Probate Order Book 2, 1831-1837;, pp. 328, 346, 366, 387, 430, 456, 503; and *Switzerland County, Indiana Probate Order Book 3, 1837-1843*; pp. 42, 68, 99, 125, 145, 179, 206, 243, 281.
Abstract of Administration for: NATHAN MORGAN of Craig Township
State & County where recorded: Switzerland Co., Indiana
Book/volume where recorded: Probate Order Book 2 and 3.
Date entered in probate: 17 Oct 1835
Administration:
Date began – 17 Oct 1835
Name of Administrator- Lewis H. Morgan
Date of Death: Proven by the Oath of Robert McKay that 15 days had elapsed since the death of Nathan Morgan.
Place of Death: Switzerland County, IN
Bonded by and amount of bond: Charles B. Frieman for $600.00
Names of Heirs and others mentioned in will (also signed receipts of division of estate) and relationship if shown: None. Administrator is probably related.
Date of Division & Disbursement , or final Return: 14 August 1838 report filed.
Final return is not indexed, and has not been located by the author.

Abstract of Final Payment Voucher; General Services Administration, Washington, DC
LAST FINAL PAYMENT VOUCHER RECEIVED FROM
THE GENERAL ACCOUNTING OFFICE
NAME   Morgan, Nathan
AGENCY OF PAYMENT   Indiana
DATE OF ACT   1832

DATE OF PAYMENT   Sept 3, 1834
DATE OF DEATH
GENERAL SERVICES ADMINISTRATION
National Archives and Records Service   NA-286
GSA-WASH DC 54-4891   November 1953

Annals of Southwest Virginia 1769-1800; Lewis Preston summers; Genealogical Publishing Co., Inc. p. 771.
At a Court held and cond. For Montgomery County May 8th 1782 ..produced sufficient proof to this Court that he ought to be paid for provisions furnished himself when on duty in North Carolina to join G. Green also for Blankett lost in action at Reedy Fork. Nathan Morgan 10/ also 1 Blankett 25/

Virginia Militia in the Revolutionary War; J.T. McAllister, McAllister Publishing Co., Hot Springs, VA, 1913. p. 283..
Part V, Pensioners Residing Outside of Virginia in 1835 who Received Pensions as Virginia Militiamen.
Morgan, Nathan   74 [age]   Switzerland   Indiana

Virginia Revolutionary Publick Claims in three volumes; compiled and transcribed b Janice L. Abercrombie and Richard Slatten; Iberian Publishing Co., Athens, GA, 1992.
p. 687. Montgomery County – Montgomery County Court Booklet – Account of claims (torn) the county court of Montgomery in the year 1782 and 1783.
Pg. 24 Montgomery May Court 1782 – The following persons proved to the satisfaction of the court that they ought to be paid the following sums for provisions furnished themselves on their march to join Gen. Green in North Carolina.
Nathan Morgan 10s [shillings] for 10 days provisions and 1 blanket lost.
p. 688. Nathan Morgan for 10 days provisions.

Historical Register of Virginians in the Revolution, Soldiers, Sailors, Marines, 1775-1783; John H. Gwathmey; The Dietz Press, Richmond, VA, 1938. p. 564.
Morgan, Nathan, 74, Switzerland Co., Ind., mpl.

Register of Certificates Issued by John Pierce, Esquire, Paymaster General and Commissioner of Army Accounts for the United States, to Officers and Soldiers of the Continental Army Under Act of July 4, 1783; Originally Published as Senate Documents, Vol.9, No. 988, 63rd Congress, 3d Session, Washington, 1915; Seventeenth report of the National Society of the Daughters of the American Revolution; Genealogical Publishing Co., Inc, Baltimore, MD, 1984. p. 363.
Men listed in this volume with the same name.

No. of Certificate	To whom issued	Amount
41511	Morgan, Nathaniel	26.11

Second Census of Kentucky, 1800; Clift G. Glenn; Genealogical Publishing Co., Baltimore, MD, 1954.

An alphabetical list of 32,000 taxpayers based on original tax lists on file at the Kentucky Historical Society. Information given includes the county of residence and the date of the tax list in which the individual is listed.
Morgan, Nathan   Campbell   9/1/1800

Indiana Territory, Switzerland Circuit Court Records, Order Book, October Term 1814 to March Term 1815. p.6.
He is listed in county records for the first time on 27 March 1815, as a juror. Court held at the house of John Francis Dufour in the Town of Vevay.

Roster of Soldiers and Patriots of the American Revolution Buried in Indiana, Vol. I; compiled by Mrs. Roscoe C. O'Byrne.; Indiana Daughters of the American Revolution, 1981; p.261.
MORGAN, NATHAN   Switzerland County
Born 22 Oct 1752, Delaware
Service – Volunteered 1777, served 2 terms, 6 mos. in all as pri. in Capt. Wm. Love's CO. Preston, Vir. Regt. Most of his service he was stationed at "Chizels" Lead Mine in Montgomery Co., Vir.
Proof – Pension claim S. 16985.
Died 4 Sep 1839 Buried in McKay Cemetery, Craig Twp. Stone
Married - Unknown
Children - Lewis Howell, married Elizabeth Freeman
Collected by Mrs. A. V. Danner, Vevay, Indiana.

Roster of Soldiers and Patriots of the American Revolution Buried in Indiana, Vol. III; 1980; p.70.
MORGAN, NATHAN   Roster I, p. 261   Switzerland County
Additional data or corrections.
Died – Court records in Switzerland Co., Ind. Nov. 18, 1836, p. 455 state Lewis H. Morgan reported death of his father, Nathan Morgan, on Aug. 27, 1835 in Craig Twp., Switzerland Co., Ind.
Children – Samuel; Rachel; Nancy; Lewis H.; Wallus.
By Mrs. A. G. Charlton, 310 Sunnyside Avenue, Aurora, Indiana 47001.

Abstract of Graves of Revolutionary Patriots (4 volumes); by Patricia Law Hatcher; Pioneer Heritage Press, Dallas, TX, 1987. Vol. 3, p. 100.
This is an abstract and an index to information reported to the Daughters of the American Revolution and published in their annual reports to the Smithsonian Institution, printed as Senate Documents (1900-1974) and published annually in the DAR magazine (1978-1987).
Published 1972 (Senate Doc. 54)
MORGAN, Nathan   Mckay Cem, Craig Twp, Switzerland Co., IN

The Vevay Reveille-Enterprise; Vol. 122, No. 37, 22 Sep 1935, p. 3, col. 2.
Roster of Revolutionary Soldiers Who Resided in Switzerland County
By Mrs. Effa M. Danner

The data which follows are obtained from the papers on file in Revolutionary War pension claim, S16985, upon the military service in the war of Nathan Morgan.

Nathan Morgan – was born October 22, 1752 in the state of Delaware. The names of his parents are not shown.

While residing in Virginia, Nathan Morgan volunteered in 1777 or 1778, exact date not shown, and served three tours, at least six months in all, as a private in Captain William Love's Company, Col. Preston's Virginia Regiment and during a considerable part of his service was stationed at "Chizel's" Lead Mines in Montgomery County, Virginia.

After the Revolution, he continued to reside in Virginia for about two years, then moved to Georgia and lived about eight years; thence to South Carolina and lived three years; thence to Kentucky and lived about two years; thence to the state of Indiana, in which state he had resided about twenty years when he was allowed pension on his application executed November 14, 1832, while residing in Switzerland County, that state.

There are no data as to soldier's family.

Probate court, Switzerland Co., 1832, p. 91 petition for pension, signed by Rev. Samuel Pavy and Chas. B. Freeman, witnesses.

Nov. 19, 1836, p. 455, Lewis B. Morgan reports death of his father, Nathan Morgan on 27th day of Aug. 1835 in Craig township.

Children, Samuel, Rachel, Nancy, Lewis H. and Wallas Morgan, no widow.

Lewis Howell Morgan, Elizabeth Freeman, April 4, 1829.

Nathan Morgan is buried in the McKay cemetery, Craig township, Switzerland County.

MOSS, ZEALLY

Patriot: Zeally Moss
Birth: 6 Mar 1755
Married Spouse 1: 1776   Martha Elizabeth "Marty" Berry
                          (b. 1756 VA, d. abt. 1790)
Married Spouse 2: 2 Oct 1790 Fauquier Co., VA
                          Jennette "Jane" "Jenny" Glascock
                          (b. 17 May 1776/1777, d. 7/9 Jan 1864)
Service state(s): VA
Service description: Quartermaster Claiborne, of Virginia
Rank: Asst. Quartermaster (Captain)
Proof of Service: Pension application W24164
Pension application No.: W24164
Residences: Loudoun Fauquier Co., VA; Indiana Territory;
            Switzerland Co., IN; Peoria Co., IL
Died: 31 Oct 1839 Peoria Co., IL
Buried: Springdale Cemetery, Peoria, Peoria Co., IL
DAR Ancestor No.: None
Daughter: Lydia (Moss) Bradley

Virginia Marriages, Fauquier County, No. 447.
02 Oct 1790, Zealy Moss to Jane Glascock.

Pension Application Abstracted from National Archives microfilm Series 805, Roll 603, File W24164.
Abstracted from pension application – Zeally Moss
Service – Virginia
Rank – Assistant Quartermaster (captain)
m. (marr. record) 28 Oct 1790, Fauquier Co., VA to Jane Clascock (on same record Jenny and Jennett Glascock).
Soldier applied 8 Apr 1832(?), aged seventy-nine.
d. 31 Oct 1839
Widow applied for pens.1848, in Peoria Co., IL.

National Archives microfilm Series 805, Roll 603, File W24164
Letter from War Dept. in Pension File – Zeally Moss
November 27, 1933
Mary Ranney   BA-J/MMHF/cal
670 Lexington Avenue   Zeally Moss-S.31464
Stockton, California
Dear Madame:
    Zeally Moss was a native of Virginia; the date of his birth is not shown in the papers in the pension claim, nor are names of his parents given.
    In March or April, 1777, while residing in Loudoun County, Virginia, he was appointed assistant quartermaster (graded as captain) and served under Quartermaster Claiborne, of Virginia, until he was appointed wagon master in 1780 and served as such until after the surrender of Cornwallis at which he was

present. In 1783 and 1784, he was engaged in building forts in Kentucky and in defending that country against Indian invasions.

Pension was allowed on his application executed April 8, 1824, while a resident of Switzerland County, Indiana, aged seventy-nine years.

He died October 31, 1839, in Peoria County, Illinois.

Soldier married October 28, 1790, Jenny (the name also appears as Jennett and Jane) Glascock. They were married in Fauquier County, Virginia.

Soldier's widow, Jenny, was allowed pension on her application executed March 19, 1851, while a resident of Peoria County, Illinois, aged eighty-one years.

Two sons were referred to: William S. Moss, the only one stated.

There are no further family data.

In order to obtain the date of last payment of pension, the name and address of person paid and possibly the date of death of the Revolutionary pensioner, Jenny Moss, widow of Zeally Moss (W.24164) you should address the Comptroller General, General Accounting Office, Records division, this city, citing the following data:

Jennie Moss, widow of Zeally Moss, Certificate No.5849, issued September 10, 1852, rate $600 per annum, commenced March 4, 1848, Act of February 2, 1848, Illinois Agency.

        Very truly yours,
        A.D. HILLER
        Assistant to Administrator

Abstract of Final Payment Voucher; General Services Administration, Washington, DC
LAST FINAL PAYMENT VOUCHER RECEIVED FROM
THE GENERAL ACCOUNTING OFFICE
NAME   Moss, Zealy
AGENCY OF PAYMENT   Illinois
DATE OF ACT   1832
DATE OF PAYMENT   1st qtr. 1852
DATE OF DEATH   Oct 1, 1839
GENERAL SERVICES ADMINISTRATION
National Archives and Records Service   NA-286
GSA-WASH DC 54-4891   November 1953
&

Abstract of Final Payment Voucher; General Services Administration, Washington, DC
LAST FINAL PAYMENT VOUCHER RECEIVED FROM
THE GENERAL ACCOUNTING OFFICE
NAME   Moss, Jenny (Leally)
AGENCY OF PAYMENT   Illinois, Springfield
DATE OF ACT   1848
DATE OF PAYMENT   3rd qtr. 1864 pd in full
DATE OF DEATH   Jan 9, 1864
GENERAL SERVICES ADMINISTRATION
National Archives and Records Service   NA-286

GSA-WASH DC 54-4891   November 1953

Early Ohio Settlers, Purchasers of Land in Southwestern Ohio, 1800-1840;
Compiled by Ellen T. Berry & David A. Berry; Genealogical Publishing Co.,
Inc., Baltimore, MD, 1986. p.233.

Purchaser	Year	Date	Residence	R – T - S
Moss, Zealley (B)	1814	Oct. 13	Ind Territory	01-02-17
Moss, Zealley (B)	1814	Oct. 13	Ind Territory	01-02-28
Moss, Zealley (B)	1816	Feb. 12	Switzerland	01-02-17

(B) Indiana Survey: Land lying west of a meridian drawn west of the Great
Miami (known as the "Gore"). Switzerland, Dearborn, Franklin, Ohio, Union and
Randolph Counties (all or only a part of each county) – all in Indiana.

Early Settlers of Indiana's "GORE" 1803-1820; Compiled and Edited by Shirley
Keller Mikesell; Heritage Books, Inc., 1995.
p. 183
Switzerland County - Township 2, Range 1W
Section 18 – Zeally Moss – 1817 – pg. 2.
p. 191.
Switzerland County Deed Book A.
Deed dated 1815. Zealy Moss to Barney Barnum. S 34, T 16, R 1. "being James
Truesdell's corner..with John Langlay's line". Signed Zeally Moss. Witness:
Wm. Campbell, Wm. McCorkhill. P. 15, 16.
p. 201.
Switzerland County Deed Book A.
Deed dated 1817. Zeally Moss, Jenny Moss, Barna Barnum & Polly, his wife, to
John Smith. Bounds given in Posey Twp., no S-T-R. Signed Zeally Moss, Janet
Moss, Barna Barnum, Polly Barnum. Witness: Richard Woods, Wms. Peirson.
Pp. 152, 153.

Indiana Land Entries Vol. 1 Cincinnati District, 1801-1840; Margaret R. Waters;
Originally Published Indianapolis 1948, Second Reprint 1979 by The Bookmark,
P.O. Box 74, Knightstown, In 46148. p.3(3), 4.
CINCINNNATI LAND DISTRICT – VOL. 1
Page 3. Bottom torn. From Vol. II, page 3. (Twp. & Range not given)
SWITZERLAND CO.
Zeally Moss   NW ¼ - S17; 2-12-1916.
and –
Page 3. Bottom torn. From Vol. II, page 3. (Twp. & Range not given)
SWITZERLAND CO.
Zeally Moss   SW ¼ S-17, 2-12-1816.
and –
Page 3. Twp. 2 N, Range 1 W of 1st Principle Meridian SWITZERLAND CO.
Zeally Moss   NE ¼ - S18; 1-7-1817. Relinquished W ½.
and –
Page 3. Twp. 2 N, Range 1 W of 1st Principle Meridian SWITZERLAND CO.
Zealley Moss   NE ¼ - S28; 6-11-1813.

301

-- Note: The tract books for the land offices in Indiana are deposited in the office of the Auditor of State, Indianapolis. They and are in the custody of the State Land clerk. --

U.S. Department of Interior, Bureau of Land Management, General Land Office Records; Land Patent Search – accessed 27 June 2012.
MOSS, ZELLY
Accession Nr. CV-0012-381; Document Type – Credit Volume Patent; State – Indiana; Issue Date – 2/20/1812; Cancelled – No
Names on Document: Trusdale, Nathan; Moss, Zelly; Baum, Martin
Land Office – Cincinnati; Authority – April 24, 1820 Sale-Cash Entry (3 Stat. 566); Total Acres – 0.00
Land Descriptions: State – IN; Meridian – 1st PM; Twp-Rng – 002N-001W; Aliquots - _; Section – 34; County - Switzerland
&
Accession Nr. CV-0031-369; Document Type – Credit Volume Patent; State – Indiana; Issue Date – 12/6/1816; Cancelled – No
Land Office – Cincinnati; Authority – April 24, 1820 Sale-Cash Entry (3 Stat. 566); Total Acres – 0.00
Land Descriptions: State – IN; Meridian – 1st PM; Twp-Rng – 002N-001W; Aliquots – NE1/4; Section – 28; County - Switzerland
&
Accession Nr. CV-0032-334; Document Type – Credit Volume Patent; State – Indiana; Issue Date – 2/7/1817; Cancelled – No
Land Office – Cincinnati; Authority – April 24, 1820 Sale-Cash Entry (3 Stat. 566); Total Acres – 0.00
Land Descriptions: State – IN; Meridian – 1st PM; Twp-Rng – 002N-001W; Aliquots – W1/2; Section – 17; County - Switzerland
&
Accession Nr. CV-0059-104; Document Type – Credit Volume Patent; State – Indiana; Issue Date – 7/19/1824; Cancelled – No
Land Office – Cincinnati; Authority – April 24, 1820 Sale-Cash Entry (3 Stat. 566); General Remarks – Patent Record Imperfect; Document Nr. 214; Total Acres – 79.33
Land Descriptions: State – IN; Meridian – 1st PM; Twp-Rng – E1/2-NE1/4; Section – 18; County - Switzerland

1820 U.S. Census, Indiana, Switzerland, Posey, Series: M33 Roll: 14 Page: 260
Zealy Moss 45 and up, also in household 1 male under 10, 1 male 10-16, 1 male 16-26, 1 female under 10, 1 female 16-26, 1 female 45 and up.

Rejected or Suspended Applications for Revolutionary War Pensions; Reprinted *for Clearfield Company Inc. by Genealogical Publishing Co., Inc., Baltimore, MD, 1998, p. 408.*
A list of the names of persons residing in Indiana who have applied for pensions under the act of June 7, 1832, whose claims have been rejected; prepared in conformity with the resolution of the Senate of the United States of September 16, 1850.

Names	Residence	Reasons for rejection
MOSS, ZEALLY	New York, Switzerland	He did not serve in a military capacity.

1860 U.S. Census, Illinois, Peoria, 5-WD Peoria, Series: M653 Roll: 216 Page: 351, Family No. 2833.
Moss, Jennet, Age: 95, Female, Race: White, Born: VA
Author's note: The CHILDREN OF THE AMERICAN REVOLUTION ZEALLY MOSS CHAPTER was named after this patriot. From the chapter web page - http://www.peoriadar.org/car.html: "Zeally Moss fought in the American Revolution. His daughter, Lydia Moss Bradley, was one of [DAR] Peoria Chapter's earliest members. They are both buried at the Springdale Cemetery in Peoria."
The Zealy Moss C.A.R. Chapter was the first established in Illinois in 1905. Later it became inactive, but was started again in 1970 and continues to be a viable group to this day. (2012).

Illinois State Historical Society Journal; Springfield, IL; Oct 1913, Vol. 6, Iss. 3, p. 247-248.
Peoria County
Zealy Moss was a wagon-master and assistant quarter-master in the Virginia troops; he enlisted in Loudon County in the spring of 1777, and served two years in the quarter-master's department. He re-enlisted in 1780 and served to the close of the war. Zealy Moss was born in Loudon County, Virginia, March 5, 1755; died in Peoria, Illinois, October 30, 1835, and is buried in Springdale cemetery, Peoria. His grave is marked.

Soldiers of the American Revolution Buried in Illinois; Illinois State Genealogical Society, Springfield, Il, 1976
MOSS, ZEALLY
Born: March 6, 1775 [OBVIOUS ERROR], Loudoun County, Virginia
Died: October 31, 1839
Buried: Springdale Cemetery, Peoria, Peoria County, Illinois; Private Headstone
Spouses: (1) Elizabeth Berry
          (2) Jeannette Glascock
Service: Captain Wagoneer: Virginia Continental line. He enlisted in 1777 from Loudoun County, Virginia, and served two years. He re-enlisted in 1780 and served to the close of the war.
Pension: Jenny W24164 (Cont. Va.); Moss, Jenny, widow of Zeally (Wagon master, Va.) on Illinois pension roll October 1, 1839.
Marker: The grave has been marked by the Zeally Moss Society, Children of the American Revolution, Peoria.
Sources: DAR, HR, NSDAR, PI, PENSION, W

Abstract of Graves of Revolutionary Patriots (4 volumes); by Patricia Law Hatcher; Pioneer Heritage Press, Dallas, TX, 1987. Vol. 3, p. 107.
This is an abstract and an index to information reported to the Daughters of the American Revolution and published in their annual reports to the Smithsonian

Institution , printed as Senate Documents (1900-1974) and published annually in the DAR magazine (1978-1987).
3.107 – 15
Published 1915, Serial set 6924, Volume 14.
MOSS, Zeally   Peoria IL

National Society of the Sons of the American Revolution - Revolutionary War Graves Register; Compiled and Edited by Clovis H. Brakebill, Published by db Publications, Dallas, TX, 1993. p. 439.
Moss   Zeally; ? – 1839; Springdale Cem, Peoria, IL; Captain, VA; (1)Elizabeth Berry (2)Jennette Glascock.

Springdale Cemetery, Peoria, Peoria Co., IL
Tombstone inscriptions –
    OUR FATHER
    CAPTAIN ZEALLY MOSS
    MAR 6, 1756 – OCT 30, 1839

    OUR MOTHER
    JENNET MOSS
    APR 17, 1766 – JAN 2, 1864

Inscription of plaque on stone -
    IN MEMORY OF
    ZEALLY MOSS
    A SOLDIER OF
    THE AMERICAN
    REVOLUTION

    THIS TABLET
    IS ERECTED BY THE
    ZEALLY MOSS CHAPTER
    OF THE
    CHILDREN OF THE
    AMERICAN REVOLUTION
    DECORATION DAY 1915

The Vevay Reveille-Enterprise; Vol. 122. No. 39, 28 Sep 1935, p.3, col. 4.
Roster of Revolutionary Soldiers Who Resided in Switzerland County
By Mrs. Effa M. Danner
Zeally Moss – Served in the Revolution and was at the siege of Yorktown. He stood on parade when Cornwallis surrendered the British army to Washington. He came to Switzerland County and entered 1000 acres of land in Posey Township. He served on the grand jury 1815. Norman B. Magruder was also a member. Again in 1817 when John Protsman was foreman, John Bray and Joseph Todd were members of the jury.
Zeally Moss removed to Peoria, Ill. He is the only one of our soldiers who is honored by having a D.A.R. chapter named for him.
Zeally Moss Society Children of American Revolution, Peoria, Ill. (National Report D.A.R. 1912, p. 194.)
Children of Zeally Moss: Sallie Moss married Richard Goddard, Nov. 1, 1821; William S. married Mary Cheat, Nov. 16, 1824; Lydia married Tobias Bradley, April 10, 1837; Mary; Nancy married Thomas Chambers; Micaja removed to Oregon.

MOUNTS, THOMAS
aka MOUNCE

Patriot: Thomas Mounts
Birth: 8 Jul 1764   near Cumberland, Frederick Co., MD
Married Spouse 1: 1785 Nancy Crawford (possibly Connell)
                 (b. 22 Dec 1767, d. 28 Feb 1842 Switzerland Co., IN)
Service state(s): PA
Service description: Lt. Fleming, Capts. Wallace, Mentor
Rank: Private
Proof of Service: Pension application S17594
Pension application No.: S17594
Residences: Cumberland Co., MD; Westmoreland Co., PA; KY;
           Indiana Territory; Switzerland Co., IN
Died: 8 Jul 1842   Switzerland Co., IN
Buried: Lostetter Cemetery (aka Grant's Creek Cemetery), Posey Twp.,
       Switzerland Co., IN
DAR Ancestor No.: A134882

Pension Application Abstracted from National Archives microfilm Series 805, Roll 604, File S17594.

Pension abstract for – Thomas Mounts   Service state(s): Pennsylvania
Date: 18 September 1832
County of: Switzerland   State of: Indiana
Declaration made before a Court.
Age: 68 years   Record of age: In Bible given by his father.
Residence when he entered service: Westmoreland Co., PA
Residence(s) since the war: Westmoreland Co., PA about 27 years, Kentucky
                 about 15 years, Indiana about 26 years.
Residence now: Switzerland Co., IN
Volunteer or Drafted or Substitute: Drafted
Rank(s): Private
Statement of service-

Period	Duration	Names of General and Field Officers
1779 or 80	3 months	Col. Caleb Mounts, Lt. Lewis Fleming, Ensign Joseph Davis, Pennsylvania Militia
May 1780 or 81	3 months	Capt. Jas. Wallace, Ensign Thos. Watson, Pennsylvania Militia
1781 or 82	3 months	Same

Battles: Was in McIntosh's Campaign and in a battle with the Indians.
       [8th Pennsylvania]
Service: 1st tour - Placed at Caleb Mount's Mill where they built 2 military store
                 houses.
2nd tour – Wallace's Mill in Ligonier Valley at place called Wallace's Fort.
3rd tour – same place
Names of Regular officers in troops where served: Col. Crawford afterwards

killed by the Indians; John Stevens was a Continental Captain and went to Boston.
Discharge received: No written discharge
Statement is supported by –
Evidence: Traditional
Clergyman: John Pavy
Persons in neighborhood who certify character: Samuel Jack, John F. Dufour, John D. Morerod, Henry Wallick, Joseph M. Henry.
No family information in file.

Pennsylvania Archives, Series 3, Volume XXIII. p. 600.
Muster Rolls of the Navy and Line, Militia and Rangers, 1775-1783. with List of Pensioners, 1818-1832.
Switzerland County
Mounts, Thomas, pr. P.T., March 26, 1833: 73.

Switzerland County, Indiana Civil Order Book Vol., A, Oct. 19, 1829-April 16, 1837, p. 178.
In the matter of Robert Ricketts, Thomas Mounts, Ebenezer Humphrey, Daniel Heath, William Coy and Isaac Levi, An application to obtain a pension.
      Personally appeared in open Court before the Switzerland Circuit Court now Sitting The above named applicants who being first duly Sworn doth in their several oaths make their several declarations in order to obtain the benefit of the Act of Congress of the 7th June Ad 1832 that they entered the Service of the United States under the Officers named in their several declarations (here insert them) And the said Court do hereby declare their opinion after the investigation of the matter and after putting the interrogations prescribed by the War Department that the above named applicants were Revolutionary Soldiers and Served as they have stated And the Court further certifies that is appears to them that John Pavy who signed the several Certificates is a Clergyman resident in Switzerland County and State of Indiana and the other persons who has also signed the same are credible persons and that their Statement is entitled to credit.

Abstract of Final Payment Voucher; General Services Administration, Washington, DC
LAST FINAL PAYMENT VOUCHER RECEIVED FROM
THE GENERAL ACCOUNTING OFFICE
NAME   Mountz, Thomas
AGENCY OF PAYMENT   Indiana
DATE OF ACT   1832
DATE OF PAYMENT   Sept 3, 1848
DATE OF DEATH
GENERAL SERVICES ADMINISTRATION
National Archives and Records Service   NA-286
GSA-WASH DC 54-4891   November 1953
&
Abstract of Final Payment Voucher; General Services Administration, Washington, DC

LAST FINAL PAYMENT VOUCHER RECEIVED FROM
THE GENERAL ACCOUNTING OFFICE
NAME   Mountz, Thomas
AGENCY OF PAYMENT   Indiana
DATE OF ACT   1832
DATE OF PAYMENT   March 2, 1849 (dead)
DATE OF DEATH
GENERAL SERVICES ADMINISTRATION
National Archives and Records Service   NA-286
GSA-WASH DC 54-4891   November 1953
of division & disbursement, or final return: 14 Jan 1830

Second Census of Kentucky, 1800; Clift G. Glenn; Genealogical Publishing Co., Baltimore, MD, 1954.
An alphabetical list of 32,000 taxpayers based on original tax lists on file at the Kentucky Historical Society. Information given includes the county of residence and the date of the tax list in which the individual is listed.
Mounts, Thomas   Harrison   1800

Census of Indiana Territory for 1807; Indiana Historical Society, 1980. p. 25.
A list of free males above the age of twenty one in Dearborn County in March 1807 ~~
336   Thomas Mounts

Early Ohio Settlers, Purchasers of Land in Southwestern Ohio, 1800-1840; Compiled by Ellen T. Berry & David A. Berry; Genealogical Publishing Co., Inc., Baltimore, MD, 1986. p.234.

Purchaser	Year	Date	Residence	R – T - S
Mounts, Thomas (B)	1812	Aug. 17	Dearborn Ind	01-03-28
Mounts, Thomas (B)	1814	Aug. 06	Dearborn Ind	01-03-28

(B) Indiana Survey: Land lying west of a meridian drawn west of the Great Miami (known as the "Gore"). Switzerland, Dearborn, Franklin, Ohio, Union and Randolph Counties (all or only a part of each county) – all in Indiana.

Early Settlers of Indiana's "GORE" 1803-1820; Compiled and Edited by Shirley Keller Mikesell; Heritage Books, Inc., 1995. p. 183.
Switzerland County - Township 3, Range 1W
Section 28 – Thomas Mounts – 1812 – pg. 3.

U.S. Department of Interior, Bureau of Land Management, General Land Office Records; Land Patent Search – accessed 27 June 2012.
MOUNTS, THOMAS
Accession Nr. CV-0038-542; Document Type – Credit Volume Patent; State – Indiana; Issue Date – 4/27/1818; Cancelled – No
Land Office – Cincinnati; Authority – April 24, 1820 Sale-Cash Entry (3 Stat. 566); Total Acres – 0.00
Land Descriptions: State – IN; Meridian – 1st PM; Twp-Rng – 003N-001W; Aliquots – NE1/4; Section – 28; County - Switzerland

&
Accession Nr. CV-0063-112; Document Type – Credit Volume Patent; State – Indiana; Issue Date – 4/1/1825; Cancelled – No
Names on Document: White, Jacob; Mounts, Thomas
Land Office – Cincinnati; Authority – April 24, 1820 Sale-Cash Entry (3 Stat. 566); General Remarks – Patent Record Imperfect See Serial Patent Nr. 1225250; Document Nr. 1118; Total Acres – 160.68
Land Descriptions: State – IN; Meridian – 1st PM; Twp-Rng – 003N-001W; Aliquots – SW1/4; Section 28; County - Switzerland

Indiana Territory, Switzerland Circuit Court Records, Order Book, October Term 1814 to March Term 1815. p.6.
He is listed in county records as a member of the Grand Jury at the first court held in the county, on 28 October 1814. Court held at the house of Robert M. Trotter, in the Town of Vevay.

1820 U.S. Census, Indiana, Switzerland, Jefferson, Series: M33 Roll: 14 Pg: 261
Thomas Mounts 45 and up; also in household 1 male 10-16, 1 male 16-18, 4 males 16-26,
1 female 10-16, 2 females 16-26, 1 female 45 and up.

A Census of Pensioners for Revolutionary or Military Services with their Names, Ages, and Places of Residence Under the Act for Taking the Sixth Census in 1840; Genealogical Publishing Co., Inc., Baltimore, Maryland, 1965. p.185.

INDIANA, SWITZERLAND, POSEY Names of Pensioners for Revolutionary or Military services	Ages	Names of heads of families with whom pensioner resided June 1, 1840
Thomas Mounts	76	Thomas Mounts

Revolutionary Soldiers of Switzerland County; Copied by Mary Hill, John Paul Chapter-Daughters of the American Revolution; January, 1958;
http://www.ingenweb.org/inswitzerland/switzrevsoldiers.html- Viewed June 2012.
MOUNTS, THOMAS   Pension S.17594
Born July 8, 1764, near Fort Cumberland, Maryland
Names of parents are not shown.
While living in Westmoreland Co. Pennsylvania, Thomas Mounts enlisted in Captain John Mentor's company under Colonel Providence Mounts or Mountz (no relationship shown) in the Pennsylvania troops; Marched from Mounts' Mill to Pittsburgh, where they joined General McIntosh's command, and went against the Delaware & Shawnee Indians on Big Beaver Creek; soldier stated that he was in one engagement with the savages; length of this tour not shown.
He enlisted in 1779 or 1780, served as a private under Lieutenant Lewis Flemming & Colonel Caleb Mounts (no relationship shown) in the Pennsylvania troops & acted as a guard over some military stores at Caleb Mounts' mill; length of this tour, three months.
Enlisted in 1780 or 1781, and served three months as a private in Captain James Wallace's Pennsylvania company and in 1781 or 1782, served another tour of

three months under same captain; on both these tours, he was stationed at Wallace's Fort in Ligonier Valley.
Soldier stated that he resided twenty-seven years in Pennsylvania, fifteen years in Kentucky, after which he moved to Indiana, where he had resided twenty six years when he was allowed pension on his application executed September 18, 1832, while residing in Switzerland County, Indiana.
Married Nancy Crawford (b. 27 Dec 1767; d. 22 Feb 1842)
Children: Nancy married Henry Wallick; Rachael married William Scott; Cynthia married John Lampton; Mary married Alexander Leggett; Thomas married Vina Palmer; Josena married Isaac Pogue.
Pension Certificate No. 7559, issued Apr. 26, 1833, rate $40 per annum, commenced Mar. 4, 1831, Act. of June 7, 1832, Indiana Agency."
Died 8 Jul 1842
Indianapolis Star, June 12, 1932:
Thomas Mounts, wife, 2 sons & 6 dau came to Indiana 1806; settled on banks of the Ohio, mouth of Grants Creek, NE 28-3-1, Switzerland Co. where he lived the rest of his life and he and his wife are buried there. Farm now the property of Mrs. James Humphrey. Thomas Mounts born near Ft. Cumberland, Pa. July 8, 1764, enlisted at age of 15 in company of Pa. Militia; served 3 mo. again enlisted under Capt. John Menton, Pa. Mil. served 3 mo. 1781, three months more in 1782 under Capt. James Wallace in Westmoreland Co. Wife Nancy Crawford, oldest dau. of Col. Wm. Crawford, who was burned at the stake in Ohio by Indians. The 6 dau. married: Henry Wallack, William Scott, John Lampton of Switz. Co. and Isaac Paugh, A. G. Hunter & Alex Liggett of Ripley Co.
Family Bible: Thomas Mounts, b July 8, 1764; d July 8, 1842. Nancy Crawford Mounts, b Dec. 27, 1767; d Feb. 22, 1842.

History of Switzerland County Indiana 1885; Reproduced by the Switzerland County Historical Society, Vevay, Indiana, 1999. The portion of the book relating to Switzerland County in the 1885 printing of the "History of Dearborn, Ohio, and Switzerland Counties, Indiana". p.1179.
In the passage about William Scott of York Township – "He (Scott) came into this county about 1809-1811, and married Rachel Mounts, daughter of Thomas Mounts, the pioneer of Posey Township, near North's Landing, on Grant's Creek."

Roster of Soldiers and Patriots of the American Revolution Buried in Indiana, Vol. I; compiled by Mrs. Roscoe C. O'Byrne.; Indiana Daughters of the American Revolution, 1981; p.262.
MOUNTS, THOMAS   Switzerland County
Born – July 5, 1764.
Service – Enlisted from Westmorland Co., Penn, 1779, and served 3 mos. under Lieut. Lewis Fleming and Col. Caleb Mounts. From May, 1780-1781, 3 mos. in Capt. James Wallace CO. and 3 mos. in Capt. John Minters' CO, and under Col. Providence Mounts in 1781-82.
Proof – Pension claim S. 17594.
Died – July 8, 1822. Buried Lostetter Cemetery near Grant's Creek Baptist Church. Stone.

Married – Nancy Crawford. Ch. Nancy, m. Henry Wallick; Rachael, m. Wm. Scott; Cynthia, m. John Lampton; Mary, m. Alexander Leggett; Thomas, m. Vina Palmer; Josena, m. Isaac Pogue.
Collected by Mrs. A. V. Danner, Vevay, Indiana.

Abstract of Graves of Revolutionary Patriots (4 volumes); by Patricia Law Hatcher; Pioneer Heritage Press, Dallas, TX, 1987. Vol. 3, p. 108.
This is an abstract and an index to information reported to the Daughters of the American Revolution and published in their annual reports to the Smithsonian Institution, printed as Senate Documents (1900-1974) and published annually in the DAR magazine (1978-1987).
Published 1932, Serial set 9661, Volume 7.
MOUNTS, Thomas   Nr Grant's Creek, Switzerland Co IN

The Vevay Reveille-Enterprise; Vol. 122, No. 37, p. 7, col. 2.
Roster of Revolutionary Soldiers Who Resided in Switzerland County
By Mrs. Effa M. Danner
Thomas Mounts – Pension claim S17594. Born July 5, 1764 near Fort Cumberland, state not given. While residing in Westmoreland County, Pa., he served as private in the Fall of 1779, three months under Lieut. Lewis Fielding and Col. Caleb Mounts from May 1780-81, three months, Capt. James Wallace Co., same year in Capt. John Minter's Co., in Col. Providence Mounts Regiment and was in McIntosh's campaign and in battle with the Indians from May 1781 or 1782, three months in Capt. James Wallace Co. Pension granted September 18, 1832 while living in Switzerland County, having moved there from Kentucky.
Family records – Thomas Mounts, born 1764, died July 28, 1849. Wife, Nancy Crawford born 1767, died in 1842. Children, Nancy Mounts married Henry Wallick; Rachel Mounts married Wm. Scott, Switzerland Co. Records, Cynthia Mounts married John Lampton, Nov. 25, 1824; Thomas Mounts, Jr., married Vina Palmer, Jan. 18, 1822; Josina Mounts married Isaac Pough, July 2, 1817; Polly Mounts, married Alexander Liggett, Dec. 20, 1814.
Providence Mounts made oath for her father, Thomas Mounts consent.
1820 census listed he and wife over 45; family, six boys and three girls.
Land grants entered 1812-1814 on Grant's Creek.
He served on the first grand jury of this county. He with Heathcott Picket were appointed road reviewers by the court, which is now part of Highway 156.
He and his wife are buried at Lostetter's cemetery, Grants Creek.
Personal description of Thomas Mounts is found in History of Dearborn, Switzerland, and Ohio Counties, p. 440-696-776. "Always a scout who always wore buckskins."
Deed, Thomas Mounts – wife, Nancy Mounts to Providence Mounts, $300, August 1822, Book B, p. 331. Nancy Crawford is said to be the daughter of Col. William Crawford burned at the stake by the Indians at Sandusky Plains, 1782.

The Vevay Reveille Enterprise; Vol. 122, No. 37, 22 Sep 1935, p. 3, col.3-4.
Roster of Revolutionary Soldiers Who Resided in Switzerland County
By Mrs. Effa M. Danner

In the article about William Coy – "William Coy Jr., married Catherine Charmel in Kentucky. Their daughter Sinae Elizabeth Coy in Francis Marion Scott, February 17, 1851 [error in original publication]. His father, William Scott born in Virginia 1785 came to Switzerland Co., 1809, married Rachel Mounts, daughter of Thomas Mounts and Nancy Crawford, Rev. Soldier."

NEAL, CHARLES

Patriot: Charles Neal
Birth: 27 Aug 1762 Orange Co., VA
Married Spouse 1: 23 Aug 1785 Orange Co., VA   Ann Miller
        (b. 7 Jun 1768 Orange Co., VA
        d. 30 Jul 1854 Switzerland Co., IN)
Service state(s): VA
Service description: Capt. William Barrett, Col. William Washington, Regt. Continental Dragoons
Rank: Private
Proof of Service: Pension application W9587
Pension application No.: W9587
Residences: Orange Co., VA; Madison Co., KY, Scott Co., KY, Switzerland Co., IN
Died: 27 Aug 1831 poss. Scott Co., KY [Final Payment Voucher paid in KY]
Buried: Unknown Switzerland Co., IN
DAR Ancestor No.: A081721

Pension Application Abstracted from National Archives microfilm Series 805, Roll 610, File W9587
Pension abstract for – Charles Neal Service state(s): Virginia
Continental
Date: 22 April 1818
County of: Scott   State of: Kentucky
Declaration made before a Circuit Judge.
Age: 55 years, is infirm and poor.
Statement of service-

Period	Duration	Names of General and Field Officers
1779 or 1780		Col. William Washington's regiment of Light Dragoons.

Battles: Cowpens, Guilford Courthouse, Eaton Springs
Discharge received: at Nelson's Ferry on Santie, 12 June 1782 or 1783.
&
Date: 7 August 1820 (presented schedule of property)
County of: Scott   State of: Kentucky
Declaration made before a Court.
Age: 58 years
Statement of service-

Period	Duration	Names of General and Field Officers
		Capt. William Barrett in the 3rd regiment of Light Dragoons commd. by Col. William Washington.

Occupation: Farmer but not able to do much of it.
Wife: Ann   Wife's age: 52 years
Marriage date and place: Not stated
Names and ages of children: Betsey Neal age 20; Ann Neal age 18, William A. Neal age 16; Sucy Neal age 14, all who able to support themselves.

&
Widow, Ann Neal, Application for Pension
Date: 8 October 1838
County of: Switzerland State of: Indiana
Declaration made before a Judge of the Circuit Court
Age: 70 years and upwards
Soldier's residence(s) since the war: Orange Co., VA, Madison Co., KY, Scott Co., KY, Switzerland Co., IN
Widow's residence: Switzerland Co., IN
Rank(s): Private in the regular service
Statement of service- She will not undertake to state the particulars of service.
Soldier died: August, 1831 in Switzerland Co., IN
Marriage date and place: August in 1784 or 1785, in Orange Co., VA
Proof of marriage: Mordaci McKenza and Edward Patton gave Oath that Charles Neal was reputed to be a soldier of the revolution and pensioner, who departed his life in the year 1831, left a widow Ann Neal who has remained a widow.
Names and ages of children: from Family Record in the file –
Robert M. Neal, b. 4 July 1786; Margaret M. Neal, b. 2 February 1788; Charles Neal b. 12 February 1790; Fielding Neal, b. 24 August 1793; John Neal, b. 20 November 1794; Poley Neal, b. 13 June 1797; Betsy Neal, b. 1 September 1799.
Ann Neal, widow of Charles Neal, Certificate #2744, Issued 2 Jan 1849, Madison Agency, Indiana.
Widow died 30 July 1854.

Virginia Marriages, Orange County, No. P15.
23 Aug 1785, Charles Neal to Ann Miller, daughter of Robert Miller

Abstract of Final Payment Voucher: General Services Administration, Washington, DC
NAME   Neal, Charles
AGENCY OF PAYMENT   KY
DATE OF ACT   1818
DATE OF PAYMENT   4th qtr. 1831
DATE OF DEATH   Aug 27, 1831
LAST FINAL PAYMENT VOUCHER RECEIVED FROM
THE GENERAL ACCOUNTING OFFICE   Form
General Services Administration   GSA DA 70-7035   GSA Dec 69   7068
&
Abstract of Final Payment Voucher: General Services Administration, Washington, DC
NAME   Neal, Ann widow of Charles
AGENCY OF PAYMENT   Madison [IN]
DATE OF ACT   1848
DATE OF PAYMENT   4th Qr. 1854
DATE OF DEATH   July 30, 1854
LAST FINAL PAYMENT VOUCHER RECEIVED FROM
THE GENERAL ACCOUNTING OFFICE   Form
General Services Administration   GSA DA 70-7035   GSA Dec 69   7068

Revolutionary War Records – Virginia; Virginia Army and Navy Forces with Bounty Land Warrants for Virginia Military District of Ohio, and Virginia Military Script, from Federal and State Archives; by Gaius Marcus Brumbaugh, M.D, M.s., Litt.D; Genealogical Publishing Co., Inc., Baltimore, 1995.
p. 192
List of Officers and Soldiers, Who Have Been Allowed Bounty Land by the Executive of Virginia, and Who Have Not Received Warrants. The Orders for the Same on File in the Land Office.

No.	Names	Rank	Line	Number of Acres, $Ec.
80.	Neal, Charles	Private	Cont'l	100

p. 483
Virginia Military Land Warrants, Virginia Military District of Ohio, Granted for Revolutionary War Services, State Continental Line, Beginning August 8, 1782.

Number	Warrantees	Rank & Service	
6370	Neal, Charles	Private	War

Historical Register of Virginians in the Revolution, Soldiers, Sailors, Marines, 1775-1783; John H. Gwathmey; The Dietz Press, Richmond, VA, 1938. p. 578.
Neal, Charles (Neel) 12 CL.
Neal, Charles, 1st Light Dragoons.
[?] Neale, Charles, Fauquier Mil., served as substitute for Joshua King in Mch., 1780.

Revolutionary War Bounty Land Grants Awarded by State Governments; Lloyd DeWitt Bockstruck; Genealogical Publishing co., IN, Baltimore, MD, 1996. p. 388.
Neal, Charles. Va. Private. 22 Apr 1820. 200 acres.

Muster and Pay Rolls of the War of the Revolution 1775-1783, Collections of The New-York Historical Society for the Years 1914 an 1915; Printed for the Society, New York, 1914. p. 641.
Return of Men Considered as Part of the Quota – Settled
Neal, Charles........War

Second Census of Kentucky, 1800; Clift G. Glenn; Genealogical Publishing Co., Baltimore, MD, 1954.
An alphabetical list of 32,000 taxpayers based on original tax lists on file at the Kentucky Historical Society. Information given includes the county of residence and the date of the tax list in which the individual is listed.
Neal, Charles   Pulaski   7/29/1800

Revolutionary Soldiers in Kentucky, containing a roll of the officers of Virginia line who received land bounties, a roll of the Revolutionary pensioners in Kentucky, a list of the Illinois regiment who served under George Rogers Clark in the Northwest campaign, also a roster of the Virginia Navy. Reproduction of the original which appeared in Sons of the American Revolution Kentucky Society Year Book, Louisville, 1896.; Anderson Chenault Quisenberry; Southern Book Co., Baltimore, MD, 1959. p. 221.

Roll of Pensioners – Scott County
Pensioners Under the Act of March 18, 1818
Neal, Charles, private Virginia line February 13, 1819; April 22, 1818; $96.
Age 69. Died Aug. 27, 1831

The Pension List of 1820 [U.S. War Department] Reprinted with an Index; by Murtie June Clark; Genealogical Publishing Co., Inc., Baltimore, 1991. Originally published 1820 as Letter from the Secretary of War. p. 612.
Names of the Revolutionary Pensioners which have been placed on the Roll of Kentucky, under the Law of the 18th of March, 1818, from the passage thereof, to this day, inclusive, with the Rank they held, and the Lines in which they served, viz.

Names	Rank	Line
Charles Neal	private	Virginia

1850 U.S. Census, Indiana, Switzerland, Pleasant Twp., Series: M432 Roll: 174 Page: 335, Family No. 160.
Ann Neal, Age 85, Born VA

Revolutionary Soldiers of Switzerland County; Copied by Mary Hill, John Paul Chapter-Daughters of the American Revolution; January, 1958; http://www.ingenweb.org/inswitzerland/switzrevsoldiers.html- Viewed June 2012.
NEAL, CHARLES
Born 1762 - 1763; died Aug. 27, 1831
Married Aug. 1764 Ann_____ b about 1768, Orange Co. Virginia
Revolutionary service: Continental Line, VA
Children from Bible: Libbert M. b 7-4-1786, Margaret M. f 2-2-1788, Charles b 2-22-1790, Fielding b 8-24-1792, John b 11-30-1794, Poley, b 6-13-1797, Betsy b 9-1-1799, plus (not in Bible: ages 8-7-1820) Anny, age 18, William A., age 16, Lucy age 14,
Pension Application 4-22-1818, age abt. 55 Scott Co. Ky.
After War, living in Madison and Scott Co. Ky. then Switzerland Co. Ind.
Affidavit, 12-31-1818 Scott Co. Ky. of John Jacobs, that he served in same Regt; service enlisted about 1779-1780; Col. William Washington's Regt. of Light Dragoons, 3rd Virginia Regt.
Again application 8-7-1820, age 58, six in family incl. Anny, 52, Betsy, 20, Anny, age 18, William A. 16, Lucy 14.
Died July 30, 1854
Widow's pension application age 70 Switzerland Co. Ind. 7-6-1844, Pleasant twp. Switz. Co. Ind. age 76; 9-18-1848, age 80.

Roster of Soldiers and Patriots of the American Revolution Buried in Indiana, Vol. II; 1966; p.77-78.
NEAL, CHARLES   Switzerland County
Born – 1762 or 1763
Service – Enl. Ca. 1778/80; Col. William Washington's Regt. of Light Dragoons, 3rd Vir. Regt.
Proof – Penn. W. 9587 Cont. (Vir.). Appl. for Pens., Switzerland Co.
Died – Aug. 27, 1831.

Married – Aug., 1784, Ann _____, b. ca. 1768, d. July 30, 1854. Ch. (from Bible) Libbert M., b. July 4, 1786; Margaret M., b. Feb. 2, 1788; Charles B., b. Feb. 22, 1790; Fielding, b. Aug. 24, 1792; John, b. Nov. 30, 1794; Poley, b. June 13, 1797; Betsy, b. Sept. 1, 1799, and those not in Bible: Anny; William A.; Lucy.

<u>Revolutionary Soldiers Buried in Indiana A Supplement</u>; *485 Names Not Listed in the Roster of Soldiers and Patriots of the American Revolution Buried in Indiana (1938) nor in Revolutionary Soldiers Buried in Indiana (1949); Margaret E. Waters; Indianapolis, 1954. p.75.*

NEAL, CHARLES   Switzerland
b. 1762-1763; d. 8-27-1831;
m. Aug. 1784, Orange Co., Va., Ann ---, b. ca. 1768; d. 7-30-1854;
chn (from Bible): Libbert M., b. 7-4-1786; Margaret M., b. 2-2-1788; Charles, b. 2-2-1790; Fielding b. 8-24-1792; John b. 11-30-1794; Poley b. 6-13-1797; Betsy b. 9-1-1799; plus (not in Bible; ages 8-7-1820): Anny 18; William 16; Lucy 14. Pens appl. 4-22-1818, ae. 55, Scott Co., Ky. After War liv. Madison Co., Ky.; Scott Co., Ky; then Switzerland Co., Inc; again appl. 8-7-1820, ae. 58; 6 in fam., incl.: Anny 52, Betsy 20, Anny 18, William A. 16, Lucy 14. Wid's pens. Appl., ae 70, Switzerland Co., Ind. 7-6-1844. Pleasant Twp., Switzerland Co., ae. 76; 9-18-1848, ae. 80. Affid. 12-31-1818, Scott Co., Ky., of John Jacobs; that he serv. in same Regt.
Service: enl. ca. 1779-1780; Col. William Washington's Regt. of Light Dragoons, 3rd Va. Regt.
REF: Pens. W.9587. Cont. Va.

<u>The Weekly Reveille, Vol. XXXVII, No. 21, p. 3, Col. 3.</u>
Notice of Administration – Notice is hereby given that the undersigned has been appointed administrator of the estate of Ann Neal, late of Switzerland county, deceased. Said estate is suppose to be insolvent.   Nov 16   William A. Neal,
                                                                                                 Adm'r

NIGHSWONGER, SOLOMON

Patriot: Solomon Nighswonger
Birth: Est. 1757 "native of Virginia"
Married Spouse 1: 1818 Switzerland Co., IN   Jemima (d. aft. Nov. 1833)
Service state(s): VA
Service description: Virginia Line
Rank: Private
Proof of Service: Pension Application – Switzerland Co., IN
Pension application No.: Not in War Dept. records
Residences: VA; Indiana Territory; Switzerland Co., IN
Died: 16 Sep 1832 Switzerland Co., IN   d. at age 75
Buried: Unknown – Switzerland Co., IN
DAR Ancestor No.: None

Document contributed by Judy Kappes
Pension Application Abstracted from Switzerland County, Indiana Probate Record Book Vol. A, Mar 1827-Nov 1834; p. 413.
Widow Jemima Nighswonger Application
Soldier: Solomon Nighswonger   Service state(s): VA
Alternate spelling(s):
Date: 10 Nov 1833
County of: Switzerland   State of: Indiana
Declaration made before a Probate Court.
Where and year born: Age 75 at death, "native of Virginia" [estimated b.1757]
Residence when he entered service: VA
Residence(s) since the war: VA; Switzerland Co., IN
Residence now: Widow residing in Switzerland Co., IN
Volunteer or Drafted or Substitute: Enlisted
Rank(s): Private
Statement of service-

Period	Duration	Names of General and Field Officers
	1 yr, 6 mos.	Virginia Line

Persons in neighborhood who certify character and belief he served:
Affidavit of Joseph Bosseau – said deceased was 75 years old when he died; said served as a private soldier, served full term one year and six months.
Affidavit of William Fancher – states same as Bosseau, served full term of one year and six months (including several tours), and Jemima is the widow of Solomon Nighswonger.
Soldier died: 16 Sep 1832
Widow's age: 51
Marriage date and place: 1818 "in aforesaid county" Switzerland Co., IN

Switzerland County, Indiana Probate Order Book 2(A), 1831-1837; p. 172.
16 November 1833
NIGHSWONGER, JEMIMA PENSIONERS WIDOW
In the matter of Jemina Nighswonger   } An Applicant for her husbands
Widow of Solomon Nighswonger Dec'd } pension under the act of Congress of

the 7th June 1832.
Come now here into Court before the Probate Court of Switzerland County now Sitting it being a court of record Jemima Nighswonger in order to obtain the pension due to her husband a pensioner of the Revolutionary War, under the act of Congress of 7th June makes the following report (here insert it) And the Said Court do hereby declare their opinion after the investigation of the matter that the Said Solomon Nighswonger was a Solider of the Revolution and Served as above States, and the Court further Certifies that is appears to them that Jemima Nighswonger, Joseph Boeflea and William Fancher who has Sworn to the above Affidavits are residents in Switzerland County & State of Indiana and are credible persons and that their Statement is entitled to Credit.

Indiana Territory, Switzerland Circuit Court Records, Order Book, October Term 1814 to March Term 1815. p.6.
He is listed in county records for the first time on 27 March 1815, as a juror. Court held at the house of John Francis Dufour in the Town of Vevay.

Early Ohio Settlers, Purchasers of Land in Southwestern Ohio, 1800-1840; Compiled by Ellen T. Berry & David A. Berry; Genealogical Publishing Co., Inc., Baltimore, MD, 1986. p.241.

Purchaser	Year	Date	Residence	R – T - S
Nighswonger, Solomon (B)	1814	Jan. 26	Jefferson	02-03-36
Nighswonger, Solomon (B)	1815	July 20	Switzerland	02-02-32

(B) Indiana Survey: Land lying west of a meridian drawn west of the Great Miami (known as the "Gore"). Switzerland, Dearborn, Franklin, Ohio, Union and Randolph Counties (all or only a part of each county) – all in Indiana.

Early Settlers of Indiana's "GORE" 1803-1820; Compiled and Edited by Shirley Keller Mikesell; Heritage Books, Inc., 1995.
p. 185.
Switzerland County – Township 2, Range 2W
Section 32 – Solomon Nighswonger – 1815 – pg. 7.
p. 188.
Switzerland County – Township 3, Range 3W
Section 36 – Solomon Nighswonger – 1814 – pg. 13.

U.S. Department of Interior, Bureau of Land Management, General Land Office Records; Land Patent Search – accessed 27 June 2012.
NIGHSWONGER, SOLOMON
Accession Nr. CV-0040-562; Document Type – Credit Volume Patent; State – Indiana; Issue Date – 8/17/1818; Cancelled – No
Names on Document: McKinster, William; Nighwonger, Solomon
Land Office – Cincinnati; Authority – April 24, 1820 Sale-Cash Entry (3 Stat. 566); Total Acres 0.00
Land Descriptions: State – IN; Meridian – 1st PM; Twp-Rng – 003N-003W; Aliquots – NW1/4; Section – 36; County - Switzerland

Revolutionary Soldiers of Switzerland County; Copied by Mary Hill, John Paul Chapter-Daughters of the American Revolution; January, 1958; http://www.ingenweb.org/inswitzerland/switzrevsoldiers.html- Viewed June 2012.
NIGHSWONGER, SOLOMON
Switzerland Co. Probably died in 1820's. married Jemima _____. Children possibly sons, Solomon and Joh?. Widow's pension appli. supported by affidavits signed by William Fancher & Joseph Bosea. Solomon Nighswonger entered the SE 1/2 of Sec. 32-2-2 on July 20, 1815; later relinquished it and it was reentered by Isaac Watts, the W 1/2 of Sec. 36-3-3 on Jan. 26, 1814. (It may be that these entries were made by son Solomon. 1820 census of Switz. Co. has a John Nighswonger and 1830 a Solomon.
Ref. Switz. Co. Ind. Probate bk. A pg. 413;
Probate Order bk. A, (1831-1837) pg. 172, widow's pension application;
Waters "Ind. Land Entries" v. 1 (1949) pg. 43, 72.

Revolutionary Soldiers Buried in Indiana A Supplement; 485 Names Not Listed in the Roster of Soldiers and Patriots of the American Revolution Buried in Indiana (1938) nor in Revolutionary Soldiers Buried in Indiana (1949); Margaret E. Waters; Indianapolis, 1954. p. 77.
NIGHSWONGER, SOLOMON – see p. 118.

Revolutionary Soldiers Buried in Indiana A Supplement; 485 Names Not Listed in the Roster of Soldiers and Patriots of the American Revolution Buried in Indiana (1938) nor in Revolutionary Soldiers Buried in Indiana (1949); Margaret E. Waters; Indianapolis, 1954. p. 118-119.
NIGHSWONGER, SOLOMON   Switzerland
(Uncertain). Name obtained too late to get data. Died prob. in 1820's;
m. Jemima -------;
chn.: possibly sons John & Solomon.
Wid's pens. appl. is supported by affids. signed by William Fancher (see this Suppl.) & Joseph Boesea (sp?) Solomon Nighswonger entered the SE1/4 of Sec. 32 in Twp. 2N, Range 2W of the 1st P.M. on 7-20-1815; he later relinquished it & it was re-entered by Isaac Matts. The W1/2 on 8-20-1828, the E1/2 on 9-10-1828. Solomon Nighswonger entered the NW1/4 of Sec. 36 in Twp. 3N, Range 3W of 1st P.M. on 1-26-1814. It is poss. That these entries may have been made by a son, Solomon, Jr.& that soldier may have died elsewhere (even before the fam. Mov. to Ind.); the 1820 Cens. of Switzerland Co., Ind., has a John Nighswonger & the 1830 a Solomon.
REF: Switzerland Co., Ind., Probate Book A, p. 413; Probate Order Book A (1831-1837) p. 172 (widow's pens. appl.); Waters—"Ind. Land Entries", v. 1 (1949) pp. 43, 72; Miss Mary Hill, Madison, Indiana.

NORRIS, DANIEL

A pension record has not been located for Daniel Norris, nor has a Final Payment Voucher (IN) been found. Without a pension record it is difficult to determine his rank and where he served. Service records have been located for a Daniel Norris in Maryland and Virginia (all state records have been searched by the author), and a Bounty Land Grant was awarded to a soldier of that name in South Carolina. Entries that have been located are listed at the end of this record.

Patriot: Daniel Norris
Birth: abt. 1762
Married Spouse 1: Eleanor (d. 10 Jul 1840 Switzerland Co., IN)
Service state(s): ?
Service description: ?
Rank: ?
Proof of Service: -
Pension application No.: None located
Residences: ?, Switzerland Co., IN
Died: 11 Mar 1828 Switzerland Co., IN
Buried: Lostetter Cemetery (aka Grant's Creek Cemetery),
   Posey Twp., Switzerland Co., IN
DAR Ancestor No.: None

Revolutionary Soldiers of Switzerland County; Copied by Mary Hill, John Paul Chapter-Daughters of the American Revolution; January, 1958; http://www.ingenweb.org/inswitzerland/switzrevsoldiers.html- Viewed June, 2012.
NORRIS, DANIEL
Born about 1762
Child: Hugh L, married Nancy Powell, May 8, 1830.
Buried Loshetter Cemetery
Collected by Mrs. A. V. Danner, Vevay, Indiana

Roster of Soldiers and Patriots of the American Revolution Buried in Indiana, Vol. I; compiled by Mrs. Roscoe C. O'Byrne.; Indiana Daughters of the American Revolution, 1981; p.280.
NORRIS, DANIEL   Switzerland County
Born – About 1762.
Service - Inscription on marker reads "Daniel Norris, a Revolutionary Soldier, Died March 11, 1828, in the 66th year of his age."
Died – Buried Loshetter Cemetery, Posey Twp.
Ch. Hugh L., m. Nancy Powell May 8, 1830.
Collected by Mrs. A. V. Danner, Vevay, Indiana.

Switzerland County Indiana Cemetery Inscriptions 1817-1985; Wanda L. Morford; Cincinnati, Ohio, 1986, p. 430.
Grants Creek Cemetery, Posey Twp., Switzerland Co., IN
Norris, Daniel, a Revolutionary soldier, D. Mar. 11, 1828 in the 66th year

Eleanor, wife of Daniel, d. Jul. 10, 1840 in the 87th year – (stone is down)

Abstract of Graves of Revolutionary Patriots (4 volumes); by Patricia Law Hatcher; Pioneer Heritage Press, Dallas, TX, 1987. Vol. 3, p. 125.
This is an abstract and an index to information reported to the Daughters of the American Revolution and published in their annual reports to the Smithsonian Institution, printed as Senate Documents (1900-1974) and published annually in the DAR magazine (1978-1987).
Published 1972 (Senate Doc. 54)
NORRIS, Daniel   Loshetter Cem, Posey Twp, Switzerland Co IN

The Vevay Reveille-Enterprise; Vol. 122, No. 37, 22 Sep 1935, p. 7, col. 3.
Roster of Revolutionary Soldiers Who Resided in Switzerland County
By Mrs. Effa M. Danner
Daniel Norris – "A Revolutionary Soldier died March 11, 1828 in the 66 year of his age". Grave stone inscription in the Lostutter cemetery, Posey Township a few paces from David Reamer's grave.
This grave was located by H. Fenton Emerson and since Daniel Norris is not listed for pension and we do not know in what state he enlisted we have not been able to obtain his military record. If anyone knows anything about him I would be very glad to hear from you.
This cemetery is near the Grants Creek Baptist church on the extreme edge of Switzerland county line next to Ohio county. There are three Revolutionary soldiers buried there, Daniel Norris, Thomas Mounts, and David Reamer, and Wm. Kelly may be there. This old graveyard should be a special pride of the neighborhood with all these historic dead.

MARYLAND service records for a man named Daniel Norris:
The Maryland Militia in the Revolutionary War; by S. Eugene Clements and F. Edward Wright; Published by Family Line Publications, Westminster, MD 21157, 1987.
p. 164.
Charles County, 26th Battalion
1777/A List of Capt. Sinnett's Comp. of Militia, 26th Battalion; Jno. Muskett, 1st Lt.; Wm. Maconchie, 2nd Lt.; Wm. Barnes, Sergt.; Mattew. Rigg, Sergt.
Daniel Norris (in this list of privates)
p. 172.
Frederick County
Captain John Taylor's Company – No. 7
Witness our hands and seals this 9th day of September 1775: John Taylor, Captain; Smuel Caldwell, Lieut.; Thomas Hutchins, 2nd Lt.; Vincent Richardson, Ensign..
Daniel Norris (in this list of privates)

Muster Rolls and other records of service of Maryland Troops in the American Revolution; Archives of Maryland, reprinted with permission by Genealogical Publishing Co., Inc., Baltimore, 1972.
p. 26

Muster Roll of the 6th Independent Maryland Company (Dorchester County)
Commissd. Jan 5th, 1776,   Thomas Woolford, Capt.   present
"   "   "   John Eccleston, 1st Lieut.   "
"   "   "   Hooper Hodson, 2nd "   "
"   Mch. 2nd, 1776   Lilburn Williams, 3rd "   "

Records of Maryland Troops in the Continental Service

Date of Enlistment	Names	Remarks
Jan 8	Daniel Norris	present

p.386

Chester Town, Kent County, Aug. 23rd, 1781.
Kent County. A List of Recruits.   (Enlisted for 3 yrs.)
Daniel Norris (included in list)
p.411

An Alphabetical List of discharged Soldiers of the two Battalions of Militia raised to serve in the Continental Army in the year 1781.

County	Names
Kent	Norris, Daniel

p.642

First Battalion – Captain Samuel Smith
6th Independent Company. (Dorchester County) Captain Thos. Woolford

Date	Name	Remarks
Feb 8th	Daniel Norris	present

VIRGINIA service records for a man named Daniel Norris:
Historical Register of Virginians in the Revolution, Soldiers, Sailors, Marines, 1775-1783; John H. Gwathmey; The Dietz Press, Richmond, VA, 1938. p. 588.
Norris, Daniel, 8 CL, E.
Norriss, Daniel, 8 CL.

SOUTH CAROLINA service records for a man named Daniel Norris:
Revolutionary War Bounty Land Grants Awarded by State Governments; Lloyd DeWitt Bockstruck; Genealogical Publishing co., IN, Baltimore, MD, 1996. p. 394.
Norris, Daniel. S.C. Soldier. 2 May 1785. 200 acres.

NORTH, ABIJAH

Abijah and his brothers Lot and Thomas were frequently in contact with each other. Abijah lived in Gallatin Co., KY, Lot in Ohio Co., IN, and Thomas in Switzerland Co., IN. Records for all three brothers are included in this publication as they all were a part of the beginnings of Switzerland County.

Patriot: Abijah North
Birth: 8 Feb 1759   Hartford Co., CT
Married Spouse 1: 20 Jul 1786 in Fayette Co., KY (now Bourbon Co.)
             to Sarah Marsh (b. abt. 1766 d. 1857 Gallatin Co., KY)
Service state(s): CT
Service description: Capt. Bray, Col. Enos
Rank: Private
Proof of Service: Pension application W2232
Pension application No.: W2232
Residences: Farmington, CT; Bourbon Co., KY; Harrison Co., KY; Boone Co., KY; Gallatin Co., KY; Dearborn Co., IN
Died: 23 Mar 1850 Gallatin Co., KY
Buried: Unknown
DAR Ancestor No.: A084488

Pension Application Abstracted from National Archives microfilm Series 805, Roll 617, File W2232/BLWT28632-160-55.
Abstracted from Pension Application for Abijah North & widow's pension for wife Sarah –
Date: 10 December 1832, Gallatin Co., KY in Open Court.
Service: Entered into service May 1776 at Farmington, CT as private, Co. commanded by Capt. Hooker; marched to Ft. Ticonderoga in NY under command of Gen. Gates; marched thither for 5 mos. Returned to Farmington. Drafted as private in militia some time in 1777; engaged in defending the sea coast of CT; forgot number of months, where, and name of captain. Returned to Farmington. June or July 1778 enlisted as private under command of Capt. May, for one year. Called to perform duty for three month; stationed at West Point, NY, under Capt. Malcollm. Following October 1778 he quit said company and enlisted for three year term in company commanded by Capt. Richard Farow (?); marched from Farmington to Town of Springfield in MA where he entered the army of the United States, as a blacksmith, under Col. ??? , at the rate of thirty dollars per month until September or October 1781. Received a regular discharge from Col. Bliss.
Evidence: He has no documentary evidence; can produce no one to testify to his service except the widow of his deceased brother who served with him. That this witness lives in the State of Indiana and is too aged and infirmed to attend before a court of justice, but an affidavit has been taken before a JP (produced).
Affidavit of Silence North (widow of Abijah's brother Lot North): 4 December 1832, State of Indiana, Switzerland County, personally appeared before Samuel Jack, JP the aforesaid Silence North a resident of Dearborn County.

She is the widow of Lot North who was the brother of Abijah North now residing in Gallatin co., KY. At and before the time of the Revolution she resided in Hartford Co., CT, that the said Abijah North was absent from home for a considerable length of time during the Revolution and it was her own and the general understanding of the neighborhood that he was a Soldier the greater part of the Revolutionary War.

She further states she often heard her deceased husband speak of the campaigns in which himself and the said Abijah served together and particularly the campaign of 1776 which her said husband informed her he served as a drummer and the said Abijah served as a private in the company commanded by Capt. ???diah Hooker of Farmington in the State of Connecticut that marched to Lake Champlain and were there under the command of General Gates. And she recollects her husband frequently told her that himself and the said Abijah served in the United States army at another time for three years during which time they were employed as blacksmiths in the Arsenal at Springfield MA.

She believes the said Abijah is about 73 years if age.

Born: County of Hartford, CT on the 8th day February 1759. Has no record of his age other than kept by himself and recorded by his parents (not named).

Residences: After his last term returned to CT, continued there until 17?? (smudged). Emigrated to Bourbon Co., Kentucky until 1788, commenced to Harrison Co., KY until 1825, when he removed to Gallatin Co., KY where he still resides.

Died: Gallatin Co., KY, in March, 1850.

Wife: Sarah, 8 May 1855, Gallatin Co., KY states she is now a pensioner, certificate in her possession dated 10 Feb 1851, receives $144.50 annually. Married in Fayette Co., KY(now Bourbon Co.), on 26th day of July 1786. Her name before marriage was Sarah Marsh. Stated her said husband died in Gallatin Co., KY, in March 1850.

Abstract of Final Payment Voucher; General Services Administration, Washington, DC

NAME   North, Abijah
AGENCY OF PAYMENT   KY
DATE OF ACT   1832
DATE OF PAYMENT   4th qtr. 1850
DATE OF DEATH   March 23, 1850
FINAL PAYMENT VOUCHER RECEIVED FROM
THE GENERAL ACCOUNTING OFFICE   Form
General Services Administration   GSA DA 70-7035   GSA Dec 69 7068

Rolls and Lists of Connecticut Men in the Revolution, 1775-1783; Originally published by the Connecticut Historical Society 1901; Reprint by Heritage Books, Inc, Westminster, MD, 2008.
p. 39.
Continental Regiments, 1776, Capt. Watson's Company
A Pay role of Capt Titus Watson's Comp^y being the 8th Compy in Col Charles Burrell's Battallion –

Names & Quality	Time Enlisted
Abjah North	Feb 6

p. 87.
Col. Flower's Artificers
A Return of the names of the Officers & men in Military Department at Springfield under the Direction of Col. Ezekiel Cheevers D Commissary General Military Stores and who are Lawful Inhabitantss of the State of Connecticut together with the time of their Engagements in the Department also the towns and Counties to which they Severally Belong.

Name	Time of Engagement	Towns
Abijah North Blacksmith	Oct. 20, 1779	Farmington

Second Census of Kentucky, 1800; Clift G. Glenn; Genealogical Publishing Co., Baltimore, MD, 1954.
An alphabetical list of 32,000 taxpayers based on original tax lists on file at the Kentucky Historical Society. Information given includes the county of residence and the date of the tax list in which the individual is listed.

North, Abijah	Harrison	1800

A Census of Pensioners for Revolutionary or Military Services with their Names, Ages, and Places of Residence Under the Act for Taking the Sixth Census in 1840; Genealogical Publishing Co., Inc., Baltimore, Maryland, 1965. p. 162.

KENTUCKY, GALLATIN COUNTY Names of Pensioners for Revolutionary or Military services	Ages	Names of heads of families with whom pensioner resided June 1, 1840
Abijah North	80	Abijah North

National Society of the Sons of the American Revolution - Revolutionary War Graves Register; Compiled and Edited by Clovis H. Brakebill, Published by db Publications, Dallas, TX, 1993. p. 451.
North   Abijah; 1759-1850; Gallatin Co., KY; Private; KY.

NORTH, LOT

Lot and his brothers Abijah and Thomas were frequently in contact with each other. Lot lived in Ohio Co., IN, Abijah lived in Gallatin Co., KY, and Thomas in Switzerland Co., IN. Records for all three brothers are included in this publication as they all were a part of the beginnings of Switzerland County. Lot is buried in Switzerland County.

Patriot: Lot North
Birth: 20 Jan 1756 Farmington, CT
Married Spouse 1: 7 Dec 1780   Silence Horsford (b. 11 Feb 1762, d. 14 Aug 1835 Switzerland Co., IN)
Service state(s): CT
Service description: Capt. Hooker of Farmington, CT
Rank: Drummer Boy; Private
Proof of Service: Affidavit of Silence North for Abijah North
Pension application No.: None
Residences: Farmington, CT; Boone Co., KY; Dearborn Co., IN; Switzerland Co., IN
Died: 8 Oct 1825 North's Landing, Switzerland Co., IN
(Will probated 25 Sept 1825)
Buried: North Cemetery, Posey Twp., Switzerland Co., IN
DAR Ancestor No.: A084548

Abstracted from Pension Application for Lot's brother, Abijah North & his widow Sarah.
Service of Lot North:
Affidavit of Silence North (widow of Lot North) on behalf of Abijah North: 4 December 1832, State of Indiana, Switzerland County, personally appeared before Samuel Jack, JP the aforesaid Silence North a resident of Dearborn County.
She is the widow of Lot North who was the brother of Abijah North now residing in Gallatin co., KY. At and before the time of the Revolution she resided in Hartford Co., CT, that the said Abijah North was absent from home for a considerable length of time during the Revolution and it was her own and the general understanding of the neighborhood that he was a Soldier the greater part of the Revolutionary War.
She further states she often heard her deceased husband speak of the campaigns in which himself and the said Abijah served together and particularly the campaign of 1776 which her said husband informed her he served as a drummer and the said Abijah served as a private in the company commanded by Capt. ???diah Hooker of Farmington in the State of Connecticut that marched to Lake Champlain and were there under the command of General Gates. And she recollects her husband frequently told her that himself and the said Abijah served in the United States army at another time for three years during which time they were employed as blacksmiths in the Arsenal at Springfield MA.

Early Settlers of Indiana's "GORE" 1803-1820; Compiled and Edited by Shirley Keller Mikesell; Heritage Books, Inc., 1995. p. 17.
Dearborn County: Original Land Entries Tract Book.
Dearborn County Township 3, Range 1W
Section 21 & 22 – Lot North – 1813 – pg. 2.

U.S. Department of Interior, Bureau of Land Management, General Land Office Records; Land Patent Search – accessed 27 June 2012.
NORTH, LOT
Accession Nr. CV-0039-477; Document Type – Credit Volume Patent; State – Indiana; Issue Date – 7/1/1818; Cancelled – No
Land Office – Cincinnati; Authority – April 24, 1820 Sale-Cash Entry (3 Stat. 566); Total Acres – 0.00
Land Descriptions:

State	Meridian	Twp-Rng	Aliquots	Section	County
IN	1st PM	003N-001W	-	21	Ohio
IN	1st PM	003N-001W	-	22	Ohio

Second Census of Kentucky, 1800; Clift G. Glenn; Genealogical Publishing Co., Baltimore, MD, 1954.
An alphabetical list of 32,000 taxpayers based on original tax lists on file at the Kentucky Historical Society. Information given includes the county of residence and the date of the tax list in which the individual is listed.
North, Lot   Harrison   1800

Early Dearborn County, Indiana Wills, Abstracted from Will Books I and II (Including Ohio County before 1845) and Perpetuated Testimony Books C; Compiled by Chris McHenry, Lawrenceburg, Indiana, 1976. p. 2.
Page 13: Lot North; Wife, Silence; sons, Sidney, Abijah, Rufus, Asahel, Levi; daughters, Maria(?) Miller, Abi Marsh, Huldah North, Nancy Bennett. Executrix, wife; witnesses Silas Howe, Andrew Emerson, Amy Emerson. Dated Oct. 31, 1822; Prob. Sept. 25, 1825. Left wife "ferry across the river", left daughter land "adjoining Thomas Bennett".

Switzerland County Indiana Cemetery Inscriptions 1817-1985; Wanda L. Morford; Cincinnati, Ohio, 1986, p. 436.
North Cemetery, Posey Twp., Switzerland Co., IN
Tombstone inscriptions –
In memory of Lot, who purchased from Congress the land where he lies 1813 and died Oct. 8, 1825 in his 70th year – born in Farmington, Connecticut
Silence, consort of Lot, d. Aug. 14, 1835 – aged 73y 6m 3d.

Roster of Soldiers and Patriots of the American Revolution Buried in Indiana, Vol. I; compiled by Mrs. Roscoe C. O'Byrne.; Indiana Daughters of the American Revolution, 1981; p. 280.
NORTH, LOT (Brother of Thos. of Switzerland Co.)   Ohio County
Born – Jan. 10, 1756, Farmington, Connecticut
Service – Drummer boy in Conn. Regt.

Proof – Hist. Dearborn, Switzerland, and Ohio Cos., 1885.
Died – Oct. 8, 1825. Graveyard on North's farm near Co. line runs through graveyard.
Married – Silence Horsford.
Collected by Mrs. Walter Kerr, Aurora, Indiana.

Roster of Soldiers and Patriots of the American Revolution Buried in Indiana, Vol. II; 1966; p. 129.
NORTH, LOT   (Also see Roster, Vol. I, p. 280)   Ohio County
Children – Sydney, b. Jan. 12, 1782, m. Jan. 26, 1809, Mary Hawthorne;
Almira, b. March 18, 1784, m. April 1, 1806, Beverly Miller;
Abijah, b. Dec. 25, 1787, m. Aug. 10, 1810, Margaret Wilson;
Rufus, b. Sept. 5, 1789, m. Feb. 16, 1815, Catherine Burns;
Abi, b. May 21, 1791, m. Jan. 25, 1813, Wm. Marsh;
Asavel, b. Nov. 3, 1792, m. Elizabeth Burns;
Levi, b. March 11, 793, m. Feb. 11, 1819, Rachel Rood;
Olive, b. Oct. 18, 1794, d. 1795;
Huldah, b. June 20, 1796, d. 1830;
Nancy, b. Jan 5, 1800, m. Jan. 16, 1817, Thomas Bennett,
By Mrs. J. Oscar Phillips, 523 E. Locust St., Boonville, Ind.

North Cemetery, Randolph Twp., Ohio Co. & Posey Twp., Switzerland Co., IN
[The Ohio & Switzerland County line runs through this cemetery.]
Tombstone inscriptions –

Memory of	IN
LOT NORTH	Memory of
Who purchased from	SILENCE NORTH
Congress the land	consort of
where he lies 1813	LOT NORTH
& died oct 8th 1825	who died
In his 70th year.	August 14th,1835
Born in Farmington	aged 73 years
Connecticut.	6 months & 3 days

Switzerland County Health Department, Switzerland County Cemeteries 1800-1980; Church of Latter Day Saints Microfilm No. 1460119302. p. 77.
North Cemetery, North Landing, Posey Twp., Switzerland Co., IN
NORTH, Lot, D: 10/8/1825 Age: 70 yrs.
     Silence, Consort of Lot, D: 8/1/1835 Age: 73-6-3

Abstract of Graves of Revolutionary Patriots (4 volumes); by Patricia Law Hatcher; Pioneer Heritage Press, Dallas, TX, 1987. Vol. 3, p. 125.
This is an abstract and an index to information reported to the Daughters of the American Revolution and published in their annual reports to the Smithsonian Institution, printed as Senate Documents (1900-1974) and published annually in the DAR magazine (1978-1987).
Published 1972 (Senate Doc. 54)
NORTH, Lot   Fam Farm, nr North's Landing, Ohio Co IN

The Vevay Reveille-Enterprise; Vol. 122, No. 37, p. 7, col. 3.
Excerpt from Roster of Revolutionary Soldiers Who Resided in Switzerland County   By Mrs. Effa M. Danner
Article regarding Thomas North – "His brother, Lot North is buried in Ohio County. Has many descendants in this county."

NORTH, THOMAS

Thomas and his brothers Abijah and Lot were frequently in contact with each other. Abijah lived in Gallatin Co., KY, Lot in Ohio Co., IN, and Thomas in Switzerland Co., IN. Records for all three brothers are included in this publication as they all were a part of the beginnings of Switzerland County.

Patriot: Thomas North
Birth: 29 Aug 1748 Farmington, CT
Married Spouse 1: Bathsheba (b. 3 Jun 1773,
                d. 24 Mar 1847 Switzerland Co., IN)
Service state(s): CT
Service description: Capts. Samuel Wylls, Ezekiel Scott; 2d Regt.
                     Col. Joseph Spencer, Samuel Wylls.
Rank: Private
Proof of Service: Record of Service of Conn. Men in Revolution, Adj. Gen.
                Office, Hartford, 1889 pg. 46.;
                Conn. Archives 1st ser. Vol. 11. Document 46.
                     Conn. State Library
Pension application No.: None
Residences: Farmington, CT; possibly KY; Switzerland Co., IN
Died: 22 Oct 1830 Switzerland Co., IN
Buried: North Cemetery, Posey Twp., Switzerland Co., IN
DAR Ancestor No.: None

Record of service of Connecticut men in the War of the Revolution, Vol. 1.; Connecticut Adjutant-General's Office; Adjutant-General's Office publisher, Hartford, CT, 1889. P. 46.
Second Regiment – Gen. Spencer's – 1775
Regiment raised on the first call for troops by the Legislature April-May, 1775. Recruited mainly in present Middlesex Co. and eastern part of the Colony. Marching by companies to the camps around Boston, it took post at Roxbury and served during the siege until expiration of term of service Dec. 1775.
Detachments of officers and men engaged at the battle of Bunker Hill, June 17, and in Arnold's Quebec Expedition, Sep.-Dec. 1775. Adopted as Continental in July. The regiment was re-organized for service in 1776, under Col. Wyllys.
2nd Company - Capt. Samuel Wyllys, Captain Ezekiel Scott,
                Lieutenant Samuel Cooper, Ensign Marcus Cole

Men's Names And Ranks	Time Enlisted	When Discharged & c.
Privates		
Thomas North	May 12	Dec 18

U.S. Department of Interior, Bureau of Land Management, General Land Office Records; Land Patent Search – accessed 27 June 2012.
NORTH, THOMAS

Accession Nr. CV-0069-562; Document Type – Credit Volume Patent; State – Indiana; Issue Date – 1/22/1828; Cancelled – No
Land Office – Cincinnati; Authority – April 24, 1820 Sale-Cash Entry (3 Stat. 566); Document Nr. 2287; Total Acres – 570.72
Land Descriptions; State – IN; Meridian – 1st PM; Twp-Rng – 003N-001W; Aliquots - _; Section – 27; County - Switzerland

Switzerland County, IN, Will Book Vol. 1, 3 Jan 1823-10 Nov 1847, p. 29.
Abstract of will for:Thomas North
State & county where recorded: Switzerland Co., Indiana
State & county where will was made: Posey [Township], Switzerland Co., IN
Book/volume where recorded: Vol. 1, p. 29
Date will made: 3 April 1830
Date entered in probate: 2 May 1831
Name(s) of executors: Royal F. North
Witnesses/appraisers: (in some cases, purchasers at sale of estate may be listed on another page and attached hereto): Asahel North, Levi North, James Miller,
Names of heirs and others mentioned in will (also signed receipts of division of estate) and relationship if shown: Wife, Bathsheba one just third part of all real & personal household property during her lifetime, and one third part of personal & moveable property to her heirs; son Royal F. North three hundred and thirty five acres of land (described in full) & his assigns & heirs forever; son George W. North & heirs forever the remainder of described fraction of land

Early Settlers of Indiana's "GORE" 1803-1820; Compiled and Edited by Shirley Keller Mikesell; Heritage Books, Inc., 1995. p. 183.
Switzerland County - Township 3, Range 1W
Section 28 – Thomas North – 1814 – pg. 3

Indiana Land Entries Vol. 1 Cincinnati District, 1801-1840; Margaret R. Waters; Originally Published Indianapolis 1948, Second Reprint 1979 by The Bookmark, P.O. Box 74, Knightstown, In 46148. p.6.
CINCINNNATI LAND DISTRICT – VOL. 1
Page 4. Twp. 3 N, Range 1 W of 1st Principle Meridian SWITZERLAND CO. Thomas North Pt. S27; 570.72 acres; 5-31-1814.
-- Note: The tract books for the land offices in Indiana are deposited in the office of the Auditor of State, Indianapolis. They and are in the custody of the State Land clerk. --

1830 U.S. Census, Indiana, Switzerland, No Twp., Series: M19 Roll: 32 Page: 58
North, Thomas age 80-90; others in household 1 female 50-60.

Revolutionary Soldiers of Switzerland County; Copied by Mary Hill, John Paul Chapter-Daughters of the American Revolution; January, 1958; http://www.ingenweb.org/inswitzerland/switzrevsoldiers.html- Viewed June 2012.
NORTH, THOMAS
Born Aug. 29, 1746, Farmington, Conn.

Private from May 12 to Dec. 18, 1775 in 2d Co. Capts. Samuel Wylls, and later Ezekiel Scott; 2d Regt. Col. Joseph Spencer - later Samuel Wylls.
See Conn Men in Revolution pg. 46 (Adj. Gen. Office, Hartford, 1889 pg. 46.
Conn. Archives 1st ser. Vol. 11.c document 46. Conn. State Library
Married Bathsheba (1773-1847)
Children: Royal F.
George W. married 1827 Saby B. Lanton
Died Oct. 30, 1830
Buried: Cemetery on North's farm, North's Landing, Switz. Co. Ind.
Inscription: Thomas North, Aug. 27, 1748 - died Mar. 24, 1847
Switz. Co. records Will bk. 1-29 Thomas North
Will written Apr. 1830 rec. May 2, 1831, Posey twp.
Wife, Bathsheba, sons Royal F. and George W.
signed by Asahel and Levi North

Roster of Soldiers and Patriots of the American Revolution Buried in Indiana, Vol. I; compiled by Mrs. Roscoe C. O'Byrne.; Indiana Daughters of the American Revolution, 1981; p.280.
NORTH, THOMAS   Switzerland County
Born – Aug. 29, 1748, Farmington, Connecticut
Service – Pri. from May 12 – Dec. 18, 1775, in 2nd CO., Capts. Samuel Wylls, and later Ezekiel Scott; 2nd Regt., Cols. Joseph Spencer and later Samuel Wylls.
Proof – Record of Conn. Men in the Rev., p. 46.
Died – Oct. 30, 1830. Cemetery on North's farm near North's Landing. The cemetery is in Switzerland Co. Stone.
Married – Bathsheba _____, 1773-1847. Ch. Royal F.; George W., m. 1827 Saby B. Lampton.
Collected by Mrs. A. V. Danner, Vevay, Indiana.

The Vevay Reveille-Enterprise; Vol. 122, No. 37, 22 Sep 1935, p. 7, col. 3.
Roster of Revolutionary Soldiers Who Resided in Switzerland County
By Mrs. Effa M. Danner
Thomas North – Connecticut, State Library, Hartford, Conn., Lillian b. Grant, Librarian, Jan. 18, 1938.
Service, Thomas North served as a private May 12-Dec. 18, 1778 in Company of Capt. Samuel Wylly, later Ezekial Scott, 2nd Regiment Colonel's Joseph Spencer and Samuel Wylly's as shown in published "record of Conn. men in Revolution" Adjutant's General's office, Hartford 1889, p. 49. Also in manuscripts, Conn. Archives Relating to Revolutionary War, First series, Vol. II, C. document 46. "Half of the regiment was at Bunker Hill and half went with General Arnold to Quebec, Canada."
Family records – Thomas North born Dexter North, 1748 in Farmington, Conn., son of Timothy and Hannah North.
Inscriptions on grave stones copied by H. Fenton Emerson – "Thomas North, born Aug. 29, 1748, died Oct. 30, 1830. His wife – Bathshebal North born June 3, 1773, died Mar. 24, 1747." They are buried in the North graveyard in Switzerland Co. just below North's Landing.

Will of Thomas North recorded Book E., p. 82. Mentions his beloved wife Bathshebal and sons, Royal F. North and George W. North.
His brother, Lot North is buried in Ohio County. Has many descendants in this county.

Switzerland County Indiana Cemetery Inscriptions 1817-1985; Wanda L. Morford; Cincinnati, Ohio, 1986, p. 436.
North   Thos., b. Aug. 29, 1748 d. Oct. 30, 1830   } single
          Bathsheba, wife of Thos., b. Jun. 3, 1773 d. Mar. 24, 1847 } stone

*Switzerland County Health Department, Switzerland County Cemeteries 1800-1980;*Church of Latter Day Saints Microfilm No. 1460119302. p. 77.
North Cemetery, North Landing, Posey Twp., Switzerland Co., IN
NORTH, Thomas 8/1/1748 – 10/20/1830
        Bathsheba, wife of Thomas, 6/3/1773 – 3/24/1842

Abstract of Graves of Revolutionary Patriots (4 volumes); by Patricia Law Hatcher; Pioneer Heritage Press, Dallas, TX, 1987. Vol. 3, p. 126.
This is an abstract and an index to information reported to the Daughters of the American Revolution and published in their annual reports to the Smithsonian Institution, printed as Senate Documents (1900-1974) and published annually in the DAR magazine (1978-1987).
Published 1972 (Senate Doc. 54)
NORTH, Thomas   Fam Farm, nr North's Landing, Ohio Co IN

North Cemetery, Randolph Twp., Ohio Co. & Posey Twp., Switzerland Co., IN
[The Ohio & Switzerland County line runs through this cemetery.]
Tombstone inscription –

IN
memory of
THOMAS NORTH
who died
Oct. 22, 1830
aged 82 years 1 mo.
& 23 days.

PARKINSON, ABRAHAM
aka PARKINSON, ABRAM

Patriot: Abraham Parkinson
Birth: abt. 1758   poss. Ireland
Married Spouse 1: Elizabeth (b. 1770-1780, d. aft. 1830)
Service state(s): PA
Service description: Capt. Thomas Lookus, 14th Regt. Penn. Line,
         Col. Richard Butler, Capt. Thomas Campbell
Rank: Private
Proof of Service: Pension Application – Switzerland Co., IN
Pension application No.: Not in War Department records
Residences: PA; IN
Died: Aug. 30, 1827   Switzerland Co., IN
Buried: Cotton Cemetery, Jefferson Twp., Switzerland Co., IN
DAR Ancestor No.: None

Document contributed by Judy Kappes
Pension Application Abstracted from Switzerland County, IN Civil Order book, 1820, pg. 377-8.
Pension abstract/schedule of property for – Abraham Parkinson
                                       Service state(s): Pennsylvania
Date: 16 Sep 1820
County of: Switzerland   State of: Indiana
Declaration made before a Circuit Court.
Presented property schedule valued at $553.50, and declaration of service.
Age: 62 years
Residence when he entered service: PA
Residence(s) since the war: PA; IN
Residence now: Switzerland Co., IN
Volunteer or Drafted or Substitute: Enlisted
Rank(s): Private
Statement of service-

Period	Duration	Names of General and Field Officers
9 Jul 1777	2 yrs	Capt. Thomas Lookus, 14th Regt. Pennsylvania Line, commonly called the Blues, commanded by Col. Richard Butler.
????	2 yrs	Capt. Thomas Campbell, same Regt.
????	1 yr, 5 mos.	----

Battles: Long Island, Stony Point, Brandywine.
Discharge received: in Amboy, NJ
Wife: Elizabeth   Wife's age: 47 yrs
Names and ages of children: daughter Peggy aged 17 yrs; Ester age 14; John age 10; Martin & Samuel age 8; Abraham age 20 mos.; Joseph Branham, a grandchild age 6; James H???, a bound boy age 14;

Pennsylvania Archives, Series 2, Volume X. p. 531.
Continental Line. Fourth Pennsylvania. January 1, 1777-November 3, 1783.
Non-Commissioned Officers and Privates of the Fourth Pennsylvania Regiment, Continental Line.
Parkinson, Abraham, Capt. Campbell's company; resided at Printers' Retreat, Indiana, 1827.

Pennsylvania Archives, Series 5, Volume II. p. 1087.
Arrangement of the Officers of the Fourth Regiment of Penna.
Parkinson, Abraham, Capt. Campbell's company; resided at Printers' Retreat, Indiana, 1827.

Pennsylvania Archives, Series 5, Volume XXVI. p. 490.
Provincial Papers: Warrantees of Land in the Several Counties of the State of Pennsylvania. 1730-1898.
Parkinson, Abraham   300 acres Survey date Jan. 10, 1794

Indiana Territory, Switzerland Circuit Court Records, Order Book, October Term 1814 to March Term 1815. p.92.
Henry Langham is listed in county records for the first time on 15 September 1820, as a plaintiff.
Author's note: There are entries in this volume that are not within the range of dates shown on the binder cover.

1820 U.S. Census, Indiana, Switzerland, Craig, Series: M33 Roll: 14 Page: 249
Abraham Parkinson 45 and up; others in household 4 males under 10, 2 males 10-16, 1 female 10-16, 1 female 16-26, 1 female 26-45, 1 female 45 and up.

1830 U.S. Census, Indiana, Switzerland, No Twp, Series: M19 Roll: 32 Page: 60.
Elizabeth Parkinson, Age 50-60.

Revolutionary Soldiers of Switzerland County; Copied by Mary Hill, John Paul Chapter-Daughters of the American Revolution; January, 1958; http://www.ingenweb.org/inswitzerland/switzrevsoldiers.html- Viewed June 2012.
PARKINSON, ABRAHAM
Born about 1758.
Enlisted July 1777 under Capt. Thomas Lookus, 14th Regt. Penn. Line, called "Penn Blues", Col. Richard Butler. Capt. Thomas Campbell. Served 5 years, 3 months, 11 days.
Discharged at Amboy, N. J. In battles of Long Island, Stony Point and Brandywine.
See Switzerland Co. Civil Order book, 1820, pg. 378.
Married Elizabeth _____
Children: Peggy , Ester, John, Martin, Samuel, Abram.
Collected by Mrs. A. V. Danner, Vevay, Indiana.

Roster of Soldiers and Patriots of the American Revolution Buried in Indiana, Vol. I; compiled by Mrs. Roscoe C. O'Byrne.; Indiana Daughters of the American Revolution, 1981; p.284.
PARKINSON, ABRAHAM   Switzerland County
Born – About 1758.
Service – Enlisted July, 1777, under Capt. Thomas Lookus, 14th Regt. Penn. Line, called "Penn Blues", Col. Richard Butler, Capt. Thomas Campbell. Served 5 yrs. 3 mos. 11 days. Discharged at Amboy, N.J. In the Battles of Long Island, Stony Point and Brandywine.
Proof – Switzerland Co. Civil Order Book 1820, p. 378.
Married – Elizabeth _____. Ch. Peggy; Ester; John; Martin; Samuel; Abram.
Collected by Mrs. A. V. Danner, Vevay, Indiana.

History of Switzerland County Indiana 1885; Reproduced by the Switzerland County Historical Society, Vevay, Indiana, 1999. The portion of the book relating to Switzerland County in the 1885 printing of the "History of Dearborn, Ohio, and Switzerland Counties, Indiana". p. 1038.
"A squirrel hunt took place in Craig Township March 17 and 18, 1824, and on the 19th they met at Johnson Brown's, on Long Run, to count the game with the following result:"
Included on this list is Abraham Parkinson with the count of 82.

The Swiss Settlement of Switzerland County; by Perrett Dufour; published by the Indiana Historical Commission, Indianapolis, IN, 1925. p.214.
During the days in which Camp meetings were annually held in this part of the country there lived an old man by the name of Abraham Parkinson in the neighborhood of Vevay he was a son of the Emerald Isle.

Tombstone photographed 22Oct 2011 by Marlene McDerment
Cotton Cemetery, Jefferson Twp., Switzerland Co., IN
Inscription -   Memory of
                         ABRAM PARKERSON
                         He departed this life
                            Aug. 30, 1827
                         in the 70th year of
                              his age

The Vevay Reveille-Enterprise; Vol. 122, No. 37, 22 Sep 1935, p. 7, col. 3.
Roster of Revolutionary Soldiers Who Resided in Switzerland County
By Mrs. Effa M. Danner
Abraham Parkinson – Switzerland C0., Petition, Order Book C., p. 378, Sept. 1820, age 62. Enlisted in Rev. War, July 1777 under Capt. Thomas Kookus, 14 Regiment Pa., Line called the "Pa. Blues". Col. Richard Butler under Capt. Thomas Campbell same Regiment served 5 years, 3 months and 11 days. Discharged at Amboy, N.J., 9th of Aug. year not recollected. In the battles of Long Island, Stony Point and Brandywine.
Family – wife, Elizabeth, age 47.

Children , Peggy, 17, Ester, 14, John 10, Martin 8, Samuel 6, Abram 6 months. Lonat Branham, grandson, 6 and James Welsh, a bound boy 19.
He was a Master Mason by trade but unable to work.
Marriage Record – Margaret Parkinson married Wm. Cassaday, Aug. 25, 1827.
Switzerland County Census 1820 – Abram Parkinson lived in Craig township, wife 45, family, six boys and three girls.

PEABODY, STEPHEN G.

Patriot: Stephen G. Peabody
Birth: 22 Jul 1753   Boxford, MA
Married Spouse 1: 8 Dec 1795, Haverhill, Sussex County, MA   Elizabeth Clark
(b. 1 Nov 1760 NY d. 8 Jul 1816)
DAR record has marr. 1 Feb 1781
Service state(s): MA
Service description: Capt. Stephen Webster, Col. Jacob Gerrish
Rank: Private
Proof of Service: Massachusetts Soldier & Sailors, Vol. 12, p. 10.
Pension application No.: None
Residences: MA; Switzerland Co., IN
Died: 6 Feb 1838   Vevay, Switzerland Co., IN
Buried: Unknown
DAR Ancestor No.: A086830

Massachusetts Marriages, Haverhill, Sussex County,
08 Dec 1795, Stephen Peabody to Elizabeth Clark.

Massachusetts Soldiers and Sailors of the Revolutionary War, A Compilation from the Archives; prepared and published by the Secretary of the Commonwealth in accordance with Chapter 100, Resolves of 1891, Vol. XII; Wright & Potter Printing co., State Printers, Boston, MA, 1904. p. 10.
PEABODY, STEPHEN. Private, Capt. Stephen Webster's co., Col. Gerrish's regt.; enlisted Oct. 14, 1779; discharged Nov. 22, 1779; service 1 mo. 19 days., at Claverack, including travel (220 miles) home; regiment raised in Suffolk and Essex counties to reinforce army under Gen. Washington.
Comment by Marlene McDerment - There are 5 other entries for Stephen Peabody on this page. Further research would be required to determine if the entries are for this man.

Early Ohio Settlers, Purchasers of Land in Southwestern Ohio, 1800-1840; Compiled by Ellen T. Berry & David A. Berry; Genealogical Publishing Co., Inc., Baltimore, MD, 1986. p. 250.
(B) Indiana Survey: Land lying west of a meridian drawn west of the Great Miami (known as the "Gore"). Switzerland, Dearborn, Franklin, Ohio, Union and Randolph Counties (all or only a part of each county) – all in Indiana.

Purchaser	Year	Date	Residence	R – T - S
Peabody, Stephen (B)	1817	Aug 22	Switzerland	03-03-03
Peabody, Stephen (B)	1817	Aug 22	Switzerland	03-03-03
Peabody, Stephen (B)	1818	Jan 14	Switzerland	03-03-14

Early Settlers of Indiana's "GORE" 1803-1820; Compiled and Edited by Shirley Keller Mikesell; Heritage Books, Inc., 1995. p. 187.
Switzerland County – Township 3, Range 3W
Section 3 – Stephen Peabody – 1817 – pg. 10.

Indiana Land Entries Vol. 1 Cincinnati District, 1801-1840; Margaret R. Waters; Originally Published Indianapolis 1948, Second Reprint 1979 by The Bookmark, P.O. Box 74, Knightstown, In 46148. p.70.
CINCINNNATI LAND DISTRICT – VOL. 1
Note: --The tract books for the land offices in Indiana are deposited in the office of the Auditor of State, Indianapolis. They and are in the custody of the State clerk. –
SWITZERLAND CO.
Stephen Peabody SW1/4 S3; 8-22-1817
Stephen Peabody SW1/4 S13; 8-22-1817
Stephen Peabody SW1/4 S14; 1-14-1818

U.S. Department of Interior, Bureau of Land Management, General Land Office Records; Land Patent Search – accessed 27 June 2012.
PEABODY, STEPHEN
Accession Nr. CV-0038-587; Document Type – Credit Volume Patent; State – Indiana; Issue Date – 4/29/1818; Cancelled – No
Names on Document: Peabody, Stephen; Dickason, William
Land Office – Cincinnati; Authority – April 24, 1820 Sale-Cash Entry (3 Stat. 566); Total Acres – 0.00
Land Descriptions: State – IN; Meridian – 1st PM; Twp-Rng – 002N-002W; aliquots – NE1/4; Section – 8; County - Switzerland
&
Accession Nr. CV-0038-595; Document Type – Credit Volume Patent; State – Indiana; Issue Date – 4/29/1818; Cancelled – No
Land Office – Cincinnati; Authority – April 24, 1820 Sale-Cash Entry (3 Stat. 566); Total Acres – 0.00
Land Descriptions: State – IN; Meridian – 1st PM; Twp-Rng – 003N-003W; Aliquots – SW1/4; Section – 3; County - Switzerland
&
Accession Nr. CV-0038-596; Document Type – Cash Volume Patent; State – Indiana; Issue Date – 4/29/1818; Cancelled – No
Land Office – Cincinnati; Authority – April 24, 1820 Sale-Cash Entry (3 Stat. 566); Total Acres – 0.00
Land Descriptions: State – IN; Meridian – 1st PM; Twp-Rng – 003N-003W; Aliquots SW1/4; Section – 13; County - Switzerland
&
Accession Nr. CV-0057-282; Document Type – Credit Volume Patent; State – Indiana; Issue Date – 12/5/1823; Cancelled - No
Names on Document: Peabody, Stephen; Backus, Marvin
Land Office – Cincinnati; Authority – April 24, 1820 Sale-Cash Entry (3 Stat. 566); Document Nr. 145; Total Acres – 160.00
Land Descriptions: State – In; Meridian – 1st PM; Twp-Rng – 002N-002W; aliquots – SE1/4; Section – 7; County - Switzerland
&
Accession Nr. CV-0057-283; Document Type – Credit Volume Patent; State – Indiana; Issue Date – 12/5/1823; Cancelled – No

Land Office – Cincinnati; Authority – April 24, 1820 (3 Stat. 566); Document Nr. 146; Total Acres 139.34
Land Descriptions: State – IN; Meridian – 1st PM; Twp-Rng – 003N-003W; Aliquots – SE1/4; Section – 14; County - Switzerland

<u>*1820 U.S. Census, Indiana, Switzerland, Cotton, Series: M33 Roll: 14 Page: 269*</u>
Stephen Peabody 45 and up; others in household 1 male under 10, 1 male 6-18, 2 males 16-26, 1 female under 10, 1 female 16-26.

PEAKE, NATHAN
aka PEAK

Patriot: Nathan Peake
Birth: c. 1752
Married Spouse 1: Catherine X (possibly Catherine Logan)
          (b. abt. 1756 d. aft. 15 Aug 1821 Switzerland Co., IN)
Service state(s): MD
Service description: Capts. Michael Cresap, Barton Lucas, Nathaniel Ewing,
          Col. Stone, Brig. Gen. Wm. Smallwood, 1st MD Regt, Cont.
          Line
Rank: Private, Sergeant; Patriotic Service
Proof of Service: Pension application S35550
Pension application No.: S35550
Residences: Enlisted Annapolis, Anne Arundel Co., MD; Indiana Territory, Switzerland Co., IN
Died: 25 Jan 1825 Switzerland Co., IN
Buried: On his farm later owned by Charles Haskell
DAR Ancestor No.: A203768

Pension Application Abstracted from National Archives microfilm Series 805, Roll 639, File S35550.

Pension abstract for – Nathan Peak   Service state(s): None shown
Date: 13 May 1818
County of: Switzerland   State of: Indiana
Declaration made before a Judge of the Circuit Court
Residence now: Jefferson Twp., Switzerland, IN
Volunteer or Drafted or Substitute: Not stated
Rank(s): Private & Sergeant
Statement of service-

Period	Duration	Names of General and Field Officers
1775 as Private	Not stated	Company of rifle commanded by Capt. Michael (illegible) in Maryland in Gen. Montgomery's army.
1776 as Private	1 year	Capt. Parton Linear, Col. Smallwood
1777	3 years	Capt. Nathan Ewing, brigade commanded By William Smallwood. Capt. Morse took command before the Battle of Gilford in NC.
1782		Prisoner at Charleston, SC

Battles: Wounded at Battle of Gilford
Discharge received: Paroled by Gen. Lasley at Charleston, SC.
&
Date: 14 September 1820
County of: Switzerland   State of: Indiana
Declaration made before the third judicial circuit of the State of Indiana
Age: 68
Residence now: Switzerland Co., IN

Volunteer or Drafted or Substitute: Not stated
Rank(s): Not stated
Statement of service- Same as above
Wife: Residing with him – Catherine Peak   Wife's age: 64 years

Switzerland County, Indiana Civil Order Book 4, 1820 – 1823; pg. 70.
Sept. 1820
Nathan Peake, Revolutionary soldier & U.S. pensioner---$187.25.

Author's note: Nathan, and his wife, Catherine Peak of Indiana sold land on 15 Ag 1821. This indicates that Catherine was still living at this time. See *Switzerland County, Indiana Deeds, Vol. B., p. 142.*

Switzerland County, IN, Will Book Vol. 1, 3 Jan 1823-10 Nov 1847, p. 4.;
Switzerland County, Indiana Probate Record Book Vol. A, Mar 1827-Nov 1834; p. 7.
Abstract of will and/or administration for: Nathan Peak
State & county where recorded: Switzerland Co., Indiana
State & county where will was made: Switzerland Co., IN
Book/volume where recorded: Will Book Vol. 1
Date will made: 14 October 1824
Date entered in probate: 25 January 1825
Name(s) of executors: Samuel Peak
Witnesses to Will – John Pavy, Samuel Peak, Gabriel Johnston, Richard Johnston.
Administration:
Name of administrator – Samuel Peak & William Keith
Witnesses: John Pavy, Gabriel Johnston, Richard Johnston
Bonded by and amount of bond: Gabriel Johnston & John Pavy for $300.00.
Appraisers: Samuel Peak, William Keith, Nathaniel Cotton, Barnabas Newkirk.
Names of heirs and others mentioned in will and relationship if shown: Beloved wife Catherine; Son Samuel Peak; Daughter Elizabeth Peak alias Fenton; granddaughters Elizabeth Peak, Alice Fenton; heirs (relation not stated) Ellenor Keith, Nancy Fenton, Catherine Keith, Samuel Peak.
Date of division & disbursement, or final return: 3 Nov 1829

Abstract of Final Payment Voucher; General Services Administration, Washington, DC
FINAL PAYMENT VOUCHER RECEIVED FROM
THE GENERAL ACCOUNTING OFFICE
NAME   Peak, Nathan
AGENCY OF PAYMENT   Indiana
DATE OF ACT   1818
DATE OF PAYMENT
DATE OF DEATH   Died Nov. 24, 1824 Paid
GENERAL SERVICES ADMINISTRATION
National Archives and Records Service   NA-286

Maryland Revolutionary Records; Harry Wright Newman; Tuttle Publishing, Rutland, VT, 1928. p. 41.
Revolutionary Pensioners
Peak, Nathan   1752   Lieut.   Maryland Line   Prisoner

Muster and Pay Rolls of the War of the Revolution 1775-1783, Collections of The New-York Historical Society for the Years 1914 an 1915; Printed for the Society, New York, 1914. p. 147.
Maryland Line – First Regiment

Dates	No.	Names	3 yrs
10 Feb '80	31	Nathan Peake	1

Muster Rolls and other records of service of Maryland Troops in the American Revolution; Archives of Maryland, reprinted with permission by Genealogical Publishing Co., Inc., Baltimore, 1972.
p. 10.
Records of Maryland Troops in the Continental Service
Third Company
Commd. Jan 3d, 1776　　　Barton Lucas, Capt.　　　present
　"　　　　　　　　　　　Wm. Sterrett, 1 Lt.　　　on furlough
　"　　　　　　　　　　　Alex. Roxburgh, 2 Lt.　　"
　"　　　　　　　　　　　Wm. Ridgely, Ensign　　 "

Rank	Date of Enlistment	Names	Remarks
Private	Feb 13	Nathan Peake	present

p. 149.
Musters of Maryland Troops, Vol. I.

Names	Rank	Time of Service Enlisted	Discharged	Remarks

Peake, Nathan
   certified by Ensign B. Burgess that his time of service expired 17 Nov 82
p. 313.
Voluntary Enlistments for 3 years, Dec. 3rd, 1776.
Darby McNamarra　　　　Terrence Duffey
A List of Recruits passed by James Brice, Lieut. of Annl. County.
Nathan Peak [included in list]
p. 432.

Name and Rank	When Commenced	When Left Service and the Reasons	Remarks
Nathan Peeke P		disch'd 14 Nov '82	-

p. 550.

	Served between 1 Aug 80	Served between 1 Jan 82	Served between 1 Jan 83	Served between 15 Nov 83

Rank	Names	Remarks	1 Jan 82	1 Jan 83	15Nov83	10 July '84
Serjt.	Nathan Peak	Dischd. 14 Nov '82	"	"	"	-

Register of Certificates Issued by John Pierce, Esquire, Paymaster General and Commissioner of Army Accounts for the United States, to Officers and Soldiers of the Continental Army Under Act of July 4, 1783; Originally Published as Senate Documents, Vol.9, No. 988, 63rd Congress, 3d Session, Washington, 1915; Seventeenth report of the National Society of the Daughters of the American Revolution; Genealogical Publishing Co., Inc, Baltimore, MD, 1984. p. 393.
Men listed in this volume with the same name.

No. of Certificate	To whom issued	Amount
85939	Peake, Nathan	136.60
86865	Peake, Nathan	69.70

Revolutionary War Bounty Land Grants Awarded by State Governments; Lloyd DeWitt Bockstruck; Genealogical Publishing co., IN, Baltimore, MD, 1996. p. 411.
Peak, Nathan. Md. Sergeant. 50 acres.

A Partial Census For Indiana Territory 1810; Compiled by John D & E. Diane Stemmons; Census Publishing LC, Sandy, UT, 2004. p.423.
Peak, Nathen, Historical Locality: Indiana Territory, Current State: Indiana, Jefferson County,- Name on recommendation list, 1813, to the President asking that Eijah Sparks be appointed to fill the vacancy on the General Court that existed because of the death of Judge Vanderburgh (pages 244-50).- Territorial Papers of the US, vol. 8 pg. 247.
Peak, Nathen, Male

Indiana Territory, Switzerland Circuit Court Records, Order Book, October Term 1814 to March Term 1815. p.90 .
He is listed in county records for the first time on 14 September 1815, as a juror.

Early Settlers of Indiana's "GORE" 1803-1820; Compiled and Edited by Shirley Keller Mikesell; Heritage Books, Inc., 1995. p. 202.
Switzerland County Deeds; Book A
Deed dated 1818. John James Dufour to Stephen C. Stevens. S12, T2, R3. "surveyed by John Gilliland for John David Dufour…to Nathan Peak's eastern boundary". Signed John James Dufour. Witness: Truman Richards, John Francis Dufour. Pp. 163, 164.

The Pension List of 1820 [U.S. War Department]Reprinted with an Index; by Murtie June Clark; Genealogical Publishing Co., Inc., Baltimore, 1991. Originally published 1820 as Letter from the Secretary of War. p. 658.
Names of the Revolutionary Pensioners which have been placed on the Roll of Indiana, under the Law of the 18th of March, 1818, from the passage thereof, to this day, inclusive, with the Rank they held, and the Lines in which they served, viz.

Names	Rank	Line
Nathan Peak	Sergeant	Maryland

1820 U.S. Census, Indiana, Switzerland, Jefferson; Series: M33 Roll: 14 Pg: 267. Nathan Peak 45 and up; others in household 1 female 26-45.

Revolutionary Soldiers of Switzerland County; Copied by Mary Hill, John Paul Chapter-Daughters of the American Revolution; January, 1958; http://www.ingenweb.org/inswitzerland/switzrevsoldiers.html- Viewed June 2012.
PEAK, NATHAN
Born about 1752
Enlisted at Annapolis under Capt. Henry Saitor, Col. Stone.
In battles of White Plains and Trenton. Auditors Office, Annapolis, shows he enlisted as private in Md. Regiment, Dec. 10, 1776.
Discharged near Philadelphia, Nov. 14, 1780.
Received $136.60 from John Hamilton, Agent MD. Line for pay from August 1, 1780 to Jan. 1, 1782. Also $69.70 from Jan. 1, 1782 to Jan. 1, 1783.
Married Catherine _____
Children: Samuel m Polly Butler; Eleanor m. a Keith; Nancy m. a Fenton; Catherine m. Wm. Keith, Jr.
Died Dec. 1824 Buried on his farm now owned by Charles Haskell.
Will of Nathan Peak
Written Jan 25, 1818
Probate Oct. 12, 1826
Names wife Catherine, son Samuel, granddaughter Elizabeth Peak alias Fenton, 1 chest, etc. dau. Eleanor Keith, Nancy Fenton, Catherine Keith.

Roster of Soldiers and Patriots of the American Revolution Buried in Indiana, Vol. I; compiled by Mrs. Roscoe C. O'Byrne.; Indiana Daughters of the American Revolution, 1981; p.288.
PEAK, NATHAN   Switzerland County
Born – About 1752.
Service – Enlisted at Annapolis under Capt. Henry Gaitor, Col. Stone. Discharged near Philadelphia. In Battles of White Plains and Trenton. Auditors Office, Annapolis shows he enlisted as pri. in Md. Regt. Dec. 10, 1776. Discharged Nov. 14, 1780. Received $136.60 from John Hamilton, Agent Md. Line for pay from Aug.1, 1780, to Jan. 1, 1782. Also, $69.70 from Jan. 1, 1782, to Jan 1., 1783.
Proof - Pension claim S. 35550.
Died – Dec. 1824. Buried on his farm now owned by Charles Howell.
Married – Catherine _____. Ch. Samuel, m. Polly Butler; Eleanor, m. _____ Keith; Nancy, m. _____ Fenton; Catherine, m. Wm. Keith, Jr.
Collected by Mrs. A. V. Danner, Vevay, Indiana.

History of Switzerland County Indiana 1885; Reproduced by the Switzerland County Historical Society, Vevay, Indiana, 1999. The portion of the book relating

to Switzerland County in the 1885 printing of the *"History of Dearborn, Ohio, and Switzerland Counties, Indiana". p.1042.*
First Schools of the County – "Nathan Peak, who lived on a twenty acre piece of land in Section 12 which twenty acres were owned by William Protsman, taught school at his house."

The Swiss Settlement of Switzerland County; by Perrett Dufour; published by the Indiana Historical Commission, Indianapolis, IN, 1925. p.30.
Nathan Peak who lived on a 20 acre piece of land in Section 12 which 20 acres of land is now owned by William Protsman taught school at his house.

The Vevay Reveille-Enterprise; Vol. 122, No. 37, 22 Sep 1935, p. 7, col. 3.
Roster of Revolutionary Soldiers Who Resided in Switzerland County
By Mrs. Effa M. Danner
Nathan Peak, Sergeant – Certificate No. S35550, Switzerland County, Ind., 1819. Thomas Youngs, Joseph Oglesby (Jefferson Co.) Harvey Innes, all testify that Nathan Peak served in the Maryland line and was wounded at the battle of Guilford, in hand and leg. That he served under Col. Thomas Stone, Md. line and Gen. Wm. Smallwood. 1819, age about 67. Enlisted at Annapolis under Capt. Henry Gaiter, Col. Stone. Discharged near Philadelphia. In the battles of White Plains and Trenton.
Wife, Catherine Peak, age 64.
Auditor's office, Annapolis. Nathan Peak enlisted private in Md. line, Dec. 10, 1776. Discharged Nov. 14, 1780. Received $136.60 from John Hamilton, agent of Md. line for pay August 1, 1780 to Jan. 1, 1782, also $69.70 from Jan. 1, 1782-Jan. 1, 1783.
Service, seven years. Pension list rank of Sergeant, 1818.
Switzerland County probate Nov. 1823, Estate of Nathan Peak, Samuel Peak, administrator and Wm. Keith. Assessors, Nathaniel Cotton and Banabas New Kirk.
Nathan Peak taught school in his cabin in the 20 acres, Sect. 12, Jefferson Township in 1812-13.
Perret Dufour, Swiss Settlement, Switzerland County, page, "When I was a boy there was a Peak orchard on the hill side just south of the farm of my parents and on the hill was a grave George Protsman said was the grave of Nathan Peak, a Revolutionary Soldier." This 20 acres was owned by the Protsmans – Archibald Shaw, letter.
1938 this land is now owned by Charles Haskell.
Samuel Peak married Peggy Butler, Dec. 20, 1815; Catherine Peak married Wm. Keith Jr., July 9, 1817; Caroline Peak married Richard Martin, October 11, 1828. Samuel Peak was in the county militia in 1812.
Vevay Records, p. 365, 1820 Order Book C. He writes his petition in the book and signs the same. Miles Eggleston, Pres. Judge.

PENMETENT, JOHN

Patriot: John Penmetent
Birth: abt. 1748
Married Spouse 1: Catherine (d. 22 Jun 1837)
Service state(s): VA
Service description: Lieut. Samuel Bell; 16th Regt.
                      Col. Graceham, General Scott's brigade;
                      Capt. Porter, Lieut. Thomas Bell, & Ensign Green
Rank: Private
Proof of Service: Pension application S35554
Pension application No.: S35554
Residences: VA; Switzerland Co., IN; Ripley Co., IN;
               widow to McDonald Co., SW Missouri.
Died: 24 Oct 1821 Ripley Co., IN
Buried: prob. Ripley Co., IN
DAR Ancestor No.: None

Pension Application Abstracted from National Archives microfilm Series 805, Roll644, File S35554.

Pension abstract for – John Pennetent   Service state(s): VA
Date: 3 September 1818
County of: Switzerland   State of: Indiana
Declaration made before a Court.
Age: Abt. 70
Where he entered service: 1. Staunton, Augusta Co., VA
                               2. Botetourt Co., VA
Volunteer or Drafted or Substitute: Volunteered
Statement of service-

Period	Duration	Names of General and Field Office
1. 1776	18 months	Lieut. Samuel Bell; 16th Regt. commanded by Col. Graceham of General Scott's brigade.
2. ----	18 months	Capt. Porter, Lieut. Thomas Bell, & Ensign Green.

Battles: Monmouth, NJ; Guilford, NC; at the taking of Ft. Friday in SC; at the Siege of Ninety-Six in SC. He was wounded severely at the Siege of Ninety-Si.
Discharge received: 1. Yes
                        2. Yes
Signed by: 1. Col. Graceham, written by Col. James Woods of the 8th Regiment
              2. Adj. Gen. Williams at the Highlands of Santee in South Carolina
What became of it?: Does not have papers and certificates.
Statement is supported by – He has Scars and is indigent.
Documentary proof: None
Persons in neighborhood who certify character: William Cotton, Associate Judge &
Date: 6 June 1821
County of: Switzerland   State of: Indiana

Declaration made before a Court
Age: 73 or 74
Statement of service-

Period	Duration	Names of General and Field Officers
	For 3 years	Company commanded by Capt. John McGuire in The 16th Virginia Regiment, Commanded by Col.William Griegan in the Virginia Line.

Statement is supported by – His original Certificate for Pension , No. 11,999
Wife: Not named   Wife's age: Abt. 41
&
Heirs (Inquiry) Application for Pension – by Catherine Pennetent
Date: 15 June 1854
County of: McDonald   State of: Southwest Missouri
Declaration made before a Court.
   Author's note: Application Rejected – Not married before 1894.
   Catherine Pennetent d. 22 Jun 1837.

Switzerland County, Indiana Civil Order Book 4, 1820 – 1823; pg. 192.
June 1821
John Penmetent, Revolutionary soldier and U.S. pensioner---$184.12 1/2

Revolutionary War Records – Virginia; Virginia Army and Navy Forces with Bounty Land Warrants for Virginia Military District of Ohio, and Virginia Military Script, from Federal and State Archives; by Gaius Marcus Brumbaugh, M.D, M.s., Litt.D; Genealogical Publishing Co., Inc., Baltimore, 1995. p. 608
A List of the Men's Names in Dunmore County Militia Under the Command of Capt. John Holeman.
Penneitt (Pinnett?), John

Historical Register of Virginians in the Revolution, Soldiers, Sailors, Marines, 1775-1783; John H. Gwathmey; The Dietz Press, Richmond, VA, 1938. p. 615.
Penetant, John, Pvt., WD.

The Pension List of 1820 [U.S. War Department] Reprinted with an Index; by Murtie June Clark; Genealogical Publishing Co., Inc., Baltimore, 1991.
Originally published 1820 as Letter from the Secretary of War. p. 658.
Names of the Revolutionary Pensioners which have been placed on the Roll of Indiana, under the Law of the 18th of March, 1818, from the passage thereof, to this day, inclusive, with the Rank they held, and the Lines in which they served, viz.

Names	Rank	Line
John Pennetent	private	Virginia

Pensioners of the Revolutionary War Struck Off the Roll with an Added Index to States; Reprinted by Genealogical Publishing Co., Baltimore, MD for Clearfield Company, Inc., 1989. p.100 .

Pensioners in Indiana who have been dropped under the act of 1st May, 1820; prepared in conformity with a resolution of the House of Representatives of the United States of the 17th December, 1835.

Names	Acts under which restored	Remarks
John Pennetent	March 1, 1823	-

Roster of Soldiers and Patriots of the American Revolution Buried in Indiana, Vol. I; compiled by Mrs. Roscoe C. O'Byrne.; Indiana Daughters of the American Revolution, 1981; p.290

PENNETENT, JOHN   Ripley County
Born – About 1748.
Service – Pri. in Regt. commanded by Cols. Bluford and Haws of Vir. Line, 18 mos. service.
Proof – Pension claim S. 35554.
Died – Oct. 24, 1821, Ripley Co.
Married – Catherine _____ d. 1834. [should be 1837]

The Vevay Reveille-Enterprise; Vol. 122, No. 37, 22 Sep 1935, p. 7, col. 3-4.
Roster of Revolutionary Soldiers Who Resided in Switzerland County
By Mrs. Effa M. Danner
John Pennetent – S35554. Switzerland County, May 22, 1819. Served in Company under Capt. John McQuire who resigned at Valley Forge, enlisted, Winchester, Virginia – 15th Reg. Gen. Scott's brigade in May or June, 1780. Discharged by Col. Gracehemp of Gen. Scott's Brigade. Col. James Wood wrote discharge. Enlisted in Boutetort Co., Vir., attached to Capt. Thos. Bell's Co., at Staunton, Augusta Co., Virginia. Reg. attached to Col. Bluford's line in Hillsboro, N.C. Served 18 months and discharged at highlands of Santee (Col. Thompson's plantation, Oct. 31, 1781) signed by Adj. Gen. Williams. December 3, 1819, about 70 years of age. In battles of Monmouth, Guilford, Camden, Fort Friday in S.C., Siege of 96. Mentions wife about 41 has rheumatic pains. Died October 24, 1821 in Ripley Co.
Loomesville, McDonald Co., S.W. Mo., July 3, 1850 letters written in relation to claim of Catherine Pennetent's heirs (none named). ~~Widow~~ died June 22, 1834. Ind. Cert. 11999, John P., private in Regiment of Cols. Bluford and Haws of Virginia line, 18 months, inscribed on rolls of Indiana at rate of $8.00 per a. to commence Dec. 3, 1819. Cert. issued June 17, 1819, sent to Wm. Keen, Vevay, Jefferson Township, Indiana.
No records here.

PICKETT, HEATHCOTE

Patriot: Heathcote Pickett
Birth: poss. b. 29 Mar 1746, Jamestown, Caroline Co., VA.
Married Spouse 1: Rachael
Service state(s): PA
Service description: See Pennsylvania Archives citations
Rank: Private
Proof of Service: Pennsylvania Archives – multiple citations
Pension application No.: None
Residences: NC; PA; Indiana Territory; Switzerland Co., IN
Died: d. 1820 near Mt. Sterling, Switzerland Co., IN (family records)
Buried: poss. Hiram Ogle farm, Switzerland Co., IN
DAR Ancestor No.: None

Pennsylvania Archives, Series: Series 3, Volume: XXIII,
Chapter: Muster Rolls of the Navy and Line, Militia and Rangers, 1775-1783.
with List of Pensioners, 1818-1832., Page: 234.
RANGERS ON THE FRONTIER
Heathcot Picket

Pennsylvania Archives, Series: Series 5, Volume: IV,
Chapter: List of "Soldiers of the Revolution who received pay for their services,"
Taken from Manuscript Record, having neither date nor title, but under "Rangers
on the Frontiers, 1778-1783" was published in (end of description) Page: 611.
SOLDIERS OF THE REVOLUTION
Picket, Heatheat, private

Pennsylvania Archives, Series: Series 6, Volume: III,
Chapter: Militia Rolls- 1783-1790., Page: 451.
HUNTINGDON COUNTY
#69 on list – Haithcot Picket.

Pennsylvania Archives, Series: Series 5, Volume: IV,
Chapter: Soldiers Who Received Depreciation Pay as Per Cancelled Certificates
on File in the Division of Public Records, Pennsylvania State Library., p: 248.
CONTINENTAL LINE
Picket, Heathcut, private

Pennsylvania in 1780, A Statewide Index of Circa 1780 Pennsylvania Tax Lists,
Compiled by John D and E. Diane Stemmons; Self published, 1978. p. 143.
Picket, Hethcott   BDFE: DB   [Bedford Co: Dublin Twp.]

Census of Indiana Territory for 1807; Indiana Historical Society, 1980. p. 25.
A list of free males above the age of twenty one in Dearborn County in March
1807 ~~
413   Heathcoat Picket

A Partial Census For Indiana Territory 1810; Compiled by John D & E. Diane Stemmons; Census Publishing LC, Sandy, UT, 2004. p.423.
Picket, Hethcoat, Historical Locality: Indiana Territory, Current State: Indiana, Jefferson County,- Name on recommendation list, 1813, to the President asking that Eijah Sparks be appointed to fill the vacancy on the General Court that existed because of the death of Judge Vanderburgh (pages 244-50).-
Territorial Papers of the US, vol. 8 pg. 247.
Picket, Hethcoat, Male

Indiana Territory, Switzerland Circuit Court Records, Order Book, October Term 1814 to March Term 1815. p. 83.
Heathcoat Pickett is listed in county records for the first time on 11 September 1820, as a witness for the plaintiff. *Author's note:* There are entries in this volume that are not within the range of dates shown on the binder cover.

Revolutionary Soldiers Buried in Indiana A Supplement; 485 Names Not Listed in the Roster of Soldiers and Patriots of the American Revolution Buried in Indiana (1938) nor in Revolutionary Soldiers Buried in Indiana (1949); Margaret E. Waters; Indianapolis, 1954. p. 81.
PICKETT, HEATHCOTE   Switzerland
Rev. sold. who died there.
REF: Mr. Schrum

Switzerland County, Indiana Cemetery Locator; By Ellyn R. Kern; Published by Switzerland County Historical Society, Vevay, IN, 1998 (2011). p. 11.
It is claimed that Heathcoate Pickett, the earliest white man to live in Switzerland County was buried on the Hiram Ogle farm which is believed to be on SR 56 about .6 mile north of Bennington Pike across from Brooks Road.

History of Switzerland County Indiana 1885; Reproduced by the Switzerland County Historical Society, Vevay, Indiana, 1999. The portion of the book relating to Switzerland County in the 1885 printing of the "History of Dearborn, Ohio, and Switzerland Counties, Indiana". p. 990.
The First Settlers – "The first settler in the county of whom any definite account can be given, was Heathcoat Pickett, who located above Plum Creek, about three miles above Vevay, in 1795, and there built a cabin and resided for several years"….."The family consisted of the father, mother, two sons and one daughter, who endured many privations, and often narrowly escaped the tomahawks and scalping knives of the savage Indians."

Vevay Switzerland County Indiana 1795-1999; no author or publisher. p. 1.
The first settler in the county of whom any definite account is given was Heathcoat Pickett, a Revolutionary War veteran, who located here is 1795, followed in 1798 and 1799 by the Cotton, Dickason and Gullion families.

The Swiss Settlement of Switzerland County; by Perrett Dufour; published by the Indiana Historical Commission, Indianapolis, IN, 1925.p.7
Indiana Historical Collections VOL. XIII, The Swiss Settlement of Switzerland Co., Indiana; Peret Dufour; Indianapolis 1923;
p. 7.
"The first settlers, of the county, or rather of the territory embraced in the limits of the county, were the Cottons, Dickason, Ricketts, Drakes, Maguire, Rayl, David and Stewart, who severally settled within a few miles of the present location of Vevay. William Cotton, and Griffith Dickason settled on Indian Creek sometime in 1798 or 1799, Heathcoat Pickett above the mouth of Hunts Creek about the year ------ Robert and Benjamin Drake two brothers about 1799 or 1800. Maguire whose Christian name is not known about 1800, John Rayl about 1801, and James Stewart about the year 1799 or 1800, and then a part [of] the Swiss colony became their neighbors in the spring of 1803...."

Vevay Reveille Enterprise, 9 Feb1952 - 6 Mar 1952, p.3, column 1-7; by Guy Walden.
Excerpts from the series – full text is on microfilm at the Switzerland County Public Library, Vevay, IN.
...before the Revolutionary War, they were living in North Carolina. The people in sympathy with the colonies were so distressed by their property being taken from them daily and the Picketts in constant danger of their lives by the Tories and robbers, protected by the British, were obliged to leave their habitation every night to take rest or fall prey to the villains so the Picketts as did others, moved to Cumberland County, Va.
Later they moved to Bedford County, Pennsylvania. The Picketts saw the great caravans moving to the west. So in 1789 a company of seven families at Bedford, Pa., proceeded to Fort Pitt.
They spent the winter months in preparation for the trip, building boats, collecting supplies....
In March 1790 Heathcoate Pickett found himself with his wife Rachel, two sons [Heathcoate II and James], and six daughters [Mary Polly), Sally, Rachael, Eliza, Nancy, Keziah] drifting into practically a new world.

PIERCE, JAMES
aka PEARCE, JAMES

Documentation has not been found to place this man in the Revolutionary War or in Switzerland County. Prior references to his being a Revolutionary ancestor are in error. The current (2012) DAR Ancestor Database does not show a James Pierce who served in New York, nor do they show anyone by that name having died in Indiana. There are no Revolutionary War pension applications for this man. James Pierce did serve in the War of 1812. Prior erroneous and correct records pertaining to this man are shown on these pages.

Patriot: James Pierce
Birth: -
Married Spouse 1: -
Service state(s): NY ?
Service description: NY Militia ?
Rank: ?
Proof of Service: None
Pension application No.: None
Residences: -
Died: -
Buried: -
DAR Ancestor No.: None

Erroneous records -
Revolutionary Soldiers Buried in Indiana A Supplement; *485 Names Not Listed in the Roster of Soldiers and Patriots of the American Revolution Buried in Indiana (1938) nor in Revolutionary Soldiers Buried in Indiana (1949);* Margaret E. Waters; Indianapolis, 1954. p. 26.
PIERCE, JAMES   Fayette Co.
Bur. Orange Twp., Cem., Connersville, Ind., gr. Loc. By Connersville Chap., DAR. REF: DAR 15, p. 85, DAR 18, p. 240; Bowen's Hist. of Fayette Co., Ind. (1917), p. 320.
[This DAR reference does not exist.]

Abstract of Graves of Revolutionary Patriots (4 volumes); by Patricia Law Hatcher; Pioneer Heritage Press, Dallas, TX, 1987. Vol. 3, p. 173.
This is an abstract and an index to information reported to the Daughters of the American Revolution and published in their annual reports to the Smithsonian Institution , printed as Senate Documents (1900-1974) and published annually in the DAR magazine (1978-1987).
Published 1915, Serial set 6924, Volume 14.
PIERCE, James   Orange Twp Cem, Connersville IN   [Fayette County]

History of Fayette County Indiana, Her People, Industries and Institutions, With Biographical Sketches of Representative Citizens and Genealogical Records of Many of the Old Families, Illustrated; Frederic Irving Barrows, Editor-in-Chief; B. F. Bowen & Company, Inc., Indianapolis, Indiana, 1917. p. 320.

"The chapter [Connersville Chapter Daughters of the American Revolution]has made an effort to locate the graves of all the Revolutionary War soldiers who are buried in the county, and thus far has located ten: Jonathan Davis (1760-1845), Springersville cemetery; James Hamer,
Union cemetery; Daniel Bloomhart (died in 1837), Jonathan Gillian (1758-1833), James Justice (1742-1832), Nicholas Keemar (died in 1828) and James Pierce, Orange township cemetery: Amos Milner (died in 1851), Mt. Garrison cemetery: Robert Groves (died in 1855) and Samuel Isles (died in 1855), Fairview cemetery."

The Vevay Reveille-Enterprise; Vol. 122, No. 37, 22 Sep 1935, p. 7, col. 3.
Roster of Revolutionary Soldiers Who Resided in Switzerland County
By Mrs. Effa M. Danner
Sergeant James Pierce – His name is on the pension lists of 1814. Sergeant in New York Militia. *Author's note:* His name has not been located on this list.

Correct record -
Roster of Soldiers and Patriots of the American Revolution Buried in Indiana, Vol. I; compiled by Mrs. Roscoe C. O'Byrne.; Indiana Daughters of the American Revolution, 1981; p.406.
List of Indiana Pensioners in Other Wars,
Giving the County in Which They Were Living When Pensioned
Pierce, James   Switzerland Co.   War of 1812
Author's note: Not Revolutionary War

PORTER, THOMAS

Patriot: Thomas Porter
Birth: 29 Nov 1761 near New Haven, CT
Married Spouse 1: Unknown
Service state(s): CT
Service description: CT Militia, Capt. Chapman, Capt. Beelee
Rank: Private
Proof of Service: Pension application S17640
Pension application No.: S17640
Residences: Wyoming, PA; Bethlehem Society, near Woodbury, CT; NY; KY; OH; Cotton Twp., Switzerland Co., IN
Died: aft 1840
Buried: Unknown
DAR Ancestor No.:

Pension Application Abstracted from National Archives microfilm Series 805, Roll 660, File S17640.

Pension abstract for – Thomas Porter   Service state(s): Connecticut
Date: 21 August 1832
County of: Switzerland   State of: Indiana
Declaration made before a Judge. Unable to appear in court in consequence of bodily infirmary caused by a rupture on both sides of the groin.
Recorded in Book A, pg. 280.
Age: 70 years   Record of age: None except this which I made myself containing the names of my own children.
Where and year born: near New Haven, CT on 29 November 1761
Residence when he entered service: 1778 in Wyoming, PA; 1780/1781 in the Bethlehem Society near Woodbury, CT
Residence(s) since the war: 5 or 6 years in New York State, then in Kentucky about 10 years, about 20 years in Ohio, 13 in Indiana.
Residence now: Cotton Twp., Switzerland Co., IN
Volunteer or Drafted or Substitute: 1778 Volunteered; 1780/1781 Enlisted.
Rank(s): Private
Statement of service-

Period	Duration	Names of General and Field Officers
1778	short term	Served under a man named Jenkins.
13 April 1780/81	9 months	Company of Connecticut Militia commanded by Capt. Chapman in regiment commanded by Col. Beelee

Battles: 1778 - pursuit of savages who had massacred two brothers named Hardin.
    1780/1781 -None, in a place called Horseneck pretty much during the full term of service.
Discharge received: 1778 – none; 1780/1781 - on 1st January at Horseneck.
Statement is supported by –
Documentary proof: Has none.
Evidence: Traditional evidence
Person now living who can testify to service: Knows of no one

Clergyman: Luther Gilmore, resident of Switzerland Co., IN
Persons in neighborhood who certify character: Allen Wiley, David Lee, Charles Leatherberry, John Tague, Hiram Peabody, Augustus A. Peabody, Jeremiah Thomas.
Wife: Not shown
Names and ages of children: Not listed

Abstract of Final Payment Voucher; General Services Administration, Washington, DC
#1 of 2
LAST FINAL PAYMENT VOUCHER RECEIVED FROM
THE GENERAL ACCOUNTING OFFICE
NAME   Porter, Thomas
AGENCY OF PAYMENT   Indiana
DATE OF ACT   1832
DATE OF PAYMENT   Sept 1, 1850 Jan. 1, 1851
DATE OF DEATH
GENERAL SERVICES ADMINISTRATION
National Archives and Records Service   NA-286
GSA-WASH DC 54-4891   November 1953
&
Abstract of Final Payment Voucher; General Services Administration, Washington, DC
#2 of 2
LAST FINAL PAYMENT VOUCHER RECEIVED FROM
THE GENERAL ACCOUNTING OFFICE
NAME   Porter, Thomas
AGENCY OF PAYMENT   Indiana
DATE OF ACT   1818 (Invalid)
DATE OF PAYMENT   1st qr. 1855
DATE OF DEATH   Feb 6, 1854
GENERAL SERVICES ADMINISTRATION
National Archives and Records Service   NA-286
GSA-WASH DC 54-4891   November 1953

Register of Certificates Issued by John Pierce, Esquire, Paymaster General and Commissioner of Army Accounts for the United States, to Officers and Soldiers of the Continental Army Under Act of July 4, 1783; Originally Published as Senate Documents, Vol.9, No. 988, 63rd Congress, 3d Session, Washington, 1915; Seventeenth report of the National Society of the Daughters of the American Revolution; Genealogical Publishing Co., Inc, Baltimore, MD, 1984. p. 508.
Men listed in this volume with the same name.

No. of Certificate	To whom issued	Amount
85990	Porter, Thomas	80.00
93180	Porter, Thomas	80.00

Second Census of Kentucky, 1800; Clift G. Glenn; Genealogical Publishing Co., Baltimore, MD, 1954.
An alphabetical list of 32,000 taxpayers based on original tax lists on file at the Kentucky Historical Society. Information given includes the county of residence and the date of the tax list in which the individual is listed.
[There are two entries for Thomas Porter – which entry is for this man has not been determined.]
Porter, Thomas   Muhlenberg   1800
Porter, Thomas   Nicholas   1800

A Census of Pensioners for Revolutionary or Military Services with their Names, Ages, and Places of Residence Under the Act for Taking the Sixth Census in 1840; Genealogical Publishing Co., Inc., Baltimore, Maryland, 1965. p.185.

INDIANA, SWITZERLAND, COTTON Names of Pensioners for Revolutionary or Military services	Ages	Names of heads of families with whom pensioner resided June 1, 1840
Thomas Porter	78	James Porter

Roster of Soldiers and Patriots of the American Revolution Buried in Indiana; 1938; p.297.
PORTER, THOMAS
Born 29 Nov 1761
Pension Application – CT Militia
Age 70 in Aug. 1832, b. 29 Nov 1761, near New Haven, CT
National Archives, pension application

Roster of Soldiers and Patriots of the American Revolution Buried in Indiana, Vol. I; compiled by Mrs. Roscoe C. O'Byrne.; Indiana Daughters of the American Revolution, 1981; p.297.
PORTER, THOMAS   Switzerland County
Born – Nov. 29, 1761.
Service – Pri. in CO. under Capt. Chapman in Conn. Line, for 9 mos.
Proof – Pension claim S. 17640.

The Vevay Reveille-Enterprise; Vol. 122, No. 37, 22 Sep 1935, p. 7, col. 4.
Roster of Revolutionary Soldiers Who Resided in Switzerland County
By Mrs. Effa M. Danner
Thomas Porter – Switzerland Co., Thomas Porter, Dearborn Co., same, so they say at pension office, S17640. Switzerland County, Ind., Cotton Township, 1832. He was unable to appear in court. Testimony taken by Wm. Keen. Age 70 years. In 1780 or 81 in a Company of Conn. Militia under Capt. Chapman in Reg. of Col. Beebee, 9 months.
Born Nov. 29, 1761 near New Haven, Conn. When called into service lived in Bethlehem Society near Woodbury, Conn. Since war lived 5 or 6 years in New York, 10 years in Kentucky, 20 years in Ohio, 13 in Indiana. When he enlisted, marched to a place called Horseneck, stationed there most of the time.
No record of family or children.

Indiana 7650, Thomas Porter, Switzerland Co., Ind., private in Co. of Capt. Chapman in Conn. line, 9 months. Inscribed on rolls of Indiana $30.00 per a cert. issued Apr. 26, 1833.

Military Census 1840, resident of Cotton Township, age 78. James Porter, guardian.

James Porter married Susan Renols, Jan. 8, 1833. Thomas Porter married Jane Adkins, Sept. 12, 1826.

POTTER, DAVID

Patriot: David Potter
Birth: 26 Jun 1760 Coventry, Kent Co., RI
Married Spouse 1: 4 Dec 1785 RI   Elizabeth Vaughan
                        (b. 9 Oct 1762 East Greenwich, Kent Co., RI
                        d. 5 Feb 1831 Salisbury, Herkimer Co., NY)
Service state(s): CT & RI
Service description: Capts. Ely, Shapley, Calvin, Whitmarsh, Brayton,
                     Wheaton, Green, Kirtland
Rank: Private
Proof of Service: Pension application S14189
Pension application No.: S14189
Residences: Saybrook, CT; Coventry, RI; Pittstown, Rensselaer Co., NY;
              Salisbury, Herkimer Co., NY; Switzerland Co., IN
Died: 13 May 1838   Switzerland Co., IN
Buried: poss. Allenville Cemetery, Cotton Twp., Switzerland Co., IN
        (son David is buried there)
DAR Ancestor No.: A091550

Pension Application Abstracted from National Archives microfilm Series 805, Roll 661, File S14189.; Switzerland County, Indiana Probate Record Book Vol. A, Mar 1827-Nov 1834; p. 280.
Pension abstract for – David Potter
                        Service state(s): Connecticut & Rhode Island
Date: 9 October 1832
County of: Herkimer   State of: New York
Declaration made before an Open Court.

Age: 72 and upwards   Record of age: At home in Salisbury.
Where and year born: Coventry, Kent Co., RI on 26 June 1760.
Residence when he entered service:
1776 - Saybrook, New London Co. (now Middlesex)
May 1777 – Coventry, Kent Co., CT
Dec 1777 – Coventry, Kent Co., CT
1779 – Brooklyn, Windham Co., CT
Residence(s) since the war: 5 or 6 years in Kent Co., RI; about eleven years
              in Pittstown, Rensselaer Co., NY; more than 30 years in
              Salisbury, Herkimer Co., NY where he now resides.
Residence now: Salisbury, Herkimer Co., New York
Volunteer or Drafted or Substitute: 1776 - Enlisted as a volunteer; May 1777 – Drafted; Dec 1777 – Drafted; Jan 1778 – drafted; Dec 1778 – drafted; Jun 1778 – drafted; Jul 1778 – drafted; Aug 1778 – drafted; 1779 substitute for Dr. Baker at Brooklyn.
Statement of service-

Period	Duration	Names of General and Field Officers
1 Feb 1776	10 months	Capt. John Ely's company, New York

Late May 1777	1 month	State Troops. Built a fort at New London called Fort Trumbell. Marched by Capt. Martin Kirtland to White Plains. Benedict Calvin's company, Col. Archibald Carson's Connecticut regiment.
December 1777	1 month	Capt. Calvin's company, Col. Carson's regiment in the state service.
Abt. 1 Jan 1778	1 month	In the state service under command of Capt. Whitworth at Widow Spencer's house in East Greenwich.
June 1778	1 month	Capt. Brayton's company, Col. Carson's regiment in the state service.
July 1778	1 month	Capt. Calvin's company, Col. Carson's regiment in the state service, stationed at Thomas Nichol's house in East Greenwich.
1 Aug 1778	1 month	Capt. Wheaton's company, Col. Carson's regiment in the state service.
1 Jun 1779	3 months	Capt. Green's company, Col. Leo Yard's regiment in the state service.

Battles: White Plains; Butt's Hill
Discharge received: 1 Dec 1776 – not in writing; 1777- late Jun, not in writing; 1778 – in Jan 1778, not in writing; Mar 1778 – not in writing; Jul 1778 – not in writing; Aug 1778 – not in writing; Sep 1778 – not in writing; Aug/Sep 1779 – not in writing.
Statement is supported by: Testimony of living witnesses.
&
Date: 5 September 1837
County of: Switzerland   State of: Indiana
He moved to Cotton Twp., Switzerland Co., IN, and wishes his name to be transferred from the New York agency to the agency of the State of Indiana.
&
Date: 14 April 1841
Treasury Department, Second Comptroller's Office.
Under the act of 6th April 1838, entitled "An act directing the transfer of money remaining unclaimed by certain Pensioners, and authorizing the payment of the same at the Treasury of the United States, " the child of David Potter dec'd, a Pensioner in the Roll of the Albany, New York Agency at the rate of Sixty three Dollars and thirty three Cents per annum, under the law of the 7th June 1832, has been paid at this Department, from the 4th of March 1837, to the 13th May 1838.

Switzerland County, Indiana Probate Order Book 3, 1837-1843; p. 86.
(noted in the left margin is: Certify under the Seal made for M. Potter.)
16 May 1838
In the matter of the Proof of the death }
Of David Potter Deceased

Now on this day comes Martin Potter and proved to the Satisfaction of the Court that David Potter late of Switzerland Indiana who was a pensioner of the United States at the rate of   Dollars. Pensioner died in Cotton township County aforesaid on the 13th day of May 1838, and that he left no widow and that Said Martin Potter is the executor named in a will left by the Said deceased.

Switzerland County, IN, Will Book Vol. 1, 3 Jan 1823-10 Nov 1847, p. 133.
Abstract of will and/or administration for: David Potter
State & county where recorded: Switzerland Co., Indiana
State & county where will was made: Switzerland Co., IN
Book/volume where recorded: Will Book Vol. 1.
Date will made: 25 April 1838
Date entered in probate: 26 May 1838
Witnesses/appraisers: (in some cases, purchasers at sale of estate may be listed on another page and attached hereto): Witnesses to Will – Eliza Andrews & William Andrews.
Names of heirs and others mentioned in will (also signed receipts of division of estate) and relationship if shown: Son Martin Potter.

Lists and Returns of Connecticut Men in the Revolution, 1775-1783; Connecticut Historical Society, 1909; Heritage Books, 2008. p. 323.
Continental Line, 1781-1783   Seventh Company – Capt. Riley
Muster Roll of Captain John Rileys Company of the 3rd Connecticut Regiment in the service of the United States commanded by Colonel Samuel B. Webb for the month of February 1782

Inlisted	Term	
May 16, 1781	3 years	David Potter

The Rhode Island 1777 Military Census; Transcribed by Mildred M. Chamberlain; Published Under the Direction of the Rhode Island Genealogical Society, Genealogical Publishing Co., Baltimore, 1985.
p. 15
Page 1.   Coventry, Rhode Island   David Potter   16-50 A
p. 77
Page 2.   Richmond, Rhode Island   David Potter   16-50 A
p. 80
Page 1.   Scituate, Rhode Island   (D)avid Potter   16-50 A

Register of Certificates Issued by John Pierce, Esquire, Paymaster General and Commissioner of Army Accounts for the United States, to Officers and Soldiers of the Continental Army Under Act of July 4, 1783; Originally Published as Senate Documents, Vol.9, No. 988, 63rd Congress, 3d Session, Washington, 1915; Seventeenth report of the National Society of the Daughters of the American Revolution; Genealogical Publishing Co., Inc, Baltimore, MD, 1984. p. 408.
Men listed in this volume with the same name.

No. of Certificate	To whom issued	Amount
2492	Potter, David	14.34
11835	Potter, David	10.79

27202	Potter, David	40.60
27436	Potter, David	80.00
31626	Potter, David	80.00
32027	Potter, David	25.50

<u>*1830 U.S. Census, New York, Herkimer, Salisbury, Series: M19 Roll: 91 Pg: 73.*</u>
David Potter, Age 60-70. Also female (wife?) in household age 60-70, and others.

<u>*The Vevay Reveille-Enterprise*</u>; *Vol. 122, No. 37, 22 Sep 1935, p. 7, col. 4.*
Roster of Revolutionary Soldiers Who Resided in Switzerland County
By Mrs. Effa M. Danner
David Potter – "Revolutionary Soldier in Pleasant Township, died May 13, 1838, age 78." Vevay Times 1838.

PRESTON, WILLIAM

There is no doubt that William Preston lived in Switzerland County where he was enumerated in the 1840 census as a Revolutionary pensioner. Where he served has not been determined. William Preston is a fairly common name. Numerous records have been located for men by that name in Maryland, Massachusetts, Pennsylvania, and Virginia. Additional records were found in New Hampshire and New York soldiers but these men died there as evidenced by pension applications. The exact service for this man has not been determined.

Patriot: William Preston
Birth: abt. 1765 [Estimated from 1840 census where he is age 75.]
Married Spouse 1: Unknown
Service state(s): Not determined
Service description: Not determined
Rank: ?
Proof of Service: Not determined
Pension application No.: None
Residences: ?; Switzerland County, IN
Died: aft. 1840, prob. Switzerland Co., IN - listed in 1840 Federal Census
(see below)

Buried: Unknown
DAR Ancestor No.: None

A Census of Pensioners for Revolutionary or Military Services with their Names, Ages, and Places of Residence Under the Act for Taking the Sixth Census in 1840; Genealogical Publishing Co., Inc., Baltimore, Maryland, 1965. p.185.

INDIANA, SWITZERLAND, POSEY Names of Pensioners for Revolutionary or Military services	Ages	Names of heads of families with whom pensioner resided June 1, 1840
William Preston	75	William Preston [b. abt. 1765]

1840 U.S. Census, Indiana, Switzerland, Posey, Series: M704 Roll: 95 Page: 166, Line 1.
William Preston age 70-80; others in household 1 female 20-30, 1 female 50-60.
&
Pensioners for Revolutionary or Military Services Included in the Foregoing

Names	Age
William Preston	75

Register of Certificates Issued by John Pierce, Esquire, Paymaster General and Commissioner of Army Accounts for the United States, to Officers and Soldiers of the Continental Army Under Act of July 4, 1783; Originally Published as Senate Documents, Vol.9, No. 988, 63rd Congress, 3d Session, Washington, 1915;

Seventeenth report of the National Society of the Daughters of the American Revolution; Genealogical Publishing Co., Inc, Baltimore, MD, 1984. p. 412.
Men listed in this volume with the same name.

No. of Certificate	To whom issued	Amount
27606	Preston, William	11.07
52660	Preston, William	73.30
56816	Preston, William	16.34

<u>*The Vevay Reveille-Enterprise;* Vol. 122, No. 37, 22 Sep 1935, p. 7, col.4.</u>
Roster of Revolutionary Soldiers Who Resided in Switzerland County
By Mrs. Effa M. Danner
Wm. Preston – Listed on Switzerland Co., list U. S. Military Census 1840.
Record not available.

PROTSMAN, JOHN
(PROTZMAN) (PRUTSMAN)

Patriot: John Protsman
Birth: 10 Jul 1763 NJ
Married Spouse 1: 1790 Pennsylvania Nancy Barbara Reckner
                               (b. 1766, d. 19 Aug 1841)
Service state(s): PA
Service description: Capt. Alshouse, Cpl. Roup.
Rank: Private, Ensign
Proof of Service: See citations
Pension application No.: None in War Department records or in Switzerland Co.
Residences: Northampton Co., PA; KY; OH; Indiana Territory;
               Switzerland Co., IN
     Died: 10 Aug 1841 Switzerland Co., IN
Buried: Vevay Cemetery, Section 2, Jefferson Twp., Switzerland Co., IN
DAR Ancestor No.: None

Pennsylvania Archives, Series 5, Volume VIII. p. 369.
Fifth Battalion Northampton County Militia.
Associators and Militia County of Northampton
A Return of the Officers of the 5th Battalion of Militia in the County of Northampton, with the Rank of the Companies.
Colonel – Abraham Labar; Lieut. Col'o – Isaac Sidman; major – Robert Traill; Adjutant – Christopher Hartzel.
2d Comp'y: Captain – Jacob Weygandt; 1st Lieut – George Stacher; 2d Lieut – John Rambach; Ensign – John Protzman

Pennsylvania Archives, Series 2, Volume XIV. p. 572.
Muster Rolls and Papers Relating to the Associators and Militia of the County of Northampton.
Associated Battalions and Militia of the Revolution Fifth Battalion
A Return of the Officers of the Fifth Battlion of Militia in the County of Northampton, with the Rank of the Companies.
Colonel – Abraham Lavar, May 21, 1777
Second Company
Captain - Jacob Weygandt, May 21, 1777; First Lieutenant – George Stacker, May 21, 1777; Second Lieutenant – John Rambach, May 21, 1777; Ensign – John Protzman, May 21, 1777

Pennsylvania Archives, Series 5, Volume IV. p. 724.
List of "Soldiers of the Revolution who received pay for their services," Taken from Manuscript Record, having neither date nor title, but under "Rangers on the Frontiers, 1778-1783"
Continental Line Soldiers of the Revolution
Prottsman, John, private

Pennsylvania Archives, Series 5, Volume VIII. p. 141.
Associators and Militia County of Northampton
Second Battalion, Northampton Militia
A List of Captain Henry Alshouses Company of Militia in Easton as they are now Class'd. April ye 30th, 1781. (c)
Lieut. Abraham Horn
6th Class
John Brotsman [in the list of privates]

Pennsylvania Archives, Series 5, Volume VIII. p. 121.
Associators and Militia County of Northampton
Second Battalion, Northampton Militia
Associators and Militia County of Northampton
A List of Easton Company with their Names and Classes where they belong to. (c)
Capt. Alshouse
6th Class
John Brotsman [in list of privates]

Pennsylvania Archives, Series 5, Volume VIII. p. 133.
Associators and Militia County of Northampton
Second Battalion, Northampton Militia
6th Class
John Bretzman [in list of privates]

Pennsylvania Archives, Series 5, Volume VIII. p. 135.
Associators and Militia County of Northampton
Second Battalion, Northampton Militia

Appointed	A substitute In the Place of	Batt	Belongs to Class	Remarks
Nov. 18	John Brotsman			Served 30 days before

Indiana Territory, Switzerland Circuit Court Records, Order Book, October Term 1814 to March Term 1815. p.66.
He is listed in county records for the first time on 16 February 1820, as a juror.
Author's note: There are entries in this volume that are not within the range of dates shown on the binder cover.

Early Ohio Settlers, Purchasers of Land in Southwestern Ohio, 1800-1840; Compiled by Ellen T. Berry & David A. Berry; Genealogical Publishing Co., Inc., Baltimore, MD, 1986. p.262.

Purchaser	Year	Date	Residence	R – T - S
Protsman, John (B)	1814	July 30	Dearborn Ind	03-03-31
Protsman, John 3rd (B)	1836	June 13	Switzerland	03-03-08

(B) Indiana Survey: Land lying west of a meridian drawn west of the Great Miami (known as the "Gore"). Switzerland, Dearborn, Franklin, Ohio, Union and Randolph Counties (all or only a part of each county) – all in Indiana.

Early Settlers of Indiana's "GORE" 1803-1820; Compiled and Edited by Shirley Keller Mikesell; Heritage Books, Inc., 1995.
p. 188.
Switzerland County Original Land Tract Book
Township 3, Range 3W
Section 31 & 32 – John Pratsman – 1814 – pg. 12.
p. 203.
John Protsman witness –
Switzerland County Deeds; Book A
Deed dated 1818. Amos Gilbert & Sally, his wife, to Gabriel Johnson. S11, T2, R3W. Signed Amos Gilbert, Sally (x) Gilbert. Witness: John Gilliland, John Protsman. pp. 178, 179, 80.
p. 212.
Switzerland County Deeds; Book A
Deed dated 1818. Amos Gilbert & Sally, his wife, to John Protsman. S11, T2, R3. "corner to Gabriel Johnson." Signed Amos Gilbert, Sally (x) Gilbert. Witness: John Gilliland, Lyman Gilbert. pp. 308, 309, 310.
p. 220.
Switzerland County Deeds; Book A
Bond dated 1818. James Bolens to Philo Averill. Bond on lots in town of Mt. Sterling. S35, T3, R3W. Lots sold to George W. Sampson, Benjamin Heady, Jacob L. Carlow, Caldwell Hines, Alexander Hatton, John Protsman Sr, John Dumont, Samuel Roberts, John Dunsroth, George Coggshell, P.D. Manville, Samuel Davis. Signed J. Bolens. Witness: Wm. C. Keen, John Brown. pp.469, 470.

Indiana Land Entries Vol. 1 Cincinnati District, 1801-1840; Margaret R. Waters; Originally Published Indianapolis 1948, Second Reprint 1979 by The Bookmark, P.O. Box 74, Knightstown, In 46148. p.71, 144.
CINCINNNATI LAND DISTRICT – VOL. 1
Page 67. Twp. 3 N, Range 3 W of 1st Principle Meridian SWITZERLAND CO. John Protsman NE ¼ - S32; 5-1-1817. Relinquished E ½.
and
Page 118. Twp. 3 N, Range 3 W of 1st Principle Meridian SWITZERLAND CO. John Protsman SE ¼ - SE ¼ - S8; 6-13-1836.
-- Note: The tract books for the land offices in Indiana are deposited in the office of the Auditor of State, Indianapolis. They and are in the custody of the State Land clerk. --

U.S. Department of Interior, Bureau of Land Management, General Land Office Records; Land Patent Search – accessed 27 June 2012.
PROTSMAN, JOHN
Accession Nr. CV-0063-089; Document Type – Credit Volume Patent; State – Indiana; Issue Date – 4/1/1825; Cancelled – No
Land Office – Cincinnati; Authority – April 24, 1820 Sale-Cash Entry (3 Stat. 566); General Remarks – Patent Record Imperfect; Document Nr. 1093; Total Acres – 335.28
Land Descriptions:

State	Meridian	Twp-Rng	Aliquots	Section	County
IN	1ST PM	003N-003W	SE1/4	31	Switzerland
IN	1st PM	003N-003W	SW1/4	32	Switzerland

1820 U.S. Census, Indiana, Switzerland, Cotton, Series: M33 Roll: 14 Page: 266
John Protsman 45 and up; others in household 3 males under 10, 1 male 16-18, 4 males 16-26, 1 female under 10, 1 female 16-26.

History of Switzerland County Indiana 1885; Reproduced by the Switzerland County Historical Society, Vevay, Indiana, 1999. The portion of the book relating to Switzerland County in the 1885 printing of the "History of Dearborn, Ohio, and Switzerland Counties, Indiana".
p. 1004.
"Of the horse-mills of early days, …one on the farm which Samuel Protsman owned, which was built by John Protsman, the father of Samuel and William Protsman."
p. 1258.
In the passage about William R. Protsman – "Grandfather, John Protsman, was born in New Jersey; grandmother, Nancy (Rechner) Protsman, in Philadelphia, Penn, and came to Indiana in 1814. He was a teamster in the Revolutionary war."

Revolutionary Soldiers of Switzerland County; Copied by Mary Hill, John Paul Chapter-Daughters of the American Revolution; January, 1958;
http://www.ingenweb.org/inswitzerland/switzrevsoldiers.html- Viewed June 2012.
PROTZMAN, JOHN
Born 10 Jul 1763, New Jersey
Service under Capt. Henry Alshouse, Col. Roup. Received pay from 1778 to 1783.
Penn. Archives, 5th Series, Vol. 8 pg. 369, 121, 135, 133; vol. 13, pg. 217.
Married Nancy Barbara Reckner (1766-1841)
Children:
David b. 1791 married Maxey McMillen (War of 1812)
John b. 1793 married Elizabeth Mitchell (War of 1812)
Elizabeth b. 1795 married Stephen Stewart
Samuel b. 1797 married Jemiman Campbell
Nancy b. 1799
William b. 1801 married Polly Campbell
Died Aug. 10, 1841
Buried Vevay Cemetery. Stone
From D.A.R. Magazine, Dec. 1922:
Lawrence and John Protzman owned property in Ky. John came from Washington Co. Md. Apr. 1814 Michael McJiernan, son-in-law, & Catherine Protzman, decd, deed their remaining interest in land on which Paris, Ky. now stands to the town trustees.
Mrs. W. N. Whitley, 525 Vine St. Paris, Ky.
D.A.R. Magazine, Aug. 1922:
State of Pa. granted 2 patents of land to John Protzman, one for 353 acres, other for 37 acres (Apr. 1, 1791) John Protzman did convey 350 acres to David Martin in May 1784, & by his last will empower executors to sell the rest--land was on

Welsh Run, Franklin Co. Pa.
See Court records, Hagerstown, Md. for Protzman wills & records.
Indianapolis Star, May 18, 1930:
John Protzman came to America from Germany, 1740: died in Pennsylvania, 1788: lived in N. J. several years, where his sons were born John, Jr. July 10, 1763 and Jacob, July 4, 1776. John, Jr. hauled supplies to Washington's army with oxen when only 15 years old; his father was a soldier in the army. John, Jr. married Nancy Barbary Rickner, 1790; moved to Ky. that year, and to Ohio, 1802, and to Switz. County, Ind. 1813.
Their children were; David B. b 1791; John b 1793; Elizabeth b 1795; Samuel b 1797; Nancy b 1799; William b 1801.
Nancy Barbary Richner was born 1765, the dau. of Daniel or David Richner; both served in the 5th Pa. Regiment, enlisting from Allentown, Northampton Co. 1778-1783.

Roster of Soldiers and Patriots of the American Revolution Buried in Indiana, Vol. I; compiled by Mrs. Roscoe C. O'Byrne.; Indiana Daughters of the American Revolution, 1981; p.300-301.
PROTSMAN (PROTZMAN), JOHN   Switzerland County
Born – July 10, 1763, New Jersey.
Service – Serve in 5th CO., 2nd Battalion, Northampton, Penn. Militia under Capt. Henry Alshouse, Col. Roup. Received pay for service from 1778-1783.
Proof – Penn. Archives, 5th Series, vol. 8, pp. 369, 121, 135, 133, vol. 13, p. 217.
Died – Aug. 10, 1841. Buried Vevay Cemetery. Stone
Married – Nancy Barbara Reckner (1766-1841). Ch. David b. 1791, m. Maxey McMillen; John b. 1793, m. Elizabeth Mitchell (both were soldiers of 1812); Elizabeth b. 1795, m. Stephen Stewart; Samuel, b. 1797, m. Jemima Campbell; Nancy, b. 1799; William b. 1801, m. Polly Campbell.
Collected by Mrs. A. V. Danner, Vevay, Indiana., and Nellie Protsman Waldenmaier, Washington, D.C.

Vevay Cemetery, Switzerland County, IN
Tombstone inscriptions –

IN	IN
memory of	memory of
JOHN PROTSMAN	NANCY
(rest of stone is weather damaged)	consort of
	JOHN PROTSMAN
	(rest of stoen is weather damaged)

Abstract of Graves of Revolutionary Patriots (4 volumes); by Patricia Law Hatcher; Pioneer Heritage Press, Dallas, TX, 1987. Vol. 3, p. 192.
This is an abstract and an index to information reported to the Daughters of the American Revolution and published in their annual reports to the Smithsonian Institution, printed as Senate Documents (1900-1974) and published annually in the DAR magazine (1978-1987).
Published 1972 (Senate Doc. 54)
PROTSMAN, John   Vevay Cem, Switzerland Co IN

Switzerland County Indiana Cemetery Inscriptions 1817-1985; Wanda L. Morford; Cincinnati, Ohio, 1986, p. 148.
Vevay Cemetery, Section 2, Jefferson Twp., Switzerland Co., IN
Protsman John, Sen. d. Aug. 10, 1841   aged 78y 1m
    Nancy B., consort of John Sen., d. Aug. 19, 1841 aged 75y 10m

Indiana Historical Collections VOL. XIII, The Swiss Settlement of Switzerland Co., Indiana; Peret Dufour; Indianapolis 1923; p. 104.
Of the horse mills of early days, the writer recollects ...., one on the farm which Samuel Protsman owned, which was built by John Protsman the father of Samuel and William Protsman;.....

The Vevay Reveille-Enterprise; Vol. 122, No. 37, 22 Sep 1935, p. 7, col. 4.
Roster of Revolutionary Soldiers Who Resided in Switzerland County
By Mrs. Effa M. Danner
John Protsman or Protzman, Ensign – born July 10, 1768 in New Jersey, removed to Pa. in 1776.
Military record – He served in 5th Co., 2nd battalion, Northampton Co., Pa., Militia, Capt. Henry Alshouse, Col. Roup.
His name appears, private, 6th class undated muster roll, published Vol. XIII, p. 217, 5th series, Pa. Archives and on muster roll dated Nov. 18, 1780, found page 133, lance Vol. State Library, Harrisburg. Also Series 5, Vol. 8, p. 369.
"In regard to officers returning of the 5th Battalion, 2nd Co., Northampton Co., Militia, May 21, 1777, Ensign John Protsman."
Also Vol. 4, p. 724, John Protsman received pay for service 1778, 1783. Series 5, Vol. 8, p. 121-135, 133, 217, Militia May 16, 1780, Nov. 18, 1780.
Congressional Library, Nellie P. Waldenmaier, Researcher.
Switzerland Co., John Protsman married in Pennsylvania in 1790, Miss Nancy Barbara Reckner. They lived in Danville, Ky., 1790-1802, Cincinnati 1802-1814 moved to Vevay, Ind., Switzerland County.
Land Patent dated 1814 – 490 acres of land. He lived one mile North of Vevay. He died Aug. 10, 1841. Buried in Vevay cemetery – sand stone marker.
Wife, Nancy Barbara, born Oct. 19, 1766 in Pennsylvania. Died Aug. 19, 1841. Epedemic of fever. Burial at Vevay.
Children – David Protsman born 1791, married 1812, Maxey McMillen. John born Aug. 4, 1793, married 1820, Elizabeth Mitchel. Elizabeth, born April 5, 1795, married 1816, Stephen Stewart. Samuel, born Feb. 18, 1797, married 1824, Jemima Campbell. Nancy, born May 12, 1799. Infant, born March 1, 1800. William born Feb. 5, 1801, married Polly Campbell.
Effa M. Danner research.

RANSTEAD, JAMES
aka RAMSTED

Patriot: James Ranstead
Birth: c. 1762
Married Spouse 1: Unknown
Married spouse 2: Aug 1793 Franklin, Ostego Co., NY   Jane McMullen
(b. 5 Jan 1778 d. 12 May 1867 Polk Twp., Marshall Co., IN)
Service state(s): MA
Service description: Capt. John Kilby Smith, Cols. Smith, Tupper, Sprout
Rank: Private
Proof of Service: Pension application W26352
Pension application No.: W26352
Residences: Montague, Hampshire Co., MA; Switzerland Co., IN;
St. Joseph Co., IN
Died: 20 Aug 1836 St. Joseph Co., IN
Buried: Hamilton Church Cemetery, Hamilton, St. Joseph County, IN
DAR Ancestor No.: A094579

Pension Application Abstracted from National Archives microfilm Series 805, Roll 676, File W26352/BLWT57784-160-55.

Pension abstract for – James Ranstead   Service state(s): Massachusetts
Alternate spelling(s):   Ransted
Date: 5 May 1818
County of: Switzerland   State of: Indiana
Declaration made before a Judge.
Residence when he entered service: Montague, Hampshire Co., MA
Rank(s): Private
Statement of service –

Period	Duration	Names of General and Field Officers
1780	3 mos.	Capt. Pierce's Massachusetts company
1781	2 yrs., 9 mos.	Capt. John Kilby Smith's company, Col. Smith

Battles: None stated
Wife: Jane McMullen   Wife's age: born January 1777
Marriage date and place: August 1793 in Franklin, Orange Co., NY
&
Date: 15 September 1820
County of: Switzerland   State of: Indiana
Declaration made before the Circuit Court. He received pension certificate no. 9314 under the act of Congress 18 March 1818. On this date his schedule of property was submitted to the court.
Age: about 58 years
Residence now: Switzerland Co., IN
Statement of service – see 1818 paper
Wife: Jane, being crippled and unable to work.   Wife's age: about 39
Names and ages of children: Sarah, Leonard, aged 16; John, aged 14, in poor health; Almira, aged 10; Joel aged 8; Jane, aged 6; James Jr., aged 4 years.

&
Date: In 1849, Elizabeth Hyde (or Hide), stated she was the oldest daughter of James Ransted and his first wife (her name not stated), and was about 7 years old when her father married Jane McMullen (McMullin).
&
Declaration for Widow Who has never received Bounty Land
Date: 25 October 1850
County of: Marshall   State of: Indiana
Declaration made before a Justice of the Peace
Widow's age: 75 (? – illegible)
Affidavit was filed declaring they were well acquainted with James Ransted and his wife Jane.
Affidavit of John Ranstead declaring he is the child of James and Jane, and cannot now remember the date of marriage. His father late of Switzerland County died in St. Joseph's Co., IN.
Soldier died: 30 August 1836 at St. Joseph's Co., IN
Marriage date and place: Unknown, in Oswego Co., NY. Married by Thomas Walters, JP.
Proof of marriage & family record: In Bible losing much to worm and defaced now entirely destroyed.

Switzerland County, Indiana Civil Order Book 4, 1820 – 1823; pg. 77.
Sept. 1820 - James Ramstead, Rev. soldier and U.S. pensioner filed his schedule--valued at $94.50.

Abstract of Final Payment Voucher: General Services Administration, Washington, DC
NAME   Ranstead, James
AGENCY OF PAYMENT   Cincinnati, Ohio
DATE OF ACT   1818
DATE OF PAYMENT   (act 6 Apr.)
DATE OF DEATH   Aug 20, 1836
FINAL PAYMENT VOUCHER RECEIVED FROM
THE GENERAL ACCOUNTING OFFICE   Form
General Services Administration   GSA DA 70-7035 GSA Dec 69 7068
&
Abstract of Final Payment Voucher: General Services Administration, Washington, DC
NAME   Ranstead, Jane Widow of James
AGENCY OF PAYMENT   Fort Wayne, Ind
DATE OF ACT   1853 2d Sect
DATE OF PAYMENT   March 1862
DATE OF DEATH
LAST ~~FINAL~~ PAYMENT VOUCHER RECEIVED FROM
THE GENERAL ACCOUNTING OFFICE   Form
General Services Administration   GSA DA 70-7035 GSA Dec 69 7068

Massachusetts Soldiers and Sailors of the Revolutionary War, A Compilation from the Archives; prepared and published by the Secretary of the Commonwealth in accordance with Chapter 100, Resolves of 1891, Vol. XII; Wright & Potter Printing co., State Printers, Boston, MA, 1904. p. 975.
RANSTED, JAMES. Descriptive list of men raised in Hampshire Co. to serve in the Continental Army, ad returned by Noah Goodman, Superintendent; age, 16, yrs.; stature, 5ft. 1 in.; complexion, light; hair, light; occupation, farmer; engaged for town of Montague; engaged March 29, 1781; term, 3 years; also, Private, Capt. J.K. Smith's (3rd) co. (formerly Capt. Peter Clayes's en.), Lieut. Col. Calvin Smith's (6th) regt.; return for wages for the year 1781; wages allowed said Ransted from March 29, 1781, to Dec. 31, 1781, 9 mos. 3 days; also, Capt. John K, Smith's co.., Lieut. Col. Calvin Smith's regt.; return for wages for the year 1782; wages allowed said Ransted for 12 mos.; also, order on John Pierce, Paymaster General, or the Agent of (late) 6th Mass. regt., payable to Roger Savage, dated West Point, Oct. 2, 1783, signed by said Ransted, for wages due him for service in the Mass. regt. in 1781; certificate signed by Capt. John K. Smith is appended to order, certifying that said Ransted served in the 6th Mass. regt. in 1781, and that pay was due him for eight mos. and some days service.

Register of Certificates Issued by John Pierce, Esquire, Paymaster General and Commissioner of Army Accounts for the United States, to Officers and Soldiers of the Continental Army Under Act of July 4, 1783; Originally Published as Senate Documents, Vol.9, No. 988, 63rd Congress, 3d Session, Washington, 1915; Seventeenth report of the National Society of the Daughters of the American Revolution; Genealogical Publishing Co., Inc, Baltimore, MD, 1984. p. 418.
Men listed in this volume with the same name.

No. of Certificate	To whom issued	Amount
25646	Ranstead, James	53.30
26263	Ranstead, James	23.12
12520	Ransted, James	57.66
13000	Ransted, James	80.00

Indiana Territory, Switzerland Circuit Court Records, Order Book, October Term 1814 to March Term 1815. p.46.
He is listed in county records for the first time on 10 March 1819, as a witness for the plaintiff.
Author's note: There are entries in this volume that are not within the range of dates shown on the binder cover.

U.S. Department of Interior, Bureau of Land Management, General Land Office Records; Land Patent Search – accessed 27 June 2012.
RANSTED, HENRY
Accession Nr. IN1610_.039; Document Type – State Volume Patent; State – Indiana; Issue Date – 3/15/1837; Cancelled – No
Land Office – LA Porte; Authority – April 24, 1820 Sale-Cash Entry (3 Stat. 566); Document Nr. 540; BLM   Serial Nr. – IN NO S/N; Total Acres – 160.00

Land Descriptions: State – In; Meridian – 2nd PM; Twp-Rng – 038N-002E; Aliquots – NE1/4; Section – 24; County – St. Joseph&
&
Accession Nr. IN1610_.40; Document Type – State Volume Patent; State – Indiana;
Issued Date – 3/15/1837; Cancelled – No
Land Office – LA Porte; Authority – April 24, 1820 Sale-Cash Entry (3 Stat. 566); Document Nr. 542; BLM Serial Nr – IN NO S/N; Total Acres – 40.00
Land Descriptions: State – IN; Meridian – 2nd PM; Twp-Rng – 038N-001E; Aliquots – NE1/4-NE-1/4; Section – 29; County – St. Joseph
&
Accession Nr. IN1730_.275; Document Type – State Volume Patent; State – Indiana;
Issued Date – 8/10/1837; Cancelled – No
Land Office – LA Porte; Authority – April 24, 1820 Sale-Cash Entry (3 Stat. 566); Document Nr. 7050; BLM Serial Nr – IN NO S/N; Total Acres – 80.00
Land Descriptions: State – IN; Meridian – 2nd PM; Twp-Rng – 038N-001E; Aliquots – W1/4-NE1/4; Section – 28; County – St. Joseph
&
-Possible additional record-
Accession Nr. IN400_.424; Document Type – State Volume Patent; State – Indiana;
Issued Date – 4/1/1823; Cancelled – No
Names on Document: Ransted, James; Vanderur, Thomas
Land Office – Brookville; Authority – April 24, 1820 Sale-Cash Entry (3 Stat. 566); Document Nr. 2996; BLM Serial Nr – IN NO S/N; Total Acres – 80.00
Land Descriptions: State – IN; Meridian – 2nd PM; Twp-Rng – 010N-010E; Aliquots – W1/2-NW1/4; Section – 17; County – Decatur

The Pension List of 1820 [U.S. War Department] Reprinted with an Index; by Murtie June Clark; Genealogical Publishing Co., Inc., Baltimore, 1991.
Originally published 1820 as Letter from the Secretary of War. p. 658.
Names of the Revolutionary Pensioners which have been placed on the Roll of Indiana, under the Law of the 18th of March, 1818, from the passage thereof, to this day, inclusive, with the Rank they held, and the Lines in which they served, viz.

Names	Rank	Line
James Ranstead	private	Massachusetts

1820 U.S. Census, Indiana, Switzerland, Craig, Series: M33 Roll: 14 Page: 249
James Ranstead 45 and up; others in household 3 males under 10, 1 male 10-16, 1 male 26-45, 2 females under 10, 1 female 26-45.

The "Lost" Pensions, Settled Accounts of the Act of 6 April 1838; by Craig R. Scott; Willow Bend Books, Lovettsville, VA, 1996. p. 268.
An Act directing the transfer of money remaining unclaimed [for the term of eight months] by certain pensioners, and authorizing payment of the same at the Treasury of the United States.

Name – Ranstead, James, wife of; Pension Office - Ohio; Box - 21; Account - #9743.

1860 U.S. Census, Indiana, Marshall, German Twp., Series: M653 Roll: 278 Page: 514, Family No. 576.
Jane Ransted, Age 80, Housekeeper, Born NY, Over 90 cannot read or write.

Roster of Soldiers and Patriots of the American Revolution Buried in Indiana, Vol. I; compiled by Mrs. Roscoe C. O'Byrne.; Indiana Daughters of the American Revolution, 1981; p.305.
Ranstead, Joseph   *Author's note:* Given name is corrected in Vol. II.
St. Joseph County
Born – 1767.
Service – Pri. in regt. commanded by Col. Sprouts in Mass. Line, 2 yrs., 9 mos.
Proof – Pension claim W.26352. B.L.Wt. 57784-160-55.
Died – Aug. 20, 1836. Buried Hamilton Cemetery. Bronze tablet placed by Schuyler Colfax Chapter, D.A.R.
Married – First W. unknown. Dau. Elizabeth; second W. 1793, Jane McMullen. Ch. Leonard; Minerva; Joel; Jane; James; Sarah; Susan, m. Jesse Frame; Mary Ann.
Collected by Miss Amanda McComb, South Bend, Indiana, and Mrs. Orville Dailey, Albany, Ohio.

Roster of Soldiers and Patriots of the American Revolution Buried in Indiana, Vol. II; 1966; p. 131.
Roster, Vol. I, p. 305
RANSTEAD, JAMES   St. Joseph County
Soldier's name should be James instead of Joseph. Verified by grave stone and Court Records.
Married – First w. unknown but had a son, Henry A., and a dau., Elizabeth, b. 1886. Married (2) 1793, Jane McMullen. Ch. Sarah; Leonard; John B., m. Matilda Layton; Almyra; Joel; Jane; James; Susannah, m. Jesse Frame; Mary Ann.
By Mrs. Rue Green, 1405 Jefferson St., LaPorte, Ind. 46350, and William Tuffs Chapter, Elkhart, Ind.

The Vevay Reveille-Enterprise; Vol. 122. No. 39, 28 Sep 1935, p.3, col.1.
Roster of Revolutionary Soldiers Who Resided in Switzerland County
By Mrs. Effa M. Danner
JAMES RANSTEAD - age 56, 1820, enlisted under the command of Capt. John R. Smith (Col. Smith later) and Col. Tupper, Col. Sprouts, Continental Establishment in Mass. line, served 2 years and 9 months. He was granted pension in 1818 while a resident of Switzerland County, No. 9314, p. 367, Sept. 1820 Order Book.
Family, Jane Ranstead, age 39, crippled. Children, Leonard 16, John 14, Almera 10, Joel 8, Jane 6, James 4.
James Ranstead died 1837 and is buried in Hamilton Cemetery, South Bend, Ind., St. Joseph Co., has stone and bronze D.A.R. marker.

1820 Switzerland County census, James Ranstead lived in Craig Township, age 45 upward, wife
under 45, four boys and 3 girls. Record Book C., p. 367 Court Orders.

Abstract of Graves of Revolutionary Patriots (4 volumes); by Patricia Law Hatcher; Pioneer Heritage Press, Dallas, TX, 1987. Vol. 3, p. 202.
This is an abstract and an index to information reported to the Daughters of the American Revolution and published in their annual reports to the Smithsonian Institution, printed as Senate Documents (1900-1974) and published annually in the DAR magazine (1978-1987).
Published 1972 (Senate Doc. 54)
RANSTEAD, James   Hamilton Cem, nr New Carlisle, St. Joseph Co IN

Hamilton Church Cemetery, Hamilton, St. Joseph Co., IN
Inscription on top of marker–   DAR Marker –
    JAMES   REVOLUTIONARY
    RANSTEAD   SOLDIER
                                      1775   1783
                                 PLACED BY THE
                               SCHUMBER COLFAX
                                   CHAPTER
                                      DAR

REMER, DAVID
aka, REAMER, REIMER

Patriot: David Remer
Birth: Dec 1754   Somerset Co., NJ
Married Spouse 1: Sep 1780 Carlisle, Cumberland Co., PA   Nancy Smith
            (b. abt. 1762/1765 d. 2 Jan 1848 Switzerland Co., IN)
Service state(s): PA
Service description: The Regiment of Artillery Artificers in Continental Line,
            Capts. Thomas Wylie, Gibson
Rank: Private
Proof of Service: Pension application W9621
Pension application No.: W9621
Residences: Cumberland Co., PA; KY; Indiana Territory; Switzerland Co., IN
Died: 17 Sep 1836 Posey Twp., Switzerland Co., IN
Buried: Lostetter Cemetery (aka Grant's Creek Cemetery),
            Posey Twp., Switzerland Co., IN
DAR Ancestor No.: A095291

Pension Application Abstracted from National Archives microfilm Series 805, Roll 679, File W9621.; Switzerland County, Indiana Probate Record Book Vol. A, Mar 1827-Nov 1834; p. 316.
Pension abstract for – David Reamer   Service state(s): Pennsylvania
                                                                  Continental

Alternate spelling(s): Remer, Reemer
Date: 5 September 1832
County of: Switzerland   State of: Indiana
Declaration made before a Judge. Unable to appear in court because of bodily infirmity caused by general debility and old and severe nature...
Age: 78 years
Where and year born: December 1754 in Somerset Co., NJ
Residence when he entered service: Carlisle, Cumberland Co., PA
Residence(s) since the war: In Pennsylvania about 15 years, in Kentucky about
            22 years, since that in Indiana.
Residence now: Cotton Twp., Switzerland Co., IN
Volunteer / Drafted / Substitute: Enlisted as an Artificer, a blacksmith by trade.
Rank(s): Artificer
Statement of service-

Period	Duration	Names of General and Field Officers
Fall 1779	2 yrs, 9 mos.	Company of artificers commanded by Thomas Wiley of Pennsylvania

Battles: None – worked with other artificers (blacksmiths).
Discharge received: Written discharge received
What became of it?: Lost
Statement is supported by – Traditionary evidence
Clergyman: George Dugan, resident of Dearborn Co., IN

Persons in neighborhood who certify character: Henry Wallicks, John Gibbons, William Kelly, Pascal Early
Wife: Nancy Smith
&
Widow's application for pension
Date: 5 November 1838
County of: Switzerland   State of: Indiana
Declaration made before a Judge or Court.
Widow: Nancy Reamer
Widow's age: 76 years
Widow's residence now: Posey Twp., Switzerland Co., IN
Soldier died: 21 September 1836
Marriage date and place: Carlisle, Cumberland Co., PA, no date stated.
Proof of marriage: Rev. Kincade married then, he has been dead for a long time.
Personally appeared Henry Kelly, of Switzerland Co., was acquainted with David and Nancy Remer since 1808. Shows family record of David Remer containing names and ages of all his children. Pages from family record are in the file.
Names and ages of children: Catherine b. 28 Dec 1782; Jane b. 22 Jul 178?; George b. 10 Oct 1786; Betsy b. 11 Sep 1788; James b. 22 Jan 1791; Mary b. 16 Aug 1793.
Additional testimony in writing:
Elizabeth Lostetter in Ohio Co., N states she is the daughter of David and Nancy Reamer. David died 19 September 1836, that he left no widow now living, and he left 5 children now living, Elizabeth, David, Sarah, Permelia and Malinda.
Peter Lostetter of Randolph Twp., Ohio Co., IN, states same as Elizabeth Lostetter.
&
Date: 26 November 1851
County of: Ohio   State of: Indiana
Declaration made before a Court of record.
It was proven by exhibition of testimony that David Reimer deceased, late a resident of Switzerland County, was a Revolutionary Pensioner. He died 20 Sep 1836; widow died 2 Jan 1848; left 5 children now living. Elizabeth Lostutter, formerly Elizabeth Reimer, aged 63 years; David Reimer aged 53 years; Parmelia Hodges, formerly Parmelia Reimer, aged 44 years; Malinda Smith, formerly Malinda Reimer, aged 42 years.
More family information is in the letter from the War Department, addressed to Rev. Harmon Kelly, is in the file.

Switzerland County, Indiana Probate Order Book 3, 1837-1843; p. 121.
12 November 1838
In the matter of Nancy Remer widow
of David Remer a Pensioner of the United States }
            Now on this day comes into open Court George Marche and proved to the satisfaction of the Court now here that David Reamer of Said County Deceased, was a Pensioner of the United States and at the rate of one hundred and forty five dollars per annum, that he was a resident of Switzerland County aforesaid, and died in Posey Township in Said County on the 21st day of

September 1836, that Said David Reamer left a widow whos name is Nancy Reamer.
-on the same page-
In the matter of Nancy Remer Widow   }
of David Remer Dec'd a Pensioner of the U.S. } The Report of the Said Nancy Remer taken by the Judge of this Court in vacation under the act of Congress of 1838 is verified which a part reads in the words and figures following to wit (here insert it) and the Court now here orders the Same to be opened upon the Records of the Court.

Pennsylvania Archives, Series 3, Volume XXIII. p. 597.
Muster Rolls of the Navy and Line, Militia and Rangers, 1775-1783. with List of Pensioners, 1818-1832.
Statement Showing the Names of Pennsylvanians Residing in the State of Indiana, Who Have Been Inscribed on the Pension List under the Act of Congress Passed June 7th, 1832.
Dearborn County
    Reamer, David, artificer P.M., July 30, 1833; 80.

Author's note: Muster Rolls are absent for Company E, commanded by Capt. Thomas Wylie.

Second Census of Kentucky, 1800; Clift G. Glenn; Genealogical Publishing Co., Baltimore, MD, 1954.
An alphabetical list of 32,000 taxpayers based on original tax lists on file at the Kentucky Historical Society. Information given includes the county of residence and the date of the tax list in which the individual is listed.
Remer, David   Montgomery   8/22/1800

Early Ohio Settlers, Purchasers of Land in Southwestern Ohio, 1800-1840; Compiled by Ellen T. Berry & David A. Berry; Genealogical Publishing Co., Inc., Baltimore, MD, 1986. p.269.

Purchaser	Year	Date	Residence	R – T - S
Remer, David (B)	1815	March 07	Kentucky	01-03-20

(B) Indiana Survey: Land lying west of a meridian drawn west of the Great Miami (known as the "Gore"). Switzerland, Dearborn, Franklin, Ohio, Union and Randolph Counties (all or only a part of each county) – all in Indiana.

Early Settlers of Indiana's "GORE" 1803-1820; Compiled and Edited by Shirley Keller Mikesell; Heritage Books, Inc., 1995. p. 17.
Dearborn County: Original Land Entries Tract Book.
Dearborn County Township 3, Range 1W.
Section 20 – David Remer – 1815 – pg. 2.

*Switzerland County Health Department, Switzerland County Cemeteries 1800-1980;*Church of Latter Day Saints Microfilm No. 1460119302. p. 66.
Grants Creek Cemetery
Remer, David Artificer Gibson's Co., Rev. War died Sept. 17, 1836
    Born Dec. 1754 Somerset Co., N.J. age 83 yrs.
  Nancy, wife of David Remer died Jan. 2, 1848

The "Lost" Pensions, Settled Accounts of the Act of 6 April 1838; by Craig R. Scott; Willow Bend Books, Lovettsville, VA, 1996. p. 269.
An Act directing the transfer of money remaining unclaimed [for the term of eight months] by certain pensioners, and authorizing payment of the same at the Treasury of the United States.
Name – Reamer, David, wife of; Pension Office - Ind; Box - 97; Account - #2367.

Revolutionary Soldiers of Switzerland County; Copied by Mary Hill, John Paul Chapter-Daughters of the American Revolution; January, 1958; http://www.ingenweb.org/inswitzerland/switzrevsoldiers.html- Viewed June 2012.
REAMER, DAVID
Born Dec. 1754 Somerset Co. N. J.
Enlisted in fall of 1779.
Served until March or April, 1783 in Capt. Thomas Wylies' Company of Artificers, Continental Army. Also served under Col. Gibson.
Married 1780 to Nancy Smith (d 1848)
Children: Catherine b 1782, m George March; Jane b. 1784; George b. 1786; Elizabeth b. 1788, m Peter Lostetter; James b 1791; Mary b. 1783; David; Rebecca m Calib Hayes; Henry b. 1812
Sarah m Henry Kelley; Nancy m James A. Kelley.
Switzerland County Pension claim, W.9621; Dec. 1st Session of 23d Congress.
Died Sept. 21, 1836 Buried Lostetter's cemetery, near Ohio Co. Line. Stone.
Collected by Mrs. A. V. Danner, Vevay, Indiana

Roster of Soldiers and Patriots of the American Revolution Buried in Indiana, Vol. I; compiled by Mrs. Roscoe C. O'Byrne.; Indiana Daughters of the American Revolution, 1981; p.307.
REAMER, DAVID   Switzerland County
Born – Dec, 1754, Somerset Co., New Jersey.
Service – Enlisted in fall of 1779. Served until March or April, 1783, in Capt. Thomas Wylies' CO. of Artificers, Continental Army. Also served under Col. Gibson.
Proof – Pension claim W. 9621; Doc. 1st Session of 23rd Congress.
Died – Sept. 21, 1836. Buried Lostutter's Cemetery, near Ohio Co. Line. Stone.
Married – 1780, Nancy Smith d. 1848. Ch. Catherine b. 1782, m. George March; Jane b. 1784; George b. 1786; Elizabeth b. 1788, m. Peter Lostutter; James b. 1791; Mary b. 1783; David; Rebecca, m. Calip Hayes; Henry b. 1812; Sarah, m. Henry Kelly; Nancy, m. James A. Kelley.
Collected by Mrs. A. V. Danner, Vevay, Indiana.

Roster of Soldiers and Patriots of the American Revolution Buried in Indiana, Vol. II; 1966; p.131.
REAMER (REIMER, REMER), DAVID   Switzerland County
Additional Data On Some Of The Soldiers Listed In Volume I
Further Proof – Penn. Arch., Vol. III, pp. 1087-1088, 1091-1093; Vol. II Penn. In the War of the Revolution, Battalions and Line, 1775-1783, Linn & Egle, p. 249.
Children restated – Mary, b. 1783; Catherine, b. 1782, m. Georg March; Jane, b. 1784; George, b. 1786; Elizabeth, b. 1788, m. Peter Lostutter; James, b. 1791; David, b. Feb. 1, 1798; Rebecca, b. June 25, 1802, m. Calip Hayes; Sarah, m. Henry Kelley; Nancy, m. James A. Kelley; Parmelia, b. 1807, m. Andrew Hodges; Malinda, b. 1810, m. Michael Smith; Henry, b. 1812.
By Rev. Harmon Kelly, 405 E. Sale St., Tuscola, Ill.

Switzerland County Indiana Cemetery Inscriptions 1817-1985; Wanda L. Morford; Cincinnati, Ohio, 1986, p. 430.
Grants Creek Cemetery, Posey Twp., Switzerland Co., IN
Remer   David, Artificer Gibsons Co., Rev. War. Sep 1836 born in Somerset Co., N.J. Dec. 1754 erected 1941 there is also an old stone for David, but it is broken and down
        Nancy, wife of David Remner, d. Jun. 2, 1848 aged 82y 10m – down have seen the last name also spelled Reamer, do not know which is correct

Abstract of Graves of Revolutionary Patriots (4 volumes); by Patricia Law Hatcher; Pioneer Heritage Press, Dallas, TX, 1987. Vol. 3, p. 205.
This is an abstract and an index to information reported to the Daughters of the American Revolution and published in their annual reports to the Smithsonian Institution, printed as Senate Documents (1900-1974) and published annually in the DAR magazine (1978-1987).
Published 1933, Serial set 9787, Volume 5.
REAMER. David   Lostetter Cem, Dearborn Co IN

Lostetter Cemetery (aka Grant's Creek), Posey Twp., Switzerland Co., IN

Tombstone inscription (old stone) -	Inscription on (newer) stone -
IN	DAVID REMER
Memory of	ARTIFICER GIBSON'S CO.
DAVID REMER	REV. WAR
Who died Sept 17th 183	SEPTEMBER 1836
In the 82d year of his	BORN
(rest of stone is missing)	SOMERSET CO. N. J.
	DEC 1754
	ERECTED 1941

The Vevay Reveille-Enterprise; Vol. 122. No. 39, 28 Sep 1935, p.3, col. 1.
Roster of Revolutionary Soldiers Who Resided in Switzerland County
By Mrs. Effa M. Danner

David Reamer (Remer) – Born in 1754, Sumerset Co., New Jersey. Enlisted in Pa., service certificate. Pension granted 1831, certificate No. 7508 while a resident of Dearborn County, Ind.

Died in Switzerland County, Sept. 21, 1836, buried in Lostutter's cemetery, Posey Township. Inscription from stone, "David Reamer died September 11, 1836 in the 82nd year of his age". Stone broken beside him is his wife's head stone in good condition. Nancy, wife of David Reamer, died Jan. 2, 1848, age 83 years and 10 months. Located by H. F. Emerson.

D.A.R. Lineage Books, "David Reamer's daughter Elizabeth born 1788, married 1808, Peter Lochetter (Lostutter) Boone County, Ky., Peter was born in 1784". Children of Elizabeth and Peter Lochetter: William Lochetter married Elizabeth Robertson, April 29, 1839; Nancy married Hiram Robertson, Dec. 26, 1839; Peter married Rose Robertson, Oct. 4, 1841; Samuel married Elizabeth Wallick; John married Delilah Robertson; Christian married Nancy Robertson; David and Wilson. Five Lostutter brothers and sisters married five Robertson brothers and sisters; very unusual record.

Probate Court p. 121, Vol. 1838-40, Nancy Remer, widow of David Remer pensioner, allowed a pension Nov. 1838. This record endorsed by D.A.R. Chapter at Terre Haute, Ind., descendant, Mary E. Jack Ramsey.

RENNO, GEORGE
aka RENEAU, RENO

Patriot: George Renno
Birth: 1 Sep 1751   Prince William Co., VA
Married Spouse 1: Unknown
Service state(s): PA
Service description: Ranger on the Frontier for several tours.
Rank: Private
Proof of Service: Pension Application in Switzerland Co., IN
Pension application No.: Not in War Department records
Residences: PA; NC; KY; OH; IN
Died: aft 1834
Buried: Unknown
DAR Ancestor No.: None

Document contributed by Judy Kappes
Pension Application Abstracted from Switzerland County, Indiana Probate Record Book Vol. A, Mar 1827-Nov 1834, p. 429.

Pension abstract for – George Renno   Service state(s): Pennsylvania
Date: 3 Apr 1834
County of: Switzerland   State of: Indiana
Declaration made before a Judge. Unable to appear in court due in consequence of bodily infirmity, general debility, and old age.
Age: 83 years   Record of age: No record of age in this county
Where and year born: Prince William Co., VA on 1 Sep 1751
Residence when he entered service: Pittsburg in Pennsylvania
Residence(s) since the war: Pittsburg, Pennsylvania; North Carolina 6 yrs; to Kentucky in 1793 for 2 yrs; Ohio 20 yrs; 19 yrs in Indiana (Dearborn Co. & Switzerland Co.)
Residence now: Cotton Twp, Switzerland Co., IN
Volunteer or Drafted or Substitute: Drafted 6 times, served as a volunteer on several scouts.
Rank(s): Private; served as a Ranger
Statement of service-

Period	Duration	Names of General and Field Officers
1776	2 mos.	Capt. Drennen
1776	2 mos.	Capt. Zadac Wright
1777	2 mos.	Capt. Philip Ross
1778	2 mos.	Capt. Capt. P. Ross
1779	2 mos.	Capt. Z. Wright [Second Battalion Washington County Militia.]
------		Served as a Ranger – tours forgotten

Served for a full term of 18 months
Battles: Indian conflicts as a Ranger on the Frontier
Discharge received: Never received a written discharge
Living witness, name(s): None
Documentary proof: None

Clergyman: Francis Whitcom, resident Switzerland Co., IN
Persons in neighborhood who certify character: Ezra Gaul, David Gard, Thomas Miller, Levi Miller, Job Miller, Jas. Hayes all of Dearborn Co., IN
No family information

Revolutionary Soldiers of Switzerland County; Copied by Mary Hill, John Paul Chapter-Daughters of the American Revolution; January, 1958; http://www.ingenweb.org/inswitzerland/switzrevsoldiers.html- Viewed June, 2012.

RENNO, GEORGE
Uncertain. He may not have died in Indiana, though he did apply for pension here.
A Presley Renno entered the E 1/2 of the NW 1/4 of Sec. 2 of twp. 3 E., Range 3 ? of the 1st P.M. on 2/26/1818, and a Presley ? Reno, the NW 1/4 of the SW 1/4 of sec. 28, in twp 4 N Range 3 W of 1st. P.M. on 2/10/1837.
Reference; Switz. Co. Ind. Probate book A. pg. 429
Waters "Indiana Land Entries." v 1 (1949) pg. 69; 148.

Revolutionary Soldiers Buried in Indiana A Supplement; 485 Names Not Listed in the Roster of Soldiers and Patriots of the American Revolution Buried in Indiana (1938) nor in Revolutionary Soldiers Buried in Indiana (1949); Margaret E. Waters; Indianapolis, 1954. p. 119.

Renno, George   Switzerland
(Uncertain)   Name received too late to get data. He may not have died in Ind. although he appl. for pens. here. A Presley Reno entered the E 1/2 of the NW 1/4 of Sec. 2 of Twp. 3N, Range 3W of the 1st P.M. on 2-26-1818, & a Presley Q. Reno the NW 1/4 of the SW 1/4 of Sec. 28 in Twp. 4N, Range 3W of 1st P.M. on 2-10-1837. Ref: Switzerland Co., Ind. Probate Bk. A, p. 429; Waters—Ind. Land Entries: v.1 (1949) pp. 69, 148.

Author's note: Thomas Reneau, Revolutionary soldier born in VA, enlisted near Pittsburgh, PA, is probably George's brother. His Pension Application is No. S32477. DAR Roster of Soldiers and Patriots Buried in Indiana, p. 312, shows he died in Harrison Co., IN.

RICKETTS, NATHAN

Patriot: Nathan Ricketts
Birth: 26 Aug 1759 or 1760   Antietam, MD
Married Spouse 1: Jane Wilson
Service state(s): PA
Service description: Capts. Alexander McCormick; Captains James Johnson, John Thornton, Piper, Edward Ricketts, Thomas Ricketts, David Caldwell, John Beaty, Col. Piper.
Rank: Private
Proof of Service: Pension application S32480
Pension application No.: S32480
Residences: On frontier in Cumberland County, PA; KY; Indiana Territory; Dearborn Co., IN
Died: 10 Jan. 1847, Ohio Co., IN (will probated there)
Buried: Mt. Carmel Cemetery, Aberdeen, Posey Twp., Switzerland Co., IN
DAR Ancestor No.: None

Pension Application Abstracted from National Archives microfilm Series 805, Roll 689, File S32480.

Pension abstract for – Nathan Ricketts   Service state(s): PA
Date: 17 September 1832
County of: Switzerland   State of: Indiana
Declaration made before a Court.
Age: 72 years
Where and year born: Antietam, Maryland on August 26, 1759 or 1760
Residence when he entered service: In Pennsylvania on the Frontier in Cumberland County.
Residence(s) since the war: Pennsylvania for 30 years, Kentucky for 9 years then to Indiana.
Residence now: Dearborn County, Indiana
Volunteer or Drafted or Substitute : Enlisted & Volunteered
Rank(s): Private
Statement of service-

Period	Duration	Names of General and Field Officers
Summer 1779	3 mos.	Capt. Alexander McCormick, Cumberland Co. Pennsylvania Militia.
1780	3 mos.	Capt. J. L. Johnson and John Thornton, or Thorton, of Col. Piper's Regt. Pennsylvania Militia.
1781 and 1782	12 mos.	Edward Ricketts & Thomas Ricketts were Captains in command at Frankstown and the Lead Mines. Capt. David Caldwell, Major Francis Clugeorge

Discharge received: Never received a written discharge
Statement is supported by –
Living witness, name(s): Robert Ricketts

Evidence: No documentary evidence. My nephew (Robert Ricketts) served 3 mos. with me under Capt. Johnson.
Clergyman: John Pavy
Persons in neighborhood who certify character: Robert Ricketts, James Dill, Abel C. Pepper, David V. Cully, John Spencer.
Note: Nathan Ricketts testified for the Pension Application of Robert Ricketts, stating that he had known him since his birth in 1765, and served 3 mos. with Robert in a Company Commanded by Capt. James Johnson who was suspended by Lieut. John Thornton or Thorton.

National Archives microfilm Series 805, Roll 689, File S32480.
Letter from War Dept. in Pension File –
January 5, 1937   B4-J/EEL
Mrs. R. L. Ireland   Nathan Ricketts
415 West Main
Madison, Indiana
Dear Madame;

    Reference is made to your letter in which you request the record of Nathan Ricketts, who received pension in Switzerland County, Indiana, in 1834, on account of his service in the Revolutionary War.

    The data which follow are obtained from the papers on file in Revolutionary War pension claim, S.33480, based upon the military service of Nathan Ricketts in that war.

    Nathan Ricketts was born August 26, 1759 or 1760, at Antietam, Maryland. The names of his parents are not stated.

    While residing in the state of Pennsylvania, on the frontier in Cumberland County, Nathan Ricketts enlisted and served as a private with the Pennsylvania troops, as follows: from sometime in 1779, three months in Captain Alexander McCormick's Company, and was stationed in the mountains as an "Indian troop"; in 1780, three months in Captain James Johnson's and John Thornton's Companies, Colonel Piper's Regiment and was stationed at the Lead mines in Sinking Valley; soldier stated that Edward Ricketts and Thomas Ricketts were captains in command at Frankstown and the lead mines but did not give any relationships; in1781 and 1782, Nathan Ricketts served on tours, at least fourteen months in all under Captains David Caldwell, John Beaty and Edward Ricketts; he stated that he served, also, at different times, on tours of from two to twenty days each, at least eight months in all, names of officers not given.

    After the Revolution, he resided in Pennsylvania for thirty years, then moved to Kentucky and lived nine years; thence to Indiana.

    He was allowed pension on his application executed September 17, 1832, while residing in Dearborn County, Indiana. Said application was made in Switzerland County, Indiana.

    It is not stated that Nathan Ricketts was ever married.

    Soldier stated that his nephew served with him but did not give the name of said nephew. In 1832, one Robert Ricketts made affidavit in Switzerland County, Indiana, that he served with said Nathan Ricketts for three months in 1780, but gave no relationship.

                                    Very truly yours,

A.D. HILLER
Executive Assistant
to the Administrator

Switzerland County, Indiana Civil Order Book Vol., A, Oct. 19, 1829-April 16, 1837, p. 171.
In the matter of Robert Moore, Griffith Dickinson, Nathan Ricketts, Gideon Tower, and John Shaddy, An application to obtain a pension under the Act of Congress of the 7th June AD 1832.
     Personally appeared in open Court, before the Switzerland Circuit Court now sitting the above named applicants who being first duly Sworn doth on their several oaths make their several declarations in order to obtain the benefit of the Act of Congress of the 7th June AD 1832 that they entered the Service of the United States under the officers named in their several declarations (here insert them) And the said Court do hereby declare their opinion after the investigation of the matter and after putting the interrogations prescribed by the War department that the above named Applicants were revolutionary Soldiers and Served as they have stated and the Court further Certifies that it appears to them that John Pavy who Signed their several Certificates is a Clergyman Resident in Switzerland County and State of Indiana and the other persons who has also Signed the Same are credible persons and that their Statements in entitled to credit.

Abstract of Final Payment Voucher; General Services Administration, Washington, DC
FINAL PAYMENT VOUCHER RECEIVED FROM
THE GENERAL ACCOUNTING OFFICE
NAME   Ricketts, Nathan
AGENCY OF PAYMENT   Indiana
DATE OF ACT   1832
DATE OF PAYMENT   2d Qr. 1847
DATE OF DEATH   Jan 10, 1847
GENERAL SERVICES ADMINISTRATION
National Archives and Records Service   NA-286
GSA-WASH DC 54-4891   November 1953

Pennsylvania Archives, Series 3, Volume XXIII. p. 232.
Muster Rolls of the Navy and Line, Militia and Rangers, 1775-1783. with List of Pensioners, 1818-1832.
Rangers on the Frontiers – 1778-1783.
Bedford County
Nathan Ricketts – included in the list

Pennsylvania Archives, Series 5, Volume IV. p. 612.
List of "Soldiers of the Revolution who received pay for their services," Taken from Manuscript Record, having neither date nor title, but under "Rangers on the Frontiers, 1778-1783"
Continental Line Soldiers of the Revolution

Rickets, Nathan, private
[Robert Rickets is also in this list.]

Pennsylvania Archives, Series 5, Volume IV. p. 249.
Soldiers Who Received Depreciation Pay as Per Cancelled Certificates on File in the Division of Public Records, Pennsylvania State Library.
Continental Line Depreciation Pay
Rickets, Nathan, private
[Robert Rickets is also in this list.]

Second Census of Kentucky, 1800; Clift G. Glenn; Genealogical Publishing Co., Baltimore, MD, 1954.
An alphabetical list of 32,000 taxpayers based on original tax lists on file at the Kentucky Historical Society. Information given includes the county of residence and the date of the tax list in which the individual is listed.
Rickets, Nathan   Mason   1800

Census of Indiana Territory for 1807; Indiana Historical Society, 1980. p. 26.
A list of free males above the age of twenty one in Dearborn County in March 1807 ~~
426   Nathan Rickets

Early Ohio Settlers, Purchasers of Land in Southwestern Ohio, 1800-1840; Compiled by Ellen T. Berry & David A. Berry; Genealogical Publishing Co., Inc., Baltimore, MD, 1986. p.272.

Purchaser	Year	Date	Residence	R – T - S
Ricketts, Nathan (B)	1825	Sept. 22	Switzerland	02-03-25
Ricketts, Nathan (B)	1833	Aug. 22	Switzerland	02-02-01

(B) Indiana Survey: Land lying west of a meridian drawn west of the Great Miami (known as the "Gore"). Switzerland, Dearborn, Franklin, Ohio, Union and Randolph Counties (all or only a part of each county) – all in Indiana.

Early Settlers of Indiana's "GORE" 1803-1820; Compiled and Edited by Shirley Keller Mikesell; Heritage Books, Inc., 1995.
p. 17.
Dearborn County: Original Land Entries Tract Book.
Dearborn County Township 3, Range 1W.
Section 19 – Nathan Ricketts – 1816 – pg. 1.
p. 8.
War of 1812 Muster Rolls – Dearborn/3rd Regt. Capt. Charles Campbell's Co. – Nathan Ricketts is listed.

Indiana Land Entries Vol. 1 Cincinnati District, 1801-1840; Margaret R. Waters; Originally Published Indianapolis 1948, Second Reprint 1979 by The Bookmark, P.O. Box 74, Knightstown, In 46148. p 6, 45, 130.
CINCINNNATI LAND DISTRICT – VOL. 1
Page 4. Twp. 3 N, Range 1 W of 1st Principle Meridian SWITZERLAND CO.
Nathan Ricketts NE ¼ - S19; 11-18-1814.

and –
Page 42. Twp. 3 N, Range 2 W of 1st Principle Meridian SWITZERLAND CO. Cyrus Cutte NW ¼ - S25; 8-16-1817, Relinquished E ½ to Nathan Ricketts 9-22-1825; W ½ to James Shepherd 7-5-1831.
and –
Page 62. Twp. 2 N, Range 2 W of 1st Principle Meridian SWITZERLAND CO. Nathan Ricketts NW ¼ -NE ¼ - S1; 2-27-1833.
-- Note: The tract books for the land offices in Indiana are deposited in the office of the Auditor of State, Indianapolis. They and are in the custody of the State Land clerk. --

U.S. Department of Interior, Bureau of Land Management, General Land Office Records; Land Patent Search – accessed 27 June 2012.
RICKETTS, NATHAN
Accession Nr. CV-0050-286; Document Type – Credit Volume Patent; State - Indiana; Issue Date – 2/24/1820; Cancelled – No
Land Office – Cincinnati; Authority – April 24, 1820 Sale-Cash Entry (3 Stat. 566); Total Acres – 159.62
Land Description: State - IN; Meridian – 1st PM; Aliquots – 003N-001W; Section – 19; County - Ohio

Historical Register of Virginians in the Revolution, Soldiers, Sailors, Marines, 1775-1783; John H. Gwathmey; The Dietz Press, Richmond, VA, 1938. p. 663.
Ricketts, Nathan, Indiana pens.

A Census of Pensioners for Revolutionary or Military Services with their Names, Ages, and Places of Residence Under the Act for Taking the Sixth Census in 1840; Genealogical Publishing Co., Inc., Baltimore, Maryland, 1965. p. 181.

INDIANA, DEARBORN, (NO TWP.)

Names of Pensioners for Revolutionary or Military services	Ages	Names of heads of families with whom pensioner resided June 1, 1840
Rickett, Nathan	81	none named

The "Lost" Pensions, Settled Accounts of the Act of 6 April 1838; by Craig R. Scott; Willow Bend Books, Lovettsville, VA, 1996. p. 275.
An Act directing the transfer of money remaining unclaimed [for the term of eight months] by certain pensioners, and authorizing payment of the same at the Treasury of the United States.
Name – Ricketts, Nathan; Pension Office – Ind.; Box - 54; Account - #6609
&
Name – Ricketts, Nathan; Pension Office – Ind.; Box - 81; Account - #15112.

Revolutionary Soldiers of Switzerland County; Copied by Mary Hill, John Paul Chapter-Daughters of the American Revolution; January, 1958; http://www.ingenweb.org/inswitzerland/switzrevsoldiers.html- Viewed June 2012.
RICKETTS, NATHAN   Pension record S.32480.
Born August 26, 1759 or 1760, at Antietam, Maryland

While residing in the state of Pennsylvania, on the frontier, in Cumberland County, Nathan Ricketts enlisted and served as a private with the Pennsylvania troops, as follows; from sometime in 1779, three months in Captain Alexander McCormick's Company, and was stationed in the mountains on an "Indian trace"; in 1780, three months in Captains James Johnson's and John Thornton's Companies, Colonel Piper's Regiment, and was stationed at the lead mines in Sinking Valley; soldier stated that Edward Ricketts and Thomas Ricketts were Captains in command at Frankstown and the lead mines but did not give any relationship; in 1781 and 1782, Nathan Ricketts served on tours, at least fourteen months in all under Captains David Caldwell, John Beaty, and Edward Ricketts; he stated that he served, also at different times, on tours of from two to twenty days each, at least, eight months in all, names of officers not given.
After the Revolution, he resided in Pennsylvania for thirty years, then moved to Kentucky and lived nine years, thence to Indiana.
Married Jane Wilson
Children: William m Rebecca Neal, Edward,, Susanna Neal, Abram, Nathan, Elizabeth Rich, Jane Shepherd, Ann, Ephraim
(All mentioned in his will that was probated in Ohio Co., IN)
He was allowed pension on his application executed September 17, 1832, while residing in Dearborn County, Indiana. Said application was made in Switzerland County, Indiana.
Buried Mt. Carmel Cemetery, Posey Twp., Ohio County, IN. Stone.
Will probated Jan. 1847, Ohio County, IN

Roster of Soldiers and Patriots of the American Revolution Buried in Indiana, Vol. I; compiled by Mrs. Roscoe C. O'Byrne.; Indiana Daughters of the American Revolution, 1981; p.313-314.
RICKETTS, NATHAN   Switzerland County
Born – Aug. 26, 1759, Antietam, Maryland.
Service – Pri. in CO. commanded by Capt. McCormick, Regt. of Col. Piper, 11 mos., 14 days.
Proof – Pension claim S. 32480.
Died – Will probated Jan., 1847. Buried Mt. Carmel Cemetery, Posey Twp. Stone.
Married – Jane _____. Ch. William Rebecca Neal; Edward; Susannah Neal; Abram; Nathan' Elizabeth Rich; Jane Shepherd; Ann; Ephraim. (All named in Nathan St. Will, probated 1847, in Ohio Co.
Collected by Mrs. A. V. Danner, Vevay, Indiana.

The Vevay Reveille-Enterprise; Vol. 122. No. 39, 28 Sep 1935, p.3, col. 1.
Roster of Revolutionary Soldiers Who Resided in Switzerland County
By Mrs. Effa M. Danner
Nathan Ricketts – who received pension in Switzerland County, Ind., in 1834, on account of his service in the Revolutionary War.
The data which follows are obtained from the papers on file in Revolutionary War pension claim, S32480, based upon the military service of Nathan Ricketts in that war.

Nathan Ricketts was born August 26, 1759 or 1760, at Antietam, Maryland. The names of his parents are not shown.

While residing in the state of Pennsylvania, on the frontier, in Cumberland County, Nathan Ricketts enlisted and served as a private with the Pennsylvania troops, as follows: from sometime in 1779, three months in Captain Alexander McCormick's Company, and was stationed in the mountains on an "Indian Trace"; in 1780, three months in Captains James Johnson's and John Thornton's Companies, Col. Piper's Regiment and was stationed at the lead mines in Sinking Valley; soldier stated that Edward Ricketts and Thomas Ricketts were captains in command at Frankstown and that the lead mines but did not give any relationship; in 1781 and 1782, Nathan Ricketts served on tours, at least fourteen months in all under Captains David Caldwell, John Beaty and Edward Ricketts; he stated that he served also, at different times, on tours of from two to twenty days each, at least eight months in all, names of officers not given.

After the Revolution he resided in Pennsylvania for thirty years, then moved to Kentucky and lived nine years; thence to Indiana.

He was allowed pension on his application executed September 17, 1832, while residing in Dearborn County, Indiana. Said application was made in Switzerland County, Indiana.

It is not stated that Nathan Ricketts was ever married.

Soldier stated that his nephew served with him but did not give the name of said nephew. In 1832, one Robert Ricketts made an affidavit in Switzerland County, Indiana, that he served with said Nathan Ricketts for three months in 1780, but gave no relationship.

Nathan Ricketts and brother Robert Ricketts are buried on the same lot in the cemetery near Mt. Carmel church on Highway 56. The Ohio county line runs through this lot, and Robert Ricketts is buried in Ohio County.

Abstract of Graves of Revolutionary Patriots (4 volumes); by Patricia Law Hatcher; Pioneer Heritage Press, Dallas, TX, 1987. Vol. 3, p. 218.

This is an abstract and an index to information reported to the Daughters of the American Revolution and published in their annual reports to the Smithsonian Institution, printed as Senate Documents (1900-1974) and published annually in the DAR magazine (1978-1987).

Published 1972 (Senate Doc. 54)
RICKETTS, Nathan   Mt. Carmel Cem, Posey Twp,
Switzerland Co IN

Mt. Carmel Cemetery, Aberdeen, Posey Twp., Switzerland Co., IN
Tombstone inscription –
                    NATHAN RICKETTS
                PVT CO L PIPER'S REGT
                  REVOLUTIONARY WAR
            AUG 1759   JAN 1847

RICKETTS, ROBERT

Patriot: Robert Ricketts
Birth: 15 Jan 1765 Hagerstown, Frederick Co., MD
Married Spouse 1: Susanah Wilson (b. 1767 MD d. 20 Feb 1853 Ohio Co., IN)
Service state(s): PA
Service description: Col. Piper, Capt. Samuels, Cumberland Co. Militia
Rank: Private
Proof of Service: Pension application S17047
Pension application No.: S17047
Residences: Cumberland Co., PA; KY: Indiana Territory, Switzerland Co., IN
Died: 14 Feb 1853 Ohio Co., IN
Buried: Mt. Carmel Cemetery, Aberdeen, Posey Twp., Ohio Co., IN
DAR Ancestor No.: A096197

Document contributed by Judy Kappes
Pension Application Abstracted from Switzerland County, IN Civil Order Book, Sept. 1832; and *National Archives microfilm Series 805, Roll 689, File S17047*
Pension abstract for – Robert Ricketts   Service state(s): PA
Alternate spelling(s): Robert Rickets
Date: 18 September 1832
County of: Switzerland   State of: Indiana
Declaration made before a Court.
Age: 67
Where and year born: Hagerstown, MD on 15 Jan 1765
Residence when he entered service: Kishacoquillae Valley, Cumberland Co., PA
Residence(s) since the war: Lived in Pennsylvania about 10 years, then in
                             Kentucky about 15 years, then in Indiana since.
Residence now: Dearborn County, Indiana
Volunteer or Drafted or Substitute: Enlisted for 3 months and volunteered once.
Rank(s): Private
Statement of service-

Period	Duration	Names of General and Field Officers
1780	3 mos.	Capt. James Johnson of Col. Piper's Regt., a Company of Pennsylvania Militia.
1781 or 1782	3 mos. 7 days	Captain Robert Samuels and then Captain Boals Cumberland Co. Militia.

Discharge received: Never received a written discharge.
Statement is supported by – Nathan Rickets served with the said Robert Ricketts in 1780 in a Company Commanded by Capt. James Johnson who was suspended by Lieut. John Thornton or Thorton. Nathan (his uncle) has known him since his birth in 1765. (Papers of Nathan Ricketts state his "nephew" served 3 mos. with him under Capt. Johnson.)
Clergyman: John Pavy
Persons in neighborhood who certify character: Stephen Stewart, George Dugan, Caleb A. Craft, Abel C. Pepper, John Spencer, Pickney James.

Robert Ricketts was allowed pens in 1832 while residing in Dearborn Co., IN. Petitioned in Switzerland Co. He died 14 Feb 1853 leaving widow & eleven children. Wid. d. 20 Feb 1853.

National Archives microfilm Series 805, Roll 689, File S17047.
Letter from War Department in Pension File –
May 7, 1927
Rev. & 1812 Wars Section
Mrs. W. H. Shonts
203 E. Marion St.
South Bend, Ind.
Madame:
I have to advise you that it appears from the papers in the Revolutionary War pension claim, S. 17047, that Robert Ricketts was born January 15, 1765, near Hagerstown, Maryland.

   He enlisted in Cumberland County, Pennsylvania, in 1780 as a private in Captain James Johnson's Company in Colonel Piper's Pennsylvania Regiment and served three months.

   While living in Kishacoquillas Valley, Pennsylvania, he enlisted in 1782 and served three months and seven days as a private in Captains Robert Samuel's Boals' Pennsylvania Companies.

   He was allowed pension on his application executed September 18, 1832, at which time he was a resident of Dearborn County, Indiana.

   He died February 14, 1853, leaving a widow and eleven children their names not stated.

   His widow died February 20, 1853.

               Respectfully.
               WINFIELD SCOTT
               Commissioner

Switzerland County, Indiana Civil Order Book Vol., A, Oct. 19, 1829-April 16, 1837, p. 178.
In the matter of Robert Ricketts, Thomas Mounts, Ebenezer Humphrey, Daniel Heath, William Coy and Isaac Levi, An application to obtain a pension.

   Personally appeared in open Court before the Switzerland Circuit Court now Sitting The above named applicants who being first duly Sworn doth in their several oaths make their several declarations in order to obtain the benefit of the Act of Congress of the 7th June Ad 1832 that they entered the Service of the United States under the Officers named in their several declarations (here insert them) And the said Court do hereby declare their opinion after the investigation of the matter and after putting the interrogations prescribed by the War Department that the above named applicants were Revolutionary Soldiers and Served as they have stated And the Court further certifies that is appears to them that John Pavy who signed the several Certificates is a Clergyman resident in Switzerland County and State of Indiana and the other persons who has also signed the same are credible persons and that their Statement is entitled to credit.

Pennsylvania Archives, Series 5, Volume IV. p. 612.
List of "Soldiers of the Revolution who received pay for their services," Taken from Manuscript Record, having neither date nor title, but under "Rangers on the Frontiers, 1778-1783"
Continental Line Soldiers of the Revolution
Rickets, Robert, private
[Nathan Rickets is also on this list.]

Pennsylvania Archives, Series 5, Volume IV. p. 637.
List of "Soldiers of the Revolution who received pay for their services," Taken from Manuscript Record, having neither date nor title, but under "Rangers on the Frontiers, 1778-1783"
Continental Line Soldiers of the Revolution
Rickets, Robert, private

Pennsylvania Archives, Series 5, Volume VI. P. 579.
Muster Rolls Relating to the Associators and Militia of the County of Cumberland
A Pay Role of 2D and 3D Classes of the 8th Battalion of Cumberland County Militia

Names of Persons Who Performed Tour of Duty	Time when duty commenced	Time when duty expired
Robert Rickets	April 28	June 28

This is to Certify that the above Roll is a true state of my Company to the best of my knowledge, given under my hand this 27th day of Feb. 1783.
Robert Samuels, Capt.

Pennsylvania Archives, Series 5, Volume IV. p. 302.
Soldiers Who Received Depreciation Pay as Per Cancelled Certificates on File in the Division of Public Records, Pennsylvania State Library.
Continental Line Depreciation Pay
Rickets, Robert, private

Pennsylvania Archives, Series 5, Volume IV. p. 249.
Soldiers Who Received Depreciation Pay as Per Cancelled Certificates on File in the Division of Public Records, Pennsylvania State Library.
Continental Line Depreciation Pay
Rickets, Robert, private
[Nathan Rickets is also listed]

Pennsylvania Archives, Series 5, Volume VI. p. 574
Muster Rolls Relating to the Associators and Militia of the County of Cumberland
Captain Robert Samuel's Company
A Pay Book of Second and Third Classes of the Eighth Battalion of Cumberland County Militia, Commanded by Col. Alexander Brown, Who Performed a Tower of Duty in the Kischacauquillis Valley in the Year 1782. (b.)
Robert Rickets – in this list

Pennsylvania Archives, Series 5, Volume VI. p. 648.
Muster Rolls Relating to the Associators and Militia of the County of Cumberland
Capt. Robert Samuel's Pay Roll of April, May and June, 1782. (c.)
Lieut. Richard Gansalus, Ensign John Bell, 1 Sergt. John Anderson, 2 Sergt. William Duffiled, 3 Sergt. John Oliver, 4 Sergt. Amos Chapman.
Privates – Robert Rickets in the list

Second Census of Kentucky, 1800; Clift G. Glenn; Genealogical Publishing Co., Baltimore, MD, 1954.
An alphabetical list of 32,000 taxpayers based on original tax lists on file at the Kentucky Historical Society. Information given includes the county of residence and the date of the tax list in which the individual is listed.
Rickets, Robert   Mason   1800

Census of Indiana Territory for 1807; Indiana Historical Society, 1980. p. 26.
A list of free males above the age of twenty one in Dearborn County in March 1807 ~
425   Robert Rickets

Early Ohioans' Residences From the Land Grant Records; Compiled by Mayburt Stephenson Riegel; Published by the Ohio Genealogical Society, Mansfield, OH, 1976. p. 8.
Land Grants Recorded by Residents of the Indiana Territory at the Cincinnati Land Office. The original Land Grant records are in the Archives of the Ohio Historical Society. They are from the Auditor of the State of Ohio Land Office.

NAME	DATE	SEC	TWP	RANGE	VOL	PG	RESIDENCE
RICKETS, Robert	11-28-1804	S17	T3	R1W	B	196	KY Kentucky

Early Ohio Settlers, Purchasers of Land in Southwestern Ohio, 1800-1840; Compiled by Ellen T. Berry & David A. Berry; Genealogical Publishing Co., Inc., Baltimore, MD, 1986. p.272

Purchaser	Year	Date	Residence	R-T-S
Ricketts, Robert (B)	1813	Nov. 26	Dearborn Ind	02-03-24
Ricketts, Robert (B)	1813	Nov. 22	Dearborn Ind	01-03-17

(B) Indiana Survey: Land lying west of a meridian drawn west of the Great Miami (known as the "Gore"). Switzerland, Dearborn, Franklin, Ohio, Union and Randolph Counties (all or only a part of each county) – all in Indiana.

Early Settlers of Indiana's "GORE" 1803-1820; Compiled and Edited by Shirley Keller Mikesell; Heritage Books, Inc., 1995.
p. 17.
Dearborn County: Original Land Entries Tract Book.
Dearborn County Township 3, Range 1W.
Section 17 – Robert Ricketts – 1804 – pg.1.
and Section 17 – Robert Ricketts – 1813 – pg. 1.

p. 22.
Dearborn County – Township 3, Range 2W
Section 24 – Robert Ricketts – 1813 – pg. 17.

<u>Indiana Land Entries Vol. 1 Cincinnati District, 1801-1840</u>; Margaret R. Waters;
Originally Published Indianapolis 1948, Second Reprint 1979 by The Bookmark,
P.O. Box 74, Knightstown, In 46148. p.5,45.
CINCINNNATI LAND DISTRICT – VOL. 1
Page 4. Twp. 3 N, Range 1 W of 1st Principle Meridian OHIO CO.
Robert Ricketts NE ¼ - S17; 11-28-1804.
and –
Page 4. Twp. 3 N, Range 1 W of 1st Principle Meridian OHIO CO.
Robert Ricketts SE ¼ - S17; 11-22-1813.
and –
Page 42. Twp. 3 N, Range 2 W of 1st Principle Meridian OHIO CO.
<u>Author's note:</u> – page 42 also includes that portion of same township and range in Switzerland Co where Nathan Ricketts made entry.
Robert Ricketts SE ¼ - S24; 11-26-1813. Vol. II, p. 72 says Ricketty.
-- Note: The tract books for the land offices in Indiana are deposited in the office of the Auditor of State, Indianapolis. They and are in the custody of the State Land clerk. --

<u>U.S. Department of Interior, Bureau of Land Management, General Land Office Records; Land Patent Search</u> – accessed 27 June 2012.
RICKETS, ROBERT
Accession Nr. CV-0008-270; Document Type – Credit Volume Patent; State - Indiana; Issue Date – 3/23/1810; Cancelled – No
Land Office – Cincinnati; Authority – April 24, 1820 Sale-Cash Entry (3 Stat. 566); Total Acres – 0.00
Land Description: State - IN; Meridian – 1st PM; Aliquots – 003N-001W; Section – 17; County - Ohio
&
Accession Nr. CV-0037-520; Document Type – Credit Volume Patent; State - Indiana; Issue Date – 3/17/1818; Cancelled – No
Land Office – Cincinnati; Authority – April 24, 1820 Sale-Cash Entry (3 Stat. 566); Total Acres – 0.00
Land Description: State - IN; Meridian – 1st PM; Aliquots – 003N-001W; Section – 17; County - Ohio
&
Accession Nr. IN0290_.496; Document Type – State Volume Patent; State - Indiana; Issue Date – 9/9/1835; Cancelled – No
Land Office – Jeffersonville; Authority – April 24, 1820 Sale-Cash Entry (3 Stat. 566); Document Nr. -5007; BLM Serial Nr. – IN NO S/N; Total Acres – 40.
Land Description: State - IN; Meridian – 2nd PM; Aliquots – 004N-012E; Section – 9; County - Switzerland

A Partial Census For Indiana Territory 1810; Compiled by John D & E. Diane Stemmons; Census Publishing LC, Sandy, UT, 2004. p. 459.
Rickets, Robt., Historical Locality: Indiana Territory, Current State: Indiana, Dearborn County, Second Township – Name on list of electors of election held 3 April 1809,- Election returns, 1809, 1812 (Indiana Historical Society), Coll. #M98 Box 32, Folder 1 pg. 5.
Rickets, Robt., Male

A Census of Pensioners for Revolutionary or Military Services with their Names, Ages, and Places of Residence Under the Act for Taking the Sixth Census in 1840; Genealogical Publishing Co., Inc., Baltimore, Maryland, 1965. p. 181.

INDIANA, DEARBORN, (NO TWP.)

Names of Pensioners for Revolutionary or Military services	Ages	Names of heads of families with whom pensioner resided June 1, 1840
Rickett, Robert	75	none named

The "Lost" Pensions, Settled Accounts of the Act of 6 April 1838; by Craig R. Scott; Willow Bend Books, Lovettsville, VA, 1996. p. 275.
An Act directing the transfer of money remaining unclaimed [for the term of eight months] by certain pensioners, and authorizing payment of the same at the Treasury of the United States.
Name – Ricketts, Robert; Pension Office – Ind.; Box - 49; Account - #5270
&
Name – Ricketts, Robert; Pension Office – Ind.; Box - 120; Account - #5945, Card may include information about date of death or other summary information.

1850 U.S. Census, Indiana, Ohio, 2-Dist, Series: M432 Roll: 163 Page: 331, Dwelling 526, Family 543, Line 26.

Robert Rickets	Age 85	M	Farmer	$6,500	Maryland
Susan	Age 83	F			Maryland
Elloner Conover	Age 13	F			Indiana

Abstract of Final Payment Voucher; General Services Administration, Washington, DC

NAME	Ricketts, Robert
AGENCY OF PAYMENT	Indiana
DATE OF ACT	1832
DATE OF PAYMENT	-
DATE OF DEATH	-
FINAL PAYMENT VOUCHER RECEIVED FROM THE GENERAL ACCOUNTING OFFICE	Form
General Services Administration	GSA DA 70-7035 GSA Dec 69 7068

Roster of Soldiers and Patriots of the American Revolution Buried in Indiana, Vol. 1; compiled by Mrs. Roscoe C. O'Byrne.; Indiana Daughters of the American Revolution, 1981; p.314.
RICKETTS, ROBERT   Ohio County

Born – Jan. 15, 1765.
Service – Pri. in CO. commanded by Capt. Johnson, Regt. of Col. Piper, Penn. Line, 6 mos., 7 days.
Proof - Pension claim S. 17047.
Died – Feb. 14, 1853. Left widow and 11 children.
Collected by Mrs. Walter Kerr, Aurora, Indiana.

Roster of Soldiers and Patriots of the American Revolution Buried in Indiana, Vol. III; 1980; p.73.
RICKETTS, ROBERT   Roster I, p. 314.   Ohio County
Additional data or corrections.
Died – (Correction) This soldier is buried in Mt. Carmel Cemetery, Cass Twp. Ohio Co., Ind. This cemetery is very near the Ohio-Switzerland Co. line but has always been in Ohio Co.
Married – Susannah _____.
Children – Phoebe b. 1738 [1783] m. James Sheridan; Hannah b. 1790 m. William Buchanan; William; John; Susannah b. 1794 m. John Moulton; Robert, Jr. b. 1795 m. Ann Larew; Isaac m. Catherine Mounts; Edward m. Leah Cloud; Elizabeth b. 1801 m. (1) Garret Larew (2) John Blankenship; Rebecca b. 1803 m. Daniel Wining; Margaret b. 1806 m. Daniel Kelson; Sarah m. Abraham _____; Naomi.
By Mrs. A. G. Charlton, 310 Sunnyside Avenue, Aurora, Indiana47001.

Abstract of Graves of Revolutionary Patriots (4 volumes); by Patricia Law Hatcher; Pioneer Heritage Press, Dallas, TX, 1987. Vol. 3, p. 218.
This is an abstract and an index to information reported to the Daughters of the American Revolution and published in their annual reports to the Smithsonian Institution, printed as
Senate Documents (1900-1974) and published annually in the DAR magazine (1978-1987).
Published 1978
RICKETTS, Robert   Mt Carmel Cem, nr Posey Twp, Switzerland Co IN

National Society of the Sons of the American Revolution - Revolutionary War Graves Register; Compiled and Edited by Clovis H. Brakebill, Published by db Publications, Dallas, TX, 1993. p. 515.
Ricketts Robert; 1765-1853; Mt. Carmel Cem, nr Posey Twsp, Switzerland Co, IN; Soldier; PA

Mt. Carmel Cemetery, Aberdeen, Posey Twp., Switzerland Co., IN
Tombstone inscription –
ROBERT RICKETTS
PVT, PA LINE
REVOLUTIONARY WAR
JAN 15, 1765   FEB 14, 1853

The Vevay Reveille-Enterprise; Vol. 122. No. 39, 28 Sep 1935, p.3, col.1-2.
Roster of Revolutionary Soldiers Who Resided in Switzerland County
By Mrs. Effa M. Danner
Robert Ricketts – Switzerland Co., petition for pension 1832. Order Book F., p. 80. He served in Revolutionary War 1780, Pa. Militia, Capt. James Johnson, col. Piper's Regiment, again 1781-1782 Co. of Capt. Robert Samuels, Cumberland Co., Pa. He was born at Hagerstown, Md., Jan. 15, A.D. 1765, lived after the war in Pennsylvania 10 years; Kentucky 15 years, Indiana since then. Stationed at Lead Mines, Fort Bedford Co., Pa. Served as private three months under Capt. Brals, in Company of 40 men quartered at the end of Kisecoquil Valley overlook a number of Indians in Glade Valley who had taken 3 horses and were drying the meat which we destroyed. Witness, Stephen Stewart, Able C. Pepper, Pickney James.
Robert Ricketts is buried at Mt. Carmel cemetery on Highway 56, Ohio County on the same lot as his brother, Nathan Ricketts in Switzerland County as the County line runs through the cemetery lot. He died in 1840. Daughter Phoebe Ricketts married James Shadday.
History Dearborn, Ohio and Switzerland Co., 1886.

RICKETTS, WILLIAM

Patriot: William Ricketts
Birth: -
Married Spouse 1:
Service state(s): VA
Service description: Captain Baldwin Pardon (Parson)
Rank: Private
Proof of Service: Pension application X830 (Indian Wars 1781)
Pension application No.: X830
Residences: VA: KY; Indiana Territory; Dearborn Co., IN; Switzerland Co., IN
Died: abt. Nov. 1832, Switzerland Co., IN
Buried: Family cemetery, Salem Ridge, near Rising Sun, Ohio Co, IN
DAR Ancestor No.: None

Pension Application Abstracted from National Archives microfilm Series 805, Roll 689, File X830.
Notation of file cover – "NOT REV. – VA – N.W. INDIAN WARS 1791"
Pension abstract for – William Ricketts   Service state(s): VA
Alternate spelling(s): William Rickets, William Rickles
Date: 6 April 1829
County of: Dearborn   State of: Indiana
Declaration made before a Court.
Residence when he entered service: Probably Virginia
Residence(s) since the war: Kentucky from 1792 to 1814, then State of Indiana.
Residence now: State of Indiana
Volunteer or Drafted or Substitute: no information furnished
Statement of service-

Period	Duration	Names of General and Field Officers
1781		Captain Baldwin Pardon (Parson)

Battles: Against the Indians at Mingo Bottom, in the Northwest Territory, now State of Ohio
Statement is supported by:
Surgeon's Affidavit: William Rickets, a Private, in the Company of Captain Baldwin Pardon, in the State of Virginia Militia, Is rendered incapable of performing the duty of a soldier, by reason of wounds or other injuries inflicted while he was actually in the service aforesaid, and in the line of his duty, viz., and engaged against the Indians.
By satisfactory evidence and accurate examination, it appears that on the 3rd day of May in the year 1791 [should be 1781], being engaged under the command of the said Captain Baldwin Pardon against the Indians at or near a place called the Mingo Bottom in the Northwestern Territory of now State of Ohio, he received a wound in his right arm a little above the elbow which totally (illegible-seam in paper),, also a wound in the right side below the arm which took away part of two of his ribs, and he is thereby, not only incapacitated for military duty, but in the opinion of the undersigned, is also totally disabled from obtaining his subsistence from manual labor. Signed Jabez Percival, Surgeon and John S. Percival, Surgeon.

The Surgeon's Affidavit was presented to the Dearborn County, Indiana court by Thomas Palmer and John Lyons, two of the Justices of the Peace within and for the County of Dearborn. Palmer and Lyons personally came with Rickets who said the Reason he did not apply before for a pension, that he did not know until some time in January 1829 that he was entitled to draw a pension. And, that not being in the Regular army but living in a frontier settlement. That he has resided since the year 1792 until the year 1814 in the State of Kentucky, and has since lived in the State of Indiana.

Certificate of Pension issued 20 August 1833, sent to himself at the post office in Rising Sun, Indiana.

[His application had been rejected due to having served in the "Indian Wars in 1791". The battle at Mingo Bottom occurred in 1782, during the years of the Revolution. The error must have been found because William did receive his pension in August 1833. An incorrect date of service was probably acquired from the surgeon's affidavit that was either written 9-10 years later, or the doctor wrote the wrong year.]

Switzerland County, IN, Will Book Vol. 1, 3 Jan 1823-10 Nov 1847, p. 60.
Abstract of will and/or administration for: William Ricketts
Probate of estate is not indexed in Probate Order Book 2.
State & county where recorded: Switzerland Co., Indiana
State & county where will was made: Switzerland, Indiana
Book/volume where recorded: Will Book Vol. 1,
Date will made: 25 August 1832
Date entered in probate: 18 November 1832
Witnesses/appraisers: Witnesses to will – John Gibbons and James Robinson.

Virginia Soldiers of 1776; Compiled from Documents on File in the Virginia Land Office, Together with Material found in the Archives Department of the Virginia State Library, and Other Reliable Sources, 3 volumes; Compiled and Edited by Louis A. Burgess, Genealogical Publishing Co., Inc., Baltimore, MD, 1973.

p. 338.
Five Soldiers
Council Chamber, Apl. 1st, 1783. I do certify that Lewis Bigley, William Heaken, John McHenry, Richard Dunn and William Ricketts are severally entitled to the proportion of land allowed a Private of the State line for three years service. Benjamin Harrison, Gov.

p. 532.
Council Chamber, Apl 1st, 1783. Certified that Lewis Bigley, William Heaken, John McHine (McHeines), Richard Dunn and William Ricketts are severally entitled to the proportion of L.B. allowed a Private soldier of the State line for three years service. Benj. Harrison, Gov.

Catalogue of Revolutionary Soldiers and Sailors of the Commonwealth of Virginia to Whom Land Bounty Warrants Were Granted by Virginia for Military Service in the War for Independence, From Official Records in the Kentucky

State Land Office at Frankfort, Kentucky; compiled by Samuel M. Wilson; Southern Book Company, Baltimore, MD, 1953. p. 62.

Number of Warrant	Name of Officer or Soldier	Number of Acres	Dept. of Service: Continental or State Line or Navy	Number of Years in Service	Date of Warrant
274	Ricketts, William	100	Pvt. State Line	3 years	Apr 3, 1783

Historical Register of Virginians in the Revolution, Soldiers, Sailors, Marines, 1775-1783; John H. Gwathmey; The Dietz Press, Richmond, VA, 1938. p. 663.
Rickett, William 1 Va. State Reg., E.
Ricketts, William, 1 Va. State Reg., E.
Ricketts, William, BW.

Revolutionary War Records – Virginia; Virginia Army and Navy Forces with Bounty Land Warrants for Virginia Military District of Ohio, and Virginia Military Script, from Federal and State Archives; by Gaius Marcus Brumbaugh, M.D, M.s., Litt.D; Genealogical Publishing Co., Inc., Baltimore, 1995. p.354.
Virginia Military Land Warrants, Virginia Military District of Ohio, Granted for Revolutionary War Services, State and Navy, Beginning February 14, 1782.

Number	Warrantee	Person Who Performed the Service	Kind of Service
274	McClurg, James	Ricketts, William	State Line

Author's note: William was injured in 1791. Was he later in this company? Further research is needed regarding this citation.

American Militia in the Frontier Wars, 1790-1796; by Murtie June Clark; Genealogical Publishing Co., Inc., 1990. p. 73.
Kentucky Militia
Muster Roll of Commissioned, Non-Commissioned Officers and Privates, Captain Jeremiah Briscoe's Company, Major John Caldwell's Battalion, Major General Charles Scott's Command, Jul 9, 1794.

Nr	Rank	Name	Remarks
61	Private	Rickets, William	-

Register of Certificates Issued by John Pierce, Esquire, Paymaster General and Commissioner of Army Accounts for the United States, to Officers and Soldiers of the Continental Army Under Act of July 4, 1783; Originally Published as Senate Documents, Vol.9, No. 988, 63rd Congress, 3d Session, Washington, 1915; Seventeenth report of the National Society of the Daughters of the American Revolution; Genealogical Publishing Co., Inc, Baltimore, MD, 1984. p. 428.
Men listed in this volume with the same name.

No. of Certificate	To whom issued	Amount
71080	Rickets, William	33.30
71230	Rickets, William	62.60
71373	Rickets, William	80.00

Revolutionary War Bounty Land Grants Awarded by State Governments; Lloyd DeWitt Bockstruck; Genealogical Publishing co., IN, Baltimore, MD, 1996. p.
RICKETTS. William. Va. Private. 1 Apr 1783. 100 acres.

Second Census of Kentucky, 1800; Clift G. Glenn; Genealogical Publishing Co., Baltimore, MD, 1954.
An alphabetical list of 32,000 taxpayers based on original tax lists on file at the Kentucky Historical Society. Information given includes the county of residence and the date of the tax list in which the individual is listed.
Ricketts, William   Shelby   8/7/1800

Census of Indiana Territory for 1807; Indiana Historical Society, 1980. p. 26.
A list of free males above the age of twenty one in Dearborn County in March 1807 ~~
427   William Rickets

Indiana Territory, Switzerland Circuit Court Records, Order Book, October Term 1814 to March Term 1815. p. 132.
He is listed in county records for the first time on 23 October 1815, as a juror.

Early Settlers of Indiana's "GORE" 1803-1820; Compiled and Edited by Shirley Keller Mikesell; Heritage Books, Inc., 1995.
p. 215.
Switzerland County Deeds; Book A
William Ricketts is witness –
Deed dated 1820. Caleb Mounts of Posey Twp to Joseph Ritch. S6, T2, R1. Signed by Caleb Mounts, Jane Mounts. Witness: Samuel Ravenscroft, William Rickets. pp. 375, 376.
p. 222.
Switzerland County Deeds; Book A
Deed dated 1820. Daniel Miser of Posey Twp. to William Ricketts. S31, T3, R1W. Signed Daniel (x) Miser, Mary (x) Miser. Witness: Samuel Rauchdraft, Caleb Mounts. pp. 507, 508, 509.

U.S. Department of Interior, Bureau of Land Management, General Land Office Records; Land Patent Search – accessed 27 June 2012.
RICKETTS, WILLIAM
Accession Nr. CV-0062-412; Document Type – Credit Volume Patent; State - Indiana; Issue Date – 4/1/1825; Cancelled – No
Land Office – Cincinnati; Authority – April 24, 1820 Sale-Cash Entry (3 Stat. 566); General Remarks – Patent Record Imperfect; Total Acres – 155.06
Land Description: State - IN; Meridian – 1st PM; Aliquots – 004N-001W; Section - 27; County - Ohio

Abstract of Graves of Revolutionary Patriots (4 volumes); by Patricia Law Hatcher; Pioneer Heritage Press, Dallas, TX, 1987. Vol. 3, p. 218.
This is an abstract and an index to information reported to the Daughters of the American Revolution and published in their annual reports to the Smithsonian

Institution , printed as Senate Documents (1900-1974) and published annually in the DAR magazine (1978-1987).
Published 1925, Serial set 8542, Volume 4.
RICKETTS, William   Fam cem, Salem Ridge, nr Rising Sun, Ohio Co, IN

Revolutionary Soldiers Buried in Indiana (1949) With Supplement (1954) Two Volumes in One; Margaret R. Waters; Genealogical Publishing Company, Baltimore, MD, 1970. p. 29.
Ricketts, William   Ohio Co.
DAR reference below is in error; listed here to disprove Pens. file definitely states NOT Rev. War; N.W. Indian Wars, 1791; on Invalid Indian roll, 1835, Dearborn Co., Ind. File mentions Rising Sun, Ind. REF-O.W. Inv. File 26367 Va.; DAR 28, p. 158; 1835 Pens. List, v. 3, p. 3.

Surname index to Roster of soldiers and patriots of the American Revolution buried in Indiana, vol. I & II; Darlington, Jane Eaglesfield; Published by Fort Wayne Public Library, Ft. Wayne, IN, 1976. p.406.
List of Indiana Pensioners in Other Wars, Giving the County in Which They Were Living When Pensioned.
Ricketts, William   Dearborn Co.   Indian War, 1791

ROBERTS, HEZEKIAH

Patriot: Hezekiah Roberts
Birth: c. 1760
Married Spouse 1: 1783 Culpepper Co. VA   Agnes Robinson
(b. abt. 1771/4, d. 23 Sep 1843/1848 Switzerland Co., IN)
Service state(s): VA
Service description: Capts. William Fields, Thomas Bressie, James Moody,
Col. Gregory Smith, 2nd VA Regt., State Line.
Rank: Private
Proof of Service: Pension application W9631
Pension application No.: W9631
Residences: Culpepper Co., VA; Fayette Co., KY; Switzerland Co., IN
Died: 23 Feb 1826 Switzerland Co., IN
Buried: Zion Cemetery, Craig Twp., Switzerland Co., IN
DAR Ancestor No.: A207093

Pension Application Abstracted from National Archives microfilm Series 805, Roll 694, File W9631.

Pension abstract for – Hezekiah Roberts   Service state(s): Virginia
Date: 8 June 1821
County of: Switzerland   State of: Indiana
Declaration made before a Circuit Court.
Schedule of Property presented to court
Age: Not stated
Residence now: Switzerland Co., IN
Volunteer or Drafted or Substitute: Enlisted
Rank(s):
Statement of service-

Period	Duration	Names of General and Field Officers
1 March 1777	3 years	Company commanded by Capt. William Fields in the Virginia Line of the Continental establishment. Then under Capt. Bray, then under Capt. James Morley, in Mulenburg Brigade.

Battles: Monmouth and Stoney Point
Statement is supported by –
Documentary proof: Depositions of Francis Cheek and Nehimah Roberts
Occupation: Farmer but have been unable to labor for 16 years by reason of a lame hand
Wife: Agnes, affected with rheumatism   Wife's age: 51 years
Names and ages of children: Rebecca aged 15 years in good health; Hezekiah aged 13 in good health; Moses aged 12 in good health.
&
Son, William Roberts application for pension. Oldest child of Hezekiah and Agnes Roberts.
Date: 28 April 1854
County of: Switzerland   State of: Indiana

Declaration made before a Court.
Wife: Agnes died in Switzerland Co. on 23 Sep 1848, aged about 74 years.
Marriage date and place: His parents marriage, as near as he can remember from what his parents have told him, and from his own age (69), was 1783. His parents were married in Virginia either in Culpepper, Hanover, or Loudon Co. which are all adjoining counties. His father lived in Culpepper, his mother lived in Hanover Co. She was Agnes Robertson.
Proof of marriage: He knew of none such in existence . Has no family record of the marriage of his parents and the births of their children.
Names and ages of children: William (himself) b. 1788; John aged 64 in 1854; and Rebecca McKay aged about 42 years in 1854; Hezekiah Roberts aged about 40 years in 1854; Moses Perry Roberts.

Switzerland County, Indiana Civil Order Book 4, 1820 – 1823; pg. 198-199.
June 1821
Hezekiah Roberts, a Revolutionary soldier filed his Schedule and Declaration and took oath required by late Act of Congress, property valued at ninety dollars and fifty cents.

Abstract of Final Payment Voucher; General Services Administration, Washington, DC

NAME	Roberts, Agnes widow of Hezekiah
AGENCY OF PAYMENT	Madison, Ind
DATE OF ACT	1838, 1843 & 1844
DATE OF PAYMENT	3rd Qr. 1854
DATE OF DEATH	Sept. 23, 1843
FINAL PAYMENT VOUCHER RECEIVED FROM	
THE GENERAL ACCOUNTING OFFICE	Form
General Services Administration	GSA DA 70-7035 GSA Dec 69 7068

Virginia Revolutionary Militia, A List of Non-Commissioned Officers and Seamen and Marines of the State Navy, Whose names appear on the Army Register, and who have not received Bounty Land; Printed by Samuel Shepherd, Printer to the Commonwealth, Richmond, VA. 1835. p. 15.
Doc. No. 48.
Roberts, Hezekiah   Soldier   Infantry

Historical Register of Virginians in the Revolution, Soldiers, Sailors, Marines, 1775-1783; John H. Gwathmey; The Dietz Press, Richmond, VA, 1938. p. 669.
Roberts, Hezekiah, 2 Va. State Reg.

Virginia Soldiers of 1776; Compiled from Documents on File in the Virginia Land Office, Together with Material found in the Archives Department of the Virginia State Library , and Other Reliable Sources, 3 volumes; Compiled and Edited by Louis A. Burgess, Genealogical Publishing Co., Inc., Baltimore, MD, 1973. p.1265.

Non Commissioned Officers and Soldiers in Capt. Henry Garnett's Company, who ackn'd having received full pay to the 1st June, 1778.
#Hezekiah Roberts

Revolutionary War Records – Virginia; Virginia Army and Navy Forces with Bounty Land Warrants for Virginia Military District of Ohio, and Virginia Military Script, from Federal and State Archives; by Gaius Marcus Brumbaugh, M.D, M.s., Litt.D; Genealogical Publishing Co., Inc., Baltimore, 1995.p.210.
List of non-commissioned officers and soldiers of the Continental Line. List may contain names of individuals who received bounty land for services in the State Line.
Roberts, Hezekiah, Soldier, Inf.

Virginia Revolutionary Publick Claims in three volumes; compiled and transcribed b Janice L. Abercrombie and Richard Slatten; Iberian Publishing Co., Athens, GA, 1992. p. 744.
Orange County – Orange County Court Booklet – At a court held by the justices of Orange County court at the courthouse on [various dates] 1782 for adjusting the claims made to the said court agreeable to an act "For adjusting claims for property impressed or taken for public service" The following claims were allowed to be just and reasonable.
Pg. 21 – Hezekiah Roberts for 2 horses for 3rd R.L. Dragoons cert. by Benja. Garnett Cornet appraised by Andrew Shepherd and James Slone £90.

Second Census of Kentucky, 1800; Clift G. Glenn; Genealogical Publishing Co., Baltimore, MD, 1954.
An alphabetical list of 32,000 taxpayers based on original tax lists on file at the Kentucky Historical Society. Information given includes the county of residence and the date of the tax list in which the individual is listed.
Roberts, Hezekiah   Bourbon 1800

Revolutionary Soldiers of Switzerland County; Copied by Mary Hill, John Paul Chapter-Daughters of the American Revolution; January, 1958;
http://www.ingenweb.org/inswitzerland/switzrevsoldiers.html- Viewed June 2012.
ROBERTS, HEZEKIAH   Switzerland Co. Indiana
Born about 1761
Enlisted 3/1/1777, Va. Continental Line; Capt. William Fields.
Married 1783 Agnes Robinson (b. abt. 1771, d 21845/1848), in Culpeper Co., Louden Co., or Hanover Co. VA
Children: one dead, William b 1783, m 1810 Hamilton Co. Ohio Patsey Shepherd, John, Rebecca m Abisha McKay, Neely, Moses, Betsy, James, Andrew.
Hezekiah d 5/20/1852, Switz. Co., IN leaving 1 child Moses Perry Roberts Pension application 6/8/1821; age 60 yrs. Switz. Co. Ind. wife, Agnes. age 50 yrs.; children; Rebecca, age 16; Hezekiah, 13; Moses 12.
Affid. 11/4/1819 Dearborn Co. Ind. (Rev. soldier in Supplement of Margaret Waters) that he saw soldier in service.

Affid. 8/19/1819 Nicholas Co. Ky. of Nehemiah Roberts, brother of soldier, that soldier was in service.
Affid. 6/29/1852 Switz. Co. Ind. of William Roberts, age 66, and John Roberts, age 64 that mother died in 1848, age about 74 yrs. m in one of three Virginia Counties; that father lived in Culpeper Co. Va. and mother in Hanover Co. Va. that William the oldest child, except the one who died in infancy. That uncle Nehemiah had a Rev. Pension.
Two affid. that widow died in 1845. Soldier & family lived in or around Fayette Co. Ky. 1790 and Nicholas Co. Ky. 1810.
Affid. 7/18/1853, Nicholas Co. Ky of Henly Roberts (relationship not given) that he knew soldier and family from 1790 in Woodford Co. Ky. and moved to Bourbon Co. Ky.
Died 2/23/1826
Ref. Pension W.9631 VA 1831 Rej. Pension List, pg. 48-- "served in a regiment on continental establishment".

1820 U.S. Census, Indiana, Switzerland, Craig, Series: M33 Roll: 14 Page: 248
Hezekiah Roberts 45 and up; others in household 2 males 10-16, 1 male 16-18, 1 male 16-26, 1 female under 10, 1 female 16-26, 1 female 45 and up.

Roster of Soldiers and Patriots of the American Revolution Buried in Indiana, Vol. II; 1966; p.87-88.
ROBERTS, HEZEKIAH   Switzerland County
Born – Ca. 1761.
Service m- Enl. March 1, 1777, Vir. Cont. Line; Capt. William Fields.
Proof – Pens. W. 9631, Vir. Pens. Appl. 1821, age 60, Switzerland Co.
Died – Feb. 23, 1826.
Married – 1783, Agnes Robinson, 1761-1845. Ch. William, b. 1810, Patsy Shepherd; John; Rebecca, m. Abisha McKay; Neely; Moses; Betsey; James; Andrew; Hezekaih.
From Waters' Sup., pp. 85 and 86.

Revolutionary Soldiers Buried in Indiana A Supplement; 485 Names Not Listed in the Roster of Soldiers and Patriots of the American Revolution Buried in Indiana (1938) nor in Revolutionary Soldiers Buried in Indiana (1949); Margaret E. Waters; Indianapolis, 1954. p.85-86.
ROBERTS, HEZEKIAH   Switzerland
b. ca. 1761; d. 2-23-1826;
m. 1783, Culpeper Co., Va. (or Hanover Co., Va.; or Loudon Co., Va.), Agnes Robinson, b. ca. 1771; d. 9-23-1845 (2 affids.; 1848 in 1 affid.); chn: one dec'd; William b. 1788, m. 1810, Hamilton Co., O., Patsey Shepherd; John; Rebecca, m. Abisha McKay; Neely; Moses; Betsy; James; Andres; Hezekiah d. 5-20-1852, Switzerland Co., Ind.; leaving 1 ch., Moses Perry Roberts. Pens appl. 6-8-1821, ae. 60, Switzerland Co., Ind.; wife Agnes 50; chn: Rebecca 16, Hezekiah 13, Moses 12. Affid. 11-4-1819, Dearborn Co., Ind, of Francis Cheek (Rev. sold. in this Suppl.); that he saw sold. in service. Affid. 8-19-1819, Nicholas Co., Ky. Of Nehemiah Roberts, bro. of sold.; that sold. was in service. Affid. 6-29-1852, Switzerland Co., Ind. of William Roberts, ae 66, & John Roberts, ae 64; that

mother d. 1848, ae. ca. 74, m. in one of the 3 Va. Cos. given above; that father liv. Culpeper Co., Va. & mother in Hanover Co., Va; that William the oldest ch. except one that d. in infancy; that uncle Nehemiah Roberts had a Rev. pens. Two affids. that wid. d. 1845. Sold. & fam. Liv. In or around Fayette Co., Ky, 1790, & Nicholas Co., KY, 1810. Affid. 7-18-1853, Nicholas Co., Ky, of Henly Roberts (rel. not given); that he knew sold. & fam. From 1790 in Woodford Co., Ky, & mov. to Bourbon Co, KY. Service: enl. 3-1-1777, Va. Cont.. Line; Capt. William Fields. REF: Pens. W.9631 Va.; 1831 Rej. Pens. List, p. 49—"served in a regiment not on continental establishment".

History of Switzerland County Indiana 1885; Reproduced by the Switzerland County Historical Society, Vevay, Indiana, 1999. The portion of the book relating to Switzerland County in the 1885 printing of the "History of Dearborn, Ohio, and Switzerland Counties, Indiana". p. 1038.
"A squirrel hunt took place in Craig Township March 17 and 18, 1824, and on the 19th they met at Johnson Brown's, on Long Run, to count the game with the following result:"
Included on this list is Hesekiah Roberts with a count of 59.

ROBERT, JOHN
aka ROBERTS

Patriot: John Roberts
Birth: March of 1753 Morris Co., NJ
Married Spouse 1: 18 Mar 1814, Williamsburg, Clermont Co., OH
                Mary Roberts (b. abt. 1762, d. 13 Mar 1838, Switzerland Co., IN)
Service state(s): NJ
Service description: Capt. Seeley, NJ Militia
Rank: Private, Sergeant, Lieutenant
Proof of Service: Pension application S16239
Pension application No.: S16239
Residences: Morris Co., NJ, KY, abt. 1809 to Switzerland Co., IN
Died: 6 Aug 1837 Craig Twp., Switzerland Co.., IN
Buried: poss. Ebenezer Cemetery, Craig Twp., Switzerland Co., IN
             (wife buried here)
DAR Ancestor No.: None

Pension Application Abstracted from National Archives microfilm Series 805, Roll 694, File S16239.;Switzerland County, Indiana Probate Record Book Vol. A, Mar 1827-Nov 1834; p. 262.
Pension abstract for – John Roberts   Service state(s): New Jersey
Date: 16 August 1832
County of: Switzerland   State of: Indiana
Declaration made before the Probate Court.
Recorded in Book A, pg. 262
Age: 79 years   Record of age: No record
Where and year born: Morris Co., NJ in March of 1753
Residence when he entered service: Morris Co., NJ
Residence(s) since the war: In New Jersey, about 15 years in Kentucky, about 13 years in Indiana.
Residence now: Switzerland Co., IN
Volunteer or Drafted or Substitute: Drafted and volunteered
Rank(s): Sergeant, Lieutenant
Statement of service-

Period	Duration	Rank	Names of General and Field Officers
1776	1 month	Sgt.	Company commanded by Capt. Seeley of the New Jersey Militia.
1776	5 months	Sgt.	Company commanded by same captain.
1777/78	2 months	Lieut.	Under ?
1777/78	1 month	Lieut.	Under Capt. Lindley in a Militia company raised in Morris Co., NJ.
1778	3 months	Lieut.	I commanded a company of Morris Co. Militia under Capt. Brown
1778	3 months	Lieut.	Under Capt. Seeley's regiment
1779/80	1 month		Commander for a company

Battles: Long Island, retreat to New York, White Plains
No data regarding soldier's family

Soldier died: 6 August 1837. Place not shown.

Switzerland County, Indiana Probate Order Book 2, 1831-1837;p. 78.
In the matter of John Roberts by Dictation}
in order to obtain the Benefits of the act }
of Congress passed June 7th 1832. } On the 17th day of August 1833 personally appeared in open Court before the Probate Court now sitting, John Roberts a resident of the County of Switzerland and State of Indiana aged Seventy Nine years, who being first duly Sworn according to law, doth on his oath, make the following declaration in order to obtain the benefit of the act of Congress passed June 7, 1832. That he entered the Service of the United States under the following named officers and Served as herein Stated (here insert it), And the Said Court do hereby declare their opinion after the investigation of the matter, and after putting the interrogation prescribed by the war department that the above named applicant was a Revolutionary Soldier as he States, And the Court further Certifies, that it appears to them that John Pavy who has signed the preceding Certificate is a Clergyman resident in the County of Switzerland and State of Indiana aforesaid, and that Stephen Rogers who has also Signed the Same is a resident in the State & County aforesaid and is a credible person and that their Statement is entitled to Credit.

Switzerland County, Indiana Probate Order Book 3, 1837-1843; p. 59.
15 February 1838
In the matter of the Proof of the Death }
of John Roberts a resident of Switzerland } Lieutenant John Roberts
a Revolutionary Pensioner }
Now this day Comes Mary Roberts and produce to the Court, satisfactory testimony, that She is the widow of John Roberts late a revolutionary pensioner under the act of Congress of June 7th 1832, that Said John Roberts died in Craig township Switzerland County on the 6th day of August 1837, that the Said John Roberts and Mary Roberts was married in Williamsburg [Clermont County] in the State of Ohio on the 18th day of March 1814, witness was present, that his pension Certificate is dated Nov. 24, 1832 and No. 2357 & Signed by Lewis Cass Secretary of War---

Switzerland County, Indiana Probate Order Book 3, 1837-1843; pp. 5, 9, 59, 61, 78, 140, 158, 166, 169.
Abstract of will and/or administration for: John Roberts
Who died intestate leaving goods and chattels that will go to waste if they are not taken care of.
John Protsman, Jr. The guardian of Mary Roberts, the incapacitated widow, a lunatic.
State & county where recorded: Switzerland Co., Indiana
Book/volume where recorded: Probate Order Book 3, 1837-1843.
Date entered in probate: 15 August 1837
Administration:
Date began – 15 August 1837
Name of administrator – John F. Cotton

Date of death: 6 August 1837
Place of death: Craig Township, Switzerland County, Indiana
Bonded by and amount of bond: James M. Cotton for $500.00
Names of heirs and others mentioned in will (also signed receipts of division of estate) and relationship if shown: Mary Roberts, widow, Morris A. Roberts, Anna Roberts, Cornelius Bidwell and Eleanor his wife, George Stewart and Sally his wife, Daniel Stewart and Polly his wife from the county of White in the State of Illinois.
Date of division & disbursement, or final return: 14 May 1839

Abstract of Final Payment Voucher; General Services Administration, Washington, DC
FINAL PAYMENT VOUCHER RECEIVED FROM
THE GENERAL ACCOUNTING OFFICE
NAME   Roberts, John
AGENCY OF PAYMENT   Indiana
DATE OF ACT   1832
DATE OF PAYMENT   4th Qr. 1838
DATE OF DEATH   Aug 6, 1837
GENERAL SERVICES ADMINISTRATION
National Archives and Records Service   NA-286
GSA-WASH DC 54-4891   November 1953

Official Register of the Officers and Men of New Jersey in the Revolutionary War; Compiled Under Orders of His Excellency Theodore F. Randolph, Governor; by William S. Stryker, Adjutant General, Printed by the Authority of the Legislature; Wm. T. Nicholson & Co., Printers, Trenton, NJ, 1872, Facsimile Reprint by Heritage Books, Inc., Bowie, MD, 1993;
p.274.
Private - Roberts, John.
p. 275.
Private – Roberts, John. First Regiment.

Register of Certificates Issued by John Pierce, Esquire, Paymaster General and Commissioner of Army Accounts for the United States, to Officers and Soldiers of the Continental Army Under Act of July 4, 1783; Originally Published as Senate Documents, Vol.9, No. 988, 63rd Congress, 3d Session, Washington, 1915; Seventeenth report of the National Society of the Daughters of the American Revolution; Genealogical Publishing Co., Inc, Baltimore, MD, 1984. p. 431.
Men listed in this volume with the name John Roberts.
Author's note: Due to the large number of men with this name they are not listed here. "Pierce's Register" is available in most large libraries.

Revolutionary Soldiers in Kentucky, containing a roll of the officers of Virginia line who received land bounties, a roll of the Revolutionary pensioners in Kentucky, a list of the Illinois regiment who served under George Rogers Clark in the Northwest campaign, also a roster of the Virginia Navy. Reproduction of the original which appeared in Sons of the American Revolution Kentucky

Society Year Book, Louisville, 1896.; Anderson Chenault Quisenberry; Southern Book Co., Baltimore, MD, 1959. p. 86.
List of Bounty Receipts - Non-Commissioned Officers and Privates
John Roberts is in this listing

Second Census of Kentucky, 1800; Clift G. Glenn; Genealogical Publishing Co., Baltimore, MD, 1954.
An alphabetical list of 32,000 taxpayers based on original tax lists on file at the Kentucky Historical Society. Information given includes the county of residence and the date of the tax list in which the individual is listed.
There are four entries for John Roberts – it has not been determined which are for this man.

Roberts, John	Logan	1800
Roberts, John	Madison	8/12/1800
Roberts, John	Montgomery	8/22/1800
Roberts, John	Montgomery	8/22/1800

Indiana Territory, Switzerland Circuit Court Records, Order Book, October Term 1814 to March Term 1815. p.52.
He is listed in county records for the first time on 17 June 1819, as a juror.
Author's note: There are entries in this volume that are not within the range of dates shown on the binder cover.

1820 U.S. Census, Indiana, Switzerland, Posey, Series: M33 Roll: 14 Page: 262
John Roberts 45 and up; others in household 1 male 10-16, 1 female 16-26, 1 female 45 and up.

Revolutionary Soldiers of Switzerland County; Copied by Mary Hill, John Paul Chapter-Daughters of the American Revolution; January, 1958; http://www.ingenweb.org/inswitzerland/switzrevsoldiers.html- Viewed June 2012.
ROBERTS, LT. JOHN   Pension record S.16239
Born March, 1753 in Morris Co., NJ
While residing there, he enlisted in the New Jersey troops in 1776, eight months as sergeant in Captain Seeley's company, Colonel Martin's Regiment. Service being in three tours, five months and two months, during the 2d tour he was in the battle of Long Island, in the retreat to New York, and the battle of White Plains; in 1777 he was commissioned Lieutenant, his commission signed by the Governor of New Jersey. He served two months as such officer, one month stationed at Haddonfield, name of Captain not shown; one month under Captain Lindsley, during which tour he marched to New Windsor on the North River; in 1778 or 79 he served three months as Lieut. one month in command of Morris Co. New Jersey troops; one month under Captain Brown and one month under Colonel Seeley. In 1780 he served as Lieut. in command of a company stationed at Newark, time not given; another tour in command of company under Col. Seeley, on an alarm to protect the town of Springfield; length of this tour not shown.
After the Revolution he resided in Kentucky for about 15 years, then moved to Indiana.

Married Mary _____, 1814 Switzerland Co.
He was allowed pension on his application executed August 17, 1832, while residing in Switzerland County, Indiana. Pension certificate No.2557, date Nov. 24, 1832.
Lt. John Roberts died Switzerland County, Indiana August 6, 1837
Switzerland Co. Probate Court; Term February, 1838, pg. 39
In the matter of proof the death of John Roberts, Revolutionary Soldier, a Sergeant and Lieutenant, comes Mary Roberts, and produces the court satisfactory testimony that she is the widow of John Roberts, late Rev. War pensioner, under Act of Congress, Jan. 7, 1832. John Roberts died Craig twp. Aug. 6, 1837. John & Mary were married at Williamsburg, Ohio, March 18, 1814. Witness present.
Feb. term 1838
Mary Roberts, widow of John Roberts, a lunatic, incapable of managing property. John Protzman, Jr. appointed guardian.

Roster of Soldiers and Patriots of the American Revolution Buried in Indiana, Vol. I; compiled by Mrs. Roscoe C. O'Byrne.; Indiana Daughters of the American Revolution, 1981; p.315.
ROBERT, JOHN   Switzerland County
Born – March, 1753, Morris Co., New Jersey.
Service – Volunteered New Jersey Troops 1776-8, 8 mos. as Sergt. Under Capt. Seeley, Col. Martin's Regt. In battle of Long Island and White Plains, 1777, commissioned Lieut. Stationed at Haddonfield, 3 mos.
Proof – Pension claim S. 16239.
Died – Aug. 6, 1837. Buried Craig Twp.
Married – 1814, Mary _____.
Collected by Mrs. A. V. Danner, Vevay, Indiana.

Switzerland County Indiana Cemetery Inscriptions 1817-1985; Wanda L. Morford; Cincinnati, Ohio, 1986, p.60.
Ebenezer Cemetery, Craig Twp., Switzerland Co., IN
Roberts   Mary   d. Mar. 13, 1838   aged 76y

The Vevay Reveille Enterprise; Vol. 122. No. 39, 28 Sep 1935, p.3, col.2-3.
Roster of Revolutionary Soldiers Who Resided in Switzerland County
By Mrs. Effa M. Danner
John Roberts, Serg. And Lieut. – Died in Switzerland County, Ind. August 6, 1837.
The data which follows were obtained from the papers on file in Revolutionary War pension claim S16239, based upon the military service in that war of John Roberts.
John Roberts was born in March, 1758, in Morris County, New Jersey. The names of his parents are not shown.
While residing in said Morris County, John Roberts volunteered and served with the New Jersey troops, as follows: in 1776, eight months as sergeant in Captain Seeley's Company, Colonial Martin's Regiment, the service being in three tours of one month, five months and two months respectively; during the second tour

he was in the battle on Long Island, in the retreat to New York and the Battle of White Plains; in 1777 he was commissioned lieutenant, his commission signed by the Governor of New Jersey, and served two months as such officer, one month being stationed at Haddonfield, name of captain not shown; and one month under Captain Lindsley, during which tour he marched to New Windsor, on the North River; in 1778, or 1779, he served three months as lieutenant, one month in command of a company of Morris County, New Jersey troops, one month under Captain Brown and one month under Colonel Seeley; in 1780, he served as lieutenant in command of a company and was stationed at Newark, length of this tour not given, and another tour in command of a company under Colonel Seeley on an alarm to protect the town of Springfield, length of this tour not shown.
After the Revolution, he resided in Kentucky for about fifteen years, then moved to Indiana.
John Roberts was allowed pension on his application executed August 17, 1832, while residing in Switzerland County, Ind.
He died August 6, 1837, place not shown.
There are no data as to soldier's family.
In order to obtain the date of last payment of pension, and the name and address of the person paid in the case of the Revolutionary War pensioner, John Roberts (S16239) you should address The Comptroller General Account Office, Records Division, Washington, and cite the following data: John Roberts, Certificate No. 2357, issued Nov. 24, 1832. Rate, $160 per annum. Commenced March 4, 1831. Act of June 7, 1832, Indiana Agency.
Probate court, May 1839, pages 195-6-7, List of estates – John Roberts, Rev. Soldier died at the home of John Protsman Jr., near Moorefield.
Switzerland County Probate Court, Feb., 1838, p. 59. Mary Roberts, widow married at Williamsburg, Ohio, March 18, 1814. John Protsman Jr. appointed guardian.

ROBERTS, JOHN

Patriot: John Roberts
Birth: 1763 Culpepper Co., VA
Married Spouse 1: 22 Jun 1789 Culpepper Co., VA   Sarah (aka SallyHawley
(Halley or Holley)
(b 1760-69,Culpepper Co., VA   d. aft. Nov. 1839)
Service state(s): VA
Service description: Capt. Todd, VA State Troops
Rank: Private, Lieutenant
Proof of Service: Pension application R8877
Pension application No.: R8877
Residences: Culpepper Co., VA; KY.
Died: Jun 1819   Shelby Co., KY (Widow to Switzerland Co., IN)
Buried: Unknown, Shelby Co., KY
DAR Ancestor No.: None

Virginia Marriages, Fauquier County, No. 264, 446.
22 Jun 1789, John Roberts to Sarah Holly or Holley.

Author's note: He was commissioned Lieutenant in Capt. Todd's Co., Virginia State Troops. He later entered the Illinois Regiment, Virginia State Troops, commanded by Col. Geo. Rogers Clarke, in the spring of 1780 in Kentucky. He served in the Ill. Regt. until spring of 1781 when the Regt. disbanded.
He died June 1819 in Shelby Co.,,, KY.
His widow, Sarah (Hawley) Roberts made application for widow's pension in 1838. Abstract follows.

Pension Application Abstracted from National Archives microfilm Series M805, Roll 694, File R8877.
The deposition of Henry R. Roberts taken at his own house in the County of Putnam and State of Indiana to be used on behalf of Sarah Roberts who is making application for a pension – this 28th day of November 1839.
This deponent being duly Sworn States that he is now 74 years of age and upwards that he is the brother of John Roberts deceased who was the husband of said Sarah Roberts – that his said brother according to the family Register was born in Culpeper County Virginia in 1763. He further states that his said Brother married Sarah Halley more than fifty years ago – that the marriage took place at the house of George Johnston in Culpeper County Va. and this deponent was present and witnessed the ceremony. He cannot recollect the year or month of said marriage not having kept a record of it but he knows that is was more than fifty years ago from a variety of circumstances within his distinct recollection. The rites were solemnized as well as he remembers by a preacher named Pickett. This deponent further states that the said marriage of his said brother John did not take place till after the revolutionary war and that during said war his said Brother served as a soldier. I recollect distinctly of two tours of duty which he performed. I cannot say whether he was drafted in the first tour but from what I have understood believe that he was in the second tour.

I know he was a volunteer in Second tour and served three months as well as I remember. I have understood from him & others that in this last mentioned tour he served under Col. Maj Boyd and that he was at the taking of Cornwallis. In the second mentioned tour I think he was absent in the service six months or more. This deponent further says that his said Brother was out in the service on other occasions as a drafted man but how long at a time and how often he cannot say for his memory does not serve him with certainty and he does not want to state any thing which he does not certainly recollect. He is confident of his having served the six months mentioned

above in the two first tours spoken of and he may have served as much (sentence stricken out).

He further states that his said Brother died 18 or 19 years ago and that his widow the said Sarah (whom we sometimes called Sally) still living and lives in Switzerland county Indiana and has not married since his death.

Henry R. Roberts

Sworn to and subscribed the day and year aforesaid.
State of Indiana
Putnam County
&
Switzerland County
State of Indiana

Be it known that on this 28 day of March 1839 personally appeared before Newton H. Tupp one of the Judges of the Court of Common pleas in and for said county Sarah Roberts a resident of said county aged [illegible] years and upwards who being first duly sworn according to law made the following declaration in order to obtain the benefit of the act of Congress passed in 1838 allowing under certain circumstances a five years pension to the widows of Revolutionary soldiers.

This declarent states that she is a resident of said county and is now seventy [illegible] years of age & upwards, that her maiden name was Sarah Hawley, that she lived in Culpeper County Va. and was legally and duly married to John Roberts in 1788, that she does not now know what month or that year the marriage took place in and she has no record of it or memorandum in relation to it. She states that she has often understood from her husband the said John Roberts and from others that he served the United States faithfully in the war of the Revolution and that he was out in the service at one time as a common soldier 18 months, and that he served at other times but she cannot state the particular tour, nor the length of time were from information, nor does she remember the names of the officers under whom he served. She states that her memory has greatly failed her from old age and disease And that her said husband died about 18 years ago, so that lapse of time combined with the other above named circumstances she cannot remember the particulars of his statements, but she is well assured that he served his country faithfully and valiantly.

She will have to rely upon the proof which she will forward to procure in relation to his tours of service in the Revolution & the length thereof. She states she has not married since his death. She states that she is unable from bodily infirmly arising from old age and general disability to attend the proper court to make her declaration.

Sworn to & subscribed this twenty eight day of March 1839.

Tunafer X Roberts [?name?]
his mark

Document – (appears that the previous page is missing)

___ Acquainted with Reuben Redding who was sworn in and subscribed his name to the foregoing affidavit and I know him to be a man of truth and veracity: Given under my hand as a justice of the peace for the county the 21st day of Oct. 1839.
                  Henry Bohannon

Also the affidavit of Elizabeth Redding taken for the same purpose as the preceding, the deponent being duly sworn deposeth and saith: that she is the sister of John Roberts spoken of in the preceding affidavit, that he was married to Sarah Holly in Culpeper County Virginia about fifty years ago & perhaps a little over. She says she was present and saw the marriage take place. She also states that he served two tours against the British, one of six months, and another of three months. But she cannot say to what part of the county he marched, nor can she remember the names of any of the officers under whom he served, but one thing she distinctly recollects, that on his return home he brought with him a leather halter and a pair of striped pantaloons, which he said he took in a skirmish with the British. She states further that previous to his entering the service he lived in Culpeper County Virginia, and there he returned after the service was rendered. She says he has been well acquainted with the said Sarah Roberts ever since her youth, that she has remained a widow ever since the death of her husband the said John Roberts, that she now lives in Switzerland County Indiana, and further she saith not.

                her
            Elizabeth X Redding
                mark

State of Kentucky
Shelby County

  I Certify, that Elizabeth Redding came personally before me on this 21st day of Oct. 1839 and Subscribed and was sworn to the above affidavit. And I further certify that she is a woman of truth and good character.

Given under my hand as a justice of the peace for said County the day & date aforesaid.
                  Henry Bohannon

<u>Virginia Soldiers of 1776</u>; *Compiled from Documents on File in the Virginia Land Office, Together with Material found in the Archives Department of the Virginia State Library , and Other Reliable Sources, 3 volumes; Compiled and Edited by Louis A. Burgess, Genealogical Publishing Co., Inc., Baltimore, MD, 1973.*

p. 1244.
The following officers of Illinois Regt. had not rec'd land.
1834:
Roberts, John. Lieut. for the war

p. 1249
Raised in Bedford Co. Served under Gen. Andrew Lewis the Battle of Point Pleasant, 10 Oct. 1774.
Privates

John Roberts (listed with others)
p. 1430.
JOHN ROBERTS. Coun. Cham., 18 Nov., 1831. Allowed land for three years service as a Major in Cont'l line. John Floyd Gov. John Roberts appointed John S. Pendleton as Atty. Wt. 7112 issued to him 7 Dec., 1831.

Historical Register of Virginians in the Revolution, Soldiers, Sailors, Marines, 1775-1783; John H. Gwathmey; The Dietz Press, Richmond, VA, 1938. p. 669.
Roberts, John, Lieut. Clark's Ill. Reg. 1779-82. Mss. WD half pay claim states he was commissioned Lieut. in Capt. Todd's Co., and served in Kentucky in the Spring of 1780; settled first in Montgomery Co., KY., then in Shelby Co.,; died June, 1819; heirs given.

Virginia Revolutionary Publick Claims in three volumes; compiled and transcribed b Janice L. Abercrombie and Richard Slatten; Iberian Publishing Co., Athens, GA, 1992. p. 281.
Culpeper County – Culpeper County Court Booklet I – At a court held for Culpeper County 19 Aug. 1782 the Court proceeded to adjust claims for property impressed or taken for public service and made the following valuations.
Pg. 9 – John Roberts Dec. 1781 for 312# beef.

Catalogue of Revolutionary Soldiers and Sailors of the Commonwealth of Virginia to Whom Land Bounty Warrants Were Granted by Virginia for Military Service in the War for Independence, From Official Records in the Kentucky State Land Office at Frankfort, Kentucky; compiled by Samuel M. Wilson; Southern Book Company, Baltimore, MD, 1953. p. 64.

Number of Warrant	Name of Officer or Soldier	Number of Acres	Dept. of Service: Continental or State Line or Navy	Number of Years in Service	Date of Warrant
3151	Roberts, John	100	Pvt. VA State Line	3 years	Jun 11, 1784

Revolutionary War Records – Virginia; Virginia Army and Navy Forces with Bounty Land Warrants for Virginia Military District of Ohio, and Virginia Military Script, from Federal and State Archives; by Gaius Marcus Brumbaugh, M.D, M.s., Litt.D; Genealogical Publishing Co., Inc., Baltimore, 1995.
p. 113
List of Officers of the Army and Navy, Who Have Received Lands From Virginia for Revolutionary Services; the Quantity Received, the Time of Service for which each Officer Received Land, &c. Down to September, 1833.
Roberts, John   Major   Cont'l   5333-1/3   Dec. 7, 1831   3 years
p. 137
List of Officers of the Virginia Continental and State Lines and State navy, Whose Names Appear on the Army Register, and Who Have Not Received Land for Revolutionary Services, or Not in the Characters in Which They There Appear. They who are entitled to Land are distinguished from those whose claims to Bounty land are Not Satisfactorily Proved by Documents on file in the Public Offices of Virginia.

No.	Names	Rank	Line	Remarks
223.	Roberts, John	Lieutenant	State	Received land as major in the Continental Line for a service of three years.

p. 151
Army and Navy Bounty Land Warrants, Revolutionary War, Governor John Floyd's List of Officers [Part of List No. 1, p. 85]
Roberts, John, Lieut., Ill.

p. 165
List of Officers of the Illinois Regiment, who Have Not Received Lands for revolutionary Services.

Names	Rank	Remarks
10. Roberts, John	Lieutenant	Entitled to land for the war

p. 369
Virginia Military Land Warrants, Virginia Military District of Ohio, Granted for Revolutionary War Services, State and Navy, Beginning February 14, 1782.

Number	Warrantee	Person Who Performed the Service	Kind of Service
1591	Roberts, John	Roberts, John	State Line

p. 370

| 3151 | Roberts, John | Roberts, John | State Line |

p. 535
Roberts, John, Lieut. Va. State Troops, Ill. Regt.; Capt. Robt. Todd's Co. of Foot. (no. 8,706, Pension Office, Apr. 1852) Mentioned: Col. (later Gen.) Geo. R. Clarke, Pay roll Robt. Todd's Co.; Capt. Benj. Roberts, Capt. Abraham Chaplin, Lieut. Anthony Crockett, Lieut. John Roberts, Ens. Wm. Roberts, et al., of Ill. Regt.; Gen. G. R. Clarke. Entire pay roll of Capt. Robert Todd's Co., Lt. Col. Montgomery; also Stephen Chilton, "soldier," Col. Joseph Crockett's Regt.; Bland W. Ballard, Wm. Fleming, John Edwards, Thos. Quick, Maj. Inf. James Meriweather, Light Inf.; Mark Thomas, Capt. of Inf.; Lieut. Joseph Slaughter, Lieut. James Slaughter, Lieut. Wm. Clarke, Lieut. James Whitecotton, Henry Foster, "soldier."

p. 562
Roberts, John (A.G. 50,142), Lieut. Ill. Regt. Va. State Troops. He was comm.. Lieut. in Capt. Todd's Co. and later entered the Ill. Regt. in the spring of 1780 in Ky. He served to Dec. 31, 1781 when the Regt. disbanded. After the war he settled in Montgomery Co., Ky., then went to Shelby Co., same State and d June, 1819. In 1835 his heirs were Augustus Roberts, Elizabeth Gregory, John Roberts, Willis Roberts and Sally McMakin, wife of Charles McMakin. In 1842 his two daughters, Mrs. Gregory and Mrs. McMakin were living in Shelby Co., Ky. His wife was Sarah Roberts. Several affidavits were made.

p. 587

Statements of Third Auditor's Office, Revolutionary War Commutation of Interest N.D.). Statement of all payments made, under Act of July 5, 1832 "for liquidating and paying certain claims of the State of Va.," since Mar. 1, 1849.

Names of Claimants	Rank in Va. State Troops and Navy	In Commutation of Half Pay 5 yrs. Full Pay
Roberts, John	Lieut. Troops	5,986.63

A List of Officers of the Illinois Regiment, and of Crockett's Regiment, Who have received Land for their Services – A List of Officers of The Illinois Regiment Who have not received lands for Revolutionary Services – A List of Non-Commissioned Officers and Soldiers of the Illinois Regiment, and the Western Army, Under the Command of General George Rogers Clarke, who are entitled to Bounty in Land – A List of Captain Francis Charloville's Volunteers, Entitled to two hundred Acres of Land each; John H. Smith; Borderland Books, Anchorage, KY, 1962. p. 11.
A List of Officers of the Illinois Regiment and of Crockett's Regiment, Who have received Land for their Services.
Illinois Regiment

No.	Name	Rank	Remarks
10	Roberts, John	Lieutenant	Entitled to land for the war.

Register of Certificates Issued by John Pierce, Esquire, Paymaster General and Commissioner of Army Accounts for the United States, to Officers and Soldiers of the Continental Army Under Act of July 4, 1783; Originally Published as Senate Documents, Vol.9, No. 988, 63rd Congress, 3d Session, Washington, 1915; Seventeenth report of the National Society of the Daughters of the American Revolution; Genealogical Publishing Co., Inc, Baltimore, MD, 1984. p. 431.
Men listed in this volume with the name John Roberts.
Author's note: Due to the large number of men with this name they are not listed here. "Pierce's Register" is available in most large libraries.

Second Census of Kentucky, 1800; Clift G. Glenn; Genealogical Publishing Co., Baltimore, MD, 1954.
An alphabetical list of 32,000 taxpayers based on original tax lists on file at the Kentucky Historical Society. Information given includes the county of residence and the date of the tax list in which the individual is listed.
Roberts, John   Shelby   8/7/1800

The Pension List of 1820 [U.S. War Department]Reprinted with an Index; by Murtie June Clark; Genealogical Publishing Co., Inc., Baltimore, 1991. Originally published 1820 as Letter from the Secretary of War. p. 614
Names of the Revolutionary Pensioners which have been placed on the Roll of Kentucky, under the Law of the 18th of March, 1818, from the passage thereof, to this day, inclusive, with the Rank they held, and the Lines in which they served, viz.

Names	Rank	Line
John Roberts	Surgeon	Virginia

Pensioners of the Revolutionary War Struck Off the Roll with an Added Index to States; Reprinted by Genealogical Publishing Co., Baltimore, MD for Clearfield Company, Inc., 1989. p. 94.
Pensioners in Kentucky who have been dropped under the act of 1st May, 1820; prepared in conformity with a resolution of the House of Representatives of the United States of the 17th December, 1835.

Names	Acts under which restored	Remarks
John Roberts	March 1, 1823	

Revolutionary War Bounty Land Grants Awarded by State Governments; Lloyd DeWitt Bockstruck; Genealogical Publishing co., IN, Baltimore, MD, 1996. p. 449.
He may have received one or all of these Bounty Land Grants –
Roberts, John. Va. Private. 20 Aug 1783. 100 acres.
Roberts, John. Va. Private. 11 Jun 1784. 100 acres.

Revolutionary Soldiers Buried in Indiana (1949) With Supplement (1954) Two Volumes in One; Margaret R. Waters; Genealogical Publishing Company, Baltimore, MD, 1970. p.137, 140, 141.
ROBERTS, JOHN & SARAH (HAWLEY)   Switzerland
He d. ca. 1820, Henry Co., Ky. Susp. Pens. List,   or Putnam
(1852) p. 419, gives her of Putnam Co., Ind.; so she may have mov. there later. Pens. R.8877 Va.
(Not [same man as on] "Roster", p. 315)
Comment by Marlene McDerment - this is not correct. Sarah Roberts was living in Switzerland Co., Ind. The brother of John Roberts, Henry Roberts, was living in Putnam Co., Ind. and Sarah's sister, Elizabeth Redding was living in Shelby Co., KY.
p. 140 – In list of spouses buried in Indiana for Switzerland Co. – Roberts, Sarah- w. John.
p. 141 – In list of "Soldiers Who Died in Other States" (husbands of widows on list of spouses) – Kentucky – Roberts, John.

Rejected or Suspended Applications for Revolutionary War Pensions; Reprinted for Clearfield Company Inc. by Genealogical Publishing Co., Inc., Baltimore, MD, 1998, p. 409.
A list of the names of persons residing in Indiana who have applied for pensions under the act of July 7, 1838, whose claims have been suspended; prepared in conformity with the resolution of the Senate of the United States of September 16, 1850.

Names	Residence	Reasons for rejection
ROBERTS, SARAH widow of John	Greencastle, Putnam	For proof and specification of service.

Possible citation for this man -
American Militia in the Frontier Wars, 1790-1796; by Murtie June Clark; Genealogical Publishing Co., Inc., 1990. p.56.
Kentucky Militia

Pay Roll of a Company of Mounted Volunteers, Commanded by Captain John Franciscoe, major William Price's Battalion, Called into the Services by the President of the United States in 1794.

Nr	Rank	Name	Remarks
62	Private	Roberts, John	Transf to Baker's spies

ROBINSON, WINTHROP

Patriot: Winthrop Robinson
Birth: 22 Apr 1761 Stratham, Rockingham Co., NH
Married Spouse 1: 11 Sep 1784 Westborough, Westchester Co., MA
                         Beulah Rice
                         (b. 1763 Worchester, MA d. 13 Jul 1844
                         Cotton Twp., Switzerland Co., IN)
Service state(s): NH
Service description: Capts. Parsons, Worthen, Gordon,
Rank: Drummer, Private, Orderly Sergeant, Lieutenant, Privateer (buccaneer)
Proof of Service: Pension application W9637
Pension application No.: W9637
Residences: Epping, Rockingham Co., NH; MA; VT; OH; Switzerland Co., IN
Died: 5 Nov 1836 Switzerland Co., IN
Buried: Aberdeen Cemetery (aka Murray Cemetery), Cass Twp., Ohio Co., IN
DAR Ancestor No.: A097799

Massachusetts Marriages, Westborough, Worcester County, It 2, p. 341.
11 Sep 1784, Winthrop (Winthorp) Robertson to Bulah Rice.

Pension Application Abstracted from National Archives microfilm Series 805, Roll 698, File W9637.; Switzerland County, Indiana Probate Record Book Vol. A, Mar 1827-Nov 1834; p. 277.
Pension abstract for – Winthrop Robinson   Service state(s): New Hampshire
Date: 23 August 1832
County of: Switzerland   State of: Indiana
Declaration made before a Judge. Unable to appear in court because of bodily infirmity caused by the palsy…
Recorded in Book A, pg. 377.
Age: 71 years   Record of age: Shows record of himself, brothers, sisters.
Where and year born: 22 April 1761 at Stratham, Rockingham Co., NH
Residence when he entered service: Epping, Rockingham Co., NH
Residence(s) since the war: Epping, NH about 20 years, Massachusetts about 5
                years, Vermont about 3 years, Ohio about 8 years, Indiana
                about 13 years.
Residence now: Cotton Twp., Switzerland Co., IN
Volunteer or Drafted or Substitute: Volunteered four tours, enlisted last one.
Rank(s): Drummer, Private, Orderly sergeant, Lieutenant
Statement of service-

Period	Duration	Names of General and Field Officers
1777		Drummer in company commanded by Capt. Parsons in regiment of NH Militia commanded by Col. Santra.
1778		Private in company commanded by Capt. Worthern, in regiment of NH Militia commanded by Col. Peabody.
1779		Orderly sergeant in company commanded

1780   by Capt. Worthern in regiment commanded by Col. Mooney. Orderly sergeant in company commanded by Capt. Gordon in regiment commanded by Col. Bartlett.

1781 or 1782   Lieutenant on board ship Buccaneer.

Discharge received: Never received written discharge.
Statement is supported by – Traditionary evidence
Person now living who can testify to service: None
Clergyman: Samuel Pavy
Persons in neighborhood who certify character: William Smith of Switzerland Co., John K. Walker, Horace Bassett of Dearborn Co., and several other persons.
Solider died: 5 Nov 1836
Wife: Bulah Rice
Marriage date and place: 11 Sep 1784 Westborough, Westchester Co., MA
Proof of marriage: Copy of marriage record in file.
&
Widow's application for pension. Soldier's certificate No. 19052.
Date: 12 November 1838
County of: Switzerland   State of: Indiana
Declaration made before a Judge.
Widow's age: 75 years   Record of age:
Widow's residence now: Cotton Twp., Switzerland Co., IN
Soldier died: 5 December 1836 at Cotton Twp., Switzerland Co., IN
Marriage date and place: April or May 1784 at Marlborough, Massachusetts
Proof of marriage: Never had any certificate of marriage
Names and ages of children: Family record in the handwriting of Winthrop Robinson in the file shows – Isabella b. 6 Feb 1785; Algemon Sidney b. 23 Jul 1787; Winthrop b. 7 Nov 1792; William M. b. 19 Dec 1794; Anthony W. b. 22 Dec 1796; Azubah b. 8 Oct 1798, d. 26 Jan 1800; Daniel L. b. 8 Jun 1801, d. 26 Jul 1811; Eliza Little b. 22 Oct 1804, d. 12 Sep 1810; Jeremiah b. 28 Sep 1806.

Switzerland County, Indiana Probate Order Book 2, 1831-1837; p. 491.
8 May 1837
       Now on this Comes into open Court Sidney Robinson and produced to the Satisfaction of the Court the Certificate from the war department under the act of 7th June 1832 to Winthrop Robinson a revolutionary Soldier and proved to the Inspection of the Court that the Said Winthrop Robinson departed this life on the 5th day of December 1836 in Switzerland County Indiana and that he left Bulah Robinson his widow.

Switzerland County, Indiana Probate Order Book 3, 1837-1843; p. 121.
12 November 1838
In the matter of Bulah Robinson widow   }
of Winthrop Robinson a Pensioner of the U.S.   }
         Now on this day comes the Said Bulah Robinson and filed her report under the act of Congress of 1838 which report reads in the words and

figures following to wit (here insert it) which being seen and inspected by this Court is ordered of record.

Abstract of Final Payment Voucher; General Services Administration, Washington, DC
FINAL PAYMENT VOUCHER RECEIVED FROM
THE GENERAL ACCOUNTING OFFICE
NAME					Robinson, Winthrop
AGENCY OF PAYMENT		Indiana
DATE OF ACT			1832
DATE OF PAYMENT		2d Qr. 1837
DATE OF DEATH			Nov 5, 1836
GENERAL SERVICES ADMINISTRATION
National Archives and Records Service		NA-286
GSA-WASH DC 54-4891				November 1953

Composite Index to Volumes xiv-xvii (Revolutionary War rolls) of the New Hampshire State Papers; Frank C. Mevers, compiler; Heritage Books, Bowie, MD, c1993. p.237.
Robinson, Winthrop XV, 259, 262, 267-68, 270, 475, 494, 657, 678; XVI, 115, 837.
From the State Papers -
Vol. XV
p. 259 Muster Roll of Captain Joseph Parson's Company in the Service of the United States, Commanded by Lt. Col. Joseph Senter, Engaged for Six Months & five Days from June 25th 1777 taken to Decr 18th 1777.
Drums & fifer			Winthrop Robinson 5th July

The "Lost" Pensions, Settled Accounts of the Act of 6 April 1838; by Craig R. Scott; Willow Bend Books, Lovettsville, VA, 1996. p. 278.
An Act directing the transfer of money remaining unclaimed [for the term of eight months] by certain pensioners, and authorizing payment of the same at the Treasury of the United States.
Name – Robinson, Bulah; Pension Office – Madison, Ind.; Box - 96; Account - #1673.

Early Ohio Settlers, Purchasers of Land in Southwestern Ohio, 1800-1840; Compiled by Ellen T. Berry & David A. Berry; Genealogical Publishing Co., Inc., Baltimore, MD, 1986. p.276.

Purchaser	Year	Date	Residence	R – T - S
Robinson, Winthrop (B)	1833	Dec. 10	Switzerland	03-03-01

(B) Indiana Survey: Land lying west of a meridian drawn west of the Great Miami (known as the "Gore"). Switzerland, Dearborn, Franklin, Ohio, Union and Randolph Counties (all or only a part of each county) – all in Indiana.

Indiana Land Entries Vol. 1 Cincinnati District, 1801-1840; Margaret R. Waters; Originally Published Indianapolis 1948, Second Reprint 1979 by The Bookmark, P.O. Box 74, Knightstown, In 46148. p.144.

CINCINNNATI LAND DISTRICT – VOL. 1
[Likely that this transaction was made by the son, Winthrop Robinson.]
Page 115. Twp. 2 N, Range 3 W of 1st Principle Meridian SWITZERLAND CO.
Winthrop Robinson E ½ - SE ¼ - S1; 12-10-1833.
-- Note: The tract books for the land offices in Indiana are deposited in the office of the Auditor of State, Indianapolis. They and are in the custody of the State Land clerk. –

1830 U.S. Census, Indiana, Switzerland, No Twp., Series: M19 Roll: 32 Page: 63
Robinson, Winthrop age 60-70; others in household 1 female 60-70.

Revolutionary Soldiers of Switzerland County; Copied by Mary Hill, John Paul Chapter-Daughters of the American Revolution; January, 1958; http://www.ingenweb.org/inswitzerland/switzrevsoldiers.html- Viewed June 2012.
ROBINSON, WINTHROP
Born April 22, 1761 in Stratham, New Hampshire.
Served:
1777 as a drummer in co. commanded by Capt. Parsons in Col. Sentre's N.H. Militia.
1778 private in Co. commanded by Capt. Worthen, Col. Peabody's N.H. Militia.
1779 orderly-sergeant in co. commanded by Capt. Worthen, Col Mooney N. H. Militia.
1780 orderly-sergeant in co commanded by Capt. Gordon as Lieut. on board ship, "Buccanier,"
Married 1784 to Beulah Rice.
Children; Isabella b. 1785, Algernon Sidney b. 1787 - 1862 m Abigail Harding, Winthrop b. 1792, William N. b. 1794, Anthony W. b. 1796, Azubah b.1798, d.1800, Daniel L. b. 1801, d. 1811, Eliza L. b. 1804, d. 1810, Jeremiah b. 1806.
Died Dec. 5, 1836 in Cotton twp. Switz. Co., by statement of widow
Switz. Co. records Pr. Bk. A. pg. 491. Sidney Robinson comes with certificate showing Winthrop Robinson, a revolutionary soldier, departed this life, Dec. 5, 1836, Switz. Co.
Left Bulah Robinson, his lawful widow.

History of Dearborn and Ohio Counties; From Their Earliest Settlement; F. E. Weakley & Co., author & publisher, Chicago, 1885.p. 199.
List of Dearborn soldiers [Revolutionary War]
Included in this list is Winthrop Robinson

Roster of Soldiers and Patriots of the American Revolution Buried in Indiana, Vol. I; compiled by Mrs. Roscoe C. O'Byrne.; Indiana Daughters of the American Revolution, 1981; p. 316.
ROBINSON, WINTHROP   Switzerland County
Born – April 22, 1761, Stratham, New Hampshire.
Service – Served 1777 as a drummer in CO. commanded by Capt. Parsons in Col. Sentre's N. H. Militia. 1778 pri. in CO. commanded by Capt. Worthen, Col. Peabody's N.H. Militia. 1779, orderly-sergeant in CO. commanded by Capt.

Worthen, Col. Mooney, N.H. Militia. 1780, orderly-sergeant in CO. commanded by Capt. Gordon as Lieut. on board ship, "Buccaneer".
Proof – Pension claim W. 9637.
Died – Dec. 5, 1836, by statement of widow in Cotton Twp., Switzerland Co.
Married – 1784, Beulah Rice. Ch. Isabella b. 1785; Algernon Sidney (1787-1862), m. Abigail Harding; Winthrop b. 1792; William N. b. 1794; Anthony W. b. 1796; Azubah b. 1800; Daniel L. b. 1801; Eliza L. b. 1804 d. 1810; Jeremiah b. 1806. Collected by Mrs. Walter Kerr, Aurora, Indiana.

Roster of Soldiers and Patriots of the American Revolution Buried in Indiana, Vol. III; 1980; p.74.
ROBINSON, WINTHROP   Roster I, p. 316   Ohio County
Additional data or corrections.
Died – A stone marker was found in 1977 for this soldier in the Aberdeen Cemetery, Cass Twp., Ohio Co., Ind.
By Mrs. A. g. Charlton, 30 Sunnyside Avenue, Aurora, Indiana 47001.

Abstract of Graves of Revolutionary Patriots (4 volumes); by Patricia Law Hatcher; Pioneer Heritage Press, Dallas, TX, 1987. Vol. 3, p. 226.
This is an abstract and an index to information reported to the Daughters of the American Revolution and published in their annual reports to the Smithsonian Institution, printed as Senate Documents (1900-1974) and published annually in the DAR magazine (1978-1987).
Published 1978
ROBINSON, Winthrop   Aberdeen Cem, Cass Twp., Ohio Co IN

National Society of the Sons of the American Revolution - Revolutionary War Graves Register; Compiled and Edited by Clovis H. Brakebill, Published by db Publications, Dallas, TX, 1993. p. 521.
Robinson Winthrop; 1761-1836; Aberdeen Cem, Cass Twsp, Ohio Co, IN; Lieutenant, NH.

Aberdeen Cemetery, Ohio Co., IN
Tombstone inscription
                    WINTHROP   BEULAH
                    ROBINSON   Wife of
                    died   Winthrop Robinson
                    Nov. 5, 1836   died
                    aged   Feb. 5, 1848
                    75 Years   aged
                                            84 Years 11
                                            mo. & 3 ds.

The Vevay Reveille-Enterprise; Vol. 122. No. 39, 28 Sep 1935, p.3, col.2.
Roster of Revolutionary Soldiers Who Resided in Switzerland County
By Mrs. Effa M. Danner
Lieut. Winthrop Robinson – Switzerland County, Cotton Township. He served 1777 as a drummer in Company commanded by Capt. Parsons in Regiment New

Hampshire Militia by Col. Sentre. 1778 private in Company of Capt. Worthen, Reg., N.H. Militia by Col. Peabody, 1779 Orderly Sergeant in Co. Capt. Worthen, Col. Mooney. 1780 Orderly Sergeant in Company of Capt. Gordon as Lieutenant on board ship "Buccanier".
Winthrop Robinson, born April 22, 1761, at Stratham, Rockingham Co., N.H. Lived in Epping N.H. Since the war, N.H. 20 years; Mass 5 years; Vermont 27 years, Ohio 8 years and Indiana 13 years.
His officers, Gen. Lafayette on Rhode Island when French troops went to attack British. Brother Noah being a Captain of Marines and was wounded, pension granted under Pres. Jefferson.
Nov. 1838 Bulah, widow, files for pension. Married Worchester, Mass., 1784. He died Dec. 5, 1836 in Cotton Township, Switzerland County.
Algernon Sidney Robinson gives the family record. Isabella, born Feb. 6, 1787; Algernon Sidney, born July 23, 1787; Winthrop, born Nov. 7, 1792; William N., born Dec. 19, 1794; Anthony W., born Dec. 22, 1796; Azubah, born Oct. 8, 1798; Daniel, born June 8, 1801; Eliza L., born Oct. 22, 1804; Jeremiah, born Sept. 28, 1806; June 1843, Bulah, age 80.
Ezubah died January 26, 1800; Eliza L., died Sept. 12, 1810; Daniel L., died July 26, 1811.
Worchester Co., Mass., Feb. 14, 1843; Persis Sawyer, resident of Berlin Co., Mass., testifies Bulah's maiden name was Rice.
Winthrop Robinson died Nov. 5, 1836.
Switzerland County Census 1830, Winthrop Robinson listed, age between 60-70. Wife listed, age between 60-70. Sidney Robinson, age between 40-50. Sidney Robinson's wife, age between 20-30. Sidney Robinson two boys and two girls under 10.
Bulah Robinson application on file Probate Court, October 1838, p. 121.

ROGERS, STEPHEN

Patriot: Stephen Rogers
Birth: 1755 VA
Married Spouse 1: Nancy (b. 1758 d. 11 Jun 1837 Switzerland Co., IN)
Married Spouse 2: 12 May 1839, Switzerland Co., IN
        Mrs. Villa (McPhearson) Todd
        (b. abt. 1796, d. 1855 Switzerland Co., IN)
        [Widow of Joseph Todd – Rev. Soldier]
Service state(s): VA
Service description: Capt. Garland Burley, Col. Francis Taylor
Rank: Private
Proof of Service: Pension application W5729
Pension application No.: W5729
Residences: Albemarle Co., VA; Indiana Territory; Switzerland Co., IN
Died: 30 Nov 1845 Switzerland Co., IN
Buried: Long Run Cemetery, Craig Twp., Switzerland Co., IN
DAR Ancestor No.: A098241

Pension Application Abstracted from National Archives microfilm Series 805, Roll 699, File W5729/BLWT18372-160-55.

Pension abstract for – Stephen Rodgers   Service state(s): Virginia
Alternate spelling(s):   Rogers
Date: 30 May 1818
County of: Switzerland   State of: Indiana
Declaration made before a Court.
Age: Not stated
Residence now: Switzerland Co., IN
Where entered service: Albemarle Barracks, Albemarle Co., VA
Volunteer or Drafted or Substitute: Enlisted
Rank(s): Not stated
Statement of service-

Period	Duration	Names of General and Field Officers
1778		Capt. Garland Burely, Lieut. Thomas Porter, Ensign John Taylor in Col. Francis Taylor's regiment, Gen. Wood's brigade. [Virginia Line]

Discharge received: May 1781
Signed by: Gen. Wood
&
Schedule of Property presented to the court.
Date: 14 September 1820
County of: Switzerland   State of: Indiana
Declaration made before a Circuit Court.
Age: 62 years
Rank(s): Not stated
Rank: Private
Statement of service- Same as 30 May 1818 statement

Wife: Nancy Rodgers   Wife's age: 62 years
Names and ages of children: Stephen Rodgers, age about 20 years.
&
Widow's application for pension
Date: 2 April 1853
County of: Switzerland   State of: Indiana
Declaration made before a Justice of the Peace
Solider died: 30 November 1845 in Switzerland Co., IN
Wife/Widow: Villa Todd
Marriage date and place: 12 May 1839 in Switzerland Co., IN
Proof of marriage: Family record, and public record in this county
&
Widow's application for Bounty Land
Date: 13 April 1855
County of: Switzerland   State of: Indiana
Declaration made before a Justice of the Peace
Widow's age: 58 years
Widow's residence now: Switzerland Co., IN
Soldier's rank(s): Private
Wife/Widow: Villa Todd Rodgers
Marriage date and place: 10 May 1839 in Switzerland Co., IN
Proof of marriage: Certificate of marriage in pension file.

Switzerland County, Indiana, Civil Order Book - Vol.5, Feb 10, 1823 - Jun 21, 1826, p.56.
3 June 1823 – Stephen Rodgers, a revolutionary soldier and United States pensioner, now filed his schedule, made the declaration, and took the oath required by late laws and acts of Congress, providing for persons engaged in the land & navel service of the United States, in the revolutionary war, which are ordered to be recorded, and it is ordered to be certified that the property contained in said schedule is valued by the court at fifty three dollars and twenty five cents.

Switzerland County, Indiana Civil Order Book 4, 1820 – 1823; pg. 70.
Sept. 1820
Stephen Rodgers, Revolutionary soldier & U.S. pensioner---$264.00
and
Switzerland County, Indiana Civil Order Book 4, 1820 – 1823; pg. 194.
Stephen Rodgers, Rev. sol. & U.S. pensioner---$125.25

Abstract of Final Payment Voucher; General Services Administration, Washington, DC
NAME   Rogers, Villa Widow of Stephen
AGENCY OF PAYMENT   Indiana
DATE OF ACT   1853 2d Sect
DATE OF PAYMENT   Sept 3, 1855
DATE OF DEATH
LAST ~~FINAL~~ PAYMENT VOUCHER RECEIVED FROM

THE GENERAL ACCOUNTING OFFICE   Form
General Services Administration   GSA DA 70-7035 GSA Dec 69 7068

Revolutionary War Records – Virginia; Virginia Army and Navy Forces with
Bounty Land Warrants for Virginia Military District of Ohio, and Virginia
Military Script, from Federal and State Archives; by Gaius Marcus Brumbaugh,
M.D, M.s., Litt.D; Genealogical Publishing Co., Inc., Baltimore, 1995.p. 264.
List of non-commissioned officers and soldiers of the Continental Line. List may
contain names of individuals who received bounty land for services in the State
Line.
Rogers, Stephen, Soldier, Inf.

Historical Register of Virginians in the Revolution, Soldiers, Sailors, Marines, 1775-1783; John H. Gwathmey; The Dietz Press, Richmond, VA, 1938. p. 675.
Rogers, Stephen, Inf.
Rogers, Stephen, Taylor's Va. Reg.

Register of Certificates Issued by John Pierce, Esquire, Paymaster General and Commissioner of Army Accounts for the United States, to Officers and Soldiers of the Continental Army Under Act of July 4, 1783; Originally Published as Senate Documents, Vol.9, No. 988, 63rd Congress, 3d Session, Washington, 1915;
Seventeenth report of the National Society of the Daughters of the American
Revolution; Genealogical Publishing Co., Inc, Baltimore, MD, 1984. p. 435.
Men listed in this volume with the same name.

No. of Certificate	To whom issued	Amount
10049	Rogers, Stephen	15.28
10477	Rogers, Stephen	58.00
10964	Rogers, Stephen	80.00
40113	Rogers, Stephen	30.06
40936	Rogers, Stephen	53.30
47310	Rogers, Stephen	16.58

Virginia Revolutionary War Land Grant Claims 1783-1850 (Rejected); William
Lindsay Hopkins; self published, Richmond, VA, 1988, p.188.
Rogers, Stephen – Soldier – Army – Switzerland CO, Indiana
Stephen Rogers, aged 72, in Switzerland CO, Indiana on 3 Aug 1830 states that
he enlisted near Charlottesville, Albemarle CO, VA in 1777 under Capt. Garland
Burnly in the 14th VA Regt of Col. Francis Taylor. He is a pensioner.

Possible citation - his residences have not been fully determined.
Census of Indiana Territory for 1807; Indiana Historical Society, 1980. p. 33.
Randolph County

Names of Persons	No. of free male Inhabitants 21 yrs and above
Stephen Rogers	1

Indiana Territory, Switzerland Circuit Court Records, Order Book, October Term 1814 to March Term 1815. p.90 .

He is listed in county records for the first time on 14 September 1815, as a witness for the defense – he was not sworn.

Early Settlers of Indiana's "GORE" 1803-1820; Compiled and Edited by Shirley Keller Mikesell; Heritage Books, Inc., 1995. p. 188.
Switzerland County – Township 3, Range 3W
Section 30 – Stephen Rogers SR – 1817 – pg. 12.

Indiana Land Entries Vol. 1 Cincinnati District, 1801-1840; Margaret R. Waters; Originally Published Indianapolis 1948, Second Reprint 1979 by The Bookmark, P.O. Box 74, Knightstown, In 46148. p. 71.
CINCINNNATI LAND DISTRICT – VOL. 1
Page 67. Twp. 3 N, Range 3 W of 1st Principle Meridian SWITZERLAND CO. NE 1/3 – S30; 5-14-1817 Vol. II, p. 122 adds Sr.
-- Note: The tract books for the land offices in Indiana are deposited in the office of the Auditor of State, Indianapolis. They and are in the custody of the State Land clerk. --

U.S. Department of Interior, Bureau of Land Management, General Land Office Records; Land Patent Search – accessed 27 June 2012.
ROGERS, STEPHEN
Accession Nr. CV-0057-520; Document Type – Credit Volume Patent; State - Indiana; Issue Date – 12/16/1823; Cancelled – No
Land Office – Cincinnati; Authority – April 24, 1820 Sale-Cash Entry (3 Stat. 566); Document Nr. -266; Total Acres – 161.00
Land Description: State - IN; Meridian – 1st PM; Aliquots – 003N-003W; Section - 30; County - Switzerland

1820 U.S. Census, Indiana, Switzerland, Vevay, Series: M33 Roll: 14 Page: 254
Steven Rogers 45 and up; also in household 1 male 16-26, 1 female 45 and up.

The Pension List of 1820 [U.S. War Department] Reprinted with an Index; by Murtie June Clark; Genealogical Publishing Co., Inc., Baltimore, 1991. Originally published 1820 as Letter from the Secretary of War. p. 658.
Names of the Revolutionary Pensioners which have been placed on the Roll of Indiana, under the Law of the 18th of March, 1818, from the passage thereof, to this day, inclusive, with the Rank they held, and the Lines in which they served, viz.

Names	Rank	Line
Stephen Rodgers	private	Virginia

Pensioners of the Revolutionary War Struck Off the Roll with an Added Index to States; Reprinted by Genealogical Publishing Co., Baltimore, MD for Clearfield Company, Inc., 1989. p. 100.
Pensioners in Indiana who have been dropped under the act of 1st May, 1820; prepared in conformity with a resolution of the House of Representatives of the United States of the 17th December, 1835.

433

Names	Acts under which restored	Remarks
Stephen Rogers	March 1, 1823	
	-	

A Census of Pensioners for Revolutionary or Military Services with their Names, Ages, and Places of Residence Under the Act for Taking the Sixth Census in 1840; Genealogical Publishing Co., Inc., Baltimore, Maryland, 1965. p.185.

INDIANA, SWITZERLAND, PLEASANT

Names of Pensioners for Revolutionary or Military services	Ages	Names of heads of families with whom pensioner resided June 1, 1840
Stephen Rogers	80	Henry Rogers

1850 U.S. Census, Indiana, Switzerland, Pleasant Twp., Series: M432 Roll: 174 Page: 324, Family No. 367.
Villa Rogers, Age 54, Real estate value $150., Born VA; in her household is Catherine Todd, Age 19, Born IN.

Revolutionary Soldiers of Switzerland County; Copied by Mary Hill, John Paul Chapter-Daughters of the American Revolution; January, 1958; http://www.ingenweb.org/inswitzerland/switzrevsoldiers.html- Viewed June, 2012.

ROGERS, STEPHEN   Switzerland Co. Indiana.
                      Pension claim W.5729, B. L. Wt. 18372-160-55
Born 1760 [Note: DAR proof shows b. 1755]
Private in Regt commanded by Col. Taylor in Virginia Line for 3 years
Married 1st wife Nancy _____ died 1837
Children: Henry m 1829 Lucinda Crandall, Stephen m 1822 Ruth Todd; ,
Elizabeth, m 1824 John Lock, Nancy m 1830 John Graham.
Married 2nd wife Villa McPhearson Todd
Died Nov. 30, 1845
Buried Long Run cemetery. Stone.
Collected by Mrs. A. V. Danner, Vevay, Indiana

Roster of Soldiers and Patriots of the American Revolution Buried in Indiana, Vol. I; compiled by Mrs. Roscoe C. O'Byrne.; Indiana Daughters of the American Revolution, 1981; p.317.

ROGERS, STEPHEN   Switzerland County
Born – 1760.
Service – Pri. in Regt. commanded by Col. Taylor in Vir. Line, 3 yrs.
Proof – Pension claim W. 5729, B.L.Wt. 18372-160-55.
Died – Nov. 30, 1846. Buried Long Run Cemetery. Stone.
Married – First W, Nancy _____ d. 1837. Ch. Henry, m. 1829 Lucinda Crandell; Stephen, m. 1822 Ruth Todd; Elizabeth, m. 1824 John Lock; Nancy, m. 1830 John Graham.
Second W, of the soldier, Villa McPhearson Todd.
Collected by Mrs. A. V. Danner, Vevay, Indiana.

Abstract of Graves of Revolutionary Patriots (4 volumes); by Patricia Law Hatcher; Pioneer Heritage Press, Dallas, TX, 1987. Vol. 3, p. 229.
This is an abstract and an index to information reported to the Daughters of the American Revolution and published in their annual reports to the Smithsonian Institution, printed as Senate Documents (1900-1974) and published annually in the DAR magazine (1978-1987).
Published 1972 (Senate Doc. 54)
ROGERS, Stephen   Log Run Cem, Switzerland Co IN

The Vevay Reveille-Enterprise; Vol. 122. No. 39, 28 Sep 1935, p.3, col.2.
Roster of Revolutionary Soldiers Who Resided in Switzerland County
By Mrs. Effa M. Danner
Stephen Rodgers – No, W5729.
Military record, Switzerland County, Ind., 1828, age 69. Enlisted in Virginia 1777 in December. In Company of Captain Garl and Burlee and Col. Frances Taylor served until Apr. or May 1781. Discharged Albemarle Barracks, Virginia. Now resides with youngest son, Stephen Rodgers. 1820 states wife, Nancy, age 62, son Stephen, 20.
January 1854 Vella Rogers, widow of Stephen Rogers, who died Nov. 30, 1846, Married May 12, 1839 by John G. Anderson, Maiden name Vella Todd, applies for pension.
Indiana record, Stephen Rodgers, Switzerland County, Ind. Private in Regiment of Col. Taylor, Virginia line for 3 years. Inscribed on rolls $8 per month.
Switzerland County Manifest Order Book., p. 369.
Stephen Rodgers listed U.S. Military Census 1840, age 80, Henry Rodgers, guardian, Switzerland Co.
He enters land patent Switzerland County, May 14, 1817.
"Nancy Rogers, wife of Stephen Rogers died June 11, 1837, age 75 years".
Inscription on grave stone at Ebenezer M.E. Church, Moorefield – Mary Hill. Henry Rogers buried same place. He married Lucinda Crandell, Sept. 24, 1829. Stephen Rogers, Jr., married Ruth Todd, April 20, 1822. Nancy Rogers married John Graham, July 22, 1830, Elizabeth Rogers married John Lock, March 10, 1824. Their daughters Nancy and Eleanor Lock married John and Joseph Todd sons of Joseph Todd Sr. who was a soldier in the French and Indian War. His widow, Vella McPhearson Todd married Stephen Rogers, Sr. May 10, 1839. Stephen Rogers, Sr. died Nov. 20, 1846 and is buried at Lon Run Baptist church near Moorefield.

SCUDDER, ABNER
aka SCUDDER, ABRAHAM

Patriot: Abraham Scudder
Birth: 17 Jun 1764 Essex Co., NJ
Married Spouse 1: 19 Aug 1789 Rowan Co., NC   Katherine (Kitty) Barkley
                                (b. abt. 1770 KY d. Switzerland Co., IN)
Service state(s): NC
Service description: Capt. Alexander Brevard, Cols. Dickson, Blouts, NC Regt.
Rank: Private
Proof of Service: Pension application S32510
Pension application No.: S32510
Residences: Essex Co., NJ; Rowan Co., NC; KY; OH; Indiana
            Territory; Switzerland Co., IN
Died: 15 May 1842   York Twp., Switzerland Co., IN
Buried: Bethel Cemetery, York Twp., Switzerland Co., IN
DAR Ancestor No.: A100820

Pension Application Abstracted from National Archives microfilm Series 805, Roll 722, File S32510.; Switzerland County, Indiana Complete Records, Circuit Court, Vol. A, Apr ?, 1827-Mar 10, 1832; p.262.; Switzerland County, Indiana Probate Record Book Vol. A, Mar 1827-Nov 1834; p. 498.
Pension abstract for – Abner Scudder   Service state(s): North Carolina
Date: 22 Apr 1829
County of: Switzerland   State of: Indiana
Declaration made before a Circuit Court.
Schedule of personal property valued at $190.50, and declaration of service.
He states in this application that - He applied to Jesse Hunt, on 16 June 1818 at Cincinnati, OH, who promised to make application for him. Afterwards called on Hunt but got no satisfactory of his claim. In the fall of 1818 moved to Indiana and has never since heard from Hunt.
Age: 67 yrs. on the 17th June next.
Residence when he entered service: Rowan Co., NC
Residence(s) since the war: Rowan Co., NC; Cincinnati, Ohio, to Indiana in fall of 1818.
Residence now: Switzerland Co., IN
Volunteer or Drafted or Substitute: Enlisted
Rank: Private
Statement of service-

Period	Duration	Names of General and Field Officers
17 May 1781	12 mos.	Capt. Alexander Bovard, Col. Dickrow, then Col. Bloceur, Brigade commanded by Gen. Summer, in the Line of North Carolina, Continental Estab.

Battles: Eutaw Springs
Discharge received: at Bacous Bridge near Ashley, SC.
Statement is supported by –

Documentary proof: none
Occupation: Farmer, very frail not being able to get my own firewood.
Wife: Not named   Wife's age: 66 yrs
Names and ages of children: Daughter, not named, aged 27 yrs., very subject to fits and almost totally unable to support herself; two sons living in the neighborhood, one has a large family to support, the other recently married with a good prospect of having a large family. His son David, age 21, has left him.
&

Date: 12 November 1834
County of: Switzerland   State of: Indiana
Declaration made before a Court.
Recorded in Book A, pg. 498.
Age: 70 years   Record of age: Bible
Where and year born: 17 June 1764 in Essex Co., New Jersey
Residence when he entered service: Rowan Co., North Carolina
Residence(s) since the war: Rowan Co., NC for about 37 years, Kentucky about 10 years, Ohio about 11 years, then in Indiana.
Residence now: Switzerland Co., IN
Volunteer or Drafted or Substitute: Enlisted
Rank(s): Private
Statement of service-

Period	Duration	Names of General and Field Officers
May 1781	1 year	Company commanded by Capt. Alexander Bovard.

Battles: Eutaw Springs where he was wounded on 9 Sep 1781. The shot grazed the side of head.
Discharge received: Written discharge
Signed by: Col. Blount
Statement is supported by –
Living witness, name(s): None
Documentary proof: None
Clergyman: George Markland residing in Switzerland County
Persons in neighborhood who certify character: John Miller, Jesse v. Daily, Joseph Malin, Charles F. Kurtz, Robert Gullion, N.H. Tapp, Thomas Armstrong, J.R. Whitehead.
Wife: Not stated
Names and ages of children: In 1836 he was living with a daughter, not named.

Switzerland County, Indiana Probate Order Book 2, 1831-1837;p. 243.
12 November 1834
In the matter of Abner Scudder}   Under the act of 7th June 1832
an applicant for a pension   }
            Now on this day in open Court before Probate Court of Switzerland County now Sitting, And in order to obtain a pension under the act of 7th June 1832 Comes Abner Scudder on oath makes the following Declaration (here insert it) And the Said Court do hereby declare their opinion, after the investigation of the matter, and after putting the interrogations prescribed by the war department, that the above named Abraham Scudder was a Revolutionary

Soldier and Served as he States, and the Court further Certifies that it appears to them that George Markland who has also Signed the preceding Certificate is a Clergyman resident in Switzerland and State of Indiana, and that Robert Gullion who also Signed the same is a resident of Switzerland County and State of Indiana and is a credible person, and that this Statement is entitled to Credit.

North Carolina Marriages, Rowan County,
Scudder, Abner   Kitty Barkly   19 Aug. 1789   Saml. x Roberts
                                                                                                                                                        (w) W. Alexander

Switzerland County, Indiana Probate Order Book 3, 1837-1843; pp. 471, 476, 49 and *Switzerland County, Indiana Probate Orders Book, 1843-1849, p. 2, 29, 88.*
Abstract of will and/or administration for: Abner (Abraham) Scudder
State & county where recorded: Switzerland Co., Indiana
Book/volume where recorded: Probate Order Book 3, 1837-1843.
Date entered in probate: 9 August 1842
Administration:
Date began -   9 August 1842
Name of administrator - David Scudder
Date of death and place of death: On 11 August 1842, Satisfactory proof by the oath of David Miller and James Jackson that <u>Abner</u> Scudder late a Revolutionary Pensioner of the United States departed his life in Switzerland County on the 15th day of May AD1842 – and that he was the identical person named in a pension certificate now produced to the court, Granting to the Said Abner Scudder a pension of forty dollars per annum during his natural life Numbered 30450, dated the 7th March 1936 and Signed by Lewis Cass Secretary of War, and it is proven to the Court that <u>Abraham</u> Scudder left now widow.
Bonded by and amount of bond: William Scudder for $100.00.
Date of division & disbursement, or final return: 12 February 1845

Abstract of Final Payment Voucher; General Services Administration, Washington, DC
FINAL PAYMENT VOUCHER RECEIVED FROM
THE GENERAL ACCOUNTING OFFICE
NAME   Scudder, Abner
AGENCY OF PAYMENT   Indiana
DATE OF ACT   1832
DATE OF PAYMENT   3d Qr. 1842
DATE OF DEATH   May 15, 1842
GENERAL SERVICES ADMINISTRATION
National Archives and Records Service   NA-286
GSA-WASH DC 54-4891   November 1953

Roster of Soldiers from North Carolina in the American Revolution, with an appendix containing a collection of miscellaneous records; North Carolina Daughters of the American Revolution; D.A.R., Durham, NC, 1932. p. 19.
Pierce's Register – From Seventeenth Report of the National Society Daughters American Revolution. The general index of the register is preserved in MSS, in the Library of Congress N.C. Certificates 89, 501 to 91, 938.; page 150.

No. 90358   Scudder, Abner
p. 164.
Roster of the Continental Line from North Carolina; Reference North Carolina State Records, Clark, Vol. XVI, 1782-1783; Copy of a Register showing the names alphabetically (in Regiments) ranks, dates of commission and enlistment, periods of service, and occurrences, taken from the original muster and pay rolls of the North Carolina Line of the late Army of the United States.
10TH Regiment – Col. Abraham Shepard
Dates of

Name and Rank	Company	Commission	Enlistment And Service	Period of Occurrences
Scudder, Abner, Pt.	Brevard's		1781	12 mos.

Register of Certificates Issued by John Pierce, Esquire, Paymaster General and Commissioner of Army Accounts for the United States, to Officers and Soldiers of the Continental Army Under Act of July 4, 1783; Originally Published as Senate Documents, Vol.9, No. 988, 63rd Congress, 3d Session, Washington, 1915; Seventeenth report of the National Society of the Daughters of the American Revolution; Genealogical Publishing Co., Inc, Baltimore, MD, 1984. p. 350.
Men listed in this volume with the same name.

No. of Certificate	To whom issued	Amount
90358	Scudder, Abner	26.60

Second Census of Kentucky, 1800; Clift G. Glenn; Genealogical Publishing Co., Baltimore, MD, 1954.
An alphabetical list of 32,000 taxpayers based on original tax lists on file at the Kentucky Historical Society. Information given includes the county of residence and the date of the tax list in which the individual is listed.
Skudder, Abner   Madison   10/1/1800

Early Ohio Settlers, Purchasers of Land in Southwestern Ohio, 1800-1840; Compiled by Ellen T. Berry & David A. Berry; Genealogical Publishing Co., Inc., Baltimore, MD, 1986. p.286.

Purchaser	Year	Date	Residence	R – T - S
Scudder, Abraham (B)	1815	Oct. 27	Hamilton	02-02-27

(B) Indiana Survey: Land lying west of a meridian drawn west of the Great Miami (known as the "Gore"). Switzerland, Dearborn, Franklin, Ohio, Union and Randolph Counties (all or only a part of each county) – all in Indiana.

Early Settlers of Indiana's "GORE" 1803-1820; Compiled and Edited by Shirley Keller Mikesell; Heritage Books, Inc., 1995. p. 185.
Switzerland County – Township 2, Range 2W
Section 27 – Abner Scudder – 1815 – pg. 6.

Indiana Land Entries Vol. 1 Cincinnati District, 1801-1840; Margaret R. Waters; Originally Published Indianapolis 1948, Second Reprint 1979 by The Bookmark, P.O. Box 74, Knightstown, In 46148. p. 42.

CINCINNNATI LAND DISTRICT – VOL. 1
Page 40. Twp. 2 N, Range 2 W of 1st Principle Meridian SWITZERLAND CO.
Abraham Scudder SE ¼ - S27; 10-27-1815. Vol. II , p. 66, says Abner.
-- Note: The tract books for the land offices in Indiana are deposited in the office of the Auditor of State, Indianapolis. They and are in the custody of the State Land clerk. –

U.S. Department of Interior, Bureau of Land Management, General Land Office Records; Land Patent Search – accessed 27 June 2012.
SCUDDER, ABNER
Accession Nr. CV-0035-206; Document Type – Credit Volume Patent; State - Indiana; Issue Date – 8/7/1817; Cancelled – No
Land Office – Cincinnati; Authority – April 24, 1820 Sale-Cash Entry (3 Stat. 566); Total Acres – 0.00
Land Description: State - IN; Meridian – 1st PM; Aliquots – 003N-002W; Section - 27; County - Switzerland

A Census of Pensioners for Revolutionary or Military Services with their Names, Ages, and Places of Residence Under the Act for Taking the Sixth Census in 1840; Genealogical Publishing Co., Inc., Baltimore, Maryland, 1965. p.185.
INDIANA, SWITZERLAND, YORK

Names of Pensioners for Revolutionary or Military services	Ages	Names of heads of families with whom pensioner resided June 1, 1840
Abraham Scudder	77	William Scudder

1840 U.S. Census, Indiana, Switzerland, York, Series: M704 Roll: 95 Page: 189
Abner Scudder age 70-80; others in household 1 female 20-30.
Pensioners for Revolutionary or Military Services Included in the Foregoing

Names	Age
Abner Scudder	77

Revolutionary Soldiers of Switzerland County; Copied by Mary Hill, John Paul Chapter-Daughters of the American Revolution; January, 1958; http://www.ingenweb.org/inswitzerland/switzrevsoldiers.html- Viewed June 2012.
SCUDDER, ABNER
Born June 17, 1784 in Essex Co. N. J.
While residing in Roman Co. N. C. he enlisted in May 1781 and served one year as a private in Capt. Alexander Brevard's company, Cols. Dickson's (Dickerson) and Blount's N. C. regiments, was in battle of Eutaw Springs, where he was slightly wounded by a gun shot.
Left service April 18, 1782.
Married Katherine_____.
Children; William 1793 - 1872, in War of 1812 m. Kate Cox
Buried: Bethel cemetery in York Twp. Stone
Switzerland Co. Indiana. Pension record.
Collected by Mrs. A. V. Danner, Vevay, Indiana.

Roster of Soldiers and Patriots of the American Revolution Buried in Indiana, Vol. 1; compiled by Mrs. Roscoe C. O'Byrne.; Indiana Daughters of the American Revolution, 1981; p.325.

SCUDDER, ABNER   Switzerland County

Born – June 17, 1764, in Essex Co., New Jersey.
Service – While residing in Roman Co., N.C., he enlisted in May, 1781, and served 1 yr. as a private in Capt. Alexander Brevard's CO., Cols. Dickson's (Dickinson) and Blount's N.C. regiments, was in battle of Eutaw Springs, where he was slightly wounded by a gun shot. Left service April 18, 1782.
Proof – Pension record.
Buried – Bethel Cemetery in York Twp. Stone.
Married – Catherine _____. Ch. William b. 1793-1872 (War of 1812), m. Kate Cox.
Collected by Mrs. A. V. Danner, Vevay, Indiana.

History of Switzerland County Indiana 1885; Reproduced by the Switzerland County Historical Society, Vevay, Indiana, 1999. The portion of the book relating to Switzerland County in the 1885 printing of the "History of Dearborn, Ohio, and Switzerland Counties, Indiana". p. 1178.
York Township – "There are other worthy old settlers throughout the township, whose toil, hardships and privations brought about noble results in awarding and keeping alive a business industry. Among the number.....Abner Scudder."

The Vevay Reveille-Enterprise; Vol. 122. No. 39, 28 Sep 1935, p.3, col. 3.
Roster of Revolutionary Soldiers Who Resided in Switzerland County
By Mrs. Effa M. Danner
Abner Scudder – Pension Claim No. S32510. Abner Scudder enlisted May 1781, served 1 year private in Capt. Alexander Brevord's Co., Cols. Dickson's (Dickenson) and Blounts, North Carolina Regiment, was in the Battle of Entan Springs, he was slightly wounded in the side of his head by a gun shot. Left the service April 18, 1782. He was allowed pension on his application executed Nov. 12, 1834 while living in Switzerland Co., York Township. In 1836 stated he was living with his daughter, name not given. Wife's name Katherine.
Abner Scudder application in Probate Court June 7, 1832 – witnesses Rev. George Markland and Robert Gullion.
Abner Scudder's land grant, Oct. 7, 1815. He donated the land for Old Bethel church, a log church in the center of the grave yard and later for the brick church and the Scudder school house.
He is buried in Bethel grave yard – no marker.
He came from Rowan County, N. Carolina. His sons, John and William Scudder were in the War of 1812 in Hall's surrender. Two brothers, David and Walter Scudder came to Indiana. Family record, Mabel Scudder, daughter of John William Scudder.

SHADDAY, JOHN
aka SHADDY

Patriot: John Shadday
Birth: 26 Feb 1754 Orange Co., NC
Married Spouse 1: 20 Mar 1795 Orange Co., NC Mary Fogleman
(b. 23 Dec 1780 PA d. 22 Apr 1863)
Service state(s): NC
Service description: Capts. Allen, H. Perkins
Rank: Private
Proof of Service: Pension application W9647
Pension application No.: W9647
Residences: Orange Co., NC; TN; KY; OH; Switzerland Co., IN
Died: 21 Feb 1859 Bennington, Switzerland Co., IN
Buried: Slawson Cemetery, Pleasant Twp., Switzerland Co., IN
DAR Ancestor No.: A102516

Pension Application Abstracted from National Archives microfilm Series 805, Roll 727, File W9647/BLWT26115-160-55
Pension abstract for – John Shaddy   Service state(s): North Carolina
Date: 7 September 1832
County of: Switzerland   State of: Indiana
Declaration made before a Court.
Recorded in Book F, pg. 72.
Age: 78 Years   Record of age: My father's Bible that he presented to me.
Where and year born: 26 February 1754 at Hillsboro, Orange Co., North Carolina
Residence when he entered service: Orange Co., North Carolina
Residence(s) since the war: North Carolina about 25 years, Tennessee about 2 years, Kentucky about 4 years, Ohio about 2 years, Indiana about 17 years.
Residence now: Switzerland Co., IN
Volunteer or Drafted or Substitute: First I volunteered , secondly enlisted, lastly volunteered.
Rank(s): Private
Statement of service-

Period	Duration	Names of General and Field Officers
1779	5 or 6 mos.	Capt. Allen of the 14th regt. (Carolina)
1780	19 mos.	Capt. Hardin Perkins, Col. ONeal
1781 or 1782	1 mo.	Same

Battles: Guilford, Alamanse Creek
Discharge received: at Peede River in South Carolina. Second tour was thrown from the horse of a General when taking it to water, breastbone broken, discharged about 10 miles from Charleston, SC by Gen. Butler.
Statement is supported by –
Evidence: Traditionary
&
Bounty Land Claim
Date: 31 March 1855
County of: Switzerland   State of: Indiana

Declaration made before a Judge or Court.
Age: 97 years
Volunteer or Drafted or Substitute: Volunteered
Where he entered service?   Ourray Co., North Carolina
Rank(s): Private
Statement of service-
Period   Duration   Names of General and Field Officers
9 mos. as Infantry, 5 mos. as Calvary   Captain Hardin Perkins, Col. Onell
&
Widow, Mary Shaddy's application for pension
Date: 6 October 1859
County of: Switzerland   State of: Indiana
Declaration made before Open Court.
Widow's age: 83 years
Widow's residence now: Bennington, Switzerland Co., IN
Soldier died: 21 February 1859 at Bennington, Switzerland Co., IN
Marriage date and place: 20 April 1795 in Orange Co., NC
Proof of marriage: Does not know of a public or private record
&
Widow, Mary Shaddy, makes statement
Date: 13 February 1860
County of: Switzerland   State of: Indiana
Declaration made before a Notary Public
Widow's residence now: Jefferson Co., IN, with her son William & with Francis Shaddy.
Proof of marriage: No public, private, or Family Record of marriage
Names and ages of children: Catherine; Elizabeth, deceased; Polly; Barbra; Lucinda; Emsley; George W., deceased; Jacob, deceased; Jordon, deceased; William; Hardin, deceased; John, deceased; Turley, deceased; and Elizabeth, deceased. Emsley was age 56 in 1860.

Switzerland County, Indiana Civil Order Book Vol., A, Oct. 19, 1829-April 16, 1837, p. 171.
In the matter of Robert Moore, Griffith Dickinson, Nathan Ricketts, Gideon Tower, and John Shaddy, An application to obtain a pension under the Act of Congress of the 7th June AD 1832.
  Personally appeared in open Court, before the Switzerland Circuit Court now sitting the above named applicants who being first duly Sworn doth on their several oaths make their several declarations in order to obtain the benefit of the Act of Congress of the 7th June AD 1832 that they entered the Service of the United States under the officers named in their several declarations (here insert them) And the said Court do hereby declare their opinion after the investigation of the matter and after putting the interrogations prescribed by the War department that the above named Applicants were revolutionary Soldiers and Served as they have stated and the Court further Certifies that it appears to them that John Pavy who Signed their several Certificates is a Clergyman Resident in Switzerland County and State of Indiana and the other persons who

has also Signed the Same are credible persons and that their Statements in entitled to credit.

Switzerland County, Indiana Probate Order Book 3, 12 Jan 1863-20 Sep 1867; p. 88, 98, 113, 173.
Abstract of administration for: Mary Shaddy
State & county where recorded: Switzerland Co., Indiana
Date entered in probate: 2 November 1863
Name of administrator – Emsley Shaddy
Bonded by and amount of bond: John L. Shaddy for $400.00.
Petition to sell personal property filed 2 November 1863. Property – 1 chest, trunks, scissors, flat iron and dish, 1 bed and bedding, 1 calf, 1 cow, 1 yearling heifer, 1 cupboard, 1 looking glass, 1 lot sundries, wagon irons and harness.
Names of heirs and others mentioned in will (also signed receipts of division of estate) and relationship if shown: Distribution of funds to –

William Shaddy	son	$20.35
Catherine Ramseyer	daughter	$20.35
Barbara Cole	"	$20.35
Polly Leap	"	$20.35
Lucinda Thompson	"	$20.35

[Inheritance of children & grandchildren of her deceased daughter, Elizabeth Cole, are also listed.]
Date of division & disbursement, or final return: 8 March 1864

Abstract of Final Payment Voucher; General Services Administration, Washington, DC
FINAL PAYMENT VOUCHER RECEIVED FROM
THE GENERAL ACCOUNTING OFFICE
NAME   Shaddy, John
AGENCY OF PAYMENT   Indiana
DATE OF ACT   1832
DATE OF PAYMENT   1st Qr. 1860
DATE OF DEATH   Feb. 21, 1859
GENERAL SERVICES ADMINISTRATION
National Archives and Records Service   NA-286
GSA-WASH DC 54-4891   November 1953
&

Abstract of Final Payment Voucher; General Services Administration, Washington, DC
NAME   Shaddy, Mary Widow of John
AGENCY OF PAYMENT   Madison, Ind.
DATE OF ACT   1853 2d Sect
DATE OF PAYMENT   Sept 1861
DATE OF DEATH
LAST ~~FINAL~~ PAYMENT VOUCHER RECEIVED FROM
THE GENERAL ACCOUNTING OFFICE   Form
General Services Administration   GSA DA 70-7035   GSA Dec 69 7068

Indiana Territory, Switzerland Circuit Court Records, Order Book, October Term 1814 to March Term 1815. p.92.
Henry Langham is listed in county records for the first time on 15 September 1820, as a witness for the plaintiff.
Author's note: There are entries in this volume that are not within the range of dates shown on the binder cover.

1830 U.S. Census, Indiana, Switzerland, No Twp., Series: M19 Roll: 32 Page: 68
Shaddy, John age 60-70; others in household 1 male 5-10, 2 males 10-15, 1 female 5-10, 1 female 15-20, 1 female 40-50.

1860 U.S. Census, Indiana, Switzerland, Pleasant Twp., Series: M653 Roll: 299 Page: 230, Family No. 608.
Mary Shaddy, Age: 83, Female, Race: White, Born: NC

Revolutionary Soldiers of Switzerland County; Copied by Mary Hill, John Paul Chapter-Daughters of the American Revolution; January, 1958; http://www.ingenweb.org/inswitzerland/switzrevsoldiers.html- Viewed June 2012.
SHADDAY (SHADDY) JOHN
Born Feb. 29, 1754 Orange Co. N. C.
Private in Cav. and Inf. in Co. commanded by Capt. Allen, Regt. by Col. O'Neal, N. C., 14 months from 1779.
Married 1795 to Mary Fogleman
Children: Elizabeth, Polly m John Low, Barbara m Martin R. Cope, Lucinda m Alexander Thompson, Emsley m Polly Leap, George W. m Louisa Green, William Hardin m Frances Dyer, Jacob, John m Frances A. Neal, Turley, Jordan m Louise Bronson.
Pension claim W. 9647; B. L. Wt. 26115-100-55
Died Feb. 21, 1859
Buried Slawson cemetery, Bennington, Ind. Stone
Collected by Mrs. A. V. Danner, Vevay, Indiana

Roster of Soldiers and Patriots of the American Revolution Buried in Indiana, Vol. I; compiled by Mrs. Roscoe C. O'Byrne.; Indiana Daughters of the American Revolution, 1981; p.327.
SHADDAY (SHADDY), JOHN   Switzerland County
Born – Feb. 26, 1754, Orange Co., North Carolina
Service – Pri. in Cav. And Inf. In CO. commanded by Capt. Allen, Regt. by Col. O'Neal, N.C., 14 mo. from 1779. Proof – Pension claim W 9947; B.L.Wt. 26115-160-55.
Died – Feb. 21, 1859. Buried Slawson Cemetery, Bennington, Ind. Stone.
Married – 1795, Mary Fogleman. Ch. Elizabeth; Polly, m. John Low; Barbara, m. Martin R. Cope; Lucinda, m.. Alexander Thompson; Emaley, m. Polly Leap; George W., m. Louise Green; Wm. Hardin, m. Francis Dyer; Jacob; John, m. Francis A. Neal; Turley; Jordan, m. Louise Brenson.
Collected by Mrs. A. V. Danner, Vevay, Indiana.

The Weekly Messenger; Vol. II, No. 98, Col. 3. Saturday, 27 July 1833.
Newspaper article –
"LOOK AT THIS

Friends and Fellow Citizens – I am a candidate for the School Commissioner. I reside in Pleasant township – have lived in your county seventeen years – was a soldier in the Revolutionary war – bor arms in defense of my country before my opponents for this office, were thought of.

Methinks, I can hear my fellow-citizens with united voices, say "Let's to the polls and vote for the old veteran JOHN SHADDY."

How cheering the sound – how gratifying, in old age, to receive a unanimous vote for the only office I ever seriously, wished for.

My wife, who has been jogging on thro' the last fifty years with me expresses much solicitude for my success it would do your hearts grand to see the old body, when I come in from my daily labor, take her white napkin, and wipe the sweat from my face, accompanied generally with a stanza or two of an old song, altered by her - -

> Oh! Jonny Shaddy, dear John
>   When first we were acquaint,
> Your locks were like the sloe, John,
>   Your bonny brow was brent;
> But now your brow is bald, John,
>   Your locks are like the snow,
> Yet blessings on your frosty prow.
>   Dear, dear Joney, oh my Jo.

Gentlemen, permit me, to subscribe myself your humble servant.

                                                JOHN SHADDY"

Switzerland County Indiana Cemetery Inscriptions 1817-1985; Wanda L. Morford; Cincinnati, Ohio, 1986, p. 353.
Shadday John, a Revolutionary Soldier, born in Orange Co., N. Carolina Feb. 26, 1754, emigrated to this co. in 1814, d. Feb. 2(?), 18(??)/broken, reset
        Mary, wife of John, born in Orange county, North Carolina Dec. 23, 1780, d. Apr. 22, 1863.

Abstract of Graves of Revolutionary Patriots (4 volumes); by Patricia Law Hatcher; Pioneer Heritage Press, Dallas, TX, 1987. Vol. 4, p. 21.
This is an abstract and an index to information reported to the Daughters of the American Revolution and published in their annual reports to the Smithsonian Institution, printed as Senate Documents (1900-1974) and published annually in the DAR magazine (1978-1987).
Published 1972 (Senate Doc. 54)
SHADDAY, John   Slawson Cem, Bennington, Switzerland Co IN

The Indiana Reveille, Vol. XLII, March 2, 1859, pg. 2, col. 1.
Death of a Revolutionary Soldier.
       Mr. John Shaddy, aged 103 years, died near Bennington, in this county, on the 21st day of February, 1859.

Mr. Shaddy was born on the 26th day of February, 1756, in Orange county, North Carolina, and emigrated to this county in 1814. He served as a soldier in the Revolutionary war. His wife aged 80 years, survives him.

Thus one by one, the heroes of our National Independence are fast passing away, and ere long not one will remain to tell the tales that "tried men's souls."

Peace to their ashes, and may their memory ever be revered by their children and their children's children.

Tombstones were photographed by Marlene McDerment, October, 2011.
Slawson Cemetery, Pleasant Township, Switzerland Co., IN.

Tombstone inscription –
In Memory of
John Shaddy
A Revolutionary
Soldier
Born in Orange Co.
No. Carolina
Feb. 26th 1754
Emigrated to this
Co. in 1814
Died - Feb. 21st 1859
Aged 101 years 11Mo 4 Da

Tombstone inscription –
Mary
Wife of John Shaddy
Born
In Orange County
North Carolina
Dec 23, 1780
Died
Apr. 22, 1863

The Vevay Reveille-Enterprise; Vol. 122. No. 39, 28 Sep 1935, p.3, col. 3.
Roster of Revolutionary Soldiers Who Resided in Switzerland County
By Mrs. Effa M. Danner

John Shaddy (Shadday) – He brought his family to Switzerland County about 1814 and settled near Bennington. He is on the pension list of 1835, No. W9647. National Records, Sept. 7, 1832, John Shaddy, Switzerland County, Indiana, age 78. Served in 1779 for five or six months, private in Horse troops commanded by Captain Allen of Guilford, 11th, Regiment, North Carolina Militia, 1780 served 19 months, Col. William O'Neal; 1781 served six months, Captain Hardin Perkins of 14th Regiment, N. Car. Militia.

He was born near Hillsboro, Orange County, N. Car, February 26th, record in his father's handwriting in the Bible. Lived since the Revolution 25 years in North Carolina, 2 years in Tennessee, 4 years in Kentucky, 2 in Ohio and 17 in Indiana. October 6, 1859 Mary Shaddy, his widow applies for pension. Married in Orange County, N.C., April 20, 1795 by Rev. Barnhart, Presbyterian minister. Her maiden name was Fogleman. John Shadday died at Bennington, February 21, 1859, age 104 years, 11 months, 25 days. He is buried at the Slawson grave yard where a tall marble slab marks his grave. He was the last Revolutionary soldier in Switzerland County.

1860, January 12, Emsley Shaddy, 58 years old, names the children, Elizabeth, deceased; Polly, Barbara, Lucinda, Emsley, George, deceased; William Hardin, Jacob, deceased; John, Turley, deceased; Jordon, deceased.

Early marriages in Switzerland County; Polly Shaddy to John Low, Jan. 5, 1830, Emsley Shaddy to Polly Leap, July 28, 1824, George W. Shaddy to Louise Green, Feb. 27, 1832, Barbara Shaddy to Martin E. Cole, June 26, 1832, Jordan C. Shaddy to Lucinda Brinson, June 14, 1841, Lucinda Shaddy to Alexander Thompson, Dec. 2, 1843, John L. Shaddy to Frances O'Neal, Mar. 5, 1847, William H. Shaddy to Frances Dyer, Jan. 26, 1849.

The Shadday family Association has an annual meet in this county with a large membership. Mrs. Hildreth Sisson Riddle, a descendant of George W. Shaddy is a member of the D.A.R. No. 71605, Mrs. Josephine Shadday Griffith of Vevay is a member of the John Paul Chapter D.A.R. of Madison. Her picture was among those published in the D.A.R. magazine, February, 1937, p. 160, as one of the few real granddaughters of a Revolutionary Soldier, now living

SHADDY, WILLIAM

Military evidence has not been located for this man. The only reference regarding a man by this name, living in Switzerland County, is from this citation:
Abstract of Graves of Revolutionary Patriots (4 volumes); by *Patricia Law Hatcher; Pioneer Heritage Press, Dallas, TX, 1987. Vol. 4, p. 21.*
This is an abstract and an index to information reported to the Daughters of the American Revolution and published in their annual reports to the Smithsonian Institution, printed as Senate Documents (1900-1974) and published annually in the DAR magazine (1978-1987).
Published 1925, Serial set 8542, Volume 4.
SHADDY, William   Bennington Cem, Switzerland Co IN

Author's note: The incorrect name, William, was probably recorded instead of the name John Shadday. See record for John Shadday.

Patriot: William Shaddy
Birth:
Married Spouse 1:
Service state(s): -
Service description: None
Rank: -
Proof of Service: None
Pension application No.: None
Residences:
Died: -
Buried: Bennington Cemetery, Pleasant Twp., Switzerland Co., IN
DAR Ancestor No.: None

SHAVER, JOHN

Patriot: John Shaver
Birth: abt. 1766
Married Spouse 1: Nancy
Service state(s): VA
Service description: Reuben Fields, Col. Thomas Gaskinsi Regt., VA Line
Rank: Private
Proof of Service: Pension application S36753
Pension application No.: S36753
Residences: VA; KY; Switzerland Co., IN
Died: aft 1827
Buried: Unknown
DAR Ancestor No.: None

Pension Application Abstracted from National Archives microfilm Series 805, Roll 728, File S36753.
Author's note: Most of the pages of this application are illegible due to light ink that did not copy.
Pension abstract for – John Shaver   Service state(s): VA
Acts of Congress dated 18 March 1818 and 1 May 1820.
Date: 18 April 1827
County of: Switzerland   State of: Indiana
Declaration made before the Circuit Court.
Age: 61 years
Residence when he entered service: State of Virginia
Residence now: Switzerland Co., IN
Volunteer or Drafted or Substitute: Enlisted
Statement of service-

Period	Duration	Names of General and Field Officers
About 14 Feb 1781	3 years	Company commanded by Reuben Fields in the Regiment commanded by Colonel Thomas Gaskinsi in the Line of the State of Virginia.

Discharged: abt. the 1st day of Sept. 1780, on James River, Rockingham Co., VA.
Statement is supported by –
Living witness, name(s): Affidavit of Medley Shelton, sworn in the presence of Henry Harris, J.P., in Gallatin Co., KY. He stated that they (he and John Shaver) served together in the same regiment for about 19 months, commencing about the 1st day of June 1782. They served in the Virginia Line commanded by Captain Reuben Field, in the Regiment commanded by Thomas Gaskins.
Occupation: Farmer – not able to do much work owing to old age and severe affliction of rheumatism.
Wife: Not named – is affected with dropsy
Names and ages of children: Three children, one age 17, second age 14, third age 11. (Not named.)

Switzerland County, Indiana Civil Order Book Vol. 6, Oct. 17, 1825-Apr. 25, 1929, p. 249.
18 Apr 1827 -
John Shafer a Revolutionary Soldier now in open Court files his Schedule, and made the Declaration and took the Oath Required by an Act of Congress relative to pensioners which is ordered to be Recorded, and it is further ordered by the Court to be Certified that the property contained in the Said Schedule is Valued at One hundred and Twenty five Dollars.

Historical Register of Virginians in the Revolution, Soldiers, Sailors, Marines, 1775-1783; John H. Gwathmey; The Dietz Press, Richmond, VA, 1938. p. 703.
Shaver, John, Va. Battalion, 8 CL, 9 CL, 13 CL. Of Fauquier. E.

Revolutionary War Records – Virginia; Virginia Army and Navy Forces with Bounty Land Warrants for Virginia Military District of Ohio, and Virginia Military Script, from Federal and State Archives; by Gaius Marcus Brumbaugh, M.D, M.s., Litt.D; Genealogical Publishing Co., Inc., Baltimore, 1995. p.501.
Virginia Military Land Warrants, Virginia Military district of Ohio, Granted for Revolutionary War Services, State Continental Line, Beginning August 8, 1782.

Number	Warrantee	Rank & Service	
3865	Shaver, John	Soldier	3 years

Catalogue of Revolutionary Soldiers and Sailors of the Commonwealth of Virginia to Whom Land Bounty Warrants Were Granted by Virginia for Military Service in the War for Independence, From Official Records in the Kentucky State Land Office at Frankfort, Kentucky; compiled by Samuel M. Wilson; Southern Book Company, Baltimore, MD, 1953. p.47.

Number of Warrant	Name of Officer or Soldier	Number of Acres	Dept. of Service: Continental or State Line or Navy	Number of Years in Service	Date of Warrant
3865	Shaver, John	100	Pri. Va. Cont. Line	3 yrs.	May 10,1785

American Militia in the Frontier Wars, 1790-1796; by Murtie June Clark; Genealogical Publishing Co., Inc., 1990.
p. 24.
Kentucky Militia
Muster Roll of Mounted Volunteers from Kentucky under the Command of Captain John Hall, Lieut. Colo. Horation Hall's Regiment, in the Service of the United States, Commanded by Major General Charles Scott, Oct 30, 1793.

Nr	Rank	Name	Remarks
65	Private	Shaver, John	enlisted
Oct 1			

p. 66.
Kentucky Militia
Muster Roll of a Company of Mounted Volunteers Under the Command of Captain Henry Lindsey, Major William Russell's Battalion, in the Service of the United States, Commanded by Major General Charles Scott, from Jul 10 to Oct 22, 1794.

Nr	Rank	Name	Remarks
73	Private	Shaver, John	(Negro Solomon)

p. 79.
Kentucky Militia
Muster Roll of a Company of Mounted Volunteers under the Command of Captain Samuel Moore in the Service of the United States Commanded by Major General Charles Scott, July 14, 1794.

Nr	Rank	Name	Remarks
36	Private	Shaver, John	Jul 14-Oct 26, 105 days

Southwest Territory Militia (Note: the Southwest Territory, was an organized incorporated territory of the United States that existed from May 26, 1790, until June 1, 1796, when it was admitted as the State of Tennessee.)
Muster Roll of a Company of Infantry under the Command of Captain Bartley Marshall in the Second Regiment of Washington District Militia Commanded by John Scott, Esquire, Being Called into Service of the United States for the Protection of the Frontier's Territory Northwest of the Ohio for the period Oct 5 to Dec 31, 1793.

Nr	Rank	Name	Remarks
4	Sergeant	Shaver, John	-

Revolutionary War Bounty Land Grants Awarded by State Governments; Lloyd DeWitt Bockstruck; Genealogical Publishing co., IN, Baltimore, MD, 1996. p. 475.
Shaver, John. Va. Private. 10 May 1785. 100 acres.

Register of Certificates Issued by John Pierce, Esquire, Paymaster General and Commissioner of Army Accounts for the United States, to Officers and Soldiers of the Continental Army Under Act of July 4, 1783; Originally Published as Senate Documents, Vol.9, No. 988, 63rd Congress, 3d Session, Washington, 1915; Seventeenth report of the National Society of the Daughters of the American Revolution; Genealogical Publishing Co., Inc, Baltimore, MD, 1984. p. 453.
Men listed in this volume with the same name.

No. of Certificate	To whom issued	Amount
79833	Shaver, John	79.00

The "Lost" Pensions, Settled Accounts of the Act of 6 April 1838; by Craig R. Scott; Willow Bend Books, Lovettsville, VA, 1996. p. 292.
An Act directing the transfer of money remaining unclaimed [for the term of eight months] by certain pensioners, and authorizing payment of the same at the Treasury of the United States.
Name – Nancy Shaver; Pension Office - Administration of Madison, Ind.; Box - 122; Account - #8117.
Author's note: Evidence of spouse name – Nancy.

Early Kentucky Householders 1787-1811; Compiled by James F. Sutherland; Genealogical Publishing Co., Inc., Baltimore, MD, 1986. p. 166.

Lincoln County Tax Lists	Date	bk. pg.	
Shaver, John	09 Jun 96	1.11	1 male over 21

Shiffer, John	26 Jun 99	3.18	"
Shapher, John	20 Jun 00	3.27	"
Shaffer, John	02 May 01	3.31	"
Shiffer, John	08 Jun 09	1.30	"

Revolutionary Soldiers of Switzerland County; Copied by Mary Hill, John Paul Chapter-Daughters of the American Revolution; January, 1958; http://www.ingenweb.org/inswitzerland/switzrevsoldiers.html- Viewed June 2012.
SHAVER, JOHN
Enlisted for 3 years about Feb. 14, 1781, in Virginia company under Capt. Reuben Field, Col. Thomas Gaskins' Regiment. Served until Sept. 1783. Wife and three children named in pension but their names not given. Switzerland County Pension claim S. 36753.

Roster of Soldiers and Patriots of the American Revolution Buried in Indiana, Vol. I; compiled by Mrs. Roscoe C. O'Byrne.; Indiana Daughters of the American Revolution, 1981; p. 328.
SHAVER, JOHN   Switzerland County
Service – Enlisted for 3 yrs., about Feb. 14, 1781, in Vir. CO. under Capt. Reuben Field, Col. Thomas Gaskins' Regt. Served until Sept. 1783.
Proof – Pension claim S. 36753. Wife and children mentioned in application but names not given.

The Vevay Reveille-Enterprise; Vol. 122. No. 39, 28 Sep 1935, p.3, col. 3.
Roster of Revolutionary Soldiers Who Resided in Switzerland County
By Mrs. Effa M. Danner
John Shaver – Switzerland County, April 18, 1827, Enlisted for three years, about Feb. 14, 1781 in Virginia in Company of Capt. Reuben Field of Regiment commanded by Col. Thomas Gaskins. Served until September 1783, discharged on James River, Rockingham Co., Va. Farmer, three children, age 17, 14, and 11. Wife has consumption.
I have not found Shaver's name on our records. Jacob Shaver and David Shaver are listed 1830 census, may be his sons. Jacob Shaver married Nancy Williams, March 20, 1820. David Shaver married Elizabeth McCreary, April 30, 1840.

SHUPE, JOHN
Aka John SHUFF, SHUTTS, SHOOP, SHOUP

Patriot: John Shupe
Birth: 15 Apr 1764 Bucks County, PA
Married Spouse 1: Unknown
Service state(s): PA
Service description: Capt, John Jameson, Col. Weichlein's or S. Dean, PA Regt.
Rank: Private, Ensign
Proof of Service: Pension application S16247
Pension application No.: S16247
Residences: PA; Cincinnati, Hamilton Co., OH; Switzerland Co., IN
Died: 24 Feb 1833 Switzerland Co., IN
Buried: prob. Vevay Cemetery, Jefferson Twp., Switzerland Co., IN
DAR Ancestor No.: None

Switzerland County, Indiana Probate Record Book Vol. A, Mar 1827-Nov 1834; p.437.

Pension abstract for – John Shupe   Service state(s): PA
Date: 16 Aug 1832
County of: Switzerland   State of: Indiana
Declaration made in Open Court.
Age: 68 years   Record of age: Lost it a few years ago.
Where and year born: Bucks Co., PA on 15 Arp 1764
Residence when he entered service: Bucks Co., PA
Residence(s) since the war: In PA for abt. 40 years; in Cincinnati for 1 year; IN
                              balance of time.
Residence now: Switzerland Co., IN
Volunteer or Drafted or Substitute: Enlisted
Rank(s): Private
Statement of service-

Period	Duration	Names of General and Field Officers
1776 or 1777	8 mos.	Company of PA troops commanded by Capt. John Jameson of Col. Hendricks Regt.

Battles: none stated
Discharge received: In Bucks Co., PA
Signed by: Col. S. Dean
What became of it?: Lost or destroyed.
Clergyman: John Pavy
Persons in neighborhood who certify character: John Daniel Morerod, Joseph Malin, John F. Siebenthall, Andrew C. Forbes, John Mendenhall.

National Archives microfilm Series 805, Roll 73, File S16247.
Letter from War Dept. in Pension File – John Shupe
February 18, 1938
Mrs. Mary Hill
801 E. First Street   John Shupe

S.16247
Madison, Indiana
Re: John Shupe, S.16247
Dear Madam:
Reference is made to your request for information relative to Revolutionary War soldier, John Shupe, who was pensioned while living in Switzerland County, Indiana.
The data which follow were obtained from papers on filed in the pension claim S.16247, based upon the military service of John Shupe.
He was born April 15, 1764, in Bucks County, Pennsylvania. The names of his parents were not given.
While a resident of Bucks County, he enlisted in 1776 or 1777 and served eight months as private in Captain John Jameson's company in Colonel Weichlein's or S. Dean's Pennsylvania regiment.
After the Revolution he lived about forty years in Pennsylvania, one year in Cincinnati, Ohio, and the remainder of the time in Indiana.
He was allowed pension on his application executed August 16, 1832, at which time he was living in Switzerland County Indiana.
He was allowed pension on his application executed August 16, 1832, at which time he was living in Switzerland County, Indiana.
There are no data relative to the family of John Shupe.
Very truly yours,
A. D. Hiller
Executive Assistant
to the Administrator

Switzerland County, Indiana Probate Order Book 2, 1831-1837; p. 78.
In the matter of John Shupe an applicant to obtain a Pension}
    Now on this 17th day of August 1832 personally appears in open Court before the Probate Court of Switzerland County now Sitting John Shupe a resident of Switzerland County in the State of Indiana aged Sixty eight years who being first duly Sworn according to law doth on his oath make the following Declaration in order to obtain the benefit of the act of Congress passed June 7th 1832. That he entered the Service of the United States under the following named officers and Served as herein Stated (here insert) And the Said Court do hereby declare their opinion after the investigation of the matter and after putting the interrogations prescribed by the War Department, that the above named applicant was a Revolutionary Soldier and Served as he States and the Court further Certifies it appears to them that John Pavy who Signed the preceding Certificate is a Clergyman resident in Switzerland County in the State of Indiana and that Jean D. Morerod who has also Signed the Same is a resident of the Same County and State and is a credible person, and that their Certificate or Statement is entitled to Credit.

Switzerland County, Indiana Probate Order Book 2, pp. *117, 119, 125, 169, 187, 194.; Switzerland County, IN, Will Book Vol. 1, 3 Jan 1823-10 Nov 1847,* p. *66.;*

Switzerland County, Indiana Probate Record Book Vol. A, Mar 1827-Nov 1834; p.437.
Abstract of will & administration for: John Shupe
State & county where recorded: Switzerland Co., Indiana
Book/volume where recorded: Probate Order Book 2.
Date will made: 21 February 1833
Date entered in probate: 2 March 1833
Name(s) of executors: William D. Cox relinquished executorship, 2 March 1833
Administration:
Date began – 26 March 1833
Name of administrator – Norman Bruce Magruder and Nancy his wife
Date of death: 24 February 1833
Place of death: Switzerland County
Bonded by and amount of bond: Amos Hilbert, Jr. for $200.00
Names of heirs and others mentioned in will (also signed receipts of division of estate) and relationship if shown: To "my friend" Nancy Magruder, wife of Norman B. Magruder, a chest of tools, one shot gun & appurtenances, one bed and bedding, one trunk and clothing, also my claim of pension money due during my natural life, upon the authority of the War Department granted the 7th day of June 1832, for her services rendered me in sickness and for other considerations.
Date of division & disbursement, or final return: Estate settled 12 May 1834

Abstract of Final Payment Voucher; General Services Administration, Washington, DC
LAST FINAL PAYMENT VOUCHER RECEIVED FROM
THE GENERAL ACCOUNTING OFFICE
NAME   Shupe (or Shape), John
AGENCY OF PAYMENT   Indiana
DATE OF ACT   1832
DATE OF PAYMENT   3d Qr. 1833
DATE OF DEATH   Feb 24, 1833
GENERAL SERVICES ADMINISTRATION
National Archives and Records Service   NA-286
GSA-WASH DC 54-4891   November 1953

Pennsylvania Archives, Series 2, Volume XIV. p. 168.
Muster Rolls and Papers Relating to the Associators and Militia of the County of Bucks.
Associated Battalions and Militia of the Revolution
August, 1775 – Whereas, It appears from authentic Accounts Received from England that it is the Design of the Present Ministry to Enforce the Great unjust and Cruel acts of parliament Complained of in the Most Loyal and Dutiful manner by the congress, And whereas, an Additional Number of Troops with a fleet have been ordered for America to assist the Troops now in Boston, in the Execution of Said acts, We the Subscribers agreed that we will associate of the Purpose of Learning the military Exercise and for Defending our Property, Liberty and Lives against all attempts to Deprive us of them.
Roll of the Associated Company for the Township of Tinicum, Bucks county

Captain Nicholas Patterson; 1 Lt. Henry Douty; 2 Lt. Thomas Ramsey; Ensign William Means.
John Shupe is included in the list of privates.

Pennsylvania Archives, Series 5, Volume V. p. 396.
Muster Rolls and Papers Relating to the Associators and Militia of the County of Bucks.
Associators and Militia County of Bucks
Tinicum Company (a.)
Captain Nicholas Patterson; 1 Lt. Henry Douty; 2 Lt. Thomas Ramsey; Ensign William Means
In the list of privates is John Shupe.

Pennsylvania Archives, Series 3, Volume XXIII. p. 600.
Muster Rolls of the Navy and Line, Militia and Rangers, 1775-1783. with List of Pensioners, 1818-1832.
Switzerland County
Shupe, John, pr. P.M., Nov. 21, 1832; 90.

Pennsylvania Archives, Series 3, Volume XIII. p. 89.
Provincial Papers Proprietary and Other Tax Lists of the County of Bucks for the Years 1779,1781,1782,1783,1784,1785,1786.
Bucks County Transcript – 1779
John Shoop, still   239 Acres   3 Horses 2 Cattle   0 Servants

Pennsylvania Archives, Series 5, Volume V. p. 417.
Muster Rolls and Papers Relating to the Associators and Militia of the County of Bucks.
Associators and Militia County of Bucks
A Return of the Men that Marched in Capt. William Erwins Company out of the two First Classes of Tinicum. October 1st, 1781.
Third Class Marched
John Shoup in this list.

Pennsylvania Archives, Series 5, Volume V. p. 444.
Muster Rolls and Papers Relating to the Associators and Militia of the County of Bucks.
Associators and Militia County of Bucks
         Bucks County, May Ye 12th, 1783.
A Return of Militia Officers elected agreeable to the Militia Law, and now returned to the Supreme Executive Council for Commissions Pr Joseph Hart Lieut. of sd. County. (c.)
Battalion No. 3
Captains Nathan Evens, Wm. McHenry, Robert Gibson, Thos. Sebring, William Hines, William Erwin, John Thomas, Mathew Greer.
Lieutenants Josiah Lunn, Nicholas Gares, George Geats, Garret Cavender, Thomas Stewart, Ludwick Worman, Adam Barr, Evan Griffith.

Ensigns Joseph Wilson, Henry Wisel, James Nuckiman, Joseph Caryell, Isaac James, <u>John Shoop</u>, Samuel Simpson, James Ledom.

Pennsylvania Archives, Series 3, Volume XIII. p. 546.
Provincial Papers Proprietary and Other Tax Lists of the County of Bucks for the Years 1779,1781,1782,1783,1784,1785,1786.
Bucks County Transcript 1785
John Shoop   241Acres 3Horses 2Cattle   0 Servants

Pennsylvania Archives, Series 3, Volume XIII. p. 785.
Provincial Papers Proprietary and Other Tax Lists of the County of Bucks for the Years 1779,1781,1782,1783,1784,1785,1786.
Bucks County Transcript – 1787
John Shoop   Amount of tax 17.1

Author's note: John Shupe, Shoop, Shoup, etc. appears in several more citations in the Pennsylvania Archives. There are too many to list here.

Pennsylvania in 1780, A Statewide Index of Circa 1780 Pennsylvania Tax Lists, Compiled by John D and E. Diane Stemmons; Self published, 1978. P. 165.
Shoop, John   BUCK:TN   [Bucks Co.: Tinicum Twp.]

American Militia in the Frontier Wars, 1790-1796; by Murtie June Clark; Genealogical Publishing Co., Inc., 1990. p.103.
Southwest Territory Militia (Note: the Southwest Territory, was an organized incorporated territory of the United States that existed from May 26, 1790, until June 1, 1796, when it was admitted as the State of Tennessee.)
Muster Roll of a Detachment of Mounted Infantry in the Service of the United States in the Southwestern Territory under the command of Cornet George Lee Davidson from Nov 19, 1792 to Jan 20, 1793.

Nr	Rank	Name	Remarks
9	Private	Shute, John	-

1820 U.S. Census, Indiana, Switzerland, Jefferson, Series: M33 Roll: 14 Pg: 261
John Shuff (Shupe) 45 and up; also in household 2 males 10-16, 1 male 16-26, 1female 16-26, 1 female 45 and up.

Indiana Territory, Switzerland Circuit Court Records, Order Book, October Term 1814 to March Term 1815. p.74. He is listed in county records for the first time on 8 May 1820, as a witness for the defendant.
Author's note: There are entries in this volume that are not within the range of dates shown on the binder cover.

Revolutionary Soldiers of Switzerland County; Copied by Mary Hill, John Paul Chapter-Daughters of the American Revolution; January, 1958;
http://www.ingenweb.org/inswitzerland/switzrevsoldiers.html- Viewed June 2012.
SHUPE, JOHN   Pension record: S.16247   Switzerland County, Indiana
John Shupe was born April 15, 1764, in Bucks Co. Pennsylvania

While a resident of Bucks Co. he enlisted in 1776 or 1777 and served eight months as private in Captain John Jameson's Company in Colonel Keichline's or S. Dean's Pennsylvania regiment.
After the Revolution he lived about 40 years in Pennsylvania, one year in Ohio, at Cincinnati, and the remainder of the time in Indiana.
He was allowed pension on his application executed August 16, 1832, at which time he was living in Switzerland County, Indiana.
There are no data relative to the family of John Shupe.
Probate bk. A-pg. 76 Switz. Co.
John Shupe age 68 in 1832
Roster says he died Feb. 24, 1833, probably buried in Vevay cemetery.
Buried: Probably Vevay Cemetery

Roster of Soldiers and Patriots of the American Revolution Buried in Indiana, Vol. I; compiled by Mrs. Roscoe C. O'Byrne.; *Indiana Daughters of the American Revolution,1981; p.331.*

SHUPE, JOHN   Switzerland County
Born – April 14, 1764, Berks Co., Pennsylvania
Service – Enlisted Bucks Co., Penn., 1776 or 77, served 8 mos. pri. in John Jameson's CO. in Col. Keichline's of S. Dean's Penn. Regt.
Proof – Pension claim S. 16247.
Died – Feb. 24, 1833, probably buried Vevay Cemetery.
Collected by Mrs. A. V., Danner, Vevay, Indiana.

The Vevay Reveille-Enterprise; Vol. 122. No. 39, 28 Sep 1935, p.3, col. 4.
Roster of Revolutionary Soldiers Who Resided in Switzerland County
By Mrs. Effa M. Danner
John Shupe – The data which follows were obtained from papers on file in the pension claim, S10247, based on the military service of John Shupe.
He was born April 15, 1764, in Bucks County, Pennsylvania. The names of his parents were not given.
While a resident of Bucks County, he enlisted in 1776 or 1777 and served eight months as private in Captain Jameson's company in Colonel Keichline's or S. Dean's Pennsylvania regiment.
Sallie Burns, William Hannis, Aug, [error in original article]
After the Revolution he lived about forty years in Pennsylvania, one year in Cincinnati, Ohio and the remained of the time in Indiana.
He was allowed pension on his application executed August 16, 1832, at which time he was living in Switzerland County, Ind.
There are no data relative to the family of John Shupe.
John Shupe, Switzerland County Records, Switzerland Monitor (Vevay paper) March 2, 1833, Obituary, "Died in this vicinity on Sunday last, February 24, at an advanced age, Mr. John Shupe. He was a soldier in defense of his county in the Revolutionary War and by act of Congress June 1st was entitled to receive a pension from the Government. But the destroyer came and his soul summoned to the Court of Heaven where we trust it may finally be located and enjoy the felicity of the just made perfect."

Probate Court Record Jan. 3, 1816, Estate of Patrick King – bill allowed of John Shupe for making coffin $6, Allowed of John Shupe for making coffin $5 for Michael Wilson, Nov. 5, 1824 – Rev. soldier also.

Estate of John Shupe – 1834, p. 194 N.B. Magruder and Nancy Magruder administrators – final settlement, will annexed. (I have not found this will.)

Life of Washington – Washington Irving, p. 241. Kechline's riflemen were under Lord Sterling at the Battle of Long Island.

SIX, JOHN
aka SYKE, SYKES

Patriot: John Six
Birth: 18 Aug 1758 VA (prob. Shenandoah Co.)
Married Spouse 1: KY 1785- 1794   possibly -
Mary or Maria DeWald/Duvall/Devault
(d. 3 Sep 1825 Switzerland Co., IN)
Service state(s): VA
Service description: Capt. Matthew Arbuckle, Col. John Newell, 12th VA Regt.
Rank: Private
Proof of Service: Pension application S36758
Pension application No.: S36758
Residences: VA; KY; Switzerland Co., IN; Posey Co., IN
Died: 22 Jun 1842 Posey Co., IN
Buried: Maple Hill Cemetery, New Harmony, Posey Co., IN
DAR Ancestor No.: None

Pension Application Abstracted from National Archives microfilm Series 805, Roll 740, and File S36758; Switzerland County, Indiana Complete Records, Circuit Court, Vol. ?, Sep 3, 1821-Apr 18, 1827; p. 513.

Pension abstract for – John Six   Service state(s): Virginia
Date: 17 October 1825
County of: Switzerland   State of: Indiana
Declaration made before a Circuit Court.
Age: 67 years
Where and year born: born 18 August last [1758]
Residence(s) since the war: to Kentucky then to Indiana
Residence now: Switzerland Co., IN
Volunteer or Drafted or Substitute: Enlisted
Rank(s): Private
Statement of service-

Period	Duration	Names of General and Field Officers
5 Aug 1776	12 months	Company commanded by Capt. Matthew Arbuckle
	and 2 additional months	in 12th Virginia regiment commanded by Col. John Newell.

Discharge received: at the "great Kanawah" in VA, by Arbuckle.
Occupation: Farmer but unable to make a living owing to old age.
I have no family.
Schedule of property presented.
Wife: Not named, died 3 Sep 1825
Marriage date and place: No date, in Kentucky
Names and ages of children: Referred to daughters who were married but not named. States – residing in house belonging to my son-in-law which he loaned to me for residence.

Additional note in file: In the Report of the Secretary of War, printed in 1835, the name of the soldier was erroneously recorded on the list of pensioners of Dearborn County, Indiana.

Switzerland County, Indiana Civil Order Book Vol. 6, Oct. 17, 1825-Apr. 25, 1829, p. 6.
17 Oct 1825 –
Now John Six a Revolutionary Soldier files here in Court his Schedule of Property, and made the Declaration, and took the Oath Required: And it is ordered by the Court to be Certified that the Property contained in the Said Schedule is Valued by the Court to Twenty Seven Dollars and Fifty Cents.

Abstract of Final Payment Voucher; General Services Administration, Washington, DC
FINAL PAYMENT VOUCHER RECEIVED FROM
THE GENERAL ACCOUNTING OFFICE
NAME   Six, John
AGENCY OF PAYMENT   Indiana
DATE OF ACT   1818
DATE OF PAYMENT   4th Qr. 1842
DATE OF DEATH   June 29, 1842
GENERAL SERVICES ADMINISTRATION
National Archives and Records Service   NA-286
GSA-WASH DC 54-4891   November 1953

Virginia Revolutionary Militia, A List of Non-Commissioned Officers and Soldiers of the Virginia Line on Continental Establishment, Whose names appear on the Army Register, and who have not received Bounty Land; Printed by Samuel Shepherd, Printer to the Commonwealth, Richmond, VA. 1835. p. 44.
Doc. No. 44.
Sicks, John   Soldier   Infantry

Revolutionary War Records – Virginia; Virginia Army and Navy Forces with Bounty Land Warrants for Virginia Military District of Ohio, and Virginia Military Script, from Federal and State Archives; by Gaius Marcus Brumbaugh, M.D, M.s., Litt.D; Genealogical Publishing Co., Inc., Baltimore, 1995. p.270.
List of non-commissioned officers and soldiers of the Continental Line. List may contain names of individuals who received bounty land for services in the State Line.
Sicks, John, Soldier, Inf.

Draper Series, Volume III - Frontier Defense On The Upper Ohio, 1777-1778, Compiled from the Draper Manuscripts in the Library of the Wisconsin Historical Society of the Sons of the American Revolution; Edited by Reuben Gold Thwaites, LL.D, Superintendent of the Society and Louise Phelps Kellogg, Ph.D. Editorial Assistant on the Society's Staff; Madison Wisconsin Historical Society, 1912. p. 305.

Pay Abstract of Capt. John Witsell's (Wetzel's) company of Rangers, Monongahala County under command of Col. Daniel McFarland. Ranging in Monongahala and Ohio Counties from the 22nd day of April to the 25th July 1778 both days included:
John Six is included in the list of Privates [his name is entered twice]

Historical Register of Virginians in the Revolution, Soldiers, Sailors, Marines, 1775-1783; John H. Gwathmey; The Dietz Press, Richmond, VA, 1938. p. 716.
Six, John, WD. Monongalia Mil. E.

Register of Certificates Issued by John Pierce, Esquire, Paymaster General and Commissioner of Army Accounts for the United States, to Officers and Soldiers of the Continental Army Under Act of July 4, 1783; Originally Published as Senate Documents, Vol.9, No. 988, 63rd Congress, 3d Session, Washington, 1915; Seventeenth report of the National Society of the Daughters of the American Revolution; Genealogical Publishing Co., Inc, Baltimore, MD, 1984. p. 462.
Men listed in this volume with the same name.

No. of Certificate	To whom issued	Amount
77091	Sisk, John	100.00
77412	Sisk, John	80.00
77678	Sisk, John	50.75
76778	Sisk, John	135.56

Second Census of Kentucky, 1800; Clift G. Glenn; Genealogical Publishing Co., Baltimore, MD, 1954.
An alphabetical list of 32,000 taxpayers based on original tax lists on file at the Kentucky Historical Society. Information given includes the county of residence and the date of the tax list in which the individual is listed.
Six, John   Montgomery   8/22/1800

1810 Federal Census, Kentucky, Montgomery County, Roll: 7; Page: 360
John Six – 1 male under 10; 1 male 10-15; 2 males 16-25; 1 male over 45; 1 female under 10; 1 female over 45.

1820 U.S. Census, Indiana, Switzerland, Pleasant, Series: M33 Roll: 14 Pg: 255
John Six 45 and up; also in household; also in household 1 male under 10, 1 male 10-16, 1 female under 10, 1 female 26-45.

Indiana Territory, Switzerland Circuit Court Records, Order Book, October Term 1814 to March Term 1815. p.86.
He is listed in county records for the first time on 13 September 1820, as a juror.
Author's note: There are entries in this volume that are not within the range of dates shown on the binder cover.

A Census of Pensioners for Revolutionary or Military Services with their Names, Ages, and Places of Residence Under the Act for Taking the Sixth Census in 1840; Genealogical Publishing Co., Inc., Baltimore, Maryland, 1965. p.184.

INDIANA, POSEY COUNTY, NEW HARMONY

Names of Pensioners for Revolutionary or Military services	Ages	Names of heads of families with whom pensioner resided June 1, 1840
John Six	80	John Six [b. abt. 1760]

Roster of Soldiers and Patriots of the American Revolution Buried in Indiana, Vol. I; compiled by Mrs. Roscoe C. O'Byrne.; Indiana Daughters of the American Revolution, 1981; p.332.
SIX, JOHN   Posey County
Born – Aug. 18, 1758.
Service – Enlisted in Vir., Aug. 5, 1776, served as a pri. in Capt. Matthew Arbuckle's CO., Col. John Nevill's Vir. Regt. and was discharged at "the great Kanawha", having served 14 mos.
Proof – Pension claim S. 36758.
Died – 1826. Buried Maple Hill Cemetery. Marked by New Harmony Chapter D. A. R.
Married – Wife died 1825. Daughter, m. John Grant.
Collected by New Harmony Chapter D.A. R.
Author's note: The death date shown in this record is probably in error.

Abstract of Graves of Revolutionary Patriots (4 volumes); by Patricia Law Hatcher; Pioneer Heritage Press, Dallas, TX, 1987. Vol. 4, p. 37.
This is an abstract and an index to information reported to the Daughters of the American Revolution and published in their annual reports to the Smithsonian Institution , printed as Senate Documents (1900-1974) and published annually in the DAR magazine (1978-1987).
Published 1923, Serial set 8234, Volume 2; Published 1972 (Senate Doc. 54).
SIX, John   Maple Hill Cem, New Harmony, Posey Co IN

Maple Hill Cemetery, New Harmony, Posey Co., IN
Tombstone inscription –   JOHN SIX
                                  VA. MIL.
                                  REV. WAR

Posey County Cemetery Records; Carroll O. Cox and Posey County Burials, Vol. II; Darlene McConnell . Both books list John Six, Va. Mil. Rev. War in Maple Hill Cemetery (no dates).
In 1977, the General Thomas Posey Chapter Daughters of the American Revolution erected a marker In Memory of Soldiers of the American Revolution 1775-1783 Buried in Posey County. John Six is listed 2nd name from the bottom. The marker that is located at the west entrance of the Posey County Courthouse in Mount Vernon, IN.

The Vevay Reveille-Enterprise; Vol. 122. No. 39, 28 Sep 1935, p.3, col.3-4.
Roster of Revolutionary Soldiers Who Resided in Switzerland County
By Mrs. Effa M. Danner

John Six removed to Posey County, Switzerland Coun- [transcribed as written - error in original article]
Pension Certificate No. 19653. Switzerland County 1820 census, he lived in Pleasant Township, 2 boys, 1 girl and wife.
Marriage record p. 42, Joseph Six, Ruth McPhearson, June 4, 1820, John Six gave consent. Margaret Six, Colin Grant, Nov. 18, 1820, [error in original article] 28, 1819, John Six, stepfather of lady, giving consent. Wm. J. Stewart J. of P. John Six removed to Posey County, Ind. and died there. U. S. Military Census 1840, residence, New Harmony, Posey County, John Six, age 80.

SMYTH, PHILLIP D.
aka SMITH

Patriot: Phillip D. Smyth
Birth: 19 Oct 1759
Married Spouse 1: Unknown
Service state(s): MD
Service description: Capt. William Hirer, Col. Hooicker, MD Line,
                Gen. Mecklinberg, Continental Line; Gen. Sullivan
Rank: Private
Proof of Service: Pension application S40466
Pension application No.: S40466
Residences: Hagerstown, MD; Switzerland Co., IN; Hamilton Co., OH
Died: 20 Jan 1837 Hamilton Co., OH
Buried: Hamilton Co., OH
DAR Ancestor No.: None

Pension Application Abstracted from National Archives microfilm Series 805, Roll 752, and *File S40466; Switzerland County, Indiana Complete Records, Circuit Court, Vol. ?, Sep 3, 1821-Apr 18, 1827; p. 527.*

Pension abstract for – Philip D. Smith   Service state(s): Maryland
                                                               Continental
Alternate spelling(s): Phillip D. Smyth, Philip Smith
Date: 10 October 1825
County of: Switzerland   State of: Indiana
Declaration made before a Circuit Court.
Age: 66 years on 19 Oct 1825
Residence when he entered service: Hagerstown, Maryland
Residence now: Switzerland Co., IN
Volunteer or Drafted or Substitute: Enlisted for 3 years, then volunteered for 2-3 months.
Rank(s): Not stated
Statement of service-

Period	Duration	Names of General and Field Officers
1 Aug 1776	3 years	Company commanded by Capt. William Hirer, regt. commanded by Col. Hooicker, in Line of State of Maryland attached to Gen. Mecklinberg's regt. of Continental establishment.
Abt. 1779	2-3 mos.	Gen. Sullivan into the Indian country up the Susquehanna.

Battles: Princeton, Brandywine, Germantown, Monmouth.
Discharge received: from second tour at Wyoming, State of Pennsylvania
Wife: aged about 75 (not named)
&
Request for transferred of Pension
Date: 10 March 1828
City of: Cincinnati   County of: Hamilton   State of: Ohio

Declaration made before the Mayor of Cincinnati.
States his name was placed on the Pension Roll of the State of Indiana from whence he has lately removed, that he now resides in Hamilton County in the State of Ohio where he intends to remain and wishes his pension to be there payable in future, and that his reason for removing to the State of Ohio was that he might be among his friends.
Note: Transferred to Ohio 3 May 1828.

Switzerland County, Indiana Civil Order Book Vol. 6, Oct. 17, 1825-Apr. 25, 1929, p. 22.
19 Oct 1825 -
And now here comes Phillip D. Smyth, a Revolutionary soldier, and files his Schedule of Property and Made the Declaration, and took the Oath Required by a Late act of Congress, relative to pensioners which are ordered to be Recorded. And it is Ordered to be Certified that the property contained in said Schedule is Valued by the Court to Seven Dollars and fifty cents.

Abstract of Final Payment Voucher; General Services Administration, Washington, DC
NAME   Smith, Philip D.
AGENCY OF PAYMENT   Cincinnati, Ohio
DATE OF ACT   1818
DATE OF PAYMENT   2d qr 1837
DATE OF DEATH   Jan 20, 1837
FINAL PAYMENT VOUCHER RECEIVED FROM
THE GENERAL ACCOUNTING OFFICE   Form
General Services Administration   GSA DA 70-7035 GSA Dec 69 7068

Index of Revolutionary War Pension Applications; by Max Ellsworth Hoyt & Frank Johnson Metcalf, Agatha Bouson Hoyt, Mabel Van Dyke Baer & Sadye Giller; National Genealogical Society, Washington, DC, 1966;p. 1073.
SMYTH (or SMITH), PHILIP D., Cont. (Md.)
b. 4/26/1759, enl. at Hagerstown, Md.
res. in 1825 Switzerland, Ind. S40466

The Maryland Militia in the Revolutionary War; by S. Eugene Clements and F. Edward Wright; Published by Family Line Publications, Westminster, MD 21157,1987. p. 241.
Washington County
A List of the Officers & men in Capt. Joseph Chapline's Compy. 1 Lieut. James Chapline; 2 Lieut Thomas Crampton; Ensign James Stewart
6th Class: Phillip P Smith (on list)

Muster Rolls and other records of service of Maryland Troops in the American Revolution; Archives of Maryland, reprinted with permission by Genealogical Publishing Co., Inc., Baltimore, 1972. p. 72.
Records of Maryland Troops in the Continental Service

Frederick County – Middle District.
    10 September 1776.
Vallentine Creager, Capt.   George Need, (Neet), 2nd Lieut.
Phillip Smith, Jr., 1st Lieut. John Parkinson, (Pirkinson), Ensign
Register of Certificates Issued by John Pierce, Esquire, Paymaster General and Commissioner of Army Accounts for the United States, to Officers and Soldiers of the Continental Army Under Act of July 4, 1783; Originally Published as Senate Documents, Vol.9, No. 988, 63rd Congress, 3d Session, Washington, 1915; Seventeenth report of the National Society of the Daughters of the American Revolution; Genealogical Publishing Co., Inc, Baltimore, MD, 1984. p. 470.
Men listed in this volume with the same name.

No. of Certificate	To whom issued	Amount
36861	Smith, Phillip	24.00
37206	Smith, Philip	72.60
38011	Smith, Philip	80.00
38428	Smith, Philip	80.00
38985	Smith, Philip	40.60
72493	Smith, Philip	33.30
72709	Smith, Philip	14..60

Revolutionary Soldiers of Switzerland County; Copied by Mary Hill, John Paul Chapter-Daughters of the American Revolution; January, 1958; http://www.ingenweb.org/inswitzerland/switzrevsoldiers.html- Viewed June 2012.
SMYTH, PHILIP D.
Born: -
Enlisted for 3 years, Aug. 13, 1776 in Hagerstown, Maryland, under Capt. William Hirer, Regt. of Col. Hoociker, Col Sticker, Major Wiltner, Maryland Line, attached to Gen. Mechlinberg's Brigade, Continental Establishment. Volunteered for 2 or 3 months tour under Gen. Sullivan to go up Susquehanna River. In battles of Princeton, Brandywine and Germantown and Monmouth.
Married: In 1825 his wife was 75 years old.
Died:
Collected by Mrs. A. V. Danner, Vevay, Indiana

Official Roster III, Soldiers of the American Revolution Who Lived in the State of Ohio; Daughters of the American Revolution, 1959. p. 329.
Smith, Philip D. - Hamilton Co
Pvt. drew pens in Ind, Cert No 19628. May 26, 1826. To O[hio] May 3, 1828.
Ref: DAR Magazine, July 1949, p. 614.

The Official Roster of the Soldiers of the American Revolution Buried in the State of Ohio; Compiled under the direction of Frank D. Henderson, the adjutant-general, John R. Rea, military registrar, Daughters of the American revolution of Ohio. Jane Dowd Dailey (Mrs. O. D.) state chairman; The F. J. Heer Printing Co., Columbus, OH, 19229-1959. p. 342.
SMITH, PHILIP D., (Hamilton Co.)
Br 1759, Maryland. D 1837. Ref: S. A. R. Fur infor Cincinnati Chap.

National Society of the Sons of the American Revolution - Revolutionary War Graves Register; Compiled and Edited by Clovis H. Brakebill, Published by db Publications, Dallas, TX, 1993. p. 561.
SMITH, Philip D.; 1759-17=837; Hamilton Co., OH; Soldier, MD.

Roster of Soldiers and Patriots of the American Revolution Buried in Indiana, Vol. 1; compiled by Mrs. Roscoe C. O'Byrne.; Indiana Daughters of the American Revolution, 1981; p.337.
SMYTH, PHILLIP D.   Switzerland County
Service – Enlisted for 3 yrs. Aug. 18, 1776, in Hagerstown, Md., under Capt. Wm. Hirer, Regt. of Col. Hooicker, Col. Sticker, Maj. Wiltber, Md. Line, attached to Gen. Mechlenberg's Brigade, Continental Establishment. Discharged. Volunteered for 2 or 3 mos. tour under Gen. Sullivan to go up Susquehanna River. In battles of Princeton, Brandywine and Germantown, and Monmouth.
Proof - Switzerland County Court – Order Book D., p. 627. Declaration made Oct. 5, 1825. His wife was 75 yrs. old.
Collected by Mrs. A. V. Danner, Vevay, Indiana
Author's note: Smyth did not die in Indiana – he died in Hamilton Co., Ohio.

The Vevay Reveille-Enterprise; Vol. 122. No. 39, 28 Sep 1935,p.3, col. 4.
Roster of Revolutionary Soldiers Who Resided in Switzerland County
By Mrs. Effa M. Danner
Phillip D. Smyth – Declaration listed October 9, 1825, Switzerland Co. Court Book D. Record Book, p. 627. He enlisted for a term of three years August 18, 1776 in Hagerstown, Maryland in the Company of Wm. Hirer, Regiment of Col. Hooicker and Col. Sticker, Major Wilton, Maryland line attached to General Mechlenbergs Brigade, Continental Establishment. After three years service was discharged and volunteered for 2 or 3 months tour under Gen. Sullivan into Indian country on the Susquehanna river, discharged from service at Wyoming, Pa. by Capt. Baiser who was in command of regiment. He was at the battles of Prinstown, N.J., Brandywine and Germantown and Monmouth.
He was a farmer and shoemaker but unable to work. His wife is 75 years old.

STEPLETON, ANDREW

Patriot: Andrew Stepleton
Birth: 1752   Romney, VA
Married Spouse 1: Barbara X (b. 1761 d. aft. 5 Jan 1820)
Service state(s): VA
Service description: Capt. William Voss, Cols. Wood, Neville,
                     Gen. Scott, 12th Regt.
Rank: Private
Proof of Service: Pension application S36799
Pension application No.: S35799
Residences: Romney, VA; Indiana Territory; Switzerland Co., IN
Died: 20 Nov 1843 Switzerland Co., IN
Buried: Allensville, Cotton Twp., Switzerland Co., IN
DAR Ancestor No.: A108476

Pension Application Abstracted from National Archives microfilm Series 805, Roll XXX, File S36799.
Pension abstract for – Andrew Stepleton   Service state(s): Virginia
Date: 5 May 1818 & 13 Feb 1820
County of: Switzerland   State of: Indiana
Declaration made before a Circuit Court.
Age: 69 years
Residence when he entered service: Virginia
Residence now: Jefferson Twp., Switzerland Co., IN
Volunteer or Drafted or Substitute: Enlisted at Romney, VA
Rank(s): Private
Statement of service-

Period	Duration	Names of General and Field Officers
1777-1783	6 yrs, 2 mos.	Capt. William Vause, Col. James Wood's 12th Regt. of the Virginia Line.

Battles: Brandywine – wounded in the left arm;
          Monmouth – wounded in the thigh
Discharge received: at Winchester, VA
Signed by: Col. Neville
Occupation: Farmer and am much afflicted with rheumatism
Wife: Not named   Wife's age: about 59 years
Names and ages of children: daughter Betsey age 18 yrs. , and John Cole age 9 yrs.

Switzerland County, Indiana Civil Order Book 4, 1820 – 1823, pg. 116.
Feb. 1821
Andrew Stepleton, Revolutionary soldier & U.S. pensioner---$81.62 ½

Historical Register of Virginians in the Revolution, Soldiers, Sailors, Marines, 1775-1783; John H. Gwathmey; The Dietz Press, Richmond, VA, 1938. p. 739.
Stepleton, Andrew E.

Virginia Revolutionary War Land Grant Claims 1783-1850 (Rejected); William Lindsay Hopkins; *self published, Richmond, VA, 1988, p. 207-208.*
Stepleton, Andrew – Soldier – Army - Switzerland CO, Indiana
Andrew Stepelton, aged 73, of Switzerland CO, Indiana on 5 Aug 1830 states that he enlisted under Capt. William Voss of the 12th VA Regt of Col. James Wood of Winchester, VA. He enlisted at Fort Pleasant near Winchester, VA and is now a pensioner.

A Partial Census For Indiana Territory 1810; Compiled by John D & E. Diane Stemmons; Census Publishing LC, Sandy, UT, 2004. p.515.
Stepleton, Andrew, Historical Locality: Indiana Territory, Current State: Indiana, Dearborn County, First Township – Name on list of electors of election held 3 April 1809 at the house of Daniel Dufour.- Election Returns, 1809, 1812 (Indiana Historical Society), Coll. #M98 Box 32, Folder 1 pg 9.
Stepleton, Andrew, Male

Early Ohio Settlers, Purchasers of Land in Southwestern Ohio, 1800-1840; Compiled by Ellen T. Berry & David A. Berry; *Genealogical Publishing Co., Inc., Baltimore, MD, 1986. p.311.*

Purchaser	Year	Date	Residence	R – T - S
Stepleton, Andrew (B)	1813	June 07	Jefferson	03-03-19

(B) Indiana Survey: Land lying west of a meridian drawn west of the Great Miami (known as the "Gore"). Switzerland, Dearborn, Franklin, Ohio, Union and Randolph Counties (all or only a part of each county) – all in Indiana.

Early Settlers of Indiana's "GORE" 1803-1820; Compiled and Edited by Shirley Keller Mikesell; *Heritage Books, Inc., 1995. p. 188.*
Switzerland County Original Land Entries Tract Book
Township 3, Range 3
Section 26 – Andrew Stepleton – 1813 – pg. 12.

Indiana Land Entries Vol. 1 Cincinnati District, 1801-1840; Margaret R. Waters; *Originally Published Indianapolis 1948, Second Reprint 1979 by The Bookmark, P.O. Box 74, Knightstown, In 46148. p. 71.*
CINCINNNATI LAND DISTRICT – VOL. 1
Page 66. Twp. 3 N, Range 3 W of 1st Principle Meridian SWITZERLAND CO. SW ¼ - S26; 6-7-1813.
-- Note: The tract books for the land offices in Indiana are deposited in the office of the Auditor of State, Indianapolis. They and are in the custody of the State Land clerk. --

U.S. Department of Interior, Bureau of Land Management, General Land Office Records; Land Patent Search – accessed 27 June 2012.
STEPLETON, ANDREW
Accession Nr. CV-0035-248; Document Type – Credit Volume Patent; State - Indiana; Issue Date – 8/11/1817; Cancelled – No
Land Office – Cincinnati; Authority – April 24, 1820 Sale-Cash Entry (3 Stat. 566); Total Acres – 0.00

Land Description: State - IN; Meridian – 1st PM; Aliquots – 003N-003W; Section - 26; County - Switzerland

Indiana Territory, Switzerland Circuit Court Records, Order Book, October Term 1814 to March Term 1815. p.74.
He is listed in county records for the first time on 8 May 1820, as a juror.
Author's note: There are entries in this volume that are not within the range of dates shown on the binder cover.

Author's note: Andrew Stepleton, and his wife Barbary, sold land on 5 Jan 1820. This indicates she was living at this time. See *Switzerland County, Indiana Deeds, Vol. A., p. 492.*

1820 U.S. Census, Indiana, Switzerland, Pleasant, Series: M33 Roll: 14, p. 255
Andrew Stepleton 45 and up; also in household 1 male under 10, 1 female 16-26, 1 female 45 and up.

The Pension List of 1820 [U.S. War Department] Reprinted with an Index; by Murtie June Clark; Genealogical Publishing Co., Inc., Baltimore, 1991. Originally published 1820 as Letter from the Secretary of War. p. 658.
Names of the Revolutionary Pensioners which have been placed on the Roll of Indiana, under the Law of the 18th of March, 1818, from the passage thereof, to this day, inclusive, with the Rank they held, and the Lines in which they served, viz.

Names	Rank	Line
Andrew Stepleton	private	Virginia

A Census of Pensioners for Revolutionary or Military Services with their Names, Ages, and Places of Residence Under the Act for Taking the Sixth Census in 1840; Genealogical Publishing Co., Inc., Baltimore, Maryland, 1965. p.185.
INDIANA, SWITZERLAND, COTTON

Names of Pensioners for Revolutionary or Military services	Ages	Names of heads of families with whom pensioner resided June 1, 1840
Andrew Stepleton	96	Andrew Stepleton

Revolutionary Soldiers of Switzerland County; Copied by Mary Hill, John Paul Chapter-Daughters of the American Revolution; January, 1958; http://www.ingenweb.org/inswitzerland/switzrevsoldiers.html - Viewed June 2012.
STEPLETON, ANDREW   Switzerland County. Pension claim S.26799
Born about 1752
Enlisted at Romney, Virginia, 1777
Served in Capt. William Vause's company, Col. James Wood's 12th Virginia Regiment. In battles of Brandywine and Monmouth. Wounded
Served 6 years and 2 months.
Discharged at Winchester, Va. by Col. Neville.
Married: Barbara _____.

472

Children: John m Polly Johnson; Betsy m Daniel Cole; Andrew m Huldah Spencer
Buried: Probably at Allensville, Cotton twp.
Collected by Mrs. A. V. Danner, Vevay, Indiana.

Roster of Soldiers and Patriots of the American Revolution Buried in Indiana, Vol. I; compiled by Mrs. Roscoe C. O'Byrne.; Indiana Daughters of the American Revolution, 1981; p.342.
STEPLETON, ANDREW   Switzerland County
Born – About 1752.
Service – Enlisted at Romney [Romney], Vir. Served in Capt. William Vause's CO., Col. James Wood's 12th Vir. Regt. Vir. Regt. In battle of Brandywine and Monmouth. Wounded. Served 6 yrs. and 2 mos. Discharged at Winchester, Vir. by Col. Neville.
Proof – Pension claim S. 36799.
Buried – Probably at Allensville, Cotton Twp.
Married – Barbara _____. Ch. John, m. Polly Johnson; Betsy, m. Daniel Cole; Andrew, m. Huldah Spencer.
Collected by Mrs. A. V. Danner, Vevay, Indiana.

Roster of Soldiers and Patriots of the American Revolution Buried in Indiana, Vol. II; 1966; p.135.
STEPLETON, ANDREW   Switzerland County
Additional Data On Some Of The Soldiers Listed In Volume I
Son, John Stepleton, m. Sarah Dow.
By Mrs. Belle Dufour Stepleton, Vevay, Ind.

History of Switzerland County Indiana 1885; Reproduced by the Switzerland County Historical Society, Vevay, Indiana, 1999. The portion of the book relating to Switzerland County in the 1885 printing of the "History of Dearborn, Ohio, and Switzerland Counties, Indiana". p. 1143.
Cotton Township – "Andrew Stepleton, a Revolutionary pensioner, was in business in the village about 1828. He kept liquor to sell by the quart in those days of sobriety."

The Vevay Reveille-Enterprise; Vol. 122. No. 39, 28 Sep 1935, p.3, col. 4.
Roster of Revolutionary Soldiers Who Resided in Switzerland County
By Mrs. Effa M. Danner
Andrew Stepleton – The data which follow are obtained from the papers on file in Revolutionary War pension claim S36799, based upon the military service in that war of Andrew Stepleton.
The date and place of birth and the names of parents of Andrew Stepleton are not shown.
Andrew Stepleton enlisted at Romney, Virginia, in the spring of 1777, served in Captain William Vause's Company, Colonel James Wood's 12th Virginia Regiment, was in the battle of Brandywine, September 11, 1777, where he was wounded in the left arm and in the battle of Monmouth here wounded in the

thigh; he served six years and two months and was discharged at Winchester, Virginia, by Colonel Neville.

He was allowed pension on his application executed May 25, 1818, while residing in Jefferson Township, Switzerland County, Indiana.

In 1821, he gave his age as sixty-nine years and stated that his family then residing with him consisted of his wife, aged 59 years, a daughter Betsy, aged 18 years, and john Cole, aged 9 years. He gave no further particulars in regard to his wife nor did he state any relationship to the said John Cole.

He is listed on the U.S. Military Census 1840, age 96. Entered land patent S.W. qt. Sect. 26, T3, R3W, signed Jas. Monroe, August 11, 1817. He lived at Allensville and kept stire – license dated 1836.

Deed – Book A., p. 794 signed by his wife, Barbara, 1820. Children, John Stepleton married Polly Johnson, Dec. 19, 1815. Elizabeth married Daniel Cole, Sept. 18, 1826. Andrew married Hulda Spencer, Nov. 30, 1830. May have been others.

This family has given soldiers to every war of the U.S. Jesse Stepleton, Mexican War; Capt. Andrew Stepleton, Civil War; Wm. Stepleton, Spanish War; Bert Stepleton, Battleship Virginia, World War.

STEWART, CHARLES
aka STEWARD

Patriot: Charles Stewart
Birth: 1759 VA
Married Spouse 1: Nancy Ann Beckley
                 (b.1760/1762 VA, d. 5/7 Nov 1837 Ripley Co., IN)
Service state(s): VA
Service description: Capt. Jones; Col. Gibson
Rank: Private Marine 18 mos.
Proof of Service: Pension application S16261
Pension application No.: S16261
Residences: Spotsylvania Co., VA; Switzerland Co., IN; Ripley Co., IN
Died: 4 or 6 Feb 1845 Switzerland Co., IN
Buried: Cross Plains Methodist Church Cemetery, Cross Plains, Ripley Co., IN
DAR Ancestor No.: A135172

National Archives microfilm Series 805, Roll 772, File S16261.
Letter from War Dept. in Pension File – Charles Steward

Mrs. Iva Hisle   March 6, 1936
410 East Main Street   Charles Steward – S.16261
Madison, Indiana   BA-J/AWF
Dear Madam:

     Reference is made to your letter in which you request the Revolutionary War record of Charles Stewart, who was pensioned in 1832, while living in Indiana.

     The data furnished herein were obtained from the papers on file in the pension claim, S.16261, based upon the service of Charles Steward in the Revolutionary War.

     The date and place of birth of this soldier are not given, nor are the names of his parents stated.

     Charles Steward (as the name is found in the claim), while residing in Spotsylvania County, Virginia, enlisted in 1775 and marched down to Hobbs Hole under Lieutenant Stubblefield, and there went into the marine service and served eighteen months. He enlisted December 20, 1776, for three years, served in Captain Gabriel Jones' company, Colonel George Gibson's Virginia regiment, was furloughed, May 17, 1779 on account of sickness.

     He was allowed pension on his application executed August 13, 1833, then aged seventy-three years and living in Ripley County, Indiana.

     The papers in this claim contain no reference to the family of Charles Steward.

                                              Very truly yours
                                              A.D. HILLER
                                              Executive Assistant to the
                                              Administrator

Author's note: He made application in Jefferson County, Indiana. Certificate of Application was issued in Madison, Jefferson Co., Switzerland Co., IN, 19 Nov 1832.

Abstract of Final Payment Voucher; General Services Administration, Washington, DC
FINAL PAYMENT VOUCHER RECEIVED FROM
THE GENERAL ACCOUNTING OFFICE
NAME   Stewart, Charles
AGENCY OF PAYMENT   Indiana
DATE OF ACT   1832
DATE OF PAYMENT   4th Qr. 1845
DATE OF DEATH   Feb 6, 1845
GENERAL SERVICES ADMINISTRATION
National Archives and Records Service   NA-286
GSA-WASH DC 54-4891   November 1953

Pennsylvania Archives, Series 3, Volume XXIII. p. 597.
Muster Rolls of the Navy and Line, Militia and Rangers, 1775-1783 with List of Pensioners, 1818-1832.
Statement Showing the Names of Pennsylvanians Residing in the State of Indiana, Who Have Been Inscribed on the Pension List under the Act of Congress Passed June 7th, 1832.
Dearborn County   Reamer, David, artificer P.M., July 30, 1833; 80.

Register of Certificates Issued by John Pierce, Esquire, Paymaster General and Commissioner of Army Accounts for the United States, to Officers and Soldiers of the Continental Army Under Act of July 4, 1783; Originally Published as Senate Documents, Vol.9, No. 988, 63rd Congress, 3d Session, Washington, 1915; Seventeenth report of the National Society of the Daughters of the American Revolution; Genealogical Publishing Co., Inc, Baltimore, MD, 1984. p. 483.
Men listed in this volume with the name Charles Steward & Charles Stewart & Charles Stuart.
Author's note: Due to the large number of men with this name they are not listed here. "Pierce's Register" is available in most large libraries.

Muster and Pay Rolls of the War of the Revolution 1775-1783, Collections of The New-York Historical Society for the Years 1914 an 1915; Printed for the Society, New York, 1914. p. 6.
ARTILLERY 1ST REGIMENT, Capt. William Brown's Company 1780, Payroll of Capt. William Brown's Company in the first Regiment of Artillery commanded by Colonel Charles Harrison, for September, October & November 1780.

Names	Rank	Time in Service		Pay pr	Amount
		Mo	Days	Mo.	
Charles Stewart	Sergeant	3	-	10	30

Historical Register of Virginians in the Revolution, Soldiers, Sailors, Marines, 1775-1783; John H. Gwathmey; The Dietz Press, Richmond, VA, 1938. p. 741.
Steward, Charles (Stuart) 1 CL, 1 Va. State Reg., 1 and 10 CL, 3 and 4 CL, 7 CL, 15 CL.

Stewart, Charles, (Stuart) 1 CL, 1 Va. State Reg., 1 and 10 CL, 3 CL, 3 and 4 CL, 5 CL, 5 and 9 CL, 15 CL.

Revolutionary War Bounty Land Grants Awarded by State Governments; Lloyd DeWitt Bockstruck; Genealogical Publishing co., IN, Baltimore, MD, 1996. p. 505.
Stewart, Charles, Va. Private. 6 Feb 1797 100 acres.

Revolutionary War Records – Virginia; Virginia Army and Navy Forces with Bounty Land Warrants for Virginia Military District of Ohio, and Virginia Military Script, from Federal and State Archives; by Gaius Marcus Brumbaugh, M.D, M.s., Litt.D; Genealogical Publishing Co., Inc., Baltimore, 1995.
p. 116
List of Officers of the Army and Navy, Who Have Received Lands from Virginia for Revolutionary Services; The Quantity Received, The Time of Service for which each Officer Received Land, &c. Down to September, 1833.
Stewart, Charles   Ensign   Cont'l   2666-2/3 Apr. 10, 1819   3 years
p. 503
Virginia Military Land Warrants, Virginia District of Ohio, Granted for Revolutionary War Services, State Continental Line, Beginning August 8, 1872.

Number	Warrantees	Rank & Service	
4768	Stewart, Charles	Soldier	3 years

p. 617
Original Bounty Land Warrants Located in Virginia Military District in Ohio
Stewart, Charles

U.S. Department of Interior, Bureau of Land Management, General Land Office Records; Land Patent Search – accessed 27 June 2012.
STEWART, CHARLES
Accession Nr. CV-0022-487; Document Type – Credit Volume Patent; State - Indiana; Issue Date – 10/3/1814; Cancelled – No
Names on Document: Stewart, Charles; Lane, Joseph
Land Office – Jeffersonville; Authority – April 24, 1820 Sale-Cash Entry (3 Stat. 566); Total Acres – 0.00
Land Description: State - IN; Meridian – 2nd PM; Aliquots – 005N-011E; Section - 19; County - Jefferson
&
Accession Nr. CV-0040-205; Document Type – Credit Volume Patent; State - Indiana; Issue Date – 7/15/1818; Cancelled – No
Names on Document: Stewart, Charles; Lander, John
Land Office – Jeffersonville; Authority – April 24, 1820 Sale-Cash Entry (3 Stat. 566); Total Acres – 0.00
Land Description: State - IN; Meridian – 2nd PM; Aliquots – 005N-012E; Section - 9; County - Switzerland
&
Accession Nr. CV-0040-207; Document Type – Credit Volume Patent; State - Indiana; Issue Date – 7/15/1818; Cancelled – No
Names on Document: Stewart, Charles; Lander, John

Land Office – Jeffersonville; Authority – April 24, 1820 Sale-Cash Entry (3 Stat. 566); Total Acres – 0.00
Land Description: State - IN; Meridian – 2nd PM; Aliquots – 005N-012E; Section - 4; County - Switzerland
&
Accession Nr. CV-0053-362; Document Type – Credit Volume Patent; State - Indiana; Issue Date – 12/6/1820; Cancelled – No
Land Office – Jeffersonville; Authority – April 24, 1820 Sale-Cash Entry (3 Stat. 566); Total Acres – 160.00
Land Description: State - IN; Meridian – 2nd PM; Aliquots – 006N-012E; Section - 21; County - Ripley

A Census of Pensioners for Revolutionary or Military Services with their Names, Ages, and Places of Residence Under the Act for Taking the Sixth Census in 1840; Genealogical Publishing Co., Inc., Baltimore, Maryland, 1965. p.185.
INDIANA, SWITZERLAND, PLEASANT

Names of Pensioners for Revolutionary or Military services	Ages	Names of heads of families with whom pensioner resided June 1, 1840
Charles Steward	82	Charles Steward

1840 U.S. Census, Indiana, Switzerland, Pleasant, Series: M704 Roll: 95 Pg: 131
Charles Stewart age 80-90; others in household 1 male under 5, 2 males 5-10, 1 male 10-15, 1 male 30-40, 1 female 10-15, 1 female 30-40.
Pensioners for Revolutionary or Military Services Included in the Foregoing

Names	Age
Charles Steward	82

Roster of Soldiers and Patriots of the American Revolution Buried in Indiana, Vol. I; compiled by Mrs. Roscoe C. O'Byrne.; Indiana Daughters of the American Revolution, 1981; p. 343.
STEWART, CHARLES   Jefferson County
Born - 1759
Service – While residing in Spotsylvania Co., Vir., enlisted in 1775, marched to Hobbs Hole under Lt. Stubblefield, went into the marine service, served 18 mos. Enlisted Dec. 20, 1776, for 3 yrs. served in Capt. Gabriel Jones' CO., Col. George Gibson's Regt. Was furloughed May 17, 1779, on account of sickness, Proof – Penn. Archives, Series 2, vol. 10, p. 637. Pension claim S16261.
Died – 1840, in Switzerland Co. May be buried across the line in Ripley or Switzerland.
Married – Ann ------.
Collected by John Paul Chapter D.A.R., Madison, Indiana.

Roster of Soldiers and Patriots of the American Revolution Buried in Indiana, Vol. III; 1980; p. 76.
From a Roster of Revolutionary Ancestors of the Indiana Daughters of the American Revolution, Vol. 1, p. 608.
STEWART, CHARLES   Roster 1, p. 343   Ripley County

Proof – Ripley Co., Ind. Probate C:375 dated Nov. 3, 1845.
Died – Feb. 4, 1845 age 85 yrs., 3 mos. Buried Methodist Church, Cross Plains, Ripley Co., Ind.
Married – Nancy Ann Beckley d. Nov. 7, 1837 age 77.
Children – Sally m. John Copeland; Rebecca m. James Hukill; Charles; John d. Oct. 8, 1852 age 50; Levi d. Mar. 5, 1847 age 18.
By Mrs. David Gibbs, RR #2, Box 58, Holton, Indiana 47023.

<u>Roster Soldiers and Patriots of the American Revolution Buried in Indiana</u>; Compiled and Edited by Mrs. Roscoe C. O'Byrne; Published by Indiana Daughters of the American Revolution, 1938.
Stewart, Charles
b. 1759; d. 1840, Switzerland Co., IN; may be bur. across the line in Ripley or Switzerland Co; m. Ann ____.

<u>Cross Plains Cemetery, Cross Plains, Ripley Co., IN</u>
Charles Stewart (Senior) & wife tombstone inscriptions -

Newer tombstone –	Original tombstone -	
CHARLES STEWART PVT REGT VA LINE REV WAR FEB 4 1845	CHARLES STEWART SEIGNOR died February 4th, 1845 Aged 85 Years & ? months	NANCY STEWART Consort of Charles Stewart died November 5th 1847 Aged 75 Years

479

TODD, JOSEPH

His service has erroneously been attributed as being the Revolutionary War as seen in some of the following records. Joseph Todd served in a Kentucky unit at the Battle of the Wabash, aka St. Clair's Defeat that was a part of the Northwest Indian War. The battle began on 4 November 1791. This conflict was a lingering aspect of the Revolutionary War therefore Joseph Todd's record in included in this volume.

Patriot: Joseph Todd
Birth: 27 Feb 1769   Place unknown
Married Spouse 1: 13 Sep 1810 Bath Co., KY   Katherine Ferguson
Married Spouse 2: 11 Jul 1817 Switzerland Co., IN   Villa McPhearson
          Prior to 9 November 1841, Villa (McPhearson) Todd was married to Stephen Rogers (Revolutionary Soldier). See will/administration abstract on this page.
Service state(s): KY
Service description: KY
Rank: Private
Proof of Service: Pension application X811
Pension application No.: X811
Residences: KY; Switzerland Co., IN
Died: . Mar. 20, 1837 Switzerland Co., IN aged 68y 29d
Buried: Long Run Cemetery, Craig Twp., Switzerland Co., IN
DAR Ancestor No.: None

Pension Application Abstracted from National Archives microfilm Series 805, Roll 806, File X811.
The pension file for Joseph Todd pertains to his service at the Battle of the Wabash, aka St. Clair's Defeat that was part of the Northwest Indian Wars. The file has been re-constructed because the original papers were "burned". He received "Invalid Pension" beginning 14 Jan 1812 for the wound he received during that service.

Switzerland County, Indiana Probate Order Book 2, 1831-1837; p. 492.
8 May 1837   Now on this day comes into Villa Todd and addressed to the Court Satisfaction that Joseph Todd late of this County of Switzerland in the State of Indiana, was an invalid pensioner and that he was placed on the pension list rolls of the Indiana agency, that he departed this life in said County of Switzerland on the 26th day of March 1837 leaving Villa Todd his lawful widow.

Switzerland County, Indiana Probate Order Book 2, p. 492; and *Switzerland County, Indiana Probate Order Book 3, 1837-1843;* pp. 24, 96, 129, 140, 169, 170, 181, 267, 289, 313, 347, 412, 452. & Cotton Admin. pp. 187, 197, 198, 212, 236; and *Switzerland County, Indiana Probate Orders Book, 1843-1849,* p. 42, 408, 430, 450, 464-5.
Abstract of will and/or administration for: Joseph Todd
State & county where recorded: Switzerland Co., Indiana

Date entered in probate: 26 March 1837
Administration:
Date began – 26 March 1837
Name of administrator – Villa Todd & Ralph B. Cotton
November Term, 1837 – John Todd brings amicable suit vs. Villa Todd & Ralph B. Cotton.
14 November 1837 - Villa Todd appointed guardian of minor heirs of Joseph Todd, being Jesse Todd & Adalina Todd, Joseph Todd, and Catherine Ann Todd.
14 November 1838 – R.B. Cotton filed his account of the estate.
Citation ordered by the Court that Villa Todd be notified and citing her to appear in court on the first day of the next term.
12 February 1839 - On the motion of Villa Todd notice be given to the heirs of said estate, by publication in the Vevay Times a paper printed and published in Vevay for three weeks previous to the first day of the next term of the Court, that this estate will be settled on the third day of the next term of the Court.
14 May 1839 -   Villa Todd files her account of the estate, and pays $239.43, the amount of assets that has come into her hands belonging to said estate. Court orders $230.00 be divided among the several heir being Henry Rogers as assignee of Elizabeth Windsor, Ruth Rogers, and David H. Todd $76.65, and to John Todd $25.00.
15 May 1839 -   Distribution is receipted.
17 May 1839 -   John F. Cotton appointed Administrator.
11 November 1839 - Villa Todd files her account for services as administratrix and resigns her services.
12 May 1840 -   R. B. Cotton late administrator files his account of the estate.
9 November 1841 - John F. Cotton and Villa Rogers the widow of said decedant and former administratrix of estate. By agreement the Court orders all proceedings in the collection of a judgment until the amount that may be coming to the said Villa Rogers shall be ascertained.
10 May 1842 -   Judgment against Villa Rogers and other is dissolved and case is continued.
Bonded by and amount of bond:
26 Mar 1837 - David Lewyallen & A. H. Grimes & Joseph Dow for $(not stipulated)
17 May 1839 – John F. Cotton to James M. Cotton for $500.00.
Names of heirs and others mentioned in will (also signed receipts of division of estate) and relationship if shown: Henry Rogers as assignee of Elizabeth Windsor, Ruth Rogers and David H. Todd, & John Todd.
Date of division & disbursement, or final return: 15 May 1839; March 1849 distribution to Villa.

Abstract of Final Payment Voucher; General Services Administration, Washington, DC
FINAL PAYMENT VOUCHER RECEIVED FROM
THE GENERAL ACCOUNTING OFFICE
NAME   Todd, Joseph
AGENCY OF PAYMENT   Indiana

DATE OF ACT 1818
DATE OF PAYMENT 4th Qr. 1837
DATE OF DEATH March 4, 1837
GENERAL SERVICES ADMINISTRATION
National Archives and Records Service NA-286
GSA-WASH DC 54-4891 November 1953

Index to U.S. Invalid Pension Records 1801-1815; by Murtie June Clark; Genealogical Publishing Co., Inc., 1991; p.98.
Joseph Todd received Invalid Pension due to the wound he received during the Battle of Wabash. KENTUCKY

Name	Rank	Page	Remarks
Todd, Joseph	Private	133	began Jan 14, 1812

Note: This book is an index to the ledger titled: "Revolutionary War and Acts of Military Establishment, Invalid Pensioners Payments, March 1801 through September 1815, containing pensions paid by the United States to invalid soldiers who served in the Revolutionary War and the frontier wars after 1783."
Description : "This ledger is an important substitute for lost claim files, composed of evidence and testimony of Revolutionary War soldiers together with judicial certification and War Department confirmation, that perished in the catastrophes in the capital city."A soldier received an invalid pension if he was wounded, injured, or contracted a disease in the service.

Second Census of Kentucky, 1800; Clift G. Glenn; Genealogical Publishing Co., Baltimore, MD, 1954.
An alphabetical list of 32,000 taxpayers based on original tax lists on file at the Kentucky Historical Society. Information given includes the county of residence and the date of the tax list in which the individual is listed.
There are four entries for Joseph Todd. The enties in Madison Co. are probably not this man. Another Joseph Todd (Pension W3055) resided in Madison Co.

Todd, Joseph	Barren	1800
Todd, Joseph	Madison	8/12/1800
Todd, Joseph	Madison	10/1/1800
Todd, Joseph, Sr.	Madison	10/1/1800

Early Settlers of Indiana's "GORE" 1803-1820; Compiled and Edited by Shirley Keller Mikesell; Heritage Books, Inc., 1995.
p. 198.
Switzerland County Deeds; Book A
Joseph Todd is witness -
Deed dated 1818. John Francis Dufour & Polly his wife, to Abner K. Starr of Butler Co., OH. Vevay lots 123, 183. Signed John Francis Dufour, Polly Dufour. Witness: Truman Richards, Joseph Todd. pp. 119, 120.
p. 207.
Switzerland County Deeds; Book A
Joseph Todd is witness -

Deed dated 1819. Henry Hannis & Hannah, his wife, to James Bell. S36, T3, R4W. "to Sarah Bell". Signed Henry Hannis, Hannah (x) Hannis. Witness: Joseph Gilliand, <u>Joseph Todd</u>. pp. 232, 233.
p. 211.
Switzerland County Deeds; Book A
Joseph Todd is witness -
Deed dated 1819. Henry Hannis & Hannah, his wife, to Sarah Bell. S36, T3, R4W. Signed Henry Hannas, Hannah (x) Hannis. Witness: John Gilliand, <u>Joseph Todd</u>. pp. 299, 300, 301.

<u>U.S. Department of Interior, Bureau of Land Management, General Land Office Records; Land Patent Search</u> – accessed 27 June 2012.
TODD, JOSEPH
Accession Nr. CV-0050-438; Document Type – Credit Volume Patent; State - Indiana; Issue Date – 3/21/1820; Cancelled – No
Names on Document: Todd, Joseph; Vandine, Henry
Land Office – Jeffersonville; Authority – April 24, 1820 Sale-Cash Entry (3 Stat. 566); Total Acres – 315.52
Land Description:

State	Meridian	Aliquots	Section	County
IN	2nd PM	004N-012E	11	Switzerland
IN	2nd PM	004N-012E	14	Switzerland

<u>Indiana Territory, Switzerland Circuit Court Records, Order Book, October Term 1814 to March Term 1815.</u> p.74.
He is listed in county records for the first time on 8 May 1820, as a juror.
<u>Author's note:</u> There are entries in this volume that are not within the range of dates shown on the binder cover.

<u>The Hoosier Genealogist;</u> Fifth year (issue unknown); Switzerland county Marriages 1814-1830; Credited to Louise A. L. Knox.
Marriage – Todd, Joseph – Villa McPhearson 7-11-1817

<u>Switzerland County, Indiana Early Marriage Records 1814-1825;</u> by. Colleen Alice Ridlen; Copyright by Walter R. Gooldy, Ye Olde Genealogie Shoppe, Indianapolis, IN, 2001. p. 24.
Todd, Joseph   Villa McPhearson   July 1, 1817

<u>1820 U.S. Census, Indiana, Switzerland, Vevay, Series: M33 Roll: 14 Page: 254</u>
Joseph Todd 45 and up; also in household 1 male under 5, 1 male 10-16, 1 male 16-26, 1 male 26-45, 2 females 16-26.

<u>1850 U.S. Census, Indiana, Switzerland, Pleasant Twp., Series: M432 Roll: 174 Page: 324, Family No. 367.</u>
Villa Rogers, Age 54, Real estate value $150., Born VA; in her household is Catherine Todd, Age 19, Born IN.

Revolutionary Pensioners, A Transcript of the Pension List of the United States for 1813; Southern Book Company, Baltimore, 1959. p. 45.

		No on Roll	Rank or Quality	Annual Stipend
Kentucky	Joseph Todd	20	Private	24

Revolutionary Soldiers of Switzerland County; Copied by Mary Hill, John Paul Chapter-Daughters of the American Revolution; January, 1958; http://www.ingenweb.org/inswitzerland/switzrevsoldiers.html- Viewed June 2012.
TODD, JOSEPH
Pension record is listed in Roster of Indiana Soldiers of the Revolution but later information says he did not serve in that war.
*See Vevay Reveille, Sept. 28, 1938
Born abt 1769 (Source: The Vevay Reveille-Enterprise; 28 September 1938 issue.)
Married--1st wife unknown.
Children: Nancy m James McClanahan, John m Nancy Lock, David
Married: 2d wife, Villa McPherson
Children: Jesse, Adaline, Catherine.
Died in 1837.
Buried in Long Run cemetery.
Stone: Inscription reads "Revolutionary Soldier"
Collected by Mrs. A. V. Danner, Vevay, Indiana.
Switzerland County Court records have material on Joseph Todd.

Roster of Soldiers and Patriots of the American Revolution Buried in Indiana, Vol. I; compiled by Mrs. Roscoe C. O'Byrne.; Indiana Daughters of the American Revolution, 1981; p.356.
TODD, JOSEPH
Service – Inscription on stone reads "Revolutionary Soldier".
Died – 1834. Buried Long Run Cemetery. Stone
Married – First W. unknown. Ch. Nancy, m. James McClanahan; Ruth, m. Stephen Rogers, Jr.; Joseph Jr., m. Eleanor Lock; John, m. Nancy Lock; David. Second W., Villa McPhearson. Ch. Jesse; Adaline; Catherine.
Collected by Mrs. A. B. Danner, Vevay, Indiana.

The Vevay Reveille-Enterprise; Vol. 122. No. 39, 28 Sep 1935, p.3, col. 3.
Roster of Revolutionary Soldiers Who Resided in Switzerland County
By Mrs. Effa M. Danner
Joseph Todd is listed as a Revolutionary Soldier but it is a mistake the Revolutionary War closed in 1783 and the French and Indian War followed and Joseph Todd fought in this war. He served in Captain George Madison's Co. in Regiment of Col. Oldham and wounded at St. Claire's defeat in the waist, Nov. 4, 1781. Switzerland County, Ind., Nov. 1819, late of Montgomery Co., Ky. Invalid pension increased from $2.00 to $3.00 on Kentucky rolls February 1820. Original papers burned. Old War, Indian file – 25886.
He died Mar. 26, 1837, buried at Long Run Baptist churchyard.

Census 1820, Pleasant township, four boys, one girl and wife. First wife unknown. Children John Todd married Nancy Lock; Nancy Todd married James McClanahan, July 1, 1815; Ruth Todd married Stephen Rogers, Jr., April 20, 1822; Joseph Todd Jr., married Eleanor Lock, Aug. 13, 1850. Joseph Todd Jr. [error – should be Joseph Todd, Sr.] married Vella McPhearson July 11, 1817 by Wm. Keen. Probate Court 1837, p. 492. Jesse Todd, Joseph Todd, Sena and Catherine Todd, infant heirs of Joseph Todd, also Hugh, Mary, Jerry and Susan McClanahan, minor heirs of James and Nancy Todd McClanahan. Evaline Todd Tower, wife of Daniel Tower, minor heir of Joseph Todd, 1843, p. 523. Mrs. Vella Todd, widow, married Stephen Rogers, Jr. May 10, 1839.

Switzerland County Indiana Cemetery Inscriptions 1817-1985; Wanda L. Morford; Cincinnati, Ohio, 1986, p. 70.
Todd Joseph, d. Mar. 20, 1837 aged 68y 29d

Abstract of Graves of Revolutionary Patriots (4 volumes); by Patricia Law Hatcher; Pioneer Heritage Press, Dallas, TX, 1987. Vol. 4, p. 119.
This is an abstract and an index to information reported to the Daughters of the American Revolution and published in their annual reports to the Smithsonian Institution, printed as Senate Documents (1900-1974) and published annually in the DAR magazine (1978-1987).
Published 1972 (Senate Doc. 54)
TODD, Joseph   Long Run Cem, Switzerland Co   IN

Long Run Cemetery, Craig Twp., Switzerland Co., IN
Tombstone inscription –
JOSEPH
TODD
CAPT
G. MADISON'S CO
COL OLDHAM'S
REGT
INDIAN WARS
FEB 27 1769
MAR 26 1837

Author's notes:
There are several references to Joseph Todd in the Pennsylvania Archives that might be attributable to this man. Some citations are in Chester County where Owen Todd served. I have not determined if Owen and Joseph Todd are related. Joseph Todd has been proven for the lineage society "First Kentucky Ancestors" See Kentucky Ancestors (periodical); Frankfort, KY; Winter 1990, Vol. 25, Iss. 3. pg. 177.
Joseph Todd
Born 27 Feb. 1769, Va. Resided in Clark, Warren/Baren (now Monroe), Montgomery/Bath cos. of Ky. Moved to Switzerland Co., Ind., where he died 26 Mar. 1837.; buried Long Run Baptist Cemetery, Switzerland Co., Ind. Married 2nd, 13 Sept. 1810, Bath Co., Ky., to -

TODD, OWEN

Patriot: Owen Todd
Birth: 20 Apr 1762 Philadelphia Co., PA
Married Spouse 1: Elizabeth X
Married Spouse 2: 9 Jun 1790 Rockbridge Co., VA   Maria Jane Paxton
(b. 22 Apr 1771 d. 1834 Madison, Jefferson Co., IN)
Her father, Col. Thos. Paxton, Rev. War
Service state(s): PA
Service description: Pennsylvania Archives, *Ser. 2, Vol. XIV. p. 126;* 5th Series, Vol. 5, p. 862. Capt. Alexander Johnson, Col. John Gardner, 1st Battalion, Chester Co. Militia, Light Horse
Rank: Private
Proof of Service: Pennsylvania Archives
Pension application No.: None
Residences: Hanover Twp., Lancaster Co., PA; Chester Co., PA; Switzerland Co., IN
Died: 15 Jan 1817 Switzerland Co., IN
Buried: Vevay Cemetery, Jefferson Twp., Switzerland Co., IN
DAR Ancestor No.: A114381

Switzerland County Probate Order Book 1, Nov 1814 - Sept1824; p. 43, 58, 68, 238, 246 and *Switzerland County, Indiana Probate Order Book 2, 1831-1837; p. 5, 13;* and *Switzerland County, Indiana Probate Record Book Vol. A, Mar 1827- Nov 1834; p. 193.*
Abstract of will and administration for: Owen Todd
State & county where recorded: Switzerland Co., Indiana
Date will made: 28 November 1816, in Vevay, Switzerland County, Indiana
Witnesses: John Mendanhall, Joshua Smithson, Jane Steel.
Date entered in probate: 15 January 1817
Name(s) of executors: Wife, Jane Todd
Administration:
Name of administrator – Executrix, wife Jane Todd
15 January 1817 – Administration began
21 July 1816 - Jane Todd produced inventory of the goods & chattels of Owen Todd, dec'd. Inventory filed.
14 April 1824 - Court grants motion for John Todd, one of the heirs of Owen Todd, to be Administrator, so soon as Timothy Beebe and Jane Beebe late Jane Todd relinquish their right of Administration.
24 April 1824 - Timothy Beebe and Jane Beebe, wife of Timothy Beebe, late Jane Todd relinquish the right of Administration of the estate of Owen Todd.
May 1831 - Citation ordered to Sheriff of Jefferson County citing David Todd, Admin. to appear at the next term of the court,
July 1831 - Estate settled.
Bonded by and amount of bond: Jane Todd to Paxton W. Todd for $1,200.00
John Todd to Hiram Ogle & Francis G. Lindley for $800.00

Names of heirs and others mentioned in will: Wife, Jane; Children, Owen, Maria, Paxton Warren, Robert, David, John, Isabella, Nancy, Levi, Eliza & Elijah Smith, & Hannah Redd.
Date of division & disbursement, or final return: July 1831

Marriage - The Hoosier Genealogist; Fifth year (issue unknown); Switzerland county Marriages 1814-1830; Credited to Louise A. L. Knox.
Beebe, Timothy to Jane Todd 11-3-1823
[Jane Todd is the widow of Owen Todd - also see will/estate abstract]

Pennsylvania Archives, Series 2, Volume XIV. p. 126.
Muster Rolls and Papers Relating to the Associators and Militia of the County of Chester.
Associated Battalions and Militia of the Revolution
Light Horse, 1780-1781
A Return of the names and number of the Volunteer Militia Light Horse for the County of Chester, with a State of their equipment and the Battalions to which they respectively belong.
Captain Alexander Johnson. Lieutenant Samuel Vanleer; Cornet James Clarke.
First battalion, Colonel Gardner
Owen Todd is in this list.

Pennsylvania Archives, Series 5, Volume V. p. 862.
Muster Rolls Relating to the Associators and Militia of the County of Chester.
Light Horse, 1781
Captain Alexander Johnson; Lieutenant Samuel Vanleer; Cornet James Clarke
First Battalion, Colonel John Gardner
Owen Todd is in this list.

American Militia in the Frontier Wars, 1790-1796; by Murtie June Clark; *Genealogical Publishing Co., Inc., 1990.* p. 42.
Kentucky Militia
Muster Roll of the Staff, Commissioned and Noncommissioned of General Robert Todd's Brigade of Mounted Volunteers from Kentucky in the Division Commanded by General Charles Scott, mustered at Fort Washington, Oct 23, 1794. [Located in now Newport, KY across the Ohio River from Cincinnati.]

Nr	Rank	Name	Remarks
24	QM Sgt	Todd, Owen	-

Kentucky Ancestors (periodical); Frankfort, KY; Winter 1990, Vol. 25, Iss. 3. pg. 217.
Some Residents of Virginia and Other "Persons Chargeable with Tax" in Kentucky Counties, 1794-95.
Owen Todd   400 acres (2nd rate) in Bourbon County, Kentucky

Early Settlers of Indiana's "GORE" 1803-1820; Compiled and Edited by Shirley Keller Mikesell; Heritage Books, Inc., 1995. p. 218.
Switzerland County Deeds; Book A

487

Deed dated 1819. John James Dufour to Jane Todd, widow of Owen Todd. S22, T2, R3. Signed J.J. Dufour. Witness: Truman Richards, Elisha Golay. Pp. 433, 434, 435.

1820 U.S. Census, Indiana, Switzerland, Posey, Series: M33 Roll: 14 Page: 262.
Jane Todd (wid. of Owen) female 45 and up; others in household 2 males under 10, 1 male 10-16, 1 male 16-18, 2 males 16-26, 1 female under 10, 1 female 10-16.

History of Switzerland County Indiana 1885; Reproduced by the Switzerland County Historical Society, Vevay, Indiana, 1999. *The portion of the book relating to Switzerland County in the 1885 printing of the "History of Dearborn, Ohio, and Switzerland Counties, Indiana". p. 1212.*
In the passage for Francis S. Dupraz who married Julia L. Dumont - "Mrs. Durpaz's, father Abram B. Dumont, was born in New Brunswick, N.J., September 2, 1789; her mother, Isabella R. (Todd) Dumont, was born in Lebanon, Ohio, November 24, 1804. They were married in December 1820, and raised ten children. They moved to this county in 1814, and here Mrs. D. died February 2, 1879. Her grandparents Owen and Jane (Paxton) Todd, moved to this county in 1816. Owen Todd at the age of fourteen, acted as a guide to Gen. Washington on his retreat from Valley Forge, for which at the insistence of Washington, David Todd, his father, presented him a horse, which he rode to Kentucky, and kept as a war horse. He was the youngest son and remained with his father until his death December 6, 1817, at the age of fifty-five years."

Switzerland County Indiana Cemetery Inscriptions 1817-1985; Wanda L. Morford; Cincinnati, Ohio, 1986, p. 155.
Vevay Cemetery Section 2, Jefferson Twp., Switzerland Co., IN
TODD, Owen d. Dec. 6, 1817 age 55

Vevay Cemetery, Jefferson Twp., Switzerland Co., IN
Tombstone inscription –

> In memory of
> OWEN TODD
> who departed his life
> Dec. 6, 1817
> aged 55 Years
> (rest of tombstone is illegible)

Author's note: There is an article posted at www.findagrave.com regarding this man. Evidence is not shown so the material is not included here.

TOWER, GIDEON

Patriot: Gideon Tower
Birth: 30 Apr 1753 Cumberland, Providence Co., RI
Married Spouse 1: Mar 1775 Abigail Perkins
                        (b. 28 Nov 1754 d. May 1847 Dearborn Co., IN)
Service state(s): CT & RI
Service description: Capts. Clift, Hutchins, Wilcox, Noble, Cols. Parsons,
                     Herrick, Dyer
Rank: Private, Non-commissioned officer, Orderly Sgt.
Proof of Service: Pension application S17735
Pension application No.: S17735
Residences: Windham Co., CT: Bennington Co., VT; Coventry, Kent Co., RI;
            NY; KY; Switzerland Co., IN; Dearborn Co., IN
Died: Sep 1847 Cesar Creek Twp., Dearborn Co., IN
Buried: Caesar Creek Twp., Dearborn Co., IN
DAR Ancestor No.: A115277

Pension Application Abstracted from National Archives microfilm Series 805, Roll 808, File S17735.

Pension abstract for – Gideon Tower   Service state(s): Connecticut
                                                       Rhode Island
                                                       Vermont

Date: 1832
County of: Dearborn   State of: Indiana
Declaration made before a Judge or Court.
Age: 79 years
&
Date: 17 September 1832
County of: Switzerland   State of: Indiana
Declaration made before a Circuit Court.
Recorded in Book F, pg. 70.
Age: 79 years   Record of age: In town record books. No copy here.
Where and year born: 30 April 1753 at Cumberland Co., Rhode Island
Residence when he entered service: Not stated
Residence(s) since the war: About 16 years in New York, about 2 years in Kentucky, 16 years in Dearborn County, Indiana.
Residence now: Dearborn Co., IN
Volunteer or Drafted or Substitute: Enlisted 1775, 1775, Substitute 1778, Enlisted 1779, 1780.
Rank(s): 1775, 76, 78, 79 Private; 1780 Orderly sergeant.
Statement of service-

Period	Duration	Names of General and Field Officers
1775		Company of Connecticut Militia commanded by Capt. Cleft of Parson's regiment.
1776		Company of Rhode Island troops

489

	commanded by Capt. Wilcox of Dyer's regiment.
1778	Substitute for Av Boober in same company.
1779	Company of Vermont Militia commanded by Capt. Noble in Herrick's regiment.
1780	Company of Vermont Militia commanded by Capt. Hutchins of Herrick's regiment.

Battles: None stated
Discharge received: No written discharge.
Statement is supported by –
Documentary proof: None
Person now living who can testify to service: None
Clergyman: John Pavy, resident of Switzerland County
Persons in neighborhood who certify character: Samuel Pavy resident of Switzerland County, James Murray, Joel Pearce, James T. Pollock, Joseph Wood, Esq., Ezra Lampkins, Dr. Gillespie, Benj. Livew.
No data regarding family

Switzerland County, Indiana Civil Order Book Vol., A, Oct. 19, 1829-April 16, 1837, p. 171.
In the matter of Robert Moore, Griffith Dickinson, Nathan Ricketts, Gideon Tower, and John Shaddy, An application to obtain a pension under the Act of Congress of the 7th June AD 1832.

    Personally appeared in open Court, before the Switzerland Circuit Court now sitting the above named applicants who being first duly Sworn doth on their several oaths make their several declarations in order to obtain the benefit of the Act of Congress of the 7th June AD 1832 that they entered the Service of the United States under the officers named in their several declarations (here insert them) And the said Court do hereby declare their opinion after the investigation of the matter and after putting the interrogations prescribed by the War department that the above named Applicants were revolutionary Soldiers and Served as they have stated and the Court further Certifies that it appears to them that John Pavy who Signed their several Certificates is a Clergyman Resident in Switzerland County and State of Indiana and the other persons who has also Signed the Same are credible persons and that their Statements in entitled to credit.

Abstract of Final Payment Voucher; General Services Administration, Washington, DC
LAST FINAL PAYMENT VOUCHER RECEIVED FROM
THE GENERAL ACCOUNTING OFFICE
NAME	Tower, Gideon
AGENCY OF PAYMENT	Indiana
DATE OF ACT	1832
DATE OF PAYMENT	March 1, 1847

DATE OF DEATH
GENERAL SERVICES ADMINISTRATION
National Archives and Records Service   NA-286
GSA-WASH DC 54-4891   November 1953

Rolls and Lists of Connecticut Men in the Revolution, 1775-1783; Originally published by the Connecticut Historical Society 1901; Reprint by Heritage Books, Inc, Westminster, MD, 2008. p. 170.
Militia Regiments, 1776   Lieut. Parke's Company
Pay Roll of Lt Robart Parke Company in col Douglas Regt who Joined the American army in the Stat of Newyork Sept
Elisha Hall and Gideon Tower Recd 20s each & were left sick on the Road & Returned home & nothing Drawn for them.
Jany 31, 1777   Test Robert Parke Lieut

1840 U.S. Census, Indiana, Switzerland, Pleasant, Series: M704 Roll: 95 Pg: 128
Gideon Tower age 80-90; others in household 1 male 5-10, 1 male 10-15, 1 male 40-50, 1 female 10-15, 1 female 15-20, 1 female 80-90.
Gideon was not listed as a pensioner on the next page.

Roster of Soldiers and Patriots of the American Revolution Buried in Indiana, Vol. I; compiled by Mrs. Roscoe C. O'Byrne.; Indiana Daughters of the American Revolution, 1981; p.357.
TOWER, GIDEON   Dearborn County
Born – April 11, 1753, Cumberland, Providence Co., R.I.
Service – Enlisted 1775 in CO. of Conn. Militia under Capt. Cleft, Parson's Regt.; 1776, pri. in CO of R.I. Troops under Capt. Wilcox, Dyer's Regt.; 1778, substitute; 1779, pri. in CO of Vt. Militia, Capt. Noble; 1780, orderly-sergt. In CO. of Vt. Militia, Capt. Hutchins.
Proof – Pension claim S. 1735.
Died – 1847. Probably buried in Ceasar Creek Twp.
Married – 1775, wife unknown, had 13 ch.: John and Gideon are only names known.
Collected by Mrs. Walter Kerr, Aurora, Indiana.

Roster of Soldiers and Patriots of the American Revolution Buried in Indiana, Vol. III; 1980; p.77.
TOWER, GIDEON   Roster I, p. 357.   Dearborn County
Additional data or corrections.
Married – Mr. 1775, Abigail Perkins b. Nov. 28, 1754 d. 1845 age 91.
Children – Hannah b. Jan 1776 m. ____ Pease; Nancy b. 1777 m. ____ Millard; Jonathan d. Switzerland Co., Ind. 1855; Robert d. 1813/15 m. Rebecca Stone; Abigail b. June 21, 1787 d. 1844 Dearborn Co., Ind. M. William Lemon; Mary; Gideon b. 1794 m. Roxana Scranton; Clarissa b. Aug. 7, 1797 m. Benjamin Larue; Alphus P. b. Jan. 21, 1800 m. Orpha Hunter.
By Mrs. A. G. Charlton, 310 Sunnyside Avenue, Aurora, Indiana 47001.

The Vevay Reveille-Enterprise; Vol. 122. No. 39, 28 Sep 1935, p.3, col. 3
Roster of Revolutionary Soldiers Who Resided in Switzerland County
By Mrs. Effa M. Danner
Gideon Tower – Sept. Court, Switzerland County 1832 he personally appeared in open court and made manifest for pension for Revolutionary War service.
He enlisted as private in 1775 in Connecticut Militia under Capt. Cleft, Col. Parsons Regiment. 1776 enlisted private in Rhode Island troops, Capt. Wilson, Col. Dyers Regiment. 1778 as substitute for Wm Barker, Quaker, same officers. 1779 private in Vermont Militia, Capt. Noble, Col. Herrick's Regiment. 1780 Orderly Sergeant Co. of Vermont Militia, Capt. Hutchens of Herrick's Regiment, under Gen. Patman, Col. Warner, Gen Sullivan, Gen. Ethan Allen. Enlisted May A.D. 1775 at Windham, Conn. Marched to New London where the news of battle of Bunker Hill reached us. Ordered to Roxbury, Mass. Stationed at Fort Castleton head quarters. He was selected as a scout under Gen. Allen's command. Discharged at Castleton after serving 25 months and one month as substitute for Quaker.
Order Book F, p. 70-71, Switzerland County.
Gideon Tower was a resident of Dearborn County, age 79 – 1832.

TRAINER, ISAAC

Isaac Trainer was not a participant in the Revolutionary War. Confusion has arisen because of the appearance of his children in Switzerland County Probate Court where they state they are heirs of Isaac Trainer who was a Rifleman in the Army of the United States. They were awarded land for his service in the War of 1812 (see Bounty Land Warrant below). Also, there is no indication that Isaac Trainer had ties to Switzerland County.

Patriot: Isaac Trainer - not a Revolutionary War patriot
Birth: -
Married Spouse 1: Elizabeth
Service state(s): N/A
Service description: None
Rank: N/A
Proof of Service: None
Pension application No.: None
Residences: Switzerland County, IN
Died: 1819
Buried: Unknown
DAR Ancestor No.: None

Switzerland County, Indiana Probate Order Book 2, 1831-1837; p. 444.
16 Nov 1836
    Now on this day Comes into Court James H. Trainer addressed to the Court Satisfaction evidence & proof that Maria, Cynthia, John, James H., Jane, Hiram and Amaline Trainer, are the children and heirs of the late Isaac Trainer deceased; together with Elizabeth Trainer widow, are the heirs at law in fee to Isaac Trainer late a private in the Second Regiment of Rifleman, in the army of the United States who departed this life some time in the year 1819.

U.S. War Bounty Land Warrants, 1789-1858
Isaac Trainer Heirs War of 1812 Warrants – Warrant No. 1073
Pursuant to the second section of an Act of Congress, passed 6th of May, 1812, authorizing the Secretary of War to issue Land Warrants to the noncommissioned Officers and Soldiers enlisted in the service of the United States, and in conformity with the 4th section of an Act of the 10th of December, 1814,
    Maria, Cynthia, John, James H., Jane, Hiram and Emeline Trainer, children & the only heirs at law of Isaac Trainer, a Private of the 2^{d} Regiment of Riflemen are entitled to Three Hundred and Twenty Acres of Land, to be located agreeably to the said act on any unlocated parts of the six millions of acres appropriated by law for the original grantees of such military warrants; and this warrant is not assignable or transferable in any manner whatever.
    Given at the War Office of the United States,
    This Seventeenth day of May A.D.
    one thousand eight hundred and thirty seven.

The following records are in error –
Revolutionary Soldiers of Switzerland County; Copied by Mary Hill, John Paul Chapter-Daughters of the American Revolution; January, 1958
TRAINER, ISAAC
Married: Elizabeth _____
Children: Maria, Cynthia, John, James H. , Jane, Hiram, Amaline.
Service, private in 2d Regiment of Rifleman in U.S. Army.
Reference; Switz. Co. Ind. Probate Order Bk. A 1831 – 1837, pg. 444
He died in 1819 - perhaps not in Switzerland Co.

Revolutionary Soldiers Buried in Indiana A Supplement; 485 Names Not Listed in the Roster of Soldiers and Patriots of the American Revolution Buried in Indiana (1938) nor in Revolutionary Soldiers Buried in Indiana (1949); Margaret E. Waters; Indianapolis, 1954. p. 119.
TRAINER, ISAAC   Switzerland
(Uncertain). Name received too late to get full data. He died in 1819 (but poss. not here); m. Elizabeth -------; chn. (at least): Maria; Cynthia; John; James . (deposition in ref. below); Jane; Hiram; Amaline. Service: pvt. in 2nd Regt. of Riflemen in U.S. Army. REF: Switzerland Co., Ind., Probate Ord. Bk. A (1831-1837) p. 444; Miss Mary Hill, Madison, Ind.

TURNER, ROBERT

Patriot: Robert Turner
Birth: 8 Oct 1760   near Oxford, Chester Co., PA
Married Spouse 1: Ann Carlisle (b. 1760/2 d. 2 Feb 1850)
Service state(s): PA & MD & NJ
Service description: See abstract of pension application
Rank: Teamster
Proof of Service: Pension application R10762
Pension application No.: R10762
Residences: Chester Co., PA; Switzerland Co., IN
Died: Oct 1838   Murray's Mills, Switzerland Co., IN
Buried: Murray Cemetery (aka Aberdeen Cemetery), Aberdeen, Ohio Co., IN
DAR Ancestor No.: A117193

Pension Application Abstracted from National Archives microfilm Series 805, Roll 816, File R10762.
Pension Abstract for: Robert Turner
County & state: Switzerland Co., IN
Date: 18 Apr 1827, and 28 June 1832.
Service: Maryland.
Volunteered in Dec. 1777, as private in Chester Co., PA, Capt. James McDowell's Co. 3 mos. June 1778 contracted as a teamster finding his own wagon and team of horses under Capt. Saunderson attached to Maj. Montgomery's battalion in the command of Col. Henry Hollingsworth of Maryland (Pennsylvania crossed out and Maryland written in), served under said Capt. for several months. Was transferred, with his wagon and team, to the company commanded by Capt. John McClanahan of the same battalion until Capt. McClanahan was wounded and left the service. Transferred, with his wagon and team, to the company commanded by Capt. James Mackey same battalion and served upwards of 1 yr. Was attached and engaged as a teamster for the full term of 4 yrs. and when not attached to the above company being variously employed by different officers. Discharged in Maryland. Did not receive promised pay, lost one valuable horse for which he never received any pay, had to buy another at his own expense. In 1827 he is much afflicted, wife is 75 and one son is age 20. Household and kitchen furniture presented by his son on whose charity he has lived for 9 yrs.

Switzerland County, Indiana Civil Order Book Vol. 6, Oct. 17, 1825-Apr. 25, 1929, p. 250.
18 Apr 1827 –
Robert Turner a Revolutionary Soldier now in open court files his Schedule of property, and made the Declaration and took the Oath required by an Act of Congress Relative to Pensioners which is ordered to be Recorded: and it is further ordered by the Court to be Certified that the property contained in Said Schedule is Valued at Twenty five Dollars.

Official Register of the Officers and Men of New Jersey in the Revolutionary War; Compiled Under Orders of His Excellency Theodore F. Randolph, Governor; by William S. Stryker, Adjutant General, Printed by the Authority of the Legislature; Wm. T. Nicholson & Co., Printers, Trenton, NJ, 1872, Facsimile Reprint by Heritage Books, Inc., Bowie, MD, 1993; p.868.
Turner, Robert. Teamster, "Captain Hallybirt's Team Brigade."

Roster of Soldiers and Patriots of the American Revolution Buried in Indiana, Vol. I; compiled by Mrs. Roscoe C. O'Byrne.; Indiana Daughters of the American Revolution, 1981; p. 361-362.
TURNER, ROBERT   Ohio County
Born – Oct. 8, 1760, Penn.
Service – Volunteered in Chester Co., Penn., under Capt. James McDowell, Col. Montgomery, using his own team. He was wagon master 1778-1781 under Henry Saunderson.
Proof – Pension claim R. 10762; D.A.R. No. 29138.
Died – 1838. Buried at Aberdeen. [9 Oct. 1838]
Married – Ann Carlisle (1760-1850) Had a son. [Son William shown in D.A.R. No. 29138]

Rejected or Suspended Applications for Revolutionary War Pensions; Reprinted for Clearfield Company Inc. by Genealogical Publishing Co., Inc., Baltimore, MD, 1998, p. 409.
A list of the names of persons residing in Indiana who have applied for pensions under the act of June 7, 1832, whose claims have been rejected; prepared in conformity with the resolution of the Senate of the United States of September 16, 1850.

Names	Residence	Reasons for rejection
TURNER, ROBERT	Printer's Retreat	Only three months service as a soldier.

Early Ohio Settlers, Purchasers of Land in Southwestern Ohio, 1800-1840; Compiled by Ellen T. Berry & David A. Berry; Genealogical Publishing Co., Inc., Baltimore, MD, 1986. p.332.

Purchaser	Year	Date	Residence	R – T - S
Turner, Robert (B)	1835	April 17	Dearborn Ind	03-05-35 [Son?]

(B) Indiana Survey: Land lying west of a meridian drawn west of the Great Miami (known as the "Gore"). Switzerland, Dearborn, Franklin, Ohio, Union and Randolph Counties (all or only a part of each county) – all in Indiana.

1840 U.S. Census, Indiana, Dearborn, No Twp., Series: M704 Roll: 77 Page: 89.
Ann Turner, Age 70-80.

The Vevay Reveille-Enterprise; Vol. 122, No. 39, 28 Sep 1935, p.3, col. 3.
Roster of Revolutionary Soldiers Who Resided in Switzerland County
By Mrs. Effa M. Danner
Robert Turner, soldier, manifest 1825-29, Book 6, Switzerland Co.

Abstract of Graves of Revolutionary Patriots (4 volumes); by Patricia Law Hatcher; Pioneer Heritage Press, Dallas, TX, 1987. Vol. 4, p. 131.
This is an abstract and an index to information reported to the Daughters of the American Revolution and published in their annual reports to the Smithsonian Institution, printed as Senate Documents (1900-1974) and published annually in the DAR magazine (1978-1987).
Published 1972
TURNER, Robert   Aberdeen Cem, Cass Twp, Ohio Co IN

National Society of the Sons of the American Revolution - Revolutionary War Graves Register; Compiled and Edited by Clovis H. Brakebill, Published by db Publications, Dallas, TX, 1993. p. 611.
Turner   Robert; 1769-1838; Aberdeen Cem, Cass Twsp, Ohio Co, IN; Wagonmaster, NJ.

Murray Cemetery (aka Aberdeen Cemetery), Aberdeen, Ohio Co., IN
Tombstone inscriptions -

IN	ROBERT	ANN
memory	TURNER	Wife of
of	CONTINENTAL	ROBERT TURNER
ROBERT TURNER	LINE	DIED
who departed his	REV WAR	Feb. 2, 1850
life Oct. 9th 1838	OCT 8 1760	in the 88th year
aged 78 years	OCT 9 1838	of her age

497

TURNER, SMITH

Patriot: Smith Turner
Birth: -
Married Spouse 1: 30 Oct 1797 Accomack Co., VA   Abigail Prewit
Service state(s): VA
Service description: Capt. Thomas Palmer, 9th VA Regt., Gen. Muhlenburg,
                     On board the schooner Sally, captured British schooner
                      commanded by Capt. Carey.
Rank: Private
Proof of Service: Pension application S36832
Pension application No.: S36832
Residences: VA; NC; KY; Switzerland Co., IN
Died: 7 Mar 1831 Switzerland Co., IN
Buried: prob. Jefferson Twp., Switzerland Co., IN
DAR Ancestor No.: None

Virginia Marriages, Accomack County,
30 Oct 1797, Smith Turner to Abigail Prewit.

Pension Application Abstracted from National Archives microfilm Series 805, Roll 816, and *File s36832;Switzerland County, Indiana Complete Records, Circuit Court, Vol. ?, Sep 3, 1821-Apr 18, 1827;* p. 318.

Pension abstract for – Smith Turner   Service state(s): Virginia
Date: 12 May 1818
County of: Switzerland   State of: Indiana
Declaration made before a Circuit Court.
Age: Not stated
Residence now: Switzerland Co. IN
Volunteer or Drafted or Substitute: Enlisted
Rank(s): Private
Statement of service-

Period	Duration	Names of General and Field Officers
1776	Until March 1778	Capt. Thomas Palmer of the 9th Virginia Regiment commanded by Gen. Muhlenburg.
After discharge		On board the schooner Sally, was captured by the British King's schooner, commanded by Capt. Carey who destroyed his discharge.

Battles: Brandywine, and Germantown.
Discharge received: Honorably discharged by Gen. Muhlenburg
                     at Valley Forge in Pennsylvania.
&
Date: 15 September 1820
County of: Switzerland   State of: Indiana
Declaration made before a Circuit Court.
He received pension Certificate No. 9469, dated 20 May 1818.

Schedule of property submitted.
Age: about 76 years
Residence now: Switzerland Co., IN
Rank(s): Not stated
Statement of service-

Period	Duration	Names of General and Field Officers
		Served under Capt. Thomas Palmer of the 4th Regiment of the Virginia Line.

Occupation: Farmer
Wife: Abigail   Wife's age: about 65 years
Soldier died: 7 March 1831
&
Date: 5 Jun 1823
County of: Switzerland   State of: Indiana
Declaration made before a Circuit Court.
Age: abt. 73 yrs
Residence when he entered service: State of Virginia
Residence now: Switzerland Co., IN
Volunteer or Drafted or Substitute: Enlisted
Statement of service-

Period	Duration	Names of General and Field Officers
	2 yrs	Capt. Thomas Palmer, Col. George Mathews, VA State Line, Continental establishment.

Battles: none stated
Discharge received: At Valley Forge, PA
Wife: Abigail Turner   Wife's age: abt. 70 years   Has rheumatism and
        is unable to make a living for herself or contribute to mine.

Switzerland County, Indiana, Civil Order Book - Vol.5, Feb 10, 1823 - Jun 21, 1826, p.66.
5 June 1823 – Smith Turner, a revolutionary soldier and United States pensioner, now files his schedule and declaration and took the oath required by the several acts of congress, providing for certain persons engaged in the land and navel service, of the United States, in the revolutionary war, which was ordered to be recorded, and it is further ordered that it be certified that the property contained in the schedule aforesaid is valued by the court at ninety six dollars and fifty cents.

Switzerland County, Indiana Civil Order Book 4, 1820 – 1823; pg. 78.
Sept. 1820
Smith Turner, Revolutionary soldier and U.S. pensioner filed his schedule, valued at $275.75.

Switzerland County, Indiana Civil Order Book 4, 1820 – 1823; pg. 199.
June 1821
Smith Turner, Rev. soldier & U.S. pensioner---$183.56¼

Switzerland County, Indiana Probate Order Book 2, 1831-1837, pp. 7, 13, 18, 24, 34, 46, 52, 74, 110.; *Switzerland County, IN, Will Book Vol. 1, 3 Jan 1823-10 Nov 1847*, p. 27.; and *Switzerland County, Indiana Probate Record Book Vol. A, Mar 1827-Nov 1834*; p. 374.
Abstract of will and/or administration for: Smith Turner
State & county where recorded: Switzerland Co., Indiana
Book/volume where recorded: Probate Order Book 2, 1831-1837;
Will Book Vol. 1.
Date will made: 26 July 1830
Date entered in probate: 2 April 1831
Name(s) of executors: Abigail Turner
Name(s) of executors: Abigail Turner, wife of the deceased
Administration:
Date began – 12 Feb 1833
Appraisers: executrix, Abigail Turner
Witnesses to Will – Joseph Dow, James Malcomson, James Stewart.
Bonded by and amount of bond: Joseph Dow for $500.00.
Names of heirs and others mentioned in will (also signed receipts of division of estate) and relationship if shown: Wife Abigail Turner, son William Turner.
Date of division & disbursement, or final return: 13 Feb 1833

Abstract of Final Payment Voucher; General Services Administration, Washington, DC
LAST FINAL PAYMENT VOUCHER RECEIVED FROM
THE GENERAL ACCOUNTING OFFICE
NAME   Turner, Smith
AGENCY OF PAYMENT   Indiana
DATE OF ACT   1818
DATE OF PAYMENT   March 1, 1831
DATE OF DEATH   March 7, 1831
GENERAL SERVICES ADMINISTRATION
National Archives and Records Service   NA-286
GSA-WASH DC 54-4891   November 1953

Revolutionary War Records – Virginia; Virginia Army and Navy Forces with Bounty Land Warrants for Virginia Military District of Ohio, and Virginia Military Script, from Federal and State Archives; by Gaius Marcus Brumbaugh, M.D, M.s., Litt.D; Genealogical Publishing Co., Inc., Baltimore, 1995.p. 272.
List of non-commissioned officers and soldiers of the Continental Line. List may contain names of individuals who received bounty land for services in the State Line.
Turner, Smith, Soldier, Inf.

Historical Register of Virginians in the Revolution, Soldiers, Sailors, Marines, 1775-1783; John H. Gwathmey; The Dietz Press, Richmond, VA, 1938. p. 786.
Turner, Smith. Inf. 9 CL. E.

Second Census of Kentucky, 1800; Clift G. Glenn; Genealogical Publishing Co., Baltimore, MD, 1954.
An alphabetical list of 32,000 taxpayers based on original tax lists on file at the Kentucky Historical Society. Information given includes the county of residence and the date of the tax list in which the individual is listed.
Turner, Smith   Clark   7/22/1800

Early Settlers of Indiana's "GORE" 1803-1820; Compiled and Edited by Shirley Keller Mikesell; Heritage Books, Inc., 1995. p. 215.
Switzerland County Deeds; Book A
Deed dated 1819. William Turner & Tabitha, his wife, to Smith Turner. S3, T2, R3W. Signed William (x) Turner, Tabitha (x) Turner. Pp. 373, 374.

The Pension List of 1820 [U.S. War Department] Reprinted with an Index; by Murtie June Clark; Genealogical Publishing Co., Inc., Baltimore, 1991. *Originally published 1820 as Letter from the Secretary of War. p. 658.*
Names of the Revolutionary Pensioners which have been placed on the Roll of Indiana, under the Law of the 18th of March, 1818, from the passage thereof, to this day, inclusive, with the Rank they held, and the Lines in which they served, viz.

Names	Rank	Line
Smith Turner	private	Virginia

1820 U.S. Census, Indiana, Switzerland, Posey, Series: M33 Roll: 14 Page: 262
Smith Turner 45 and up; others in household 1 female under 10, 1 female 45 and up.

Pensioners of the Revolutionary War Struck Off the Roll with an Added Index to States; Reprinted by Genealogical Publishing Co., Baltimore, MD for Clearfield Company, Inc., 1989. p. 100.
Pensioners in Indiana who have been dropped under the act of 1st May, 1820; prepared in conformity with a resolution of the House of Representatives of the United States of the 17th December, 1835.

Names	Acts under which restored	Remarks
Smith Turner	March 1, 1823	-

Revolutionary Soldiers of Switzerland County; Copied by Mary Hill, John Paul Chapter-Daughters of the American Revolution; January, 1958; http://www.ingenweb.org/inswitzerland/switzrevsoldiers.html- Viewed June 2012.
TURNER, SMITH   Pension S.36832
Born 1750
Enlisted 1776 under Captain Thomas Palmer of 9th Virginia Regiment under Gen. Muhlenburg, served to March 1778.
Discharged by Gen. Muhlenburg at Valley Forge. In battles of Brandywine and Germantown.
Married Abigail _____
Children:
Daughter - unknown

Son - William.
Died March 7, 1832, Probably buried in Jefferson twp. [Date should be 7 Mar 1831]
Buried: prob in Jefferson Twp.
Abstract of Will in Switzerland Co. Indiana; July 16, 1830, probated April 2, 1831
Wife Abigail; son William
Witnesses; Joseph Dow, James Malcomson, James Stewart

Roster of Soldiers and Patriots of the American Revolution Buried in Indiana, Vol. 1; compiled by Mrs. Roscoe C. O'Byrne.; Indiana Daughters of the American Revolution, 1981; p. 362.

TURNER, SMITH   Switzerland County
Born – 1750.
Service – Enlisted 1776 under Capt. Thomas Palmer of 9th Vir. Regt. under Gen. Muhlenburg, served to March, 1778. Discharged by Gen. Muhlenburg at Valley Forge. In battles of Brandywine and Germantown.
Proof – Pension claim S. 36832.
Died – March 7, 1831. Probably buried in Jefferson Twp.
Married – Abigail _____. Had a daughter.

The Vevay Reveille-Enterprise; Vol. 122. No. 39, 28 Sep 1935, p.3, col. 4.
Roster of Revolutionary Soldiers Who Resided in Switzerland County
By Mrs. Effa M. Danner
Smith Turner – is listed in the Switzerland County Census of 1830 which states that he and wife are over 45 years of age. Family – one girl.
He was granted a pension for his Revolutionary service May 1818, No. S36832.
He enlisted 1776 under Captain Thomas Palmer of the 9th Virginia Regiment commanded by Gen. Muhlenburg at Valley Forge. He was in the battles of Brandywine, Germantown. After his discharge he entered on board the schooner "Sally" at Musquito Point, Va. It was captured by the British King's Schooner commanded by Captain Carey, who destroyed his discharge. His wife, age 65, name Abigain (1820), 1823 Smith Turner gives his age 78 years.
William Turner testifies that Smith bought and paid for articles of him. 1822 sold land to Joseph Dow, Indiana certificate No. 9469 issued April 19, 1819, sent to Vevay. Died March 7, 1831.
Switzerland County Probate Court 1831, April 2, page 634 comes his widow, Abigail Turner sole executor of Smith turner's will and administrator, she being sole legatee, except William Turner $1.00. Joseph Dow security for $500.00 Estate settled p. 110-1831, Book H, p. 242, deeds signed by Wm. Turner and wife Tabitha Turner.

WARDEN, BARNARD
aka WORDEN

Patriot: Barnard Warden
Birth: abt. 1764
Married Spouse 1: Not stated
Service state(s): NY
Service description: Company of New York Militia commanded by Capt. Froman, Col. Wisenfelt's regiment; Capt. Norton of 4th NY regiment; Capt. Williams of the Flying Camp
Rank: Private
Proof of Service: Pension application R21899
Pension application No.: R21899
Residences: Johnston, NY; Duchess Co., NY; Switzerland Co., IN
Died: aft 1826 prob. Switzerland Co., IN
Buried: Unknown
DAR Ancestor No.: None

Pension Application Abstracted from National Archives microfilm Series 805, Roll 838, and *File R21899; Switzerland County, Indiana Complete Records, Circuit Court, Vol. ?, Sep 3, 1821-Apr 18, 1827; p. 660.*

Pension abstract for – Barnard Warden
Alternate spelling(s): Worden
Date: 25 November 1818
County of: Switzerland
Declaration made before a Judge.
Age: 54 years
Where he entered service: 1st & 2nd tour at Johnston, NY;
                            3rd tour in Duchess Co., NY
Residence now: Switzerland Co., IN
Volunteer or Drafted or Substitute: Enlisted
Rank(s): Private
Statement of service-

Service state(s): New York
Old War Invalid
State of: Indiana

Period	Duration	Names of General and Field Officers
Apr 1780	3 months	Company of New York Militia commanded by Capt. Froman, Col. Weisenfelt's regiment.
Abt. Jul 1780	4 months	Capt. Norton of 4th NY regiment.
Spring 1781	9 months	Capt. Williams of the Flying Camp

Battles: Valentine's Hill in New York
No family data in file.

Switzerland County. Switzerland Co. IN. Circuit Court Complete Record, Sept 1821 – Sept 1826, pg. 660.
Date: 20 Oct 1826
County of: Switzerland
Declaration made before a Circuit Court.
Age: about 65 years

State of: Indiana

Residence when he entered service: New York
Residence now: Switzerland County, IN
Volunteer or Drafted or Substitute: 1st tour - Enlisted in July of the year that Major Andre was hung at Johnstown on the Mohawk River State of New York.
2nd tour – at Duchess Co., New York
Statement of service-

Period	Duration	Names of General and Field Officers
July ----	9 mos.	Recruited by Capt. Norton of the 4th New York, Regiment, served in company commanded by Capt. Smith, regiment commanded by Col. Wisenfelt in the Line of the State of New York in the Continental establishment.
May ----	9 mos.	Capt. Williams. A short time after his enlistment Capt. Williams was arrested for striking Barnard with his sword. Then under command of Capt. Sacket in Regt. commanded by Col. Sheldon, Line of New York Continental establishment.

Discharge received: 1st tour – in Albany, NY; 2nd tour – in Middle Patton in NY
Signed by: Capt. Sacket
I have nothing under heaven except these his ragged clothes which cover my feeble body."
The court appraised his schedule of property at $5.00.

Switzerland County, Indiana Civil Order Book Vol. 6, Oct. 17, 1825-Apr. 25, 1929, p. 190.
20 Oct 1826 -
And now Bernard Worden a Revolutionary Soldier here in Open Court files his Schedule and made the Declaration, and took the Oath Required by an act of Congress Relative to Pensioners, and it is ordered the same be Recorded, and it is further Ordered, by the Court, to be certified that the Property Contained in Said Schedule is by the court valued at Five Dollars.

New York in the Revolution as Colony and State, Second Edition, 1898; by James A Roberts, Comptroller; Genealogical Publishing Co., Baltimore, MD. p. 70.
The Levies
Colonel	John Harper	Quarter Master		Barent Roseboom
Major	John Chipman			Barent TenEyck
	James M. Hughes	Pay Master		Isaac Paris
Adjutant	John Bateman	Surgeon		William Petrie

Additional Name on State Treasurer's Pay Books
Ensign Thomas Boyce
Enlisted Men – Warden Barnerd (in this listing)

Early Settlers of Indiana's "GORE" 1803-1820; Compiled and Edited by Shirley Keller Mikesell; Heritage Books, Inc., 1995.
p. 215.

Switzerland County Deeds; Book A
Deed dated 1819. John Francis Siebenthal & Jane Marie, his wife, to Barnard Warden. S15, T2, R3W. Signed John F. Siebenthal, J. Maria Siebenthal. Witness: Sam'l Fallis, A. B. Dumont, Wm. C. Keen. Pp. 363, 364.
p. 218.
Switzerland County Deeds; Book A
Deed dated 1819. Barnard Warden to Rawleigh Day. S15, T2, R3W. Signed Barnard Warden. Witness: Wm. C. Keen, David McCormick. pp. 431, 432, 433.

1820 U.S. Census, Indiana, Switzerland, Jefferson, Series: M33 Roll: 14 Pg: 264
Barnard Worden 45 and up; others in household 1 male 10-16, 1 female 45 and up.

Revolutionary Soldiers of Switzerland County; Copied by Mary Hill, John Paul Chapter-Daughters of the American Revolution; January, 1958; http://www.ingenweb.org/inswitzerland/switzrevsoldiers.html- Viewed June 2012.
WARDEN (WORDEN). BARNARD
Enlisted in July, the year Major Andre was hanged (1780) at Johnstown on the Mohawk River, N. Y. in Capt. Norton's company, 4th N. Y. Regt. Capt. Smith, Col. Wisenfelt's Regt. Continental Establishment.
Discharged at Albany, N.Y.
Enlisted again in May for 9 months, in Dutchess Co. N. Y.
Switzerland County. Switzerland Co. Ind. Civil Order bk. 1826, pg. 660
Collected by Mrs. A. V. Danner, Vevay, Indiana

Roster of Soldiers and Patriots of the American Revolution Buried in Indiana, Vol. 1; compiled by Mrs. Roscoe C. O'Byrne.; Indiana Daughters of the American Revolution, 1981; p.372.
WARDEN (WORDEN), BARNARD   Switzerland County
Service – Enlisted in July, the year Maj. Andre was hanged at Johnstown on Mohawk River, N.Y., in Capt. Norton's CO., 4th N.Y. Regt., Capt. Smith, Col. Wisenfelt's Regt., Cont'l Establishment. Discharged at Albany, N.Y. Enlisted again in May for 9 mos. in Dutchess co., N.Y.
Proof – Switzerland Co., Ind., Civil Order book, 1826, p. 660.
Collected by Mrs. A. V. Danner, Vevay, Indiana.

The Vevay Reveille-Enterprise; Vol. 122. No. 39, 28 Sep 1935, p.3, col. 3-4.
Roster of Revolutionary Soldiers Who Resided in Switzerland County
By Mrs. Effa M. Danner
Barnard Worden – He enlisted in July, the year Major Andre was hung at Johnstown on the Mohawk River, New York under Capt. Norton, 4th New York Regiment, was on recruiting service. In the Company of Capt. Smith, Reg. of Col. Wisenfelt Continental establishment. Discharged at Albany, N.Y. Again enlisted in may for 9 months in Duchess Co., N.Y. Capt. Williams who was arrested for striking said Barnard with his sword and sent to Poughkeepsie for trial.
Barnard was put under command of Capt. Sacket, Col. Sheldon. Term 9 months.

He swore in open court Switzerland County, "I have nothing under heaven except these ragged clothes which cover my feeble worn out body." P. 660, Oct. 1826, Order book D. Civil Court, 1830 Switzerland County Census, Jesse Worden, 6 boys, 1 girl and wife.

Note – the best history available on the movement of these troops is <u>Life of Washington</u> by Washington Irving at the Library, Vevay.

WEIST, HENRY

Patriot: Henry Weist
Birth: 1 Jan 1754   York Co., PA
Married Spouse 1: abt. 1773/1774   Elizabeth Reister
             (b. 3 Jul 1755/1756 d. 3 Jul 1838 Switzerland Co., IN)
Service state(s): PA
Service description: Capt. John Travis, York Co. Militia
Rank: Private
Proof of Service: Penn. Archives, 6th S., Vol. 2, p 620;
             3rd S., Vol. 21, pp. 46, 479, 541, 780.
Pension application No.: None
Residences: York Co., PA; Indiana Territory; Switzerland Co., IN
Died: 18 Nov 1845 Switzerland Co., IN
Buried: Davis Cemetery, near Patriot, Posey Twp., Switzerland Co., IN
DAR Ancestor No.: A121779

Pennsylvania Archives, 6th Series, Volume 2. p. 620.
Battalions Not Stated – York County Militia
Associators and Militia County of York
The Within Return Made by Me May 27, 1778 – John Travis (h)
Henry Wiest in this list.

Pennsylvania Archives, Series 3, Volume XXI. p. 46.
Return of Taxables County of York - 1779
Henry Weast   100 Acres   0 Negroes 1 Horses   2 Cattle   Tax 36.0.0

Pennsylvania Archives, Series 3, Volume XXI. p. 479.
Transcript of Taxables County of York – 1781
John Henry Wist   Amount of Tax 4.11.S

Pennsylvania Archives, Series 3, Volume XXI. p. 541.
Transcript of Taxables County of York - 1782
John Henry West   150 Acres   0 Negroes   2 Horses   2 Cattle   Tax 4.15.0

Pennsylvania Archives, Series 3, Volume XXI, p. 780.
Number of Inhabitants, Etc. County of York – 1783
Weist, Henry   200 acres 7 Inhabitants   0 Servants   0 Negroes

Early Ohio Settlers, Purchasers of Land in Southwestern Ohio, 1800-1840;
Compiled by Ellen T. Berry & David A. Berry; Genealogical Publishing Co., Inc., Baltimore, MD, 1986. p.346.

Purchaser	Year	Date	Residence	R – T - S
Weist, Henry (B)	1816	June 19	Dearborn Ind	01-02-04
Weist, Henry (B)	1816	June 19	Dearborn Ind	01-02-22
Weist, Henry (B)	1818	Jan. 08	Switzerland	01-02-22
Weist, Henry (B)	1827	Aug. 21	Switzerland	01-02-22

(B) Indiana Survey: Land lying west of a meridian drawn west of the Great Miami (known as the "Gore"). Switzerland, Dearborn, Franklin, Ohio, Union and Randolph Counties (all or only a part of each county) – all in Indiana.

Early Settlers of Indiana's "GORE" 1803-1820; Compiled and Edited by Shirley Keller Mikesell; Heritage Books, Inc., 1995.
p. 182.
Switzerland County - Township 2, Range 1W
Section 4 – Henry Weist – 1816 – p. 1.
p. 183.
Switzerland County - Township 2, Range 1W
Section 22 – Henry Weist – 1818 – pg. 3.

Indiana Land Entries Vol. 1 Cincinnati District, 1801-1840; Margaret R. Waters; Originally Published Indianapolis 1948, Second Reprint 1979 by The Bookmark, P.O. Box 74, Knightstown, In 46148. p.2 (2), 4 (2).
CINCINNNATI LAND DISTRICT – VOL. 1
Page 2. Twp. 2 N, Range 1 W of 1st Principle Meridian SWITZERLAND CO. Henry Weist NW ¼ - S4; 6-19-1816.
and –
Page 2. Twp. 2 N, Range 1 W of 1st Principle Meridian SWITZERLAND CO. Henry Weist SE ¼ - Sr; 6-19-1816.
and -
Page 5. Twp. 2 N, Range 1 W of 1st Principle Meridian SWITZERLAND CO. NW ¼ - S22; 1-8-1818. Relinquished. Note adds to Henry Weist.
-- Note: The tract books for the land offices in Indiana are deposited in the office of the Auditor of State, Indianapolis. They and are in the custody of the State Land clerk. --

U.S. Department of Interior, Bureau of Land Management, General Land Office Records; Land Patent Search – accessed 27 June 2012.
WEIST, HENRY
Accession Nr. Cv-0062-403; Document Type – Credit Volume Patent; State - Indiana; Issue Date – 4/1/1825; Cancelled – No
Names on Document: Weist, Henry; Larew, William
Land Office – Cincinnati; Authority – April 24, 1820 Sale-Cash Entry (3 Stat. 566); General Remarks – Patent Record Imperfect; Document Nr. -958; Total Acres – 159.26
Land Description: State - IN; Meridian – 1st PM; Aliquots – 002N-001W; Section - 3; County - Switzerland
&
Accession Nr. CV-0066-473; Document Type – Credit Volume Patent; State - Indiana; Issue Date – 2/18/1826; Cancelled – No
Land Office – Cincinnati; Authority – April 24, 1820 Sale-Cash Entry (3 Stat. 566); Document Nr. -1708; Total Acres – 158.70
Land Description: State - IN; Meridian – 1st PM; Aliquots – 002N-001W; Section - 4; County – Switzerland
&

Accession Nr. CV-0072-535; Document Type – Credit Volume Patent; State - Indiana; Issue Date – 8/2/1833; Cancelled – No
Names on Document: Davis, Margaret; Weist, Margaret; Weist, Henry
Land Office – Cincinnati; Authority – April 24, 1820 Sale-Cash Entry (3 Stat. 566); Document Nr. -2732; Total Acres – 158.70
Land Description: State - IN; Meridian – 1st PM; Aliquots – 002N-001W; Section - 4; County – Switzerland

Indiana Territory, Switzerland Circuit Court Records, Order Book, October Term 1814 to March Term 1815. p.52.
He is listed in county records for the first time on 17 June 1819, as a juror - excused.
Author's note: There are entries in this volume that are not within the range of dates shown on the binder cover.

1820 U.S. Census, Indiana, Switzerland, Jefferson, Series: M33 Roll: 14 Pg: 264
Henry Weist 45 and up; others in household 1 female 16-26, 1 female 45 and up.

Roster of Soldiers and Patriots of the American Revolution Buried in Indiana, Vol. II; 1966; p.105.
WEIST, HENRY   Switzerland County
Born: 1 Jan 1754, Hopewell Twp., York Co., PA
Service – Name appears on list of John Travis' Comp. of York Co., Penn., Militia, May 27, 1775.
Proof – Penn. Archives, 6th S., Vol. 2, p 620; 3rd S., Vol. 21, pp. 46, 313, 471, 541, 750; 1820 and 1830 census of Switzerland Co.
Died: 18 Nov 1845 in his 91st year. Bur. near Patriot. Stone
Married: In his 20th yr., [abt. 1774] Elizabeth Reister, b. 3 Jul 1775, d. 3 Jul 1838, Switzerland Co. Ch. Margaret b. Jan 7, 1795, d. Nov 3, 1873, m. Oct 1, 1827, Peter Davis, 1805-1866.
From Water's Sup. P. 107.

Revolutionary Soldiers Buried in Indiana A Supplement; 485 Names Not Listed in the Roster of Soldiers and Patriots of the American Revolution Buried in Indiana (1938) nor in Revolutionary Soldiers Buried in Indiana (1949); Margaret E. Waters; Indianapolis, 1954. p. 106.
WEIST, HENRY   Switzerland
b. 1-1-1754, Hopewell Twp. (formerly Shrewsbury Twp. Till 1767), York co., Pa.; d. 11-18-1845, in 91st yr. (obit says he died in Ohio; this might be an error for Ohio Co., Ind.); anyhow was bur. near Patriot, Ind, with tombstone, now nearly illegible; elderly relatives remember as children that stone stated he was a Rev. sold. & gave the Regt.; obit also says Rev. sold.);
m. in 20th yr. (prob. York Co., Pa, or Baltimore Co., Md.) Elizabeth Reister, b. 7-3-1755; d. 7-3-1838, Switzerland Co., Ind.; dau. Of John Reister;
chn: Margaret b. 1-7—1795, Md. (prob. Baltimore Co.); d. 11-3-1873, Switzerland Co., Ind.; m. 10-1-1827, Switzerland Co., Ind. (as 1st wife), Peter Davis, b. 1805-1806, N.Y.; d. 1886 (will pr. Aug 4.), Posey Twp., Switzerland Co., Ind.; son of James & Catherine Davis.

Henry Weist (Wiest-Weast-Weest) lived in the disputed Penna.—Md. Region settled by the Mason-Dixon Line in 1768. Titles to land in this region were granted by Maryland. He appears in the 1779-80 Tax Lists of Hopewell Twp., York Co., Pa. By 1790 had moved to Baltimore Co., Md. where he later was executor of the estate of his father-in-law, John Reister. One of John Reister's heirs was Margaret Trine (dau.?) & Henry Weist as executor, conveyed land to Peter Trine of York Co., Pa. It is not known when Henry Weist came West. His obit states he helped build the Block House at Cincinnati. He is said to have come to Switzerland Co., Ind. In 1813, from Reistertown, Baltimore Co., Md.
Service: name is on list of John Travis' Comp. of York Co., Pa., Mil., 5-27-1778.
REF: "Pa. Arch.". 6th Ser., v. 2, p. 620; 3rd Ser., v. 21, pp. 46-312-471-541-780; 1790 Cens., Baltimore Co., Md., p. 32; 1820 Cens. Switzerland Co., Ind., v. 5, p. 282 A, Posey Twp.; 1830 Cens., Switzerland Co., Ind. v. 14, p. 1144; Waters— "Ind. Land Entries", v. 1, pp.2, 4; Knox---
"Switzerland Co., Ind., Marriages" , p. 7; Switzerland Co., Ind Will Bk. 3, pp. 1, 301, 317; Will Bk. 4, p. 237; "Western Christian Advocate", v. 12, p. 188; 3-6-1846 (obit); Miss Dorothy Mae Davis, Dallas, Tex.

Switzerland County, Indiana, Will Records, 1825-1903; compiled by Ruth M. Slevin; self published, 197?. (Allen County Public Library)Book 3, p.43.
Weist, Henry   Dtd: 23 April 1833   Rec 27 Aug 1874
                                                                          [Note this recording date.]
        Wife -   Elizabeth Weist
        Dau -   Margaret Davis and her heirs
        Note -   At time of probate of will, all the witnesses below were deceased, so Perrit Dufour proved the will. Also, Scott Carter swore that signatures were genuine.
        Exec -   Son-in-law Peter Davis
        Wit -   Thomas Armstrong
                          John R. Cotton
                          Edward Fulton

Switzerland County Indiana Cemetery Inscriptions 1817-1985; Wanda L. Morford; Cincinnati, Ohio, 1986, p. 400.
Weist   Henry   d. Nov. 18, 1845 aged 91y 10m 7d
             Elizabeth "an unusual stone in the wording: 1838 (at top) Here lies the body of Elizabeth Weist aged 83y 7m 3d lived a married life 63 years

Abstracts of obituaries in the Western Christian Advocate, 1834-1850; Compiled by Margaret R. Waters, Dorothy Riker, and Doris Leistner, in observance of the Northwest Ordinance of 1787; Indiana Historical Society, Indianapolis, IN, 1988. p. 39.
12 Oct 1838 [Note spelling error of surname.]
Wrist, Elizabeth, Mrs.; d. 8 Aug 38, age 83y.6m.4d., Switzerland Co., IN; mar. 1775 (husband survives); Was married 63y.7m. {5-100; 12 Oct 38}.

Abstract of Graves of Revolutionary Patriots (4 volumes); by Patricia Law Hatcher; Pioneer Heritage Press, Dallas, TX, 1987. Vol. 4, p. 171.
This is an abstract and an index to information reported to the Daughters of the American Revolution and published in their annual reports to the Smithsonian Institution, printed as Senate Documents (1900-1974) and published annually in the DAR magazine (1978-1987).
Published 1972 (Senate Doc. 54)
WEIST, Henry   Nr Patriot, Switzerland Co IN

WILSON, MICHAEL

Patriot: Michael Wilson
Birth: abt. 1757
Married Spouse 1: Unknown
Service state(s): VA
Service description: Capt. William Voss, 12th Regt. VA,
        Col. Wood, Gen. Scott's brigade.
Rank: Private
Proof of Service: Pension application S36849
Pension application No.: S36849
Residences: Hampshire Co., VA; Switzerland Co., IN
Died: aft 1824
Buried: in Vevay, Switzerland Co., IN
DAR Ancestor No.: None

Pension Application Abstracted from National Archives microfilm Series 805, Roll 878, File S36849.
Pension abstract for – Michael Wilson Service state(s): Virginia
Date: 2 June 1818
County of: Switzerland   State of: Indiana
Declaration made before a Judge.
Age: Not stated
Where he entered service: Romley town, Hampshire Co., VA
Residence(s) since the war: Not stated
Residence now: Switzerland Co., IN
Volunteer or Drafted or Substitute: Not stated
Rank(s): Private
Statement of service-

Period	Duration	Names of General and Field Officers
1777	3 years	Capt. William Voss of the 12th regiment of Virginia commanded by Wood, in Gen. Scott's brigade.

Battles: Brandywine, Germantown, Monmouth, and Stoney Point.
Discharge received: 1780 in Philadelphia by Col. Phebecker.
&
Schedule of property presented
Date: 15 September 1820
County of: Switzerland   State of: Indiana
Declaration made before a Circuit Court.
Age: about 63 years
Residence now: Switzerland Co., IN
Statement of service- Same as testimony of 2 June 1818
Occupation: House carpenter; unable to support himself by his labor.
He has no family residing with him.

Switzerland County, Indiana Civil Order Book 4, 1820 – 1823; pg. 76.
Sept. term 1820
Michael Wilson: A revolutionary soldier and U.S. Pensioner filed his schedule of property----valued at $18.63 1/2.

Historical Register of Virginians in the Revolution, Soldiers, Sailors, Marines, 1775-1783; John H. Gwathmey; The Dietz Press, Richmond, VA, 1938. p. 837.
Wilson, Michael. Ind. pens.

The Pension List of 1820 [U.S. War Department] Reprinted with an Index; by Murtie June Clark; Genealogical Publishing Co., Inc., Baltimore, 1991. Originally published 1820 as Letter from the Secretary of War. p. 658.
Names of the Revolutionary Pensioners which have been placed on the Roll of Indiana, under the Law of the 18th of March, 1818, from the passage thereof, to this day, inclusive, with the Rank they held, and the Lines in which they served, viz.

Names	Rank	Line
Michael Wilson	private	Virginia

Revolutionary Soldiers of Switzerland County; Copied by Mary Hill, John Paul Chapter-Daughters of the American Revolution; January, 1958; http://www.ingenweb.org/inswitzerland/switzrevsoldiers.html- Viewed June 2012.
WILSON, MICHAEL   Switzerland County. Pension claim S.36849
Born: abt. 1757, probably Virginia.
Service; enlisted at Romney, Hampshire Co. Va. in 1777, as private in Capt. William Voss's company, Col. Wood's Virginia Regt. in battles of Brandywine, Germantown, Monmouth, Stoney Point.
Discharged 1780 by Col. Fegeger. Served three years.
Died 1824; estate settled in Switzerland Co. Buried Vevay, Ind.
Buried: in Vevay, IN
Collected by Mrs. A. V. Danner, Vevay, Indiana

Roster of Soldiers and Patriots of the American Revolution Buried in Indiana, Vol. I; compiled by Mrs. Roscoe C. O'Byrne.; Indiana Daughters of the American Revolution, 1981; p.386.
WILSON, MICHAEL   Switzerland County
Born – About 1787, probably Vir.
Service – Enlisted at Romney, Hampshire Co., Vir., in 1777 as pri. in Capt. William Voss's CO., Col. Wood's Vir. Regt. In battles of Brandywine, Germantown, Monmouth, Stony Point. Discharged 1780 by Col. Febeger. Served 3 yrs.
Proof – Pension claim S. 36849.
Died – 1824 (estate settled Switzerland Co.). Buried Vevay, Ind.
Collected by Mrs. A. V. Danner, Vevay, Indiana.

The Vevay Reveille-Enterprise; Vol. 122. No. 39, 28 Sep 1935, p.3, col. 3.
Roster of Revolutionary Soldiers Who Resided in Switzerland County
By Mrs. Effa M. Danner

Michael Wilson – Record as found in papers on file in this soldier's pension claim, S36849. The date and place of his birth and the names of his parents were not given.

He enlisted at Romney, Hampshire County, Virginia in 1777 as private in Captain William Voss' Co. in Colonel Wood's Virginia Regiment; he was in the battles of Brandywine, Germantown, Monmouth and Stony Point and was discharged in 1780 by Colonel Febiger, having served three years.

Michael Wilson was allowed pension on his application executed June 2, 1818 at which time he was living in Switzerland County, Ind.

In 1820 he was living in Switzerland County, Indiana, aged 63 years, and he stated that he has no family then residing with him. There are no further data relative to family.

Probate Court Record p.4, Nov. 5, 1824, Michael Wilson's estate, Amos Gilbert and McGruder, administrators. John Fox and Wm. Brandenburg assessors.

Page 64 final settlement – To cash paid to Dr. T.C. Forbes $6.50; J. Shupe for coffin $5.00; Abner Webb, grave digger $1.25; J. Fox, crying sale $1.50, care in last illness $5.00; 16 weeks board $1.25 per week $20. Other bills, all total $66.18 1/2.

To cash received, being pension, $44.75; amount of sale 410.81 1/4; note, John Conner, $3.00 Total $59.56 1/4.

Amos Gilbert and Norman B. McGruder are creditors and heirs of Michael Wilson, p. 275, Vol. 1818-1824.

Research Effa Morrison Danner.

Amos Gilbert, wife Agnes, came from Virginia and built one of the first hotels in Vevay, "The National". Norman B. McGruder is a Revolutionary Soldier.

WHITTEKER, JOHN
aka WHITACAR, WITTAKER

Patriot: John Whitteker
Birth: 1758/1760
Married Spouse 1: Unknown
Service state(s): VA
Service description: Capt. George McCormick, 13th VA Regiment; Maj. Taylor.
Rank: Private
Proof of Service: Pension application S36845
Pension application No.: S36845
Residences: VA; Switzerland Co., IN
Died: 12 Sep 1828 prob. Switzerland Co., IN
Buried: Unknown
DAR Ancestor No.: None

Pension Application Abstracted from National Archives microfilm Series 805, Roll 865, File S36845.
Abstracted Pension Application – John Witteker
23 June 1818
The State of Indiana, Switzerland County
Appeared John Whitteker, of Ross township of aforesaid county, aged about fifty-eight years.
Enlisted 17th day of December, 1776 on Peters creek in the state of Virginia, under Capt. George McCormick of the 13th Virginia regiment which was commanded by Colonel John Gibbons of
General Hand's brigade, and served about three years.
He received no discharge in consequence of the neglect of his captain in making a correct return.
He quit the service in Pittsburg in 1779.
18 Feb 1820 - District of Indiana, Dearborn County, being a court of Reason (?) for the County of Switzerland in the then(?) Judicial Circuit of the State of Indiana.
Appeared John Whitaker, resident in said county, aged about sixty-two years. Served in the Revolutionary War as follows – that he enlisted near Pittsburg, Capt. George McCormick's Company in the thirteenth Virginia Regiment, afterwards company was commanded by Maj. Taylor.
That he enlisted on the 13th Dec. 1776 and continued in the service three years.
That he has a previous certificate numbered 12571 the date which is the 22nd July 1819 to commence on the 23rd day of June 1818.
He is by occupation a farmer can make but little that family residing with him consists of his wife Martha and his granddaughter Maria Whitaker two years of age.
& *also from this pension file* -
Letter from War Dept. in Pension File –
May 19, 1937

Miss Pearl Scotts   RA-J/EEL

Madison
Indiana
Dear Madame:

John Whitteker-S.36845

    Reference is made to your letter in which you request the Revolutionary War record of John Whitteker, who received pension while residing in Switzerland County, Indiana.

    The data which follows are obtained from the papers on file in the Revolutionary War pension claim, S.36845, based upon the military service in that war of John Whitteker,

    The date and place of birth and names of the parents of John Whitteker are not shown.

    John Whitteker enlisted in the state of Virginia, in December, 1776, served as a private in Captain George McCormick's Company, Colonel John Gibson's Virginia Regiment: length of service, three years.

    He was allowed pension on his application executed June 23, 1818, at which time he was a resident of Ross Township, Switzerland County, Indiana. He gave his age at that time as about fifty-eight years.

    In 1820, soldier stated that he was aged about sixty-two years, and that his family then residing with him consisted of his wife, Martha, aged sixty-three years and a granddaughter, Maria Whitaker, aged two years. He gave no further data in regard to his wife nor do the names of the parents of the granddaughter appear nor are the names of any children given.

    The soldier died September 12, 1828, place not shown.

    Very truly yours,
    A. D. HILLER
    Executive Assistant
    to the Administrator.

Author's note: There are hand-written notations on the War Dept. copy.

Virginia Revolutionary Militia, A List of Non-Commissioned Officers and Soldiers of the Virginia Line on Continental Establishment, Whose names appear on the Army Register, and who have not received Bounty Land; Printed by Samuel Shepherd, Printer to the Commonwealth, Richmond, VA. 1835. p. 49. Doc. No. 44.

Whitacar, John   Soldier   Infantry

Revolutionary War Records – Virginia; Virginia Army and Navy Forces with Bounty Land Warrants for Virginia Military District of Ohio, and Virginia Military Script, from Federal and State Archives; by Gaius Marcus Brumbaugh, M.D, M.s., Litt.D; Genealogical Publishing Co., Inc., Baltimore, 1995.p. 276. List of non-commissioned officers and soldiers of the Continental Line. List may contain names of individuals who received bounty land for services in the State Line.

Whitacar, John, Soldier, Inf.

Historical Register of Virginians in the Revolution, Soldiers, Sailors, Marines, 1775-1783; John H. Gwathmey; The Dietz Press, Richmond, VA, 1938. p. 820.

Whitaker, John (Whitacre) 9 CL, 13 CL, 15 CL.

The Pension List of 1820 [U.S. War Department] Reprinted with an Index; by Murtie June Clark; Genealogical Publishing Co., Inc., Baltimore, 1991. Originally published 1820 as Letter from the Secretary of War. p. 658.
Names of the Revolutionary Pensioners which have been placed on the Roll of Indiana, under the Law of the 18th of March, 1818, from the passage thereof, to this day, inclusive, with the Rank they held, and the Lines in which they served, viz.

Names	Rank	Line
John Whitacar	private	Virginia

Abstract of Final Payment Voucher; General Services Administration, Washington, DC
WHITEKER, JOHN
LAST FINAL PAYMENT VOUCHER RECEIVED FROM
THE GENERAL ACCOUNTING OFFICE
NAME   WHITEKER, JOHN
AGENCY OF PAYMENT   INDIANA
DATE OF ACT   1818
DATE OF PAYMENT   Sept. 1, 1825
DATE OF DEATH   Sept. 12, 1825   [Note date error.]
GENERAL SERVICES ADMINISTRATION   na-286
NATIONAL ARCHIVES AND RECORDS SERVICE   November 1953
GSA-WASH DC 54-4891

Revolutionary Soldiers of Switzerland County; Copied by Mary Hill, John Paul Chapter-Daughters of the American Revolution; January, 1958; http://www.ingenweb.org/inswitzerland/switzrevsoldiers.html- Viewed June 2012.
WITTAKER, JOHN   Pension S.36845
The data which follow are obtained from the papers on file in Revolutionary War pension Claim, S.36845, based upon the military service in that war of John Whittaker.
Born: 1758-1760 (estimated from his age of 58 in 1818, age 62 in 1820) The date and place of birth and the names of the parents of John Whittaker are not shown. John Whittaker enlisted in the state of Virginia, in December, 1776, served as a private in Captain George McCormick's Company, Colonel John Gibson's Virginia Regiment; Length of service three years.
Married: Martha _____
Children:
Son (granddaughter, Maria Whittaker mention in 1820 pension appl.)
Possibly others
23 June 1818 He was allowed pension on his application executed at which time he was a resident of Ross Township, Switzerland Co. Indiana. He gave his age at that time as about fifty-eight years.
1820 Soldier stated that he was aged about sixty-two years, & that his family then residing with him consisted of his wife, Martha, aged sixty-three years, and a grand-daughter Maria Whittaker, aged two years. He gave no further data in regard to his wife, nor do the names of the parents of the grand-daughter appear nor are the names of any children given.

The soldier died September 12, 1825, place not shown.
Buried: According to Roster of Rev. Soldiers, John Whittaker is buried at Benham, Indiana. Name on bronze tablet in Versailles Court House. [This is the "other" John Whitacar – see note at the end of this record.]

Author's note: There is another patriot by the name of Whitacar (Whitacer), John, who applied for pension in 1818 and in 1822 in Ripley County. His pension application number is S36844, served in VA; b. 175?/1757, d. 1833 in Ripley Co.; wife not named, son and daughter not named.

Possible burial information for this Ripley County man –
Abstract of Graves of Revolutionary Patriots (4 volumes); by Patricia Law Hatcher; Pioneer Heritage Press, Dallas, TX, 1987. Vol. 4, p. 189..
This is an abstract and an index to information reported to the Daughters of the American Revolution and published in their annual reports to the Smithsonian Institution, printed as Senate Documents (1900-1974) and published annually in the DAR magazine (1978-1987).
Published 1972 (Senate Doc. 54)
Whittaker, John   Benham Cem., Benham, Ripley Co., IN.

Also this land record –
U.S. Department of Interior, Bureau of Land Management, General Land Office Records; Land Patent Search – accessed 27 June 2012.
WHITAKER, JOHN
Accession Nr. IN0210_.305; Document Type – State Volume Patent; State - Indiana; Issue Date – 10/4/1824; Cancelled – No
Land Office – Jeffersonville; Authority – April 24, 1820 Sale-Cash Entry (3 Stat. 566); Document Nr. -825; BLM Serial Nr. – IN NO S/N; Total Acres – 80.00
Land Description: State - IN; Meridian – 2nd PM; Aliquots – 006N-012E; Section - 19; County – Ripley.]

WOOLCOTT, JOSEPH
aka WALCOTT

Patriot: Joseph Woolcott
Birth: 27 Jul 1764 Newton, CT
Married Spouse 1: Unknown
Service state(s): NY
Service description: Capt. Ichabod Turner, Lieut. Joel Peas, NY Militia;
                         Capt. Downs, NY Militia; Capt. Breadbreak, NY Militia;
                         Capt. Young, NY Militia; Capt. Capt. Newell or Wright,
                         NY Militia Capt. Tierce or Tass
Rank: Militiaman; Private
Proof of Service: Pension application S32610
Pension application No.: S32610
Residences: Newton, CT: Stephentown, Albany Co., NY; Rennsselaer Co. NY;
               KY; Switzerland Co., IN
Died: aft 1836, prob. Switzerland Co., IN
Buried: Unknown
DAR Ancestor No.: None

Pension Application Abstracted from National Archives microfilm Series 805, Roll 889, File S32610.; Switzerland County, Indiana Probate Record Book Vol. A, Mar 1827-Nov 1834; p. 381.

Pension abstract for – Joseph Woolcott   Service state(s): New York
Date: 17 May 1833
County of: Switzerland   State of: Indiana
Declaration made before a Probate Court.
Recorded in Book A, pg. 384.
Age: 68 years   Record of age: Recorded in the town news of Newton, CT
Where and year born: Newton, Connecticut on 27 July 1764.
Residence when he entered service: Stephentown, Albany Co., NY
Residence(s) since the war: about 29 yrs. in New York, thence to Indiana.
Residence now: Switzerland Co., IN
Volunteer or Drafted or Substitute: 1776 drafted; *1777 substitute for his father
         Augustus Woolcott; volunteered, and enlisted. *Father called out for
         nine months, Joseph served 6 mos., his father served balance of time.
Rank(s): Private – 7 mos. as a militia man, 18 as an enlisted soldier.
Statement of service- [terms of service conflict in this application]

Period	Duration	Names of General and Field Officers
1776	3 weeks	Capt. Ichabod Turner, Lieut. Joel Peas, NY Militia
1777	6 mos.	Capt. Downs, NY Militia
1778 or 1779	3 mos.	Capt. Breadbreak, NY Militia
1779 or 1780	7 mos.	Capt. Young, NY Militia
1780 or 1781	4 mos.	Capt. Capt. Newell or Wright, NY Militia
1781	7 mos.	Capt. Tierce or Tass

Officers in troops where served: Lieut. Thornton, Cole, Moore; Capt. James
                     Cannon, Wright; Sgt. Maj. Cone.

Discharge received: Verbal discharge
Statement is supported by – Traditionary evidence
Persons in neighborhood who certify character: Caleb Wright, Thomas Davis, John Clark, Dudley Linwell, Payton Bear, David Brown.
This application was rejected for the reason "he was too young to have performed the services set forth previous to the year 1781", 28 Feb 1834, War Department.
&
Affidavit of brothers Norman and Charles Woolcott.
Date: 13 January 1834
County: Steuben   State: New York
Declaration made before Justice of the Peace
"Personally came Norman Woolcott and Charles Woolcott" "that they were brothers of Joseph Woolcott and at the time of and during the Revolutionary War between the United States and Great Britain they and their brother Joseph and the whole of their fathers family resided in the County of Rensselaer in Said State and that Joseph Woolcott is about 10 or 11 years older than they, and they were then about fifteen years of age and that Joseph Woolcott as they understood served in the Revolutionary War for the space of Six years at Different periods that they knew him to Equip himself and go into the Army and remain three months and at other times more than two months and during the whole time he was not at home at any time more than two weeks and they understood and verily believe that he Served….(description of service follows)."

Switzerland County, Indiana Probate Order Book 2, 1831-1837; p. 129.
17 May 1833 – May Term
In the matter of   } An applicant for a pension under the act of Congress of
Joseph Wolcott   } the 7 June AD 1832
          Now here in open Court before the Probate Court of Switzerland County now Sitting comes Joseph Wolcott and files his report which he is now Sworn to in open Court and is in the words and figures following to wit (her insert it) and the Court do hereby declare their opinion after the investigation of the matter, and after putting the interrogations prescribed by the war department that the above named Joseph Wolcott was a Revolutionary Soldier and Served as he states, and the Court further certifies that it appears to them that Caleb Wright who Signed the above Certificate is a resident of Switzerland County State of Indiana and a credible person, and that his Statement is entitled to Credit, and that there is no Clergyman in Said Joseph Wolcotts neighborhood.

New York in the Revolution as Colony and State, Second Edition, 1898; by James A Roberts, Comptroller; Genealogical Publishing Co., Baltimore, MD.
p. 96.
The following men (according to the certificates of the muster-masters) served either in the Line of the Levies, having been hired by the several classes under the Land Bounty Rights; but there is nothing to indicate in which regiment of the Line of the Levies they served.
Lieut. Abraham Ten Eyck
          Enlisted Men - Woolcot Joseph (in this listing)

p. 107,
Albany County Militia – Fourth Regiment
Colonel Kilian Van Rensselaer   Major Cornelius Van Buren
Lieut. Col. John H. Beeckman   Adjutant John E. Lansing
Major Jacob C. Schermerhorn   Quarter Master Jacob Statts
          Enlisted Men - Woolcot Joseph

New York in the Revolution as Colony and State, Volume II, 1901 (Supplement);
Compiled by Frederick G. Mather; Genealogical Publishing Co., Baltimore, MD.
p. 211.
Land Bounty Rights
The names of all persons who appear in connection with the Land Bounty Rights have been classified; and they may be found in the six lists given below: -
          Assignees -   Woolcott Joseph (in this listing)

Register of Certificates Issued by John Pierce, Esquire, Paymaster General and Commissioner of Army Accounts for the United States, to Officers and Soldiers of the Continental Army Under Act of July 4, 1783; Originally Published as Senate Documents, Vol.9, No. 988, 63rd Congress, 3d Session, Washington, 1915; Seventeenth report of the National Society of the Daughters of the American Revolution; Genealogical Publishing Co., Inc, Baltimore, MD, 1984. p. 561.
Men listed in this volume with the same name.

No. of Certificate	To whom issued	Amount
4233	Woolcott, Joseph	80.00

Revolutionary Soldiers of Switzerland County; Copied by Mary Hill, John Paul Chapter-Daughters of the American Revolution; January, 1958;
http://www.ingenweb.org/inswitzerland/switzrevsoldiers.html- Viewed June 2012.
WOOLCOTT, JOSEPH   See Pension records in text
Born: July 27, 1764, Newington, Conn (pension appl.) or July 27, 1760 Stuben Co. N. Y. (see below); son of August Woolcott
At enlistment lived Stephentown, Albany Co. N. Y. there for about 29 yrs.
After War continued to live in Rennsselaer Co. N. Y. for many years
Then to Kentucky
Then to Indiana.
May 17, 1833 Pension application, age 68 yrs. Switzerland Co. Ind.
Jan. 30, 1834 Affidavit of Charles Woolcott, age 66 and of Norman Woolcott, age 68 yrs. that they are brothers of Joseph; that they now (I think) live in Rennsselaer Co. N. Y.; that soldier made his home at their father's house in Rennsselaer Co. N. Y.; that soldier is 6 yrs. older than Norman, and 8 yrs older than Charles; that soldier served as a substitute for father Augustus Woolcott, who had been called out for 9 months; Joseph substituted 6 months and father served the balance.
May 16, 1836 Pension application, age about 74, Switz. Co. Ind.
Ref.; Pension S.32610, N. Y.
Switz. Co. Ind. Probate Order bk. A. 1831 - 1837, pg. 129.

1830 U.S. Census, Indiana, Switzerland, No Twp., Series: M19 Roll: 32 Pg: 75
Woolcut, Joseph age 60-70; others in household 1 male 5-10, 1 female 20-30, 1 female 60-70.

Revolutionary Soldiers Buried in Indiana A Supplement; 485 Names Not Listed in the Roster of Soldiers and Patriots of the American Revolution Buried in Indiana (1938) nor in Revolutionary Soldiers Buried in Indiana (1949); Margaret E. Waters; Indianapolis, 1954. p. 112.
WOOLCOTT, JOSPEH   Switzerland
b. 7-27-1764, Nowington, Conn (pens. Appl.) or b. 7-27-1760, Steuben Co., N.Y. (see below); son of Augustus (or Justus) Woolcott. Pens. Appl. 5-17-1833, ae. 68, Switzerland Co., Ind.; & 5-16-1836, ae. Ca. 74, Switzerland Co., Ind. After War, continued to live in Rensselaer Co., N.Y., for many years. Affd. 1-30-1834 of Charles Woolcott, 66, & of Norman Woolcott, 68; that they are bros. of Joseph; that they now (I think) live in Rensselaer Co., N.Y.; that Joseph was b. 7-27-1760, not 1764, in Steuben Co., N.Y.; that sold. made his home at their father's house in Rensselaer Co., N.Y.; that said sold. is 6 yr. older than Norman & 8 yr. older than Charles; that said sold. served as a subst. for their father, Justus Woocott.
Service: enl. 1776; Capt. Turner; later serv. as subst. for father Augustus Woolcott, who had been called out for 9 mo.; Joseph subst. 6 mo. & father serv. the balance. At enl. liv. Stephentown, Albany Co., N.Y.; there for ca. 29 yr; to Ky.; then to Ind.
REF: Pens. Appl. S. 32610 N.Y. (see p. 119).

Revolutionary Soldiers Buried in Indiana A Supplement; 485 Names Not Listed in the Roster of Soldiers and Patriots of the American Revolution Buried in Indiana (1938) nor in Revolutionary Soldiers Buried in Indiana (1949); Margaret E. Waters; Indianapolis, 1954. p. 119.
WOOLCOTT, JOSEPH – p. 112. Switzerland Co., Ind. Probate Order Book A. (1831-1837), page 129.

Roster of Soldiers and Patriots of the American Revolution Buried in Indiana, Vol. II; 1966; p. 109.
WOOLCOTT, JOSPEH   Switzerland County
Born – July 27, 1760 or 1764, Newington, Conn.
Service – Enl. 1776 under Capt. Turner; later served as substitute for his father, Augustus Woolcott.
Proof – Penn. S. 32610, N. Y.; Probate Order book A (1831-37), p. 129, Switzerland Co., Ind.
From Waters' Sup., p. 112.

APPENDIX A

Soldier	State of Service	Soldier	State of Service
Cross, Ebenezer	CT	Woolcott, Joseph,	NY
Harris, Robert	CT	Andrews, Arthur	PA
Moore, Roderick	CT	Christy, James	PA
North, Abijah	CT	Cotton, Ralph	PA
North, Lot	CT	Davis, David	PA
North, Thomas	CT	Dewitt, William	PA
Porter, Thomas	CT	Gray, Moses	PA
Buck, William	CT	Gullion, Jeremiah	PA
Potter, David	CT, RI	Gullion, John	PA
Tower, Gideon	CT, RI	Gullion, Robert	PA
Todd, Joseph	KY	Harris, Daniel	PA
Boisseaux, Jean B.	Lafayette	Leap, John W.	PA
Bassett, Joseph	MA	Mounts, Thomas	PA
Humphrey, Ebenezer	MA	Parkinson, Abraham	PA
Mellen, John	MA	Pickett, Heathcote	PA
Peabody, Stephen	MA	Protsman, John	PA
Ranstead, James	MA	Remer, David	PA
Blades, John Levy	MD	Renno, George	PA
Coy, Christopher	MD	Ricketts, Nathan	PA
Coy, William	MD	Ricketts, Robert	PA
Griffith, William	MD	Shupe, John	PA
Hufman, Henry	MD	Todd, Owen	PA
Lanham, Henry	MD	Weist, Henry	PA
Magruder, Robert B.	MD	Hall, Benjamin	RI
Peake, Nathan	MD	Abney, George	SC
Smyth, Phillip D.	MD	Knox, Robert	SC
Turner, Robert	MD,NJ,PA	Bray, John	VA
Carver, Christian	NC	Brown, Samuel	VA
Critchfield, John	NC	Burns, John	VA
Green, Richard	NC	Chandler, William	VA
Scudder, Abner	NC	Conine, Andrew	VA
Shaddy, John	NC	Dickinson, Griffith	VA
Robinson, Winthrop	NH	Drake, Benjamin	VA
Butler, Richard	NJ	Goddard, Joseph	VA
Deisky, Leiman	NJ	Hammond, Lewis	VA
Dumont, Peter	NJ	Kelly, William	VA
Haycock, Daniel	NJ	Lancaster, William	VA
Lee, John	NJ	Landers, Kimbrow	VA
Robert(s), John	NJ	Levi, Isaac	VA
Ayer, Thomas	NJ,NY	Lewis, Thomas	VA
Fancher, William	NY	McKay, Robet	VA
Gazley, James	NY	Morgan, Nathan	VA
Hannis, Henry	NY	Moss, Zeally	VA
Heath, Daniel Jr.	NY	Neal, Charles	VA
Jennings, Solomon	NY	Nighswonger, Solomon	VA
Warden, Barnard	NY	Continued	

APPENDIX A (Continued)

Soldier	State of Service
Pennetent	VA
Ricketts, William	VA
Roberts, Hezekiah	VA
Roberts, John	VA
Rogers, Stephen	VA
Shaver, John	VA
Six, John	VA
Stepleton, Andrew	VA
Stewart, Charles	VA
Turner, Smith	VA
Wilson, Michael	VA
Whittaker, John	VA

APPENDIX B

Revolutionary Soldiers Who Lived in Switzerland County

George Abney
Arthur Andrews
Thomas Ayer
Joseph Bassett
Jean Baptiste Boisseaux
John Bray
Samuel Brown
William Buck
John Burns
Richard Butler
Christian Carver
William Chandler
James Christie
Ralph Cotton
Christopher Coy
William Coy
John Critchfield
Ebenezer Cross
David Davis
Leiman Deisky
William Dewitt
Griffith Dickinson
Benjamin Drake
Peter Dumont
William Fancher
Daniel Field
James Gazley
Moses Gray
Richard Green
William Griffith
John Gullion
Robert Gullion
Benjamin Hall

Lewis Hammond
Henry Hannis
Daniel Harris
Robert Harris
Daniel Haycock
Daniel Heath
Henry Hufman
Ebenezer Humphrey
William Kelly
Robert Knox
William Lancaster
Kimbrow Landers
Henry Lanham
John Leap
John Lee
Isaac Levi
Thomas Lewis
Robert Magruder
John Mellen
Roderick Moore
Nathan Morgan
Zeally Moss
Thomas Mounts
Charles Neal
Solomon Nighswonger
Daniel Norris
Lot North
Thomas North
Abraham Parkinson
Stephen Peabody
Nathan Peake
John Pennetent
Heathcote Pickett

Thomas Porter
David Potter
William Preston
John Protsman
James Ranstead
David Remer
George Renno
Robert Ricketts
William Ricketts
Hezekiah Roberts
John Roberts
Winthrop Robinson
Stephen Rogers
Abner Scudder
John Shaddy
John Shaver
John Shupe
John Six
Phillip Smyth
Andrew Stepleton
Charles Stewart
Joseph Todd
Owen Todd
Gideon Tower
Isaac Trainer
Robert Turner
Smith Turner
Barnard Warner
Henry Weist
Michael Wilson
John Whittaker
Joseph Woolcott

Wives Who Settled in Switzerland County After the Death of the Soldier

Sarah, wife of John Blades
Lydia, wife of Andrew Conine
Frances Glasscock, wife of Joseph Goddard
Polly Reading, wife of Solomon Jennings
Sarah Hawley, wife of John Roberts

APPENDIX C
Interesting observations discovered during compilation of this work.

Jane Glascock, of Fauquier Co., VA, married Zeally Moss. She was b. c1770.
&
Francis Glascock, of Fauquier Co., VA, married Joseph Goddard. She was b. 1762/3.

Andrew Stepleton & Michael Wilson are from Romney, VA. Both were in Capt. Voss' (Vause's) Co., under Col. Woods.

Leaman Deisky and John Lee served together in NJ militia. John Lee's widow refers to Leaman in her application for widow's pension.

John Mellen and Ebenezer Humphrey were both from Oxford, MA.

William Dewitt and William Fancher were in Bracken County, KY on 11/22/1799 when they were taxed.

Stephen Rogers signed the Certificate for John Roberts (sp. of Mary) pension application.

William Fancher signed the Certificates for Solomon Nighswonger's widow Jemima.

Robert Gullion and Robert Knox may have attended the same church in Gallatin County, Ky. James Cox, Clergyman of Gallatin County signed their Certificates, for Revolutionary pensions, in Switzerland County on 13 August 1832.

Christopher Coy signed certificate for his brother William Coy. Christopher and William served in the same unit – Montgomery Co., MD, Middle Battalion, 4th Company. Christopher Coy and William Coy were in Madison Co., KY in 1800 where they were taxed.

Nathan & Robert Rickets were in Mason Co., KY in 1800 where they were taxed. Also, a Roclif Rickets is listed who is a possible relation.

Abijah & Lot North were in Harrison Co., KY in 1800 where they were taxed.

Michael Wilson's heir is Norman B. McGruder.
Norman Magruder was an administrator for Michael Wilson's estate.

N. B. McGruder & wife Nancy were administrators for John Shupe's estate. John Shupe made coffin for Michael Wilson (& others).

Norman McGruder & Zeally Moss served on Switz. Grand jury in 1815.
Zeally Moss, John Bray, Joseph Todd, & foreman John Protzman served on Switz. Grand jury in 1817.

www.ingramcontent.com/pod-product-compliance
Lightning Source LLC
Chambersburg PA
CBHW060908300426
44112CB00011B/1386